Praise for *American Patriots*

"Black Americans have participated in every American war, to the benefit of us all. Despite overt discrimination and crude racism, they produced many heroes and did great deeds. This is a triumphant American success story, from slaves in the Revolutionary War to Colin Powell as the top military man of Desert Storm. Gail Buckley tells it well. She has done the research, done the interviews, read the literature, thought about her subject, and knows how to write, how to engage her reader. A triumph."

—Stephen E. Ambrose, author of *D-Day*

"An unabashed patriot and a child of World War II . . . Buckley brings an enthusiasm to the subject informed in part by family history, but shaped most notably by her desire to set the historical record straight. . . . In her capable hands, a narrative emerges rich in historical detail and carefully crafted anecdotes. . . . The stories that she tells (many of them based on interviews she conducted with twentieth-century black veterans during the fourteen years she worked on the book) are compelling and often inspiring."

—James A. Miller, *The Boston Globe*

"*American Patriots* adds an unforgettable chapter to the saga of race relations in America. The author's exhaustive chronicle of the black American military experience yields both a compelling historical narrative and an encyclopedic resource on an important branch of American history."

—Rick Harmon, Portland *Oregonian*

"Most Americans don't know that one out of seven men in George Washington's army was black or that a black soldier stopped Benedict Arnold from handing West Point to the British. That's just part of the history Gail Buckley uncovered in the fourteen years she spent writing *American Patriots.*"

—*Parade*

"What an extraordinary history it is . . . in both its grandeur and its tragedy. . . . Buckley has written a book to fill a significant gap in our history. She has recounted a remarkable human drama, one of struggle, betrayal and ultimate redemption."

—*The New York Times Book Review*

"A salute to the courage, valor, and patriotism of America's black military, from the Buffalo Soldiers to Desert Storm."

—*Vanity Fair*

"Gail Buckley has written an important and readable book on a topic that should be of interest to all Americans."

—John Whiteclay Chambers II, *The Star-Ledger*

"*American Patriots* is a long-overdue work that is full of revelations and bitter ironies. Buckley . . . has written a book that finally pays homage to the hundreds of thousands of African American men and women who serve and die for their country. . . . *American Patriots* is a scholarly triumph."

—Bill Maxwell, *St. Petersburg Times*

"Gripping . . . They are great stories, and Buckley tells them well."

—Anne Stephenson, *The Arizona Republic*

"Gail Buckley has given us a powerful account of a long and shamefully overlooked part of American military history—the heroic efforts of African Americans to serve honorably and courageously in the armed forces when they were subjected to the worst kinds of racism. The full story is at once uplifting and deeply disturbing. We should all be grateful to Gail for bringing us these stories—and to the people about whom she writes for their determined patriotism."

—Tom Brokaw, author of *The Greatest Generation*

"Gail Buckley's *American Patriots* gathers in one place the record of black American soldiers and sailors who for centuries heroically served a nation that despised them. 'A black Marine who survived boot camp could go through hell singing a song,' recalled one World War II–era Marine. With their blood and courage, they lift us all up. Buckley has written a fascinating, stirring, and important book."

—Mark Bowden, author of *Black Hawk Down*

"No group in our nation's history was more eager to prove their loyalty and courage. Sometimes treated worse than our enemies, they perservered to become American patriots, as Gail Buckley reveals in this powerful and illuminating book."

—Henry Louis Gates, Jr.

"Gail Buckley's *American Patriots* unveils a forgotten but essential strand in the fabric of American history. This fine book recalls the bravery and sacrifice of black soldiers who believed in the ultimate promise of American life—and fought and died for a nation that systematically denied them that promise. *American Patriots* is a noble work of recovered memory."

—Arthur Schlesinger, Jr.

"Gail Buckley tells a gripping story about an unsung group of American heroes. In Korea and Vietnam, I fought alongside the sorts of warriors who make up her story. They were America's best. At last their story is told, and told brilliantly. *American Patriots* should be required reading for soldier and civilian alike."

—Colonel David H. Hackworth, author of *About Face*

"A compulsive and humbling history of nobility in the face of American prejudice, and courage in the face of America's enemies. Buckley writes with grace and authority—and an almost unearthly restraint."

—John le Carré

PHOTO: © STAR BLACK

GAIL BUCKLEY'S family history, *The Hornes,* was a national bestseller. She collaborated on an *American Masters* documentary with her mother, Lena Horne, and narrated a documentary on black families for PBS. She has written for the *Los Angeles Times, Vogue,* the New York *Daily News,* and *The New York Times.* She is married to the journalist Kevin Buckley and lives in New York.

ALSO BY GAIL BUCKLEY

The Hornes: An American Family

AMERICAN PATRIOTS

AMERICAN PATRIOTS

The Story of Blacks in the Military from the Revolution to Desert Storm

Gail Buckley

Random House Trade Paperbacks · New York

Grateful acknowledgment is made to the following for permission to reprint previously published material:

BANTAM BOOKS, A DIVISION OF RANDOM HOUSE, INC.: Excerpts from *It Doesn't Take a Hero,* by General H. Norman Schwarzkopf and Peter Petre. Copyright © 1992 by H. Norman Schwarzkopf. Used by permission of Bantam Books, a division of Random House, Inc.

BENJAMIN BENDER: Excerpt from a letter published in *The New York Times* on April 22, 1985. Copyright © 1985 by Benjamin Bender. Reprinted by permission of the author.

HOWARD UNIVERSITY PRESS: Excerpts from *GI Diary,* by David Parks (Washington, D.C.: Howard University Press, 1984). Copyright © 1984 by David Parks. Reprinted by permission of Howard University Press.

RANDOM HOUSE, INC.: Excerpts from *My American Journey,* by Colin Powell with Joseph E. Persico. Copyright © 1995 by Colin L. Powell. Reprinted by permission of Random House, Inc.

RANDOM HOUSE, INC.: Excerpt from "Spain 1937," by W. H. Auden, from *W. H. Auden: Collected Poems.* Copyright © 1940 and copyright renewed 1968 by W. H. Auden. Reprinted by permission of Random House, Inc.

RANDOM HOUSE, INC.: Excerpts from *Bloods,* by Wallace Terry. Copyright © 1984 by Wallace Terry. Reprinted by permission of Random House, Inc.

REGNERY PUBLISHING, INC.: Excerpts from *Memoir of an American Patriot,* by Hamilton Fish (Washington, D.C.: Regnery Publishing, Inc., 1991). Copyright © 1991 by Lydia Ambrogio Fish. Reprinted by special permission of Regnery Publishing, Inc., Washington, D.C. All rights reserved.

SIMON AND SCHUSTER, INC.: Excerpt from *About Face,* by Colonel David H. Hackworth and Julie Sherman. Copyright © 1989 by David Hackworth and Julie Sherman. Reprinted by permission of Simon and Schuster, Inc.

TEXAS A&M UNIVERSITY PRESS: Excerpts from *One Woman's Army,* by Charity Adams Earley. Copyright © 1989 by Charity Adams Earley. Reprinted by permission of the Texas A&M University Press.

Library of Congress Cataloging-in-Publication Data

Buckley, Gail Lumet.
American patriots : the story of blacks in the military from the Revolution to Desert Storm / Gail Buckley.
p. cm.
Includes bibliographical references and index.
ISBN 0-375-76009-1 (acid-free paper)
1. Afro-American soldiers—Biography. 2. Afro-American soldiers—History. 3. United States—History, Military. 4. United States—Armed Forces—Afro-Americans—History. 5. United States—Race relations. I. Title.

E185.63 .B93 2001
355'.008996'73—dc21 00-051825

Random House website address: www.atrandom.com
Printed in the United States of America on acid-free paper
9 8 7 6 5 4 3 2
First Trade Paperback Edition

Book design by Mercedes Everett

For Kevin

Foreword

David Halberstam

One of the remarkable aspects of the often painful and amazingly complicated story of blacks in this country is that they remained loyal to concepts of freedom and democracy even when they were the most marginal beneficiaries of the very ideals they were defending. Their loyalty has proven to be, as Gail Buckley shows in *American Patriots,* a source of strength not merely to the nation but also to the blacks who committed themselves to these American ideals, even if their promise remained elusive in their own lives. There are eloquent voices in *American Patriots.* "'My military career gave me the ability to search out a problem,' said William DeFossett of the 369th Regiment, which went to the Pacific in World War II. 'It taught me how to plan, how to examine things, when to improve upon them. It taught me about teamwork, physical fitness—pride.' 'Civilians don't understand the meaning of leadership,' said Gene Doughty, a veteran of Iwo Jima." This book is first and foremost a great American story—and one long overdue.

I remember spending time with Martin Luther King, Jr., in 1967, when I was writing a magazine article about him for *Harper's.* We were in a car going to the airport one day and he was talking about black loyalty and willingness to serve in a war he had already criticized, a phenomenon that both amazed him (and I think made him covertly proud as a black man) and greatly irritated him as a committed pacifist. It was about earning your place as an American, he said, no small touch of bitterness in his voice, that this, serving in the Army in what he considered to be a bad war, was the easiest way to show your loyalty.

Buckley makes this seeming paradox, which so puzzled Dr. King, a powerful narrative thread of American history. Throughout most of American history, blacks have never ceased trying to claim their birthright. There is something enduring and powerful about their role in America: so much taken from them, so little given in return. It makes their American journey unique, their history our most absorbing. Rarely has any author caught the contradictions inherent in this special story, the heartbreaking irony of it all, as skillfully as Gail Buckley, who shows us how blacks were the only Americans who had to don uniforms and go to war in order to claim what was for all others a natural birthright.

Why blacks displayed such loyalty is not easily explained. Listen to Capt. David J. Williams II, a young, white company commander of the World War II 761st Tank Battalion, the first black armored combat unit in the U.S. Army. "These guys were better than heroes because they weren't supposed to be able to fight, and they were treated worse than lepers. I can tell you, it took a rare sort of character to go out there and do what they did. I used to ask myself, why the hell should these guys fight? Why?"

I have my own partial explanations. In part, my thinking goes back to something that Hodding Carter, Jr., the longtime editor of the Greenville, Mississippi, *Delta Democrat-Times* and perhaps the most courageous editor in Mississippi at mid-century, told me when I was a twenty-one-year-old reporter. We had been sitting at his house in Greenville late one night, and he had begun a rumination on what he considered the amazing shrewdness and resilience of black Americans. Because of their long, hard journey in America, they had become involuntarily astute and wise, he thought. Far too many people had come along and promised them too much over the years, and then had departed without much in the way of fulfillment of those promises. As such they had become very good judges of quality, wary of anyone promising too much too quickly. Everything that works for them, they had decided long ago, must be earned, and earned twice over. They were particularly suspicious of promises from strangers who did not share their hard condition.

In turn, I was reminded of something that Mike Heningburg told me, much later, when I was working on a magazine article about Colin Powell, when Powell was Chairman of the Joint Chiefs of Staff. Heningburg, also black, became pals with Powell when they were both young Army officers in the early sixties; Heningburg too had a highly successful Army career. The young black officers of their era, when things were still extremely difficult, were bonded together by two things, Heningburg told me. The first and most obvious was that they were black in a white man's world. The second was that all of them had had drummed into them by their parents that if they were to succeed in this difficult world, they had to be better, much better, than any white person. If that is true, and I think it is, we have here a partial explanation of this remarkable story of black loyalty; for the military in all times, whatever its own momentary prejudices, offers codes and standards and rules that mark those in uniform as men and citizens.

That loyalty, often so poorly deserved by those running the country, has sometimes proven to be, as Buckley shows in this remarkable book, a source of bitter awareness of the uses of adversity—as well as strength, albeit more often than not a strength born of sorrow. It has often given blacks, in lieu of direct improvement in their own condition, an inner strength as well as an odd faith that somehow, eventually, there would be a better day for those who came after them. In the words of one of our best anthems, "America the Beautiful," this story is about the "patriot dream that sees beyond the years."

All of this has been, over the torturous years, an amazing story. *American Patriots* is a dazzling mosaic of American patriotism, a compelling account of this unique story of honor and courage.

Contents

Introduction

As a World War II child, I was indelibly marked with a sense of American history as a home to heroes. The first books I remember reading are the Ingri and Edgar D'Aulaire lives of George Washington and Abraham Lincoln; I can still conjure up images of little George in his wig and frock coat, and young Abe studying by candlelight. The glorification of America's heroic past was part of the World War II propaganda effort. It was easy to contrast the founding fathers of democracy with the founding fathers of Axis dictatorships.

I was patriotic to the core. I knew the hymn of every armed service and had my own victory garden (I remember radishes). My great-uncle John Burke Horne was a sergeant in the Army, where my mother, his niece Lena, sang for GIs. Uncle Burke was already a hero to me because he was engaged to my personal military role model, Lieutenant Harriet Pickens, a Navy Wave, dazzling in her white dress uniform. I had no idea then that Uncle Burke was a sergeant in the *segregated* Army or that Harriet was the first *black* Wave; but I knew that I wanted the war to last long enough for me to wear the uniform. Like any other World War II child, I aspired to heroism. I also equated victory with virtue. I had no idea then that there were wartime race riots in northern cities, often over black war workers. And I had no idea that black GIs often sat behind German prisoners of war at United Service Organizations shows, although my mother was banned from the USO for refusing to sing at such an event.

Later on, when I began to research *The Hornes,* a family history, I found another hero, Burke's much older brother Errol. The oldest of four brothers and a city boy, despite the farm at the end of the street (a token of Brooklyn's bucolic roots), Errol was the product of an integrated neighborhood as well as an integrated education. There was no military tradition in the family, but somehow he decided to make a career in the Army, then based in the faraway vastness of the West, home of the 9th and 10th Cavalries and 24th and 25th Infantries: the legendary Buffalo Soldier Regiments.

Always a superb athlete, Errol was taught to ride and shoot by old Indian-fighters at Fort Huachuca, in the Arizona desert. Among the very few nonsegregated activities in the Army, all-unit marksmanship and riding competitions regularly awarded top prizes to blacks. By 1916, handsome twenty-six-year-old Sergeant Horne was at the top of his profession. (In those days, sergeant was the highest rank to which a black soldier could aspire.) But Errol was about to be promoted. My mother always remembered being told that Uncle Errol had chased Pancho Villa into Mexico.

In March 1916, a punitive expedition of some five thousand U.S. Army troops under the command of Brigadier General John J. Pershing crossed the Rio Grande, pursuing Pancho Villa in what was the fourth Mexican Revolution since 1910. Among those seeking the bandit-revolutionary, and revenge for the seven soldiers killed in his raid on Columbus, New Mexico, were members of the black, Texas-based 24th Infantry and 10th Cavalry Regiments: heroes of the Indian Wars, the Spanish-American War of 1898, and the Philippine Insurrection of 1899–1906. Pershing's strategy was to rapidly move three columns southward. Two of the three columns were made up of squadrons of the 10th Cavalry, an indication of Pershing's high regard for the black cavalry troops he had led in the Spanish-American War.

In April, sounding familiar bugle calls of help on the way, Major Charles Young and members of the 10th Cavalry raced to the rescue of a large ambushed unit of the white 13th Cavalry at Santa Cruz de Villegas. "By God, Young, I could kiss every black face out there," Major Frank Tompkins said to his 10th Cavalry counterpart. "If you want," Young said, "you may start with me."[1] Villa's incursion made national heroes of the 10th and of one of its few black officers, the forty-two-year-old Major Young, the third black graduate of West Point.

War with Mexico was averted only by America's entry into the First World War. Because of Mexico, Pershing (who owed his nickname, Black Jack, to the color of his troops) was promoted to major general and named chief of the American Expeditionary Forces in France. Major Young, a hero of the Philippine Insurrection as well as of the pursuit of Villa, was promoted to lieutenant colonel—but then declared physically unfit for further combat and retired from active duty. The reason was simple: if Young went to France as a full colonel, he might come back home as a brigadier. And the American military would never countenance a black general. To prove his fitness, Young mounted his cavalry horse, Charlie, for a nonstop "Pony Express" dash from Wilberforce University in Ohio to the Department of the Army in Washington. The Army was forced to surrender, more or less. Young was promoted to full colonel—but not recalled to active duty until the last week of the war.

While the Mexican campaign meant the end of Charles Young's career, it was a breakthrough and a new beginning for Sergeant Errol Horne. Junior officers were needed for the new black labor divisions scheduled to be sent to France, and Errol was called to the First World War as a second lieutenant. He got his lieutenant's bars and, at almost the same time, married a lovely young woman named Lottie. He took her picture sometime in 1917 before setting off for active duty. His shadow holding the box camera is clearly visible, as Lottie poses in a white middy dress that seems almost translucent in the harsh glare of the desert sunlight.

Within a year, twenty-eight-year-old Lieutenant Horne was dead, a victim of the influenza pandemic that swept the ranks of the American Expeditionary Forces and much of the world in the winter of 1918. "Everything possible was done for him, and he was buried with every military honor, but O, it is a deep, deep sorrow," my great-grandmother wrote in a black-bordered note to a cousin. "Am here in the country trying to rest mind and body," she said. "I have Lottie with me and she is a wreck." It is impossible to know how much of the war Errol actually saw: his records were among those destroyed in the tragic 1973 fire in the U.S. Army archives.

* * *

American history is full of heroes. For a long time, it seemed that none of them were black. Yet there have been black heroes from the beginning; they were simply cut out of the picture. What do heroes do? They fight dragons. And blacks have been fighting the dragons of racism since the country began. One of their most powerful weapons, I learned, was military service. In going to war, black men and women believed they could both better their own lives and make their country true to its own best promise.

I discovered Crispus Attucks, the first black hero of the Revolution, in my World War II childhood when our propaganda effort (in contrast to the Axis powers) celebrated multicultural heroes. For a long time, I assumed that Crispus Attucks was the only black hero of the Revolution. Researching this book I found a world of black heroes, many connected to the most treasured and sacrosanct images of the Revolution. All the heroes of the Revolution, white and black, were founders of our nation.

Midway through the Revolutionary War, some 15 percent of the Continental Army was black. They "mix, march, mess and sleep with the Whites," wrote the eighteenth-century historian William Smith of the integrated American ranks. Only half-disapproving, Washington ultimately called his army a "mixed multitude." It would be the last "mixed multitude" for 175 years, until the Korean War.

Prince Estabrook, a Massachusetts slave and militiaman, stood with his musket on Lexington Green in April 1775 on America's "first glorious morning." Later that morning he was wounded at Concord Bridge, where the "shot heard round the world" was fired. In May, Barzillai Lew, a free Massachusetts cooper, was one of Ethan Allen's Green Mountain Boys at Ticonderoga, the first American victory of the war. In June, Lew, who was also a fifer-drummer, kept American spirits lively at Bunker Hill by playing "Yankee Doodle." In the winter of 1776, "the times that try men's souls," Prince Whipple, a New Hampshire slave, was an oarsman in Washington's boat at the crossing of the Delaware. A few days later at Princeton, Primus Hall, son of Prince Hall, a free Boston tanner who supplied leather drumheads to the Continental Army, single-handedly captured a number of British soldiers. A Connecticut slave, Nero Hawley, was one of the starving, ragged band who spent the terrible winter of 1777–1778 with Washington at Valley Forge. In June 1778, in hundred-degree heat (eased only by "Molly Pitcher's" jugs of water), Adam Pierce, a free New Jersey militiaman, was victorious with Washington at Monmouth Court House. The only all-black regiment of the war, the 1st Rhode Island, were heroes of the Battle of Newport in August. In the summer of 1779, Pompey Lamb, a New York slave, was key to General "Mad" Anthony Wayne's victory at Stony Point. At the British surrender at Yorktown in October 1781, which essentially marked the end of the war, James, a Virginia slave, was Lafayette's spy—astonishing the British general Cornwallis, who thought he was a British spy. James won his freedom at Yorktown and renamed himself James Lafayette in honor of the man who later wrote, "I would never have drawn my sword in the cause of America if I could have conceived that thereby I was helping to found a nation of slaves."

"In considering the services of the Colored Patriots of the Revolution," wrote Harriet Beecher Stowe in her preface to William Cooper Nell's *Colored Patriots of the American Revolution,* published in 1855, "we are to reflect upon them as far more magnanimous, because rendered to a nation which did not acknowledge them as citizens and equals . . . but for a land which had enslaved them, and whose laws, even in freedom, oftener oppressed than protected. Bravery, under such circumstances, has a peculiar beauty and merit."

* * *

The Emancipation Proclamation of January 1, 1863, brought the first black division into the Civil War, the United States Colored Troops, or USCT, which took part in the costly but victorious battles for Vicksburg and Richmond. In June, at Milliken's Bend outside Vicksburg, the 5th USCT Heavy Artillery lost 45 percent of its men—the highest proportion of deaths suffered by a single regiment in the course of the war. Emancipation also brought the first regiment of free northern blacks: the 54th Massachusetts (subject of the film *Glory*), who were essentially sacrificed in July 1863 at Fort Wagner, in South Carolina. Lewis and Charles Douglass, the two sons of Frederick Douglass, fought with the 54th at Fort Wagner, as did Sergeant William H. Carney, a New Bedford seaman in civilian life, who became the first black soldier to win the new Congressional Medal of Honor. Zimri Lew, grandson of the Revolutionary veteran Barzillai Lew, fought in the 55th Massachusetts, the 54th's sister regiment, at the final siege of Charleston in May 1865. By the end of the war, blacks would make up 10 to 12 percent of the Union Army.

At its peak in the 1870s and early 1880s, the post–Civil War period of Reconstruction was a golden age for American blacks as well as poor southern whites. The promise of freedom was finally being fulfilled. Thanks to military protection, southern blacks participated in state and local government and elected black senators and representatives to Congress. Contrary to southern propaganda, most black congressmen were either lawyers or Civil War veterans, like Captain Robert Smalls, who became a U.S. representative from South Carolina.

Civil War veterans also formed the nucleus of four new black regiments, the 9th and 10th Cavalries and the 24th and 25th Infantries, part of the New Army created in 1866 to tame the West. One out of every five western soldiers was black. The mission of western regiments, white and black, was to tame whatever stood in the way of "progress" and "civilization," from flora and fauna to native Indians. A fierce two-day battle in Kansas in 1867 saw some eight hundred Cheyenne defeated by ninety troopers of the 10th Cavalry, which lost only three men. The Cheyenne, who prized black scalps, called them Buffalo Soldiers, for an animal they considered sacred. Sergeant Emanuel Stance of the 9th Cavalry became the first black winner of the Medal of Honor in the Indian Wars when his detachment of ten troopers drove off some thirty Kickapoos in Texas in 1870.

Between 1870 and 1877, eight blacks were admitted to West Point; only one, Lieutenant Henry O. Flipper, would graduate. Like all black cadets, Flipper was ostracized and undermined at almost every turn. But he believed in the officer code, and deflected his tormentors with great dignity and gentlemanly forbearance. Flipper was, in fact, an ideal cadet. Crediting Academy instructors with surprising fairness, he managed to so impress his fellow engineering students that he was never "silenced" in the classroom. By the time of his graduation in June 1877, Flipper was a national celebrity. General Sherman himself led the applause when America's first black officer received his diploma. After graduation, Flipper went to the Indian Wars, where he was victorious against Apaches. In 1881, betrayed by a combination of racism and jealousy, he was expelled by the Army on false charges of embezzlement. It would take almost a hundred years for his name to be cleared, and for Lieutenant Flipper to return to his rightful place in military history.

Crispus Attucks and the black revolutionaries, the 54th Massachusetts in the Civil War, and the Buffalo Soldiers were all celebrated in the nineteenth century. But by the early twentieth century they were expunged from textbooks and erased from history. Now black soldiers were replaced with images of the happy slave, Reconstruction was vilified, and, according to Frances FitzGerald's admirable *America Revised,* textbooks used for sixty years in American public schools even questioned the value of the Fourteenth Amendment. W.E.B. Du Bois called southern revisionism "one of the most stupendous efforts the world ever saw to discredit human beings, an effort involving universities, history, social life and religion." With revisionism, the military exploits of blacks in the Revolution, the War of 1812, the Civil War, and the Indian Wars were buried and consigned to obscurity.

* * *

My great-grandparents were children of Reconstruction. Cora Calhoun and her younger sister, Lena (my mother's namesake), were born in Atlanta, the daughters of Moses Calhoun, a domestic slave who prospered in freedom as the owner of a grocery-catering establishment. The Calhoun sisters attended new schools created to foster an educated black middle class in the South. Cora went to Atlanta University and Lena to Fisk, where her classmate W.E.B. Du Bois fell hopelessly in love with her. Cora, Lena, and "Willie" were members of what Du Bois later called the Talented Tenth.

By the time handsome, twice-widowed Edwin Horn married young Cora Calhoun in 1887, he had been principal of an Indianapolis "colored" school and had cofounded the *Indianapolis World,* a long-lived black weekly. He had twice been a delegate to the Republican National Convention: in 1880 and 1884. When Indiana's favorite son, Benjamin Harrison, was elected president in 1888, Edwin was short-listed for the position of recorder of deeds of Washington, D.C.

The U.S. Supreme Court decision in *Plessy v. Ferguson* (1896) marked the end of Republican influence in the South. *Plessy* solidified white supremacy and legitimized the exclusionary race laws known collectively, after a popular minstrel song, as Jim Crow laws. Cora and Edwin, who had moved to Tennessee, now moved their growing family of sons to New York. Like any refugee, Edwin reinvented himself. He added an "e" to Horn, and became a Democrat, doing such excellent political work for Tammany Hall that he was appointed an inspector in the Brooklyn fire department, unheard of for a "colored" man (or even, it was said, a Protestant). Edwin's greatest political moment came in the 1910 election, when his anti–Theodore Roosevelt pamphlets convinced New York blacks to vote Democratic for the first time in history. Among other things, the pamphlets called for a black National Guard regiment.

The 369th Regiment, the eventual outgrowth of Edwin Horne's political demand, became the most decorated American unit of World War I. Two soldiers from the regiment, Sergeant Henry Johnson and Private Needham Roberts, were the first American enlisted men to win the Croix de Guerre. The 369th fought in French uniforms under the French flag because President Woodrow Wilson and former Buffalo Soldier commander Black Jack Pershing, who headed the American Expeditionary Forces, did not want blacks to bear arms for America.

The 369th won French hearts, as well as gratitude, when its famous Regimental Band, led by the black recording star Lieutenant James Reese Europe, toured the devastated country with America's new gift of jazz. William Layton, whom I met in 1990, was a seventeen-year-old boy bugler in the 369th Band. He was gassed in the Meuse-Argonne offensive and won the Croix de Guerre for battlefield valor; five of his children served in the Second World War.

One of the most remarkable American heroes of World War I, Eugene Bullard, ran away from home in Georgia at the age of eight to make his way to France. At the onset of war (he was then a boxer in Paris) he volunteered for a special French Foreign Legion battalion for foreigners. Sent to the Somme, he joined the unofficial Christmas cease-fire of 1914 when both sides stopped, infuriating their commanding officers, to sing carols. By the spring of 1915, Bullard's special battalion was essentially wiped out and he joined the French army. In February 1916 he went to Verdun, where he received two wounds and two medals: the Croix de Guerre and the Médaille Militaire. Out of the infantry with a leg wound, he learned to fly on a bet. In November 1917 he joined the French flying corps, and later that month, making a pass at the Red Baron's Flying Circus, got a reported kill. Some ten days after the kill, Bullard, a sergeant, was accused of striking an officer. He had no idea that the soldier in the troop truck whom he had pulled off and punched for kicking him and saying "No room for your kind" was a lieutenant. He was dismissed from the Air Corps, but escaped court-martial because of his combat record.

Still in France in May 1940, where he doubled as a nightclub host and spy for the Deuxième Bureau, he joined his old Verdun regiment at Orléans for a last stand against the Germans. Bullard was wounded again and decorated in his second war. Now he fled back to America via Lisbon. He was working as an elevator man in New York City in 1959 when he was made a Knight of the Legion of Honor and was finally discovered by the newspapers of his native land.

Although the U.S. government was officially neutral in Ethiopia and the Spanish Civil War, most American blacks were not. When fascist Italy invaded Ethiopia, blacks poured into the streets of every major northern city. Raising funds and medical supplies for Ethiopia became a priority for blacks, who saw no way of getting there but were determined to fight Fascism, which they regarded as an international form of Jim Crow. A year later, when General Franco's armies attacked the new socialist Spanish Republic, black Americans, recruited by the Communist Party, volunteered to fight for Spain. Many who joined the integrated Abraham Lincoln Brigade were Communists, including a cadre of black World War I veterans who won leadership positions. Vaughn Love, godson of Sergeant Henry Johnson, the first American winner of the Croix de Guerre, went to Spain because he considered Fascism to be the "enemy of all black aspirations."[2] James Yates, who ran away as a teenager from a near lynching in Mississippi to join the Harlem Communist Party, collected medical supplies for Ethiopia with Salaria Kee, a young black nurse from Harlem Hospital. In Spain Yates was wounded after volunteering to drive a truck for the German Republican brigade when all their drivers were killed. Salaria Kee, the only black female volunteer in Spain, became an enormous propaganda asset as a nurse for the short-lived Republic. James Peck, a black American who was not permitted to fly in his own country, joined the Republican air force, becoming one of three American aces in Spain and a friend of Ernest Hemingway.

Although not an American war, the Spanish Civil War was the first war since the Revolution in which black and white Americans fought side by side as equals. It was the first war, ever, in which white Americans were led into battle by a black commander: Captain Oliver Law, a veteran of the Buffalo Soldier 24th Infantry. During the McCarthy era in the 1950s, decorated veterans of World War II who also fought in Spain were, until the courts ruled in their favor, denied burial in Arlington National Cemetery.

* * *

World War II was even more rigidly segregated than World War I. In neither war were any blacks awarded the Medal of Honor (although there were black honorees in every war before and after). But World War II was nevertheless a war of enormous black firsts: fighter pilots, female soldiers and sailors, armored combat personnel, paratroopers, Navy officers and U.S. Marines. I met and became friends with some of these pioneers as they shared stories with me of their fifty-years-younger selves.

The 332nd Fighter Squadron, the first black Army Air Force unit, known as the Tuskegee Airmen for their Alabama training base, was led by Colonel Benjamin O. Davis, Jr., the son of America's first black general and the most celebrated black West Point graduate since Lieutenant Flipper. Captain Lee Archer, with five victories, was the first black "Ace."

In February 1945, Major Charity Adams, a black graduate of the first class of the new Women's Army Corps (which, unlike the male Army, had integrated training), was commanding officer of the "Six Triple Eight" Central Postal Directory Battalion. With one of the most important jobs in the war in terms of morale, the 6888 redirected all "V-Mail" for Europe. Sallie Smith joined the WACs halfway through college because they sounded "exciting" and she wanted to be near her boyfriend in Italy. In Birmingham, England, in 1945, civilian aides called her "Sergeant Sallie." Back home, she returned to college on the GI Bill and became the first black woman to receive a master's degree from the University of West Virginia.

In February 1945, Gene Doughty, a member of the first black Marine Corps unit, the Montford Point Marines, was acting platoon sergeant in the 8th Ammunition Company, on his way to the "hellish" landscape of Iwo Jima. In the single fiercest Pacific contest, lasting more than a month, Doughty saw the American flag raised on Mount Suribachi, overcame a night attack by Japanese who sprang from underground caves, and celebrated his twenty-first birthday.

Most Americans are unaware that the very first hero of World War II was Dorie Miller, a Navy messman at Pearl Harbor who became the first black winner of the Navy Cross, and you would never know from Hollywood that there were black GIs at Normandy Beach. The Spanish Civil War veteran Vaughn Love landed on D-Day with the Quartermaster Corps, and New York Supreme Court Justice Bruce M. Wright, then a twenty-five-year-old poet and infantry medic, won a Purple Heart at Normandy. Less than a year later, he won a Bronze Star, and another Purple Heart, in the Battle of the Bulge. On November 2, 1944, having just arrived in France's Saar Basin with the black 761st Tank Battalion, Private E. G. McConnell was personally exhorted by General George S. Patton to "shoot every damn thing you see." Three weeks later McConnell earned a Purple Heart. Between March and May 1945, the 761st, spearheading the Third Army, cracked the Siegfried Line and, crossing the Danube, took over 100,000 German prisoners, liberated a concentration camp, and beat the Red Army into Austria.

* * *

In 1948, President Harry Truman, a veteran of the First World War, integrated the armed forces by executive order, much to the displeasure of most of the military brass, including General Eisenhower. Truman's motives were partly humanitarian (he was appalled by the rampant lynchings of black veterans in the postwar South) and partly political. Despite its presidential seal, the integration process was slow. Thus the Korean War, which began in June 1950 and ended in July 1953, opened as a segregated war.

In August 1950, Private First Class William H. Thompson of the 24th Infantry became the first GI to win the Medal of Honor in Korea and the first black Medal of Honor winner since the Spanish-American War. In June of the following year, Sergeant Cornelius H. Charlton became the 24th Infantry's second Medal of Honor winner. By October, however, the regiment had been accused of wholesale cowardice and deactivated. The sad end of the once-proud Buffalo Soldier regiment was seen by many as the inevitable result of an immoral and unjust system. But the end of the 24th also marked the birth of the integrated military.

Halfway through, the Korean War became the first officially integrated war since the Revolution. Lieutenant Ellison C. Wynn of the 9th Infantry, the first integrated regiment in Korea, was one of the few black officers to win a Distinguished Service Cross. The World War II pilot Major Daniel "Chappie" James (who became the first black four-star general) was one of the illustrious new fighter jocks of the integrated Air Force.

Reflecting the thinking of many younger combat officers that military segregation was inefficient as well as unfair, President John F. Kennedy, a World War II Navy veteran, used executive orders to destroy the last traces of institutionalized military racism. His Committee on Equal Opportunity in the Armed Forces issued the revolutionary directive that military commanders must oppose discriminatory practices against military personnel both on and off base. It came just in time for Vietnam, the first war since the Revolution in which blacks and whites served together from the outset as equals under the American flag.

There were really two Vietnams. Those who were there in the early 1960s, products of Eisenhower social moderation as well as Kennedy social justice, were mostly volunteers and full of patriotic idealism. My friend Colonel John Cash, then a young captain in the 1st Battalion of the 7th Cavalry and one of the few black company commanders in the division, recalled Vietnam in 1965 as a time of "tremendous" military morale and a racial atmosphere that was "sweetness and light." Heroism in the 1965 Army seemed marked by a spirit of selflessness. In October, eighteen-year-old Private First Class Milton L. Olive became Vietnam's first black Medal of Honor winner when he saved the lives of fellow 173rd Airborne Brigade soldiers by falling on a live grenade and absorbing the blast with his body. That same month, Colonel Fred V. Cherry, who had been inspired by the Tuskegee Airmen, was shot down over North Vietnam to become the first black prisoner at the "Hanoi Hilton." He spent eight years, tortured twice a day for many of those years, as a POW.

The first great Vietnam battle, in November 1965 at Ia Drang, marked the beginning of the end of U.S. idealism. It was a horrifically costly American victory that caused many younger officers to question the efficacy and direction of the war and its leadership. Nonetheless, selfless heroism continued to be the rule. A twenty-four-year-old combat medic, Calvin Bouknight, a conscientious objector who refused to carry a weapon, sacrificed his life by going to the aid of wounded men in the midst of a terrifying firefight. Captain George Forrest, another Ia Drang hero, made a six-hundred-yard football-trained dash through a gauntlet of enemy fire to form his men into a defensive perimeter—thereby saving most of his company, while other companies around him were slaughtered. He won a Silver Star. Some thirty years later, Forrest told me that Ia Drang was the beginning of both his "guilt" and his disillusion about a war that "turned warriors into bounty hunters."

By 1968, the war in Vietnam had changed, and the American soldier had, too. High morale and racial "sweetness and light" had been swept aside in a climate of political assassinations, civil rights martyrdoms, urban riots, and violent war protests. As the streets of America changed, so did the jungles of Vietnam, now infected by drugs, racial conflicts, and crimes like the massacre at My Lai. There was a new black GI: an angry draftee who was, above all, "black"—which, again, did not preclude heroism.

Duery Felton was drafted in November 1968. Emulating his father, who was a veteran of World War II, he tried to enlist in the Navy but was rejected because of a heart murmur and joined the Army instead. As a radio operator he never saw the men in the field, but he felt as if they were part of his family. In December, in Cambodia, where Americans were not supposed to be, he was nearly crushed by an American tank. Seriously wounded, he was sent home, where he never wore his uniform in the streets and found that the only people he wanted to see were other vets. In 1989, he became curator of the Vietnam Veterans Memorial Collection, overseeing the thousands of objects left by visitors at the Wall.

Wayne Smith enlisted in 1968 at eighteen, to become a combat medic. He came to hate the war and became a conscientious objector, but extended his tour anyway because he wanted to continue to help the men. "No one wanted to die alone in Vietnam," he told me. "The men always said, 'Doc, stay with me.' " After the war he became executive director of the Justice Project, a veterans' advocacy organization.

* * *

Vietnam was the most unpopular war in American history, with social ramifications far beyond its time span. It was also America's first loss. But out of it came the military "miracle." For by the early 1970s, the Army understood that it could afford no more Vietnam-style breakdowns and no more losing wars. It was determined to reshape itself, as well as its image, on the basis of that understanding. There would be no more angry draftees, because the new American military would be all-volunteer. Drug use was to be eradicated, and so was all overt racism. Stressing cohesion, inclusion, and diversity, the armed forces opened doors for women, as well as for black men. The New Army solved the problems of diversity through a strict code of behavior and a refusal to see any color but Army green. The bottom line was respect for the uniform, whoever was wearing it. The Army was interested in changing behavior, not minds. The New Army reached its apogee in President George Bush's 1990 war in the Persian Gulf, the first American war whose chief military leader was black and whose recognized heroes came in all colors and both sexes.

With the Gulf War, America found a new hero. General Colin L. Powell, the first black chairman of the Joint Chiefs of Staff, was both a combat officer of the early Eisenhower–Kennedy era Vietnam and one of the fathers of the New Army. His appointment as chairman was symbolic on several levels: as the culmination of President Truman's forty-year-old executive order; as the ultimate embodiment of the military's commitment to reshape itself; and as the furthest extension of the New Army's recruitment call, "Be All You Can Be." Powell, who had ranked first in nearly every Army test of skills since he was seventeen, was more Army green than black, although he clearly saw himself as indebted to the black officers who had struggled through the system before him. In 2001, he was chosen by President George W. Bush as the first black secretary of state in American history.

Once one of the most racist public institutions in America, the military came to afford blacks personal, cultural, and social validity far above the American norm. Pursuing excellence as well as heroism, they were integrated within themselves and the larger community because of their military experience. It is always easy to quarrel with military aims, but the military ethos, with its appeal to integrity, discipline, loyalty, selfless service, personal courage, honor, and respect, is powerfully compelling. Its impact on the men and women who served in the armed forces has reached far beyond the battlefield. "All the hunters, gatherers, defenders, knights, samurais and swordsmen," wrote the Franciscan priest Richard Rohr, "are, in fact, telling us something good about focus, determination, and courage for the common good."[3]

"My military career gave me the ability to search out a problem," said William DeFossett of the 369th Regiment, which went to the Pacific in World War II. "It taught me how to plan, how to examine things, when to improve upon them. It taught me about teamwork, physical fitness—pride." "Civilians don't understand the meaning of leadership," said Gene Doughty, a veteran of Iwo Jima. "They don't understand human behavior and how to alter it to accomplish the mission." Doughty said that he learned "courage, poise, self-confidence, and self-discipline" in the Marine Corps. Major Flossie Satcher, an admittedly "scared" young lieutenant in Operation Desert Storm, told me that her military experience had made her "braver"; she also believed that Army values were not unlike those instilled by her mother.

* * *

It took me fourteen years to research and write this book, and in the course of those years I met some extraordinary people. I wanted to know how they felt about being a part of history. I wanted to know what made them risk their lives for their country, often at a time when they were not accepted as full American citizens. I wanted to know where they found their courage and how military service had affected the rest of their lives. Finally, I wanted to know what their experiences were, to hear and record their stories. Every veteran I met, no matter what age, remembered his or her war as if it were yesterday.

Writing this book at a time when many black Americans had become Afrocentric, I found myself becoming America-centric. Learning about fourteenth-century Africa is good; but showing blacks their place in American history is vital. There are spiritual ancestors at home, whom most Americans have been deprived of knowing. "In self-segregation," wrote Albert Murray in *The Omni-Americans,* modern blacks "capitulate too easily to a con game which their ancestors never fell for, and they surrender their birthright to the propagandists of white supremacy, as if it were of no value whatsoever, as if one could exercise the right of redress without first claiming one's constitutional identity as a citizen!"[4] When we realize how many fought and died for the right to a constitutional identity, we see that these are the roots that matter.

* * *

My focus in writing this book has been on people: how America's wars affected black Americans both on and off the battlefield and how black Americans participated in America's history. Research, as well as the many veterans I spoke to, taught me that this sense of making history carried over into civilian life. From the Revolution onward, black veterans have effected change in their communities, usually by means of civic leadership, community service, or civil rights activism. The military made a difference in people's lives, and the differences were reflected in society.

Vast numbers of soldiers throughout history have been defeated by war and carried its scars for the rest of their lives, but most of the veterans I spoke to seem to have valued their experiences. No matter how terrible, these were seen either as life lessons learned or as a fair contribution to the common good. Their heroism belongs as much to white Americans as to blacks.

AMERICAN PATRIOTS

1 The Revolution

SLAVERY AND INDEPENDENCE

I served in the Revolution, in General Washington's army. . . . I have stood in battle, where balls, like hail, were flying all around me. The man standing next to me was shot by my side—his blood spouted upon my clothes, which I wore for weeks. My nearest blood, except that which runs in my veins, was shed for liberty. My only brother was shot dead instantly in the Revolution. Liberty is dear to my heart—I cannot endure the thought, that my countrymen should be slaves.[1]

—*"Dr. Harris," a black Revolutionary veteran, in an address to the Congregational and Presbyterian Anti-Slavery Society of Francestown, New Hampshire, 1842*

Crispus Attucks: The First Martyr of the Revolution

BLOODY MASSACRE," screamed the March 12, 1770, issue of the *Massachusetts Gazette,* Paul Revere's four-color illustrated broadsheet, depicting redcoats with muskets firing into a crowd of well-dressed Boston citizens. Four victims lie bloodied on the ground. One, closest to the soldiers, the only one dressed in rough seaman clothes instead of a waistcoat and three-cornered hat, lies in the center foreground in a pool of blood. "The unhappy Sufferers," Revere wrote, were "Sam'l Gray, Sam'l Maverick, James Caldwell, Crispus Attucks Killed." (Revere omitted Patrick Carr, an Irish leather worker, who was also killed.) Gray was a rope maker, Maverick an apprentice joiner, Caldwell a ship's mate; the seaman Attucks, "killed on the Spot, two Balls entering his Breast," was described as "born in Framingham, but lately belonging to New Providence [the Bahamas]." The victims would lie in state in Faneuil Hall. "All the Bells tolled a solemn Peal" when they were buried together in one vault "in the middle burying-ground."[2]

Calling himself Michael Johnson, Attucks, the son of an African father and a Massachusetts Natick Indian mother, had spent the past twenty years at sea, having run away to escape slavery.[3] Ten pounds' reward had been offered in 1750 by Deacon William Brown of Framingham for the return of "a Molatto Fellow, about 27 years of age, named Crispas, 6 Feet two Inches high, short, curl'd Hair, his Knees nearer together than common: had on a light colour'd Bearskin coat."[4] In port in Boston on the night of March 5, 1770, Attucks was in a King Street tavern when an alarm bell was heard from the street's British sentry. When, leading a stick- and bat-wielding gang from the tavern, he discovered that the sentry was under "attack" only from snowball-throwing boys, he and his mob immediately took the side of the boys against the "Lobster Backs"—using heavy sticks instead of snowballs. Witnesses said that Attucks, striking the first blow, caused arriving British soldiers to open fire and hit eleven civilians—five of whom, including Attucks, were killed.

At the cost of public scorn (and to cover up his cousin Samuel Adams's role in inciting riots), the Boston lawyer John Adams, a radical "Son of Liberty" who disapproved of violence, defended the British soldiers. Contradicting Paul Revere's presentation of the dead as respectable Bostonians, Adams declared that Attucks had been the leader of a "motley rabble of saucy boys, negroes and molattoes, Irish teagues and outlandish jack tarrs."[5] The merchant John Hancock also accused Attucks of provoking the so-called "Boston Massacre," but from a different point of view. "Who set the example of guns?" Hancock asked later. "Who taught the British soldier that he might be defeated? Who dared look into his eyes? I place, therefore, this Crispus Attucks in the foremost rank of the men that dared."[6] The British soldiers were acquitted, but Americans won the propaganda battle. Attucks and his companions became the first popular martyrs of the Revolution.

"You will hear from Us with Astonishment," read an anonymous letter to Governor Thomas Hutchinson in 1773, which John Adams copied in his diary. "You ought to hear from Us with Horror. You are chargeable before God and Man, with our Blood— The Soldiers were but passive Instruments. . . . You acted, cooly, deliberately, with all that premeditated Malice, not against Us in particular but against the People in general. . . . You will hear further from us hereafter."[7] It was signed "Crispus Attucks"—a new symbol of resistance.

* * *

On the eve of the Revolution, the black population of the British North American colonies was 500,000, out of a total population of 2,600,000.[8] Only a fraction of that population went to war. Some five thousand blacks served under George Washington, and about a thousand, mostly Southern runaways, fought for George III.[9] Although the percentage of the black population who served was small, by 1779 as many as one in seven members of Washington's never very large army were black. According to the historian Thomas Fleming, the Continental Line was "more integrated than any American force except the armies that fought in the Vietnam and Gulf Wars."[10]

THE GREAT AMERICAN "FIG TREE"

At the end of the French and Indian Wars, Britain controlled North America from the Atlantic to the Mississippi, as well as most of the West Indies. It had reached the zenith of its empire just as the colonies were beginning to have a sense of nationhood. "Cast your eyes with me a little over this globe to view the deplorable state of your fellow creatures in other countries," wrote the Philadelphia lawyer John Dickinson in 1768. "In Russia, Poland, Bohemia, Hungary, and many parts of Germany there is no such thing as free-holders. . . . But how different is the case amongst us. We enjoy an unprecarious property, and every man may freely taste the fruits of his own labors under his vine and under his fig tree."[11]

The debt Britain had incurred in the Seven Years' War ensured taxation of the colonies and threatened life under the idyllic American fig tree. In British eyes, the American colonies existed only for the benefit of the mother country, but Americans saw any form of taxation as slavery. New England's objections to the Sugar Act, the Stamp Act, and all the other unpopular acts fueled the fires of independence. John Adams and his failed businessman cousin Samuel, leading radicals in the Continental Congress, were outspoken "Sons of Liberty," a term coined in the British Parliament in 1765 to describe American Stamp Act protestors. Samuel Adams created the Committees of Correspondence, an underground movement with branches springing up throughout New England, to encourage resistance against the British.

The fires of independence were fueled among blacks as well as whites. A Massachusetts petition of 1773 from "a Grate Number of Blacks . . . who . . . are held in a state of slavery within the bowels of a free and Christian Country" asked for freedom and "some part of the unimproved land, belonging to the province, for a settlement, that each of us may there sit down quietly under his own fig tree."[12]

Quaker Philadelphia was the heart of early eighteenth-century abolitionism. Massachusetts Puritans preached against slavery, but only Quakers argued for justice and equality for blacks on every level of life. In 1727, the twenty-one-year-old Philadelphia printer Benjamin Franklin started a discussion group, the Junto, in which antislavery ideals figured large. Two years later he printed, anonymously, the first of his many antislavery tracts. "A Caution and a Warning to Great Britain and Her Colonies," a pamphlet published in 1766 by a Philadelphia Quaker named Anthony Benezet, was widely circulated. "How many of those who distinguish themselves as Advocates of Liberty remain insensible," he wrote, "to the treatment of thousands and tens of thousands of our fellow men, who . . . are at this very time kept in the most deplorable state of slavery." Meanwhile, Boston's James Otis, another outspoken opponent of Britain's "Intolerable Acts," wrote: "The colonists are by the law of nature free born, as indeed are all men, white or black."

The upper South seemed to agree with the North that slavery would eventually be abandoned, and in the meantime ameliorated. In 1762, George Washington told his new overseer to "take all necessary and proper care of the Negroes, using them with proper humanity and discretion."[13] Young Thomas Jefferson's first legislative action in the 1769 Virginia House of Burgesses was an emancipation measure.[14] With so many important advocates, many believed that the new American nation would be free.

Slavery was abolished in the British Isles in 1772. The decision resulted from the suit of one slave, James Somerset, who ran away from his American master in England. Somerset's lawyer, the British abolitionist Granville Sharp, won the case by arguing that since no positive law creating slavery existed in England, it could not be practiced there. Three days after the judgment, a group of two hundred blacks "with their ladies" held a public entertainment in Westminster "to celebrate the triumph of their Brother Somerset."[15] British emancipation was a major propaganda coup, but it freed only the twenty thousand–odd slaves living in Britain itself, leaving American and West Indian slavery untouched. Benjamin Franklin wrote to Anthony Benezet about the "hypocrisy" of Britain "for promoting the Guinea trade, while it piqued itself on its virtue . . . in setting free a single Negro."[16]

By 1774, Boston—whose port was closed until the eighteen thousand pounds of tea dumped in the harbor the previous December was paid for—was the center of abolition as well as revolution. "No country can be called free when there is one slave," wrote James Swan, a Boston merchant and Son of Liberty who had disguised himself as an Indian in the Boston Tea Party.[17] "It has always appeared a most iniquitous scheme to me," Abigail Adams wrote to her husband, John, "to fight for what we are daily robbing and plundering from those who have as good a right to freedom as we have."[18]

In November 1774, the thirty-seven-year-old Tom Paine arrived in Philadelphia with a letter of introduction to Benjamin Franklin. Paine, a former corsetmaker's apprentice and low-level tax collector, was drawn to abolition as much by his sympathy for antigovernment politics as by his Quaker background. Franklin helped Paine become editor of *The Pennsylvania Magazine,* where his first published article, "African Slavery in America," appeared on March 8, 1775. "With what consistency, or decency," he wrote, could colonists "complain so loudly of attempts to enslave them, while they hold so many hundred thousand in slavery."[19] Paine advocated abolition, land redistribution, and economic opportunity. Two weeks later Patrick Henry, a slave owner who called slavery "repugnant to humanity," raised the American battle cry with "Give me liberty or give me death!" America's first antislavery society met in Philadelphia on April 14, 1775. Five days later, America was at war with Britain.

LEXINGTON AND CONCORD

New England towns and villages had been preparing for war since the winter of 1774. Weapons and gunpowder were stored and militia and Minutemen (an elite militia in existence only since the Boston Tea Party) were armed and ready. The war began in Massachusetts, where the British were greatly outnumbered.

Boston's ever more rebellious population outnumbered Governor Thomas Gage's troops by a factor of four, and his request for more men had been rejected. In April 1775, British intelligence learned that a secret meeting in Concord of the illegal Massachusetts Congress had determined to establish an army to fight the Crown. On April 18, Gage ordered troops, under Colonel Francis Smith, to proceed to Concord to seize all weapons and ammunition as Major John Pitcairn, Smith's second in command, led an advance guard to Lexington.

American intelligence was equally alert. (Many believed that Gage's American wife was supplying information to Dr. Joseph Warren, Samuel Adams's closest associate on Boston's Committee of Correspondence.[20]) As British soldiers left by boat across Back Bay late on the night of April 18, the Committee of Correspondence dispatch rider Paul Revere, under instructions from Warren, hung two signal lamps ("One if by land, two if by sea") in the steeple of the Old North Church. Then, having been silently rowed across the Charles under the guns of a British man-of-war, he mounted one of the fastest horses in the colony, to warn first Lexington (where Samuel Adams and John Hancock were distancing themselves from Boston and possible arrest) and then Concord that the British were coming. In Lexington, Revere, joined by another Committee of Correspondence dispatch rider, was briefly stopped by a British patrol. After supplying "information" (with a gun to his head), the printer-silversmith-revolutionary and his partner managed to break away by galloping off in opposite directions. Armed with Revere's "information," the British patrol rode back to say that at least five hundred Minutemen were waiting on Lexington Green. The several hundred British soldiers who approached the green early the next morning were probably surprised to find a motley army of seventy-seven, including boys, old men, and a slave.[21]

Ordering British troops not to fire, Pitcairn told the Americans to drop their weapons and disperse. Lexington's militia, led by Captain John Parker, a farmer and a veteran of the French and Indian Wars, was not eager for battle, either. But just as Parker gave the order to withdraw, a musket (American or British) flashed in the pan. There were now scattered shots from both sides. Eight Americans died and nine were wounded before the firing stopped. "O what a glorious morning is this!" said Samuel Adams, hearing the guns from his refuge near Lexington.

Prince Estabrook, a Lexington slave and member of Captain Parker's company, was one of the Americans who fought on Lexington Green that first morning of the Revolution. Later in the day other black militiamen from neighboring towns met the British at Concord, Arlington, Lincoln, and points on the road back to Boston.

According to the historian Howard Peckham, the Battle of Lexington lasted about fifteen minutes and the Battle of Concord lasted about five.[22] Entering Concord without resistance at around eight A.M., Smith's men found some four hundred Minutemen waiting at North Bridge, including the Reverend William Emerson, whose grandson Ralph Waldo Emerson would write of the "rude bridge" and the "shot heard round the world." In Concord, the British fired first. Three British and two Americans were killed before the Americans retreated. Prince Estabrook, veteran of Lexington, was wounded. He was listed on the official roster of "Provincials" killed or wounded at Concord as "a Negro man"—the only victim not called "Mr."[23] The American casualties were 41 wounded and 49 dead. The British counted 73 dead, 174 wounded, and 26 missing.[24]

There were other black militiamen defending North Bridge: Peter Salem of Framingham, who had been freed to enlist; Samuel Craft, of Newton; Caesar Ferrit and his son John, of Natick; Pompy, of Braintree; Pomp Blackman; and Prince, of Brookline (the slave of Joshua Boylston).[25] The twenty-two-year-old Lemuel Haynes had marched all the way to Concord with his Connecticut militia regiment.

Haynes had just missed Lexington: his company was en route from Granville, Connecticut, when the battle broke out. But he made it to Concord, and shortly after the battle the "former indentured servant and patriot versus bruit Tyranny" wrote a poem, "The inhuman tragedy perpetrated 19th of April 1775 by a number of the British Troops under the command of Thomas Gage," signed "Lemuel a Young Mollato": "For Liberty, each Freeman Strives / As its a gift of God / And for it willing yield their Lives . . . Much better there, in Death Confin'd / than a Surviving Slave."[26]

Born in West Hartford of an African father and a white mother, Lemuel Haynes had been indentured at the age of five months to Deacon David Rose of Granville. Raised like a son, he worked the farm, attended the local public school, and studied theology and the Bible. As a youth he experienced a religious conversion at the sight of the aurora borealis (he believed it a "presage of the day of judgment," wrote an early biographer), after which he often led church services, reading from his own sermons. As a member of Captain Lebbeus Ball's Granville militia, he trained one day a week on the Granville green, learning crude military drills and Indian stealth-fighting techniques.

Marching back to Boston, the red-coated "victors" of Lexington and Concord were perfect targets for waiting militiamen, who outraged the British by being better at Indian-style warfare than even their elite light infantrymen, who also learned from the Indians. British uniforms, heavy with linings and piping and brass buttons, not to mention 60 to 125 pounds of gear, had been designed for "splendor, not comfort," wrote A. J. Langguth in *Patriots: The Men Who Started the American Revolution.*[27] Americans fired at will from behind trees and stone walls at rows of shiny black hats and bright red coats, aiming at officers as well as men. Europeans never fired at officers. "The soldiers were so enraged at suffering from an unseen enemy that they forced open many of the houses from which the fire proceeded and put to death all those found in them," wrote the British lieutenant Frederick Mackenzie.[28] Black militiamen Cato Stedman and Cato Bordman of Cambridge, Cato Wood of Arlington, and Job Potoma and Isaiah Bayoman of Stoneham joined the fighting as the British reached Lincoln.

Again revealing America's talent for propaganda, stories of Lexington and Concord describing the Redcoats as savages were sent to England and circulated throughout the colonies even before the British had sent their official report. The Massachusetts Congress authorized the raising of 13,600 troops. Connecticut promised six thousand, New Hampshire two thousand, and Rhode Island fifteen hundred. As the New England army, headquartered at Cambridge, prepared to besiege British-held Boston, Governor Gage considered raising a regiment of freed slaves: "Things are now come to that Crisis," he wrote to his government, "that we must avail ourselves of every resource, even to raise the Negroes in our cause."[29]

YANKEE DOODLE: BARZILLAI LEW

On May 6, 1775, Barzillai Lew, a black man described as "30 yrs old and 6 ft tall," with the occupation of cooper, enlisted as a fifer and drummer in Captain John Ford's company of Colonel Ebenezer Bridge's 27th Massachusetts Regiment.[30] Lew was a veteran of the French and Indian Wars, where he had served in His Majesty's service under the command of Captain Thomas Farrington. A month after Lexington, he joined the hardy band of volunteers for Ticonderoga, under the dual leadership of Ethan Allen and Benedict Arnold. The raid on the old Lake Champlain fort was the first American victory of the war. The poet Lemuel Haynes was in Benedict Arnold's Connecticut company. Primas Black, Epheram Blackman, Abijah Prince, Jr. (son of Lucy Terry, the Deerfield poet), and Barzillai Lew were black members of Ethan Allen's Green Mountain Boys.

Barzillai Lew had been born in Dracut, outside Boston, in 1743. The marriage of his parents, two free blacks—"Primus, Captain Boyden's negro manservant to Margaret, a mulatto formerly a servant of Samuel Scripture, both of Groton"—was recorded in the Groton, Massachusetts, church registry in December 1742. While Primus Lew's place of birth was not officially recorded, according to Lew family legend he was born in West Africa. Still a boy, he was about to be captured by warriors from an enemy tribe when he dived into the sea and was picked up by a ship headed for Massachusetts.

Shortly after their marriage, Primus and Margaret Lew moved to Dracut's "Black North," where Anthony Negro and his wife, Sary, had established a black settlement in 1712. After their son Barzillai (a biblical name) was born, the Lews moved across the Nashua River to Pepperell and had three more children. Sometime in 1745, during the next-to-last French and Indian war, Primus joined New England troops under the command of William Pepperell to take the French fortress of Louisbourg on Cape Breton Island in French Canada. Primus Lew would establish a seven-generation musical and martial dynasty.

In 1768, Barzillai Lew married Dinah Bowman, a pianist from Lexington, whose freedom he bought from her owner. They would have eight children, all of whom became musicians. In May 1775, Barzillai went off to the Revolution.

Peter Salem, Salem Poor, and Cuff Whitemore at Bunker Hill

In the early morning of June 17, 1775, Boston took to the rooftops to watch the show when British ships in Boston Harbor opened fire on Bunker Hill just north of the city, which American militiamen had been fortifying since late the night before. If the British could be driven from Boston, the Americans would control Massachusetts. With a hundred times as many ships and far less manpower than the colonists, the British were trying to destroy the American army. Despite the bombardment, Americans under the command of Colonel William Prescott, a Pepperell farmer, continued to fortify their position until late in the afternoon, then waited behind their parapets for the British to come ashore and storm the hill. Prescott ordered his men to pick out officers and to aim at the crossings of their belts. Anxious about their small stores of ammunition, General Israel Putnam of Connecticut famously added, "Don't fire till you see the whites of their eyes."

Initially repulsed in heavy fighting on the beach, the British now assaulted Prescott's fort. Rows of Redcoats, led by Major Pitcairn, marched up the hill, firing at intervals but receiving no return fire. The Americans finally fired, to devastating effect, when the British were within fifty yards. A British officer would recall "an incessant stream of fire from the rebel lines . . . Most of the grenadiers . . . the moment of presenting themselves lost three-fourths and many nine-tenths of their men."[31] The British fell back, but regrouped and advanced again, marching over their dead and wounded. More British fell in the second advance. By the third advance, the Americans were almost out of ammunition. Offering brief but fierce resistance, they began to retreat as ship-based British marines swarmed over the parapet. Officially a British victory, Bunker Hill eventually became a great American propaganda coup.

"Retreat was no flight; it was covered with bravery and even military skill," said the British general John Burgoyne, praising the Americans. The British lost 1,150 of the 2,500 men who marched up Bunker Hill. The Americans lost more than 400 (140 killed, 271 wounded, 30 prisoners) out of 1,500. One of the British officers killed at Bunker Hill was Major Pitcairn, the leader of the offensive.

The major's death is credited to Peter Salem, a black veteran of Concord Bridge. Dr. Jeremy Belknap, the son of Salem's first owner, noted in his diary that someone at the battle had reported a "Negro man belonging to Groton, took aim at major Pitcairn, as he was rallying the dispersed British troops and shot him thro' the head."[32] Samuel Swett's *Historical and Topical Sketch of Bunker Hill Battle* (1818) was the first published account of the battle. "Among the foremost of the [British] leaders was the gallant Maj. Pitcairn," wrote Swett, "who exultingly cried 'the day is ours,' when Salem, a black soldier, and a number of others shot him through and he fell." Salem was rewarded by a group of American officers, who later presented him to General Washington.

John Trumbull, who had watched the battle from Roxbury, painted *The Battle of Bunker Hill* in London in 1786. ("My whole frame contracted, my blood shivered," wrote Abigail Adams to a friend when she saw the painting.) A black musket bearer is depicted in the right foreground, standing behind a sword-wielding officer, while another black soldier is visible under the flag. The black musket bearer appeared in the 1801 engraving of Trumbull's painting, but later engravings left him out.

Trumbull's black musket bearer in *The Battle of Bunker Hill* was first identified as Salem Poor. Poor, a twenty-eight-year-old free black from Andover, is credited with the death at Bunker Hill of the British lieutenant colonel James Abercrombie. In December 1775, fourteen American officers petitioned the General Court of Massachusetts to ask the Continental Congress to give Poor "the Reward due to so great and Distinguished a Caracter." They declared that "a Negro Man Called Salem Poor . . . behaved like an Experienced Officer, as Well as an Excellent Soldier."[33] There is no record that Poor ever received any reward from the Congress.

Cuff Whitemore, veteran of Concord, "fought bravely in the redoubt," wrote Samuel Swett, although he was wounded and had "a ball through his hat." Compelled to retreat, Whitemore "seized the sword [of a British officer] slain in the redoubt . . . which in a few days he unromantically sold"; and "served faithfully through the war, with many hairbreadth 'scapes from sword and pestilence." Other black Bunker Hill soldiers were Jude Hall, of Exeter, who fought in New Hampshire's Second Battalion under Captain Nathan Hale; Seasor and Pharoh, of York County; Job Potama and Isaiah Bayoman, of Arlington; Pompy, of Braintree; and Robin, of Sandowne, New Hampshire. There were also Cato Tufts, Caesar Dickenson, Grant Cooper, Cuff Hayes, Titus Coburn, Seymour Burr, Cato Howe, Charlestown Eads, Alexander Eames, Caesar Jahar, Cuff Blanchard, Pomp Fisk, Caesar Post, a seventeen-year-old named Sampson Talbot, from Chelsea—and soldier-fifer Barzillai Lew, veteran of Ticonderoga, who kept American morale high by playing "There's Nothing Makes the British Run Like Yankee Doodle Dandy."[34] (In 1767, "Yankee Doodle" was the hit song in *The Disappointment; or, The Force of Incredulity,* by Andrew Barton, the first ballad opera published in America. It was sung by the opera's leading character, a free black called Racoon. Played by a white actor in blackface, Racoon had a white mistress and equal status with comic Irish and Scottish characters.[35])

For Duke Ellington, Barzillai Lew was the real ragtag fifer in Archibald Willard's iconic revolutionary painting, *The Spirit of '76.* A 1943 radio broadcast of Ellington's "Black, Brown and Beige" suite (in the record collection of the writer Albert Murray) included an homage to Lew, with piano "Liberty" bells, drum artillery, and a bit of "Yankee Doodle." According to family tradition, Barzillai played in New York City at Washington's first inauguration. His Bunker Hill powder horn can be found in Chicago's Du Sable Museum of African-American History.

George Washington's "Mixed Multitude"

After Bunker Hill, the Continental Congress agreed to help Massachusetts by raising an army and choosing a commander. John Adams proposed the forty-three-year-old Virginia militia leader George Washington, a veteran of the French and Indian Wars and Continental Congress delegate. Six foot three and "straight as an Indian," Washington refused to accept any pay for his services beyond expenses. He took command of New England's army of fourteen thousand troops on July 3, 1775, in Cambridge, Massachusetts, and told his wife he would be home by Christmas.

Besides the reputed gift of Indian-style warfare, amateur American soldiers had other immediate advantages over their professional opponents, fighting a war that soon became highly unpopular both at home and in the field. Americans were better paid by Congress than British troops were paid by the king, and they were seasonal soldiers. Most New England militiamen signed up for six months, then went home to plant, harvest, or ply their trades. Americans were as revolutionary in their idea of warfare as they were in their concept of government. With no British military class system, they elected their own officers. Punishments and courts-martial were rare, and officers and men fraternized freely. Their weapons were mostly self-supplied. Pennsylvania, Virginia, and Maryland riflemen joined the New England militiamen, bringing the "Pennsylvania rifle," a frontier weapon superior in accuracy to "Brown Bess," the British musket. With varied equipment, and no uniforms except hunting shirts, the only insignia the Americans shared was a sprig of laurel in the hat.

Eighteenth-century armies often traveled with women. American wives, daughters, mothers, sisters, and camp followers made bandages, melted pewter for musket balls, and nursed wounded soldiers in camps or homes. A few disguised themselves as men and fought. Washington called his army "this mixed multitude of people."[36]

"In the regiments at Roxbury," wrote the American general John Thomas, "we have some Negroes; but I look on them, in General, Equally Serviceable with other men . . . many of them have proved themselves brave." Not everyone shared his opinion. General Philip Schuyler complained to John Hancock that one-third of the New England troops were old men, boys, or blacks. And the wealthy Pennsylvanian Alexander Graydon wrote of the poor discipline of Continental troops: "The only exception I recollect to have seen, to these miserably constituted bands from New England, was the regiment of Glover from Marblehead [Colonel John Glover led an amphibious regiment of Massachusetts fishermen]. . . . But even in this regiment there were a number of Negroes, which, to persons unaccustomed to such association, had a disagreeable, degrading effect."[37]

Soon after George Washington, a Virginia slaveholder, took command of the Continental Army in July 1775, blacks were forbidden to serve (although Washington's favorite slave, William Lee, his "black shadow," fought by his side throughout the war). Most southern slaveholders opposed the arming of blacks, who would, they feared, set a dangerous example for slaves. On July 10, Horatio Gates, an adjutant general of the American army, instructed recruiting officers not to enlist "any deserter from the Ministerial army, nor any stroller, negro, or vagabond."[38] That same day, orders were issued that blacks already serving—veterans of Lexington, Concord, Ticonderoga, and Bunker Hill—could complete their tour of duty.

In September, Edward Rutledge, South Carolina's delegate to the Continental Congress, introduced a resolution barring all blacks from fighting. A new directive was issued a month later: no "negroes, Boys unable to bear Arms nor Old men unfit to endure the Fatigues of the Campaign" would be accepted in the Continental Army. Washington issued a final order banning blacks from recruitment or reenlistment. "Many northern blacks were excellent soldiers," wrote Samuel Swett, "but southern troops would not brook equality with whites."[39]

In October 1775, Washington received a letter and poem from Phillis Wheatley, a well-known young poet-slave of Boston, titled "His Excellency General Washington" and including these lines: "Proceed, great chief, with virtue on thy side, / Thy ev'ry action let the goddess guide. / A crown, a mansion, and a throne that shine, / With gold unfading, WASHINGTON! be thine." The general responded to "Miss Phillis": "I thank you most sincerely for your polite notice of me, in the elegant lines you enclosed. . . . If you should ever come to Cambridge, or near headquarters, I shall be happy to see a person so favored by the Muses, and to whom nature has been so liberal in her dispensations."[40] Wheatley, who had carried on a public flirtation with John Paul Jones, visited headquarters later that year, and was received with "marked courtesy." In February 1776, Washington wrote to a friend: "At first, with a view of doing justice to her great poetical genius, I had a great mind to publish the poem; but not knowing whether it might not be considered rather as a mark of my own vanity, than as a compliment to her, I laid it aside." In April 1776, the poem and Washington's letter appeared together in Tom Paine's *Pennsylvania Magazine.*

In January 1776, Paine's pamphlet *Common Sense* had electrified the colonies. There were twenty-five printings in 1776 alone, roughly some 150,000 copies.[41] Paine, who called himself a "citizen of the world," spoke a new national language ("language as plain as the alphabet") embracing revolution, republicanism, secularism, and belief in human perfectibility. "We have it in our power to begin the world over again. . . . O! ye that love mankind! Ye that dare oppose not only tyranny but the tyrant, stand forth!" Calling *Common Sense* "sound doctrine and unanswerable reasoning," Washington had it read to all the ranks. Congress made Paine the first paid propagandist of the American government, hiring him to rouse public opinion for the war.

British Blacks: Lord Dunmore's Ethiopian Regiment

On November 7, 1775, John Murray, Earl of Dunmore, Royal Governor of Virginia, issued a proclamation from Norfolk harbor inviting slaves to leave their masters and join the Royal forces. Black response was enormous, even though the proclamation applied only to male, able-bodied slaves of rebels. (Tories' slaves were returned to their masters.) By December 1, 1775, three hundred blacks—Lord Dunmore's "Ethiopian Regiment"—were in uniform, with the words "Liberty to Slaves" inscribed across their chests. They were part of the British force routed by American militiamen later that month at Great Bridge, known as the Lexington of the South.

Slaves who escaped to the British lived on the water. With no mainland base after Great Bridge, Dunmore created a virtual floating city of ships in Norfolk harbor. In early 1776, Americans accused Dunmore of opening a "promiscuous ball" with "one of the black ladies" in his "floating town."[42] By March 1776, recruitment was going well among the Ethiopian Regiment, but "a fever crept in amongst them which carried off a great many Very fine fellows." By early summer there were only 150 "effective Negro men" left. "The shores are full of dead bodies, chiefly negroes," stated the Maryland Council of Safety in July, reporting a smallpox outbreak among some black British deserters.[43] Dunmore wrote that if fever had not killed the Ethiopian Regiment, it would have grown to two thousand men. In August 1776, the British, faced with smallpox, insufficient water, and no reinforcements, sailed out of the Potomac.

Dunmore's proclamation, and the fact that Washington had raised less than half the force needed for his new army, caused the American command to change its mind about black soldiers again. On December 31, 1775, Washington wrote to John Hancock, president of the Continental Congress: "Free Negroes who have served in this Army, are very much dissatisfied at being discarded." On January 17, the Continental Congress announced: "The free Negroes who have served faithfully in the army at Cambridge, may be re-enlisted, but no others."[44] Free blacks, as well as slaves substituting for their masters, would now fight until the end of the war.

Independence and Slavery

The first version of the Declaration of Independence sent to Congress by the Committee of Five—John Adams, Benjamin Franklin, Thomas Jefferson, Robert R. Livingston, and Roger Sherman (with Jefferson chosen to draft the document)—contained an antislavery statement: "He [the king] has waged cruel war against human nature itself, violating its most sacred rights of life and liberty in the persons of a distant people who never offended him, captivating and carrying them into slavery in another hemisphere, or to incur miserable death in their transportation thither. This piratical warfare, the opprobrium of *infidel* powers, is the warfare of this *Christian* king of Great Britain determined to keep open a market where *men* should be bought and sold." The passage was deleted at the request of South Carolina, Georgia, and New England slave-trading interests.

"Our slaves being our property," said Thomas Lynch of South Carolina, in the July Continental Congress slavery debate, "why should they be taxed more than land, sheep, cattle, horses, etc?" Benjamin Franklin pointed out one difference: "Sheep will never make any insurrection."

With the Declaration of Independence, Americans were fighting for a new America, not just fighting against Britain. Blacks were fighting for the same thing. Inspired by the Declaration, the soldier-poet Lemuel Haynes wrote an essay late in 1776, "Liberty Further Extended": "Liberty, & freedom, is an innate principle, which is unmovably placed in the human Species. . . . I think it not hyperbolical to affirm, that even an African, has Equally as good a right to his Liberty in common with Englishmen . . . consequently, the practice of slave-keeping, which so much abounds in this land is illicit."[45]

THE BATTLE OF LONG ISLAND

In the late summer of 1776, the British general Sir William Howe, who had retreated to Nova Scotia from Boston, was preparing to attack New York. His first goal was to capture Long Island. Washington called for help from all the colonies. Pro-Tory Manhattan was of little help: a Loyalist plot there to poison Washington had been uncovered in June. By August, the British were ready to attack. Facing some twenty thousand British and Hessian mercenary troops, Washington urged his men to "shew our enemies, and the whole world, that free men, contending on their own land, are superior to any mercenaries on earth."[46] But despite Washington's incantations, the Battle of Long Island was the most devastating American loss of the early war. Some Hessians bayonetted surrendering Americans and won a reputation as "butchers," although they were known for singing hymns as they went into battle.

The Americans retreated to Brooklyn Heights, having lost fourteen hundred men, many of whom were wounded or captured. Ordering every boat "from Hellgate on the Sound to Spuyten Duyvil Creek [on the Hudson] that could be kept afloat and had either sails or oars," Washington assembled a makeshift fleet. Colonel John Glover's "Massachusetts Fishermen" joined this ragged armada, which gathered in the East River on the night of August 26 to transport troops to lower Manhattan. There were at least 150 blacks in Glover's regiment of land- and sea-fighting Massachusetts Fishermen, the earliest American marines (and the "only exception" to Alexander Graydon's appraisal of the New England troops as shoddy). The amphibious evacuation of men, horses, guns, ammunition, and supplies continued throughout the night. It was so quiet that the British never knew what was happening. At dawn, with a sudden fog, Washington stepped into one of the last boats and the escape, with a third of the army left behind, was accomplished.

The British occupied Manhattan for much of the war, with no complaints from the island's Tory establishment. (New York was the most pro-British city in America, and even its patriots had a slightly Tory mind-set.) "The mob begins to think and reason," the prominent New Yorker Gouverneur Morris had written in 1774. "Poor reptiles! It is with them a vernal morning; they are struggling to cast off their winter's slough, they bask in the sunshine and ere noon they will bite."[47] Morris, an American aristocrat, was anti-British and pro-Revolution—but he was also suspicious of democracy, equating it with mob rule.

Black veterans of the Battle of Long Island included London Citizen, who was listed among the dead or missing; Julius Cezar and Timothy Prince, both evacuated; and Samuel Sutphin, a slave substituting for his master. After the battle, Sutphin hid for several days before being taken across the water by a local black man. Later wounded in a skirmish with Hessians, he had joined the army on the promise of freedom. When he returned to New Jersey to collect his manumission papers after his discharge, his master sold him. He was sold four times in the next twenty years, until he finally earned enough to buy his freedom.[48]

(A note on black Revolutionary names: In the eighteenth century the most popular slave names were either Anglicized African names such as Cuffe and Cajoe, or classical names such as Pompey, Caesar, and Quato. Place-names, such as London or York, were also fashionable. In New England, unlike the South, the most popular slave names were biblical.)

"Land of the Blacks"

Revolutionary New York had the highest percentage of blacks of any northern colony. There were eleven blacks on the Dutch West India Company ship that arrived in 1626 to establish New Netherlands and the Manhattan Island trading post. In the seventeenth century, under the Dutch, slaves were granted half-freedom and land grants to clear and cultivate lower Manhattan. The eighteenth-century British forbade blacks to own land—thereby encouraging the 1741 slave plot to burn the city.

In October 1991, an eighteenth-century Negro burial ground was unearthed by a New York City construction crew. Besides skeletons buried with their heads to the west (to face the rising sun on Judgment Day), there were British military buttons.

This was not the first time that the Negro Burial Ground had been disturbed. In the early 1850s, the Boston minister and abolitionist Theodore Parker wrote (with some exaggeration, since probably no more than a dozen black soldiers were killed in the Battle of Long Island):

> Not long ago, while the excavations for the vaults of the great retail dry goods store of New York [Macy's] was going on, a gentleman

> from Boston noticed a large quantity of human bones thrown up by the workmen. . . . They were shoveled up with the earth they had rested in, carted off and emptied into the sea . . . these were the bones of colored American soldiers, who fell in the disastrous battles of Long Island, in 1776. . . . Three quarters of a century have passed by since the retreat from Long Island. What a change since then! . . . Briton has emancipated every bondman. . . . America has a population of slaves greater than the people of all England in the reign of Elizabeth. Under the pavement of Broadway, beneath the walls of the Bazaar, there still lie the bones of the colored martyrs to American Independence.

AMERICAN CRISIS

The summer and early autumn of 1776 saw a series of defeats for the Continental Army, and winter was the Revolution's darkest hour. In November, Washington fell back across New Jersey, plagued by desertions and losses of equipment. On December 18, Congress was evacuated from Philadelphia to Baltimore. "In a passion of patriotism," Tom Paine, now an aide-de-camp to General Nathanael Green, wrote "The American Crisis": "These are the times that try men's souls. The summer soldier and the sunshine patriot will, in this crisis, shrink from the service of his country; but he that stands it Now, deserves the love and thanks of man and woman. Tyranny, like hell, is not easily conquered; yet we have this consolation with us, that the harder the conflict the more glorious the triumph." On Christmas Eve, Washington had Paine's "American Crisis" read to all the troops, just before they retreated toward Trenton.

It was a time of crisis, but it was also a turning point. Washington was becoming a great general and, after the Battle of Long Island, he had formed a strategy to defeat the British. Henceforth, the war would be "defensive," he wrote to Congress. He would "avoid a general action"—he would also, to bedevil the British, "protract the war."[49]

The combination of Washington's military genius and Paine's words had the power to stir men's fighting passions. Washington turned retreat into a major American victory, once again getting his army out of a trap. The Americans reached Trenton in the dawn of December 26, just as the Hessians were sleeping off their drunken Christmas celebration. After overrunning the town from two directions, Washington retreated with some 2,400 men, all the men he had left, across the Delaware River into Pennsylvania. Generals Nathanael Greene, John Sullivan, and Henry Knox and Colonel John Glover's Massachusetts Fishermen led the evacuation.

In the 1851 painting by Gottlieb Leutze of Washington standing in his boat as it crosses the Delaware, there is one recognizable black oarsman—Prince Whipple, a slave of Washington's aide Commodore William Whipple. The commodore was a former slave ship captain from Portsmouth, New Hampshire. Prince Whipple (also depicted in Thomas Sully's 1819 painting of Washington at the Delaware) had been sent to study in colonial America by his wealthy West African parents, but was sold into slavery by the captain of the ship he sailed on. Whipple would be one of nineteen "natives of Africa" from Portsmouth who in 1799 petitioned the state legislature to restore their freedom "for the sake of justice, humanity, and the rights of mankind."[50]

Oliver Cromwell, a twenty-four-year-old New Jersey farmer, was another one of the free black soldiers who crossed the Delaware with Washington. Cromwell fought at Princeton, Brandywine, Monmouth, and Yorktown. His 1783 honorable discharge was signed by Washington, as was his "Badge of merit for Six Years faithful service." On his hundredth birthday, the *Burlington Gazette* recounted Cromwell's Revolutionary experiences: "He was with the army at the retreat of the Delaware, on the memorable crossing of the 25th of December, 1776, and relates the story of the battles of the succeeding days with enthusiasm. He gives the details of the march from Trenton to Princeton and told us, with much humor, that they 'knocked the British about lively' at the latter place."[51]

The Battle of Princeton took place in an orchard outside of town. Washington's men followed him to within thirty yards of the Redcoats before he gave the order to fire. "It's a fine fox chase, my boys!" Washington is said to have shouted, standing in his stirrups, as the British, under Cornwallis, fell back. "His march through our lines is allowed to have been a prodigy of generalship," wrote Horace Walpole of Washington. Frederick the Great considered Washington's Princeton campaign the most brilliant of the century.[52]

A number of British soldiers were captured single-handedly at Princeton by Primus Hall, a free Boston black whose father, Prince Hall, a Boston tanner, furnished leather drumheads to the Continental Army. Prince Hall had been freed by his master, William Hall, one month after the Boston Massacre. Shortly before Lexington and Concord, Hall and fourteen others became the first black Masons in America, members of a lodge attached to a Boston British regiment.

Hall, who would be listed as a Massachusetts voter in 1780, was one of eight Boston blacks who signed a January 1777 petition for the abolition of slavery: "A Great Number of Negroes who are detained in a State of slavery in the Bowels of a free & Christian country . . . they can not but express astonishment that every principle from which America has acted in the course of her unhappy difficulties with Great-Britain pleads stronger than a thousand arguments . . . [that] they may be restored to the enjoyment of that freedom which is the natural right of all Men"—signed Prince Hall, Lancaster Hill, Peter Bess, Brister Slenser, Jack Pierpont, Nero Funelo, Newport Sumner, and Job Look.[53] That same month, Vermont became the first American state to abolish slavery.

Brandywine Creek in Pennsylvania in September 1777 was another defeat for the Continental Army. Oliver Cromwell, who had crossed the Delaware with Washington, was among Brandywine's brave. But folklore tells of one Black Samson, a giant figure, who had witnessed the brutal murder by the British of his friend, a white schoolmaster. The next day, Samson had volunteered to fight at Brandywine. Armed with a scythe, he single-handedly wreaked havoc among the British. "The giant Negro armed with a scythe, swept his way through the red ranks like a sable figure of time," read a contemporary account. The late nineteenth-century black poet Paul Laurence Dunbar wrote of Samson: "Straight through the human harvest, / Cutting a bloody swath, / Woe to you, soldier of Britain! / Death is abroad in his path. / Flee from the scythe of the reaper, / Flee while the moment is thine, / None may with safety withstand him, / Black Samson of Brandywine."

The tide turned again in October, when General John Burgoyne surrendered at Saratoga, the first major British defeat. Among the black victors of Saratoga were Peter Salem, hero of Bunker Hill, Brister Freeman, and Ebenezer Hill. (General Burgoyne would rather have been killed than considered a coward. "I have had some narrow personal escapes, having been shot through my hat & waistcoat, & my horse hit," he wrote of Saratoga. "If my reputation suffers among the respectable part of my profession, I shall think those escapes unfortunate."[54]) Discontent, desertion, and a number of suicides among the British followed, while the hated Hessians deserted heavily among the Pennsylvania Dutch. Captain James Murray, serving with the British 57th Regiment, sought only to get away from "a barbarous business in a barbarous country." The war was equally unpopular with Britons at home.

NERO HAWLEY AND VALLEY FORGE

By the end of 1777, blacks had become a familiar part of Washington's "mixed multitude." "The rebel clowns, oh what a sight / To awkward was their figure / 'Twas yonder stood a pious wight / And here and there a nigger," went a British jingle.[55]

The thirty-six-year-old Nero Hawley, the slave of a Connecticut sawmill owner named Daniel Hawley, went to Danbury in 1777 to join Captain Granger's company of the 2nd Connecticut Regiment. Nero, who worked in his master's sawmill, lived in the household of the Reverend James Beebee, for whom his wife, Peg, was a servant. The Hawleys were expecting their second child when Nero went to war. Private Hawley's pay was $6.67 monthly. His daily rations were one pound of beef or pork, one pound of bread or flour, a small quantity of vegetables when available, and one gill (4 oz.) of rum or whiskey; he got small quantities of vinegar, salt, soap, and candles each week.[56] In November 1777, Nero's regiment joined Washington's army in Pennsylvania. In the first week of December, he participated in a skirmish at Whitemarsh, about twelve miles from Valley Forge, on the other side of the Schuylkill River where the American army encamped for the winter of 1777–1778.

The terrible winter at Valley Forge could be blamed as much on William Buchanan, the congressionally appointed head of the Commissary Department, as on the weather. Thanks to mismanagement, graft, and greed, uniforms and supplies simply never arrived. On December 23, 1777, Washington wrote to Congress that 2,900 men were "unfit for duty because they were barefoot and otherwise naked."[57] By February, the number of barefoot and seminaked had risen to four thousand. The camp ran out of food three times. Five hundred horses starved to death. Men, living in freezing huts, died at the rate of four hundred per month of "putrid fever, the itch, bloody flux or smallpox." As many as 2,500 died in six months—and hundreds more deserted for home, or went over to the British. Fortunately for the Americans at Valley Forge, the British general, Sir William Howe, was thought to be enjoying himself too much in Tory Philadelphia, only eighteen miles away, to plan an attack. There was a Loyalist song: "Awake, arouse, Sir Billy, / There's forage in the plain, / Ah, leave your little filly, / And open the Campaign." Actually, a "filly" had nothing to do with it—Howe believed that Washington's Valley Forge defenses were too strong to attack. Howe's resignation was soon accepted by the king, and General Sir Henry Clinton, his replacement, ordered the evacuation of Philadelphia.

Among the blacks who survived Valley Forge were Salem Poor, veteran of Bunker Hill; Timothy Prince, veteran of the Battle of Long Island; Prince Whipple and Oliver Cromwell, who had crossed the Delaware with Washington; and Connecticut's Nero Hawley. From January 1 to March 1, 1778, Nero Hawley was "on command," attached to a headquarters unit under Captain James Beebee (son of the Reverend) with "Extraordinary Pay 6⅔ Dollars." In March, sixty-three members of the elder Beebee's congregation sent relief, money, and provisions (including cheese and gammon) "for the Continental soldiers in the southern army, Valley Forge belonging to this place . . . being fifteen in number, to be divided between them."[58] Nero Hawley was among the beneficiaries.

FOREIGN AID

In February 1778, France became the first country to recognize the new American Republic. But the rich and idealistic young Frenchman Marie-Joseph-Paul-Yves-Roch-Gilbert du Motier, Marquis de Lafayette, who spent the winter at Valley Forge, was not the only foreign volunteer. Johann Kalb, a self-styled baron from Bavaria, would be killed in action. The Prussian baron Friedrich von Steuben (a former staff captain to Frederick the Great), speaking French to an interpreter who in turn translated for the troops, gave Americans at Valley Forge their first formal training in the art of war. Count Casimir Pulaski (killed at the Battle of Savannah) and the engineer Thaddeus Kosciuszko, who supervised the fortification of West Point, were Poles who believed in America's revolutionary ideas about freedom. Kosciuszko, like Lafayette, was an ardent abolitionist. "I would never have drawn my sword in the cause of America if I could have conceived that thereby I was helping to found a nation of slaves," Lafayette wrote later of his Revolutionary experience.[59]

Spain entered the war in 1779 as a partner of France, without officially recognizing America. Young Bernardo de Gálvez, governor of the Spanish colony of Louisiana, America's best Spanish friend, drove the British from Louisiana and Alabama. Gálvez mobilized a task force of 670 men of all nationalities, including eighty free New Orleans blacks, to take Mobile in March 1780. These troops and a company of Louisiana *pardos* (mulattos) and *morenos* (blacks) also helped capture Baton Rouge, Pensacola, and Natchez. Nearly half of Gálvez's Mississippi Valley force was black, among them two companies of black Louisiana militia. "No less deserving of eulogy are the companies of Negro and Free Mulatoes," who conducted themselves "with as much valor and generosity as the white," he wrote.[60] Gálvez turned Louisiana into a vital source of money and guns for the Americans by shipping ammunition and supplies up the Mississippi under the Spanish flag. In 1781, when the Spanish established the city of Los Angeles ("El Pueblo de Nuestra Señora la Reina de los Angeles"), more than half of the tiny cluster of eleven families recruited in Mexico were black.

GOULDTOWN AND THE PIERCE FAMILY MILITARY DYNASTY

Adam Pierce, a black soldier in the company of Captain John Noble Cummings of the 2nd New Jersey Regiment, fought in the June 1778 Battle of Monmouth Court House in New Jersey, claimed as an American victory because it drove the British back to New York. New Jersey, which generally proved lucky for Washington's army, saw the most fighting of the war. The Americans were on a winning streak, but Monmouth was fought in hundred-degree weather. At least thirty-seven Americans died of heatstroke—despite the famous "Molly Pitcher" and her jugs of water—and Washington's horse dropped dead.

Adam Pierce's father and uncle had won their freedom and became seamen, marrying and freeing Dutch indentured-servant sisters. Both families settled in southern New Jersey in a place called Gouldtown, forty-two miles from Philadelphia, where Adam Pierce was born in 1756.[61]

Gouldtown was created when John Fenwick, lord proprietor of Fenwick's Colony and the biggest landowner in New Jersey, all but disinherited his daughter for marrying a black man, leaving her just 500 acres, where she and her husband settled. One of the oldest black settlements in the United States, it furnished three Revolutionary soldiers: Adam Pierce and his cousins Richard and Anthony Pierce. It also produced a privateering sailor in the War of 1812, and a number of soldiers of the Civil War.

Members of the Pierce family have served in every major U.S. war. Two of Adam's descendants, Brigadier General Harold E. Pierce, U.S. Air Force, and Circuit Judge Lawrence W. Pierce, were active members of the Sons of the American Revolution—and their aunt, Mildred Pierce Dart, was one of the very few black members of the DAR. Judge Lawrence Pierce named his younger son Mark, believing that their Revolutionary ancestor's full name was Adam Mark Pierce. They discovered later that "Mark" actually meant "X," because Adam Pierce, like many other Revolutionary soldiers, could neither read nor write.

THE 1ST RHODE ISLAND REGIMENT

As the war went on, most states found it increasingly difficult to meet their recruiting quotas. Rhode Island was desperate; Newport was occupied by British troops, and a blockade was strangling commerce, including the slave trade. Because Newport was the chief eighteenth-century slaving port, Rhode Island had the largest population of blacks in New England. General James M. Varnum, one of Washington's brigadiers and a former officer of the Rhode Island militia, suggested that a black regiment be raised, and Washington agreed.

The first all-black American regiment—the 1st Rhode Island—was formed in 1778. Colonel Christopher Greene, a Rhode Island native and one of Washington's best young officers, was chosen to command the new 132-man regiment. In February 1778, the Rhode Island legislature announced that any slave volunteering for the new battalion would be "absolutely free," with the same wages and bounties as regular soldiers. Blacks and whites fought side by side throughout the Revolution; Rhode Island provided the only battleground where blacks were conspicuous as a distinct racial group.

That August, in the only Revolutionary engagement fought in Rhode Island, Hessians directed their main assault against the new black regiment. They "experienced a more obstinate resistance than they had expected," finding "large bodies of troops . . . chiefly wild looking men in their shirt sleeves, and among them many Negroes."[62] A Rhode Island history of 1860 reported that Colonel Greene's regiment "distinguished itself by deeds of desperate valor." A 1st Rhode Island veteran, one "Dr. Harris," recalled the battle in an address to a New Hampshire antislavery society in 1842: "When stationed in the State of Rhode Island, the regiment to which I belonged was once ordered to what was called a flanking position . . . it was a post of imminent danger," he recalled. "They attacked us with great fury, but were repulsed. Again they reinforced, and attacked us again, with more vigor and determination, and again were repulsed. Again they reinforced, and attacked us the third time, with the most desperate courage and resolution, but a third time were repulsed. The contest was fearful. Our position was hotly disputed and as hotly maintained."[63]

By holding the line against four hours of British-Hessian assaults, the 1st Rhode Island helped the American army to escape and be ferried to the mainland, another skillfully executed rescue-retreat by the Massachusetts Fishermen. The Americans lost the Battle of Rhode Island, but British casualties were five times greater. Lafayette called it the best-fought action of the war. The 1st Rhode Island, with black women camp followers, went on to fight at Points Bridge and Yorktown. "At the ferry crossing I met with a detachment of the Rhode Island regiment," wrote the Marquis de Chastellux in his journal of January 1781. "The majority of the enlisted men are Negroes or mulattoes; but they are strong, robust men, and those I saw made a very good appearance."[64] William Cooper Nell described the death of Colonel Greene at Points Bridge, New York, in May 1781: "Colonel Greene, the commander of the regiment, was cut down and mortally wounded: but the sabres of the enemy only reached him through the bodies of his faithful guard of blacks, who hovered over him to protect him, *and every one of whom was killed.*"[65]

STONY POINT: "THE FORT'S OUR OWN"

In the summer of 1779, Nero Hawley and his Connecticut regiment were at Camp Robinson's Farm, a hospital and generals' quarters high above the Hudson River, opposite the newly fortified West Point. Hawley had joined General "Mad" Anthony Wayne's attempt to storm Stony Point, a nearby British-held fort. Other blacks among Wayne's 1,500 elite "picked troops" were Peter Bonet; Bristol Budd, a veteran of Saratoga, Whitemarsh, and Monmouth; Julius Cezar, a veteran of Long Island, Trenton, and Brandywine; Primus Tyng, a veteran of Saratoga and Monmouth; and Peter Salem, a veteran of Bunker Hill. Stony Point was Salem's last battle. After the war, he became a cane weaver in Leicester, Massachusetts, and died in the poorhouse in 1816. In 1882, the citizens of Leicester erected a memorial to "Peter Salem / A Soldier of the Revolution / Concord / Bunker Hill / Saratoga."

Wayne's mission hinged on the complicity of a black spy, Pompey Lamb, the slave of a patriot, who regularly delivered fruit and vegetables to the British in the fort and passed on information to the Americans. The British agreed, at Lamb's request, to a night delivery—and gave him the password. "The fort's our own!" he exclaimed, late on the night of July 15, accompanied by Wayne and two officers disguised as farmers. The gates were opened, the "farmers" subdued the guards, and the rest of Wayne's regiment charged the fort. In the brief and bloody battle, fifteen Americans were killed and eighty-three, including Wayne, were wounded. Sixty-three British were killed and seventy-one wounded before they surrendered. The assault on Stony Point was the last major battle in New York State. Wayne wrote to Washington on the night of the victory: "Our officers & men behaved like men who are determined to be free."[66] Pompey Lamb won his personal freedom and a horse (no small thing) for his services.

Nero Hawley was forty-one years old on November 4, 1782, when he received his freedom from Daniel Hawley. He continued to work in Hawley's brick factory, but in 1785 he started his own brick-making business, and later went into the timber business. In 1801 he bought the freedom of his four children. He died in January 1817, aged seventy-five.

The Siege of Charleston and Southern Resistance

"All our misfortunes," wrote John Adams to General Horatio Gates in March 1776, "arise from a single source—the reluctance of the Southern colonies to republican government."[67] Most Revolutionary slave owners in the South wanted their slaves neither to fight nor to be freed.

In the spring of 1779, John Laurens, Washington's aide-de-camp and the son of the president of the Continental Congress, asked permission to raise three thousand black South Carolina soldiers. Before the war, Laurens had studied in Switzerland, where he developed abolitionist opinions. (His father, Henry Laurens, a landowner and importer, had abandoned the slave trade in 1770.) Congress approved the Laurens plan and agreed to pay slaveholders up to $1,000 for "each active able-bodied negro man of standard size, not exceeding thirty-five years of age," who would himself receive no pay or bounty, but freedom and fifty dollars at the end of the war.[68] Colonel Alexander Hamilton, John Laurens's close friend, wrote to President of Congress John Jay in March 1779:

> I have not the least doubt that the Negroes will make very excellent soldiers, with proper management. . . . I hear it frequently objected to the scheme of embodying Negroes, that they are too stupid to make soldiers. This is so far from appearing to me a valid objection . . . for their natural faculties are as good as ours . . . The contempt we have been taught to entertain for the blacks, makes us fancy many things that are founded neither in reason nor experience.[69]

Hinting that it would rather lose the war than any slaves, the South Carolina council rejected the Laurens plan eight to one. The plan died, wrote Laurens, at the hands of "the triple-headed monster, in which prejudice, avarice and pusillanimity were united."

The siege and fall of Charleston, in May 1780, was the greatest British victory of the war. America surrendered six thousand soldiers, sailors, and armed citizens, as well as five ships and over three hundred cannon. During the siege, a Charleston slave named Duncan furnished Major John André, Britain's chief intelligence officer and former aide-de-camp to British commander Lord Howe, with full reports on American ships and troops. Charleston slaveholders were right to worry about their slaves.

On New Year's Eve, 1781, a group of British officers in Charleston "put aside the cares of the days to attend an 'Ethiopian Ball,' " organized by three "Negro Wenches assuming their Mistress's names . . . dressed up in taste, with the richest silks, and false rolls in their heads," wrote Charleston slaveholder Daniel Stevens in a letter of February 1782. An American prisoner of war wrote, "This Ball was held at a very capital private House in Charleston, and the supper cost not less than 80 pounds Sterling, and these tyrants danced with these Slaves until four o'clock in the morning."[70] To Americans, such behavior would be deemed typical of British immorality and licentiousness.

"YE ABLE BACKED SAILORS"

Blacks had served on merchant ships and whaling vessels since long before the Revolution. There were hundreds of blacks in the Continental Navy, where any able-bodied hand was accepted, regardless of race. A 1775 recruiting poster in Newport sought "ye able backed sailors, men white or black, to volunteer for naval service in ye interest of freedom." Besides ordinary seamen duties, blacks in the Continental Navy served as marine sharpshooters and gunmen. The navy tempted recruits with prize money from captured ships, but state navies, with shorter enlistments, were generally more popular. Even South Carolina showed less resistance to black sailors, who had been common since early colonial days, than to black soldiers. Most of the Chesapeake Bay and river pilots of Virginia's navy were black men who had grown up on the bay or its tributaries.

Joseph Ranger served longer than any other black Virginia seaman. He served on a ship that was blown up by the British navy, and on another whose entire crew was captured and held by the British until the end of the war. Caesar Tarrant, the slave of Carter Tarrant of Hampton, Virginia, who "behaved gallantly" at the wheel of the schooner *Patriot* when it captured the British brig *Fanny,* was freed for his wartime efforts in 1789, when the legislature purchased him from his owners. His daughter later received 2,667 acres in Ohio's Western Reserve, land set aside for Revolutionary veterans. Tarrant is a rare example of a black man who received the maximum rewards for serving his country. As states began to have trouble filling their quotas for Continental service, it was "obvious," as the historian Benjamin Quarles wrote, "that the best way to prevent the Negro from going over to the British was to give him sufficient inducement to fight for America."[71]

Remembering the war in old age, Commodore James Barron wrote of his days as captain of the armed schooner *Virginia,* and of the "courageous patriots who had served on board her during the war. Amongst these, I take pleasure in stating there were several colored men who, I think, in justice to their merits should not be forgotten." Among those "zealous and faithful soldiers in the cause of freedom" was a man named Aberdeen, who "distinguished himself so much as to attract the notice of one of our first officers and citizens . . . Patrick Henry who befriended him as long as he lived." Commodore Barron also remembered Mark Starlins, a black Virginia pilot who called himself "Captain." "He was brought up as a pilot, and proved a skillful one, and a devoted patriot," Barron wrote; Starlins was held in high estimation "by all worthy citizens, and, more particularly, by all the navy officers of the state."[72]

As freelancers, going where they wanted, privateers (private vessels of war commissioned by the states as agents for Congress) were most popular with runaway slaves, and New England privateers were the most successful. Titus, the slave of Mrs. Joseph Cabot of Salem, Massachusetts, enlisted crews as a business agent for privateers, and brought his owner a tidy income. In William Pynchon's diary of August 13, 1781, Titus was described as wearing "cloth shoes, ruffled shirts, silk breeches and stockings and dancing minuets at Commencement."

A fourteen-year-old named James Forten, born free in Philadelphia, signed on in 1781 as a powder boy on the Pennsylvania privateer *Royal Louis,* under Captain Stephen Decatur, Sr. On Forten's second cruise, the *Royal Louis* (with a crew of two hundred, including twenty blacks) was captured by a British frigate. Black prisoners were usually sold in the West Indies, but Forten (thanks to his talent for shooting marbles) became a playmate of the captain's son. Refusing to give up his American allegiance and join the British, however, he was sent to spend the last seven months of the war on *Old Jersey,* a notorious floating dungeon in New York. More than eleven thousand Americans died on that "floating and pestilential hell"; prisoners died with such regularity that when British jailers opened the hatches in the morning, their greeting to the men below was "Rebels, turn out your dead!" Forten himself wrote that he was "made to suffer not a little." At the end of the war, a skeletal Forten, his hair fallen out from malnutrition, was released in the general exchange of prisoners, and walked home barefoot to Philadelphia.[73]

THE FONTAGES LEGION

The French forces of the ill-fated Franco-American siege of Savannah of October 1779 included seven hundred free black Haitians, the Fontages Legion (named for their French commander). Georgians asked the French to prevent contact between their free black men and American slaves. The

Fontages Legion included several future leaders of the Haitian Revolution: André Rigaud, Louis Jacques Beauvais, Martial Besse (wounded in battle), and Jean-Baptiste Mars Belley. Haiti's future king, twelve-year-old Henri Christophe, a powder boy, was wounded at Savannah.

In 1793, all French colonial slaves were freed. Former slaves became "overseas" ("outre-mer") Frenchmen, civilly and legally equal with their fellow citizens. Martial Besse became a general in the French army (a parallel would have been inconceivable in America). That year, Jean-Baptiste Mars Belley, a captain in the French army, was one of three "free citizens of Saint Domingue," a white, a black (Belley), and a mulatto, elected to the French Assembly. Traveling to France by way of the United States in September 1793, Belley was a conspicuous figure in Philadelphia in his French officer's uniform. Wearing a sash of office and holding a hat with a tricolor panache (an ornamental plume), Belley was the subject of a stunning 1797 portrait by the Romantic painter Girodet-Trioson.

FORT GRISWOLD: JORDAN FREEMAN AND LAMBERT LATHAM

In September 1781, British soldiers under the command of traitor Benedict Arnold, who had tried to sell West Point to the British the year before, set fire to New London, Connecticut, not far from Arnold's birthplace. Then, with eight hundred troops, Arnold attacked Fort Griswold, held by a hundred and fifty Americans under Colonel William Ledyard. The Americans surrendered as the British invaded the fort. But Ledyard was killed as he offered his sword to the British—whereupon Jordan Freeman, Ledyard's black orderly, avenged his master's death by bayoneting the British officer who killed him. About eighty Americans were shot, stabbed, or bludgeoned to death in the ensuing massacre. Jordan Freeman was found with more than thirty-three bayonet wounds in his body. Another black hero, Lambert Latham, was with his owner, Captain William Latham, inside the fort, where, according to Latham family tradition, he "fought manfully by his master's side up to the time he was slain."

The forty-minute battle of Fort Griswold, or Groton Heights, came to be known for its segregated memorial tablet: a 134-foot granite shaft, dedicated in 1830, "in memory of the brave patriots who fell in the massacre at Fort Griswold." The names of eighty-four patriots are inscribed on the shaft. At the top is Colonel William Ledyard, commander; at the bottom, segregated under "Colored Men," are "Sambo" Latham and Jordan Freeman. William Anderson, a New London black man who was in the crowd the day the memorial was dedicated, was angry that Latham, known as Lambo, had been turned into "Sambo."

Twenty-five years later, Parker Pillsbury, a white New Hampshire abolitionist, wrote about the Fort Griswold memorial to the black historian William Cooper Nell. "The names of the colored soldiers last, and not only last, but a blank space left between them and the whites; in genuine keeping with the 'Negro Pew' distinction—setting them not only below others, but by themselves," he wrote. "They were not the last in the fight. . . . Jordan Freeman stands away down, last on the list of heroes—perhaps the greatest hero of them all."[74]

The Siege of Yorktown and Surrender

Between January and April 1781, General Cornwallis lost over fifteen hundred men. In September, he found himself besieged by a Franco-American army at Yorktown, on the Chesapeake in northeastern Virginia. Worn down by smallpox, lack of food, and protracted war, his men were in no condition to break out. Despite quarrels with General Clinton over being in Virginia in the first place, he had been promised reinforcements. Although he always referred to Lafayette dismissively as "the boy," Cornwallis had no choice but to respect the presence of the large Franco-American force, encamped at Williamsburg under Washington and Count Jean de Rochambeau, the commander of the French army, and the smaller American camp at Richmond, under Von Steuben and Lafayette.

Cornwallis had to know that he was outnumbered. The British had some eight thousand men; the Americans had about nine thousand. Thanks to the support of a newly arrived French army of seventy-eight hundred, the Allies at Yorktown now had twice as many men as the British. Excellent French-American relations were another disadvantage for Cornwallis. The British generals quarreled, but Washington, the American commander-in-chief, would write: "It may, I believe, with much truth be said that a greater harmony between two armies [his and Rochambeau's] never subsisted."[75] The harmony extended to the French navy, which had sailed from the Caribbean to the Chesapeake under Admiral François-Joseph-Paul de Grasse in early September, just in time to encircle Cornwallis at Yorktown.

The siege lasted from late September until mid-October. On the night of October 6, a French-American force stormed the advance British defense post. French infantry and artillery joined forces with an American division led by Von Steuben. Lafayette commanded a light infantry division, of which Colonel Alexander Hamilton led a detachment. Mad Anthony Wayne and his Stony Point troops, now famed for their night attacks with bayonets, were in the vanguard. Washington, ever courteous, had made "Rochambeau" the battle watchword—it was transformed by the Americans to "Rush-on-Boys."

The British and Hessian defenders of the redoubt were easily overwhelmed. An American-French bombardment followed. "I now want words to express the dreadful situation of the garrison," wrote a lieutenant of the Royal Navy. "Upwards of a thousand shells were thrown into the works this night, and every spot became alike dangerous."[76] Cornwallis's headquarters was destroyed. After a week of intense bombardment, his officers told him that he owed it to his men to surrender.

On the morning of October 17, a red-coated drummer boy was seen on the ramparts of the British camp. The drummer's call to parley could not at first be heard above the bombardment. When the guns finally died down, a British officer appeared next to the boy waving a white handkerchief. The only sound now was the drummer. "I thought I never heard a drum equal to it," said one American officer. "It was the most delightful music to us all."[77]

James, a Virginia slave who won his freedom acting as Lafayette's Yorktown spy, "properly acquitted himself with some important communication I gave him," wrote Lafayette. "His intelligence from the enemy's camp were industriously collected and more faithfully delivered."[78] After the surrender, Cornwallis was surprised to find James at Lafayette's headquarters; the British had believed he was *their* spy.

★ ★ ★

On October 19, 1781, 6,850 British and Hessian soldiers and seamen, many of whom were drunk, took part in the Yorktown surrender ceremony. Cornwallis, a shamed and very sore loser, refused to attend. The ramifications of surrender, from the point of view of career and country, were probably more than he could contemplate. The British second-in-command, General Charles O'Hara, offered his sword to Rochambeau, who gestured toward Washington, who, in turn, indicated that O'Hara should surrender his sword to the American second-in-command, General Benjamin Lincoln.

Muskets were piled in an open field. The British and Hessians had new uniforms for the ceremonies, and the French officers and troops were, typically, well uniformed. But the Americans were ragged, and many were barefoot—an archetypal rebel army. A British band played the melancholy and somewhat ironically titled tune "The World Turned Upside Down."

"Universal silence was observed amidst the vast concourse, and the utmost decency prevailed," wrote an American officer, Henry "Light-

Horse Harry" Lee, "exhibiting in demeanor an awful sense of the vicissitudes of human life, mingled with commiseration for the unhappy."[79] The British, apparently, were so humiliated by the defeat that they refused to look at the Americans until Lafayette ordered his drummers and fifers to play "Yankee Doodle"—then, wrote the historian Thomas Fleming, every head turned as if "on a string" in the direction of the ragged, hollow-eyed victors.[80]

The black 1st Rhode Island Regiment (obviously with rich patrons) was one of the few American units in full uniform. A French sublieutenant, Jean-Baptiste Antoine de Verger, was impressed enough to make a watercolor sketch of a 1st Rhode Island light infantryman. "Three-quarters of the Rhode Island regiment consists of Negroes, and that regiment is the most neatly dressed, the best under arms, and the most precise in its maneuvres," observed Baron von Closen, as the Continental Army passed in review.[81]

"The war over, and peace restored, these men returned to their Respective states; and who could have said to them, on their return to civil life, after having shed their blood in common with whites in the defense of liberties of the country: 'You are not to participate in the rights secured by the struggle, or in the liberty for which you have been fighting,'" wrote the American army surgeon William Eustis, future governor of Massachusetts.[82] Eustis was writing of the 1st Rhode Island, but his words could have referred to any black soldier.

* * *

America claimed victory in the war, but King George, whom many thought mad, refused to recognize American independence or accept the idea of surrendering to a former colony. In February 1782, the parliamentary opposition proposed that the "war in America be no longer pursued for the impracticable purpose of reducing the inhabitants to obedience by force."[83] The motion first lost by one vote. A week later, it won by nearly twenty. The prime minister resigned and the king offered to abdicate.

The American Revolution continued to exist in name only, without fighting, for another year. On April 19, 1783, it officially ended, eight years to the day after Lexington and Concord. Washington wrote to General Nathanael Greene that his men had sometimes been "half-starved; always in rags, without pay, and experiencing, at times, every species of distress which human nature is capable of undergoing."[84]

Soldiers started coming home in the summer of 1783. The peace was formally signed in Paris that September. The American negotiators, seventy-six-year-old Benjamin Franklin, with John Jay and John Adams, almost had more trouble with their former allies France and Spain over territorial demands than with their British enemy. On November 25, the British army and navy began to evacuate New York City. On December 4, "With a heart full of love and gratitude," Washington bade farewell to his remaining officers at New York City's Fraunces Tavern and went home for Christmas, eight years later than he had planned.

EXODUS AND AFTERMATH

"The chief concern of Americans about Negroes in the thirty months after Yorktown was their disappearance," wrote the historian Benjamin Quarles. "Whenever the defeated British made their final withdrawals, whether by land or sea, thousands of slaves went with them."[85] It was estimated that the South lost something like 100,000 slaves. South Carolina lost some 25,000 of its 110,000 slaves; Georgia lost 75 to 85 percent of its slaves; and Thomas Jefferson wrote that Virginia lost 30,000 slaves in 1778 alone. Some slaves joined the British out of hatred of America, but most, especially in the South, simply because it seemed the easiest road to freedom.

In the immediate postwar period, many ex-slaves accepted the British offer of free emigration to Britain or its colonies. They could not "in justice be abandoned to the merciless resentment of their former masters," wrote the British general Alexander Leslie to General Sir Guy Carlton.[86] British ships leaving New York, Charleston, and Savannah after the war carried well-known Tories, and up to twenty thousand blacks—all en route to Britain, Nova Scotia, Jamaica, Florida, or Africa. One corps of black drummers, who served in Baron Friedrich von Riedesel's Brunswick forces, chose to go to Germany. Other black British soldiers stayed behind to continue the war. A Georgian corps of three hundred ex-slaves, calling themselves the King of England's Soldiers, plundered by night and disappeared by day into the Savannah River swamps, to be burned out in May 1786 by South Carolina and Georgia militia.

Some three thousand former slaves chose to emigrate to Nova Scotia. The British had promised ex-slaves farms in Nova Scotia after the war, but when they arrived there were no farms, only wretched hovels, barely adequate against the harsh winters, and slavelike work for refugees. In 1781, David George, an ex-slave preacher from Virginia, sailed from Nova Scotia to Britain to plead the black cause. British abolitionists, led by William Wilberforce and Thomas Clarkson, established the Sierra Leone Company to enable destitute blacks to settle in West Africa. They persuaded the British secretary of state to order the governor of Nova Scotia to either give land to some two hundred black families, or send them to Sierra Leone at government expense. In January 1792, David George led about twelve hundred settlers from Halifax to Freetown to start a colony.

After the war, many black veterans had trouble getting pensions, as well as their promised freedom. Gad Asher, a substitute for his East Guilford, Connecticut, owner, won his. Asher's 1783 disability pension called him "unfit for any further duty, either in the field, or in garrison, being blind." His blind grandfather's war stories almost made him believe that he "had more rights than any white man in the town," wrote Jeremiah Asher, a Baptist minister and Civil War chaplain, in 1862. "Because of lessons taught by old black soldiers of the Revolution, neither my father nor my mother could persuade me that white boys were allowed to insult me because I was colored," he wrote. "I invariably felt justified in defending myself. Thus, my first ideas of the right of the colored man to life, liberty and the pursuit of happiness, were received from these old veterans and champions for liberty."[87]

All Revolutionary veterans, black and white, could consider themselves as founders of a nation, and their descendants heirs to the freedoms they had won.

"E Pluribus Unum"

In June 1782, with less than a year of war remaining, the nascent country created a motto: "E pluribus unum"—"Out of many, one." Some Americans, New Englanders especially, thought that the "one" included blacks.

In 1781, Elizabeth Freeman, a Revolutionary widow living in Stockbridge, Massachusetts, ran away when her slave mistress tried to hit her with a hot shovel. On the basis of the new state constitution and the "Bill of Rights," which she had learned about by listening as she served at table, Freeman, known as "Mumbet," sought help from the young lawyer Theodore Sedgwick, a member of the town's most important family. Arguing before the county court in Great Barrington, Sedgwick won her case in 1783, and slavery throughout New England began to collapse. In 1784 it was abolished in Massachusetts, and Connecticut and Rhode Island passed gradual emancipation acts. (Freeman was an ancestor of W.E.B. Du Bois.)

Revolutionary ideas of racial equality were also alive in the upper South. "Holding fellow men in bondage and slavery is repugnant to the golden law of God and the inalienable right of mankind, as well as every principle of the late glorious revolution," wrote Philip Graham of Maryland, who freed his slaves in 1787.[88] "I have for some time past been convinced that to retain them in Slavery is contrary to the true principles of Religion & Justice," wrote Robert Carter III of Virginia, one of the richest men in America, as he freed more than five hundred slaves in 1791.[89] Another upper South master asserted that he had freed his slaves on the authority of Tom Paine and God: "REASON THE FIRST: Agreeability to the RIGHTS OF MAN, every human being, be his or her color what it may, is entitled to freedom . . . Reason the second: My CONSCIENCE, the great criterion, condemns me for keeping them in slavery. Reason the third: The golden rule directs us to do unto every creature as we would be done unto. . . . Reason the fourth and last: I wish to die with a clear conscience."[90] And Richard Randolph, brother of John Randolph of Virginia, wrote to his guardian at his coming of age: "With regard to the division of the estate, I have only to say that I want not a single Negro for any other purpose than his immediate liberation. I consider every individual thus unshackled as the source of future generations, not to say nations, of freemen; and I shudder when I think that so insignificant an animal as I am is invested with this monstrous, this horrible power."[91]

Washington himself seemed to be of the slavery-is-distasteful-but-useful school. In April 1786, he wrote to Robert Morris: "There is not a man living who wishes more sincerely than I do, to see a plan adopted for the gradual abolition of [slavery]." Five months later, he wrote to John F. Mercer that he was determined never "to possess another slave by purchase, it being among my first wishes to see some plan adopted by which slavery may be abolished by law."[92] Washington's Revolutionary colleague General Horatio Gates freed all his slaves with generous provisions in 1790, but Washington himself remained of two minds. Typically, in 1791, when some of his slaves were taken to Pennsylvania and officials refused to return them to Virginia, Washington instructed Tobias Lear, his estate manager, to bring the slaves back in a manner that would "deceive both the slaves and the public." Washington's slaves were freed when he and his wife died. William Lee, who accompanied him into battle, received an annuity of thirty dollars, "as a testimony of my sense of his attachment to me, and for his faithful services during the Revolutionary War."[93]

Thomas Jefferson, who of course never led a "mixed multitude" in battle, saw blacks as a foreign element in the new American nation. While conceding the probable advisability of future emancipation, he thought that blacks and whites should be separated afterward, because of "deep-rooted prejudices entertained by the whites" and "ten thousand recollections, by the blacks, of the injuries they have sustained," he wrote in *Notes on the State of Virginia.* By southern lights a benevolent master, Jefferson nonetheless found blacks inferior in "endowments of both body and mind . . . dull, tasteless and anomalous. . . . Never yet could I find that a black had uttered a thought above the level of plain narration; never saw even an elementary trait of painting or sculpture."[94] In 1791, Washington appointed the black mathematician and astronomer Benjamin Banneker to the District of Columbia surveying commission. As a mathematical challenge, without ever seeing a clock (although he had examined a pocket watch), Banneker constructed the first clock entirely made in America. In 1792, when he was sixty-two, Banneker published the first of his six popular almanacs, and sent a copy to Jefferson, who was then secretary of state. Jefferson forwarded his copy to the Marquis de Condorcet, of the French Amis des Noirs ("Friends of the Blacks"), with a properly nationalistic accompanying letter: "I am happy to be able to inform you that we have now in the United States a negro . . . who is a very respectable mathematician." Taking credit for Washington's action, he told Condorcet that he had "procured [Banneker] to be employed under one of our chief directors in laying out the new federal city of the Potomac." Jefferson's private opinion was different: "I have a long letter from Banneker, which shows him to have a mind of a very common stature indeed." Banneker's "long letter" asked Jefferson to reconcile the proposition that all men were "created equal" with "detaining by fraud and violence so numerous a part of my brethren, under groaning captivity."[95]

Jefferson, who fathered children by his slave Sally Hemings, his father-in-law's "mighty near white" daughter, was, of course, a man in conflict. "I tremble for my country when I reflect that God is just—that his justice cannot sleep forever," he wrote. *Notes on the State of Virginia* decried slavery's "bad" influence. "The whole commerce between master and slave is a perpetual exercise of the most boisterous passions . . . the most unremitting despotism," he wrote. "Our children see this, and learn to imitate it . . . the child . . . puts on the same airs in the circle of smaller slaves . . . and thus nursed, educated, and daily exercised in tyranny, cannot but be stamped by it with odious peculiarities. The man must be a prodigy who can retain his manners and morals undepraved by such circumstances."[96]

* * *

The post-Revolutionary golden age for American blacks ended in Philadelphia in the summer of 1787, when the Constitutional Convention, led by conservatives who planned to entrench both slavery and southern political power, debated abolition. Most American radicals were not in Philadelphia. Jefferson, Paine, Patrick Henry, and John and Samuel Adams were all absent; New York's Gouverneur Morris (not overly fond of democracy) spoke for the radicals. Calling slavery "the curse of heaven," he swore he would rather "pay taxes to free all the Africans in America" than see it tolerated in the Constitution.[97] But the South threatened secession unless it got its way. "The true question at present," said South Carolina's John Rutledge, "is whether the Southern States shall or shall not be parties to the Union." As with the Declaration of Independence, the South put sectional interests first. Of the fifty-five convention delegates, sixteen had "productive" slaves and nine more had a least "a few slaves around the house."[98]

Northern states demanded that slaves be excluded from representation, as they were neither citizens nor voters, but included in taxation as property. The South won the compromise: each slave would count as three-fifths of a person. Thanks to the three-fifths clause, the South gained extra congressional representation, and won a more powerful vote than the North in the Electoral College. The "compromise" also guaranteed the right to import new slaves for at least twenty years, and ensured federal aid to the South in suppressing slave rebellions. "Religion and humanity have nothing to do with the question," Rutledge explained to the northerners. "Interest alone is the governing principle with nations. . . . If the Northern states consult their interests they will not oppose an increase of slaves, which will increase the commodities of which they will become carriers."[99]

Six years later, in 1793, Eli Whitney's cotton gin was introduced in the South. It condemned the vast majority of American blacks to slavery without hope of freedom for generations to come. A fierce new Fugitive Slave Law arrived with the cotton gin. Runaways could be seized in any state, slave or free, and returned to their owners on the owner's word alone. This license to kidnap made it a crime to harbor a fugitive or prevent his arrest. James Forten, free black Philadelphia sailmaker and former Revolutionary powder boy, signed a petition to Congress for modification of the act. It was tabled out of hand.

But hope was reborn in the same year when it seemed lost. In 1793, the Canadian Upper Legislature abolished slavery. Despite the Fugitive Slave Law, runaways now had a true goal in the "North Star." Freedom was no longer merely a hope, it was a reality at the northern U.S. border. As the nineteenth century began, the drama of flight—and freedom—would take on new meaning.

In his 1842 address to the New Hampshire antislavery society, Revolutionary veteran Dr. Harris expressed the nineteenth-century concept of freedom as colored by eighteenth-century ideals. "It surprises me," he said, "that every man does not rally at the sound of liberty, and array himself with those who are laboring to abolish slavery in our country. The very mention of it warms the blood in my veins, and, old as I am, makes me feel something of the spirit and impulses of '76. *Then* liberty *meant* something. Then, liberty, independence, freedom, were in every man's mouth. They were the sounds at which they rallied, and under which they fought and bled . . . The word slavery then filled their hearts with horror. They fought because they would not be slaves. Those whom liberty has cost nothing, do not know how to prize it."[100]

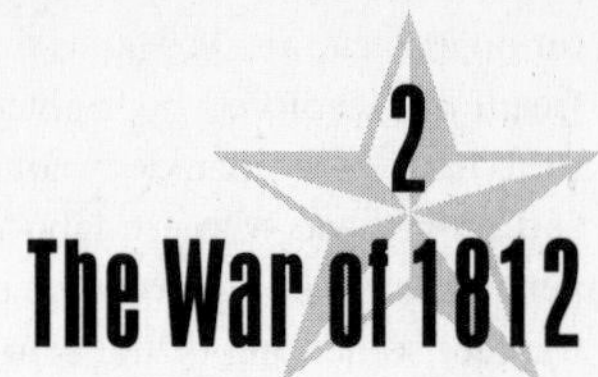

2 The War of 1812

RALLY ROUND THE EAGLE

I have nothing more to offer than what General Washington would have had to offer had he been taken by the British and put to trial by them. I have adventured my life in endeavoring to obtain the liberty of my countrymen, and am a willing sacrifice to their cause.[1]

—a Virginia slave executed in 1804 for poisoning whites

THE COMMON WIND

In 1791, America's slave owners, and many of their slaves, paid close attention to Haiti's revolution against France. More than 100,000 Haitian slaves had participated in a monthlong uprising against their colonial masters. "Good God, who makest the sun to light us from on high, who raisest up the sea and makes the storms to thunder—Good God, who watches over all, hidden in a cloud, protect us and save us from what the white men do to us. . . . Good God, give us vengeance, guide our arms, give us help. Good God, grant us that freedom which speaks to all men!" went the Haitian revolutionary Creole prayer.[2]

The American Revolutionary veteran Henri Christophe was Haiti's first king, but the rebel army chief Toussaint-Louverture, idolized by nineteenth-century romantic revolutionaries, became its great leader in the eight-year battle with Napoleon. Toussaint, who did not participate in the initial arson-and-murder phase of the revolt, would abolish slavery, establish schools, build roads, integrate the white minority into government life, and encourage Catholicism. Rumored to sleep only two hours a night, he was considered a military genius. "He disappears—he has flown—as if by magic. Now he reappears again where he is least expected. He seems to be ubiquitous. One never knows where his army is, what it subsists on, how he manages to recruit," wrote one Frenchman. "He, on the other hand, seems perfectly informed concerning everything that goes on in the enemy camp."[3] Napoleon tried to retake the island beginning in 1799, but resistance was so strong that he agreed to a treaty. France lost sixty thousand men in Haiti, including Karl Marx's brother-in-law.

Shortly after the peace treaty was signed, Toussaint-Louverture was kidnapped and taken to France. At Toussaint's death in a French prison in 1803, Napoleon restored slavery in Haiti, Martinique, and Guadeloupe—but later that same year, Haiti's Jean-Jacques Dessalines defeated the French yet again. Having been put off the Americas by the experience of Haiti, Napoleon sold the Louisiana Territory to the United States at the rock-bottom price of four cents an acre. "Thus," wrote De Witt Talmadge, a nineteenth-century white cleric, "all of Indian Territory, all of Kansas and Nebraska, Iowa and Wyoming, Montana and the Dakotas, and most of Colorado and Minnesota, and all of Washington and Oregon states, came to us as the indirect work of a despised Negro."[4]

Toussaint was a hero to the British because he had defeated Napoleon. His death inspired Wordsworth to write:

TOUSSAINT, the most unhappy man of men! . . .
Though fallen thyself, never to rise again,
Live, and take comfort. Thou hast left behind
Powers that will work for thee; air, earth, and skies;
There's not a breathing of the common wind
That will forget thee; thou hast great allies;
Thy friends are exultations, agonies,
And love, and man's unconquerable mind.

The first quarter of the nineteenth century saw America as godparent to domestic rebellion, as well as international revolution. Haiti had inspired horror among whites, north and south, and the country was by now wary of revolutions and revolutionaries. In 1806, Tom Paine, who first used the words "United States of America," was denied American citizenship.[5] Commercial expansion now seemed more important in the founding colonies than the rights of man. Yet the new Northwest Territory, carved out of the Louisiana Purchase and stretching from Kentucky to Canada, the greatest commercial boon of all, proved that revolutionary principles and commercial expansion could coexist. The Territory's charter was pure Rights of Man: mandating trial by jury, public education, freedom of religion, and the permanent prohibition of slavery.[6] To many, it represented the American future. Establishing the idea of "free men and free land," the Northwest Territory became a cradle of nineteenth-century abolitionism. As sectional politics on the issue of slavery became more and more entrenched, Kentucky to Canada would become the main line of the Underground Railroad. The slave system, entering its prime, had all the muscle, but the antislavery movement was alive and growing.

According to the U.S. Census of 1800, 90 percent of the country's 1,002,037 blacks, 18.9 percent of the American population, were enslaved—and annual cotton exports were approaching twenty million pounds.[7] Slave revolts increased steadily over the next decade. Having heard "the breathing of the common wind," as well as the cry of the American Revolution, slaves fought for freedom as a right given by God, not only by man. Leaders of slave revolts, some of them veterans of the Revolution, would be motivated by extraordinary courage and conviction, and, often as not, by apocalyptic visions.

Conspiracies and Rebellions

Early in 1800, Gabriel Prosser began to organize a rebellion to free all Virginia slaves and create a black Virginia nation, with himself as leader. Taught to read by the wife of his owner, Gabriel believed that God, speaking to him through the Bible, had told him to free his people. Imitating Samson, he refused to cut his hair. The twenty-four-year-old blacksmith would oversee the making of weapons and bullets and eventually recruit over a thousand slaves from at least three counties around Richmond, making Revolutionary veterans among them group leaders. Gabriel assembled his followers at a brook on his owner's property on Saturday night, August 20, 1800 (there was no work the next day, and it was harvest time, so his troops could live off the land). They were organized to march on Richmond, about six miles away. The city was short on men and muskets—the surprise attack might have succeeded—but the plan was doomed by nature and by human treachery. As the slave troops gathered, there was a sudden heavy rainstorm, washing out all roads and bridges to Richmond—where, because two house slaves had already informed authorities, Governor James Monroe's Virginia military was waiting. Most of Prosser's band escaped capture because of the storm. Gabriel initially escaped but was found a month later in Norfolk, hiding in the hold of the ship that had brought him from Richmond. He had been betrayed, once again, by a fellow slave.[8]

Gabriel "expected that the poor white people would join him, and . . . two Frenchmen had actually joined," read the trial testimony of a slave known as Prosser's Ben. Gabriel had ordered that "none were to be spared of the whites except Quakers, Methodists, and French people."[9] Gabriel and some thirty-five fellow conspirators were hanged for insurrection, with compensation paid to their owners. Gabriel "seemed to have made up his mind to die," wrote Governor Monroe, "and to have resolved to say but little on the subject of the conspiracy."

In 1802, a slave named Arthur from Henrico County, Virginia, began recruiting for another armed rebellion. A recruitment leaflet was intercepted by an anonymous slave informer and passed on to a Mr. Matthews of Norfolk. "Black men if you have now a mind to join with me now is your time for freedom," wrote Arthur. "I have taken it on myself to let the country be at liberty. . . . I have joined with both black and white which is the common man or poor white people, mulattoes will join with me to help free the country, although they are free already. I have got 9 or 10 white men to lead me in the fight on the magazine, they will go before me and hand out guns, powder, pistols, shot . . . black men I mean to lose my life in this way if they will take it." The informer's note read: "White pepil be-ware of your lives, there is a plan now forming and intend to put in execution this harvest time—they are to commence and use their sithes as weapons until they can get possession of other weapons. . . . I am a confident of the leaders and cannot give you my name. I am also a greater friend to some of the Wites, and wish to preserve their lives. I am a favorite servant of my Master and Mistis, and love them dearly."[10]

Nine years later, in 1811, Charles Deslondes, a free mulatto from Santo Domingo, led a rebellion of more than four hundred slaves outside New Orleans. They destroyed several plantations and killed at least two whites, including the son of Major Andry, the owner of the plantation where the uprising began. The slaves fled to the woods, where Andry's posse followed and summarily executed them. The next day, Governor William Claiborne called out troops, including the battalion of the Free Men of Color, or Corps d'Afrique, the New Orleans black militia, to quell any possible slave uprising. Under Spanish rule during the Revolution, they had helped Bernardo de Gálvez drive the British from the lower Mississippi and were seen as useful in hunting runaway slaves. Of the four hundred slaves, some sixty-six were executed; their severed heads were strung up at intervals from New Orleans to the Andry plantation.[11]

* * *

The years leading up to the War of 1812 saw both the British and American slave trades officially abolished. In 1807, President Thomas Jefferson signed the bill that ended American participation in the slave trade as of January 1, 1808. There was too much money involved for the law to be a great deterrent, however. Now the kidnapping of free border-state blacks became rampant, and an illegal slave trade continued with impunity.

Slavery in America was stronger than ever, and slave laws were entrenched and intensified, although some powerful voices spoke out in opposition.

"It appears that American citizens are instrumental in carrying on a traffic in enslaved Africans, equally in violation of the laws of humanity, and in defiance of those of their own country," said President James Madison in an 1810 address to Congress. "The same just and benevolent motives which produced the interdiction in force against this criminal conduct will doubtless be felt by Congress, in devising further means of suppressing the evil."[12] Even Jefferson, in an 1810 letter to the French abolitionist the Abbé Grégoire, agreed that "whatever be their degree of talent, it is no measure of their rights."[13]

"DOVES" AND "HAWKS"

The historian Samuel Eliot Morison called the War of 1812 "the most unpopular war that this country has ever waged, not even excepting the Vietnam conflict."[14] Like that of Vietnam, it was a highly politicized war that raised conflicts between generations. It was bitterly contested between antiwar Federalists from New England, called Doves, and southern and western Hawks. Largely belonging to the Revolutionary generation, Doves had seen war; most Hawks had not.

The Doves generally supported Jefferson's policy of economic "peaceable coercion" in dealing with Britain, although they also generally disliked and ignored the embargo on British goods. Hawks preferred expansion to peace. Southerners wanted the Spanish, who were then British allies, out of Florida, and westerners wanted the British out of western Canada. New England opposed the war partly out of loyalty to Britain and opposition to Napoleon, but mostly because war would completely destroy American shipping, the already crippled chief industry. New England Federalists talked of secession—of separating the thirteen original colonies from the Louisiana Purchase, and negotiating a separate peace with Britain.

While British naval policy had almost no effect on the South and West, Hawks wanted action against Britain. "Is the rod of British power to be forever suspended over our heads?" asked Representative Henry Clay, of Kentucky.[15] Clay and Senator John C. Calhoun of South Carolina, the congressional War Hawk leaders, envisioned a war that could win America Florida, Mexico, and *all* of Canada. Unlike most New Englanders, the ever rebellious John Adams was a Hawk—believing that war against England was "necessary to convince France that we are something; and above all necessary to convince ourselves, that we are not-Nothing." This war was the first expression of America's bid to become a world power.

The War of 1812 was essentially fought for freedom of the seas. The chief American complaints against Britain were interference with American shipping and naval impressment (forcing men into the Royal Navy). For some time, British sailors had been escaping the terrible conditions of their service and fleeing to American ships (although these were only slightly better). In response, Britain claimed the right to stop all neutral vessels on the high seas and remove sailors of British birth, impressing them into service—but too many Americans were taken by "mistake."

The roots of war lay in Britain's ongoing conflict with Napoleon. After Nelson's celebrated defeat of the French at the Battle of Trafalgar in 1805, France had tried to stop British trade with Europe. The British had retaliated by blockading French ports. British and French blockades naturally had a disastrous effect on American shipping, prompting complaints to both sides. In 1808, when a British man-of-war outside Norfolk fired on the U.S. frigate *Chesapeake,* whose captain, the Revolutionary veteran James Barron, had refused to let his ship be searched, anti-British feeling soared. Three U.S. sailors were killed, eighteen wounded, and four seized as deserters from the British navy. Three of the so-called deserters were black: William Ware, John Strachan, and David (or Daniel) Martin.[16] The four sailors were soon released, but President Thomas Jefferson ordered all British vessels out of U.S. harbors.

An American war with Britain was of great advantage to France. Seeking to woo Americans to the French side, in 1810 Napoleon exempted the United States from all French shipping restrictions. The following year, although Britain apologized for the *Chesapeake* incident and paid damages, President James Madison, now Napoleon's good friend, shut off all British trade. In exchange for congressional Hawk support in the 1812 election, Madison asked Congress for a declaration of war on June 1; and Congress finally declared it on June 18, 1812. Two days before the American declaration, Britain announced that it would repeal the shipping and impressment laws that were the chief basis for the conflict. But it was too late: "Free Trade and Seamen's Rights" had already become the battle cry.

"UNCLE SAM"

When the war broke out, the U.S. treasury was nearly empty. The Navy had fewer than twenty seagoing ships. While the War Department had been authorized to recruit fifty thousand one-year volunteers, it only managed to obtain ten thousand men.[17] New England, the country's richest region, protested the war by withholding troops and money—although it still raised more regiments than the Hawkish middle and southern states. Henry Clay's Kentucky sent only four hundred recruits. New York organized two regiments of approximately two thousand blacks, slave and free, promising freedom to the former at the end of the war. Philadelphia also organized a black regiment, but too late for action.[18]

The American defense industry was born when the War Department contracted the cotton gin's inventor, Eli Whitney, to manufacture assembly-line muskets at his Whitneyville, Connecticut, factory. The name of "Uncle Sam" was also born in the War of 1812: a government inspector, Samuel "Uncle Sam" Wilson, was responsible for stamping "U.S." approval on boxes of military provisions. Workers and loaders joked that the initials stood for "Uncle Sam."

"SUCH TARS"

The U.S. naval position looked bad on paper. Britain had a thousand fighting ships, with more than a hundred battleships; the United States had no battleship-class vessels, and only seventeen frigates and sloops-of-war. But the British were in for a surprise. Three U.S. frigates, the *Constitution* (nicknamed *Old Ironsides* by its sailors), the *President,* and the *United States,* were faster, and had heavier broadsides, than any ship of their class in the world.

One-sixth of the U.S. Navy seamen who fought in the War of 1812, serving on warships and privateers, were black. They fought conspicuously in the only two American naval victories that directly affected the course of the war—Captain Oliver Hazard Perry's on Lake Erie, on September 10, 1813, and Lieutenant Thomas McDonough's on Lake Champlain, on September 11, 1814. Both victories permitted U.S. inroads into Canada. ("Backside Albany" was a popular song about a black sailor at Lake Champlain: "Backside Albany stan' Lake Champlain, / One little pond half full a water . . .")

More than a hundred blacks were among the four hundred men in Perry's 1813 Great Lakes Armada, dispatched to spearhead an invasion of Canada. Perry had complained at being sent only "blacks, soldiers, and boys" for nine new ships, but Commodore Isaac Chauncey replied that Perry should be happy with blacks: "They are not surpassed by any seamen we have in the fleet and I have yet to learn that the color of a man's skin or the cut and trimmings of the coat can affect a man's qualifications or usefulness. I have nearly fifty blacks on board this ship, and many of them are among my best men."[19] Perry's Lake Erie victory forced the British to pull out of Detroit, and much of what is now Michigan came under U.S. control, allowing Major General William Henry Harrison to cross Lake Michigan and defeat the retreating British at Canada's Battle of the Thames. (By 1814, however, Napoleon had lost in Europe and the British were able to send new troops to Canada, thus ending U.S. hopes of Canadian conquest.)

Blacks served on American privateers as well as warships. Commander Nathaniel Shaler, of the privateer schooner *Governor Thompkins,* described the heroism of his black men in an encounter with three British ships on January 1, 1812:

> Her first broadside killed two men and wounded others. . . . The name of one of my poor fellows who was killed ought to be registered in the book of fame, and remembered with reverence as long as bravery is considered a virtue; he was a black man by the name of John Johnson; a 24 lb. shot struck him in the hip and took away all the lower part of his body; in this state the poor brave fellow lay on the deck, and several times exclaimed to his shipmates, "Fire away my boys, no haul a color down." The other was also a black man, by the name of John Davis, and was struck in much the same way; he fell near me, and several times requested to be thrown overboard, saying he was only in the way of others. While America has such tars, she has little to fear from the Tyrants of the ocean.[20]

The Royal Navy had black sailors, too. The British vice admiral Sir Alexander Cochrane, whose expeditionary force from Bermuda landed in Chesapeake Bay in the summer of 1814, offered fleeing slaves the choice of bearing arms for Britain or emigrating as free men to Canada or the West Indies. As many as five thousand Chesapeake Bay slaves fled to the British, who now controlled the Atlantic coastal waters. Rear Admiral George Cockburn organized the "Black Marines," a hard-fighting unit of runaway slaves. ("The Guinea Boy" was a popular British song about a black volunteer on the Chesapeake with the "redoubtable Admiral Cockburn."[21]) In August, the "Black Marines" were part of the fifteen-hundred-member British invading force in Bladensburg, Maryland. A humiliating American defeat, Bladensburg saw some five thousand Virginia and Maryland militia run away, terrified by the sight and sound of the new British rockets. Fortunately for national honor, six hundred sailors and marines from a gunboat flotilla, including several blacks, stayed with their guns.

"Black Marines" were in the British advance a few days later that captured the Federal City. President James Madison and his glamorous wife,

Dolley, had been forced to evacuate, escaping only with Gilbert Stuart's portrait of George Washington, the President's House silver, a wagonload of official papers, and Dolley Madison's parrot. Meanwhile, all able-bodied Washington citizens, including "free men of color," were ordered to build redoubts. "An immense crowd of every description of persons attended to offer their services," reported *The National Intelligencer* of August 21, 1814. "It is with much pleasure also we state that on this occasion the free people of color in this city acted as became patriots conducting themselves with the utmost order and propriety."[22] The Capitol was burned, and the President's House was looted before it was torched. Cockburn himself took some souvenirs: one of Madison's hats, and Dolley's favorite chair cushion (which he made the object of rude jokes).

Americans had their revenge a month later, when they defeated the British at the Battle of Baltimore. The Washington lawyer Francis Scott Key (a prisoner on a British ship) was inspired to express his joy at seeing at first light, after a night of "rockets' red glare" and "bombs bursting in air," the tattered, but still flying, American flag over Fort McHenry. "'Tis the star-spangled banner," he wrote in September 1814. "O, long may it wave / O'er the land of the free and the home of the brave."

JOSEPH SAVARY AND THE NEW ORLEANS FREE MEN OF COLOR

Blacks were basically eliminated from the military after the Revolution. In 1792, Congress restricted militia service to "free able-bodied white male citizens."[23] Most states followed suit—but Louisiana had special circumstances. In 1805, New Orleans had thirty-five hundred whites and sixteen hundred free blacks. By 1809, there were some two thousand more free blacks, refugees from Santo Domingo, many of whom had supported the French in the Haitian Revolution.[24] Louisiana was a slave territory, but its constitution permitted a free black militia, formerly recognized by both France and Spain, as useful in hunting runaway slaves.

The New Orleans free black militia first offered its services to the United States in 1803. It was initially ignored, then ordered disbanded. In the midst of the threat of British invasion in 1812, however, when Louisiana officially became a state, Governor William Claiborne wrote to President James Madison that New Orleans's black militia was "esteemed a very serviceable corps . . . not to re-commission them would disgust them, and might be productive of future mischief." The Louisiana military now recruited free blacks who had either paid taxes for the previous two years, or who owned $300 worth of property. The new Battalion of Free Men of Color was organized around the earlier militia group. The law specified that all militia officers be white, but there were three black second lieutenants: militia veterans Isidore Honoré and Vincent Populus, and Joseph Savary, who had been an officer in the Santo Domingo army.

In the autumn of 1814, General Andrew Jackson, who had retaken Pensacola from the British and was currently defending Mobile, was called to save New Orleans from imminent invasion. Writing to Jackson, Governor Claiborne reiterated the fact that under the Spanish, New Orleans free blacks "were always relied on in time of difficulties, and on several occasions evinced in the field the greatest firmness and courage."[25] Jackson had already used black troops in Mobile. When an American charge was repulsed at the Battle of Fort Boyer, near Mobile, a black soldier from Tennessee named Jeffrey had leaped onto a horse and rallied his fellow Americans to keep fighting. Jackson made him an honorary major. When the assistant paymaster of the Seventh Military District objected to paying black troops in cash, Jackson wrote: "Be pleased to keep to yourself your opinions upon the policy of making payment to particular corps. It is enough for you to receive my order for the payment of troops with the necessary muster rolls, without inquiring whether the troops are white, Black, or Tea."

On September 21, 1814, Jackson called on New Orleans's "free men of color" to "rally round the standard of the eagle, to defend all which is dear in existence." He acknowledged military injustice:

> Through a mistaken policy you have heretofore been deprived of participation in the glorious struggle for national rights in which our country is engaged. This no longer shall exist. As sons of freedom, you are now called upon to defend our most inestimable blessing. To every noble-hearted, generous freeman of color, volunteering to serve during the present contest with Great Britain . . . there will be paid the same bounty in money and lands now received by the white soldiers of the United States, viz: one hundred and twenty-four dollars in money, and one hundred and sixty acres of land.[26]

The men of color would be segregated, however. "As a distinct, independent battalion, or regiment pursuing the path of glory," Jackson said, "you will, undivided, receive the applause and gratitude of your countrymen."

* * *

Major General Sir Edward Pakenham's British invasion armada was gathering in Jamaica and preparing to move on New Orleans as Second

Lieutenant Isidore Honoré's new battalion reported to duty on December 12, 1814. Honoré's was one of two black battalions (including a twelve-piece band) organized and equipped by Colonel Michel Fortier, Sr., a wealthy New Orleans merchant. Both were commanded by white officers. The militia veteran Vincent Populus became the first black officer of field-grade rank (major or above) recognized by the United States. Joseph Savary became a hero of the war, and Jackson, who would make him a major, usually referred to him as Colonel. Savary had sided with whites during the Santo Domingo uprising; he and his family, including his brother Belton Savary, were among the refugees of 1809. Savary's reputation was distinctly enhanced by his association with the piratical Lafitte brothers, of Galveston, Texas. Governor Claiborne described Lafitte's black pirates as "Santo Domingo negroes of the most desperate character, and no worse than most of their white associates."[27] Savary's force of two hundred free men of color included Creoles, Choctaws, and Lafitte pirates.

On December 18, Jackson addressed his six thousand troops, some five hundred of whom were free blacks. A special address was read to the blacks:

> To the Men of Color, Soldiers! From the shores of Mobile I collected you to arms; I invited you to share in the perils and to divide the glory of your white countrymen. I expected much from you for I was not misinformed of those qualities which must render you so formidable to an invading foe. I knew that you would endure hunger and thirst and all the hardships of war. I knew that you loved the land of your nativity, and that, like ourselves, you had to defend all that is most dear to man; but you surpass my hopes. I have found in you, united to those qualities, that noble enthusiasm which impels to great deeds. Soldiers! The President of the United States shall be informed of your conduct on the present occasion, and the voice of the representatives of the American Nation shall applaud your valor, as your General now praises your ardor. The enemy is near; his sails cover the lakes; but the brave are united; and if he finds us contending among ourselves, it will be for the prize of valor, and fame its noblest reward.

The Battle of New Orleans began on New Year's Day, 1815. Jackson had misjudged the British. Thinking they would come in overland, he sent the black battalions to join in guarding the vulnerable route from Mobile. When he discovered that the British had come by water, through the bayous, and were now encamped nine miles outside the city, he ordered a night assault. "There was, at times, considerable confusion on both sides," wrote Marcus Christian in his monograph on the one hundred and fiftieth anniversary of the battle. "When the fight came close, it often developed into a series of duels between regiments, battalions, companies, squads and even individuals. Under such circumstances the Negro troops fared well, although some of the guns which Colonel Fortier had repaired for the free men of color failed at the crucial moment, and in the hand-to-hand fighting they were used as clubs."[28] Savary's young drummer boy, Jordan Noble, beating incessantly "in the hottest hell of fire," was the rallying point in the dark for the black troops. With overtones of the French Revolution, Savary himself could be heard above the battle, crying in Santo Domingo French, "March on, my friends, march on against the enemies of the country!" Jackson, praising Savary's troops for "great bravery," was said to have hugged him on the battlefield.

The outcome was a stalemate, but the British were held off. All New Orleans men, white and black, slave and free, were called to help fortify Rodriguez Canal, on the right bank of the Mississippi. When the British finally marched on the city, on January 8, they met a fortified line on the Chalmette Plains, opposite the canal—and the largest black army ever seen in America. The two black battalions stood side by side in the middle of the "Jackson Line," and blacks were scattered throughout the other regiments. "The New Orleans colored regiment were so anxious for glory that they could not be prevented from advancing over our breastworks and exposing themselves," wrote Vincent Nolte, a white veteran of the battle and noted soldier of fortune (the inspiration for Hervey Allen's *Anthony Adverse*). Savary and his men fought like "desperados," he added, and they deserved distinguished praise.[29]

One-third of the wounded were from the black battalions, including Sergeant Belton Savary, Major Savary's brother, who died two days after the battle. The British lost two thousand men, including General Pakenham. "I have always believed he fell from the bullet of a free man of color, who was a famous rifle shot and came from the Attacaps region of Louisiana," Jackson wrote to President Monroe.[30]

"The two corps of colored volunteers have not disappointed the hopes that were formed of their courage and perseverance in the performance of their duty," said Jackson in tribute to his black battalions. He singled out Joseph Savary for special mention.[31] Meanwhile, a furious Savary defied a postbattle order forbidding blacks to join in the victory parade, and marched his men through the city. Expressing hatred of ungrateful Americans, he returned to Jean Lafitte in Texas to continue his career of smuggling, privateering, piracy, and revolution, eventually fighting with Simón Bolívar.

Most of the free men of color who fought in New Orleans were soon disillusioned, regarding themselves as *objets de mépris* (objects of contempt) in the eyes of white society. Although a few, or their descendants, won pensions, it is doubtful that any received their promised bounties and land. Savary requested, and received, a pension in 1819 "for the services by him rendered . . . under command of major general Jackson during the invasion of the British."[32]

New Orleans was the worst British military defeat since the Revolution and a psychological high point for the American people. The Revolution had given America independence and a national identity; the War of 1812 gave it a place in the larger world—proving, in John Adams's words, that America was "not nothing." The new country was fighting for a continent, not just thirteen colonies. Both Britain and the United States ultimately saw the war as wasteful and counterproductive to their real military and commercial interests. And both could claim victory. The terms of the Treaty of Ghent specified that all lands captured by either side were to be returned. Everything would be exactly as it was before the war, with commissions from both countries to settle any boundary issues. (In this pretelegraph war, the Battle of New Orleans was actually fought two weeks after the treaty was signed.) But the war not only consolidated American independence and identity; it also strengthened southern slavery. The treaty mandated that blacks who fled to the British be returned to their masters or sold in the West Indies, with compensation to American owners.

COLONIZATION

By the first quarter of the nineteenth century, free American blacks had become a beleaguered group. In the North, they now had to compete with urban immigrants for employment, and in the South they were perceived as a threat to slavery. The first quarter of the century saw the development of what the black historian John Hope Franklin called "a set of defenses of slavery that became the basis for much of the racist doctrine to which some Americans have subscribed from then to the present time."[33] The idea that free blacks were a menace to themselves as well as society was advanced and theorized by a coalition of southern politicians and pseudo–social scientists.

In the early years of the eighteenth century, Quakers and others had discussed the idea of returning blacks to Africa—of restoring them to their native land. In the Revolutionary years, Thomas Jefferson headed a Virginia legislative committee that produced a plan for gradual emancipation and restoration to Africa. After the Revolution, Dr. Samuel Hopkins and the Reverend Ezra Stiles (a future president of Yale) discussed the possibility of sending well-educated American blacks to colonize and Christianize Africa. In 1800, after the Gabriel Prosser insurrection, the Virginia legislature took up the question of colonizing "persons obnoxious to the laws, or dangerous to the peace of society." By the early years of the nineteenth century, colonization of free blacks had ceased to be a humanitarian effort and become a police action for slave owners.

Late in 1816, the southerners Bushrod Washington, Francis Scott Key, and John Randolph were among the founders of the American Colonization Society. At the first meeting, Henry Clay praised the society's aim "to rid our country of a useless and pernicious, if not dangerous portion of its population—the free Negro." The society purchased territory near Cape Mesurado, on the West African coast, for the resettlement of freed American slaves. They named the colony Liberia, and its capital city Monrovia, in honor of President James Monroe. Some Colonization Society members, perhaps hoping to deflect black fears of enforced exportation, freed some of their own slaves specifically to colonize Liberia.

In January 1817, three thousand free blacks met in St. Thomas A.M.E. (African Methodist Episcopal) Church in Philadelphia to protest Colonization Society attempts to exile them from the land of their "nativity." The leaders of the meeting were the Revolutionary veteran and sailmaker James Forten and two A.M.E. Church founders, the Reverends Richard Allen (also a Revolutionary vet) and Absalom Jones. "Whereas our ancestors (not of choice) were among the first successful cultivators of the wilds of America, we their descendents feel ourselves entitled to participate in the blessings of her luxuriant soil, which their blood and sweat manured; and that any measure or system of measures, having a tendency to banish us from her bosom, would not only be cruel, but in direct violation of those principles, which have been the boast of this republic," read the group's resolution. The resolution further resolved "that we never will separate ourselves voluntarily from the slave population in this country; they are our brethren by the ties of consanguinity, of suffering, and of wrong."[34]

Free blacks had few friends. Even that so-called ally of the blacks James Madison succumbed to the lure of colonization: "To be consistent with existing and probably unalterable prejudices in the United States, the freed blacks ought to be permanently removed beyond the region occupied by, or allotted to, a white population. . . . The objections to a thorough incorporation of the two people are insuperable."[35] Although new free states had joined the union and the power of the abolitionist movement was growing, legal doors were closing. This was so even in the North, where new economic and social tensions were surfacing. In 1818, Connecticut blacks were disenfranchised. In 1819, three white women stoned a black woman to death in Philadelphia. And in 1820, the U.S. government announced: "No Negro or mulatto will be received as a recruit of the Army."[36]

Blacks could not be American soldiers, but they could still wage domestic war on slavery. Insurrections continued to simmer, and arson was a favorite weapon. "I am to inform you that this company, for the present, declines to make insurance in any of the slave states," wrote a northern fire insurance executive to a Georgia subscriber in 1820.[37]

DENMARK VESEY

Denmark Vesey, a successful free Charleston carpenter, began to organize his underground army during Christmas in 1821, when neighboring plantation slaves could traditionally visit each other. Originally planned for July 14, 1822—not because of the French Revolution, but because that night, a Sunday, would be moonless, and because most of Charleston's important citizens would be away for the summer—the revolt was pushed up to June 16, and plans were made apace. "Vesey said we were to take the Guard-House and Magazine to get arms; that we ought to rise up and fight against the whites for our liberties," said his fellow leader Rolla, describing a meeting. "He read to us from the Bible, how the Children of Israel were delivered out of Egypt from Bondage."[38] According to the nineteenth-century black historian William Cooper Nell, Vesey's men planned to "sweep the town with fire and sword, not permitting a single white soul to escape."[39]

In 1800, some twenty years after he arrived in Charleston from French Santo Domingo as a fourteen-year-old slave, Denmark Vesey won a $1,500 lottery and bought his freedom for $600. Denmark (an approximation of his French slave name, "Télémaque"), the former favorite slave of a Charleston slave trader named Captain Vesey, became a successful carpenter, with possibly two wives and several children, eventually amassing property worth $8,000. A pillar of black Charleston, he was also a charismatic lay preacher in the city's A.M.E. Church. Inspired by Haiti and Santo Domingo, he preached revolution on just about every plantation around Charleston.

He made plans and held meetings—often in churches, where slaves could legitimately gather on Sundays—creating a network of recruiters, agents, cells, and assignments. According to Rolla, who was owned by the governor of South Carolina, Vesey listed thousands of recruits—each man contributing "12 and ½ cents" to make or buy arms.[40] Blacksmiths made daggers, pikes, and bayonets, and a white barber was recruited to make wigs and whiskers out of European hair. Vesey's army of nine thousand or so Charleston-area plantation slaves was organized and led by a distinctly dangerous (to slave-owning eyes) coalition: free Charleston blacks and slaves of Charleston's white leadership. What was even more dangerous, two of Vesey's major lieutenants—Gullah Jack, "a man of magic" whose followers believed he could not be killed, and a mystic known as Blind Phillip—were leaders of plantation slaves. They bridged the historic gap between house and field.

Vesey had wanted to recruit all blacks, but the carpenter Peter Poyas, another lieutenant, warned against "favorite" house servants—especially "those waiting men who received presents of old coats, etc. from their masters."[41] The conspirators ignored their own rules. Vesey was betrayed on May 30, 1822, by Peter Devany, "favorite and confidential slave of Col. J. C. Prioleau." A second house slave also furnished information. Both informers received freedom and a lifetime annuity from the South Carolina legislature.

Four whites and 131 blacks were arrested; thirty-seven blacks (including Rolla) were hanged. Vesey was captured on June 22, after another slave, under torture, revealed his whereabouts. "It is difficult to imagine what infatuation could have prompted you to attempt an enterprise so wild and visionary," the judge said before sentencing him to death. "You were a free man; were comparatively wealthy; and enjoyed every comfort. . . . You had, therefore, much to risk, and little to gain."[42] But Vesey, who was hanged before a large crowd, "died silent." At first, official versions of the revolt were widely circulated; very soon, however, all information about Vesey's insurrection was suppressed, although he was said to have inspired a young John Brown.

After Vesey, the free blacks of Charleston were required to wear diamond-shaped badges on their clothing, and to carry "free" papers at all times. Because whites believed that black Methodists aided the rebellion, the flourishing African Methodist Episcopal Church of Charleston was crushed. Slavery's despotic rule now extended to all blacks, slave and free. "Let it never be forgotten," wrote Edwin C. Holland, of Charleston, in 1822, "that our Negroes are freely the JACOBINS of the country."[43]

It would take almost another half-century for the aim of Vesey's rebellion to be accomplished—not by insurrection, but by war.

3 The Civil War

LIKE MEN OF WAR

Once let the black man get upon his person the brass letters, U.S., let him get an eagle on his buttons, and a musket on his shoulder and bullets in his pocket, and there is no power on earth which can deny that he has earned the right to citizenship in the United States.[1]

—*Frederick Douglass, 1863*

The Civil War, like the Revolution, was born in Boston. Charleston might not have fired on Fort Sumter if John Brown had not fired first at Harpers Ferry, with guns from Boston's "Secret Six." Brown's Virginia raid, with an integrated "army" of twenty-two, was financed by six prominent Boston abolitionists: the clergymen Thomas Wentworth Higginson and Theodore Parker; the editor Franklin B. Sanborn; the former New York congressman Gerrit Smith; the merchant George L. Stearns; and Dr. Samuel Gridley Howe, head of the Perkins School for the Blind.[2] That righteous abolitionists had become quixotic terrorists was symptomatic of the sea change that occurred in the abolitionist movement in the 1850s: armed struggle had replaced the Quaker pacifism of earlier years.

In the seamless garment of nineteenth-century social justice were woven together abolition, feminism, temperance, and peace—but abolition was the sacred thread. "To the outside world a set of pestilent fanatics," wrote Sidney Howard Gay, managing editor of the antislavery *New York Tribune,* of abolitionists, "among themselves the most charming circle of cultivated men and women that it has ever been my lot to know."[3]

By the mid-nineteenth century, many white abolitionists, influenced by the second Great Awakening, the religious revival of the 1820s, had come to regard the war against slavery as a crusade. "Evangelical abolitionists" from New England, western New York, and the Ohio frontier saw themselves, in the words of the historian Merton L. Dillon, as actors in "a cosmic drama of sin and redemption."[4] Many other white Americans, however, regarded them as dangerous fanatics. To the Irish working class, they were hypocrites taking bread from the mouths of poor white babies—a concept promulgated by the northern Democratic Party. Republican Boston, the Athens of the New World, produced abolition's great apologists: Emerson, Whittier, Longfellow, Thoreau, Wendell Phillips, Theodore Parker, Richard Henry Dana, Horace Mann, the Lowells, the Jameses, the Beechers, the Alcotts, and the Adamses. (Boston-born Edgar Allan Poe was the only nineteenth-century writer of any note who was proslavery.)

Boston women also contributed much to the abolitionist and, later, the Union cause. "All through the conflict, up and down / Marched Uncle Tom and Old John Brown," wrote Supreme Court Justice Oliver Wendell Holmes, a Civil War veteran.[5] Both of these figures were immortalized by women. If Harriet Beecher Stowe was, in Lincoln's words, the "little woman who wrote the book that made this great war," then Julia Ward Howe, wife of Secret Sixer Samuel Gridley Howe, was the "little woman" who gave the North, in "The Battle Hymn of the Republic," a better anthem than "Dixie."

Boston abolitionists not only wanted to fight the Slave Power, they wanted black soldiers in the vanguard of the crusade. Led by the Secret Six, they got their way. Thomas Wentworth Higginson, one of the six, became colonel of the 1st South Carolina Volunteers, the first regular Army regiment of runaway slaves. Another "Sixer," George L. Stearns, organized the 54th Massachusetts, the first regiment of free black northerners. Frederick Douglass, America's first national black leader, was the 54th's principal recruiter. Douglass traveled all over the North calling on blacks to enlist—often encouraging them by singing "John Brown's Body." His two sons were 54th volunteers.

* * *

By 1860 there were four million slaves in America. One out of every seven people in the country was a slave. "They are deceived who flatter themselves that the ignorant and debased slave has no conception of the magnitude of his wrongs," wrote the ex-slave Solomon Northrup in 1854. "A day may come—it WILL come, if his prayer is heard—a terrible day of vengeance, when the master in his turn will cry in vain for mercy."[6]

"The citizen of the Southern states becomes a sort of domestic dictator from infancy," wrote the French traveler and cultural historian Alexis de Tocqueville in 1833 in *Democracy in America.* "The first notion he acquires in life is, that he was born to command, and the first habit he contracts is that of ruling without resistance. His education tends, then, to give him the character of a haughty and hasty man—irascible, violent, ardent in his desires, impatient of obstacles but easily discouraged if he cannot succeed in his first attempt."[7] Tocqueville's prediction seems to have been borne out by the testimony of William Wells Brown, the son of a slave and her Kentucky master. In his historical work *The Black Man* (1863) Brown described his life under his five-year-old white "master": "William had become impudent, petulant, peevish and cruel. Sitting at the tea table, he would often desire to make his entire meal out of the sweetmeats, the sugar bowl, or the cake; and when mistress would not allow him to have them, he, in a fit of anger, would throw anything within his reach at me; spoons, knives, forks, and dishes would be hurled at my head, accompanied with language such as would astonish any one not well versed in the injurious effects of slavery upon the rising generation."[8] Jefferson, too, had warned that the children of slave owners were "nursed, educated, and daily exercised in tyranny."

The master ruled his slaves with "all the rights that he, as a warrior, could exercise over a vanquished foe," wrote Richard Hildreth in 1840 in his antislavery tract "Despotism in America." Certainly, slaves saw their bodies as a battleground. Ella Wilson described her beatings at the hands of her master: "He would put my hands together and tie them. Then he would strip me naked. . . . He would whip me on one side till that was sore and full of blood and then he would whip me on the other side till that was all tore up."[9] And then, of her mistress, "I got a scar big as the place my old mistress hit me. She took a bull whip once. The bull whip had a piece of iron in the handle of it. . . . She was so mad she took the whip and hit me over the head with the butt end of it and the blood flew. It ran all down my back and dripped off my heels."

Hinton Helper's 1857 book, *The Impending Crisis of the South,* would outrage southerners by pointing out that poor whites, as well as slaves, were slavery's victims. Because there were few jobs for landless white men, it was said in the South that the only people who worked were blacks and poor white women. Although cotton forced landless whites into rocky hollows, and out of the economy, the racial basis of slavery gave the South a unique means of keeping white populism at bay. "If he had no worthwhile interest in slavery," wrote W. J. Cash, describing the poor white, "if his real interest ran the other way about, he did nevertheless have that, to him, dear treasure of his superiority as a white man, which was conferred on him by slavery; and so was determined to keep the black man in chains."[10] For the South, there were only two classes of society: white and black. "Color alone is here the badge of distinction, the true mark of aristocracy, and all who are white are equal in spite of the variety of occupation," wrote Professor Thomas R. Dew of the College of William and Mary in 1832.[11]

The entire white community in the South was involved in protecting the property interests of slave owners. All white men, whether they owned slaves or not (most did not) had "patrol" duty—riding at night, making sure that blacks were in their proper place. "One seeking military activity did not have to wait for war with Britain or Mexico," wrote John Hope Franklin. "He could find it in the regular campaign against the subversion of slavery."[12] Because of the quasi-military aspect of the slave patrol, and the fact that regular employment for white males did not exist outside of a few large southern towns, the military became the traditional outlet for poor white males—and the southern mind-set came to rule the American military.

The last organized group of black soldiers, the New Orleans Free Men of Color, was abolished in 1834. Only the Navy continued to recruit blacks: nineteenth-century life at sea appealed only to the most desperate volunteers. By 1839, black sailors were so numerous on American warships that some Europeans believed "that all Americans were black and that naval officers, all of them white, were Englishmen especially recruited by the Navy."[13] Under pressure from congressional southerners, the Navy finally imposed a quota: blacks were not to exceed 5 percent of the "whole number of white persons" enlisted weekly or monthly. John C. Calhoun waged personal warfare on black sailors, insisting, unsuccessfully, that the Navy bar all black seamen except cooks and personal servants. In 1842, Calhoun's home state of South Carolina mandated jail for any black sailor of any nationality who stepped ashore.

Through the first half of the nineteenth century, the slave states ruled Congress, the presidency, the Supreme Court, and the Democratic Party. The old Democratic Party found its ideal in Andrew Jackson, president from 1829 to 1837. A great extoller of the "common man," Jackson spoke of the "Democracy of Numbers," as opposed to the Federalist emphasis on the "moneyed aristocracy of the few."[14] The Jacksonian ideal was somewhat disingenuous: his democracy of numbers extended mostly to big northern cities and included the newest and poorest immigrants, but the party had its own "moneyed aristocracy" in land, banking, and trading interests. Both elements depended economically on slavery. By the 1850s, cotton accounted for more than half of all U.S. exports. The banking magnate J. Pierpont Morgan had been pleased to hear a British admiral say, writes Jean Strouse in *Morgan,* that the only ship that could render the superior British navy "useless" was the American vessel *Cotton.*[15] New York City, whose new immigrants were mostly Irish, and whose banks held plantation mortgages, was the bastion of the northern Democratic Party.

PROPHETS: DAVID WALKER AND WILLIAM LLOYD GARRISON

Boston produced Crispus Attucks, America's first revolutionary martyr. Boston also produced abolition's first black militant publisher. David Walker, owner of a Cambridge secondhand clothing store and co-secretary of the Prince Hall Masonic Lodge, was the Boston agent for *Freedom's Journal,* America's first black newspaper. In September 1829, the paper, founded in New York City in 1827 by John B. Russwurm, published "Walker's Appeal": "To the Colored Citizens of the World, but in particular, and very expressly to those of the United States of America." Walker asked the "candid and unprejudiced" to search the pages of history "to see if the Antediluvians . . . Greeks—the Romans—the Mohametans—the Jews . . . ever treated a set of human beings as the white Christians of America do us, the blacks, or Africans." He called on Americans to remember their Declaration of Independence:

> Do you understand your own language? Hear your language, proclaimed to the world. . . . "We hold these truths to be self-evident—that ALL men are created EQUAL! that they are endowed by their Creator with certain unalienable rights; that among these are life, liberty, and the pursuit of happiness!!" . . . Hear your language further! "But when a long train of abuses and usurpations, pursuing invariably the same object, evinces a design to reduce them under absolute despotism, it is their RIGHT, it is their DUTY, to throw off such government. . . ." Now Americans! I ask you candidly, was your sufferings under Great Britain one hundredth part as cruel and tyrannical as you have rendered ours under you?

Killing whites, Walker added, would be a matter of "self-defense."

With a price on his head in the South, dead or alive, he was urged to flee to Canada. His sudden and mysterious death in 1830, three months after the publication of the third edition of the "Appeal," raised rumors of poison, but nothing was ever proved. In 1863, Walker's son would be the first black elected to the Massachusetts legislature.

Abolition's most consistently prophetic voice before the 1840s, however, was white. "I have a system to destroy, and I have no time to waste," said twenty-four-year-old William Lloyd Garrison in 1829. Garrison could be called a white militant, but unlike David Walker, he was a militant pacifist. On New Year's Day, 1831, he published the first edition of his newspaper *The Liberator:* "I will be harsh as truth, and as uncompromising as justice," he wrote. "On this subject I do not wish to think, or speak, or write with moderation. . . . I am in earnest—I will not equivocate—I will not excuse—I will not retreat a single inch—AND I WILL BE HEARD." From that moment on, the question among abolitionists was whether or not one was a "Garrisonian."

Garrison was a pacifist who believed in militant moral persuasion. He held that abolitionists should neither vote nor run for office in a country where slavery was legal, and he publicly burned the Constitution. "No compromise with slavery! No union with slaveholders!" he thundered.[16] Quakers were Garrison's chief supporters, closely followed by the free blacks of New York, Boston, Philadelphia, and Baltimore—although free blacks in Georgetown who received copies of *The Liberator* were liable to twenty-five lashes, prison, and enslavement. By 1834, Garrison reported that three-quarters of his readers were black. Frederick Douglass, who discovered *The Liberator* ("second only to the Bible") when he escaped from bondage in 1838, expressed "love" for the paper and its editor.[17] He admired Garrison's "sinless perfection," but they broke over his militant pacifism. Douglass believed in voting, running for office, and, if necessary, waging war for freedom.

The Gag Rule

Great Britain, which had freed a handful of slaves in the British Isles proper in 1770, abolished slavery entirely in 1833 by emancipating the West Indies, offering twenty million pounds in compensation to slave owners, and with no bloodshed. Not only were British slaves free, but blacks in Canada could vote. American slavery now stood alone in Christendom, a "peculiar institution."

In 1833, the American Anti-Slavery Society was founded at the Philadelphia home of the black Garrisonian James Forten, the Revolutionary powder boy who had walked home barefoot after the war. Forten was now a rich man, with his own sail loft and a $100,000 fortune thanks to a sail-handling invention. His son-in-law Robert Purvis, a close associate of Garrison, was one of the black founding members of the American Anti-Slavery Society, along with the Philadelphia dentist James McCrumell, the Boston reformer James Barbadoes, the New York editor Samuel Cornish, and the Reverends Theodore S. Wright and Peter Williams. The white founders of the Anti-Slavery Society included Garrison, the Quaker abolitionist Evan Lewis, and Theodore Weld, a thirty-year-old self-styled "backwoodsman" who recruited college students and preached against slavery in rural areas and small towns throughout New England, where he lived with black families and taught black children.

Panic gripped the slaveholding states in 1835, when the American Anti-Slavery Society raised money to disseminate tracts to the South. "Attacking the institution of slavery means attacking the safety and welfare of our country," declared the Virginia legislature. President Andrew Jackson, a Tennessee slaveholder who had led free black soldiers in the War of 1812, agreed. He sent a message to Congress seeking severe penalties for circulation through the mails of incendiary publications. A year later, Congress passed the "Gag Rule": antislavery petitions could neither be read, discussed, nor acted upon by that body. Abolition was declared to violate the Constitution. The Gag Rule would not be withdrawn until 1845, thanks largely to the efforts of the seventy-eight-year-old John Quincy Adams, one of America's last revolutionary abolitionists.

Despite the Gag Rule, abolitionists throughout the North continued to wage an increasingly aggressive campaign to keep slavery out of the West and abolish it in the South. In 1839, abolition became an official political movement when a white newspaper editor, James G. Birney, a former Alabama slaveholder, founded the Liberty Party. But the antislavery forces faced equally aggressive anti-abolitionism in the North and South. Proslavery mob action, particularly against the abolitionist press, was common in the North. A white abolitionist editor, the Reverend Elijah Lovejoy, was murdered in 1837 by an Illinois mob while defending his fourth printing press; his three other presses had already been destroyed by such mobs.

In 1833 Prudence Crandall, the thirty-year-old white Quaker headmistress of a "Female Seminary" in Canterbury, Connecticut, opened her school to "young ladies and little misses of color." Garrison and Forten supported her enthusiastically, but Crandall became the immediate target of public outrage. She was arrested three times, the school was burned down, and she was driven out of the state—and later became a personal hero to Mark Twain.

"When the true history of the anti-slavery cause shall be written, women will occupy a large space in its pages," wrote Frederick Douglass in his *Life and Times.*[18] All abolitionists believed in emancipation, but not all believed in equality of race or sex. Sixty-four male delegates and four female observers attended the second national Philadelphia Anti-Slavery Convention, in 1834. Lucretia Mott was the only woman who dared to speak. Mott—of whom Douglass wrote, "attired in her usual Quaker dress . . . the very sight of her, a sermon"—was a founder, with the

Quaker abolitionist Susan B. Anthony and Elizabeth Cady Stanton, of the women's rights movement. Douglass would be the only male guest at the 1848 Seneca Falls Women's Rights Convention.

"THE BUSINESS OF EGYPT"

The abolitionist center of higher education was Ohio's Oberlin College, opened in 1833. Oberlin belonged to the Western Reserve, land given in bounty to Revolutionary veterans, whose counties proudly considered themselves the most abolitionist in America. Professor Asa Mahan, of Cincinnati's Lane Seminary, had accepted the presidency of Oberlin on condition that blacks and women be admitted. Cincinnati, on the Ohio River, drew fugitive slaves from five states. In the town of Oberlin, near Lake Erie, five different Underground Railroad routes converged. Oberlin knew that it was considered "peculiar"—but "peculiar in that which is good," insisted John Jay Shiperd, a town founder.[19] "Strictly temperance," the town allowed no saloons, no billiard parlors, and no public smoking. And there were black students (including the children of Frederick Douglass) in the co-ed college classrooms, black children in the public school, black families in the churches, black professionals on the main street, and black voters at the polls—conditions existing nowhere else in Ohio outside of the Western Reserve. Writing of a nearby town, a slave catcher said: "Went there and found a place worse than Oberlin. Never saw so many niggers and abolitionists in any one place in my life! . . . They gave us 20 minutes to leave and wouldn't allow us that! Might as well try to hunt the devil there as to hunt a nigger."[20] By 1837, despite the Gag Rule, Ohio's Underground Railroad stations were the busiest in America, and it had 213 antislavery societies, more than New York and Massachusetts combined. "WE GO FOR REVOLUTION!" said Ohio Quakers, who pledged to aid escaping slaves in "defiance of all the governments on earth."

Although Quakers and others had been helping blacks to freedom since the eighteenth century, the Underground Railroad, or "Business of Egypt"—Canada was known as the Promised Land—was formally organized in 1838. An estimated 75,000 slaves, helped by more than 3,000 black and white Railroad members, escaped to freedom in the 1850s alone. Most runaways traveled one of the two main lines: along the Eastern Seaboard to Canada, or through Kentucky into Ohio. "Station masters," "chief engineers," and "conductors" led fugitives north. A "safe" house identified itself by a drinking gourd hung at the door, symbolizing the Big Dipper and the North Star. The Indiana home of the Railroad's white Quaker "President," Levi Coffin (inspiration for Harriet Beecher Stowe), was known as Grand Central Station. The black station master William Still, of Snowhill, New Jersey, near Philadelphia, was one of the busiest in the East. Still was the son of slaves; one passing fugitive from Alabama turned out to be his own brother. There were few records of the Underground Railroad, but Still, author of *The Underground Railroad,* published in 1872, kept self-incriminating lists of those who passed through, so that family and friends could find them later. The Dracut, Massachusetts, home of Adrastus Lew, a great-grandson of the Revolutionary fifer Barzillai Lew, was another Eastern Seaboard station; fugitives were hidden in a compartment under the floor. With symbols, disguises, tunnels, hidden panels, and attic networks, the Underground Railroad was a model of clandestine activity.

"Liberty Line—New Arrangement—Night and Day," read a Railroad advertisement:

> The improved and splendid Locomotives . . . fitted up in the best style of accommodation for passengers, will run their regular trips during the present season, between the borders of the Patriarchal Dominion and Libertyville, Upper Canada. Gentlemen and Ladies who may wish to improve their health or circumstances, by a northern tour, are respectfully invited to give us their patronage. SEATS FREE, irrespective of color. Necessary Clothing furnished gratuitously to such as have "FALLEN AMONG THIEVES."

The Great Frederick

"In physical proportion and stature commanding and exact—in intellect richly endowed—in natural eloquence a prodigy—in soul manifestly created but a little lower than the angels," wrote William Lloyd Garrison, describing his subject in his preface to the *Narrative of the Life of Frederick Douglass.*[21] Douglass was a powerful voice and a presence for whites as well as blacks. The voice was authentic—he had escaped from slavery—and authoritative. Douglass had the great gifts of high intelligence, charisma, gravitas, and education—beginning in childhood, when his owner's wife taught him to read, until the owner stopped her because learning "spoiled even the best niggers."[22] Douglass was thereafter self-educated; he became a teacher and leader of other slaves. Albert Murray, in *The Omni-Americans,* calls him the "heroic embodiment of the American as a self-made man."[23]

Frederick Augustus Washington Bailey, son of a black mother and white father, escaped from Maryland slavery in 1838, at the age of twenty. Douglass (his new nom de guerre) had been a ship's caulker in Baltimore. He found his way north and settled among free blacks in seafaring New Bedford, Massachusetts. Hearing him speak against slavery to a black New Bedford group in 1841, the white abolitionist William Coffin invited Douglass to address the Nantucket Anti-Slavery Convention. At the end of Douglass's talk, in which he depicted life in slavery and described his escape, Garrison, who was in the audience, leaped to his feet shouting, "Have we been listening to a thing, a piece of property, or a man?" "A man! A man!" the crowd roared. Douglass was a poster boy for full black humanity—not "3⁄5" of a person. He was the answer to abolitionist prayers.

Douglass became the star of the American Anti-Slavery Society talk circuit. "As a speaker, he has few equals," wrote the Concord, Massachusetts, *Herald of Freedom,* praising his "wit, arguments, sarcasm, pathos." Abby Kelly, a pretty young Quaker, joined Douglass as a speaker in Rhode Island in 1841. "Abby Kelly . . . was perhaps the most successful of any of us," Douglass wrote. "Her youth and simple Quaker beauty . . . bore down all opposition to the end . . . though she was pelted with foul eggs and no less foul words, from the noisy mobs which attended us."[24] Abolition's most popular entertainers, New Hampshire's Hutchinson Family Singers, joined the Douglass tour in 1842. Announcing "We are the Hutchinsons and we hate oppression!" Jesse and Mary Hutchinson and their thirteen children opened the show with "Get On Board, Emancipation!" (sung in close harmony with tambourines, to the tune of "Ole Dan Tucker").

With Douglass, the voice of black America was black at last—and handsome and, at over six feet tall, imposing. Douglass would become a national moral force and the most politically powerful black in America's history. President Lincoln called him "my friend Douglass." A typical border-stater, Lincoln had fewer prejudices against blacks as individuals than as a group. "Just say that Fred Douglass is here," Douglass told a White House doorman who refused to let him in to shake the president's hand at the inaugural open house. *Narrative of the Life of Frederick Douglass,* his first book, was published in Boston in 1845. Growing up enclosed in the "dark night of slavery," he saw his mother stripped and beaten bloody, saw his younger brother's head crushed by a kick, and was himself hired out to a master who reduced him to despair. "I was broken in body, soul, and spirit," he wrote. "You have seen how a man was made a slave, you shall see how a slave was made a man."[25] The journey from slave to man began in facing down, and terrifying, the master in the next beating and ended with Douglass's successful flight north. Unlike many slave narratives of the time, the *Narrative* was not ghost-written.

Nineteenth-century slave narratives, true stories written (or more often dictated) by escaped slaves, were powerful abolitionist fund-raising and propaganda tools. Antislavery tracts were equally profitable. An 1853 tract from London, for example, simply reprinted American runaway slave ads: "TWENTY DOLLARS REWARD—Run away from advertiser, a Negro girl named MOLLY, 16 or 17 years of age; *lately branded on the left cheek, thus 'R,'* and a piece cut off her ear on the same side; the same letter on the inside of both legs."

After the publication of his book Douglass spent two years lecturing in Britain and Ireland on slavery and women's rights. In 1847, the British Quaker Ellen Richardson led a drive to raise funds to purchase his freedom, so that he would no longer be a fugitive. That year, in Rochester, New York, a center of abolition and Underground Railroad activity, Douglass founded a newspaper, *The North Star,* whose motto was "Right is of no sex—Truth is of no color—God is the father of us all, and all we are brethren."

The Politics of Free Soil and Free Men

Despite the South's grip on Congress, the presidency, and the Supreme Court, the political base of abolition strengthened and deepened throughout the 1840s and 1850s. Abolition was only the tip of the iceberg that would finally sink the S.S. *Cotton.* Radicals and do-gooders were now supported by hardheaded businessmen and western farmers: once only a moral imperative, abolition had become a matter of dollars and cents. Democratic propaganda notwithstanding, old Federalist concepts like factories with free labor, and free farmers working their own land, refused to die. With the birth of the transcontinental railroad, homestead laws, land grant colleges, and protective tariffs, politics had become entirely sectional. The question of "free soil" (equated with a strong central government and a diverse economy) versus the expansion of slavery (which meant states' rights and a one-crop system) became mid-nineteenth-century America's most urgent political issue.

The first serious challenge to Democratic power came in 1840, with the Whig Party presidential victory of General William Henry Harrison, "Old Tippecanoe," hero of the War of 1812. With its Revolutionary-era name, the new business-and-property Whig Party favored such anti-Jacksonian ideas as government roads and a new national bank. Most Whigs were not opposed to slavery in the South, but they were against its expansion anywhere else. The grand old men of the party were John Quincy Adams, Henry Clay, and Daniel Webster. Whigs, like Federalists, were accused of being anti–"common man." Harrison, a rich Ohio landowner and former senator and diplomat, portrayed himself in folksy shirtsleeves, complete with a fake log cabin. More important, he strictly obeyed the orders of his campaign manager, Nicholas Biddle: "Let no Committee, no convention—no town meeting ever extract from him a single word about what he thinks now, or what he will do hereafter."[26]

Tippecanoe won in a landslide, but caught pleurisy and died after thirty days in office. "Tippecanoe and Tyler Too" had been a catchy campaign slogan, but the new president, John Tyler, a states' rights Jeffersonian Democrat, on the ticket to appeal to northern Democrats, opposed much of the Whig philosophy. Tyler was the first in a series of so-called doughface presidents—northern politicians who thought like southerners about slavery.

Democrats officially returned to power in 1844, with James Knox Polk of Tennessee, the first "dark horse," and the first president whose election was reported by telegraph. Two smaller parties also turned up in 1844—the anti-Catholic, anti-immigrant Know-Nothing Party, and the abolitionist Liberty Party. Blacks took part in a national political gathering for the first time at the 1843 Liberty Party convention in Buffalo. The Reverend Henry Highland Garnet, a runaway slave who called for a general strike and a slave revolt, was a member of the Liberty Party nominating committee. James G. Birney, the party's founder, was its candidate. Frederick Douglass appeared at Liberty Party rallies.

Polk believed in the concept of Manifest Destiny, originally articulated in 1845 by John L. O'Sullivan, the Democratic editor of the *United States Magazine and Democratic Review:* "Our manifest destiny is to overspread and to possess the whole of the continent which Providence has given us for the . . . great experiment of liberty."[27] Manifest Destiny proponents hoped to annex Texas and California, and all of western Canada to Alaska. After a compromise with Britain on the northwestern boundaries, the biggest political issue of 1844 was the projected annexation of Texas and California. The issue, which culminated in an 1846–1847 war with Mexico, was highly divisive. Southern Democrats were strongly pro-war and pro-annexation; but northern Democrats, called Barn Burners, were strongly against. And northern "Conscience Whigs," who saw annexation as only a southern ploy to have "bigger pens to cram with slaves," disagreed with "Cotton Whigs." Horace Greeley's *New York Tribune* (which hired Karl Marx as a foreign correspondent and believed that every poor citizen deserved a piece of public land) spoke for Conscience Whigs and against slavery. Congressman Abraham Lincoln was a Conscience Whig from Illinois. In Massachusetts, Henry David Thoreau responded to his conscience and went to jail for refusing to pay a poll tax, because the money would be used to "buy a man [or] a musket to shoot one with." He was released when Emerson paid his tax. (Emerson had asked, "Why are you in there?" Thoreau had responded, "Why are you out there?")

Willing to instigate a war, Polk sent General Zachary Taylor to heat the Texas-Mexico border quarrel. Initially, it seemed a serious U.S. miscalculation. Mexico, the second largest republic in the world, not only had superior manpower, it had a great military leader: General Antonio López de Santa Ana. But Mexican manpower fell before superior U.S. weaponry—demonstrated, under Generals Zachary Taylor and Winfield Scott, at the Mexican battles of Buena Vista and Vera Cruz. The battle for California was won by the U.S. Navy.

In 1848, the Whigs nominated for president "Rough and Ready" Zachary Taylor, hero of a war they had opposed. The victorious Taylor was a doughface, but abolitionists fielded a second and larger party, the Free Soil Party, with a highly attractive candidate. Forty-six-year-old John Charles Frémont of California, a handsome ex–Army Topographical Corps officer, was no war hero but he was something of a celebrity. The illegitimate son of a French dancing master and a planter's daughter, he had explored the Oregon Trail and married the pretty daughter of Senator Thomas Hart Benton of Missouri, and would soon be earning an income of $75,000 a month from the California gold rush. With the slogan "Free Soil, Free Speech, Free Labor, and Free Men," the new party united Conscience Whigs, Barn Burners, and members of the old Liberty Party.

In 1850 the South, which had supported war with Mexico to expand slavery, was outraged when California asked to enter the Union as a free-soil state. Congressional southerners regarded this as the most dangerous attack on slavery since the Missouri Compromise, which had declared in 1820 that all land in the Louisiana Purchase north of the Ohio River (except for Missouri) would be free. Fortunately for the antislavery movement, the Wilmot Proviso, which prohibited the introduction of slavery into any new territory acquired by the war, had been passed by Congress in 1846. Introduced by David Wilmot, a Pennsylvania Barn Burner, it was the first important rider ever attached to a routine congressional bill. The battle came to a head in the Senate, with anti-Wilmot forces led by South Carolina's John C. Calhoun. To forestall full-scale conflict, the Whig leader Henry Clay carved out the Compromise of 1850. California would be free; and slave trading, though not slaveholding, would be abolished in the District of Columbia. In exchange, the New Mexico and Utah territories would be without restrictions as to slavery; and the North would agree to a drastic new Fugitive Slave Act. The compromise was attacked by hard-liners on both sides, but seen by the country at large as a means of avoiding war.

An open invitation to kidnapping, the Fugitive Slave Act of 1850 stated that an alleged runaway could be seized anywhere, could have no trial by jury, could not testify or summon witnesses on his own behalf, and could be shipped south no matter how long he had been free. Appalled by the law's blatant injustice, many more northerners were swayed to civil disobedience as well as abolition. "This filthy enactment," wrote Emerson. "I will not obey it, by God!" Free blacks in the North were no longer safe. "Caution!! Colored people of Boston, one & all," read abolitionist placards. "You are hereby respectfully cautioned and advised, to avoid conversing with the Watchmen and Police Officers of Boston, For since the recent order of the Mayor & Aldermen, they are empowered to act as Kidnappers and Slave Catchers."

THE TWO HARRIETS

John Brown called her General Tubman, but Harriet Tubman was also known as Moses. Her self-appointed task, from 1851 to 1860, was to lead as many slaves as possible to the Promised Land. "I was hopin' and prayin' all de time dat I could meets up wid dat Harriet Tubman woman," said one ex-slave, Thomas Cole. "She is a colored women, dey say, dat comes down next ter us and gits a man and his wife and takes dem out and dey didn't gits ketched, either."[28]

For the first twenty-five years of her life, Harriet Tubman, like Frederick Douglass, was a slave on the Eastern Shore of Maryland. Born in 1820, with the slave name of Araminta or Minty, the small, wiry Tubman was initially prized as a field hand. Her "feats of strength often called forth the wonder of strong laboring men," wrote the white abolitionist Sarah H. Bradford in *Scenes in the Life of Harriet Tubman,* an as-told-to biography published in 1869.[29] Hired out for housework, which she had never done, she was beaten so badly by her slave mistress that she was permanently scarred on her face and neck. Saying, "If you do not stop whipping that child, I will leave your house and never come back," the mistress's visiting sister began, patiently, to teach Harriet the rudiments of housekeeping. Because of Harriet's perceived obtuseness, however, the beatings continued, until she was finally returned to her master. When she was next hired out, she refused to help tie a man for whipping. This time, the overseer broke her skull with a scale weight, causing the first of her lifelong seizures. She was returned to her master, who tried to sell her, but no one would buy. From Christmas 1848 until the following March, she prayed, "Oh Lord, convert master!" On the first of March, she changed her prayer: "Oh Lord, if you ant nebber gwine to change dat man's heart, kill him, Lord." When he died soon after, she felt guilty; but, in fear of being sold south, she determined to escape. Traveling by night, she followed the North Star to Philadelphia. "When I found I had crossed dat *line,* I looked at my hands to see if I was the same person," she said. "There was such a glory ober eberyting."

She went on: "I was *free;* but there was no one to welcome me to the land of freedom, I was a stranger in a strange land."[30] She began, slowly but surely, to gather her family. Starting her long and celebrated "conducting" career in 1851, she returned to the South to bring back her husband, even though he had married another woman. Whenever she earned enough money, working as a hotel laundress or cook, she made her way south to bring out others, including her parents (from separate masters) and ten brothers and sisters. She always started the trip north on a Saturday night, to be well away before owners could advertise. Messages were concealed in hymns: "Hail, Oh Hail Ye Happy Spirits" meant safety; "Go Down Moses" meant danger. Babies were silenced with opium, and fearful passengers were often admonished at gunpoint to "go on or die."

Despite a $40,000 reward, dead or alive, for the unknown woman who was helping slaves to escape, Tubman returned to the South at least nineteen times, leading more than three hundred slaves out of Maryland and on to Canada. She became as celebrated and admired in the North as the eloquent Douglass, who wrote in tribute in an introduction to Bradford's book:

> The difference between us is very marked. . . . I have wrought in the day—you in the night. I have had the applause of the crowd and the satisfaction that comes of being approved by the multitude, while the most that you have done has been witnessed by a few trembling, scarred, and foot-sore bondmen and women . . . whose heartfelt "God bless you" has been your only reward. . . . Excepting John Brown (of sacred memory), I know of no one who has willingly encountered more perils and hardships to serve our enslaved peoples than you have.[31]

In 1859, in defiance of the Fugitive Slave Law, Tubman physically snatched a runaway slave from the Troy, New York, police. She was bitterly disappointed that circumstances kept her from joining John Brown at Harpers Ferry. As a nurse and a spy in the Civil War, she received glowing testimonials from Union generals. She was later active in the temperance and women's rights movements, having given up skirts for "bloomers" during the war. When she died in 1913, she was buried with full military honors.

* * *

The Fugitive Slave Act of 1850 inspired two extraordinary American women to make personal commitments to fight the law—one with her body, the other with her pen. Harriet Beecher Stowe dropped her bombshell on the South in 1852. Her *Uncle Tom's Cabin* was America's first smash hit novel. An overnight bestseller in the United States, it sold a million copies in England in eight months, and was instantly dramatized. Known in *Variety* as "U.T.C.," the play was staged regularly all over the world for seventy years. (Mrs. Stowe had only hoped to earn enough money to buy a new silk dress.) The extraordinary escape of Eliza and her child across the frozen Ohio River to the Quaker underground dramatized the evil of the Fugitive Slave Act, and the whole slave system, as nothing had before. With *Uncle Tom's Cabin,* abolitionism won the propaganda war hands down—but Harriet Tubman refused to see a performance of the play in Philadelphia. "I haint got no heart to go and see the sufferings of my people played on de stage. I've heard 'Uncle Tom's Cabin' read, and I tell you Mrs. Stowe's pen hasn't begun to paint what slavery is. . . . I've seen de *real ting,* and I don't want to see it on no stage or in no teater."[32]

Although black racial revisionism turned "Uncle Tom" into a dishonorable epithet, the real "Uncle Tom," like Stowe's hero, was a figure of strong personal character and enduring Christian virtues. He was a slave, but he was in full control of his sense of self, as well as of his soul. "I could run faster, wrestle better, and jump higher than anybody about me," wrote Josiah Henson, in his dictated 1849 pamphlet "The Life of Josiah Henson, Formerly a Slave, Now an Inhabitant of Canada as Narrated by Himself."[33] Harriet Beecher Stowe, who referred to Josiah Henson directly in her *Key to Uncle Tom's Cabin,* published in 1853, had not only read his "Life" but had met him and heard his story.

Perhaps in gratitude for sanctuary, Henson served as captain of a British regiment of "Colored Volunteers" during the Canadian Rebellion of 1837–1838. Whatever his motives for siding with the British against the bilingual rebels, led by William Lyon Mackenzie and Louis Joseph Papineau, Henson's military rank would have been unheard of in the

United States. Later, he became a successful lumber entrepreneur; his polished walnut won a prize at London's Crystal Palace Exhibition, where he met the prime minister and the Archbishop of Canterbury. Henson's seventy-six-page memoir was the most popular of all slave narratives—so popular that on another trip to England, near the end of his life, he was presented to Queen Victoria, who gave him a gold-framed, autographed photo.

"THE GLORIOUS 4TH"

Free blacks and abolitionists alike refused to celebrate Independence Day on July 4. Before 1834, blacks celebrated July 5, simply because it was not the fourth; later they chose August 1, the anniversary of British emancipation of the West Indies. John Greenleaf Whittier's editorial "The Black Man of the Revolution of 1776 and the War of 1812—A Matter Which Has Been Carefully Kept Out of Sight by Orators and Toast Drinkers," appeared in the July 4, 1847, *National Era* newspaper. "We allude to the participation of colored men in the great struggle of freedom," he wrote. As a Quaker, Whittier had no desire "to eulogize the shedders of blood, even in a cause of acknowledged justice"—but "when we see a whole nation doing honor to the memories of one class of its defenders, to the total neglect of another class, who had the misfortune to be of darker complexion, we cannot forego the satisfaction of inviting notice to certain historical facts, which for the last half-century have been quietly elbowed aside. . . . enough is known to show that the free colored men of the United States bore their full proportion of the sacrifices and trials of the Revolutionary war."[34]

"This Fourth of July is YOURS, not MINE. You may rejoice, I must mourn," said Frederick Douglass in 1852. "What to the American slave is your 4th of July? I answer; a day that reveals to him, more than all other days in the year, the gross injustice and cruelty to which he is the constant victim. . . . There is not a nation on earth guilty of practices more shocking and bloody than are the people of the United States at this very hour." Yet Douglass still believed in America. "Notwithstanding the dark picture I have this day presented. . . . I do not despair of this country. There are forces in operation, which must inevitably work the downfall of slavery. I, therefore, leave off where I began, with hope. While drawing encouragement from the Declaration of Independence, the great principles it contains, and the genius of American Institutions, my spirit is also cheered by the obvious tendencies of the age."[35]

The Revolutionary era continued to inspire blacks. Throughout the

1850s, William Cooper Nell, a close associate of Garrison and the first black to hold a federal government post, as clerk to the Boston postmaster, petitioned the Massachusetts legislature for a Crispus Attucks memorial. In 1855, the same year that he successfully petitioned to desegregate Boston's public schools, Nell published *The Colored Patriots of the American Revolution.* Inspired by Whittier's editorial, he aimed "to rescue from oblivion the name and fame of those who, though 'tinged with the hated stain,' yet had warm hearts and active hands in the 'times that tried men's souls.'" Nell called on black Americans to work with whites for a second revolution, "no less sublime than that of regenerating public sentiment in favor of Universal Brotherhood." He asked those "of every complexion, sect, sex and condition" to "nourish the tree of liberty." And he urged black Americans to "hasten the day, when they will prove valid their claim to the title, 'Patriots of the Second Revolution.' "[36] "In considering the services of the Colored Patriots of the Revolution, we are to reflect upon them as far more magnanimous," Harriet Beecher Stowe wrote in her preface to Nell's book. "It was not for their own land they fought, not even for a land which had adopted them, but for a land which had enslaved them, and whose laws, even in freedom, oftener oppressed than protected. Bravery, under such circumstances, has a peculiar beauty and merit."

The Birth of the Republican Party

By 1854, the Whigs were finished, torn apart by slavery. The Kansas-Nebraska Act, sponsored that year by Democratic senator Stephen A. Douglas, permitted new territories to decide for themselves whether to be slave or free. Most of the North was outraged: the act thus nullified the Missouri Compromise. Slavery was now legally possible in a vast new area. Before it passed, the act had been fiercely debated. When Senator George Badger of North Carolina bemoaned the fact that the North would not permit him to take his beloved "old black mammy" to Nebraska, Senator Benjamin Wade of Ohio (who was both antislavery and antiblack) asserted that Badger was troubled only because "he cannot sell the old black mammy when he gets her there."[37]

The issue of slavery was clearly dividing the country. In the North, the Democratic vote was shrinking and antislavery sentiment of every political stripe was growing. Liberty Party members, Free Soilers, Conscience Whigs, and Barn Burner Democrats were preparing to join forces. In February 1854, Alvan Bovay, a lawyer from Ripon, Wisconsin, incensed by the "wicked" Kansas-Nebraska Act, wrote to Horace Greeley of the *New York Tribune* for help in organizing a party to unite all the antislavery factions. "Urge them to forget previous political names and organizations," he wrote, "and to band together under the name I suggested to you in 1852, I mean the name REPUBLICAN."[38]

Republicans were all antislavery, but not all were abolitionists. Most considered the concepts of free soil and free labor more important than actually freeing slaves. Eric Foner points out in *Free Soil, Free Labor, Free Men,* that "free labor" was a middle-class concept as well as a working-class one. It was as much about the freedom to hire and fire as the freedom to work for wages. U.S. Representative Charles Francis Adams, who was minister to Great Britain during the Civil War, described the contrast between the Democratic and Republican constituencies. Democratic support, wrote Adams, came only from the very rich (bankers and southern planters) and "the most degraded or the least intelligent of the population of the cities." Republicans, however, drew support from "industrious farmers and mechanics" and "independent men in comfortable circumstances in all the various walks of life." The strength of the party, editorialized the Springfield, Illinois, *Republican,* was "the great middling-interest class, those who work with their hands, who live and act independently, who hold the stakes of home and family, of farm and workshop, of education and freedom. . . . They form the very heart of the nation, as opposed to the two extremes of aristocracy and ignorance."[39]

The new Republican Party represented a broad spectrum of interests: abolition, free soil, free labor, federalized government, capitalism, and expansionism. Professing a pragmatic as well as a noble purpose, Republicans sought not only to end the expansion of slavery but to promote, in their own economic interests, such anti-slave-interest ideas as protective tariffs and the expansion of industry and technology. Because they believed that states' rights, expressed in sectional power that placed its own interests above all else, could be more of a danger to individual freedom than a strong central government, Republicans made the concept of union central to their philosophy.

BLEEDING KANSAS AND DRED SCOTT

"Bleeding Kansas" earned its name in early 1855, when the territory held a "free soil" referendum to decide whether it would be slave or free, and then erupted. Armed proslavery gangs rode in from Missouri to steal the ballot. They were successful: the result showed more proslavery votes than there were registered voters in the territory. New mandates came from the hardly judicious, illegal new legislature: anyone asserting that

Kansas was "free soil" would be jailed, while death by hanging was ordained for any abolitionists who came into the territory. The antislavery faction, calling themselves Jayhawkers, set up a separate government in Topeka. Abolitionists rallied around the town. Twenty thousand new antislavery settlers went to Kansas, recruited by the New England Emigration Society. Among them were five of John Brown's sons, one of whom would die in the Kansas cause. As "Captain" of the "Liberty Guards," a quasi-militia group he had formed with a sixth son and a son-in-law, John Brown joined them in May 1855.

"Guns are a greater moral force in Kansas than the Bible," preached the charismatic Reverend Henry Ward Beecher (Harriet Beecher Stowe's brother) from his Brooklyn pulpit. The minister's rather hyperbolic assertion was typical of those for whom abolition was a holy war. The rifles that New York and New England abolitionists soon rained on Kansas were known as Beecher's Bibles. In May 1856, a proslavery gang, led by a U.S. marshal, rode into Topeka to burn the Free Soil hotel, smash the newspaper, and ransack homes. Two days later, proslavery terrorists sacked and burned the abolitionist settlement of Lawrence. "Captain" John Brown, with a group including four of his sons, now avenged Lawrence in the massacre of Pottawatomie Creek, in which five men were dragged from a proslavery camp and brutally killed. Newly notorious, "Old Pottawatomie" went on to kill a Missouri slave owner, stealing his slaves and horses. Finally, leading a few followers to Canada, he made himself "Commander in Chief" of a new revolutionary "government" of the South.

Kansas swayed many more northerners to abolition. Despite the tactics of proslavery forces, Free Soilers ultimately regained control of the legislature, repealed all proslavery laws, and rewrote the constitution to forbid slavery. Kansas asked for statehood, but southern Democrats in Congress refused to permit a new free state. Kansas did not become a state until 1861, after several southern states had already left the Union.

Eighteen fifty-six saw the election of the last doughface president, James Buchanan, of Pennsylvania. California's John C. Frémont, previously the Free Soil presidential candidate, now became the first Republican to run for that office. He and his popular wife were the first candidate couple, known as "Frémont and 'brave little Jessie.' " The leader of what the opposition called "Black Republicans," Frémont was abolition's golden boy—but Senator Charles Sumner of Massachusetts (known to Frederick Douglass as "the great and good") was its giant. In 1856, Sumner made his famous "Crime Against Kansas" speech, in which he described slavery as a "harlot" embraced by the South, and was nearly beaten to death for it on the floor of the Senate by the younger, cane-wielding Representative Preston Brooks of South Carolina. Sumner's injuries kept him out of public life for three years. Brooks resigned from Congress but was triumphantly reelected, almost at once.

In 1857, after a decade of litigation, the Supreme Court heard the case of *Dred Scott v. John F. A. Sandford.* Scott, the valet-barber slave of an Army surgeon named John Emerson, had first sued for his freedom ten years earlier in the Circuit Court of St. Louis, on the grounds that having lived on free soil, he ought to be free. Purchased by Dr. Emerson in Missouri, Scott had lived with him in free Illinois and the free Minnesota Territory, where he met and married his wife, Harriet, and where their first child was born. Later, the Scott family lived in the free Wisconsin Territory. On returning to Missouri, however, Emerson hired Scott out, and then sold him. Fearing separation from his wife and children, Scott went to court. The St. Louis Circuit Court had ruled in his favor, but Scott's new owner, John Sandford, appealed the case to the Supreme Court, where seven out of nine justices were Democrats. Chief Justice Roger B. Taney wrote for the majority in the notorious seven-to-two decision: "Negroes are a subordinated and inferior class of being with no rights which white men need respect."[40]

"My hopes were never brighter than now," wrote Frederick Douglass in the aftermath of the decision. "The Supreme Court is not the only power in this world. . . . Judge Taney cannot bail out the ocean, annihilate the firm old earth or pluck the silvery star of liberty from our Northern sky."

The Dred Scott decision denied citizenship to all blacks, slave or free, and opened federal territory to slavery—but it also drove more northern whites into the antislavery camp. Despite Taney's assertion that blacks had no rights that white men need respect, many northern whites were prepared to join blacks in asserting their right to freedom. In 1858, an integrated group of thirty-seven men and women of the town of Oberlin forcibly rescued a fugitive slave named John Price from the custody of U.S. marshals and spirited him off to Canada. The "Oberlin Rescue" became another abolitionist cause célèbre. Giving themselves up for arrest, the Rescuers were treated as honored guests of the Oberlin jail, receiving no fewer than four thousand visitors, including a disguised John Brown, while they were awaiting trial. Charles Langston, a black Rescuer, was the brother of John Mercer Langston, who in 1855 became the first black elected to public office in America, and was an ancestor of Langston Hughes. Two other black Rescuers, John Copeland and Lewis Sheridan Leary, were students at Oberlin College and future members of John Brown's army.

"Captain" John Brown

"John Brown," a name he "had heard in whispers," Frederick Douglass wrote, was "in sympathy a black man . . . as though his own soul had been pierced with the iron of slavery." Brown had sworn "eternal war" on slavery in his Connecticut childhood, when he saw a slave his own age brutally beaten with an iron shovel. As old as the century, the gray-haired, gimlet-eyed Brown had been an itinerant farmer, tanner, surveyor, shepherd, wool merchant, cattleman, and postmaster in Connecticut, Massachusetts, New York, Pennsylvania, and Ohio. He was patriarchal in fact and form (with the long white beard he grew as a disguise). His first wife died giving birth to their seventh child, and he had thirteen more with his second wife. Besides feeding his children, Brown believed his job was to free slaves. His exploits to that end in Kansas had made him revered as well as feared. Unlike Quakers and Garrisonians, Brown was "not averse to the shedding of blood," wrote Douglass, "and thought the practice of carrying arms would be a good one for the Negro people to adopt, as it would give them a sense of their manhood."[41]

In August 1859, Brown and Douglass held a secret meeting in a stone quarry near Chambersburg, Pennsylvania, where Brown sought to persuade Douglass to join his planned attack on the U.S. arsenal at Harpers Ferry, Virginia. Writing that his "discretion" or his "cowardice" made "proof against the dear old man's eloquence," Douglass refused to join. "I told him, and these were my words," Douglass wrote, "that he was going into a perfect steel trap, and that once in he would never get out alive."[42]

Offering up "a fervent prayer to God" for aid in their endeavors, "Captain" John Brown's integrated twenty-two-man "Provisional Army of the United States" met for Sunday morning Bible-reading on October 16, 1859, at a small rented farm five miles from Harpers Ferry. "The services were impressive," wrote the thirty-three-year-old free black printer Osborne Anderson, an ex–Oberlin student who joined Brown in Canada in 1858. (Anderson's eyewitness account, *A Voice from Harper's Ferry,* was published in 1861.) Brown's "Army" included three of his sons. There were seventeen whites and five blacks, including Anderson and the Oberlin Rescuers John Copeland and Lewis Sheridan Leary. The other two blacks were Shields Green and Dangerfield Newby. Green, a twenty-three-year-old illiterate runaway slave from Charleston who went by the name of Emperor, had found sanctuary with Frederick Douglass in Rochester, New York. He traveled south with John Brown's son Owen, escaping slave catchers only by swimming a river. Forty-four-year-old Dangerfield Newby, born a slave but freed by his white father, was the oldest and last recruit. Brown's spy for the past six months, Newby lived on a farm outside Harpers Ferry, but his wife and seven children were all slaves in a nearby town. When his wife wrote that she was about to be sold "down river," Newby joined the group on October 15, the day before the raid.

The surprise night attack looked at first like a success. Brown was able to seize the armory, the fire-engine house, the rifle factory, the Baltimore & Ohio Railway bridge, and several prominent citizens (including the great-grandnephew of George Washington) before the town woke up. Although, in the darkness, his bridge guards had killed a free black railway baggage man, they neglected to hold the eastbound midnight train, which quickly telegraphed the news to Washington. By mid-morning of the seventeenth, Brown's group was surrounded and besieged by federal troops and Virginia militia. Early on the eighteenth, less than thirty-six hours after the raid began, the armory was retaken. Ten of Brown's recruits, including two of his sons, were killed in the struggle. When one of his sons pleaded for a bullet to stop the agony of his wounds, Brown ordered him to "die like a man."[43] Five men were captured alive, and five escaped. Green decided to stay with "the old man," but Anderson and Albert Hazlett, a white conspirator, got to the river, where Hazlett was captured. Anderson managed to escape to Canada, and later joined the Union Army. Harpers Ferry was a prelude to war for those on the other side as well. Leading the federal and Virginia troops that captured Brown were two future officers of the Confederacy: Colonel Robert E. Lee and Lieutenant J.E.B. Stuart.

Dangerfield Newby was the first raider killed by the Virginia militia. His ears were cut off as souvenirs, hogs were set loose on his dead body, and his wife and children were sold south shortly after. Lewis Leary was killed in capture. His fellow Oberlin student, John Copeland, was taken alive and jailed with Brown. The Virginia prosecutor wanted to pardon Copeland. "From my intercourse with him," wrote the prosecutor, "I regard him as one of the most respectable persons we had," adding that Copeland "behaved himself with as much firmness as any of them, and with far more dignity."[44] Shields Green's lawyer argued that as a runaway slave, a noncitizen, Green owed no loyalty to the state of Virginia and could not be guilty of treason. The court dropped treason charges, but Green was hanged with Copeland all the same. Two captured white members of Brown's army, Edwin Coppoc, twenty-four, and Aaron Stevens, a twenty-eight-year-old veteran of Bleeding Kansas, were also hanged.

Lying on the floor of the armory, the wounded Brown had distinctly impressed the governor of Virginia, who called him "the gamest man I ever saw."[45] He also impressed the Baltimore *American and Commercial*

Advertiser. (His official interrogation was witnessed by the press.) "In the midst of enemies whose home he had invaded," the paper wrote, "wounded, and a prisoner; surrounded by a small army of officials and a more desperate army of angry men; with the gallows staring him full in the face, he lay on the floor, and in reply to every question, gave answers that betokened the spirit that animated him." Brown admitted his intention to free the slaves, "and only that." "I want you to understand, gentlemen," he said, "that I respect the rights of the poorest and weakest of colored people, oppressed by the slave system, just as much as I do those of the most wealthy and powerful." He then issued a jeremiad specifically for the benefit of the newspapers: "You had better—all you people in the South—prepare yourselves for a settlement of this question. . . . You may dispose of me very easily . . . but this question is still to be settled—this negro question I mean; the end of that is not yet."[46]

"He had the gift of establishing authority and, all through his crack-brained exploits, he maintained an indestructible dignity, a stoical fortitude, which compelled the admiration of even the paymaster of the Harper's Ferry Armory," wrote the critic Edmund Wilson in *Patriotic Gore.* "Yet it is plainly on record today that Brown's family was riddled with insanity."[47] Brown himself addressed the insanity issue in a letter written to his pastor four days before his execution: "I may be very insane. . . . But if that be so, insanity is like a very pleasant dream to me. I am not in the least degree conscious of my ravings, of my fears, or of any terrible visions whatever; but fancy myself entirely composed, and that my sleep, in particular, is sweet as that of a healthy, joyous little infant."[48]

John Brown was hanged on December 2, 1859, less than two months after the raid. The execution was another prefiguring of war. Not only were Lee and Stuart on hand, but Professor Thomas J. Jackson, the future "Stonewall," commanded a guard company of Virginia Military Institute cadets—and John Wilkes Booth was in the Virginia militia regiment that guarded the scaffold.

"I, John Brown," read a last written message, "am now quite *certain* that the crimes of this *guilty* land *will* never be purged *away;* but with Blood."[49] On the scaffold, his last words were peaceful: he remarked on the beauty of the Blue Ridge Mountains before him. The legend sprang up instantaneously, as Brown himself had predicted in a letter to his wife: "I have been *whiped* . . . but am sure I can recover all the lost capital occasioned by that disaster; by only hanging a few moments by the neck."[50]

"I would sing of how an old man, tall, with white hair, mounted the scaffold in Virginia . . . cool and indifferent, but trembling with age," wrote Walt Whitman. "Old John Brown is dead—John Brown the immortal lives," said Thoreau. For Longfellow, the execution was "the day of a new revolution, quite as much needed as the old." Even Garrison, the pacifist, called it "High Noon," and wished "success to every slave insurrection at the South, and in every slave country." Victor Hugo, in Paris, damned "the whole American Republic."[51] In London, Karl Marx believed that Brown's execution would signal the first uprising of the proletariat. As the body traveled north into New York and toward the Adirondacks for burial, bells tolled and crowds gathered in every town it passed through. War was declared a little over a year later, and "John Brown's Body," of unknown authorship (to the tune of an old camp meeting hymn, "Say, Brothers, Will You Meet Us?"), began to be sung spontaneously by Union soldiers.

In 1861, Julia Ward Howe and her husband, Dr. Samuel Gridley Howe, now a member of the U.S. Sanitary Commission (in charge of civilian assistance to military hospitals and prisons), attended a Washington military review. Driving away from the review, Mrs. Howe and others in her carriage joined soldiers walking along the road in singing "John Brown's Body." Someone in the carriage suggested that Mrs. Howe could surely compose better words for the tune. That night, awaking in a frenzy of inspiration at Washington's Willard Hotel, she lit the stub of a candle and seized her pen. She felt as if she were guided by an "unseen force"; the words of "The Battle Hymn of the Republic" "wrote themselves," she later said. The second stanza is as powerful as the first: "In the beauty of the lilies, Christ was born across the sea . . . / As He died to make men holy, let us die to make men free."

WAR: THE BIRTH OF THE CONFEDERACY

"A house divided against itself cannot stand, I believe this government cannot endure, permanently half *slave* and half *free,*" said Abraham Lincoln during his 1858 Illinois Senate campaign against Stephen Douglas. "I do not expect the house to fall; but I do expect it will cease to be divided. It will become all one thing, or all the other."[52] Two years later, by a slim margin and thanks to the Democratic Party split over slavery, he was elected president. Rather than compromise on slavery, the South preferred to destroy the Union. In December 1860, less than two months after Lincoln was elected, South Carolina, unable to accept a president and a party "whose opinions and purposes are hostile to slavery," declared itself an "independent commonwealth."

By February 1861, the Confederate States of America—Alabama, Arkansas, Florida, Georgia, Louisiana, Mississippi, North and South Carolina, Tennessee, Texas, and Virginia—were established in Montgomery, Alabama, and former U.S. senator Jefferson Davis, of Mississippi, had been chosen as president. Calling slavery the "immediate cause" of secession, C.S.A. Vice President Alexander H. Stephens, a former congressional representative from Georgia, announced in March that the "cornerstone" of the Confederacy was the idea that "the negro is not equal to the white man" and that slavery is "his natural and normal condition."[53] The new Confederate government, Stephens said, was "the first in the history of the world to be based upon this great physical, philosophical and moral truth." Meanwhile, the Confederate secretary of state, Robert A. Toombs, boasted that he would "call the roll" of his slaves at the Bunker Hill Monument.[54] Always sensitive to border states still remaining in the Union, including Kentucky and Missouri, whose proslavery governments were not secessionist, Lincoln insisted that the issue was union, not slavery. "If we aint fightin' fer slavery then I'd like to know what we are fightin' fer" was the succinct response of Nathan Bedford Forrest, Tennessee slave trader and future Confederate general, who seemed to speak for the majority of southerners.[55]

The whites of the South numbered 8,099,674; the slaves numbered 3,950,511, or almost a third of the total population. The white population of the North was 18,901,917. Northern assets included industry, finance, and the U.S. military telegraph system, with 15,398 miles of line.[56] The South's major asset was cotton, which could neither be eaten nor forged into bullets. Confident of a swift victory, the North seriously underestimated the difference between the two armies. Full of reluctant warriors, immigrants who had come to America to *escape* violence, and draftees who had never held a rifle, the Union Army could boast neither the ferocious loyalty of the rebel fighters, nor their shooting skills. And (early in the war, at least) few northern generals could approach the tactical brilliance of southerners like Jackson and Lee. "If I owned the four million slaves of the South I would sacrifice them all to the Union," said Robert E. Lee, at the onset of war. "But how could I draw my sword against Virginia?" Lee, among the southern minority who believed in the spirit of Union, seemed to be fighting more for his home state than for states' rights.

In its arrogance, the North saw no need for black soldiers, but the Confederacy used blacks from the beginning as military laborers. "Slave labor was so important to the southern war effort that the government impressed slaves into service before it began drafting white men as soldiers," wrote James M. McPherson in *Battle Cry of Freedom,* his epic history of the Civil War. The North seemed to agree with the former Georgia senator Howell Cobb: "If the black can make a good soldier," he said, "our whole system of government is wrong."[57] The War Department refused to recruit blacks: this was "a white man's war."

In July 1861, after the disastrous first Battle of Bull Run, where General "Stonewall" Jackson won his nickname, northern complacency was shaken. Lincoln now called for fifty thousand blacks to join the Union cause as commissary workers, medical assistants, engineers, pioneers, laborers, teamsters, wagoners, longshoremen, blacksmiths, carpenters, masons, laundresses, orderlies, scouts, servants, and spies—but, specifically, not as soldiers. Although Union troops were routed again in October at Ball's Bluff, Virginia, the War Department still refused to consider arming blacks. "Colored men were good enough to fight under Washington," complained Frederick Douglass. "They are not good enough to fight under McClellan."[58] General George B. McClellan, who was appointed Union general-in-chief in November, insisted that his armies be scrupulous about returning runaway slaves to their masters.

While many blacks, including Harriet Tubman, acted as Union scouts or spies, there was at least one black member of the U.S. Secret Service. Allan Pinkerton, the Scots-born Secret Service chief, had assisted runaway slaves as Chicago's first police detective and founder of Pinkerton's detective agency. "A remarkably gifted man for one of his race," wrote Pinkerton of his spy recruit, John Scobell of Memphis, Tennessee.

> He could read and write, and was as full of music as the feathered songsters. . . . In addition to what seemed an almost inexhaustible stock of negro plantation melodies he had also a charming variety of Scotch ballads, which he sang with a voice of remarkable power and sweetness. . . . Possessing the talents which he did, I felt sure, that he had only to assume the character of the light-hearted, happy darky and no one would suspect the cool-headed vigilant detective, in the rollicking negro.[59]

JAMES LANE AND THE 1ST KANSAS VOLUNTEERS

Despite the fact that both Congress and the president called it a white man's war, Union generals in the West often felt so far removed from the government that they enacted their own laws. In August 1861, the Republican-led Congress passed an essentially meaningless act declaring that all slaves used to support the Confederate military were free. That same month, the former Republican presidential candidate Major General John C. Frémont, commander of the Western Department, issued a proclamation from border-state Missouri that all slaves who took up arms for the Union would be free. Lincoln was so furious that he fired him from the Army. Eastern abolitionists, already angered by Lincoln's deference to border-state feelings, were outraged by Frémont's dismissal. Important Republican newspapers denounced the president, as did staunch abolitionists like William Lloyd Garrison, Henry Ward Beecher, James Russell Lowell, and Wendell Phillips. In response to a tearful personal visit from Jessie Frémont, Lincoln reluctantly reinstated her husband—but, to keep him as far away as possible from pronouncements on slavery, made him head of the Army Mountain Department in the far West. Still, other Union generals took up the call for border-state slaves to flee to the Union.

In October 1861, describing Brigadier James H. Lane's cavalry, the Leavenworth, Kansas, *Daily Conservative* wrote, "One peculiarity of this mounted force is curious enough to be noted down. By the side of one doughty and white cavalier rode an erect well-armed and very black man. . . . It is well known that negroes and Indians serve in the rebel army but this is the first instance which has come to our personal knowledge—although not the only one in fact—of a contraband serving as a Union soldier."[60] "Contraband of war" was what the Union Army called slaves who escaped to the northern lines. For Lane, a Jayhawker and friend of John Brown, the Civil War was only the culmination of Bleeding Kansas. Ignoring War Department directives, Lane formed the 1st Kansas Colored Volunteers, and called on slaves in Missouri and Arkansas to flee to Kansas and fight for the Union. "Give them a fair chance," he said. "Put arms in their hands and they will do the balance of the fighting in this war."[61] By August 1862, Colonel James Montgomery, another former Jayhawker (who had plotted with Thomas Wentworth Higginson to free John Brown after Harpers Ferry), had what the Emporia, Kansas, *News* called a "tri-color" battalion of Indians, blacks, and whites.

In October 1862, the Kansas Volunteers became the first black troops of the Civil War to actually engage in combat, repulsing a superior force of rebel guerrillas near Butler, Missouri. "The men fought like tigers, each and every one of them, and the main difficulty was to hold them well in hand," the Leavenworth *Conservative* reported. "These are the boys to clean out the bushwackers."[62] The 1st Kansas also had victories at Island Mound, Missouri, and at Honey Springs, against Confederate Indians, in the largest engagement in Indian territory.

The 1st South Carolina Volunteers

The Union Navy, in which blacks were already serving under integrated conditions, but with no rank higher than "Boy" (the lowest rating), took control of the major waterways, north and south, early in the war. In November 1861, black sailors were part of Commander Samuel F. DuPont's Union armada when it captured Port Royal Island and the adjacent South Carolina Sea Islands, some fifty miles southwest of Charleston. The cotton-growing Sea Islands, with large black populations and tropical vegetation, seemed to belong more to the Caribbean than the Atlantic. General Rufus Saxton's Union Army base was the palm-lined old Port Royal resort town of Beaufort. Clara Barton, future founder of the Red Cross, directed the base hospital in one of Beaufort's seafront colonnaded mansions, where Harriet Tubman was a nurse's aide.

Eight thousand slaves had been abandoned when Sea Island whites fled their cotton plantations. Hilton Head Island, a low sandy point reaching out to sea, became the refugee slave center. With high early refugee camp mortality rates, northern blacks responded by creating the Freedmen's Relief fund. New York and Boston abolitionists established the Freedmen's Bureau, essentially America's first domestic Peace Corps, sending material aid, as well as mostly white doctors, teachers, missionaries, and plantation supervisors to help former slaves become free laborers. The slaves were taught to read and write, but they also grew cotton for the Treasury Department—"contraband" agronomy working for the Union.

The former slave Elizabeth Keckley, Mrs. Lincoln's dressmaker and confidante, obtained Freedmen's Relief contributions from the president and first lady as well as from Frederick Douglass and Wendell Phillips. A former dressmaker also to Mrs. Jefferson Davis, Keckley, whose only son died fighting in Missouri under James Lane, wrote a gossipy memoir, *Behind the Scenes,* of her time in slavery and of her wartime life with the Lincolns, especially the controversial Mary Todd Lincoln. "Mr. Lincoln, as everyone knows, was far from handsome," she wrote. "He was not admired for his graceful figure and finely moulded face, but for the nobility of his soul and the greatness of his heart. His wife was different. . . . He asked nothing but affection from her, but did not always receive it. When in one of her wayward impulsive moods, she was apt to say and do things that wounded him deeply."[63] Published in 1868, *Behind the Scenes* was a bestseller.

Early in 1862, with fewer than eleven thousand men to hold the South Carolina, Georgia, and Florida coasts, General David Hunter issued a Frémont-like three-state emancipation proclamation, in order to enlist and arm blacks. Lincoln, who had ignored Hunter's appeals for reinforcements, immediately nullified the proclamation. "I have clothed, equipped and armed the only loyal regiment yet raised in South Carolina,

Georgia or Florida," Hunter (known as "Black David") complained of the president's action.[64] The first black soldier killed in action was a Hunter volunteer named John Brown.

Hunter was not permitted to emancipate slaves, but in March, Rufus Saxton was allowed to organize America's first official Union Army regiment of runaway slaves, to be based on the Sea Island of St. Helena. "These black men are slow about getting into the Army, but when they are once in they fight like fiends," said a Sea Island supervisor. "The improvement in the character and bearing of those who are now in the Army is so marked that everyone notices it." A Sea Island–based colonel was confident that the transformation, with correct leadership, could be complete: "Yesterday, a filthy, repulsive 'nigger,' today a neatly attired man; yesterday a slave, today a freeman; yesterday a civilian, today a soldier. . . . All that he has ever learned except prompt, unquestioning obedience must be unlearned."[65]

The new colonel of the 1st South Carolina Volunteers was thirty-eight-year-old Thomas Wentworth Higginson, formerly the captain of the 51st Massachusetts Infantry. "He was a born commander," a junior officer wrote, "he met a slave and made him a Man." Strong on drill and military appearance, Higginson also believed in racial equality. "This equality in war is the guarantee of that ultimate civil equality which you and I may not live to see, but for which we who knew these men in military service can never doubt their fitness," he wrote to General Saxton.[66]

Higginson—clergyman, author, aesthete, and "discoverer" of Emily Dickinson—kept a diary, which he published in 1870 as *Army Life in a Black Regiment.* He recorded the words of the ex-slave Private Thomas Long, a lay chaplain: "If we hand't become sojers, all might have gone back as it was before; our freedom might have slipped through de two houses of Congress and President Linkum's four years might have passed by and notin' been done for us. But now tings can neber go back, because we have showed our energy and our courage and our naturally manhood."[67]

In May 1862, a Beaufort native named Robert Smalls, slave pilot of the armed Confederate dispatch boat *Planter,* became a Union hero when he stole the ship from the dock while its white officers and crew were ashore. (Charleston was still barred to black sailors, even Confederates.) Spiriting his wife and two children and five other black passengers aboard, Smalls sailed the *Planter* out of Charleston harbor. Once he was in sight of Union blockade ships, the Stars and Bars came down, and the white flag of truce went up. "This man Robert Small [*sic*], is superior to any who have come into our lines, intelligent as many of them have been," wrote the Union Navy commander, Samuel F. DuPont. "His information has been most interesting, and portions of it of the utmost importance. The steamer is quite a valuable acquisition to the squadron by her good machinery and very light draught."[68] Smalls won a substantial financial reward from Congress and was made captain of the *Planter* when it was refitted as a gunboat. During the refitting, in Philadelphia, he hired tutors to teach him to read and write. In December 1863, he led his boat successfully through Confederate fire outside Charleston harbor. After the war, he became a U.S. representative to Congress from South Carolina.

ANDRÉ CAILLOUX AND THE 1ST LOUISIANA NATIVE GUARD

In March 1862, Congress officially forbade the return of fugitive slaves. A month later, compensating owners for their loss, Lincoln signed legislation abolishing slavery in Washington, D.C.—and set aside funds for the voluntary colonization of blacks in Haiti and Liberia (both recently recognized by Congress for that purpose). "I cannot make it better known than it already is, I strongly favor colonization," Lincoln said. "And yet I wish to say there is an objection urged against free colored persons remaining in the country, which is largely imaginary, if not sometimes malicious."[69]

Eighteen sixty-two opened with Union victories. In January, General Benjamin Franklin Butler's Union Army and Admiral David Farragut's Navy captured New Orleans. The Army was victorious again in February in Tennessee, led by the electrifying General Ulysses S. Grant. April brought Shiloh, a bloody stalemate—but the North claimed victory because it cleared the South out of Tennessee and began the process of dividing the Confederacy at the Mississippi. Shiloh was known as a "soldier's battle," for the seemingly poor leadership on both sides. Grant was rumored to have been drunk. "I can't spare this man—he fights!" was Lincoln's reply to post-Shiloh demands for his dismissal. Grant's pugnacity was in direct contrast to the timidity of Union General-in-Chief George McClellan, who, in May, mostly seemed to be hiding from Stonewall Jackson. Besides being a textbook case of deficient leadership, McClellan was a proslavery Democrat and nonstop political activist. In response to his constant demands for more troops, Lincoln sent the Army of the Potomac to help him out. (The Union named its armies for rivers, the James and the Potomac, for example; the Confederacy named its armies for territory, as in the Armies of the Cumberland and the Frontier.) McClellan was lucky in July, when victorious Lee failed to pursue him after the retreat at Malvern Hill. It was fortunate, in turn, for Lee that

McClellan, despite advice to the contrary, failed to counterattack in the face of greater Confederate losses. McClellan would finally be relieved of command that fall.

In July 1862, Lincoln signed the second confiscation act, providing that slaves of all who supported or aided the rebellion would be free upon coming into Union lines or territory under Union control. The act gave the president power to "employ" blacks for the suppression of rebellion. (It also provided for colonization in some "tropical country beyond the limits of the United States" for such newly freed slaves as might wish to emigrate.) In August, the repercussions began. Without sanction from Washington, General Benjamin F. Butler of Massachusetts, who had first named runaway slaves "contraband of war," called for black volunteers in newly captured New Orleans. The French-speaking 1st Regiment of Louisiana Native Guards ("Corps d'Afrique"), having offered themselves, unsuccessfully, to the rebels, were now mustered into the Union Army. The Guards, many of whose grandfathers had fought in the War of 1812, had marched in the November 1861 New Orleans Confederate Grand Review. When New Orleans fell, the 1st Louisiana presented itself to the Union. That same month, Confederate War Department General Order No. 60 branded all black troops and their white officers outlaws of war.

The 1st Louisiana's line officers were all black. Its captain, André Cailloux, was known as both the richest and the blackest member of the regiment.[70] "General, we come of a fighting race," said a spokesman, when Butler sent for regiment leaders to determine if the unit was ready to fight for the Union. "Our fathers were brought here because they were captured in war, and in hand-to-hand fights, too. Pardon me, General, but the only cowardly blood we have got in our veins is the white blood."[71] Butler, known in the South as "Beast" Butler, commissioned seventy-five black officers. His successor, General Nathaniel Banks, forced most of them to resign.

In September, Lincoln made a stupendous and long-awaited announcement: all the slaves in rebel states would be freed on January 1, 1863. Senator Charles Sumner had urged him to make the announcement on the Fourth of July, but Lincoln was waiting for a military victory. Bloody Antietam, in September, where more than twenty thousand men from both sides were killed in little more than a day, was that victory.

EMANCIPATION

"If my name ever goes into history, it will be for this act," said Lincoln on New Year's Eve afternoon, when he signed the Emancipation Proclamation with his full name instead of the usual "A. Lincoln." It was an act, "sincerely believed to be an act of justice, warranted by the Constitution, upon military necessity," on which Lincoln invoked "the considerate judgment of mankind, and the gracious favor of Almighty God."

On New Year's Day, 1863, churches and meeting halls throughout the North were packed with people awaiting official confirmation of Emancipation. When the news finally came on the wire, sometime after ten P.M., a one-hundred-voice choir broke into the "Hallelujah Chorus" at Boston's Tremont Temple, where Frederick Douglass, William Lloyd Garrison, and Ralph Waldo Emerson were waiting, and where a human chain had been formed to the telegraph office.[72] In Dracut, Massachusetts, Adrastus Lew, Underground Railroad conductor and Revolutionary descendant, and his wife were hosting an integrated party when the news was rushed in. They immediately formed a "Peace and Unity" club and decided to meet every year thereafter.

On the fiftieth anniversary of the Proclamation, in 1913, Bishop Henry McNeal Turner, of the African Methodist Episcopal Church, a freeborn former Civil War chaplain, recalled original Emancipation events in Washington. "Men squealed, women fainted, dogs barked, white and colored people shook hands, songs were sung and . . . cannons began to fire at the navy-yard, and follow in the wake of the roar that had for some time been going on behind the White House. . . . It was indeed a time of times . . . nothing like it will ever be seen again in this life."[73]

Technically the Proclamation freed only slaves in rebel states, leaving about eight hundred thousand still in bondage in West Virginia, parts of eastern Virginia, and thirteen parishes of Louisiana. Nevertheless, to the world at large, and especially to most blacks, the slaves were at last "forever free." Neither the world nor most blacks, however, considered what freedom might mean without economic compensation for people who, for the most part, had never earned a living or been farther than ten miles away from their owners' plantations.

Thunderbolts in talons, the American bald eagle, protecting the goddesses of Justice and Wisdom, soars over the word "Emancipation." A supplicant slave is freed from the devil's chains of slavery by an avenging angel, while ministering angels carry black babies to heaven. Idyllic scenes of black life, and the linked names of every state, including the Confederacy's, border the Emancipation Proclamation document. Flanked by the Stars and Stripes at the bottom of the Proclamation is Lincoln, supported by kneeling blacks, arms upraised, and the words "Give Thanks All Ye People, Give Thanks to the Lord." The penultimate paragraph of the Proclamation reads: "And I further declare and make known, that such persons of suitable condition, will be received into the armed service of the United States . . ."

CAPTAIN ROBERT GOULD SHAW AND THE 54TH MASSACHUSETTS

Swift on the heels of Emancipation, Boston abolitionists created the 54th Massachusetts, their own officially recognized state regiment. In January 1863, John A. Andrew, the governor of Massachusetts, was permitted to raise the first northern black volunteer regiment. He recruited from all over the North, the West, and Canada. Unlike the Kansas and South Carolina regiments, the 54th Massachusetts was composed predominantly of free blacks, not runaway slaves.

Frederick Douglass, working from Boston to St. Louis, led a group of black recruiters, among them William Wells Brown, Henry Highland Garnet, Dr. Martin R. Delany (prominent in the African emigration movement), and John Mercer Langston. Douglass, having accused Lincoln of fighting with his "white hand" while his "black hand" remained tied, now called passionately for black volunteers. "Men of Color, to Arms," he wrote in his paper. "We can get at the throat of treason through the State of Massachusetts. She was first in the War of Independence; first to break the chains of her slaves; first to make the black man equal before the law; first to admit colored children to her common schools. She was first to answer with her blood the alarm-cry of the nation when its capital was menaced by the Rebels. You know her patriotic Governor, you know Charles Sumner. I need add no more. Massachusetts now welcomes you as her soldiers."[74] Douglass's two sons, Charles and Lewis, were the first to enlist from New York. Lewis Douglass became the regiment's first sergeant major.

"Wanted. Good men for the Fifty-Fourth Regiment of Massachusetts Volunteers of African Descent, Col. Robert G. Shaw (commanding)," read the notice "To Colored Men," in *The Boston Journal.* It offered "$100 bounty at expiration of term of service. Pay $13 per month, and state aid for families." (Unfortunately for the 54th, they would not receive their promised $13 monthly pay until very late in the war. The Militia Act of July 1862, reflecting the initial plan to use "contraband" slaves as noncombat laborers, specified that blacks would be paid $10 a month, minus $3 deducted for clothing, while whites received $13 a month plus a clothing allowance. Black combat troops did not receive equal pay until September 1864, too late for most of the 54th.)

"Only a small proportion had been slaves," wrote Captain Luis Emilio, the regimental historian, of the 54th's recruits. "There were a large number of comparatively light complexioned men. In stature they reached the average of white volunteers." The Massachusetts surgeon general examined them himself, rejecting nearly one-third. "A more robust, strong and healthy set of men were never mustered into the service of the United States," Emilio wrote, adding that they were "gentlemen as well as soldiers."[75] The 54th Massachusetts represented a cross section of free black middle-class and working-class America: farmers, laborers, seamen, students, clerks, barbers, cooks, waiters, machinists, printers, blacksmiths, butlers, brickmakers, carpenters, dentists, and druggists. They came from Maine, Massachusetts, Connecticut, Vermont, New Hampshire, Rhode Island, New York, Pennsylvania, Ohio, Michigan, Illinois, Indiana, Kentucky, Missouri, Maryland, South Carolina, Canada, and the Caribbean.

The "Massachusetts Black Committee," prominent white Bostonians who raised $100,000 for regimental expenses, was organized by Governor Andrew and Major George Stearns (of John Brown's Secret Six). Several "Black Committee" sons would be officers in the 54th. Governor Andrew was looking for "gentlemen of the highest tone and honor . . . above vulgar contempt for color."[76] Twenty-five-year-old Captain Robert Gould Shaw, the only son of Black Committee member Francis Gould Shaw, had impeccable abolitionist credentials. His grandfather, a veteran of the Revolution, had exhorted young Shaw from his deathbed to use his influence and example "against intemperance and slavery." A member of Harvard's "Fighting Class" of 1860, Shaw had been wounded at Antietam. In April 1861, as a second lieutenant in the 2nd Massachusetts, he went to protect Washington—and made a pilgrimage to Harpers Ferry. "Isn't it extraordinary," he wrote from there to a family friend, Sidney Howard Gay, editor of the *New York Tribune,* "that the Government won't make use of the instrument that would finish the war sooner than anything else—viz the slaves? What a lick it would be to them, to call all the blacks in the country to come and enlist in our army! They would probably make a fine army after a little drill, and could certainly be kept under better discipline than our independent Yankees."[77]

Shaw initially declined Governor Andrew's offer to lead the 54th. Family friend William James believed that Shaw refused in fear of social "eclipse," having always walked on "the sunny side"—but his deeply disappointed mother called it "self-distrust," inherited from his father's side of the family. Whether social distress or self-distrust, he changed his mind overnight. "Now I feel ready to die," his mother wrote in response, "for I see you willing to give your support to the cause of truth that lies crushed and bleeding." Shaw did warn his new fiancée of possible social consequences: "Surely those at home, who are not brave or patriotic enough to enlist should not ridicule, or throw obstacles in the way of men who are going to fight for them. At any rate I shall not be frightened out of it by its unpopularity; and I hope you won't care if it is made fun of. . . . I feel convinced I shall never regret having taken this step, as far as I myself am concerned; while I was undecided I felt ashamed of myself, as if I were cowardly."[78]

The white officers of the 54th, mostly ex-Harvard students in their twenties, also had abolitionist credentials and social standing. Robertson James and Garth Wilkerson James were the younger brothers of William and Henry James; Francis Lee Higginson was the nephew of Thomas Wentworth Higginson. And Charles Bowditch, John Whittier Appleton, Cabot Russel, and the "fighting Quakers," Norwood and Edward Hallowell (Shaw's second-in-command), were Black Committee sons. Not all the officers, though, were Brahmins. Luis F. Emilio, a Portuguese American from Salem, wrote the regimental history, *A Brave Black Regiment,* published in 1894.

The Union Army had a very restrictive policy toward black officers. In February 1863, Governor Andrew wrote pleadingly to Senator Charles Sumner, one of the most influential statesmen in America: "Get me leave to commission colored chaplains, assistant surgeons, and a few second lieutenants. My discretion may be trusted."[79] The 54th was permitted two black chaplains, its only black officers: William Jackson and Samuel Harrison. In June 1863, the War Department announced that it did not intend "at present to commission colored men as line or field officers of colored regiments." Three battlefield commissions were conferred in 1865, however, all former sergeants, all wounded in action: Lieutenant Peter Vogelsang, aged forty-nine, a former New York City clerk; Lieutenant Frank M. Welch, a twenty-two-year-old barber from West Meriden, Connecticut; and Lieutenant Stephen A. Swails, a thirty-two-year-old boatman from Elmira, New York, whose wife and children were in the poorhouse, because he was serving without pay.

James Henry Gooding, a recently married whaling vessel cook from New Bedford, joined the 54th in February 1863, when he was twenty-six. Well-educated and a passionate reader (all that time in the galley), Corporal Gooding became a war correspondent, reporting on the 54th for the *New Bedford Mercury.* His first story, signed "J.H.G.," appeared on March 7, 1863, from Camp Meigs, the 54th training camp: "Immediately upon our arrival here on Wednesday afternoon, we marched to the barracks, where we found a nice warm fire and a good supper in readiness for us. During the evening the men were all supplied with uniforms, and now are looking quite like soldiers. . . . We have drill morning and afternoon, and the men are taking hold with a great deal of earnestness. . . . The men from New Bedford are the largest in camp." But two men, not of New Bedford, "attempted to skedaddle" in the second week of March, on the grounds that they had received no bounty. "You, Mssrs. editors," wrote Gooding, "may be well aware that colored men generally, as a class, have nothing to depend upon but their daily labor; so, consequently, when they leave their labors and take up arms in defense of their country, their homes are left destitute. . . . We are all determined to act like men, and fight, money or not; but we think duty to our families will be sufficient excuse for adverting to the subject."[80]

The ranks of the 54th Massachusetts were growing: Ohio sent four hundred new volunteers, and Philadelphia more than a hundred. There was now a 55th Massachusetts Regiment; Zimri Lew, a great-grandson of the Revolutionary veteran Barzillai Lew, enlisted in it. (He would die in South Carolina of acute dysentery in 1865.)

THE UNITED STATES COLORED TROOPS

By early 1863, black troops had been fighting unofficially for almost a year, although the only officially recognized black units were the 54th and 55th Massachusetts, Thomas Wentworth Higginson's 1st and 2nd South Carolina Volunteers, and the Louisiana Native Guards. In 1861, Lincoln had called for fifty thousand unarmed blacks to serve the Union. Now, in March 1863, he wrote to Andrew Johnson, who was both a slaveholder and the military governor of Union-controlled Tennessee: "The colored population is the great available, and yet unavailed of, force for restoring the Union. The bare sight of 50,000 armed and drilled black soldiers upon the banks of the Mississippi would end the rebellion at once."[81] That same month, to the horror of the South, the 1st and 2nd South Carolina captured Jacksonville, Florida. Lincoln wrote to the commanding general: "I am glad to see the account of your colored forces at Jacksonville. I see that the enemy are driving at them fiercely, as is to be expected. It is important to the enemy that such a force shall not take shape and grow and thrive in the South, and in precisely the same proportion it is important to us that it shall."[82]

In May 1863, as the North began a major southern offensive, War Department General Order 143 permitted blacks to enlist officially in the Union Army. They would belong to one central body, the United States Colored Troops, or USCT, into which all black troops, except for one new Connecticut unit and the 54th, 55th, and (new) 5th Massachusetts Cavalry, were absorbed. Thanks to Emancipation, the U.S. Army had its first black regular Army troops. But from the beginning, they were "lesser" soldiers. A white chaplain received $100 a month, a white sergeant major received $21 a month, and a white private received $13 a month. But all blacks, from chaplains to privates, earned $7 a month.[83] In November 1863, Sergeant William Walker, along with other black soldiers of the 3rd South Carolina Volunteers, refused to fight, because of unequal pay and other intolerable conditions. Walker was executed for mutiny on March 1, 1864.

In the last two years of the war, some 179,000 blacks joined the Union Army and Navy, providing 12 percent of all the North's troops.[84] According to the Official Army Register, only 110 blacks were active commissioned officers. Two-thirds of the black officers belonged to the Louisiana Native Guards, and one-fourth were chaplains or surgeons. Of 133 chaplains assigned to black regiments, fourteen were black, including the Baptist minister Jeremiah Asher, of Hartford, Connecticut, the grandson of Gad Asher, the blind Revolutionary veteran whose war stories made Jeremiah feel that he "had more rights than any white man in town." Major Alexander T. Augusta, USCT surgeon, was the highest-ranking black officer. He managed to keep his rank, but was transferred from duty when white officers complained at having to serve under him.

Major Martin R. Delany, America's foremost black nationalist and emigrationist, was also a commissioned Army surgeon. Delany had been dismissed from Harvard Medical School in 1851, when white students petitioned Dean Oliver Wendell Holmes, Sr., to rid the class of its three black members. Medical licenses not being required in 1850s America, Delany returned home as Dr. Delany, and began a busy practice. His 1852 "Condition, Elevation, Emigration and Destiny of the Colored People of the United States, Politically Considered," the first full-length formulation of black nationalism, recommended emigration. "We are a nation within a nation," he wrote. "We must go from our oppressors."[85] Delany was in Africa, seeking areas for colonization, when Emancipation brought him home to enlist. "I thank God for making me a man simply," Frederick Douglass said, "but Delany always thanks Him for making him a black man."[86]

The Confederacy branded both black troops and their white officers "outlaws." The War Department, while rejecting the idea of black officers for black troops, was extremely particular about the white officers it chose to lead them. Nine thousand whites applied for commissions in the United States Colored Troops; only a quarter that number received them. Some applied because they sought higher rank, or better pay, but many had abolitionist sympathies. Hearing a fifteen-year-old runaway describe his life under slavery, a white soldier of the 70th Indiana volunteered to join the USCT out of a newly conceived personal animus toward southerners. "To hear this child tell about the thrashing he has received from his brutal master and the chains and weights he has carried in the field," he wrote, "is enough to make a man feel like it would be in God's service to shoot them down like buzzards."[87]

On May 1, 1863, the Confederate Congress issued yet another directive against white officers commanding black troops. They would be treated as inciters of servile rebellion and would, if captured, be "put to death, or otherwise punished." The Confederate general and ex–slave trader Nathan Bedford Forrest offered $1,000 for the head of "a commander of a nigger regiment."[88]

PORT HUDSON AND MILLIKEN'S BEND

The first major engagement for black troops was the May 1863 siege of Port Hudson, Louisiana, for control of the Mississippi. The first assault, on May 27, although not a Union victory, was a victory for black soldiers. Captain André Cailloux's 1st Louisiana had asked to lead the attack, charging six times over open ground under heavy artillery fire. Cailloux was killed on the last charge, as, already wounded, he waved his sword, crying "Suivez-moi!"

In his official report, the Union general Nathaniel Banks, no friend to black officers, singled out black troops for praise. Another white officer wrote home to his family: "You have no idea how my prejudices with regard to negro troops have been dispelled by the battle. The brigade of negroes behaved magnificently and fought splendidly. . . . They are far superior in discipline to the white troops and just as brave."[89] In Massachusetts, the white abolitionist Lydia Maria Child reported another conversion: "Captain Wade of the U.S. Navy . . . has been a bitter pro-slavery man, violent and vulgar in his talk about abolitionists and 'niggers.' . . . He has been serving in the vicinity of N. Orleans, and has come home . . . an outspoken abolitionist. He not only says it privately, but has delivered three lectures in town."[90]

Early June saw U.S. Colored Troops beat back a rebel assault in hand-to-hand combat at Milliken's Bend, a Union outpost just above Vicksburg, Mississippi. The 5th USCT Heavy Artillery lost nearly 45 percent of its men—the highest proportion of deaths suffered by a single regiment in the entire war. Three days after the battle, a captain of the 9th Louisiana Volunteers wrote to his aunt in Galena, Illinois:

> We were attacked here on June 7 about 3 o'clock in the morning by a brigade of Texas troops about 2,500 in number. We had about 600 men to withstand them—500 of them negroes. Our regiment had about 300 men in the fight . . . we had about 50 men killed in the regiment and 80 wounded. . . . I never more wish to hear the expression, "the niggers won't fight." . . . The enemy charged us so close that we fought with our bayonets, hand to hand. . . . It was a horrible fight, the worst I was ever engaged in—not even excepting Shiloh.

There was even a compliment from a Confederate general, Henry McCulloch: "This charge was resisted by the negro portion of the enemy's force with considerable obstinancy . . . the white or pure Yankee portion ran like whipped curs almost as soon as the charge was made."[91]

Fort Wagner and the Glorious 54th

Meanwhile, Boston was sending its abolitionist regiment to war. The 54th was ordered to report to General "Black David" Hunter at Hilton Head, South Carolina. "Boylston, Essex . . . Tremont . . . Somerset and Beacon . . . to the State House," wrote Luis F. Emilio of the 54th's farewell parade in Boston on May 28, led by Union Army bandmaster Patrick Gilmore (composer of "When Johnny Comes Marching Home") and his musicians. "All along the route the sidewalks, windows, and balconies were thronged with spectators, and the appearance of the regiment caused repeated cheers and waving of handkerchiefs. . . . Only hearty greetings were encountered; not an insulting word was heard, or an unkind remark made." A Boston newspaper reported, "No regiment has collected so many thousands as the Fifty-fourth. Vast crowds lined the streets where the regiment was to pass, and the Common was crowded with an immense number of people such as only the Fourth of July or some rare event causes to assemble."[92]

Had they paraded through Irish Boston, the reception would have been very different—as it was at the rich Somerset Club, where some members drew the curtains as the parade neared. For abolitionist true believers, however, the parade was a beatific vision. The regiment and Shaw were elevated to adoration. "I got from him that lovely, almost heavenly smile," one Black Committee member, Dr. William Bowditch, wrote of Shaw in his diary, having watched the parade.[93] Whittier, a pacifist Quaker, later wrote to Lydia Maria Child: "The only regiment I ever looked upon during the war was the 54th Massachusetts on its departure for the South. I can never forget the scene as Colonel Shaw rode at the head of his men. The very flower of grace and chivalry, he seemed to me beautiful and awful, as an angel of God come down to lead the host of freedom to victory." Passing the balcony of Wendell Phillips's house, where William Lloyd Garrison stood with his hand on a bust of John Brown (some said weeping), Shaw saluted. When the regiment passed his own Beacon Street house, Shaw raised his sword and kissed it up to his family. Shaw's youngest sister later wrote: "My mother, Rob's wife, my sisters and I were on the balcony to see the regiment go by, and when Rob, riding at its head, looked up and kissed his sword, his face was the face of an angel and I felt perfectly sure that he would never come back."[94]

* * *

On June 3, the 54th Massachusetts marched through Beaufort, South Carolina. James Gooding, soldier-correspondent for the *New Bedford Mercury,* was not impressed with the Sea Islands, or with Beaufort's fabled resort appeal: "Talking about Southern scenery! WELL, all I have seen of it yet is not calculated to make me eulogize its beauties . . . stinkweed, sand, rattlesnakes, and alligators."[95] The regiment had arrived in time to hear the bad news from Washington that all black troops would be paid seven dollars a month, not the promised thirteen. Shaw refused to have the regiment paid at all. The men should either be "mustered out of the service or receive the full pay which was promised them," he said.[96] The Massachusetts legislature offered to make up the difference; but the regiment refused, and fought without pay for over a year. In the fall of 1863, after it was too late for many, Gooding wrote a letter to Lincoln: "Now, your Excellency, we have done a Soldier's Duty. Why Can't we have a Soldier's pay?" Early in 1864, Senator Henry Wilson of Massachusetts introduced legislation for retroactive equalization of pay. In September 1864, the U.S. paymaster finally distributed $170,000 in back pay to the men of the 54th.

Despite the salary battle, morale was high that summer in the Sea Islands. The "high tide of the Confederacy" had already begun to recede at Gettysburg in early July, and the Union continued to gain control of the Mississippi. On July 4, the day of Lee's Gettysburg retreat, the battle-scarred 1st Louisiana participated in the fall of Vicksburg, the last Confederate stronghold on the Mississippi.

Colonel Shaw had spent the Fourth of July on the island of St. Helena with Charlotte Forten, a granddaughter of the black Revolutionary veteran James Forten, a Freedmen's Bureau missionary teacher, whom he described to his family as the "belle" of the Sea Islands.[97] Shaw was a "thoroughly lovable person," Charlotte noted in her diary. On July 6, Shaw, Edward Hallowell, and another officer entertained Charlotte and two of her teaching colleagues. "What purity, what nobleness of soul," she wrote in her diary, "what exquisite gentleness in that beautiful face! As I look at it I think 'The bravest are the tenderest.' I can imagine what this must be to his mother. May his life be spared to her. . . . To-night, he helped me on my horse, and . . . said, so kindly, 'Good-bye. If I don't see you again down here I hope to see you at our house.' But I hope I shall have the pleasure of seeing him many times even down here. He and his men are eager to be called into active service."[98]

Shaw and his men met action two weeks later. About a mile and a half from Fort Sumter, Morris Island was the site of Fort Wagner—the last defense of Charleston. Landing on Morris on July 18, the 54th had just fought a hard-won diversionary action on nearby James Island. A New England correspondent wrote of that engagement: "The boys of the 10th Connecticut could not help loving the men who saved them from destruction. . . . The dark-skinned heroes fought the good fight and covered with their own brave hearts the retreat of brothers, sons and fathers of Connecticut."[99] In relieving the 10th Connecticut, fourteen members of the 54th were killed (including its "handsomest" member, Sergeant James D. Wilson, who had vowed never to retreat or surrender).

After James Island, Shaw had asked his second-in-command, Edward Hallowell, if he believed in "presentiments." According to Hallowell, Shaw "felt he should be killed in the first action."[100] He said it again, stressing the "next fight," on the steamer to Folly Island, Brigadier Quincy Adams Gillmore's appropriately named Union assault staging area.

Landing on Morris in the late afternoon, Shaw was informed by General George C. Strong that the 54th and 6th Massachusetts, with troops of the 7th Connecticut, 3rd New Hampshire, 9th Maine, 48th New York, and 76th Pennsylvania, would storm the fort that night. Two earlier Union attacks—on July 10 and 11—had failed, with 339 Union casualties to the Confederates' 12. "You may lead the column if you say yes," Strong said. "Your men, I know are worn out, but do as you choose."[101] The 54th had gone three days without rest and twenty-four hours without food. Nathaniel Paige, of the *New York Tribune,* later reported a conversation between Gillmore (the commanding general) and General Truman Seymour. Gillmore had asked Seymour how he intended to organize the assault. "Well, I guess we will let Strong lead and put those d—d niggers from Massachusetts in advance," Seymour replied. "We may as well get rid of them, one time as another."[102] Gillmore and his staff genuinely believed that only three hundred Confederates were manning Fort Wagner, instead of the actual seventeen hundred.

Heavily gunned Fort Wagner was approachable only by a narrow stretch of beach. That evening, as six hundred members of the 54th waited to open the assault, General Strong, on horseback, asked who would pick up the flag if the bearer fell. "I will," said Shaw, who was smoking a last cigar. At the signal to attack, Shaw (who seemed cheerful, Hallowell said, "ready to meet his fate") sent his horse back and led the charge on foot, sword in hand.[103] When the enemy opened fire at two hundred yards, the flag bearer was instantly hit. Seizing the flag, Shaw scrambled with it to the top of Wagner's rampart, and was hit and killed just as he shouted, "Forward, Fifty-fourth!" One hundred and fifty more members of the 54th were killed or wounded before they even reached the rampart. The regiment suffered 50 percent casualties. Five out of the assaulting brigade's six regimental commanders, including Shaw and General Strong, were killed or wounded. There were 1,515 Union casualties and 181 Confederate. "The negroes fought gallantly, and were headed by as brave a colonel as ever lived," wrote a Confederate officer, Lieutenant Iredell Jones.[104]

The national flag had tremendous importance in this war between Americans. The "Stars and Stripes" and the "Stars and Bars," of two different countries and two different philosophies, represented the difference between freedom and slavery, as well as life and death. Sergeant William H. Carney, a New Bedford seaman, picked up the flag from the fallen Shaw as he reached the top of the fort and fought his way down again, severely wounded, still holding the standard. "Boys, the old flag never touched the ground," said Carney (words soon famous all over the North) as he staggered into the hospital tent, still bearing the colors.[105] The deed made him the first black recipient of the newly created Medal of Honor. Adrastus Lew's "Peace and Unity" club was thereafter known as the Carney Circle. It would continue to celebrate Emancipation, as well as the 54th Massachusetts, well into the first quarter of the twentieth century.

"Fort Wagner is the Sebastopol of the rebels," wrote James Gooding; "we went at it, over the ditch and on to the parapet through a deadly fire; but we could not get into the fort. We met the foe on the parapet of Wagner with the bayonet—we were exposed to a murderous fire from the batteries of the fort. . . . Mortal men could not stand such a fire, and the assault on Wagner was a failure. . . . When the men saw their gallant leader fall, they made a desperate effort to get him out, but they were either shot down, or reeled in the ditch below. One man succeeded in getting hold of the State color staff, but the color was completely torn to pieces."[106] Six months later, James Gooding was wounded and captured at Olustee, Florida. He died in notorious Andersonville Prison on July 19, 1864, a year and a day after Fort Wagner.

"I escaped unhurt from amidst that perfect hail of shot and shell," wrote Sergeant Major Lewis Douglass, son of Frederick Douglass, to his fiancée: "It was terrible. I need not particularize, the papers will give a better [account] than I have time to give. . . . This regiment has established its reputation as a fighting regiment, not a man flinched. . . . Men fell all around me. A shell would explode and clear a space of twenty feet, our men would close up again, but it was no use we had to retreat, which was a very dangerous undertaking. How I got out of that fight alive I cannot tell, but I am here. . . . Remember if I die I die in a good cause. I wish we had a hundred thousand colored troops we would put an end to this war."[107]

The white officers of the 54th who had been killed received a decent burial from the Confederates, except for Shaw, whose body was stripped and dumped into an unmarked mass grave with the black troops. After the battle, the Union commander sent a flag of truce requesting Shaw's body, as was customary with high-ranking officers. It was refused. "He is buried with his niggers" was, according to the northern press, Confederate general Johnson Hagood's contemptuous reply. Although at least one Union witness denied that these were the actual words, they produced great bitterness throughout the North.

Several weeks after the assault, Union troops finally took Wagner. When a Union officer offered to search for Shaw's grave to retrieve his body, Shaw's father asked him not to, saying, "We hold that a soldier's most appropriate burial-place is on the field where he has fallen."[108]

Henry James, whose younger brothers were both wounded at Wagner, wrote to Shaw's parents: "I feel for you all, in truth exactly what I should feel for myself—profound pity: and yet such a pride in the noble and beautiful boy, such a grateful sense of his finished manhood, as disdains that pity."[109] Shaw's sacrifice was memorialized in poetry, art, and architecture. Emerson's words for Shaw were instantly memorable: "So nigh is grandeur to our dust / So near is God to man / When Duty whispers low, *Thou must,* / The youth replies, *I can.*" Augustus Saint-Gaudens, arguably the greatest American sculptor of the nineteenth century, spent almost fourteen years creating the *Shaw Memorial.* The large bronze relief on Boston Common, not far from where Crispus Attucks fell, was finally unveiled in 1897. A mounted two-dimensional Shaw, in profile, rides beside amazingly lifelike forward-striding members of the 54th. William James said that he could almost hear the soldiers breathe.

YANKEE HOSPITALS AND RETRIBUTION

Fort Wagner's captured Union wounded now faced another kind of battleground. "A chief point of attraction in the city yesterday was the Yankee hospital," the *Charleston Courier* reported on July 23, "where the principal portion of the Federal wounded, negroes and whites, have been conveyed. Crowds of men, women, and boys congregated in front of the building to speculate on the novel scenes being enacted within. . . . The wounds generally are of a severe character . . . so that amputations were almost the only operations performed. Probably not less than seventy legs and arms were taken off yesterday. . . . The writer saw eleven removed in less than an hour. Yankee blood leaks out by the bucketful. . . ."[110]

By modern lights, all Civil War hospital conditions, especially for prisoners, ranged from primitive to horrific. Besides torturous medical conditions, there was starvation. The C.S.A.'s Commissary Commission basically ran out of food for prisoners in 1862. As a prisoner of war, *New York Tribune* correspondent Albert D. Richardson was assigned to keep hospital records at the Salisbury, North Carolina, Confederate penitentiary, under typical southern prison conditions. "Nearly ten thousand prisoners of war, half naked and without shelter," he later wrote, "were crowded into its narrow limits, which could not reasonably accommodate more than six hundred."[111] Southern surgeons were "the best class of rebels we encountered," he wrote, but "to call the foul pens where the patients were confined 'hospitals,' was a perversion of the English language." Writing in the 1911 *Photographic History of the Civil War,* Major Edward L. Munson, M.D., U.S. Army, described 1860s medical conditions: "Wounds were expected—encouraged—to suppurate. . . . Nothing in the way of antiseptics was provided . . . the cleanliness of wounds, except in respect to the gross forms of foreign matter, was regarded as of little or no importance."[112] There was sometimes chloroform, or a little crude opium, but "several hundred major operations were reported during the war in which no anesthetic was employed." The South had a shortage of medical books and instruments, and no skilled instrument makers: surgical tools resembled hacksaws. The only southern resources in adequate supply were bandages (cotton) and narcotics (in good supply as a pastime of planter-class ladies). They were not to be wasted on Union prisoners—especially not on black troops, or on white officers of black troops, who were not recognized as prisoners of war. Black soldiers could expect to be enslaved, and their white officers executed.

Sergeant Robert Simmons, a twenty-six-year-old native of Bermuda, was among the twenty-nine members of the 54th who were captured and taken to Charleston's "Yankee" hospital. Simmons's arm was amputated and he died in prison a month later. Catholic Sisters of Charity provided the only care for the black wounded. The sadistic surgeon in charge, Dr. George R. C. Todd—a brother of Mary Todd Lincoln—was "considered the most degraded of all the rebels the prisoners had to do with." On July 24, in a prisoner exchange on Charleston harbor truce boats, 104 wounded white Union soldiers complained of "neglected" wounds, "unskillful" surgeons, and "unnecessary" amputations. Black prisoners, said to have received treatment last, were not released.[113]

"If our son's services and death shall have contributed in any degree towards securing to our colored troops that equal justice which is a holy right of every loyal defender of our beloved country, we shall esteem our great loss a blessing," wrote Francis G. Shaw to Lincoln, urging that immediate measures be taken for the protection of black troops.[114] On July 31, Hannah Johnson, the mother of a black member of the 54th who fought at Fort Wagner, but "thank God" was not imprisoned, also wrote to Lincoln: "Will you see that the colored men fighting now, are fairly treated . . . We poor oppressed ones, appeal to you, and ask fair play."[115]

Less than two weeks later Lincoln issued his "eye for an eye" warning: for every white or black Union prisoner killed, a rebel prisoner of war would be shot. For every black enslaved, a rebel prisoner would be sentenced to life at hard labor. The Confederate government paid grudging attention to the proclamation, but individual commanders and soldiers continued to murder captured blacks.

Gallows were erected in the yard of Charleston prison, where all black members of the 54th, including the wounded, awaited trial. Although most of the men were free, they were nevertheless charged "that being slaves, they were in insurrection against the state for fighting against slavery; and second, that they had been 'concerned and connected' with slaves in insurrection." Nelson Mitchell, a courageous and subsequently ostracized white Charleston attorney (who kept the Stars and Stripes hidden in his home), defended them free of charge. "A lawyer named Mitchell came to the jail and offered to defend us before the court," said a 54th prisoner, Private Daniel States. "He did a good deal for us, and talked with Sergeant Jeffries and Corporal Hardy, who went to trial as the two test cases. Mitchell did this without pay, and was very kind to us at all times. He worked hard and won the case, coming to us at midnight. . . . 'All of you can now rejoice. You are recognized as United States soldiers.' "[116]

The Draft Riots of 1863

In July 1863, while the 54th Massachusetts fought and died at Fort Wagner, draft riots raged in New York City. Boss William Marcy Tweed's New York was Democratic, antiwar, and antiblack; it denounced the war as a "rich man's war and a poor man's fight." The Conscription Act of 1863 permitted a man to buy his way out of the draft for $300. In the first southern draft, men with twenty or more slaves did not have to fight. In the North, Andrew Carnegie and J. P. Morgan paid for substitutes, as did the fathers of Theodore and Franklin Roosevelt. Although Daniel O'Connell, the Liberator of Ireland, refused southern contributions to the Irish cause—he said that Irish freedom could never be purchased with the labor of slaves—the New York Irish, who felt they were fighting to free blacks who would take their jobs, were another matter.

In four days of rioting, from July 13 to July 17, over one hundred people were killed and scores more injured. "The mob was composed of the lowest and most degraded of the foreign element (mostly Irish)," wrote the black historian William Wells Brown. "Having been taught by the leaders of the Democratic party to hate the negro . . . this infuriated band of drunken men, women and children . . . murdered all they could lay hands on, without regard to age or sex."[117] Black homes and shops were looted and demolished. Blacks were chased, beaten, and lynched in the streets, hanged from lampposts. The Colored Orphan Asylum was attacked and burned to the ground. Most of the orphans escaped to a nearby police station, where they stayed for several days, secretly fed by Catholic priests, but one small girl, found cowering under a bed, was said to have been killed by the mob. In describing the "unspeakable infamy of the nigger persecution," George Templeton Strong, a Republican patrician, displayed his anti-Irish bias: "They [blacks] are the most peaceable, sober and inoffensive of our poor. . . . I am sorry to find that England is right about the lower class of Irish. They are brutal, base, cruel, cowards and as insolent as base. . . . But how is one to deal with women who assemble around the lamp-post to which a Negro has been hanged and cut off certain parts of his body to keep as souvenirs?"[118] Alexander H. Newton, an African Methodist Episcopal clergyman from North Carolina, was almost captured by a mob. "I ran through the streets of New York like a wild steer, while the rioters cried out, 'Head the Nigger Off!' " he wrote in his autobiography, *Out of the Briars,* published in 1910.[119] A few months later he joined the 29th Regiment of Connecticut Volunteers.

The black-Irish battle continued after the riots. A Corporal Felix

Brannigan of the 74th New York Regiment wrote to a newspaper: "We don't want to fight side by side with the nigger. We think we are too superior a race for that."[120] The letter prompted some satirical verse in the *New York Herald,* under the signature "Private Miles O'Reilly" (aka Charles Graham Halpine, staff officer of the black South Carolina Volunteers): "Some tell us 'tis a burnin' shame / To make the naygars fight: / An' that the thrade of bein' kilt / Belongs but to the white: / But as for me, upon my soul! / So liberal are we here, / I'll let Sambo be murthered instead of myself / On every day of the year." Lincoln addressed the issue in a letter to James C. Conkling on August 26. "You say you will not fight to free negroes. Some of them seem willing to fight for you. . . . There will be some black men who can remember that, with silent tongue, and well-poised bayonet, they have helped mankind on to this great consumation; while I fear, there will be some white ones, unable to forget that, with malignant heart, and deceitful speech, they have strove to hinder it."[121]

New York was one of the last states to recruit blacks actively. When the Democratic governor, Horatio Seymour, refused state enlistment of blacks, the Union League Club and the New York Association for Colored Volunteers (whose members included William Cullen Bryant and P. T. Barnum) obtained permission from the War Department to recruit directly under national authority. When the 20th U.S. Colored Regiment, created by New York abolitionists, finally marched down Broadway on March 5, 1864, Robert Gould Shaw's young widow stood on the reviewing stand. "I think that some of the rabble, who were in the pro-slavery melee of July 13, 1863, were made to shed tears of repentance on beholding the 20th Regiment as they marched through the streets of this great city in glorious array," wrote a black journalist, "notwithstanding the outrages they suffered a few months past at the hands of the copperheads."[122]

Fort Pillow and Poison Spring

Despite Lincoln's "eye for an eye" proclamation, the early months of 1864 saw atrocities committed against black soldiers. In March, when Union troops defeated a numerically superior Confederate force under General Nathan Bedford Forrest at Fort Anderson, Kentucky, the humiliated Forrest sought revenge. "Nothing in the history of the Rebellion has equaled in inhumanity and atrocity the horrid butchery at Fort Pillow," wrote William Wells Brown.[123] In the spring of 1864, Fort Pillow was manned jointly by the 11th U.S. Colored Troops and white Unionists of the 13th Tennessee Cavalry, a force of less than six hundred. On April 12, 1864, they were surrounded and stormed by fifteen hundred men of the Confederate cavalry under the command of Forrest, who arrived mid-morning to take personal charge. Two hundred thirty-one Union soldiers, most of them black, were killed; 100 were seriously wounded, and 168 whites and 58 blacks were captured. Southern accounts insisted that the Union forces were killed fighting for the fort before their surrender. But, according to northern reports, the soldiers were massacred after they had surrendered, by Confederate cavalry shouting, "No quarter! No quarter! Kill the damned niggers; shoot them down!" Blacks were set on fire, or buried alive; bodies were mutilated. The wounded, and the black women and children inside the fort, were massacred along with the soldiers. "It will appear from the testimony that was taken, that the atrocities committed at Fort Pillow were not the results of passion elicited by the heat of conflict," reported the Committee on the Conduct of the War on the Fort-Pillow Massacre, "but were the results of a policy deliberately decided upon, and unhesitatingly announced."[124]

The Mississippi "was dyed with the blood of the slaughtered for 200 yards," wrote Forrest in his own Fort Pillow report, from which he omitted important information while expressing the hope "that these facts will demonstrate to the Northern people that negro soldiers cannot cope with Southerners."[125] (Forrest was later the first Imperial Wizard of the Ku Klux Klan. Thomas Dixon's 1905 novel *The Clansman,* which inspired D. W. Griffith's 1915 movie *Birth of a Nation,* was based on Forrest's life.)

"The Southern army, which is the Southern people, cares no more for our clamor than the idle wind," General Sherman wrote to Secretary of War Edwin M. Stanton about Fort Pillow, "but they will heed the slaughter that will follow as the natural consequence of their own inhuman acts." Black troops swore vengeance. In Memphis, Forrest's hometown, black soldiers were reported to have taken an oath "on their knees" to avenge Fort Pillow.

Six days after Fort Pillow, the 1st Kansas Volunteers were outnumbered by Confederates at Poison Spring, Arkansas. Southern troops fired on trapped and wounded blacks as Union forces retreated. Of the 438 members of the 1st Kansas, 182 were killed or missing. A sister troop, the 2nd Kansas Volunteers, resolved thereafter to take no rebel prisoners. Black troops east of the Mississippi went into battle shouting, "Remember Fort Pillow!"—as black troops in the West cried, "Remember Poison Spring!" At Jenkins Ferry, Arkansas, the 2nd Kansas overran rebel troops with 150 Confederate losses to 15 Union—and one prisoner, taken by mistake.[126]

The Battle for Richmond

Most of 1864 was devoted to the siege and capture of Richmond. U.S. Colored Troops in the Richmond campaign were consolidated under General Benjamin Butler in the Army of the James. In May, Confederates stopped the Union outside Petersburg, Richmond's transportation center. A Union engineer, head of a unit of Pennsylvania miners, evolved a plan to dig a tunnel under rebel lines, fill it with dynamite, and blow a hole in the Confederate entrenchment. On July 30, eight thousand pounds of dynamite created a five-hundred-yard tunnel—a hole sixty feet across and thirty feet deep—the longest in military history. It was planned that Union troops led by a specially trained black division would then move into the tunnel. Fearing the political implications of using blacks in such a hazardous assignment, however, the Union high command, including Grant, agreed that white troops would have to be substituted. The division commanders now drew lots to see which would lead the assault. Thanks to the Union general Ambrose Burnside, the losers faced far worse than the short end of the stick. Burnside (after whom first "burnside" then "sideburn" whiskers were named) had disregarded orders to build adequate escape passageways for the attack. Thus, troops going into the Crater were immediately trapped and blasted by Confederate cannon.

When black troops began moving in behind the whites, Confederates cried, "Take the white man, kill the nigger!" Some captured white officers of black regiments lied about their units, so angering the white Lieutenant Lemuel Dobbs of the 19th U.S. Colored Troops that when asked his unit he replied, "Nineteenth Niggers, by ———!" Black troops bore the full brunt of the final Confederate counterattack. The wounded and surrendering were shot or bayoneted. A southern journalist reported that the "sides and bottom of the chasm were literally lined with Yankee dead. . . . Some had evidently been killed with the butts of muskets as their crushed skulls and badly mashed faces too plainly indicated."[127] Grant called it "the saddest affair I have witnessed in the war." Union casualties were 3,798 to Confederate casualties of 1,500. Blacks were blamed for the defeat, but Grant faulted "inefficiency on the part of the corps commander and the incompetency of the division commander who was sent to lead the assault." Of the 180 blacks "lucky" enough to be taken prisoner at Danville detention center, only seven survived.[128]

The night before the Crater, black troops around the campfire sang the "Negro Battle Hymn": "They look like men / They look like men / They look like men of war." They never sang it again. All told, 1,327 black men were killed at Petersburg: the greatest concentrated black loss of the war. A black sergeant, Decatur Dorsey of the 39th U.S. Colored Troops, was awarded the Medal of Honor for carrying the colors and rallying his unit when Union lines were driven back.

★ ★ ★

By the fall of 1864, the failure to capture Richmond had led to political as well as military consequences. Lincoln's Democratic opponent, General George McClellan (whom Lincoln had fired in 1862), was calling for armistice and peace talks—with a virtual guarantee of southern independence and the continuation of slavery. Although General Sherman was devastating Georgia, Confederate forces under Jubal Early were threatening Washington itself.

On the morning of September 29, after two failed Union assaults, Brigadier General Charles Paine's black 3rd Division led the attack on New Market Heights, south of Richmond, to cut off reinforcements to Early. Two regiments of the 4th and 6th USCT, led by General William Birney, the Alabama-born son of the abolitionist James G. Birney, were in the vanguard. They would be decimated as waiting Confederates poured out of the trenches to kill scores in close combat—and, once again, to murder surrendering troops. Thomas Morris Chester of the *Philadelphia Press,* the war's only black correspondent of a major daily, described the action:

> In the attempt of the 4th and 6th Regiments to pass over the abattis, the 4th lost its entire color guard. Alfred B. Hilton of the 4th USCT, carried the American flag, which was presented to it by the colored ladies of Baltimore, to the very edge of the breastworks, and, lying down, held aloft the national colors. When they were ordered to fall back, this brave man was shot down, but is not dangerously wounded, and his first exclamation was, "Save the flag!" Sergeant Major Fleetwood successfully brought the colors back, riddled with some thirty rents, with no other loss to himself than a shot through his boot leg.[129]

Fleetwood was among the five members of the 4th and 6th to be awarded Medals of Honor, all for seizing the colors from fallen bearers and pressing the attack. Seven more Medals of Honor were awarded in this costly Union victory to soldiers of the 5th, 36th, and 38th Colored Regiments who led the surge into the fortification.

Immediately following New Market Heights, after two failed Union assaults, nine officers and 189 men of the 7th USCT stormed nearby Fort

Gilmer. All but one were killed, wounded, or captured. Grant himself arrived on the scene to order a coordinated attack. It was another costly Union victory. The combined engagements (also known as the Battle of Chaffin's Farm) ended the next morning—with 1,173 black casualties, and 14 black winners of the Medal of Honor. "A few more such gallant charges, and to command colored troops will be the post of honor in the American Armies," said General Benjamin Butler, as he presented specially commissioned Tiffany medals to two hundred men of the 7th USCT who had fought at New Market Heights.[130]

THE FALL OF RICHMOND AND THE END OF THE WAR

Fort Fisher, in the harbor of Wilmington, North Carolina, was General Robert E. Lee's most important supply depot and last gateway to the outside world. The Union was determined to take the fort by assault or siege. On January 15, 1865, the 1st Regiment of U.S. Colored Troops joined the amphibious attack force that ultimately brought Fisher down—a Union victory with heavy casualties on both sides. The 1st Regiment's chaplain, Henry McNeal Turner, participated in the battle, and wrote an account in the A.M.E. *Christian Recorder* that was republished in *American Heritage* in 1980. "Never had I seen grape and canister used so effectively as the rebels used it on our troops on this occasion," wrote Turner, who accompanied white troops into the battle. "At one time I thought they could never stand it; neither do I believe they would have stood, but for the fact that they knew the black troops were in the rear, and if they failed, the colored troops would take the fort and claim the honor. Indeed, the white troops told the rebels that if they did not surrender they would let the negroes loose on them."[131]

The fort surrendered. Fort Fisher finished the Confederacy: Charleston fell a month later. The first Union troops to enter the city were the 54th and 55th Massachusetts—singing "John Brown's Body," "Babylon Is Falling," and "The Battle-Cry of Freedom."

In March, the Confederate Congress finally made provisions for slaves to be enlisted as soldiers. It was "not only expedient but necessary," said Lee—adding, "it would be neither just nor wise . . . to require them to serve as slaves."[132]

Richmond finally fell on April 2, 1865. This time, the black 5th Massachusetts Cavalry was in the vanguard. Its leader, Colonel Charles Francis Adams, Jr., wrote to his father: "To have led my regiment into Richmond at the moment of its capture is the one event which I should most have desired as the culmination of my life in the Army."[133] Richmond blacks, fearing rebel ire as the city was evacuated, hid in churches until, as Thomas Morris Chester reported, "they saw colored soldiers arresting rebel soldiers found in the city."[134] Most black troops of the Army of the James that day had joined in the pursuit of Lee to Appomattox and surrender.

After Richmond's capture, the great event was Lincoln's arrival in the city, on April 3. The president, with his youngest son, walked from the wharf to Jefferson Davis's house. Most white citizens of Richmond stayed indoors, but the exultation of those whom Chester called the "loyal people" was intense. "The Union element in this city consists of negroes and poor whites," he wrote, "including all that have deserted from the army, or have survived the terrible exigencies which brought starvation to so many homes." For Richmond blacks, the occasion was a "jubilee." "I know that I am free, for I have seen Father Abraham and felt him," exclaimed one elderly black woman.[135] Elizabeth Keckley, Mrs. Lincoln's dressmaker, was in the presidential party. "The Capitol presented a desolate appearance," she wrote, "desks broken, and papers scattered promiscuously in the hurried flight of the Confederate Congress." In the Senate chamber, she looked at a paper banning free blacks from entering the state of Virginia, and she sat in Jefferson Davis's chair. When they visited Davis's mansion, she wrote, "the ladies who were in charge of it scowled darkly upon our party as we passed through and inspected the different rooms."[136]

Chester was impressed by the newly demonstrated courtesy of some Richmond whites toward blacks. "Not even the familiarity peculiar to Americans is indulged in," he wrote, "calling the blacks by their first or Christian names, but even masters are addressing their slaves as 'Mr. Johnson,' 'Mrs. Brown,' and 'Miss Smith.' A cordial shake of the hand and a gentle inclination of the body, approaching to respectful consideration, are evident in the greetings which now take place between the oppressed and the oppressor."[137]

The old Confederacy was dead. On April 15, Lincoln was dead, too. Furious because a Union victory meant "nigger citizenship," a minor actor, John Wilkes Booth (younger brother of America's great Shakespearean actor Edwin Booth), vowed to "put him through." Booth assassinated the president as he watched a play at Washington's Ford's Theatre. Black troops of the 22nd USCT led Lincoln's funeral procession, and two days later joined in the hunt for Booth.

* * *

The final engagement of the war was a Confederate victory at Palmito Ranch, Texas, on May 12. The initial Union assault was repulsed, forcing white Indiana and Texas troops, as well as men of the 62nd USCT, to retreat across the Rio Grande. Nevertheless, the 62nd won high praise from the commanding colonel: "Every attempt of the enemy's cavalry to break this line was repulsed with loss to him, and the entire regiment fell back with precision and in perfect order." The last Union soldier to be killed by a rebel bullet was black: Sergeant Bill Redman, of the 62nd USCT.[138]

By the end of the war there were 186,107 black enlisted soldiers, some 10 to 12 percent of the Union Army, and 7,122 black officers—mostly chaplains, surgeons, and battlefield commissions of 1865. There were some 30,000 black sailors—8 to 25 percent of the Union Navy—and no black Navy officers. In the last 23 months of war, black soldiers and sailors had participated in 449 engagements, 39 of which were major battles. A third, or 68,178, died: 2,751 in combat and the rest from wounds and disease. At 14 percent of the population, blacks counted for about 20 percent of total Union casualties.[139]

Despite sacrifice and loss, much had been won. In the Revolution, blacks had helped to win a country. With the Civil War, they finally won the right to live as free men in that country, and to bear arms in its defense. The future looked bright.

4 Buffalo Soldiers I

THE INDIAN WARS, 1867–1896

Perhaps no incidents in American history present a greater number of brilliant achievements, more thrilling experiences, more daring deeds, dramatic episodes and bloody tragedies than those adventures which attended the pioneers of the Western plains . . . which characterized the conquests, developments, and entire life of the United States Army in the far West, in its attempt to subdue the wild, hostile and savage Indian, for the purpose of advancing the civilization of the Western World. The great success of the Negro soldiery in this respect sufficiently vindicates their worth as efficient defenders of the country's flag and honor.[1]

—*Herschel V. Cashin, in* Under Fire with the Tenth Cavalry

The New Army

Advancing the civilization of the Western World" entailed the elimination of anything that stood in the way of "progress," from indigenous flora and fauna to indigenous people. "Take with you to the frontier your dog, your rod and gun," said General Winfield Scott Hancock, namesake of the Mexican War hero, in his address to West Point's graduating class of 1877.[2] Officers might have the leisure to hunt, but ordinary soldiers, especially black troops who served for five years without a furlough, were too busy. Exploring and charting the wilderness, they built thousands of miles of roads and telegraph lines, escorted stagecoaches, wagon trains, railroad crews, and surveying parties, and protected homesteaders, ranchers, and the U.S. Mail from outlaws—many, like themselves, Civil War veterans. Most important, from 1867 to 1890, western soldiers were busy eliminating, either by relocation or warfare, the indigenous population. The cult of the gun "civilized" the West, destroying, one way or another, most of what was native to it and, in the process, not always putting the best face on Western civilization. The Indian Wars culminated in 1890 with the massacre of the Sioux at Wounded Knee, in

South Dakota. A fact surprising to most Americans is that one out of every five soldiers in the winning of the West was black.

In July 1866, Congress established a "New Army" to fight the newest sectional war, between East and West instead of North and South. The New Army would fight a different sort of enemy than either "Johnny Reb" or "Billy Yank" was used to. In this war the enemies had names like Sitting Bull, Lone Wolf, Big Tree, Crazy Horse, and Geronimo—and armies called Sioux, Apache, Kiowa, Comanche, and Cheyenne. The Indian Wars and Indian-fighting soldiers were romanticized, commercialized, and sanitized by "Buffalo Bill" and by "penny-dreadful" adventure novels. Indians were generally demonized, and western warfare was ferocious and cruel on both sides. "We must act with vindictive earnestness against the Sioux even to their extermination, men, women and children," wrote General Sherman to General Grant in 1866, after a Sioux massacre of an Army raiding party.[3] Civilians agreed. "Exterminate the whole fraternity of redskins," wrote the *Nebraska City Press*. "Wipe them out," urged the *Montana Post*.[4] The deliberate killing of Indian children began in the seventeenth century, during the Pequot War, when an English soldier remarked, after killing an Indian baby, "Kill the nits, and you'll have no lice."[5]

The *old* Army, the Union Army, had had a million members by the end of the Civil War. The *new* Army would be smaller. "The military peace establishment of the United States," read the new congressional mandate of 1866, "shall hereafter consist of five regiments of artillery, ten regiments of cavalry, forty-five regiments of infantry, the professors and corps of cadets of the United States Military Academy, and such other forces as shall be provided for by this act, to be known as the Army of the United States." The newest thing about the New Army was that one in five of its men were black. "To the six regiments of cavalry now in service there shall be added four regiments, two of which shall be composed of colored men, having the same organization as is now provided by law for cavalry regiments," said Congress. There were also two new regiments of black infantry. The New Army, like the old, mandated complete segregation for the 12,500 or so members of the new 9th and 10th Cavalries and 24th and 25th Infantries.

By 1875, the New Army had a permanent strength of about 25,000. Civil War veterans, black and white, formed the New Army's core. But black troopers stayed longer on the frontier, deserting less and reenlisting more, than their white counterparts. They were also more abstemious. Between 1866 and 1885, their ratio of sick calls for drunkenness was only 2 per 1,000, as opposed to the white ratio of 54 per 1,000.[6] Black troops were originally sent to isolated outposts in Kansas (Fort Leavenworth), the Dakotas (Fort Rice), Nebraska (Fort Robinson), Utah (Fort Duchesne), Wyoming (Fort Washakie), New Mexico (Fort Tulersu), and Texas and the Rio Grande border (Fort McKavitt)—all far away from white populations. As Indians were subdued and white settlements grew up on the plains, black units were generally concentrated in Texas and Arizona. Frontier race relations depended on the black-white-Indian ratio. Where the Indian population was large, blacks might be treated fairly well. And despite the isolation, the danger, and the inferior horses, equipment, and food, the Army pay of thirteen dollars per month was far better than most black men could hope to see as civilians. In five years without a furlough, many made the best of it, saving money and learning to read and write. Skills could be perfected: black cavalry troopers would be put in charge of West Point riding instruction, and black military marksmanship became famous. Despite material deficiencies, black soldiers were eventually considered among the New Army's best. Eighteen Medals of Honor out of 416 awarded went to black troopers between 1866 and 1891.[7] Many of their white officers were similarly rewarded, which often indicated the quality of the troops.

Before southern revisionism, and Hollywood, erased them from history, black soldiers were an acknowledged part of the western landscape. They were featured in the sketches, paintings, and sculptures of Frederic Remington, for example, who accompanied a unit of the 10th Cavalry on Arizona patrol in the summer of 1888, and pronounced them "charming men with whom to serve."[8] One of the most popular of Remington's works was the dashing *Captain Dodge's Colored Troops to the Rescue.* Black cowboys and outlaws were as familiar as black soldiers. Black men busted broncos, roped steers, and rustled horses and cattle. "There's a yellow rose in Texas, that I am going to see / No other darkey knows her, no darkey only me," went an 1860s song. Black good guys and bad guys of the range included Nat Love ("Deadwood Dick"), Cherokee Bill, Bill Pickett, Ben Hodges, and Isom Dart. By the time Hollywood captured the West, however, mountain men, cowboys, and cavalry had all become as white as Hollywood's Indians. On rare occasions, John Ford's big sky country might shelter a token black trooper, always played by the 1930s UCLA football legend Woody Strode.

Hollywood whitewashed the West in more ways than one. No movie could capture real western warfare: bullets, arrows, thundering horses, blood, and scalping. "Black Elk himself scalped a soldier who was still alive," wrote Evan S. Connell in *Son of the Morning Star,* the story of Custer and Little Bighorn, describing a thirteen-year-old Oglala Sioux warrior and his victim. "It was hard work because the soldier's hair was short and the knife was dull. The soldier ground his teeth and made such a fuss that Black Elk had to shoot him in the head." When Black Elk offered the scalp to his mother, she uttered "a shrill tremolo in his honor."[9]

In 1867, when eight hundred Cheyenne were defeated by ninety troopers of the 10th Cavalry in a two-day battle near Fort Leavenworth, Kansas—with a loss of only three cavalrymen—black scalps became highly prized. One Cheyenne was said to have cut up a buffalo hide to make and sell black "scalps." Comparing them to an animal they considered sacred, Cheyenne called 10th Cavalry troopers buffalo soldiers. The term would come to apply to all the black western units. While Indians continued to scalp whites, it was said that they later refrained from scalping blacks and, in fact, did not relish fighting them. "Buffalo soldier no good, heap bad medicine," one brave was reported to have told a cavalry colonel.[10]

The 10th Cavalry at Fort Leavenworth

The 10th Cavalry first assembled at Fort Leavenworth, Kansas, in 1867, under Colonel Benjamin Grierson, a famous Union Army cavalry officer. A Central Plains bastion near the Nebraska and Iowa borders, Leavenworth was an unrelenting war zone for the 10th—against racist whites as well as Indians. On their arrival, the fort commander, Colonel William Hoffman, assigned them to a bog; then, calling their uniforms filthy, ordered them not to come within fifteen yards of whites, even on the parade grounds. But the men were soon too busy to worry overmuch about Leavenworth racism. By 1869, the 10th had become part of what the historian Phillip Drotning called a Central Plains "army of occupation."[11]

In 1867, the year the 10th Cavalry came to Leavenworth, the congressionally mandated Indian Peace Commission, meeting at Medicine Lodge Creek, Kansas, established the reservation system, to put an end to Plains warfare and to keep Indians as far away as possible from settlers and railroads. Treaties with the Cheyenne and Arapahoe removed them to a four-million-acre reservation in Oklahoma, between the Washita and Red rivers. A similar reservation tract of three million acres, immediately to the south of the Cheyenne-Arapahoe, went to the Comanche, Kiowa, and Kiowa-Apaches. The Indians retained the right to hunt buffalo anywhere south of the Arkansas River, and the U.S. government provided food and clothing. The reservation system would prove anything but successful, and broken treaties came to symbolize the white man's "forked tongue."

The Medicine Lodge Peace Commission provided only a brief respite from warfare. Central Plains Indians were soon furious when treaties were broken by white civilians, avid for land, as well as by government soldiers. In April 1867, white arsonists destroyed a village of some one thousand to fifteen hundred Cheyenne and Sioux on the Pawnee fork of the Arkansas River, hunting grounds guaranteed by government treaty. When Cheyenne and Arapahoe struck back with raiding parties, the Army retaliated. In November 1868, General George Armstrong Custer led a surprise attack on the Washita River encampment of Cheyenne chief Black Kettle, indiscriminately killing men, women, children, dogs, and horses.[12] The same pattern of warfare raged on the Texas border with Kiowas and Comanches, whom the 10th Cavalry would also fight in Oklahoma, Texas, New Mexico, and Arizona.

"The old Tenth had a body of noncommissioned officers that was unequalled in any regiment in the Army," wrote cavalry colonel Clarence C. Clendenen in the foreword to *Under Fire with the Tenth Cavalry.* Despite the racism of Leavenworth's commander, many white officers were appreciative of black troops. Thanks to military racism, which demanded that blacks be *better* than best, black NCOs tended to be superior soldiers. The vast majority of blacks who were awarded the Medal of Honor in the Indian Wars were NCOs, the backbone of the Army. In 1870, Sergeant Emanuel Stance of the 9th Cavalry became the first black Indian Wars Medal of Honor winner. Leading a detachment of ten troopers at Kickapoo Springs, Texas, he drove off some thirty Kickapoos by pulling ahead and repeatedly emptying and reloading his sidearm, without breaking his charge.[13]

Texas: Out from Fort McKavitt with the 24th and 25th

West Texas was known as the Soldier's Paradise, possibly because there was so much to shoot at. "Beautiful rivers, grass and grassy plains, teemed with game," wrote Captain William G. Muller of the 24th Infantry, writing in the 1920s of the landscape he remembered.

> The buffalo overran the plains in the autumn; immense herds of antelope, thousands of deer, wild turkeys, quail, duck and geese were everywhere—not to speak of cattle run wild, by the thousands, free to anyone. The wild Indian lived almost secure on the staked plains and raided the settlements every full moon. "Wild" was the characteristic of the time, place and things. All this was in a past century, a past age . . . the buffalo has been wiped off the

> face of the earth, the Indian the same in parts of our domain, while the wire fences and the railroad have cleared up the remaining fauna almost as completely.[14]

Seven companies of the 10th Cavalry were sent to Texas in 1873. Divided among Forts Richardson, Griffin, Davis, Concho, and McKavitt, they shared Indian-fighting duties with the 9th Cavalry and the 24th and 25th Infantries, all based at McKavitt. About 180 miles from San Antonio, on the edge of the great Staked Plain of west Texas and New Mexico, McKavitt was the most remote outpost of the frontier. In the spring of 1875, two companies of the 24th Infantry, one company of the 25th, nine 10th Cavalry troopers, and several Indian scouts left the fort for a seven-month expedition to explore the plains.

They marched, wrote William Muller, thirty miles a day "over a country like an ocean of waving grass," traveling with a pack train of about seven hundred mules, sixty-five six-mule wagons, and a herd of beef, as buffalo lumbered out of the way and antelope turned to gaze "in wonder." They trekked through the Texas Serengeti from early May through Christmas Eve, suffering much hardship. "During the last lap . . . the officers . . . having lost all hope, had gotten together and written messages to be taken home by any who might survive," wrote Muller. Finally reaching "civilization" at New Mexico's Pecos River, the infantry was sent out in detachments to raid Indian villages. Some five hundred to a thousand ponies were captured, with "a lot of squaws, who were taken to Fort Duncan, but subsequently escaped." The expedition, considered the "first mortal blow" to Indian domination of the territory, was mapped by a 10th Cavalry second lieutenant.[15]

In July 1875, six companies of the 10th Cavalry, two companies of the 24th Infantry, and one company of the 25th were part of Lieutenant Colonel William R. Shafter's famous expedition from Fort Duncan to Fort Concho, to explore even further the Staked Plain. According to congressional orders, the main purpose of the expedition, besides dealing, incidentally, with renegade Comanches, was to "show in detail the resources of the country, looking to its adaptability for cultivation and stock-raising." The cavalrymen discovered and mapped such well-known sites as Monument Springs and Palo Duro Canyon. Only five Comanches were captured and one killed, but the expedition did "sweep the plains clear of Indians," and cattlemen and homesteaders appeared in its wake.[16]

For actions at Florida Mountain, New Mexico, in 1877, Corporal Clinton Greaves became the second black, and the second NCO of the

9th Cavalry, to win the Medal of Honor. Two years later, three more 9th Cavalry NCOs were awarded the medal. Sergeant Thomas Boyne was honored for actions in two New Mexico battles; Sergeant John Denny was cited for valor at Las Animas Canyon, Mexico. And Sergeant Henry Thompson won his Medal of Honor for braving heavy fire to seek water for the wounded, in a battle against the Utes at Milk Creek, Colorado, in September 1879. For three days, a company of the 9th, having gone to the rescue of an outnumbered column of the white 5th Cavalry, helped keep the Indians at bay until reinforcements arrived. At the end of the siege, a white captain of the 5th referred to D Company, 9th Cavalry, in classic nineteenth-century terms as "the whitest men" he ever saw.[17]

RECONSTRUCTION: THE "MYSTIC YEARS"

The Indian Wars coincided with the era of Radical Reconstruction, what W.E.B. Du Bois called the Mystic Years. Radical Reconstruction, in the decade just after the Civil War, was a second American Revolution. The entire southern caste system was overthrown. Never before did black Americans have so much political, economic, and social freedom—freedom not to be seen again for another century. The flush of post–Civil War expansionism ushered in an era of unique good feeling for blacks. Moving ever westward (as the Army swept the path), America seemed a land of endless opportunity. The magic of Reconstruction was partly economic; black America's golden age coincided with the country's Gilded Age. And underneath all (E. L. Doctorow had it right) were the music and spirit of ragtime. For blacks this era was the first cultural Renaissance, a celebration of full citizenship, at last.

True to his border-state birth and vision, Lincoln had always had one foot in the North and one in the South. Border people often found slavery repugnant but had little interest in the plight of the slaves, and Lincoln, no exception, mishandled Emancipation. In 1863, nearly four million dependent, illiterate men and women with no knowledge of how to earn a living were suddenly liberated. Emancipation may have been a moral triumph, but with no money, no job training, and little food or shelter, it was a socioeconomic disaster. As W.E.B. Du Bois put it, ex-slaves were free "to do as they liked with the nothing they had." Congressman Thaddeus Stevens's "forty acres and a mule" proposal was sabotaged by the old oligarchy, abetted by conservative Republicans and northern Democrats. Without land, tools, capital, or access to credit, newly freed blacks became slaves of society. As sharecroppers, they were held in peonage instead of bondage. And, an important ambiguity, they were called freedmen—not *free* men.

In 1865, southerners had become the first Americans to lose a war. Edmund Wilson, in *Patriotic Gore,* describes the postwar South as a place where "fierce patriotism and pride of defeat override all mercy and reason."[18] The North could forgive the South for killing Lincoln, but the South could not forgive the North for winning the war. "You can never win us back, never, never! / Tho' we perish in the track of your endeavor," went a popular postwar Southern song.

O I'm a good old rebel
Now that's just what I am
For this "Fair Land of Freedom"
I do not care AT ALL
I'm glad I fit against it
I only wish we'd won
And I Don't want no pardon
For anything I done
I hates the constitution
This Great Republic too
I hates the freedman's Buro
In uniforms of blue.[19]

The South, in the words of the diarist Mary Chesnut, was filled with "brotherly hate."[20] This country of haters could not get at the Yankees, but it could get at blacks. Southern haters would eventually reduce the promise of freedom to a hell that almost matched slavery.

In 1865 and 1866, the old Confederacy enacted "Black Codes," effectively reestablishing slavery with vagrancy, curfew, and "apprenticeship" laws. The South Carolina Black Codes, which were typical, barred blacks from all occupations except farming and menial service. Blacks could be beaten for making "insulting" gestures at work, or for walking off the job. Any white man could arrest any black he saw commit a misdemeanor. The Ku Klux Klan (founded in 1865 by the Confederate general Nathan Bedford Forrest, of the Fort Pillow massacre) was the terrorist arm of political and economic oppression.

In 1865, President Andrew Johnson sent General Carl Schurz to investigate southern conditions. Schurz's report was hair-raising:

> Dead bodies of murdered Negroes were found on and near the highways and by-ways. Gruesome reports came from the hospitals—reports of colored men and women whose ears had been cut off, whose skulls had been broken by blows, whose bodies had been slashed by knives or lacerated with scourges. A number of

> such cases, I had occasion to examine myself. A . . . reign of terror prevailed in many parts of the South. . . . The emancipation of the slave is submitted to only in so far as chattel slavery in the old form could not be kept up. But although the freedman is no longer considered the property of the individual master, he is considered the slave of society. . . . Men who are honorable in their dealings with their white neighbors will cheat a Negro without feeling a single tinge of honor. To kill a Negro, they do not deem murder; to debauch a Negro woman, they do not think fornication; to take property away from a Negro, they do not consider robbery. The people boast that when they get freedmen's affairs into their own hands, to use their own expression, "the niggers will catch hell."[21]

President Johnson, no friend to blacks, was displeased by Schurz's report. It gave Radical Republicans the upper hand. The old abolitionists Senator Charles Sumner of Massachusetts and Representative Thaddeus Stevens of Pennsylvania created the Joint Congressional Committee of Fifteen, which radically "reconstructed" the South, dividing the former Confederacy into five military districts occupied by federal troops and controlled by generals. Congress mandated the privately funded Freedmen's Bureau to become the (short-lived) first federal welfare agency. Despite Johnson's veto, Sumner and Stevens fought for and achieved the Civil Rights Act of 1866, which conferred American citizenship on blacks. Citizenship was the cornerstone of Reconstruction. New elections, and state constitutional conventions, were ordered for the South. In Mississippi, South Carolina, Louisiana, Alabama, and Florida, blacks outnumbered whites. South Carolina's 1867 voter registration included 80,000 blacks and 46,000 whites.[22] White South Carolinians possibly regretted their ancestors' "Negro fever," the eighteenth-century mania in South Carolina for accumulating slaves. All blacks voted Republican. "The Republican Party is the ship," said Frederick Douglass, "all else is the sea."

When Thaddeus Stevens died in 1868, he chose to be buried in a small, integrated graveyard. The epitaph, which he composed himself, read: "I repose in this quiet and secluded spot, not from any natural preference for solitude, but finding other cemeteries limited by charter rules as to race, I have chosen this that I might illustrate in death the principles which I advocated through a long life, Equality of man before his Creator."[23]

Reconstruction was a high-water mark for American liberalism. Frederick Douglass, the conscience of the Civil War, now a Republican power broker, desegregated the federal government when he became the recorder of deeds and U.S. marshal for Washington, D.C. In 1866, the Civil War veteran Charles L. Mitchell and Edward G. Walker (son of David Walker, of 1829's "Walker's Appeal") made Massachusetts the first northern state to elect blacks to its legislature. A political force in the Republican Party, blacks enjoyed patronage power in civil service and consular appointments. Richard Greener, in 1870 the first black graduate of Harvard, became the U.S. consul in Vladivostok, Russia, in 1898. In the spirit of Reconstruction, the American Catholic Church named a black bishop, James Augustine Healy, the son of a Georgia Irish planter and a slave mother. (His brother, Patrick Francis Healy, became president of Georgetown University.) Women were also visible in new ways. Although they were still unable to vote, in 1872 Victoria Woodhull ran for president of the United States on the Equal Rights ticket.

If Reconstruction was radical in the North, in the South it was revolutionary. Black men could vote, hold office, and own property, and blacks could go to integrated schools, theaters, hotels, and restaurants. Poor whites also gained: imprisonment for debt was abolished; they could go to school; and all women, white and black, could petition for divorce.

In January 1868, with black Army troops as part of the northern occupying force, 84 out of 157 delegates to the first General Reconstruction Assembly of South Carolina were black. South Carolina, home of slavery's defender John C. Calhoun, was now a black Republican power base. The Civil War hero Captain Robert Smalls went from South Carolina's Assembly to the U.S. Congress.

Two former officers of the Corps d'Afrique became lieutenant governors of Louisiana: Oscar J. Dunn in 1868, and Cesar C. Antoine (whose father fought with Andrew Jackson) in 1872. There would be twenty-two blacks in Congress, including three senators of whom two were veterans. Most black Reconstruction congressmen had more formal education than Lincoln: ten had attended college, and five were lawyers. In 1870, a forty-eight-year-old former Civil War chaplain, Hiram Rhodes Revels, was elected to Jefferson Davis's old Mississippi senate seat. Revels only served one year. Mississippi Democrats argued that he could not be seated because the U.S. Constitution requires that a senator have been an American citizen for nine years before taking office—and Revels, like all blacks, became a citizen only in 1866. A former Corps d'Afrique officer, Pinckney B. S. Pinchback (a grandfather of the Harlem Renaissance writer Jean Toomer), was elected to the Senate from Louisiana in 1873. After three years of debate, that body voted 32–29, in 1876, not to seat him.

In 1874, Blanche Kelso Bruce became the second black U.S. senator from Mississippi, and the only one to serve a full term (1875–1881). One of eleven children of a slave mother and a white Virginia planter, Bruce was educated by the tutor of his master's son. Escaping to Lawrence, Kansas, during the Civil War, he was successively a schoolteacher, a printer's apprentice, a student at Oberlin, and a Mississippi riverboat porter. In Memphis, he heard a speech in which Mississippi was called the land of opportunity, and he made his way there in 1869. By 1870, he was sergeant-at-arms of the state senate in Jackson and on his way to becoming a successful planter. By 1875, he was a U.S. senator. It was a Reconstruction success story.

ANNAPOLIS AND WEST POINT: JAMES SMITH AND HENRY OSSIAN FLIPPER

After the Revolution, George Washington, among others, had proposed the idea of an official military academy. In 1802, Congress established the United States Military Academy at West Point, above the Hudson River Palisades, north of New York City. Civil War generals Robert E. Lee, Ulysses S. Grant, Stonewall Jackson, and "Little Phil" Sheridan were all graduates of West Point. The U.S. Naval School was established later, in 1845. Midshipmen were originally trained at sea, but in 1850 an old Army post at Annapolis, Maryland, became the United States Naval Academy (it was evacuated to Newport, Rhode Island, during the Civil War).

Two black natives of South Carolina entered the service academies in the early 1870s. James Webster Smith was admitted to West Point in 1870, and John Henry Conyers to Annapolis in 1872. Both resigned within a year of admission. The southern-dominated military establishment had been forced to accept black cadets and midshipmen, but it drew the line at graduating black officers. From 1870 to 1898, twenty-three blacks were appointed to West Point. Twelve actually attended, six stayed longer than one semester, and only three graduated.

The naval academy was even more successful than West Point at getting rid of black would-be officers. Alonzo McClennan followed Conyers to Annapolis in September 1873. The secretary of the Navy saved him from dismissal when a white midshipman accused him of misconduct, but he resigned in March 1874, after two faculty members promised to pay for his education anywhere else. McClennan entered medical school and became a successful physician. In September 1874, an officer had to brandish his sword to protect McClennan's Annapolis successor, Henry

E. Baker of Mississippi, from his fellow midshipmen. Baker was dismissed the following November, but also landed on his feet, becoming a clerk in the U.S. Patent Office. This was a political patronage job. Three more black candidates were appointed in the 1870s, but none actually entered. There would not be another black midshipman at Annapolis until 1949.

The Republican War Department insisted that a small black Army staff-officer cadre be created, whether the Military Academy liked it or not. So the Academy was forced to admit blacks, but it could not be forced to graduate them. In July 1870, President Grant's own cadet son swore to his father that "no d—d nigger will ever graduate from West Point."[24] The Academy's "honor system" permitted cadets to police and discipline themselves; class rank was lowered by demerits cadets gave each other. A war of terror was waged against black cadets, before a generally deaf and blind administration.

James Smith, admitted to West Point in 1870, was well-prepared academically and determined to graduate. He was told "within an hour of arrival" by several "thoughtful cadets" that he was " 'nothing but a d—d nigger.' " (Smith related his experiences in a series of letters to a black newspaper in 1874.) In the dining room, a southern cadet loudly refused to eat after he had touched the bowl, and Smith was ordered to wait until all other cadets had finished before serving himself. He had arrived with another black plebe, Michael Howard, of Mississippi, who failed his first exams and left. Howard was followed in swift succession by Henry Alonzo Napier of Nashville, admitted in 1871 and discharged in 1872 for "deficiencies in Mathematics and French"; Thomas Van Rensselaer Gibbs of Tallahassee, admitted in 1872 and discharged in 1873 for "deficiency in Mathematics"; and John Washington Williams of Hampton, Virginia, admitted in 1873 and discharged in 1874 for "deficiency in French."[25]

Meanwhile, Smith remained. He and Howard, who was his roommate during Howard's brief stay, did not have one peaceful day. "We could not meet a cadet anywhere without having the most opprobrious epithets applied to us." They complained once or twice, to deaf ears, then decided to ignore the taunts—until a slops pail was dumped over Smith while he slept, and a white cadet struck Howard in the face for being "in the way." The slops dumper remained undiscovered, and the assaulting cadet received a slap on the wrist.[26]

The abuse was psychological as well as physical. When Smith's sister and brother visited the Academy, they were publicly insulted, and Smith was placed under arrest on trumped-up charges. But Smith, who underwent one court-of-inquiry and two courts-martial within his first few months at West Point, was tough enough and good enough to become a "First Classman"—a West Pointer in his final year at the Academy. In his last year, a white visitor who called the Academy a system in which "terrorism reigned supreme" reported that Smith spoke "slowly," as if he had "lost the use of language."[27] He was dismissed in June 1874, just before graduation, for failing a philosophy course. He died two years later.

While James Smith was still at West Point, he wrote a letter to Henry Ossian Flipper, who had been appointed to the Academy from Atlanta University in 1873. "I don't think anything has affected me so or influenced my conduct at West Point as its melancholy tone," wrote Flipper in his 1878 autobiography *The Colored Cadet at West Point.* Flipper roomed with Smith the first year. "Of Smith," Flipper wrote, he preferred "to say nothing," seeming almost to take the side of the Cadet Corps. "Smith had trouble under my own eyes on more than one occasion."[28] Not one for self-pity, Flipper was consistently a figure of pluck, fortitude, and positive thinking.

Flipper was born in rural Georgia, the oldest of five brothers. His shoemaker father bought the freedom of his wife and children before the Civil War. At the end of the war, Flipper senior moved his family to Atlanta, where he began a successful shoemaking business, patronized by whites as well as blacks. As a member of the South's burgeoning black middle class, Flipper was determined to do even better for his children. He paid the wife of an ex–Confederate officer to tutor his sons. Atlanta became a hub of Reconstruction and "missionary" education as northern white abolitionists established and taught in the first black schools in the South. Atlanta University and the Storrs School—Henry Flipper's grammar school—were designed to create a black educational elite. The children of the new middle class were being trained to become teachers and "uplifters" of the great mass of rural southern blacks. W.E.B. Du Bois, a New England–born product of Fisk, a missionary college (also of Harvard and the University of Berlin), would call this elite the "Talented Tenth."

Flipper was grateful to his missionary teachers:

> I sincerely believe that all my success at West Point is due not so much to my perseverance and general conduct there as to the early moral and mental training I received at the hands of those philanthropic men and women who left their pleasant homes in the North to educate and elevate the black portion of America's citizens. . . . How they have borne the sneers of the Southern press, the os-

> tracism from society . . . the dangers of Kuklux . . . to raise up a down-trodden race, not for personal aggrandizement, but for the building up and glory of His kingdom who is no respecter of persons, is surely worthy of our deepest gratitude.[29]

Flipper's formative years were those of the Civil War, and he believed in the West Point mystique. His tenacity in pursuing an appointment impressed a white Republican congressman, J. C. Freeman. ("Freeman, the only white man in Georgia that ever disgraced the military of the United States," complained a Griffin, Georgia, newspaper at Flipper's appointment.) True to the Christian officer-gentleman code, Flipper believed in self-discipline and forbearance for all black cadets. "To be left to our own resources for study and improvement, for enjoyment in whatever way we chose to seek it, was what we desired," he wrote. "We cared not for social recognition. We did not expect it. . . . We would mark out for ourselves a uniform course of conduct and follow it rigidly. These were our resolutions."[30] Flipper's classmates included John Bigelow, Jr., son of the former U.S. minister to France, and the son of General Benjamin Butler—as well as the sons of two Confederate officers. (Confederate Army veterans were not permitted to attend West Point, but their sons were.)

Flipper was the seventh black cadet to enter the Academy. He found that only a few bullying whites were aggressive racists; many of those who ostracized him in public went out of their way to be friendly in private. "In short, there is a fearful lack of backbone," he wrote. But Flipper's engineering talent was recognized early by his white peers. "They were classmates. They listened to my voluntary instruction, and followed it without a thought of who gave it, or any feeling of prejudice." Like other black cadets, Flipper noted the general fairness of Academy instructors. He had arrived a semi-celebrity, having refused a $5,000 offer from a white man to have his son take Flipper's place, and his West Point career was tracked by the press. Flipper "sightings" were a treat for visitors. "Oh! There's the colored cadet! There's the colored cadet!" West Point "lady visitors" invariably remarked aloud.[31]

Unlike Smith, Flipper found the other cadets friendly at first. The insults and ostracism started a month or so after he arrived. "There was no society for me to enjoy—no friends, male or female, for me to visit, or with whom I could have any social intercourse, so absolute was my isolation," he wrote. Flipper relieved his loneliness by conversing with nonofficers—the Academy bugler, barber, and commissary clerk. True to his code, he tried to find, "if possible, for every insult or other offense a reason or motive which is consistent with the character of a gentleman."Unlike Smith, Flipper did not regularly fight back. He was disposed to overlook, to forgive and forget. "One must endure these little tortures—the sneer, the shrug of the shoulder, the epithet, the effort to avoid, to disdain, to ignore." Flipper complained to authorities only on very rare occasions, as when a junior cadet sought, unsuccessfully, to have him removed from his assigned seat in chapel. "If I cannot endure prejudice and persecution," he wrote, "even if they are offered, then I don't deserve the cadetship, and much less the commission of an army officer."[32]

In charge of guard duty, Flipper knew that his junior officer would find it "unpleasant" to take orders from him. "I gave him all the latitude I could, telling him to use his own discretion, and that he need not ask my permission for any thing unless he chose." This "simple act" ("forgotten almost as soon as done") was soon the talk of the Academy. "I had the indescribable pleasure, some days after, of knowing that by it I had been raised many degrees in the estimation of the corps," he wrote. The next time he was on guard duty, as junior to a white cadet, Flipper received the same "latitude" and "discretion" in almost the same words. He was proud to be "the first person of color to ever command a guard at the United States Military Academy."[33]

Flipper was a hero to black Americans. On furlough one summer Sunday in 1875, strolling with a "young lady" on New York City's Sixth Avenue (the heart of the black district), Flipper was paid a "high compliment" by an old one-legged black Civil War veteran. Seeing Flipper, the vet moved to the outside of the pavement, raised his crutch to "present arms," and saluted. "Endeavoring to be as polite as possible, both in return for his salute and because of his age," Flipper raised his cap.[34]

In June 1876, Flipper's class attended the Philadelphia Centennial (where Edward M. Bannister, a black painter, won a Centennial Medal for his Barbizon-school landscape *Under the Oaks*). "Nothing is done to make it unpleasant or in any way to discourage or dishearten me," Flipper reported. As a plebe, Flipper had often heard himself spoken of as "the nigger," "the moke," or "the thing." Now, "openly, and when my presence was not known," he heard himself described as "Mr. Flipper." His approaching graduation became a news story. *The New York Times* did not believe that he would graduate. A black newspaper was sure that he would "eventually be slaughtered" one way or another. But Flipper was reported to have passed his exams "uncommonly well"—and to have made an impression by his "modest, unassuming and gentlemanly manner."[35] His photo, handsome, confident, and splendidly uniformed, appeared in the class album, but he was not in the group picture.

"When Mr. Flipper, the colored cadet, stepped forward and received the reward of four years of as hard work and unflinching courage as any young man can be called upon to go through," wrote *The New York Times* of June 15, 1877, "the crowd of spectators gave him a round of applause."[36] General Sherman himself led the ovation when Flipper received his diploma. The *New York Herald* reported a classmate's remarks: "Flipper has certainly shown pluck and gentlemanly qualities, and I shall certainly shake his 'flipper' when we say 'Good-bye.' " Finally, the *New York Tribune* believed that Flipper had "made matters easier" for future black cadets: "Twenty years hence, if not sooner, the young white gentlemen of West Point will read of the fastidiousness of their predecessors with incredulous wonder. Time and patience will settle everything."[37]

Graduation assignments were based on choice and class standing. Black regiments were not popular. An 1876 First Classman, bound for the 10th Cavalry, wrote to his mother: "I would like much better to get into a white Regt but my class is crazy for the Cav . . . as to their being mokes I won't have near as much to do with them personally as you would with a black cook."[38] Initially, black regiments got the lowest-ranking cadets. But West Point classes of 1887 through 1891 began opting for the 9th and 10th Cavalry, for the Indian Wars had given black regiments cachet.

"Cadet Flipper has been appointed to the Tenth U.S. Cavalry (colored), now in Texas," wrote *The Sing Sing Republican.* "Secretary of State [*sic*] Bigelow's son has also been assigned to the same regiment. We wonder if the non-intercourse between the two at West Point will be continued in the army. Both have the same rank and are entitled to the same privileges. Possibly a campaign among the Indians, or a brush with the 'Greasers' on the Rio Grande, will equalize the complexion of the two.[39]" Second Lieutenant Bigelow, who opted for black troops when he could have chosen a white regiment, wrote in his diary that "dignity, grace and refinement go further . . . with colored people towards inspiring respect than they do with coarse white men."[40] Bigelow may have joined in "silencing" Flipper at West Point, but his father had been a coeditor and co-owner of the New York *Evening Post* with the abolitionist William Cullen Bryant.

Flipper had refused an offer from the government of Liberia, settled by American ex-slaves after the War of 1812, to become commander of its army, in order to be the only black officer in the U.S. Army, and the only black officer of black troops. He joined the 10th Cavalry and gave up love as well as high rank. In January 1878, when the 10th was sent to Fort Sill, Oklahoma, his fiancée's family forbade the marriage because Indian

Territory was too dangerous. Although he was an officer, Flipper would be too busy installing telegraph lines and supervising the building of the road from Fort Sill to Gainesville to take the hunting advice of his graduation speaker. His engineering skills continued to impress the Army as well as his white fellow officers. He designed a ditch to drain cesspools suspected of breeding malaria which is still known as Flipper's ditch.

Flipper served as a scout and a messenger for the 10th Cavalry's leader, Colonel Benjamin H. Grierson, in the famous 1880–1881 campaign against Victorio. (Flipper in action is captured in the print *Tracking Victorio,* by Don Stivers.) Victorio, leader of the Warm Springs Apaches, was incensed by Indian Bureau insistence that all Apaches move to the dreaded San Carlos reservation in the Arizona desert. (General John Pope had written to General Philip Sheridan that no one, red, white, or black, could expect to survive at San Carlos.) In August 1879, Victorio left the reservation to hide in the mountains of northern Mexico, and send out raiding parties. He was pursued by the U.S. and Mexican armies, the Texas Rangers, and civilian posses. His capture and killing, in October 1881, at Tres Castillos in northern Chihuahua, a combined Mexican-U.S. effort, broke the back of the Apache uprising.[41]

"Much credit is due the troops who took part in the hard work, explorations, active scouting . . . especially to those engaged in the campaign against Victorio and his band of hostile Indians who were outmarched, outmaneuvered, repeatedly headed off, disconcerted, met face to face, squarely fought, severely punished, driven into Mexico, badly crippled and demoralized," wrote Colonel Grierson in an appreciation of the 10th Cavalry at Tres Castillos.[42] Two members of the 9th Cavalry, Sergeants George Jordan and Thomas Shaw, won Medals of Honor for their actions at Tres Castillos. Four days after Sergeant Shaw won his Medal, First Sergeant Moses Williams, Sergeant Brent Woods, and Private Augustus Walley were cited for valor at Cuchillo Negro Mountains, New Mexico.

Flipper at Fort Davis and on Trial

At Fort Sill, Oklahoma, Flipper became friendly with Captain Nicholas Nolan, an Irish immigrant, and accompanied Nolan's young sister-in-law, Molly Dwyer, on rides and picnics, to the disapproval of other officers, especially one Charles Norstrom. Transferred from Fort Sill, Flipper went to the desolate outpost of Fort Davis, Texas, as quartermaster and acting commissary officer. At Fort Davis, he faced three inimical white officers—the explorer and camp commander Colonel William R. Shafter, who did not hide his dislike; Lieutenant Louis Wilheim, who had been dismissed from West Point while Flipper was there; and Charles Norstrom. In July 1881, Flipper discovered that commissary funds were missing from his trunk. As the only black officer in the Army, he was afraid to report the loss. "Never did a man walk the path of uprightness straighter than I did," Flipper wrote later, "but the trap was cunningly laid and I was sacrificed."[43]

Flipper told no one and repaid the money within two weeks, but he was arrested in August—and Shafter pressed for a court-martial. One of his jailers during his six months in solitary was Charles Norstrom (who later married Molly Dwyer). "The question before you is whether it is possible for a colored man to secure and hold a position as an officer of the Army," said Flipper's attorney, Major Merritt Barber. The answer was no. In December 1881, twenty-five-year-old Flipper was found innocent of embezzlement, but guilty of "conduct unbecoming an officer and gentleman," which automatically incurred a dishonorable discharge. The judge advocate general, who reviewed the trial record, and the secretary of the Army recommended against discharge, but President Chester A. Arthur ignored them. Fortunately, Matthew Reynolds, the U.S. attorney general, also believed in Flipper's innocence and named him a special agent for the Department of Justice. Later Reynolds wrote of his "fidelity, integrity and magnificent abilities."[44]

Flipper went on to a highly successful mining and surveying career in the Southwest and Mexico, writing several books and becoming the first black editor of a white American newspaper, the *Nogales Sunday Herald.* As a protégé of Senator Albert Fall (of the 1920s Teapot Dome scandal), he became a high-ranking Interior Department official in Alaska and Washington, and a troubleshooter for oil companies. A lifelong bachelor who lived to be eighty-three, he was always called Lieutenant. Flipper died in Atlanta in 1940, having petitioned Congress nine times to clear his name.

Thanks to a white Georgia teacher, Ray McColl, Flipper's name was finally cleared in 1976. Since discovering the case in a black history course, McColl had become "obsessed" with clearing Flipper, to the point of dreaming about him. He was encouraged by Flipper's family, as well as by West Point, which was eager to celebrate the hundredth anniversary of its first black graduate but unable to commemorate anyone who had been dishonorably discharged. The Army Board for the Correction of Military Records accepted McColl's argument that if Flipper was innocent of embezzlement, he could not be guilty of conduct unbecoming an officer and gentleman. In 1977, West Point established the Henry

O. Flipper Memorial Award for "leadership, self-discipline and perseverance in the face of unusual difficulties while a cadet." Flipper was reburied with military honors in 1978. In 1999, the work of President Chester A. Arthur was undone: Flipper received an official presidential pardon from President Bill Clinton, who called it "an event that is 117 years overdue."[45]

Until the late 1940s, Flipper's *Colored Cadet at West Point* was on the Academy's "restricted book" list, to be read only in the presence of a librarian. In 1991 West Point graduated both its thousandth black cadet and its thousandth female cadet. The Academy had been admitting blacks since 1870, and women since 1976.

Isaiah Dorman at the Little Bighorn

In June of 1876, the year before Flipper's graduation, America had been profoundly shocked by the death of a Union Army golden boy, General George Armstrong Custer (last in his West Point class), who was defeated by Sitting Bull, Crazy Horse, and three thousand Sioux at Little Bighorn, in the Montana Territory. Isaiah Dorman, a black scout and interpreter, went with Custer to Little Bighorn and also lost his life. Possibly a fugitive slave, Dorman lived with his Sioux wife near Fort Rice in the Dakota Territory and initially earned his living by supplying wood to the fort. He had been well paid during the Civil War, earning $100 a month as a War Department courier, carrying the mail once a month on foot, one hundred miles each way, between Fort Rice and Fort Wadworth, Nebraska. Said to have been a friend of Sitting Bull, Dorman appears in Sioux tribal history as early as 1850, as the "Black White Man." Known as a skilled interpreter and guide, in 1871 he was hired by the Army to lead the Northern Pacific Railroad survey. In the early summer of 1876, as official 7th Cavalry interpreter, at $75 a month, Dorman rode along with the famous white scout "Lonesome Charley" Reynolds to the Little Bighorn to meet Custer.[46]

There are several contradictory eyewitness accounts of Dorman's death. A wild-riding 5th Cavalry private named Rutten, who passed him as he knelt on one knee firing a non-regulation rifle, probably heard his last words, a shouted "Good-bye, Rutten!" A Sioux chief calmly remembered zeroing in on Dorman the target: "We passed a black man in a soldier's uniform and we had him. He turned on his horse and shot an Indian right through the heart. Then the Indians fired at this one man and riddled his horse with bullets. His horse fell over on his back, and the black man could not get up. I saw him as I rode by."[47] Custer's orderly claimed to have seen his dead body, with a dozen arrows in his breast and "a picket pin through his balls."

JOHNSON CHESTNUTT WHITTAKER

Johnson Chestnutt Whittaker, a former slave who had briefly attended the newly integrated University of South Carolina, was appointed to West Point by South Carolina Representative S. L. Hoge. He entered the Academy in 1876, as Flipper's roommate, but never went to the Indian Wars. When Flipper graduated, eighteen-year-old Whittaker became West Point's only black. He spoke to no one outside the line of duty. He had no friends and no social life. His only solace was daily Bible reading. On April 4, 1880, two months before graduation, he received a scribbled note: "You will be fixed. Better keep awake. A friend."[48] Whittaker was found unconscious in his room later that night, beaten, slashed, and tied to his bed. He reported that he had been beaten and cut during the night by three masked attackers, who burned pages of his Bible.

The Academy refused to believe him. The commandant of cadets insisted that Whittaker had slashed and bound himself, because he was afraid of failing a philosophy course. Demanding a court of inquiry to clear his name, Whittaker became the subject of national attention and congressional debate. Public opinion was generally on his side. President Rutherford B. Hayes replaced West Point's superintendent, General John M. Schofield, with General Oliver O. Howard—an ex-abolitionist, Civil War hero, and former head of the Freedmen's Bureau. But Whittaker did fail his philosophy course, and the Academy dismissed him just before graduation.

Whittaker's court-martial, January to June 1881, took place in New York City. Representing him were Daniel H. Chamberlain, a white ex-governor of South Carolina; Richard T. Greener, Harvard's first black graduate, now a lawyer; and General William Tecumseh Sherman, as a close observer. Despite his failure to arm runaway slaves in the Civil War, Sherman showed great support for black cadets. Whittaker was found guilty, but the court recommended leniency. In the fall of 1881, the judge advocate general of the Army overturned the decision on a technicality. In March 1882, Secretary of War Robert Lincoln (Abraham Lincoln's son) invalidated the trial, and President Arthur (with Whittaker safely unable to graduate) agreed. Thus, Whittaker was officially innocent, although he never became an Army officer. He gave one speech, in Buffalo, in which he said, "With God as my guide, duty as my watchword, I can, I must and I will win a place in life." He taught and practiced law in North

Carolina, and eventually became a teacher and public school principal in Oklahoma. One of his students was Ralph Ellison.

Flipper's and Whittaker's West Point careers coincided with the high and low points of Reconstruction. Senator Charles Sumner's Civil Rights Bill of 1875 originally banned discrimination in all public facilities, including schools, hospitals, cemeteries, theaters, restaurants, boats, and trains. When it finally passed, however, the school-desegregation clause was deleted. The South was not ready to cede "white superiority" in any realm, either political or social. "Whenever the Constitution comes between me and the virtue of the white women of the South," said Senator Coleman L. Blease of South Carolina, "I say to hell with the Constitution." Two 1875 Mississippi race riots saw nearly one hundred blacks and several white Republicans killed. The governor of Mississippi asked for federal troops, but was refused. "Conservatives" (Democrats) won the election. White supremacist politicians of Louisiana, South Carolina, and Alabama developed the so-called Mississippi plan, using social and economic intimidation and assassinations to overthrow Reconstruction state governments. General John McEnery of Louisiana said: "We shall carry the next election if we have to ride saddle-deep in blood to do it."[49]

THE WORMLEY COMPROMISE

In the presidential election of 1876, an ex–Barn Burner Democrat, Samuel J. Tilden of New York, received 250,000 more popular votes and 21 more electoral votes than the Ohio Republican Rutherford B. Hayes—but returns from Oregon, Louisiana, South Carolina, and Florida, representing 22 electoral votes, were disputed—with some missing, some not counted, and some with two sets of returns. A secret meeting of congressionally appointed bipartisan emissaries at Washington's Wormley Hotel (incidentally, black-owned) declared that Hayes had won all twenty-two votes and thus defeated Tilden by one vote. Tilden accepted the result to avoid a new civil war, but maintained that he had been wrongfully deprived of the presidency. The quid pro quo for a Republican presidency was the agreement to remove federal troops from the South.

With southern home rule on the "Negro question," all constitutional safeguards for blacks were suspended. Now the Democratic Congress voted to repeal the bulk of Reconstruction civil rights legislation, and the white South began the process of beating blacks back into submission. At least five thousand blacks were murdered in the mid-1870s for trying to vote. In 1878, Abbeville County, South Carolina, reported that three Republican ballots had been cast in the entire county—compared with fifteen hundred in 1874. Benjamin "Pap" Singleton led a black migration of

"Exodusters" out of the cotton states to Kansas, while planters' men stood at the border with guns trying to stop them.

In 1880, a Civil War colonel named James Garfield, an Ohio abolitionist belonging to the Radical Reconstruction, or "Half-Breed," wing of the Republican Party, successfully campaigned for president on a "bloody shirt" platform, promising protection to southern blacks. He was assassinated in July 1881, in Washington's Union Station, by a "Stalwart"—a member of the antiblack, conservative Republican wing. It was the beginning of a new dark age for black southerners.

Tennessee, birthplace of the Ku Klux Klan, segregated its railroad cars in 1881 and invented the legal system known as Jim Crow, after "Jump Jim Crow," a blackface minstrel song. Jim Crow laws swiftly followed in Florida, Mississippi, Texas, Louisiana, Alabama, Kentucky, Arkansas, Virginia, Maryland, and Oklahoma. In 1883, the U.S. Supreme Court declared Sumner's 1875 Civil Rights Bill unconstitutional on the grounds that the Fourteenth Amendment prohibited states but not individuals from discriminating. By 1884, the black vote was down by one-third in Louisiana, by one-quarter in Mississippi, and by one-half in South Carolina.

JOHN ALEXANDER AND CHARLES YOUNG

Ten years after Flipper, West Point had its second black graduate, John H. Alexander. Born in Arkansas of slave parents, Alexander was a freshman at Oberlin College when he received his appointment in 1882. He earned the highest score on the academic part of the West Point test, but was made an alternate because the son of Supreme Court Chief Justice Morrison Waite scored better on the physical. Waite failed the entrance exam, and Alexander entered the Academy. He ranked sixteenth out of one hundred in his first year, and thirty-second out of sixty-four at graduation, with the usual cadet-given demerits pulling down his class standing. (Once he was placed under close arrest for skating on the Hudson River.)

At graduation, Second Lieutenant Alexander joined the 9th Cavalry, serving in Nebraska, Wyoming, and Utah. In 1894 he became professor of military science and tactics at Wilberforce University in Ohio, a post established by President Grover Cleveland. He died the same year, at thirty, of a heart attack.

Charles Young was born in a Kentucky log cabin. His parents were former slaves, but his father had served in the Union Army. In 1873, when Young was nine years old, his family moved to Ripley, Ohio. Talented in languages and music, he graduated from high school preparing to enter a Jesuit college when he made a sudden career swerve and took the competitive entrance exam for West Point. He was the ninth black appointed and, in 1889, would be the third to graduate. (With the entrenchment of Jim Crow, he would also be the last black graduate until 1936.)

He spent five years at West Point—repeating a year because of failing a math course. He seems to have made friends with other cadets, and was possibly only "semi-silenced." When he nearly lost his diploma because of his low engineering grades, he was popular enough for a white classmate to hope that he would "get through," and to write an appreciation of "our colored classmate, Charles Young, whom we esteem highly for his patient perseverance in the face of discouraging conditions."[50] Also encouraging and assisting Young in his efforts to "get through" was the engineering instructor, Lieutenant George Goethals, who later led the construction of the Panama Canal. Graduating in 1889, Young joined the 9th Cavalry at Fort Robinson, Nebraska, and the following year went with them to Fort Duchesne, Utah. In 1893, after Alexander's death, Young became professor of military science and tactics at Wilberforce.

The Last Indian Wars

In 1885, with the Texas frontier reasonably stabilized, the 9th and 10th Cavalries were sent, respectively, to Oklahoma and Arizona. In Oklahoma, for the first time, the 9th Cavalry protected Indians from whites—in this case, settlers by the thousands determined to colonize Indian territory. Meanwhile, in Arizona, the 10th Cavalry was fighting the 1885–1886 Geronimo campaign.

"Geronimo is an Apache who belongs to the Chiracia band, and who for many years was the most vexatious and troublesome Indian with whom the government had to deal," wrote Herschel V. Cashin in 1899 in *Under Fire with the 10th Cavalry.* "He is now an old man of probably seventy years. He was born in New Mexico and for years served as a herder, working for Spaniards who owned ranches in the territory. When about twenty-one years of age he conceived the idea that he had been greatly wronged by the white man; and from that time until his final surrender to General Nelson A. Miles in 1886 he was almost continually on the warpath."[51] In old age, Geronimo admitted that it was "better to submit to great wrongs" than to fight the United States.

> For years I fought the white men, thinking that with my few braves I could kill them all off; and that we would again have the land that our Great Father gave us, and which he covered with game. I

> thought that the Great Spirit would be with us, and that after we had killed the white men, the buffalo, deer and antelope would come back. After I fought and lost . . . I knew that the race of the Indian had run, and that there was nothing left but to submit. . . . The sun rises and shines for a time and then it goes down, sinking out of sight and is lost; so it will be with the Indians. When I was a boy my old father told me that the Indians were as many as the leaves on the trees. . . . I never saw them, but I know that if they were there they have gone now, and the white man has taken all they had. . . . I am an old man and can't live many years . . . but before I die I would like to see the Indians have the same chance as the colored people or the poor whites. . . . The Indian's fighting days are over, and there is nothing left for him to do but to be a beggar and live on charity around the agency.[52]

By the last decade of the nineteenth century, except for pockets of warfare with Apache and Sioux, the wild West was basically tamed. There were still nonnative bad guys: Sergeant Benjamin Brown and Corporal Isaiah Mays, both of the 24th Infantry, won Medals of Honor for their roles in foiling the celebrated Arizona Wham Paymaster robbery attempt of 1889. The following year saw Medals of Honor awarded for bravery in the last Indian campaigns. Sergeant William McBryar, of the 10th Cavalry, was cited for actions against the Apaches in Arizona; and Corporal William O. Wilson, of the 9th Cavalry, was cited for the Sioux campaign.

"Many causes are ascribed for the outbreak among the various Indian tribes throughout Montana and the Dakotas in the winter of 1890–'91," wrote Colonel Philip Harvey, of the 25th Infantry, "but there can be little doubt that the condition of destitution . . . brought about by reduced rations and the dishonesty and mismanagement of minor government officials had a far reaching effect."[53] One major effect was that Colonel Harvey's 25th Infantry and the 9th Cavalry joined the white 7th Cavalry to fight the last Indian war, on December 29, 1890, against near-starving and destitute Sioux, near the Pine Ridge, South Dakota, agency, on a creek called Wounded Knee.

BOOKER T. WASHINGTON AND W.E.B. DU BOIS

Frederick Douglass died in March 1895 and the mantle of black leadership fell upon thirty-nine-year-old Booker T. Washington, head of Alabama's Tuskegee Institute, whom Dean Kelly Miller of Howard

University referred to in a 1903 analysis as the "natural antipode" of Douglass.[54] In September 1895, Washington's "Atlanta Compromise" speech dramatically supporting political and social inequality was highly criticized by many blacks; nevertheless it set the new tone for black leadership. Washington and Douglass had essentially the same long-term goals, full citizenship and equality for black Americans, but Washington, who lived in the South, was more pragmatic. While Douglass (who came under a political cloud in 1884 when his first wife died and he married his forty-five-year-old white secretary) continued, in old age, to call on blacks to "Agitate! Agitate! Agitate!" Washington might be said to have called on blacks to "Accommodate!" Money poured into Tuskegee from captains of industry such as Andrew Carnegie (U.S. Steel), Henry H. Rogers (Standard Oil), and Collis P. Huntington (Southern Pacific Railroad). Whatever his quarrels with black intellectuals, Washington believed in preparing his students for the world as it was, not as it should ideally be.

Washington, the author of *Up from Slavery,* a book that stressed the importance of manual training and craftsmanship for blacks, was a former child coal miner who walked barefoot many miles to get an education at Virginia's Hampton Institute. Like Douglass, Washington had escaped from slavery and renamed himself. He was the son of an unknown white father and a Virginia slave mother, and his given surname was Taliaferro. As a patriotic Virginian, he named himself "Washington" and became the most powerful black man in America. While most of middle-class black America believed in his bootstrap-pulling economic message, others refused to accept him as their leader. Harvard awarded him an honorary degree in 1896, but the Boston newspaper publisher William Monroe Trotter called him a "notorious and incorrigible Jim Crowist" who "dares to assert that the best way to get rights is not to oppose their being taken away, but to get money."[55]

Frederick Douglass attended an Election Day reception at the White House under Lincoln, but in 1901, Booker T. Washington became the first black guest invited to a White House dinner. "The most damnable outrage which has ever been perpetrated by any citizen of the United States was committed yesterday by the President, when he invited a nigger to dine with him at the White House," said the *Memphis Scimitar* of the Republican Theodore Roosevelt. A South Carolina politician, "Pitchfork Ben" Tillman, added that "the action of President Roosevelt in entertaining that nigger will necessitate our killing a thousand niggers in the South before they will learn their place again."[56] The threat appears to have been taken seriously. Roosevelt never invited another black to dine in the White House again; it was too politically dangerous. Nor, officially, would any other American president until John F. Kennedy. (Although black entertainers appeared at Harry Truman's inaugural ball.)

* * *

"The problem of the twentieth century is the problem of the color line," said the thirty-two-year-old W.E.B. Du Bois in an address to the Nations of the World Pan-African Conference in London in 1900. In contrast to Washington, William Edward Burghardt Du Bois was the voice of militant equality and full integration into all aspects of American public life. Du Bois, whose 1896 *Suppression of the African Slave Trade* was the first title in the new Harvard Historical Studies monograph series, became Washington's political and intellectual rival.

Born in Great Barrington, Massachusetts, a descendant of the Revolutionary figure Elizabeth Freeman, Du Bois was the only black member of Great Barrington High School's class of 1884. Of African, Dutch, and French Huguenot ancestry, he always said, "Thank God, no Anglo-Saxon." He graduated from Fisk University (on scholarship) in 1888, and went to Harvard as a junior with a $300 Price Greenleaf Award. Graduating cum laude in 1890, he received his master's degree in 1891, and, after two years at the University of Berlin, completed his dissertation to become Harvard's first black Ph.D. From 1895 to 1897, he taught Latin, Greek, German, and English at Wilberforce University, while writing *Suppression of the African Slave Trade.* After publishing a study of Philadelphia's black population, he became a professor of economics and history at Atlanta University. From 1896 to 1914, Du Bois led the Atlanta University Studies on black life, the first sociological studies in the South.

Atlanta University and the Tuskegee Institute were polar opposites of black thought. In 1905, Du Bois founded the Niagara Movement. "We claim for ourselves every single right that belongs to a freeborn American, political, civil and social," he said in an address to the second meeting, "and until we get these rights we will never cease to protest and assail the ears of America."[57] Four years later, he helped found the National Association for the Advancement of Colored People. From 1910 to 1934, he was among the few black members of the largely white NAACP board, and editor of its influential magazine, *The Crisis.* He became the voice and leader of the new century's "New Negro."

FROM CAKEWALK TO HARLEM

The Indian was all but eliminated, the Mystic Years were over, and the revisionist myths of the "contented slave" and "wretched freedman" were firmly entrenched in the South. But northern blacks still basked in the twilight of Reconstruction. The economic high tide of the 1890s had bolstered the black middle class and encouraged black enterprise and creativity. In keeping with the promise of a new century, blacks in the North were being woven into the fabric of American life in new and unusual ways. The Civil War veteran Lewis Latimer, a New York "Edison Pioneer," patented the first incandescent electric lamp and made drawings of the first telephone for Alexander Graham Bell. In Ypsilanti, Michigan, a machinist-inventor named Elijah McCoy made a lubricator for steam engines so good that it was known as the real McCoy. Blacks were also becoming household names in sports. Black baseball was born with the Chicago Union Giants of 1887. Between 1875 and 1902, fourteen black jockeys, including Oliver Lewis and Isaac Murphy, won the Kentucky Derby and inspired the fad for black jockey statuettes.

Despite growing political repression, the 1890s were golden years for black culture and entertainment. It was the height of the minstrel era. Callender's Spectacular Colored Minstrels, who toured Europe, were the most celebrated black troupe. White Americans may not have liked black political aspirations, but they liked black music and performers. Blacks made turn-of-the-century America sing—from James A. Bland (composer of "Carry Me Back to Old Virginny," "Oh, Dem Golden Slippers," and "In the Evening by the Moonlight") to Scott Joplin (whose "Maple Leaf Rag" was published in 1899), W. C. Handy, and Will Marion Cook. Collaborating with the poet Paul Laurence Dunbar (author of *Lyrics of a Lowly Life* [1896]), Cook wrote the first "cakewalk" musical, the 1898 Broadway hit *Clorindy, the Origin of the Cake Walk.* The cakewalk, defining black Reconstruction optimism, became the signature dance of the era. From the cakewalk (born in Jacksonville, Florida, of newly freed slaves) to ragtime (from black pianists in the brothels of Texas and the Midwest) to jazz (from New Orleans's Congo Square), black music defined the mood and essence of America. With one million immigrants arriving in America in 1900, it also helped to make that mood and essence irresistible to the rest of the world.

More serious black arts and letters were also esteemed beyond the black community. Black painters and sculptors, like their white counterparts, often chose to study and settle abroad, as much because of America's perceived lack of artistic appreciation as because of its racism. Edmonia Lewis, one of the most noted sculptors of her time, went from selling beaded moccasins at Niagara Falls to studying art in Boston when her brother struck gold in California. *Forever Free,* an 1867 marble allegory of Emancipation, was her most important early work. She later studied, and settled, in Italy, where she died just before the First World War.

The painter Henry Ossawa Tanner entered the Pennsylvania Academy of Fine Arts in 1880, when he was twenty-one, and studied under the American master Thomas Eakins, who would paint his portrait. After graduation Tanner went to Paris, where his *Daniel in the Lion's Den* won honorable mention at the Salon of 1896. He became a war-zone artist in France during World War I, was named a chevalier of the Legion of Honor in 1923, and continued to win prizes in America and Europe until his death in 1937. Meta Warrick Fuller graduated from the Philadelphia Museum of Fine Arts school in 1899. Armed with prizes, she went to Paris, where she attracted the interest of Rodin, who had seen a plaster model of her *Man Eating His Heart.*[58] When she returned to Philadelphia, she found it difficult to get attention or commissions until her work for the 1907 Jamestown Tercentennial Exposition, *The Progress of the Negro Since Jamestown,* won a gold medal. She worked steadily until her death in 1968.

There was a similar history of creativity among novelists and activist men of letters. The stories of Charles W. Chesnutt, the Ohio-born, North Carolina–bred son of a Civil War veteran, were published in *McClure's* and *The Atlantic Monthly* in the 1880s. In 1899, anthologized as *The Conjure Woman,* they were published with great success by Houghton Mifflin. The novelist–poet–editor–diplomat–civil rights activist James Weldon Johnson, author of the groundbreaking and anonymous *The Autobiography of an Ex-Colored Man* (1912), was a Renaissance figure and, like Du Bois, a quintessential New Negro. A member of the thriving black middle class of Jacksonville, Florida (his mother was a teacher and his father a headwaiter at a fashionable hotel), Johnson was educated at Atlanta University. In 1896, he became the first black lawyer admitted to the bar in Duval County and also secretary of the Atlanta University Conference on Negro Life, the first sociological research center in the South. In 1900, he wrote the lyrics for "Lift Every Voice and Sing" (music by his brother, J. Rosamond Johnson), which came to be known as "the Negro national anthem" ("Shadowed beneath Thy hand, / May we forever stand, / True to our God, / True to our native land"). Meanwhile, as one of the "Ebony Offenbachs," with Robert Cole, Johnson wrote hit songs like "Under the Bamboo Tree" and "Didn't He Ramble." In 1904, he became treasurer of the Colored Republican Club, a fiefdom of Booker T. Washington, thanks to whose influence he was named U.S. consul in Venezuela and, later, Nicaragua. In 1910, he married Grace Nail, daughter of John B. Nail, the most successful real estate entrepreneur in the burgeoning new black metropolis of Harlem.

Plessy v. Ferguson

In 1896, the Supreme Court's decision in *Plessy v. Ferguson,* which ratified the white supremacist doctrine of "separate but equal," seemed finally to bury black hopes. Homer Plessy, a New Orleans black, had been arrested and convicted for attempting to ride in a white railroad car. "The object of the [Fourteenth] Amendment was undoubtedly to enforce the absolute equality of the two races before the law, but in the nature of things it could not have been intended to abolish distinctions based on color," read the majority opinion. Sanction for segregation as the supreme law of the land was now established. But Justice John Harlan's dissent was famously eloquent: "In view of the Constitution, in view of the law, there is in this country no superior, dominant, ruling class of citizens. There is no caste here. Our Constitution is color-blind, and neither knows nor tolerates classes among citizens."

Plessy v. Ferguson enabled whites to disenfranchise blacks by means of grandfather clauses and poll taxes. Voters were required not only to have had a grandfather who voted, but also to pay for the privilege. *Plessy* also gave constitutional sanction to every form of segregation. Birmingham, Alabama, for example, forbade blacks and whites to play checkers together. In 1892, the black newspaperwoman Ida Wells-Barnett began to keep lynching statitistics in her *Red Record*. In 1896, the year of *Plessy,* more than one hundred blacks were lynched. By the first decade of the new century, all black American progress since the Civil War was at a standstill, and race riots were becoming commonplace in northern cities. True to an old American paradox, however, black soldiers were about to be raised to a new heroic status.

5 Buffalo Soldiers II

CUBA AND THE PHILIPPINES, 1898–1917

We went up absolutely intermingled, so that no one could tell whether it was the Rough Riders or the men of the 9th who came forward with the greater courage to offer their lives in the service of their country. . . . When you've been under fire with a man and fought side by side with him, and eaten with him when you had anything to eat, and hungered with him when you hadn't, you felt sort of a comradeship that you don't feel for any man that you have been associated with in other ways. I don't think that any Rough Rider will ever forget the tie that binds us to the 9th and 10th Cavalry.[1]

—*Colonel Theodore Roosevelt, in 1898*

The Spanish–American War

On February 15, 1898, 260 American sailors, of whom twenty-two were black, were killed when the battleship *Maine* blew up in Havana harbor. American popular opinion, encouraged by the press, blamed a Spanish bomb. (Later study has indicated that the real cause was probably an accidental shipboard explosion.) The *Maine* was in Havana to keep an eye on American interests during the 1895 U.S.-supported Cuban revolution. American public opinion was firmly on the side of the rebels—as were the architects of American expansionism. War's end would see former Spanish possessions—Cuba, Puerto Rico, and the Philippines—as American military protectorates.

A "splendid little war," the U.S. statesman John Hay famously called the 113-day conflict. Officially begun on April 21, 1898, the Spanish-American War may have been "little," but it loomed large in the American imagination. Fueled by ragtime and rum, the first official war since the Civil War (the Indian Wars were mere housekeeping) was a feverish exercise in jingoism, empire building, and war nostalgia. The "March King," John Philip Sousa, composer of "Stars and Stripes Forever," quickstepped the country into battle. On May 1, John Jordan, a black gunner's mate, led the crew that fired the first American shots of the war—not in Cuba, but from Commodore George Dewey's flagship in Manila Bay, in the Philippines. With the Spanish fleet obliterated, and the help of anti-Spanish insurgents, American victory in the Philippines was assured. Puerto Rico also saw fighting, but the main battle scene was Cuba. The island itself was popularized: towns named Siboney and Daiquirí entered the American vocabulary, inspiring a popular song and a popular rum drink. "Hot Time in the Old Town Tonight!," first sung by the McIntyre and Heath Minstrels, was translated into "Hot Time in Cuba!" The battle cry "Remember the *Maine,* to hell with Spain!" was equally catchy.

President William McKinley ordered an immediate Cuban blockade, and called the Army to Tampa, port of embarkation for the war zone ninety miles away. In March 1898, the black 25th Infantry became the first American troops ordered to Tampa. They had last seen action fighting civilians, in the 1892–1894 mine-labor wars of Montana and Idaho. Now, they led legendary Indian-fighting troops to Cuba. All along the way, cities and towns offered noisy demonstrations of gratitude to the men in dark blue shirts, khaki breeches, and cowboy hats—black soldiers as well as white. When the 25th Infantry troop train reached St. Paul, Minnesota, the engine was decorated with flags, and crowds gathered at the station. Suddenly there was a craze for soldiers' tunic buttons as souvenirs. (Men of the 9th Cavalry later reported having to "pin our clothes on with sundry nails and sharpened bits of wood."[2]) Their progress south "was a marked event, attracting the attention of the daily and illustrated press," wrote Chaplain Theophilus G. Steward, the only black officer of the 25th.[3] They were greeted everywhere "with enthusiastic crowds, who fully believed the war had begun."

"The streets were jammed, the people wild with enthusiasm," wrote William G. Muller of the departure of the 24th Infantry from Fort Douglas, Utah, a month later.[4] The 24th had first known Fort Douglas in the 1870s as a place of "pine forests" and "hostile Indians," wrote Muller, in his history of the regiment. When they returned in 1896 they found "civilized" Salt Lake City, which sent a deputation to Washington to have the 24th removed. The city's main newspaper now offered an editorial apology for its previous prejudice and the whole town, as well as the governor of the state, turned out to honor the troops. But good feeling toward black soldiers stopped at the Mason-Dixon Line. "It is needless to attempt a description of patriotism displayed by the liberty loving people of this country along our line of travel until reaching the South, where cool receptions told the tale of race prejudice . . . even though these brave men were rushing to the front in the very face of grim death to defend the flag and preserve the country's honor and dignity," wrote Herschel V. Cashin, traveling to Tampa with the 24th Infantry.[5]

With war officially declared, the War Department authorized four new regiments of black troops to join the Buffalo Soldiers—the 7th through 10th U.S. Volunteer Infantries, with mostly white officers. Fort Thomas, Kentucky, where the 8th Volunteers trained under old Buffalo Soldiers, had three officers' messes: one for captains and higher ranks (all white); one for lieutenants (all black); and one for field and staff officers (mostly white). Its two black staff officers, the chaplain and assistant surgeon, who were majors, ate with the lieutenants.

One of the 8th Volunteer lieutenants at Fort Thomas was eighteen-year-old Benjamin O. Davis of Washington, D.C., the son of a Treasury Department messenger. Davis had wanted to be a cavalry officer since childhood, when one of the parents at his integrated primary school, an ex–Civil War officer, organized a school drill group. His military motivation was further strengthened in 1893 by the sight of the 9th Cavalry marching in the inaugural parade of President Grover Cleveland. Later, at his segregated high school (the future Dunbar High School, whose black teachers had more higher degrees from northern colleges and universities than most teachers in Washington's white schools), Davis became captain of the Cadet Corps. He had volunteered as soon as war was declared against Spain.

In October 1898, the 8th Regiment was ordered to Chickamauga Park, Georgia, where racial hostility from white civilians extended to a cache of unexploded dynamite discovered on base. Davis so impressed the camp commander, however, an ex-Confederate officer who had served under General Nathan Bedford Forrest, that he was made the battalion adjutant. In February 1899, the 8th Regiment was mustered out without seeing service in Cuba.

Despite the dearth of black officers, the Spanish-American War was the most integrated American war since the Revolution. Cuba was a time of well-publicized black heroism, a significantly high number of black battlefield commissions, and demonstrated interracial comradeship. The "shared canteen" story was typical. "A black corporal of the Twenty-fourth Infantry walked wearily up to the 'water hole,' " wrote the black chaplain W. Hilary Coston, of the 9th U.S. Volunteer Infantry, in his memoir *The Spanish American War Volunteer.*

> He was muddy and bedraggled. He carried no cup or canteen, and stretched himself out over the stepping stones in the stream, sipping up the water and mud together out of the shallow pool. A

> white cavalryman ran toward him shouting, "Hold on, bunkie; here's my cup!" The negro looked dazed a moment, and not a few of the spectators showed amazement, for such a thing had rarely, if ever, happened in the army before. "Thank you," said the black corporal. "Well, we are all fighting under the same flag now." And he drank out of the white man's cup.[6]

The "same flag" is a reference to the black 9th and 10th Cavalries, which formed one brigade of (ex-Confederate) General Joseph "Fighting Joe" Wheeler's cavalry division.

At the onset of war, the thirty-four-year-old First Lieutenant Charles Young, 9th Cavalry, West Point class of 1889, was the only black officer in the regular Army qualified to lead troops in combat. A military instructor at Wilberforce University, Young wrote to the War Department asking to rejoin his regiment when it was called to active service. The 9th Cavalry went to Cuba, but Young did not. Instead, he became a major (wartime rank) in the 9th Ohio U.S. Volunteers, serving in Virginia, Pennsylvania, and South Carolina. West Point or not, black officers would not lead black troops in battle.

Most black Americans supported the war. Cuba was considered a "colored" country, and the Cuban rebel leader General Antonio Maceo, the African-Indian-Spanish architect of "Cuba libre," murdered by the Spanish in 1896, became a martyr to black Americans. American involvement in general, however, was clearly more about sugar, tobacco, and bananas than about liberation.

To the delight of the American press and public, the war itself was a matter of three major victories in less than three weeks, although fighting continued for three more months. The American expeditionary force landed at Daiquirí on June 22, 1898. On June 24, the Spanish outpost at Las Guásimas was destroyed. The San Juan River was forded on July 1 and 2, at El Caney, and San Juan Hill was taken. By July 15, Santiago de Cuba was besieged and bombarded, and victory was assured. It was a short war but a nasty one: 280 men were killed and 1,577 wounded in less than four months of fighting heat, mud, rainstorms, and dense tropical foothills as well as the Spanish. And when the war ended, there was still yellow fever. The New Army lost a high percentage of its younger officers in combat, but more Americans died of disease than of bullets.

Like the Civil War, the Spanish-American War was an enormous media event, covered in newspapers, magazines, and even motion pictures. What was described as "an army of correspondents and artists" arrived along with the Army and Navy.[7] Among those reporting the story were Richard Harding Davis, America's most famous foreign correspondent, and Stephen Crane, who in 1895 had published *The Red Badge of Courage.* Photography was still in its relative infancy. Action shots were impossible, so sketch artists and painters were called upon to provide action stills. *McClure's* magazine hired William Glackens, Howard Chandler Christie worked for *Leslie's,* and Frederic Remington covered the war for William R. Hearst. Sent to Cuba in 1896, Remington telegraphed Hearst that he wanted to leave; everything was quiet, he wrote, there would be no war. "Please remain" was Hearst's reply. "You furnish the pictures. I'll furnish the war."[8]

The "Rough Riders"—the 1st Volunteer Cavalry—Colonel Theodore Roosevelt's semiprivate army of Texas cowboys and eastern Ivy Leaguers, claimed the lion's share of public attention. But they owed much of their glory, as well as their lives, to Buffalo Soldiers who came to their rescue in three important battles: the 10th Cavalry, at Las Guásimas; the 25th Infantry, at El Caney ("Hell Caney"); and the 9th and 10th Cavalries, at San Juan Hill. In August 1898, *The New York World* published a poem entitled "The Rough Rider 'Remarks.' " The Rough Rider was remarking on his gratitude to the Buffalo Soldier:

> *"The cowboys always pay their debts;*
> *Them darkies saved us at Hell Caney;*
> *When we go back on the colored vets,*
> *Count Texas Bill out of the play"*
> *said the Rough Rider.*[9]

(Who also said, "You bet your sweet life them darkies is white!") The Spanish-American War represented the apotheosis of the Buffalo Soldier mystique. Unfortunately, the illustrious leader of the Rough Riders did not hesitate to "go back on the colored vets" when it became politically expedient. Roosevelt capitalized on his Rough Rider experience to become governor of New York in 1899, vice president under McKinley in 1900, and president in 1901 (when McKinley was assassinated). A man of flamboyant personality (who wished, his daughter said, to be "the bride at every wedding and the corpse at every funeral"), Roosevelt believed in the cult of personality. He was also, according to Mark Twain, "clearly insane . . . and insanest upon war and its supreme glories."[10] In order to place himself and the Rough Riders at center stage, it was necessary to betray the Buffalo Soldiers.

THE 10TH CAVALRY AT LAS GUÁSIMAS

The 10th Cavalry fought dismounted in Cuba, leaving their horses behind in Tampa. They acted as artillerymen (rare for blacks) as well as infantrymen. Sergeant Horace W. Bivens, a thirty-six-year-old Virginian, was in charge of a battery of Hotchkiss guns.

Bivens was the quintessential Buffalo Soldier. Enlisting in the 10th Cavalry in 1887, he fought in the last Apache campaigns. In 1894, he won first place in the Army-wide carbine competition at Fort Sheridan. "Buffalo Bill" Cody invited him to join his Wild West show, but Bivens declined the offer. A photograph entitled *Horace W. Bivens Equipped for Service* shows a stalwart, mustachioed western trooper, with a chest full of sharpshooting medals, his horse, his rifle, and his famous messenger dog, Booth. An Irish water spaniel born at Fort Custer, Booth was trained by Bivens on the battlefield near the Little Bighorn River. In 1898, Bivens wrote to a friend: "There is no people on earth more loyal and devoted to their country than the Negro. I believe in the doctrine of peace taught by the lowly Nazarene, but one must have liberty before abiding peace can come. Force saved the Union, kept the stars in the flag and made Negroes free. The time for God's force has come to free Cuba and avenge the Maine." Noble sentiments aside, Bivens also reported that Indian fighters were "anxious to get a whack at the Spaniards."[11]

The initial bonding of white volunteers and black professional soldiers actually involved a Rough Rider rescue of Buffalo Soldiers during the rough Daiquirí landings, when a boat carrying men of the 10th Cavalry capsized and a Rough Rider captain and several sailors dived into the sea to help. They bonded again on the fast-paced and intensely hot march from Daiquirí to Siboney, when men tossed away clothing, packs, and blankets. On June 24, two days after landing, they met the enemy at Las Guásimas. Together, fewer than a thousand Rough Riders and 10th Cavalry troopers fought two thousand Spanish and destroyed the outpost.

At Las Guásimas it was the Rough Riders who were in trouble, and 10th Cavalry troopers went to their aid. Using old Indian-fighting techniques, they saved a trapped Rough Rider squadron. The *Washington Post* correspondent at the battle scene expressed his personal gratitude: "If it had not been for the Negro cavalry, the Rough Riders would have been exterminated. I am not a Negro lover. My father fought with Mosby's Rangers and I was born in the South, but the Negroes saved that fight and the day will come when General Shafter will give them credit for their bravery."[12] The rotund, walrus-mustached old Indian-fighter

William R. Shafter, ex-tormentor of Lieutenant Flipper, was commander of the American forces. "The First and Tenth (colored) regiments of regular cavalry (dismounted) deployed and charged up the hill in front," wrote Bivens, describing Las Guásimas in *Under Fire with the Tenth Cavalry,* "driving the enemy from their position, but not until we had sustained a severe loss in both killed and wounded. . . . The conduct of the troops, both white and colored, regular and volunteer, was most gallant and soldierly."[13]

The 10th Cavalry were heroes, at least above the Mason-Dixon Line. "All the army made history during the short Cuban war; but the colored regulars in three days practically revolutionized the sentiment of the country in regard to the colored soldier," wrote T. G. Steward.[14] L. B. Channing's poem "The Negro Soldier" suggests the public's change of heart: "We used to think the Negro didn't count for very much . . . but we've got to reconstruct our views on color, more or less, / Now we know about the Tenth at Las Guasimas!"[15]

El Caney and San Juan Hill

The battle of El Caney was known as Hell Caney. William Glackens's painting *The Twelfth and Twenty-fifth Infantry Taking the Blockhouse at El Caney,* looking up the hill from a distance, has the energy and drama of an action photograph. The 25th Infantry captured the Spanish flag, but white troops of the 12th Infantry jumped their claim.

The 24th Infantry fought where white troops refused to go. In the midst of Hell Caney, when white troops from New York refused to fight, the 24th, in the rear of and supporting the white 13th Infantry, asked to take the lead. "The Thirteenth Infantry needed no further invitation but immediately stepped to the left of the road," wrote Herschel V. Cashin.[16] Passing the 13th, they met General J. Ford Kent at a fork in the road, "with tears running down his cheeks, begging, admonishing, persuading and entreating the Seventy-first New York Volunteers, 'for the love of country, liberty, honor and dignity . . . to stand up like men and fight, to go to the front.' But all in vain, they fled like sheep from the presence of wolves."[17]

Passing "the prostrated bodies of the bewildered and stampeded Seventy-first," wrote Cashin, the 24th "rushed like madmen into the river," crossing with water up to their necks.[18] Tearing through wire fences, they "rushed wildly across the open field, attracting the attention of the entire Spanish line, and drawing their concentrated fire." When the hill was taken, the commanding general sent congratulations to the

24th—ordering "that they be not required to fire another gun that day." The regiment had suffered major losses. Companies numbering one hundred men now reported as few as twenty—or fewer.

Public attention focused on the courage of the black regiments—even without their white officers. The Springfield, Illinois, *Republican* reported: "At San Juan Hill three companies of the twenty-fourth Infantry (colored) lost every one of their officers before the fighting was over. . . . It is said that the twenty-fourth bore the brunt of the battles around Santiago, the Spaniards directing their main attack upon them on the theory that the Negroes would not stand the punishment. Yet whole companies remained steady without a single officer."[19]

"White regiments, black regiments, regulars and Rough Riders, representing the young manhood of the North and South fought shoulder to shoulder, unmindful of race or color, unmindful of whether commanded by an ex-Confederate or not," wrote then Lieutenant John J. Pershing on the charge of San Juan Hill.[20] San Juan Hill was the most integrated battle of all. There were two brigades of integrated cavalry: the 9th Cavalry in the First Brigade with the white 3rd and 6th; and the 10th Cavalry in the Second Brigade with the Rough Riders, the 1st Regular Cavalry, and the Cuban general Calixto García Iñiguez's five thousand insurgents. They crossed the shallow San Juan River ("Bloody Ford"), where many Americans were wounded or killed, and were ready to charge the hill.

Sergeant Bivens, leading an artillery battery at the base of the hill, witnessed the charge. Although stunned by a bullet that grazed his temple, he had recovered, fired his gun, and watched the results through his field glasses. "The Tenth Cavalry charged up the steep hill and captured the blockhouse and San Juan Hill," he wrote.[21] One Rough Rider, Frank Knox (he would be secretary of the Navy during World War II), found himself fighting with the 10th when he was separated from his unit. Knox later wrote: "I joined a troop of the Tenth Cavalry, and for a time fought with them shoulder to shoulder and in justice to the colored race I must say that I never saw braver men anywhere. Some of those who rushed up the hill will live in my memory forever."[22]

San Juan Hill made the 9th and 10th Cavalry national heroes. Richard Harding Davis reported that "Negro soldiers established themselves as fighting men that morning."[23] *The New York Sun* reported the 9th Cavalry's charge:

> The soldiers leaped forward, charging and shooting across the field . . . to the river. . . . The steep banks were muddy, but our men dashed and slid down them, yelling like mad. Across the stream

> they went, and up the other side, the Spaniards pouring shot into them at a lively rate. They could no more stop the advance, however, than they could have stopped an avalanche. . . . The yelling and enthusiastic Americans charged on the blockhouse, driving the enemy before them. The enthusiasm of the Ninth Cavalry was at its highest pitch and so it was with the other troops. Only annihilation could drive them back; the Spaniards could not.[24]

"All honor to the black troopers of the gallant Tenth," wrote *The New York Mail and Express.*

> No more striking example of bravery and coolness has been shown since the destruction of the Maine than by the colored veterans of the Tenth Cavalry during the attack upon San Juan. . . . Firing as they marched, their aim was splendid, their coolness was superb, and their courage aroused the admiration of their comrades. Their advance was greeted with wild cheers from the white regiments, and with answering shouts they pressed onward over the trenches they had taken close in pursuit of the retreating enemy. The war has not shown greater heroism. The men whose own freedom was baptized in blood have proved themselves capable of giving up their lives that others may be free.[25]

"We officers of the Tenth Cavalry could have taken our black heroes in our arms," wrote Lieutenant John J. Pershing.[26] "Their conduct made me prouder than ever of being an officer in the American Army," wrote Captain John Bigelow, Jr., "and of wearing the insignia of the Tenth United States Cavalry."[27] The 10th Cavalry lost 20 percent of its men and half its officers at San Juan Hill. After the victory, the 10th Cavalry Band played "Hot Time in the Old Town Tonight!" The commander in chief of the Cuban army addressed the black American troops: "If you will be as brave in the future to your country as you have proved yourself to-day it will not be very long before you will have generals in the army of the United States."[28]

The 9th and 10th Cavalry and the 24th and 25th Infantry now received almost as much attention at home as the Rough Riders. New York City's West Fifties, the black section of the "Tenderloin," was renamed San Juan Hill. The 10th Cavalry marched in the Philadelphia Jubilee parade. "It is doubtful whether the members of any regiment who participated in the great military parade have been the recipients of so many encomiums as have the dusky warriors of the valiant Tenth," wrote a

Philadelphia paper.[29] The "well-behaving, self-respecting men" of the 10th were publicly contrasted with the drunken white 5th Pennsylvania Regiment, who destroyed their place of billeting.

Things were different in the South. William Payne, a twenty-two-year-old sergeant in the 10th Cavalry, had been seriously wounded at San Juan Hill and was sent home by hospital ship on July 8. After a passage in which he "suffered greatly," the ship arrived at Fortress Monroe, Virginia, where the hospital refused to treat blacks.[30] Payne and other wounded black soldiers were forced to go without medical treatment until the ship reached the U.S. Marine Hospital at Staten Island, New York.

Five 10th Cavalry troopers won Medals of Honor: Privates Dennis Bell, Fritz Lee, William H. Thompkins, and George Wanton, and Sergeant Major Edward L. Baker.

In October 1898, President McKinley made a speech in Springfield, Illinois, the home of Abraham Lincoln: "I am glad to be at the home of the martyred president," he said. "He liberated a race—a race which he once said ought to be free because there might come a time when these black men could help keep the jewel of liberty in the family of nations. If any vindication of that act or of that prophecy were needed, it was found when these brave black men ascended the hill of San Juan, Cuba, and charged the enemy at El Caney. They vindicated their own title to liberty on that field, and with other brave soldiers gave the priceless gift of liberty to another suffering race."[31]

YELLOW FEVER AND BACKLASH

"The starving time was nothing to the fever time, where scores died per day," read a letter from a black soldier to the 25th Infantry's chaplain, Theophilus G. Steward.[32] The yellow fever epidemic was officially announced in mid-July, about the time of the Spanish surrender, but men had been falling sick for several weeks. Because of the long-standing myth that blacks were impervious to yellow fever, Roosevelt found it "curious" that "the colored troops seemed to suffer as heavily as the white."[33] Doctors ordered all drinking water to be boiled, but because of the heat those orders were not strictly obeyed. Sergeant Horace Bivens discovered the only source of pure drinking water: two springs near a mango grove, which the 10th Cavalry guarded while hundreds of men stood on line waiting to drink. Bivens himself fell sick on July 26. After returning to San Juan Hill, where he saw "many places in the earth drenched in human blood," he came down with "camp dysentery" and was carried to the hospital on a litter, "to lie for twelve days at the point of death."[34]

The hospital for black soldiers was an open tent in which men lay on the ground. "It rained daily and as our tent fly did not shed water very well and both ends of course being open, we kept wet day and night," Bivens wrote. The 10th Cavalry's chaplain, William T. Anderson, who had been trained as a doctor, cared for the men until he was stricken himself—after which Dr. A. M. Brown, the only black surgeon in Cuba, was assigned to the regiment. "Words cannot tell the change of affairs in our regiment after Surgeon Brown's arrival," Bivens wrote. "He moved the hospital to where General Wheeler's headquarters were, put in bunks for all of the sick. . . . It seemed as though he was just in time to save us."[35]

Major A. C. Markley of the 24th Infantry called the yellow fever hospital at Siboney "that charnel house of the wrecked army." By the end of July 1898, men there were dying every hour. "All was pest camp; even separation of cases was impossible. All wards had it. Surgeons, nurses and hospital stewards were now among the patients," Markley wrote. The 24th Infantry was at Siboney on guard duty. The whole 24th stepped forward to a man when volunteer nurses were called for, after eight white regiments had already refused. Within two days, forty-two of the sixty men of the 24th who had been chosen were down with fever. When more nurses were needed, the regiment again stepped forward. All ranks worked together unloading supplies, raising and striking tents, moving the sick, digging graves, and cleaning up after dysentery. "Working convalescents was tried until unexpected deaths warned us to stop," wrote Markley.[36] Only 24 of the 456 members of the 24th who went to Siboney escaped yellow fever. At the end of August, patients were sent home to the military hospital at Camp Wikoff, at Montauk, Long Island. The 24th marched to the ship with the band playing and colors flying, but only nine officers and 198 men were able to walk. Back home, soldiers continued to fall sick. Thirty enlisted men of the 24th ultimately died. An old myth, born in the eighteenth century, that blacks were immune to yellow fever, was finally disproved.

Several "immune" regiments had in fact been organized in Louisiana to fight in Cuba. "Immune" regiment troops were simply recruited from places where tropical diseases were prevalent, like the Gulf States. Only officers were exempt from the geographic qualifications. Under white command, the 9th U.S. Volunteer Infantry had a mixed corps of black junior officers—either former Buffalo Soldier NCOs, or members of the new southern black middle class. The 9th Immunes arrived in Cuba in March 1899. Their assignment was to find and capture the bandits terrorizing the province of Santiago. The bandits were routed in less than a month, at which point the 9th Immunes came under attack at home. A March 19, 1899, *New Orleans Times-Democrat* editorial blamed them for a Georgia lynching:

> Gov. Allen D. Candler of Georgia, while in no way defending or excusing the lynching of negroes at Palmetto, in that state . . . rightly places the responsibility for the crime upon those who organized negro troops and placed arms in their hands. Mr. McKinley and those who instigated him into adopting this dangerous policy must bear the full responsibility for the Palmetto slaughter. . . . He was warned again and again that the arming of negroes meant race war. . . . There are negro regiments stationed in Cuba—the Ninth Immunes, for instance, from Louisiana. These regiments have been enjoying social equality in the island, where a large proportion of the population is of negro or of mixed blood, and where that race line which the Anglo-Saxon insists on does not exist. Every one of these men will come back filled with the idea that he can play this social equality racket here . . . that the theaters, hotels, restaurants and all places shall be open to him on the same terms as to the whites. We need not tell any of our readers who are southern . . . that this means many more Palmettos.[37]

Walter Stevens in Puerto Rico

Walter J. Stevens, the son of a French-Canadian mother and a black Civil War sergeant-major father who claimed kinship to Crispus Attucks, enlisted in a fever of patriotism at the age of sixteen. "It was a sudden happening which seemed to occur at the time when bands played stirring martial music," Stevens wrote in his 1946 autobiography, *Chip on My Shoulder.* Stevens was a member (at $11 a month) of black Company L of the white 6th Massachusetts Regiment National Guard. "Its history and exploits are known to every true Bostonian regardless of his color and creed," boasted Stevens. The company had played a heroic role in the Civil War and now had a waiting list, its own armory and drill hall, and annual field maneuvers in Framingham. "To have belonged to Company L was to have taken part in the West Point of America for colored youths," as Stevens put it. Company L, with the rest of the 6th Regiment, started for Florida. Their first stop south of the Mason-Dixon Line was Baltimore. The last time the 6th Massachusetts had marched through Baltimore, at the onset of the Civil War, it was stoned; now it had a black company attached. "To my great amazement, we were welcomed vociferously," Stevens wrote, "and there was not a single incident."[38]

Although Company L knew that they could call on their white Massachusetts cohorts against any southerners who wanted to refight the Civil War, men of the 6th, who normally did not receive weapons until they reached Tampa, were armed in Charleston "for our own safety." Stevens was part of a group of black soldiers led by the dauntless Sergeant Frank Turpin, who was determined to test southern hospitality. They entered a bar and demanded drinks. The bartender served them, then smashed the glasses on the floor. Later, using his bayonet, Stevens removed a "No Niggers or Dogs Allowed" sign from a park, under the eye of an armed policeman. To the policeman's question "What are you doing?" Stevens replied, "None of your damn business." When they left Charleston, the Massachusetts regiments were editorialized as an "undisciplined mob" intent on "inciting riots."[39]

Stevens's battleground was not Cuba but Puerto Rico, the Spanish-ruled island with somewhat less publicized warfare, where he became a corporal. "Being very small, slender and boyish in appearance, there was nothing sufficiently inspiring about me to make larger men in my squad obey my orders." When he complained to superiors that some of the men would not obey, he was told to make them do so or take off his stripes. Company L first saw action under fire at Guánica on July 25, 1898. There were no casualties, but Stevens realized then that he knew absolutely nothing about combat. Training had been calisthenics. Most of the company had never even marched. Now, they wore heavy blue woolen uniforms with sixty pounds of gear and a twenty-pound ammunition belt—this in hundred-degree heat. Fortunately for Stevens, the Spanish were poor soldiers. They fought in clusters. Americans fought in "open order," spaced a good distance apart, so that only one man at a time could be picked off by enemy rifle fire. Instead of holding their rifles shoulder high, the Spanish "shot haphazardly from the hip." Bullets thus went over the heads of Company L, lying in a wheat field.[40]

Puerto Rico was beautiful, but teeming with malaria, typhoid, and yellow fever. "Our boys also endured many other diseases and one of the things they suffered a great deal was diarrhea," wrote Stevens. "Some died of this dreaded ailment and many of the men, including myself, contracted it and were eventually brought home to good old Boston on the hospital ship *Bay State.*"[41]

"When the glamour of the Spanish-American War had completely worn off, the position of the colored folk in Boston was similar to its original status before the war," Stevens wrote. "I know that my father had said that his whole idea of fighting in the Civil War had been to improve the condition of his race by his own heroic sacrifice. We had thought that my going to war for the country would constitute an additional debt owed to our race." Stevens went from steward of Harvard's Signet Society (where he was a protégé of the famous professor of English literature

Charles Townsend Copeland) to private secretary to the wealthy merchant Edward A. Filene to entrepreneurship in New York and Boston. His success did not lessen his militancy. "Force, and a healthy hatred for oppression, will do more to settle the colored man's problem than anything else," he wrote in 1946.[42]

Roosevelt's Betrayal

Roosevelt, who had promised he "would never forget" the ties that bound him to the Buffalo Soldiers, began to betray them shortly after San Juan Hill. Though he once said that "no one could tell whether it was the Rough Riders or the men of the 9th who came forward with the greater courage to offer their lives in the service of their country," he now claimed that all black accomplishment was the result of white leadership. Worse, he invented a canard of encountering black troops drifting away from the battlefield, and forcing them at gunpoint to return. The account was challenged in the black press by the 10th Cavalry's Sergeant Presley Holliday, who reported that Roosevelt had actually stopped four men on their way to the supply point to pick up ammunition.

In 1899, with the war over, all black volunteer regiments were disbanded. The black officers of volunteer regiments were decommissioned. Blacks could still become NCOs, but all black officers returned to the regular Army as enlisted men. Chaplain Steward of the 25th Infantry called black commissions "too short-lived, and too circumscribed, to be much more than a lively tantalization, to be remembered with disgust by those who had worn them."[43] Fewer than ten blacks would become commissioned officers in the regular Army between 1899 and 1948.

Benjamin O. Davis, formerly of the 8th Volunteers, became one of those few black officers in 1901. Mustered out of the Volunteers in 1899, he applied for an Army commission but was rejected. He decided to enlist in the Regular Army for two years and then take the competitive Army officers exam. Sent to the 9th Cavalry at Fort Duchesne, Utah, he joined Troop I, known as "Old Soldiers Home" for its many Indian Wars veterans.[44] Many veterans were illiterate but had nevertheless memorized the entire book of drill instructions. Davis became the post teacher, teaching the men to write so that each could sign the payroll. In return, the old fighters coached Davis in riding and marksmanship.

When Charles Young returned to Fort Duchesne in 1900 from duty at Wilberforce, he not only organized a brass band and other musical groups, but he coached Davis in mathematics for the coming exam. In 1901, Davis and John E. Green were the only blacks to receive commissions—they were among the last for a very long time. Both men's future sons, however, would graduate from West Point and lead men in war.

The Philippine Insurrection

The Philippine Insurrection of 1899 to 1902 was unfinished Spanish-American War business. At the end of hostilities, the United States paid Spain $20 million for the Philippines (a payment seen as unnecessary largesse by those who considered the archipelago legitimate spoils of war). To all intents and purposes, the war against Spain in the Philippines ended when Admiral George Dewey won control of Manila Bay on May 1, 1898. But Dewey was unable to drive the Spanish out of the capital without the help of Philippine insurgents—the same insurgents who later refused to submit to U.S. control. The "Insurrectos" and their leader, General Emilio Aguinaldo, known as Aquino, set up a government on the island of Luzon, and prepared to attack Americans based in Manila.

When Philippine hostilities broke out on February 2, 1899, the American force of twelve thousand was faced with the possibility of imminent extermination at the hands of some forty thousand insurgents coming from Luzon. Among the desperately needed volunteer regiments authorized by the emergency act of March 2, 1899, were two new black regiments: the 48th and 49th Volunteer Infantries, who followed the Buffalo Soldiers across the Pacific. Approximately seventy thousand U.S. troops would eventually fight to end the Filipino independence movement and bring the islands under U.S. control. Hardly a "splendid little war," the Philippine Insurrection combined naïve jingoism, naked territorial expansionism, and rabid racism.

The Philippine Insurrection was the first war in which American officers and troops were officially charged with what we would now call war crimes. There would be some forty-four military trials between August 1898 and March 1901, all culminating in convictions for murder, rape, the burning of villages, and other crimes.[45] The sentences, almost invariably, were light. In December 1900, for example, Lieutenant Preston Brown of the 2nd Infantry pistol-whipped an unarmed, unresisting Filipino prisoner, then shot him in the back of the head when the man answered "No sabe" to a question. Brown was given a five-year sentence, which President Theodore Roosevelt later personally commuted to a fine of half-pay for nine months. Not all officers took war crimes lightly. "I deprecate this war, this slaughter of our own boys and of the Filipinos," wrote General Felix A. Reeve, "because it seems to me that we are doing something that is contrary to our principles." In an article entitled "To the

Person Sitting in Darkness," published in 1901 in *The North American Review,* Mark Twain suggested a new Philippine flag: "We can have our usual flag, with the white stripes painted black and the stars replaced by the skull and crossbones."[46]

"I want no prisoners. I wish you to kill and burn—the more you kill and burn the better you will please me," said Brigadier General Jacob H. Smith to Marine major Littleton W. T. Waller after the terrible American loss at Balangiga, on Samar, an island south of Luzon, in September 1901. Fifty-nine Americans had been killed and twenty-three wounded by guerrillas disguised, to the General's disgust, as women. The interior of the Samar, Smith said, "must be made a howling wilderness." When a nervous Waller, well aware of the rules of war, asked him to clarify what he meant by "no prisoners," Smith recommended summary execution for anyone over the age of ten. Waller's very arduous marine expeditionary trip to render Samar a "howling wilderness" even resulted in summary executions of Filipinos in the employ of the U.S. government. Marines who ran out of food and medicine during the jungle trek began to suspect that their Filipino porters had been stealing food. Eleven porters, whose names were never recorded, were executed without a trial, and without charges being filed. In the inevitable court-martial, Smith was only "admonished," and Waller, though he earned the nickname Butcher of Samar, was acquitted.[47]

In Senate hearings of early 1902, Senator Joseph Rawlins asked General Robert P. Hughes, the commander of Manila, about burning villages and the deaths of women and children. "The women and children are part of the family," Hughes replied, "and where you wish to inflict punishment you can punish the man probably worse in that way than in any other." When asked if that was considered "civilized warfare," he replied that "these people are not civilized." The senators seemed to accept this response without comment. Hughes favored the use of black troops in the Philippines. "The darky troops . . . sent to Samar mixed with the natives at once," he said. "Wherever they came together they became great friends. When I withdrew the darky company from Santa Rita I was told that the natives even shed tears for their going away."[48]

BLACK HEROES: CHARLES YOUNG AND THE 24TH AND 25TH INFANTRIES

Black America had a genuine Philippine Insurrection hero in Captain Charles Young, the third black graduate of West Point. The only black officer qualified to lead troops in combat, Young had stayed behind in the

United States when his regiment went to Cuba. In April 1901, he went to the Philippines, leading troops against rebels in the jungles of Samar, Blanca Aurora, Durago, Tobaco, and Rosano for eighteen months—and earning the nickname "Follow Me!"

Nevertheless, there was controversy in the black press as to whether black soldiers should support U.S. efforts against Philippine independence. Bishop Henry McNeal Turner, a Civil War chaplain and a bishop of the African Methodist Episcopal Church, led black protest. "I boil over with disgust when I remember that colored men from this country," he wrote, "are fighting to subjugate a people of their own color. . . . I can scarcely keep from saying that I hope the Filipinos will wipe such soldiers from the face of the earth."[49] With less apparent sympathy for the Filipino insurgent Aquino than the Cuban martyr Maceo, most black Americans would probably have agreed with the *Indianapolis Freeman,* a black newspaper (once edited by my great-grandfather), that "the enemy of the country is a common enemy and . . . the color of the face has nothing to do with it."[50]

Among the first troops to cross the Pacific from San Francisco at the end of June 1899 were the 24th and 25th Infantries. Thomas Edison, in a famous early newsreel, filmed black soldiers embarking for the Philippines. American troops would find jungle, forest, and mountain terrain even more difficult than Cuba's, and an enemy who was far more dangerous because he was everywhere and hidden. They also faced heat, rain, fever, and leeches; they wore uniforms left over from Cuba; and often there was no food, water, or medicine. The 25th had the first major engagement, in November, capturing the insurgent town of O'Donnell. They netted 128 prisoners, some two hundred rifles, and a quantity of ammunition and rice. Taking prisoners later became a rarity, of course.

The 25th had another major success in January 1900, when they "scaled heights of great difficulty" and "crawled through dense undergrowth" around the extinct volcano of Mount Arayat to capture an insurgent barracks, in the process freeing five wounded American prisoners, two of whom did not survive. "When the insurgents knew we were coming," wrote Lieutenant W. T. Schenck, "they waited until they were pretty certain we had captured the position, then the insurgents made all five men kneel and shot them." Schenck, who was himself killed shortly thereafter, described the death at Arayat of Corporal M. Washington: "The fire got hotter and some one nailed Corporal Washington through the arm, the bullet penetrating the stomach, giving him a mortal wound from which he died this morning."[51] Afterward, Schenk took the "greatest enjoyment" in burning native houses. Arayat made heroes of the 25th, inspiring the opening verse of John Dos Passos's novel *U.S.A.*: "It was that emancipated race / That was chargin' up the hill / Up to where them insurrectoes / Was afightin' fit to kill."

Some 350 men of the 24th Infantry, two companies plus a detachment, had first discovered the difficulties of Philippine terrain in November 1899, as they marched over the mountains of central Luzon, where few non-Filipinos had ever been. "Our marches had been a mere succession of fording of rivers and climbing of cliffs hardly any of them surmountable except by zigzag paths cut by shelves from a foot to eighteen inches wide," wrote Captain Joseph B. Batchelor, of the 24th Infantry.[52] Uniforms were now ragged, and many men were barefoot. Often waist deep in mud, or forced to swim across streams ("the officers in their drawers and the privates naked"), the men had little food or water. But Batchelor boasted that they had marched over three hundred miles without guides in unknown territory, following trails that were "just passable through chilling nights and sweltering days; [they] made 123 deep fords; crossed 80 miles of precipitous mountains in five days." They also forced the surrender of a thousand men, strictly within the rules of warfare. But although Batchelor may have decried acts of "ugly" Americanism, he was a confirmed jingoist. The Philippine people, he said, had become "enthusiastic advocates of American supremacy."[53] However, the Filipinos were discovering, as Batchelor and his men already knew, that "American supremacy" meant *white* supremacy.

"It kept leaking down from sources above," reported a white enlisted man, "that the Filipinos were 'niggers,' no better than Indians, and were to be treated as such."[54] If a person was not white, wrote Frederick Palmer in an article written in 1900 for *Scribner's* magazine, then Americans "include him in a general class called 'nigger,' a class beneath our notice, to which, so far as our white soldier is concerned, all Filipinos belonged." The testimony in later congressional hearings of a major of the 30th Infantry Regiment would confirm that assessment: "Almost without exception, soldiers and also many officers, refer to the natives in their presence as 'niggers' and the natives are beginning to understand what the word 'nigger' means."[55] Their designation as "niggers" seemed to mean that Filipinos could be mistreated with impunity. "The weather is intensely hot, and we are all tired, dirty and hungry," wrote a white private in a letter home, "so we have to kill niggers whenever we have a chance, to get even for all our trouble."[56]

Despite the civilized warfare of Captain Batchelor and the men of the 24th Infantry in central Luzon, other black soldiers did participate in criminal actions. An officer of the 10th Cavalry was court-martialed for ordering his men to apply the "water cure"—a commonly used American torture in which water was forced into the mouth and nose of a prisoner—to three Filipino priests. Fined $150, he was suspended three months. Captain Cornelius M. Brownell, an officer of white troops, ordered the water cure for another priest, who subsequently died when soldiers were told to "dose the nigger again." After the priest was buried in an unmarked grave in the field where Americans played baseball, the Army listed the cause of death as a heart attack, caused by his obesity.[57]

Some white soldiers opposed American actions. "We bombarded a place called Malabon," wrote one soldier, "and then we went in and killed every native we met, men, women and children. It was a dreadful sight, the killing of the poor creatures. The natives captured some of them Americans and literally hacked them to pieces, so we got orders to spare no one." Another soldier wrote to his father that he had "seen enough to almost make me ashamed to call myself an American." Other white Americans were less perturbed. "I am probably growing hard-hearted, for I am in my glory when I can sight my gun on some dark skin and pull the trigger," wrote one A. A. Barnes, of Battery G, 3rd U.S. Artillery. "Tell all my inquiring friends that I am doing everything I can for Old Glory and for America I love so well."[58]

"General" David Fagen and the Rebels

"To the Colored American Soldiers" ("soldados negros"), wrote General Aguinaldo, in a broadside appeal in 1899. "It is without honor that you are spilling your costly blood. Your masters have thrown you into the most iniquitous fight with double purpose—to make you the instrument of their ambition and also your hard work will soon make the extinction of your race. Your friends, the Filipinos, give you this good warning. You must consider your situation and your history, and take charge that the blood of . . . Sam Hose [a black man burned alive in Newnan, Georgia, in 1899] proclaims vengeance."[59]

Some black soldiers were caught in the middle. "The whites have begun to establish their diabolical race hatred in all its home rancor in Manila," wrote Sergeant Major John W. Galloway of the 24th Infantry in a letter home, "even endeavoring to propagate the phobia among the Spaniards and Filipinos so as to be sure of the foundation of their supremacy when the civil rule that must necessarily follow the present military regime is established." The highly intelligent Galloway would be jailed and subsequently dishonorably discharged when a letter from him was found in the raided house of a suspected Manila Insurrecto. The letter was relatively innocuous, stating only that Filipinos should look to education as a means of obtaining their freedom. "If it were not for the sake of the 10,000,000 black people in the United States," a black soldier wrote to the *Wisconsin Weekly Advocate* in 1900, "God alone knows on which side of the subject I would be."[60]

David Fagen decided early which side he was on. In November 1899, while other members of the 24th Cavalry were conquering the mountains of central Luzon, the twenty-four-year-old corporal defected to the Insurrectos. Fagen had enlisted in Tampa in June 1898, in the midst of war embarkation fever. Honorably discharged in January 1899, he immediately reenlisted. The following June, he sailed with the 24th from San Francisco to the Philippines. For the next few months he fought Insurrectos in central Luzon, around Mount Arayat. On November 17, with the help of an Insurrecto with a waiting horse, he defected to the rebels, who had promised commissions to any American who joined them. For the next year and a half, as lieutenant and later captain, he led troops in the insurgent forces of General José Alejandrino. The men he led called him General Fagen.

Fagen had been a model U.S. infantryman, promoted to corporal after less than eighteen months of service. He made three transfer requests in the Philippines, all refused. His decision to defect may have stemmed from quarrels with white superiors or black sergeants. From August 1900 to January 1901, Fagen clashed at least eight times with American forces and Philippine auxiliaries. His capture of a military steam launch on a river near Arayat, and subsequent escape to the jungle with his men, prompted a *New York Times* front-page story on "General Fagen." Rumors that Fagen routinely murdered American captives were contradicted by two former prisoners, both members of the 24th Infantry. Trooper George Jackson and a white lieutenant both said they were treated humanely, although Fagen took the lieutenant's West Point ring. Twenty American soldiers, black and white, eventually defected to the Insurrectos. All were captured and tried. Only two, Edmond Dubose and Louis Russell, both black privates of the 9th Cavalry, were executed.

Filipino resistance collapsed in central Luzon in the spring of 1901, when Aguinaldo was captured. For the sake of his "beloved country," Aquino acknowledged and accepted "the sovereignty of the United States throughout the entire archipelago."[61] General Frederick Funston, who had captured him, now placed a bounty of $600 on the head of David Fagen. In December 1901, a bounty hunter brought in a rebel commission in the name of Fagen, a West Point ring, and a slightly decomposed head. Fagen was presumed dead, although some Filipinos claimed that he was still alive, hiding in the mountains. "Fagen was a traitor and died a traitor's death," editorialized the black *Indianapolis Freeman,* in December 1901, "but he was a man no doubt prompted by honest motives to help a weaker side, and one with which he felt allied by ties that bind."[62]

THE "LITTLE BROWN BROTHER" AND "THE GREAT WHITE FLEET"

Troops began returning home in the summer of 1902. A few Americans, including the 24th Infantry, remained in the Philippines as troubles continued, especially among Muslims in the southern islands, until August 1906, when soldiers of the 24th and members of the new Philippine constabulary killed more than fifty insurgents on Leyte and significant opposition was destroyed.

President McKinley was assassinated in September 1901. The new president, Theodore Roosevelt, commuted the death sentences of fifteen deserters, all white. Despite his cultivation of Booker T. Washington, Roosevelt the president would be seen as an enemy to blacks.

The Philippines introduced a new racial configuration in American policies—the concept of the "Little Brown Brother," and of going to war to help peoples within the sphere of U.S. influence. Not all Americans supported the policy: "You are told he is your little Brown Brother," went the 1905 song. "And the equal of thee and thine, / Well! he may be a brother of your's, Bill Taft, / But he is no relation of mine."[63]

In 1906, as America's sphere of influence continued to grow, blacks at home saw the birth of the modern segregated Navy. When Japan defeated Russia in 1905, the United States worried about the security of the Philippines. In 1907 the "Great White Fleet," a brand-new American battle fleet, all painted white, sailed around the world, the aim being to impress Japan with the power of the Caucasian race. The Great White Fleet represented the new all-white Navy—the first Navy in American history without black sailors. Blacks became stewards and messmen, replacing Japanese Americans, who were now seen as a security risk.

As of 1906, there were four black officers, excluding chaplains, in the U.S. Army: non-active-duty Major John R. Lynch (a former Mississippi congressman) in the office of paymaster of volunteers; Second Lieutenant John E. Green, 25th Infantry; Second Lieutenant Benjamin O. Davis, 9th Cavalry; and Lieutenant Charles Young, of the 10th Cavalry. Young was the only black West Point graduate still on active duty. In 1904, after a tour as acting superintendent of Sequoia and General Grant National Parks, he was sent to Haiti as America's first black military attaché. Also accredited to the Dominican Republic, he explored and mapped both countries on horseback, sending reports back to the Army War College. (Marines would use parts of Young's monograph on Haiti in their 1915 occupation.) During his Haitian tour, Young also wrote a book, *Military Morale of Nations and Races,* published in 1912, and a play based on the life of Toussaint-Louverture.

THE BROWNSVILLE "RAID": WAR AT HOME

In 1906, the second Niagara Conference, the W.E.B. Du Bois–led forerunner of the NAACP, met at Harpers Ferry and issued an "Address to the Country." "We will not be satisfied to take less than our full manhood rights," it proclaimed. "The battle we wage is not for ourselves alone but for all true Americans."

The South refused to listen. There were several race riots that year; one of the worst was in Atlanta and some sixty blacks were lynched. (Eleven hundred blacks were lynched in America between 1900 and 1915.)

That year black soldiers were at the center of a significant domestic battle. When 170 men of the 25th Infantry's 1st Battalion were sent to Fort Brown, in Brownsville, Texas, in the summer of 1906 to train with the Texas National Guard, the Army's commanding general in Texas had warned that "Citizens of Brownsville entertain race hatred to an extreme degree." "During my whole experience in the service the only time I have been assaulted by uncivil and ribald speech by a man in the uniform of a soldier was at Fort Riley, Kansas, and the man who did so was a Texas militia man," wrote Theophilus G. Steward. "Texas, I fear, means a quasi battle ground for the Twenty-fifth Infantry."[64]

The men of the 25th were welcomed to Brownsville by silent, hostile citizens and by signs barring blacks from stores and parks. When shots were fired near Fort Brown on the night of August 13, the 25th, assuming a white attack, broke open locked rifle racks and the bugler roused the camp. Meanwhile, one civilian was dead and several others were wounded. Eight out of twenty-two self-proclaimed eyewitnesses, all local men, said that the late-night gunmen were black soldiers. Some reported seeing men with revolvers, weapons not used by the 25th. Morning revealed cartridges and clips from Army Springfield rifles lying in the street. All Fort Brown troops denied any knowledge of the shooting. Texans called it the "Brownsville Raid," and portrayed the men of the 25th as murderous savages. The *Brownsville Daily Herald* printed a poem ("destined to take its place in literature"): "Our daughters murdered and defiled, / Black fingers crooked about fair throat, / The leering fiend—the tortured breath— / Where's time for laggard red tape now, / When moments may mean life or death?"[65]

To a man, the 25th denied knowledge of the shooting. They were accused of shielding the guilty. The three companies of the 25th were now ordered by the War Department to name the gunmen or face summary dismissal. There were two Brownsville investigations. Although the final report stated that the "extreme penalty" would fall on "a number of men who have no direct knowledge of the identity" of the shooters, Roosevelt accepted the recommendation for dismissal. He added later that some members of the 25th were clearly "bloody butchers" who "ought to be hung." One hundred sixty-seven soldiers of the 1st Battalion (three were on leave) were dishonorably discharged without a public hearing, and forever barred from serving the government as either soldiers or civilians. The announcement of the presidential decision was delayed until after the 1906 congressional elections. The men were "not punished for not telling who the offenders were, but for not knowing who they were," said the Boston lawyer A. E. Pillsbury.[66] *The New York World* editorialized that "the logic of the verdict is as clear as day. As the report reads, nobody is guilty; therefore everybody is guilty; and everybody being guilty, nobody is innocent."[67]

Senator Joseph P. Foraker, a white Civil War veteran and Ohio Republican who may have been seeking the Republican presidential nomination, sided with the soldiers and conducted his own investigation. He found many discrepancies and anomalies. The most striking was that the bullets recovered after the incident did not come from any of the weapons issued to the battalion. Foraker believed that the conspiracy was perpetrated by townspeople, not the 25th. Napoleon B. Marshall, a black lawyer and member of the Constitution League (organized in 1904 as an integrated effort for the legal defense of poor blacks), served as counsel for the soldiers. He ultimately refused to submit an argument, because the trial process did not adhere to the concept of innocent until proven guilty.

In 1971 a black Democratic congressman, Augustus Hawkins of Los Angeles, introduced a bill to declare all the discharges honorable. "It was a frame-up straight through," said Dorsie W. Willis, who at eighty-seven was the only surviving member of the 25th Infantry at Brownsville. "They checked our rifles and they hadn't been fired."[68] When Brownsville was reinvestigated in 1972, under President Nixon, the men of the 25th received honorable rather than dishonorable discharges, but no other compensation. Congress, however, passed a bill granting Willis, who had earned his living since his discharge as a porter and bootblack, $25,000 and medical treatment at a Veterans Administration hospital.

In the wake of Brownsville, blacks turned away from the Republican Party as well as from their former hero, Theodore Roosevelt. "The Negroes are depleting the dictionary of adjectives in their denunciation of the President," wrote an angry Ohio black to Booker T. Washington.[69] Brownsville was fuel to racist fire. A congressional bill was introduced calling for the removal of all blacks from the Army by mid-1907. The bill did not pass. In March 1907, the U.S. Military Academy Detachment of Cavalry was changed from a white to a "colored" organization, sending black troops to West Point for the first time. A detachment of one hundred men from the 9th Cavalry arrived on March 23, in support of cadet riding instruction and mounted drill.

Neither Theodore Roosevelt, in his autobiography, nor John H. Nankivell in his 1927 history of the 25th Infantry, mentioned the Brownsville incident. But Brownsville would continue to resonate in the annals of black soldier–white town warfare.

The 25th Infantry went on to fight hostile Moro tribesmen in the Philippines in 1907 and 1908. In the summer of 1910, they fought devastating forest fires in the Pacific Northwest. They would spend 1913 to 1918 in Hawaii, sitting out World War I, like all Buffalo Soldiers.

6
The World War

LES ENFANTS PERDUS

TO THE FRENCH MILITARY MISSION STATIONED WITH THE AMERICAN ARMY—Secret Information Concerning Black American Troops: It is important for French officers who have been called upon to exercise command over black American troops, or to live in close contact with them, to have an exact idea of the position occupied by Negroes in the United States. . . . Although a citizen of the United States, the black man is regarded by the white American as an inferior being with whom relations of business or service only are possible. The black is constantly being censured for his want of intelligence and discretion, his lack of civic and professional conscience, and for his tendency toward undue familiarity. The vices of the Negro are a constant menace to the American who has to repress them sternly. . . . We must prevent the rise of any pronounced degree of intimacy between French officers and black officers. We may be courteous and amiable with these last, but we cannot deal with them on the same plane as with white American officers without deeply offending the latter. We must not eat with them, must not shake hands or seek to talk or meet with them outside the requirements of military service. We must not commend too highly the black American troops, particularly in the presence of Americans. . . . Make a point of keeping the native cantonment population from "spoiling" the Negroes. Americans become greatly incensed at any public expression of intimacy between white women with black men. . . . Familiarity on the part of white women with black men is furthermore a source of profound regret to our experienced colonials, who see in it an overwhelming menace to the prestige of the white race.[1]

General John J. Pershing's directive to the French military (written in French under Pershing's orders and translated above from the French) was issued from the headquarters of the American Expeditionary Forces (AEF) in France on August 17, 1918. Two years earlier, in Mexico, Pershing had praised black troops. Now he was stigmatizing them as foreigners. By 1918, encouraged by the Wilson administration, the military establishment had closed ranks against blacks in combat. All the pre–Civil War antiblack propaganda had been resurrected. Blacks were not soldiers. Blacks could not or would not fight. The curious logic of southern racism required that black men be seen at once as dangerous, in order to justify repression, and as cowardly, to justify contempt and exclusion.

It would be reported in March 1920, by the NAACP's magazine, *The Crisis,* that French officials had ordered copies of Pershing's directive to be burned. Racist directives against black Americans could not have been a matter of high priority for a French army whose own soldiers were deserting in droves, and whose country was a battlefield that would claim one in twenty-eight of its citizens by the end of 1918. And they could hardly impress an army with two generals, four colonels, 150 captains, and countless lieutenants who were black.[2] Moreover, Senegalese and Moroccan troops had already proven their heroism in the crucial Battle of the Marne in 1914, which stopped the Germans forty miles from the Champs-Elysées. Black French troops had also served with distinction at Verdun, the Somme, Aisne, and Compiègne. "It is because these soldiers are just as brave and just as devoted as white soldiers that they receive exactly the same treatment, every man being equal before the death which all soldiers face," read a (mildly rebuking) French official response to an American War Department query about French colonial troops.[3]

French civilians ignored warnings against fraternization. *The Crisis* noted that the citizens of Grandvillars found black Americans of Illinois's 370th Regiment to be far more polite than their white American counterparts, who called Frenchwomen Frog Janes. Arriving from January to June 1918, black combat troops were the last Americans to reach France and the only Americans to actually serve, with French weapons and uniforms, under the French flag. Last to arrive on the Western Front, blacks spent more consecutive time in the front lines—at Château-Thierry, Belleau Wood, the Vosges, Metz, Soissons, Champagne, and the Meuse-Argonne—than any other Americans. New York's 369th National Guard Regiment, the most decorated American unit of the war, could claim the longest time at the front: 191 days in the 1918 Champagne-Marne offensive, suffering a loss of some fifteen hundred men. This same unit was denied permission to march in the Paris victory parade and, thanks to U.S. pressure, denied a place in the French national war memorial.

The French were grateful to black Americans not only for their courage and good manners, but also for the gift of American jazz, first introduced by soldier-musicians of the 369th Regimental Band, which toured the war-devastated country and uplifted a grieving and war-weary people. For the next forty years, between two world wars, the French would love all things black American, and Paris would be the mecca for black American expatriates.

Despite Pershing's directive against commending blacks "too highly," entire black regiments and hundreds of individual black American soldiers were decorated by the French army. The first American soldier of any color to receive the Croix de Guerre was Sergeant Henry Johnson, of New York's 369th Regiment. More than a hundred members of the 369th won the Croix de Guerre or the even more prestigious Médaille Militaire. The French attention was important, since black Americans received so little gratitude from their own country. The Great War was the first since the inception of the award in which no black American won the Medal of Honor. Thanks to Sergeant Henry Johnson and its legendary bandmaster, Lieutenant James Reese Europe, the 369th received national attention—the only black unit to do so. They called themselves the Men of Bronze. American newspapers called them Harlem's Own. The Germans called them Hell Fighters. And the French called them the Enfants Perdus, because their mother country had abandoned them. The American military did not know what to do with 3 percent of its forces, its black combat units. They weren't really *American,* anyway, so giving them to the French seemed to satisfy both Wilson's expressed desire to serve humanity and his racism. They would be adopted with fulsome gratitude by the French Fourth Army.

When war was first declared, blacks were refused at many recruiting stations. But the new Selective Service Act of June 1917 mandated the enlistment of all able-bodied men aged twenty-one to thirty-one. Like the foreign-born, blacks would be overdrafted. By July 5, 1917, more than 700,000 blacks were registered; less than 10 percent of the U.S. population, they made up 13 percent of all U.S. draftees.[4] Of the 367,710 black draftees who ultimately served, 89 percent were assigned to labor, supply, and service units. Only 11 percent of all black military forces would see combat—the National Guard, and a few southern draftee units.

At the onset of the war, there were approximately ten thousand blacks in the regular Army, all members of the Buffalo Soldier 9th and 10th Cavalries and 24th and 25th Infantries. There were also ten thousand peacetime black National Guardsmen from Connecticut, Illinois, Maryland, Massachusetts, New York, Ohio, Tennessee, and the District of Columbia. Some ten thousand blacks were in the Navy, all members of the noncombat mess and stewards' branches (of whom a significant number would die in combat when their ships were torpedoed). There were no blacks in the Marines, the Air Corps, the Army Field Artillery, or the Army Corps of Engineers.

World War I saw the creation of two new black Army combat units: the 92nd and the 93rd Divisions. The all-draftee 92nd Division—the 365th through 368th Regiments—served under the American flag. The 93rd Division—comprising mainly National Guard Regiments: the 369th (New York), the 370th (Illinois), the 371st (South Carolina draftees), and the 372nd (Ohio, Massachusetts, Maryland, and District of Columbia Guardsmen)—served with the French. The American-led 92nd would be vilified as cowards. The French-led 93rd were extolled as heroes.

Whatever the white American assessment of black troops, the Germans feared them. According to Ralph W. Tyler of the U.S. Committee on Public Information, the only accredited black correspondent assigned to the American Expeditionary Forces, German fear of black troops was confirmed by two captured white American aviators, Lieutenants V. H. Burgin and A. L. Clark. "While they were captured at different points, and imprisoned at widely separate prisons, both state that when brought before the German military intelligence department and questioned as to the American force in France one of the first questions asked of them, and which the Germans seemed most concerned about, was how many colored troops the Americans had over here."[5] Burgin had replied thirteen million and Clark had said "several millions." Germans believed that black Americans, like French Senegalese and Algerians, took no prisoners.

"To serve in one's national army, under one's own leader, amid a great mass of men animated by a common spirit is one ordeal," wrote Winston Churchill. "To serve in isolated divisions or brigades or even regiments under the orders of foreign generals, flanked on either side by troops of different race and language and of unknown comradeship or quality, is another."[6] Fortunately for black Americans, their abandonment by the mother country was a blessing in disguise.

Over There

On June 28, 1914, a Serb nationalist in Sarajevo assassinated Archduke Franz Ferdinand, heir to the Austro-Hungarian throne. The assassin thereby ignited a European chain reaction. Within six weeks, all of Europe was at war, thanks to what the military historian John Keegan called a "nest of interlocking and opposed understandings and mutual assistance treaties."[7] Russia supported Serbia, Germany supported Austria, France supported Russia, and Britain supported France. In August, Germany declared war on Russia and France, and invaded neutral Belgium in order to attack France. Britain then declared war on Germany, and most of the European world was soon at war. The Allies, the Franco-British contingent, eventually included Montenegro and Italy. The "Central Powers," the German-Austrian contingent, eventually included Bulgaria and Turkey. America remained officially neutral until April 2, 1917, when Woodrow Wilson, stating that "the world must be made safe for democracy," asked Congress to declare war on the Central Powers. The European war lasted four years; the U.S. war in Europe lasted nineteen months.

Despite Wilson's claim of making the world "safe for democracy," America had no real ideological purpose in going to war. This was a war about kings and hegemony—everything Americans had rejected, and everything its tidal wave of new immigrants, who would fight the war, had sought to escape. German cruelty toward noncombatants, as well as toward other armies, was well documented, but the American response often degenerated into "beastly Hun" attacks on German-sounding names and inoffensive dachshunds. In the anti-German frenzy, German shepherds became "police dogs," sauerkraut became "liberty cabbage," and Bach and Wagner were banned.[8]

"We have no selfish end to serve," Wilson said in 1917. "We desire no conquest, no dominion. We seek no indemnities for ourselves, no material compensation for the sacrifices we shall freely make. We are but one of the champions of the rights of mankind." America liked to call its late entry into the war an act of disinterested generosity, the repayment of an old war debt. "Lafayette, nous sommes arrivés!" was more a pronouncement of friendship than a battle cry. The great-great-grandsons of the American Revolution saw themselves, and were seen, as saviors of European democracy. "The Yanks are coming!" was the jubilant cry of George M. Cohan's "Over There!" After two decades of small jingoistic victories, war for Americans remained the sentimental lie of popular songs. "Hot Time in the Old Town Tonight!" had become "Roses of Picardy." (On a deliberately contrary note, Irving Berlin's "I Didn't Raise My Boy to Be a Soldier" ranked a close second in Tin Pan Alley popularity.)

It was an eleventh-hour rescue for the Allies. Besides being badly outmanned, they were falling apart: Italy seemed ready to capitulate to Austria (later, the Russian Bolsheviks would demand a separate peace). On April 11, Marshal Douglas Haig of Britain issued his famous "backs to the wall" order: "There is no other course open to us but to fight it out! . . . With our backs to the wall, and believing in the justice of our cause, each one of us must fight on to the end."[9]

By April 1917, when America entered the war, "Bloody" Mons (where French soldiers claimed to have seen a vision of St. Michael the

Archangel), the Marne, Ypres (where the British lost thirteen thousand men in three hours), the Somme, and Verdun were over. There was an unpublicized epidemic of desertion and mutiny in the French ranks. ("It's finished, we've had enough," went the protest song, "We're finished forever with this filthy war.") Britain and France had together lost more than a million men; Germany had lost as many, but it had more troops. All that he wanted from America, said Marshal Joseph Joffre, the "Hero of the Marne," was "men, men, men."[10]

In April 1918, Germany predicted imminent victory. By July, with one million Americans newly on the fighting line, the Allied "Big Push" suddenly and irrevocably turned the tide of war. The German general Erich Ludendorff attributed the growing malaise in his army and the sense of "looming defeat" that afflicted it to "the sheer number of Americans arriving daily at the front," wrote Keegan. "After four years of a war in which they had destroyed the Tsar's army, trounced the Italians and Romanians, demoralised the French and, at the very least, denied the British clear-cut victory, they were now confronted with an army whose soldiers sprang, in uncountable numbers, as if from soil sown with dragons' teeth."[11]

The first Americans arrived in St.-Nazaire, the principal port of U.S. debarkation, in June 1917. The last Americans, blacks among them, arrived in the winter and spring of 1918. "The spectacle of these magnificent youths from overseas, these beardless children of twenty, radiating strength and health," wrote an aide to Marshal Philippe Pétain, symbolized "life coming in floods to reanimate the dying body of France."[12] Half of the "magnificent youths" barely spoke English (over six million new immigrants had arrived in the United States between 1907 and 1917); most were illiterate; and many had venereal disease, the leading cause of disability after influenza and before combat wounds. Americans were seen as ill-trained, ill-mannered, and sloppily uniformed—but great fighters. They were aware of German military might, but they had no idea that the war was a machine that ate men. The first U.S. casualties, whose manner of death was kept secret from the U.S. public, were three young men whose throats were cut and whose heads were nearly severed by the trench knives of a German raiding party in November 1917.

Trench warfare was one of many new horrors. Soldiers on both sides stood in muddy, rat-infested, and often corpse-filled trenches (suffering "trench feet" and "trench fever") until it was time to go "over the top." There were no generals on horseback in the field. There were no cavalry charges and no saber wounds. Wounds of a new kind were inflicted by weapons like *Minnenwerfer* (mortar filled with scrap metal), flamethrowers, machine guns (whose gunners were never taken prisoner by either side), and fearsome German 150 mm explosive shells, whose black smoke led the British and Americans to call them Jack Johnsons, for the black 1908–1915 heavyweight champion of the world.

"Humanity is mad! It must be mad to do what it is doing. . . . Hell cannot be so terrible," wrote a French officer, shortly before he was killed in 1914.[13] A sense of apocalyptic doom was shared by all nationalities at the front. Soldier poets would capture the senseless horror of "the war to end all wars." Fought mostly in the ore-rich territory of Belgium and northern France, the war was a no-man's-land of barbed wire and trenches, whose landscape was steeped in poison gas and riddled with half-buried, rotting corpses. By the end of four years of war, some nine to twelve million people on both sides would be dead.

EUGENE JACQUES BULLARD: THE BLACK SWALLOW OF DEATH

Eugene Jacques Bullard, a black American expatriate who enlisted in the French military in 1914, saw more war than any other American. Bullard, who served in both the French army and the French air corps, was the first black fighter pilot in the world. He left an unpublished memoir at his death in 1961; parts of it appear in *The Black Swallow of Death,* by P. J. Carisella and James W. Ryan.

Born in 1894, Eugene Jacques Bullard ran away from home in Columbus, Georgia, in 1902, at the age of eight, while his father was hiding from a lynch mob. His "North Star" was France—where, his father had always told his ten children, "white and black are treated the same."[14] Bullard's roots were Haitian; his ancestors had been slaves of French refugees from the Haitian revolution. He hitchhiked, stole rides, and did odd jobs all over the South (becoming a jockey and, for self-defense, a boxer) until 1906, when he finally reached the sea at Newport News, Virginia, and stowed away on a German ship bound for Aberdeen. In Aberdeen, and later in Glasgow (where he sang and danced with an organ-grinder, and became a whistling lookout for gamblers), he worried because he saw no blacks. In Glasgow they called him, not unkindly, "Darky" or "Jack Johnson." In Liverpool, as a union dock worker, he worked in an amusement park on weekends as a target for balls (soft), most of which he dodged. (His assessment of the job was worthy of the best Booker T. Washington bootstrap saga: "Just for letting customers throw balls at my head for those two days, I made 20 shillings, which was enough for my keep. And I had a small sum besides that I had saved for a rainy day."[15]) He had a third job in Liverpool, doing chores in a gym to further his bantamweight boxing career; there he finally met other black people. He became the protégé of the boxer Aaron Lester Brown, the "Dixie Kid." It was the Dixie Kid who gave Bullard a brief taste of France in November 1913, when they went over together for a match. Back in Liverpool, he set his eye on Paris. Among the guests in his Liverpool boarding house were "Freedman's Pickaninnies," a vaudeville act to which Bullard attached himself to sing, dance, and do slapstick comedy. The tour included Russia, Berlin, and, finally, the Bal Tabarin in Paris. It had taken him ten years to reach his goal.

Joining the Paris boxing world, Bullard picked up French and a little German, and discovered that his father had been right. "It seemed to me that the French democracy influenced the minds of both white and black Americans there and helped us all to act like brothers as near as possible. . . . It convinced me, too, that God really did create all men equal, and it was easy to live that way." When war came in August 1914, newspaper ads appealed to foreign "Friends of France" to enlist. Waiving its five-year enlistment rule, the French Foreign Legion was recruiting special "Marching Regiments" for the duration. (The legion, founded in 1831 to conquer and colonize Algeria, was famous for its fast-moving foot soldiers.) Bullard waited a month to be old enough to join the 3rd Marching Battalion, which included fifty-four different nationalities, mostly recruited from foreign residents in Paris. The poet Alan Seeger ("I Have a Rendezvous with Death") was among the American legionnaires, as were six other American blacks, including the boxer Bob Scanlon. "Our training was really tough for everyone, including me," Bullard wrote. "But because of my physical conditioning for boxing, I managed without too much hardship. Besides, it was all for the good of France that has been so kind to me."[16] Five weeks later, the trainees were sent to the Somme front. It was a time of terrible French losses—estimated at over 300,000 by the end of November.[17] Bullard took part in the unofficial Christmas 1914 cease-fire, when Allied and German soldiers all along the frontline trenches exchanged greetings and sang carols, to the fury of both high commands.

In April 1915, the 3rd Marching Battalion was sent to a rest area to reequip. "Anytime that we received new clothing and free quarters in the evening, we knew that we were being given fun before death," Bullard wrote. "But you would not have thought so to hear the men speak and joke as they drank." The enemy respected the legion, with its reputation for taking no prisoners. German leaflets dropped in May 1915 declared that any captured legionnaire would be shot. The legion had a special "take-no-prisoners" spur to battle: a one-hundred-proof drink called tafia. "All the dirty work was done with your bayonet," wrote Bullard, "if the machine guns didn't cut you down before you got to the German trenches." Before each bayonet attack, the men were given a drink of tafia. "You wanted to fight, sing, dance, or anything," he wrote. "We were more like mad men than soldiers. . . . I sincerely believe that if . . . the attack had been called off, it would have been impossible to stop us." They went over the top north of Arras, at the Battle of Artois Ridge. Approximately 4,000 legionnaires participated in the attack; 1,700 survived. Bullard's company of 250 had 54 survivors.[18]

In June, he was among the survivors of the hand-to-hand combat of Hill 119, which left the legion with only three hundred effectives. The 3rd Marching Battalion was dissolved after the battle, due to losses. Bullard now volunteered for the legion's famed 1st Regiment, based on the Alsace front, where he exchanged his kepi for a helmet and gas mask in the constant rain of the September Champagne Big Offensive. "In the Legion as long as you can walk or your trigger finger is not out of commission, you are good for the service," he wrote of the head wound he received.[19] Two companies of legionnaires, with 250 men each, began the battle; the first evening roll call found the companies with 31 survivors between them. After Champagne, the legion was sent back to Africa, and new volunteers had the option of enlisting in a French regiment. Bullard joined the 170th Infantry, the "Swallows of Death" (Hirondelles de la Mort), calling himself the Black Swallow of Death.

"Hell" was his destination in February 1916. Verdun—German codename "Operation Execution Place"—was the scene of a ten-month struggle whose object was not to gain ground but to kill the enemy. By December, over 250,000 men had been killed, 100,000 were missing, and 300,000 had been gassed or wounded on both sides. "I thought I had seen fighting in other battles," wrote Bullard, "but no one has ever seen anything like Verdun—not ever before or ever since."[20] He was twice wounded by shells, the second time seriously, in the thigh. In the hospital for three months, he received both the Croix de Guerre and the Médaille Militaire. "When I heard the general read my citation, I learned I had raised more hell during the Verdun battle than I had bargained for," he wrote. He was interviewed by Will Irwin of *The Saturday Evening Post:* "A year and a half at the front had made a strange creature of Private [he was in fact a corporal] Gene . . . he wasn't at all the Negro we know at home. War and heroism had given him that air of authority common to all soldiers of the line. He looked you in the eye and answered you straight with replies that carried their own conviction of truth. The democracy of the French Army had brushed off onto him; he had grown accustomed to looking at white men as equals. His race, they say, has a talent for spoken languages. Already there was a trace of French accent in his rich, Southern Negro speech; and when he grew excited, he would fall into French phrases."[21]

In Paris, on leave for his leg wound, Bullard joined the French flying corps on a bet with some friends from Montmartre. Taking lessons in a Blériot monoplane held together with wire and glue, he received his pilot's license on May 5, 1917. "It seemed to me that by midnight that same day, every American in Paris knew that an American Negro by the name of Eugene Jacques Bullard, born in Georgia, had obtained a military pilot's license."[22] For the first time since running away from home, he wrote to his father. In June, he was sent to France's Avord Flying School, the largest in the world, to join other advanced Allied student pilots.

"When I became a soldier and a flyer in France, I was treated with respect and friendship by my comrades—even by those from America," he wrote. "Then I knew at last that there are good and bad white men just as there are good and bad black men."[23] He had discovered the very real international comradeship of the first military pilots. Americans at Avord, mostly college-age members of the Lafayette Escadrille, were singularly nonracist in their relationship with Bullard. Besides the brotherhood of airmen, at least three factors, his medals, the Foreign Legion, and Verdun, would have won Bullard respect at Avord.

"I bunked next to him in the barracks at Avord . . . during June and July, 1917," said Reginald "Duke" Sinclaire, president of the Lafayette Escadrille Flying Corps Association, in a 1970 interview with Carisella and Ryan. "At that time Gene was a corporal in the First Regiment of the French Legion, having been twice wounded and having been awarded the Croix de Guerre with two stars. He was 'chef de chambre' of our barracks room (about 22 bunks) and I was 'sous chef de chambre.' Since there were only 10 inches of floor space between our bunks, I got to know Gene very well and liked him very much." George Dock, another Lafayette member, recalled a "humorous, brave, self-reliant man." And Charles Kinsolving remembered a man who "had no fear." (Bullard attributed his insouciance to his deep Catholic faith.) That he was black, for most, seemed to be just another odd fragment in the whole unbelievable mosaic of the war.[24]

In August 1917, American pilots in France were invited to join the U.S. Army Flying Corps. Bullard applied, and took the medical exam. With no enemies among his fellow pilots, he did have a bête noire in Dr. Edmond L. Gros of the American Hospital in Paris. There were "many rumors," Bullard wrote, "about a certain civilian American in a high executive position in Paris, who French and American friends said, disapproved of any American Negro being in the flying corps, and was trying to keep me out of the air."[25] Bullard waited as his fellow Americans received assignments in the U.S. Army Air Corps. When no word came, he remained with the French Service Aéronautique.

In November 1917, accompanied by his pet monkey Jimmy, Bullard was assigned to Escadrille Spad 93, part of the Groupe Brocard, with many top French pilots. "I was determined to do all that was in my power to make good, as I knew the eyes of the world were watching me as the first Negro military pilot in the world." Later that month, making a pass at "Red Baron" Manfred von Richthofen's "Flying Circus," he shot down a German triplane fighter. "I saw my adversary through the sight of my machine gun and would not give up the chase," he wrote. "I was forced to land just behind our lines while I was being machine-gunned from the ground by German infantry." The kill was not confirmed, but an "official report said that a German plane had been forced down after the battle just behind the German second-line trenches." Ten days later, after participating in eighteen more patrols, and enjoying several twenty-four-hour passes to Paris in the company of his friend Charles Nungesser (France's number three ace), Bullard, now a sergeant, was dismissed from the Service Aéronautique. He was accused of striking an officer.[26]

Returning late at night from a Paris leave, trying to climb onto a blacked-out troop truck, Bullard had found himself being pushed and kicked by an unseen French soldier saying, "There's no room for your kind." Grabbing the leg and boot in the darkness on the second kick, he pulled the man out and socked him in the jaw before seeing that his attacker was a lieutenant (who turned out to be a French colonial officer). Escaping a court-martial because of his wounds and combat record, Bullard was sent to a service battalion of his old 170th "Verdun" Regiment. After the war, the writers James Norman Hall and Charles B. Nordhoff, who both served in the Lafayette Escadrille and collaborated on *Mutiny on the Bounty,* remembered meeting him. "There was scarcely an American at Avord who did not know and like Bullard," they wrote in 1922. "He was a brave, loyal and thoroughly likeable fellow; and when a quarrel with his superiors caused his withdrawal from Aviation, there was scarcely an American who did not regret the fact. He was sent to the 170th French Infantry Regiment . . . from which date all trace of him has been lost."[27]

Bullard was lost to Americans, but not to the French. A familiar Paris figure between the wars, he was alternately a boxer, a physical fitness expert, a jazz orchestra leader, and a nightclub host. He was also known for memorable Pigalle street fights, often with racist American tourists. In 1923 he briefly married a Frenchwoman. They had two daughters, but the marriage broke up and his wife died shortly after they were separated, making him a single father. In 1924, he became host and part-owner of Le Grand Duc, a Montmartre nightclub frequented by Ernest Hemingway, F. Scott Fitzgerald, Gloria Swanson, and the Prince of Wales. The young American poet Langston Hughes was a Grand Duc busboy. In his autobiographical *The Big Sea,* he described the main celebrity attraction as Florence Embry, a beautiful young singer from Harlem, who adopted an air of "unattainable aloofness" that celebrities found irresistible.[28] Equally irresistible, and often playing for free, were Louis Armstrong and Sidney Bechet.

In 1939, the Deuxième Bureau asked Bullard, who understood German, to become a spy, giving him a partner from Alsace-Lorraine, named Kitty. The Nazis believed that "no Negro could be bright enough to understand any language except his own," he wrote, "much less figure out the military importance of whatever they said in German." When the "phony war" turned real in the spring of 1940, Bullard, with a Paris business, had the option to remain (although the club was empty except for stranded black American performers) when Americans were ordered to leave France. "I was never too crazy about walking away from danger," he wrote.[29] In May, the forty-five-year-old Bullard joined the other old poilus who marched out of Paris to find the French 51st Infantry, making a last stand against the Germans near Orléans, southwest of Paris. The veterans' march south was swept aside by the endless tide of refugees fleeing north to Paris. Fighting his way through refugees and dive-bombing Stukas, Bullard found the 51st barracks at Orléans, and its commander, an old Verdun comrade. Leading a machine-gun sector, he and his men helped hold off the Germans until Orléans was bombarded and set afire. Wounded in the back by a shell that killed eleven men, Bullard was now decorated in his second war. Knowing that he was too disabled to fight, and knowing that capture meant execution, he made his way to the U.S. consulate in Bordeaux, where he received his first American passport.

Bullard had left Paris for Orléans on May 28. He arrived in Biarritz on June 23, having lost twenty-one pounds, and crossed into Spain to make his way to Lisbon, where he caught a ship to New York in July. "I can never forget how thrilled I was at the sight of the Statue of Liberty," he wrote.[30] In February 1941, thanks to Kitty (who would be decorated after the war) and the French Underground, his daughters arrived in New York from occupied Paris.

Bullard's first American job was as a longshoreman. After the war he became an elevator man in Rockefeller Center. In 1954, he was among the Americans invited to France to relight the flame at the Tomb of the Unknown Soldier. In October 1959, the sixty-five-year-old Bullard became a Knight of the Legion of Honor (Charles Boyer was a witness) at the consulate general of France in New York City—whereupon Dave Garroway of the *Today* show discovered the hero in his own network's elevators and interviewed him on television. "Eugene Jacques Bullard is an American-born adventurer whose achievements make even Walter Mitty's daydreams look pale," wrote Anthony Shannon in *The New York World-Telegram.*[31] Forty years after the war, he was finally discovered by America. His "proudest moment" came the following year, at a reception in New York, when General Charles de Gaulle, spotting his legion uniform and his medals, singled Bullard (still an elevator man) out of the crowd for a handshake and an embrace. When he died in 1961, he was honored with a full French military funeral and was buried under the French tricolor in the cemetery of the Federation of French War veterans, in Flushing, New York.

COLONEL CHARLES YOUNG

Early in 1917, when Lieutenant Colonel Charles Young returned to Fort Huachuca, Arizona, from the Pancho Villa campaign, he started a school, entirely on his own, to prepare black enlisted men for officer training. Young clearly had an inkling of the military mind-set, since there had not been a black at West Point since his own graduation in 1889. Confident of coming war, however, he believed that black officers would be needed if Buffalo Soldier troops, as he expected, went to France with himself as their commander. The forty-three-year-old veteran of the Philippines and Mexico now prepared to take his examination for promotion to full colonel. But the military establishment and the Wilson administration joined forces to deny Young the rank. They also denied blacks the chance to become officers. At the onset of war, Congress authorized the establishment of fourteen officer training camps for whites only, and none for blacks. And on April 24, 1917, a month after war was declared, the War Department announced that "no more Negroes will be accepted for enlistment in the United States Army at present."[32]

The problem of Young would take more concerted effort. If Young went into war a full colonel, he was in danger of becoming a brigadier general. Military racism could never permit a black general. The only stumbling block was Secretary of War Newton D. Baker, a lawyer and a former mayor of Cleveland, who was racially moderate. When Albert S. Dockery, a white lieutenant of the 10th Cavalry, officially complained to the War Department that, as a southerner, he found it "distasteful to take orders from a black superior," namely Young, Baker ordered him to "do his duty or resign."[33] But President Wilson overruled Baker, giving the signal for most of the other white 10th Cavalry officer corps to file official complaints. The problem was nicely "solved" when Young's physical revealed "high blood pressure," necessitating his retirement from the Army before he could attain full colonel rank. The entire black population, starting with black leaders and the press, was outraged. When the white press began to follow Young's startling nonstop cavalry ride from Ohio to New York to prove his fitness, the Army was forced to blink. Five days before the Armistice, he was promoted to full colonel, and recalled to active duty with the Ohio National Guard. Young never got over missing World War I.

In 1919, at the special request of the State Department, Young was named the official American adviser to the Liberian government. In New York, en route for Liberia, he met Walter J. Stevens, a black Spanish-American War veteran, who introduced him to Paul Robeson, the football star, law student, and actor-singer. "The Colonel was proud of Robeson and said to him, 'I wish that young men like you would learn to speak the Spanish language fluently and go to South America,'" wrote Stevens in *Chip on My Shoulder.* "'A great future for the right kind of Negro lies in these South American countries.'" Stevens found Young "a sad man." In photographs of the time, he looks far older than his age, the mid-forties. "Colonel, what is the matter with the white folks in America?" asked Stevens, when they said good-bye. "Nothing," Young had answered, "except that they have left God out of the equation."[34]

Charles Young died in January 1922 in Lagos, Nigeria, and was buried with full British military honors. His remains arrived home four months later, and services in his honor were held at the City College of New York. "No man ever more truly deserved the high repute in which he was held, for by sheer force of character, he overcame prejudices which would have discouraged many a lesser man," said wartime Assistant Secretary of the Navy Franklin D. Roosevelt.[35] On June 1, 1923, Young became the fourth veteran, after two Confederate generals and the Unknown Soldier, to be honored with services in the Arlington National Cemetery amphitheater—fully embraced by the American military at last, in death.

LOYALTY AND THE DRAFT

On March 25, 1917, a week before war was declared, the 1st Separate Battalion, a black District of Columbia National Guard unit, was placed in charge of guarding reservoirs, power plants, and public buildings to prevent sabotage. "It was highly significant," wrote Emmett J. Scott, the Secretary of War's special assistant for Negro Affairs, in his *Official History of the American Negro in the World War,* published in 1919, "that their very *color* which was the *basis of discrimination in time of peace* was considered prima facie *evidence of unquestionable loyalty in time of war.*" The white *Baltimore Sun* editorialized: "The Afro-American is the only hyphenate, we believe, who has not been suspected of divided allegiance." The *Baltimore Afro-American* concluded that the "white regiments of the National Guard have so many foreigners and especially Germans belonging that the Government was afraid to entrust to them the task of watching over Government buildings. . . . For loyalty of this kind our country ought to be willing to pay something. . . . It ought to be willing to pay the price of having these citizens enjoying every right and privilege that German-Americans or any others enjoy."[36]

World War I was clearly conceived by the Wilson administration to be a "white man's war." In the face of black anger, political disturbance, and manpower needs, the War Department soon changed the policy. The question of blacks and wartime service was resolved on May 18, 1917, when the universal Selective Service Act went into effect. Over 24 million men were registered in 1917–1918. "Out of every 100 colored citizens called," read the Army Provost Marshal's report, "36 were certified for service and 64 were rejected, exempted or discharged; whereas out of every 100 whites called 25 were certified for service and 75 were rejected, exempted or discharged."[37]

The Question of Black Officers

In 1917, a U.S. Department of Immigration literacy test found that black immigrants arriving in America were more literate than the black U.S. population.[38] Thus, when Joel Spingarn, the white chairman of the NAACP, responded to black protests against the lack of officer training by convincing the War Department to establish a training camp for black officers, General Leonard Wood challenged him to find two hundred black college students. By May 1917, the Central Committee of Negro College Men (organized at Howard University) had enrolled fifteen hundred members. An intense congressional lobbying effort followed.

"The Negro welcomes the opportunity of contributing his full quota to the Federal Army now being organized," read a statement from the Central Committee. "He feels very strongly that these Negro troops should be officered by their own men." Over three hundred U.S. senators and representatives approved. On June 15, 1917, the first camp for training and commissioning black officers was established at Fort Des Moines, Iowa, under the command of Major General Charles C. Ballou, with a staff of twelve West Point instructors and regular Army black NCOs. Twelve hundred fifty men were admitted, 250 from the regular Army and a thousand from various states. "The race is on trial," read the Committee's letter to all submitted names. "Come to camp determined to make good. . . . If we fail, our enemies will dub us COWARDS for all time, and we can never win our rightful place. But if we succeed—then eternal success."[39]

On October 14, 1917, in a historical first, the Army commissioned 639 black officers: 106 captains, 329 first lieutenants, and 204 second lieutenants. Cheered by blacks nationwide, they were immediately subjected to attacks in the South. When the young second lieutenant George Washington Lee passed through Vicksburg, Mississippi, in uniform, white Mississippi guardsmen gave the rebel yell, and he was warned to leave town as soon as possible.[40] Another Vicksburg threat made the national newspapers. A *New York World* editorial described the case of a black officer visiting his home in Vicksburg who was "counseled by friends to put on civilian clothes, for fear that he might be mobbed if he appeared on the streets in a uniform of a United States Army officer." Lieutenant Joseph B. Saunders, the unnamed officer of the editorial, was "abused, knocked off the sidewalk, and set upon by certain residents of Vicksburg, Mississippi, where he had gone to visit his parents; and compelled to remove his uniform and escape from that city in disguise to avoid mob violence," wrote Emmett Scott in his World War I history.[41] According to the *New York Age,* whites in Vicksburg had announced that "they would allow 'no nigger' to wear a uniform that a white man was bound to honor."[42]

"The black officer feels that there was a prejudgment against him at the outset," wrote Colonel Charles Young to Scott, "and that nearly every move that has been made was for the purpose of bolstering up this prejudgment and discrediting him in the eyes of the world and the men whom he was to lead and will lead in the future." Scott called the effort to humiliate black officers "decidedly organized."[43]

EMMETT J. SCOTT AND THE WAR DEPARTMENT

On October 5, 1917, Emmett J. Scott, former confidential secretary to Booker T. Washington, was appointed special assistant for Negro affairs to Secretary of War Newton D. Baker. As "confidential advisor in matters affecting the 10,000,000 Negroes of the United States and the part they are to play in connection with the present war," he had the highest government position ever achieved by a black. Scott's appointment was a political response to rising lynchings and racial disturbances, German propaganda (which targeted blacks), and what Scott called black "hostility" to the Wilson administration. Scott was in a difficult position. His appointment, he insisted, was never intended to "effectively abolish overnight all racial discriminations and injustices."[44]

On November 30, 1917, Secretary Baker issued a public statement about the new role of blacks in the military: "As you know it has been my policy to discourage discrimination against any persons by reason of their race. This policy has been adopted not merely as an act of justice to all races that go to make up the American people, but also to safeguard the very institutions which we are now at the greatest sacrifice engaged in defending and which any racial disorders must endanger." It was a bold statement, but not one that would be made without a disclaimer: "At the same time," Baker concluded, "there is no intention on the part of the War Department to undertake at this time to settle the so-called race question."[45]

The race question, nevertheless, was unavoidable. "Should you not go personally to Camp Lee and investigate?" Baker had written in a November 1917 memo to Scott. "Then I can go and finish the job." The vast majority of black draftees, some 340,000, were assigned to service units where conditions were worse than inferior. Camp Lee, Virginia, was Scott's first major problem. The whole atmosphere, he wrote, "is one which does not inspire him [the black soldier] to greater patriotism, but rather makes him question the sincerity of the great war principles of America."[46] Camp Lee's white troops lived in barracks; blacks lived in tents without floors or bedding. Whites received intense military training, but all blacks, of whatever level of education, were assigned to labor units and forbidden to fire a gun. Sharp discrimination was shown in everything from recreation to punishment, and even in issuing leaves to visit sick relatives. The black draftees had inferior or insufficient sanitary conveniences, medical treatment, chaplain service, and clothing. Crates labeled "For the Colored Draft" arrived at another Virginia camp bearing discarded Civil War uniforms. At Camp Alexander, Virginia, black men froze to death in the terrible winter of 1917–1918 because they had no coats. "Men died like sheep in their tents," read a report to the secretary of war, "it being a common occurrence to go around in the morning and drag men out frozen to death."[47]

"It took a long time for this situation to get to the authorities," wrote Scott. It took, in fact, another year. The Camp Lee victory, although slow in coming, was Scott's greatest tangible success. Although many blacks regarded his appointment as a political concession, he stressed the real differences seen under his tenure. Before the war, blacks had been represented in only two branches of the U.S. Army—the cavalry (the 9th and 10th) and the infantry (24th and 25th). This amounted to fewer than ten thousand men, with fewer than a dozen black officers. In Scott's twenty-one-month tenure, approximately twelve hundred black officers and men were admitted to practically every branch of service except the Aviation Corps. And at least one white officer was punished for racist behavior without the punishment's being overruled by Wilson. Captain Eugene C. Rowan refused to obey an order by his brigade commander to call for a troop formation because both blacks and whites were included in the formation. At his court-martial, Rowan's defense argued that he was justified in disobeying the order on the grounds of "personal feelings," because he was born in Georgia, resided in Mississippi, and had made a "promise" to his men that he would do nothing to "compel white men to lower their self-respect." Rowan was convicted and dismissed from the Army.[48]

The 92nd Division

The new 92nd Division, officially organized on November 29, 1917, was drawn from the first contingent of black draftees arriving in camps around the country at the end of October. On October 26, it had been announced that all officers of general and field rank, including medical officers, would be white, as would all officers attached to division headquarters, except for lieutenants. Organized and trained in five months, the 92nd Division and its new black lieutenants were sent to seven different training camps in Kansas, Iowa, Illinois, Ohio, Maryland, New York, and New Jersey; its units were never joined until they reached France. No other division in the Army was trained in so many different camps.Most black draftees came from the South and it was the unwritten custom to assign men to camps nearest their homes. In the case of blacks, however, any overlarge concentration was considered dangerous, so thousands of southern black draftees were sent north to train in the fall of 1917.

Called the Buffalo Soldier Division in an effort to ensure black support for the war, the 92nd was poorly trained and poorly led. It never functioned in battle as a division until two days before the Armistice. Instead, basically untrained individual regiments were thrown into the fray. The division and its new black officers were sabotaged from the start by Major General Charles Ballou, the division commander (a post that, according to many blacks, rightly belonged to Colonel Charles Young). "It should be well known to all colored officers and men that no useful purpose is served by such acts as will cause the 'color question' to be raised," read Ballou's Command Bulletin No. 35, issued in the spring of 1918 to address a black soldier's illegal ejection from a movie theater in Kansas.[49] "It is not a question of legal rights, but a question of policy, and any policy that tends to bring about a conflict of the races . . . is prejudicial to the military interest of the colored race." The success of the 92nd, he wrote, was "dependent upon the good will of the public," and that public was "nine-tenths white." He warned the 92nd not to do "ANYTHING, no matter how legally correct, that will provoke racial animosity," and he stated that "white men made the Division, and they can break it just as easily if it becomes a trouble maker." The black press demanded Ballou's resignation. (In fairness to Ballou, although he admonished the sergeant who tried to attend the white theater he also pressed for the prosecution of the theater manager, who was fined $10.)[50]

The 92nd received its baptism of fire on August 25 in the front lines of the St. Die sector. Lieutenant Aaron Fisher of the 366th Regiment, one of the four draftee regiments of the 92nd—which included the 365th, 367th, and 368th (all serving under the American flag)—received the Distinguished Service Cross, and Lieutenant Thomas Bullock of the 367th became the first black officer of the 92nd Division to die in battle.

That August, Pershing received a request from the commanding officer of the 372nd Infantry that all black officers be replaced by whites. "The racial distinctions which are recognized in civilian life naturally continue to be recognized in military life and present a formidable barrier to the existence of that feeling of comradeship which is essential to mutual confidence and esprit de corps," he wrote. "With a few exceptions there is a characteristic tendency among colored officers to neglect the welfare of their men and to perform their duties in a perfunctory manner." The request was received and approved by Pershing in the same month as Pershing's own racist directive to the French. "In keeping with the prevailing custom at that time of discrediting Negro officers," wrote Scott, "desperate efforts were made, it seemed, to show the unusual efficiency of Negro soldiers when led by white officers, and their inefficiency when led by officers of their own race." Black officers were routinely charged with cowardice, but "too many Negro officers and soldiers won the Croix de Guerre, Distinguished Service Medals or Crosses," he wrote, "to lend any color to the charge that Negro officers were inefficient or cowards."[51]

In September, as a 366th Regiment raiding party captured five Germans, two members of the 366th were captured by Germans, who now discovered that the 92nd Division was all black. The first German propaganda arrived on September 12, in what looked like gas shells. "Hello boys, what are you doing over here," it read. "Do you enjoy the same rights as white people do in America, the land of freedom and democracy, or are you rather treated over there as second class citizens? . . . To carry a gun in this service is not an honor, but a shame. . . . Throw it away and come over to the German lines. You will find friends who will help you." There were no desertions. The 366th went on to win eighteen Distinguished Service Crosses for the twenty continuous days it spent at the front under terrifying artillery fire.[52]

Unfortunately, the reputation of the 92nd Division was irrevocably damaged that same September, in the Meuse-Argonne offensive, when the 368th, and particularly their black officers, were accused of cowardice. According to an article in *Harvey's Weekly* in 1919, the 368th had "refused to obey orders" and "did not go forward" when told to attack.[53] The failure to complete the mission was blamed on "the inefficiency and cowardice" of the black company officers. Thirty black officers of the 368th were relieved of command and sent back to America. Five faced courts-martial for cowardice in the face of the enemy. Four were sentenced to death by firing squad, one to life imprisonment. All five officers were later freed, thanks to Captain Leroy Goodman, a black lawyer, who won exoneration for the officers. According to Addie D. Hunton and Kathryn H. Johnson, authors of *Two Colored Women with the American Expeditionary Forces,* the "stigma of cowardice [was] removed but never forgotten."[54]

The secretary of war's defense of the 368th was printed in *The Crisis* in December 1919. "The circumstances disclosed by a detailed study of the situation . . . afford no basis at all for any of the general assumptions, with regard to the action of colored troops in this battle or elsewhere in France. On the contrary, it is to be noted that many colored officers, and particularly three in the very battalion here under discussion were decorated with Distinguished Service Crosses for extraordinary heroism under fire."[55]

Howard H. Long, a black first lieutenant, blamed the 368th disaster on the white 2nd Battalion commander—apparently on the verge of a documented nervous breakdown—who lost contact with some of his men. Long was at battalion command headquarters throughout the battle. "Many of the field officers seemed far more concerned with reminding their Negro subordinates that they were Negroes, than they were with having an effective unit that would perform well in combat," he wrote twenty-five years later. In a 1920 letter, division commander Major General Ballou himself seemed to agree: "It was my misfortune to be handicapped by many white officers who were rabidly hostile to the idea of a colored officer, and who continually conveyed misinformation to the staff," he wrote. "Such men will never give the Negro the square deal that is his due."[56] Ballou's chief of staff, Colonel Allen J. Greer, was one of those men. He wrote to a southern senator in 1919 that the 92nd Division had been "dangerous to no one but themselves and women."[57] When the 92nd went to France, Ballou's successor, General Erwin, would issue the notorious Order Number 40. Enforceable by military police, the order forbade black officers and enlisted men to speak to white women. Rape fears were, typically, exaggerated: during its entire stay in France, only one member of the 25,000-man 92nd Division was convicted of rape.[58]

In nine months in France, a total of 103 officers and 1,543 enlisted men of the 92nd were killed in action or died of other causes such as wounds and disease. There was even praise at the end of the war from Pershing: "I want you officers and soldiers of the 92nd Division to know that the 92nd Division stands second to none in the record you have made since you arrived in France." Fourteen black officers and forty-three enlisted men of the division received Distinguished Service Crosses. Captain Clarence Janifer, surgeon of the 372nd Regiment, was awarded a Croix de Guerre for valor at Bussy Farm in September. "Fearless to danger," read the citation, he "established his First Aid Post in the battlefield . . . following the battalion in the open fields, giving help and relief to the wounded and dying at first hand."[59]

On November 10 and 11, 1918, in the last battles of the war, twenty-four members of the 365th Regiment of the 92nd Division were commended for meritorious conduct at Bois Fréhaut. Among those who received the Croix de Guerre for that battle was seventeen-year-old Frederick White of Cambridge, Massachusetts, a great-great-great-grandson of the Bunker Hill fifer Barzillai Lew. Most of his company had been wiped out. Gassed and temporarily blinded, he had been rescued from a pile of bodies when someone noticed, "This one's breathing." He received his medal in a wheelchair. After the war White became a professional musician, like his Revolutionary ancestor.

"It is perhaps one of the most glorious epochs in the history of the race since the issuing of the Emancipation Proclamation," wrote the black correspondent Ralph W. Tyler in 1918, "that the race, represented by three regiments—crack fighting regiments—and a full artillery unit, was engaged in the last battle of the war." *Stars and Stripes,* the official organ of the American Expeditionary Forces, also saluted the 92nd for participating in the last battle of the war. "Probably the hardest fighting by any Americans in the final hour was that which engaged the troops of the 28th, 92nd, 81st and 7th Divisions of the Second American Army. It was no mild thing, that last flare of the battle, and the order to cease firing did not reach the men in the front line until the last moment, when the runners sped with it from foxhole to foxhole."[60]

The entire 367th Regiment was cited for bravery and awarded the Croix de Guerre for its heroic drive toward Metz on November 10 and 11, the last two days of the war. Sixty percent from New York, 20 percent from the South, the 367th was said to be best trained of all draftee regiments in the U.S. Army. On arrival in Brest in June 1918, they were ordered not to visit French civilians in their homes, on pain of "bread and water in pup tents for 24 hours, and being forced to hike 18 miles with pack." At the Battle of Metz, they saved the white 56th Regiment from annihilation. Later, at the Metz Thanksgiving celebration, when the six white officers and three thousand black soldiers of the 367th were requested to sing "My Country, 'Tis of Thee," the story, perhaps apocryphal, is that only the whites sang.

A. Philip Randolph and the War at Home

Like many black Americans, W.E.B. Du Bois supported the war effort. "That which the German power represents today spells death for the aspirations of Negroes and all darker races," he wrote in a *Crisis* editorial entitled "The Black Soldier" in July 1918. He asked blacks to "forget our special grievances and close our ranks shoulder to shoulder with our own white citizens and the allied nations that are fighting for democracy. . . . We make no ordinary sacrifice, but we make it gladly and willingly with our eyes lifted to the hills."[61]

Others, however, like A. Philip Randolph, a socialist journalist, saw no reason for blacks to make Europe "safe for democracy" when America was not safe for American blacks. Randolph left Jacksonville, Florida, in 1911, at the age of twenty-two, and headed for Harlem, which was about to become the black "city on a hill." Like the brothers J. Weldon Johnson and J. Rosamond Johnson, Randolph was a product of Reconstruction Jacksonville's thriving black middle class. In New York he held a series of day jobs, studied drama and public speaking at night, and attended City College, where he took courses in history, political science, and economics. Discovering Karl Marx and socialism, he said, was "like finally running into an idea which gives you your whole outlook on life."[62] He went to lectures by the white labor leader Eugene V. Debs, and heard the passionate soapbox orations of Harlem's black socialist Hubert Harrison. By 1913, Randolph and Chandler Owen, a Columbia University student, were holding their own soapbox debates on the corner of 135th Street and Lenox Avenue.

In January 1914, Randolph and Owen became the editors of *Hotel Messenger,* a black waiters' association magazine. Seven months later they were fired for printing an editorial in favor of a junior waiter over a headwaiter. With money supplied by Randolph's wife, Lucille, owner of a Harlem beauty parlor, the first issue of Randolph and Chandler's *Messenger* appeared in November 1917, calling itself "the first voice of radical, revolutionary, economic and political action among Negroes in America." Randolph wrote the manifesto: "No intelligent Negro is willing to lay down his life for the United States as it now exists." The Justice Department wanted to prosecute them for treason, but the Wilson administration feared black reaction. Instead, the magazine's office was wrecked, its second-class mailing privileges were revoked, and Randolph and Owen were put under close surveillance. Continuing to speak at socialist antiwar rallies all over the country, they were arrested by federal agents in Cleveland. The judge, looking at their boyish faces, told them to go home to their parents. In 1918, however, they were given jail sentences of one to two and a half years for printing an article entitled "Pro-Germanism Amongst the Negroes."

The combination of the May 1918 Sedition Act and J. Edgar Hoover's newly created General Intelligence Division of the Justice Department basically stamped out freedom of expression for the duration of the war. Under the rubrics of "espionage" and "sedition," the postmaster general could refuse to deliver "treasonous" mail. Socialist publications like *Messenger* and *The Masses* were closed down. Books were burned and banned from libraries. Troops were used against pacifists and labor activists: the national leadership of the International Workers of the World was arrested for being both. The controversial Overton Act, issued in May 1918, permitted Wilson "to disband, add to, or reorganize any executive or administrative agency without the approval of Congress."[63]

EAST ST. LOUIS AND CAMP LOGAN

The July 2, 1917, race riot in East St. Louis, Illinois, sparked by white protest against black workers in a factory holding government contracts, was one of the bloodiest in American history. Between forty and one hundred blacks were killed over several days, and black homes were set on fire. On July 28 the NAACP, with Du Bois and James Weldon Johnson in the vanguard, led a Silent Parade in New York City to protest East St. Louis and lynching. Ten thousand black New Yorkers—women and children in white, men with black armbands—marched down Fifth Avenue with signs reading: "Mr. President, Why Not Make America Safe for Democracy?" Nearly one hundred blacks, including five women, would be lynched in the nine months that America was at war.

A month after the silent march, what the Army called a mutiny occurred at Camp Logan in Houston, Texas, where 24th Infantry blacks were regularly insulted and assaulted by local police and civilians. The "mutiny" began when a black soldier, Private Alonzo Edwards, went to the aid of a black woman being beaten by Houston police and was himself beaten and arrested. Unarmed, like all black MPs in the South, Corporal Charles Baltimore of the 24th Infantry Military Police went to inquire about Edwards, and he, too, was beaten and arrested. When the news made its way to Camp Logan, white officers locked away all weapons. The 24th rebelled, nevertheless. A sergeant was killed, and guns were seized. Led by Sergeant Vida Henry, an eighteen-year veteran of the regiment (who had earlier warned superiors of imminent racial trouble), 24th Infantry soldiers marched on Houston's police station in company strength. Newspapers later said the men planned to kill all whites, but they marched from camp through the black neighborhood directly to the Houston police. Fifteen whites, including five Houston policemen, were killed and twelve others were seriously injured. Four black soldiers died. A whole division of Camp Logan's white troops was sent after them. Sergeant Vida Henry preferred suicide to capture, but the rest of the men surrendered.

The entire 24th Infantry was placed on a guarded troop train and shipped to Fort Huachuca, Arizona, where a summary court-martial, the largest such trial in the history of the United States, condemned thirteen men, including Baltimore, to death, and sentenced forty-one others to life imprisonment. The NAACP engaged a defense attorney for the soldiers and campaigned for clemency. Wilson ultimately commuted ten death sentences to life imprisonment, but three men were executed. After the Camp Logan riot, there was a "common feeling throughout the South," wrote Scott, "that no more colored troops should be stationed on Southern soil."[64] The governor of South Carolina himself went to Washington to protest black troops being sent to his state. Efforts on behalf of the 24th Infantry continued until 1938, when President Franklin Roosevelt released the last prisoners.

HAYWOOD HALL AND THE 8TH ILLINOIS

Haywood Hall was a member of the black National Guard regiment, the 8th Illinois, ordered to Camp Logan in August 1917. Half the regiment was in place when the 24th Infantry uprising occurred. Hall's group arrived a few days later, to hear the story from eyewitnesses. "They shot anyone who looked like a cop," he wrote, under the name Harry Haywood, in his autobiography, *Black Bolshevik.*[65] A black Houston laundress gave Hall the shirts, underwear, and starched khaki trousers left behind by the hanged MP, Corporal Baltimore.

For most of Hall's regiment it was their first time in the South. When the train arrived in Jonesboro, Arkansas, the first southern stop, 8th Illinois soldiers, Springfield rifles in plain view, blew kisses to white girls, saying "Come over here, baby, give me a kiss." Later, Hall and his friends wrecked a store that did not serve "niggahs" and beat up the owner. A black major, with an armed black guard, stared down a white sheriff who wanted to board the troop train.

The son of former slaves, Hall was born in Omaha in 1898. His father worked for Cudahy Meatpacking—blacks having been brought to Omaha from Tennessee in 1894 as strikebreakers. The Halls were among the few black families in the largely Irish and Bohemian lower-middle-class suburb of South Omaha. There were two black policemen in the neighborhood, one a 10th Cavalry veteran of the Geronimo campaign and Cuba. A self-taught student of black history, Hall's father knew about Egypt, Ethiopia, and the African kingdom of Kush; he knew about the Zulu chieftain Shaka and the Haitian revolutionary Toussaint-Louverture. He knew that Pushkin and Alexandre Dumas were what Americans would consider black. And he knew black military history: the living room wall had a Civil War "Remember Fort Pillow!" banner, and a print of the 10th Cavalry and 24th Infantry charging up San Juan Hill. Haywood's older brother Otto (destined, his teacher said, to be a "leader of his race") wrote a poem about blacks at San Juan Hill that was published in an Omaha daily.

Boll weevil–fleeing southern whites, demanding black factory jobs, drove the Halls out of Omaha in 1914. On the first day of school in Minneapolis, an all-white class singing old plantation songs broadened their accents into jeering drawls when Hall walked into the room. He turned around, walked out, and never returned to school—becoming, at the age of sixteen, a dining car waiter on the Chicago Northwestern Railway.

Working the Wolverine and the Twentieth Century Limited out of Chicago, nineteen-year-old Hall, like many of his friends, joined the 8th Illinois, "a big social club of fellow race-men." Black National Guard regiments considered themselves elite. Since the post–Civil War period, all black Guard units had some black officers, but Chicago's 8th Illinois, veterans of the Mexican incursion, had all black officers, including a black commander, Colonel Franklin A. Denison. Born in Texas, Denison was the former assistant city prosecuting attorney and assistant corporation counsel of Chicago. Blatantly contradicting the southern belief that black soldiers performed best under white southern officers, the 8th Illinois regarded their black officers as inspirational. "We men didn't let our officers down," Hall wrote. "We were out to show the whites that not only were we as good in everything as they, but better." They won Camp Logan division championships in track, boxing, and baseball, and had the highest number of marksmen, sharpshooters, and expert riflemen. "Of course, there was no socializing between Blacks and whites," he wrote, "but it was clear that we had the respect, if not the friendship, of many of the white soldiers in the division."[66]

After six weeks of training, they were ready for France. "With our excellent band playing the Illinois March, we passed the reviewing stand with our special rhythmic swagger which only Black troops could affect," Hall wrote of the military review. The *Houston Post* called them "the best looking outfit in the parade." Eighth Illinois esprit de corps was more racial than military, but Hall believed in the war. He had a personal reason to save France, which he saw as a sanctuary from American racism. "Joan of Arc" was Hall's favorite song: "Do your eyes from the skies see the foe? / Can't you see the drooping Fleur de Lis, / Can't you hear the tears of Normandy?" Hall had almost enlisted in the Canadian army because the kilted recruiting sergeant of the "Princess Pat Regiment" told him that Canada had no color line—that there were a number of "black boys" in the regiment. Still underage at sixteen, he knew his parents would never give permission. Most of the "Princess Pat" would be wiped out at Ypres and Passchendaele.[67]

The arrival of the 8th Illinois in Brest on April 16, 1918, with six black field officers, including Colonel Denison, was reported by Hunton and Johnson in *Two Colored Women with the American Expeditionary Forces*. "A new equality was tasted at this time by these American colored men," they wrote, "while their officers moved with perfect ease among the highest officials of the French Army."[68] The taste of new equality was brief. Almost immediately, all black field officers, including Colonel Denison, were sent home. The 8th Illinois was renamed the 370th Regiment of the 93rd Division, bearing the arms and uniforms of the French 59th Division. In June, the 370th distinguished itself in the St.-Mihiel sector. In July, they were in the Argonne Forest, where Corporal Isaac Vally of the 370th was awarded the Distinguished Service Cross for protecting his comrades by covering, with his foot, a hand grenade dropped among them in a trench.

The 370th would be the first Allied troops to break the Hindenburg

Line, retaking the fortress town of Laon, some eighty miles northeast of Paris, held by the Germans since 1914. In the final stages of the war, they advanced as far as thirty-five kilometers in one day. They fought the last battle of the war, in Belgium with the French 59th Division, on the morning of November 11, 1918, and probably made the last capture, a German army train of fifty wagons. Sixty-eight members of the 370th won the Croix de Guerre, and twenty-one received Distinguished Service Crosses, America's second highest honor. They went to France with 2,500 men and returned with 1,260.

"HARLEM'S OWN": ARTHUR LITTLE, WILLIAM HAYWARD, HAM FISH, AND THE 15TH NEW YORK

White officers of black troops generally came in three types: noblesse oblige liberals, ambitious younger officers, and superannuated patriots. The forty-three-year-old New York publishing heir Arthur W. Little was one of the latter. When war was declared, he tried unsuccessfully to join a white regiment, then offered his services to the 15th New York, a black National Guard regiment with mostly white officers. As Major Arthur Little, he wrote *From Harlem to the Rhine,* his own apologia for black troops. "It is probable that, of all the humorous anecdotes of the American Army in the World War, almost half of them are attributed to colored soldiers. . . . But let no man, on account of that record, put down the colored man in his mind as a comic soldier. A regiment of colored men, properly organized and properly officered, is a great regiment—for fighting or for any duty."[69] The 15th, belonging to the biggest and most culturally vibrant black community in America, was known as "Harlem's Own." Its black officers and men reflected Harlem's rich diversity, from its educated middle class to illiterate migrants newly arrived from the South.

The 15th New York, authorized in 1913, was a New York State Democratic Party payoff to black voters. In the 1910 election, Edwin Horne, my ex-Republican great-grandfather, helped sway New York's normally Republican blacks to vote Democratic with the help of propaganda leaflets such as the anti-Roosevelt "Remember Brownsville." Another Horne pamphlet, "What Do We Want?," listed a black National Guard regiment among its demands. But Tammany Hall showed little enthusiasm for making the 15th New York a reality. Tammany's regiment was the 69th, the "Fighting Irish."

When the war broke out in Europe, Charles W. Fillmore, a young black New York attorney, made serious efforts to sponsor and organize a black National Guard regiment, but the state rebuffed him. Following the gallant behavior of black troops at Carrizal, Mexico, in 1916, however, New York's governor, Charles S. Whitman, changed his mind and authorized the project, naming Colonel William Hayward, then public service commissioner, to head the new regiment. When the 15th New York was activated in June 1916, Charles W. Fillmore was commissioned a captain.

Colonel William Hayward, a former member of the Republican National Committee and veteran of both the Spanish-American and Philippine wars, was determined to make the regiment a success for two reasons: he had a healthy ego, and he believed that black soldiers should be in combat. A noblesse oblige liberal, like most Roosevelt Republicans, Hayward was also a tireless and well-connected self-promoter. New York City's "Boy" Mayor, John Purroy Mitchel, appropriated the regiment's "armory," a dilapidated former Brooklyn beer garden. The armory board's chief, Lawrence V. Meehan, supplied the office furnishings and equipment. Little's brother officers, Union League clubmen and Ivy League athletes, were men, he wrote, to whom "the easiest way" was open, "but in whom there existed no spirit apart from the determination to do their bit, and without hope or expectation of reward." Despite a keen sense of their own military "shortcomings," officers worked day and night to turn a "delightful, happy-go-lucky mob into an organization of soldiers."[70]

The regimental physician, Dr. George Bolling Lee, a grandson of Robert E. Lee, was, like Little, a firm believer in "sex hygiene" to combat the venereal disease sweeping the American military. Concerned with maintaining the health and efficiency of the regiment, Lee issued orders in August 1917, with Hayward's backing, "for the enforcement of prophylactic treatment." This was in direct opposition to Secretary of the Navy Josephus Daniels, who saw prophylaxis stations as an "invitation to sin" and refused to approve them. Fortunately, in Daniels's temporary absence, the "less prudish" assistant secretary of the navy, Franklin D. Roosevelt, ordered them installed. The Army made venereal disease a court-martial offense. VD would be high among black stevedores in Brest, Bordeaux, and St.-Nazaire; it would also be high among white officers and white military police.[71]

The popular press delighted in the regiment's officers. None was as well advertised as Colonel Hayward (James Montgomery Flagg's portrait sketch of a dashing Hayward in uniform was reprinted everywhere, making him a national celebrity), but Captain Hamilton Fish, Jr., was its most celebrated younger officer. Captain of the Harvard football team and one of the coach Walter Camp's "All-American" college football stars, he was still known as "Ham" Fish of Harvard, Class of 1910. (Other members of the class were T. S. Eliot and Walter Lippmann. And John Reed, who went off to report on the Russian Revolution, was a 1910 Harvard cheerleader.) According to his autobiography, *Hamilton Fish: Memoir of an American Patriot,* he accepted Hayward's offer to join the 15th "on the spot."[72] Arthur Little was impressed: "He was the son of Hamilton Fish, formerly Speaker of the Assembly of New York State, a nephew of Nicholas Fish and of Stuyvesant Fish, the latter for years President of the Illinois Central Railroad and husband of Mrs. Stuyvesant Fish, one of the most brilliant leaders of Society ever known to New York City. He was a great-grandson of Secretary of State Hamilton Fish . . . of President Grant's cabinet."[73] Not mentioned in this august genealogy was Fish's Revolutionary great-grandfather, Colonel Nicholas Fish, a friend of Lafayette who led the enactment of New York State's 1799 abolition of slavery, and Fish's grandfather, who signed the Fifteenth Amendment giving blacks the right to vote. Hamilton Fish, Jr., would write that his lifelong "sense of obligation for American blacks" came from his family's "legacy of public concern."[74]

Arthur Little also had words of praise for the 15th's black officers, especially its two black chaplains, Lieutenants Thomas W. Wallace and Benjamin C. Robeson (brother of Paul). "These officers, colored clergymen of high standards and of intelligent sympathy with our problems, valiantly set out upon their missions to move the hearts of men—who for months had been trained to do the business of the Devil—to the worship of God." And he had never seen "a better Summary Court officer" than Captain Napoleon Bonaparte Marshall, a Harvard graduate and lawyer (for the 1906 Brownsville defendants) who "held court under conditions of great impressiveness." Marshall, who had also been a star athlete at Harvard, was gassed and seriously wounded in October 1918; he would win the Croix de Guerre. Little's relationship with Captain Charles W. Fillmore was more problematic. Little described him as a young officer who seemed to believe "that every correction ever offered him . . . was offered on account of his being a colored man, and not on the merits of the good of the service." Perhaps Fillmore, who had made earlier efforts to sponsor a black regiment, believed he merited a higher rank than captain. Nevertheless, later in France, Little would cite him for "conspicuous bravery."[75]

Lieutenant James Reese Europe and Noble Sissle

Little's highest praise was reserved for the thirty-seven-year-old Lieutenant James Reese Europe, "a most extraordinary man without qualification or limitation as to race, color, or any other element."[76]

Regimental Band Master Europe was better known as Jim Europe, orchestra leader, recording star, and national celebrity. His was the orchestra that played behind the superstars Vernon and Irene Castle when they made America dance-mad—and his dark, intelligent face (with eyeglasses, stiff collar, and receding hairline) advertised "New Victor Records of the Latest Dance Music" in the first recordings by a black orchestra. "During the past three seasons Europe's Society orchestra of negro musicians has become very popular in . . . the homes of wealthy New Yorkers and at functions at the Tuxedo Club, Hotel Biltmore, Plaza, Sherry's, Delmonico, the Astor," read the Victor magazine and newspaper ads. "The success . . . is due to the admirable rhythm sustained throughout every number, whether waltz, turkey trot or tango . . . and the unique instrumentation, which consists of banjos, mandolins, violins, clarinet, cornet, traps and drums." Those who provided testimonials included the head of the Mannes Music School, who said Europe "has created a new sound in the orchestra world." The New York *Sunday Press* called him "the Paderewski of syncopation."[77]

Born in Alabama and raised in Washington, D.C., where he studied violin with the assistant bandmaster of the U.S. Marine Corps, Europe actually had two professional personae. As James Reese Europe, he cultivated a philosophy of music and dreamed of a National Negro Orchestra: "We colored people have our own music, that is the product of our souls. It's been created by the sufferings and miseries of our race. Some of the melodies we play were made up by slaves, and others were handed down from the days before we left Africa. We have developed a kind of symphony music that lends itself to the playing of the peculiar compositions of our race." In 1910, Europe founded New York City's Clef Club—a club, union, and hiring hall for black hotel and restaurant musicians. On May 2, 1912, his 125-member Clef Club Symphony Orchestra gave the first jazz concert at Carnegie Hall. "One of the most remarkable orchestras in the world," wrote the *New York Evening Post.* That night, the orchestra included forty-seven mandolins, eleven banjos, one saxophone, one tuba, thirteen cellos, two clarinets, one kettledrum, five trap drums, two double basses, and ten pianos.[78]

But it was Jim Europe's "Society Orchestra" (with "Too Much Mustard" and "Turkey Trot") that made him a household name. His orchestra was in the right place at the right time for America's dance craze, inspired by Irene Castle, slim, bobbed, and much photographed, and her partner-husband, Vernon. In 1914, the year that Europe became their personal conductor-arranger, they introduced the fox-trot, with Europe's orchestra playing W. C. Handy's "Memphis Blues." In April of that year, the Castles gave a benefit performance at Harlem's Manhattan Casino for the Negro National Orchestra's tour of Europe. *The New York Sun* reported: "Centered in one of the most picturesque gatherings New York has ever seen, Mr. and Mrs. Vernon Castle, wizards of the dance, who are to terpsichore what Edison is to electricity, appeared last night before the Tempo Club, one of the leading negro organizations of the city . . . they danced their latest steps surrounded by 2500 members of the club and more than a hundred white people of fame and fashion."[79]

Like most black officers, Jim Europe was educated and middle-class. He had volunteered in order to make a statement about black men as citizens and soldiers, but his impact was in the realm of music. "When dear old Jim Europe joined the regiment, and when I discovered who he was, I asked him to build a band," Hayward told Arthur Little.[80] Hayward persuaded John D. Rockefeller, Jr., and Daniel G. Reid ("The Tin Plate King") to chip in so that Europe's band would have a minimum of forty-four men—instead of the Army regulation twenty-eight. Europe was even permitted to recruit out of state, as far afield as Puerto Rico for reed players and Chicago for Frank De Broit, considered one of the best cornet players in the world. A playboy with a "Kaiser Bill" mustache, De Broit was given full rank as assistant bandleader, plus $100 a month from Rockefeller and Reid. Bill Robinson (the future Bojangles) was another member of the band. Because Europe was a line officer in charge of a machine-gun unit, the band was strictly in addition to his other duties, and officially under the command of Band Sergeant Eugene F. Mikell.

Lieutenant Noble Sissle, the son of a Methodist minister, was the regimental drum major. Sissle grew up in Cleveland, Ohio, where he was one of six black students at Central High School and the catcher on the varsity baseball team. He worked his way through Indiana's Butler University as a waiter, and wrote Butler football songs. "One day the manager sent for me," Sissle remembered in *Reminiscing with Sissle and Blake*. "He had just returned from New York for Christmas where he said Negro musicians were playing and entertaining in every café. He asked if I would organize an orchestra . . . in ten days I had a twelve-piece orchestra in the same room I'd waited tables in for a dollar a day."[81] Sissle was also his band's vocalist and a burgeoning lyricist. He quit college in 1915 for a winter engagement at a hotel in Palm Beach, where the white society hostess Mary Brown Warburton gave him a letter of introduction to Jim Europe. Sissle soon persuaded Europe to hire his young ragtime-piano composer friend, Eubie Blake. By 1917, Sissle and Blake were a piano-vocal duo for private parties, and a songwriting team for the Broadway stars Sophie Tucker and Nora Bayes.

Unlike black officers, the majority of Little's black enlisted men are described by him as speaking a convoluted southern dialect. Well-paid jobs for educated black men in Woodrow Wilson's America were few ("From Ph.D. to Pullman Porter" was the black quip); poor southern blacks in New York found little employment. "A large proportion of our men were Pullman porters and waiters . . . and apartment house and theatre doormen. These men, through force of habit, adopted a style of military salute all their own. They would first raise the right hand smartly to the visor of the cap over the right eye, as provided by regulations, but then they would bow very low in the most approved style of a Saratoga Springs hotel head waiter, and murmur, 'Mawnin' Suh—mawnin'!' "[82]

Two and a half weeks at the Peekskill, New York, training camp turned recruits into soldiers. "Our men, by the time we returned to our city, could drill in close order formations; and they could drill as well as any regiment in the New York Guard," Little wrote.

> They knew the important names of the many parts of the service rifle. They knew the functions of those parts. They could take their rifles apart and put them together again. They knew the duty of a sentinel on post upon Interior Guard duty, and could perform such duty in most exacting fashion. Every man had shot for the standard qualification score of the U.S. Rifle Association, over every range from 100 yards to 600 yards, including both deliberate and rapid fire. More than half of the men of the regiment and, I believe, all of the officers, had passed the preliminary qualification.[83]

When Governor Whitman presented the regimental colors in front of the Union League Club in the spring of 1917, Bert Williams, the great black star of Ziegfeld's *Follies* and a former National Guard officer in the West, was a mounted member of the parade. The crowd roared as the colors were marched up Fifth Avenue to Jim Europe's syncopated rendition of "Onward Christian Soldiers." In June, however, the usually ebullient Hayward was "wounded and bitter" when the 15th was denied inclusion in the new "Rainbow Division," which included the Fighting Irish of Tammany's 69th. Hayward was told that black was "not a color of the rainbow." And when, Jim Europe notwithstanding, the regiment was denied permission to march in the New York National Guard "Farewell to Little Old New York" Parade, Hayward told Arthur Little that he "wanted to cry." When the war was over, he vowed, the 15th New York would have the best homecoming parade "that New York will ever have seen." He asked Little to swear that if he, Hayward, did not survive, Little would carry out the pledge to "see to it that the glory and honor of the Negro race of America may be served by having our welcome home parade celebrated all alone—in the same manner in which we have been born and trained."[84]

WILLIAM LAYTON

A seventeen-year-old named William Layton joined the 15th New York in September 1917. Layton was a bugler; he had learned his instrument with the Newark Boy Scouts, and he wanted to be a professional. "I liked the bugle," he said when I interviewed him in 1990 and asked him to remember his military experience. By the age of ten he was playing in Sunday school concerts and at baseball games. Layton lived with his grandparents, and quit school in the seventh grade to work in a paper mill. His grandfather had escaped slavery in Virginia via the Underground Railroad and had fought in the Civil War. His grandmother was from a Delaware Indian tribe. In the summer of 1917, Layton found that all of his friends were enlisting and joining the new 15th New York. His mother and grandmother were vociferously opposed, but he was determined to volunteer.

At the recruiting station, the boyish Layton told the officer that he wanted to enlist to join his friends in the 15th. The officer told him he was too short and too skinny. After much pleading, the recruiter finally relented and told Layton to go to a nearby fruit stand, to drink a quart of milk and eat four bananas, then come back and be weighed. Layton made the weight but was told he could not join the 15th: they were already organized and on active duty, waiting to go overseas. After his physical at Camp Slocum, he was ordered to join the 24th Infantry in Texas. He said no, thanks—the Brownsville, Texas, 24th Infantry "mutiny" was still news—and insisted that the only regiment he wanted to join was the 15th New York. "So they sent me to Camp Dix, where I picked up the Fifteenth," he said.

At Camp Dix basic training, Layton remembered that all they did "was learn to fight each other." Fights broke out all the time. " 'All right, on your feet,' you would hear just as you were sitting down to dinner or breakfast," he said. Faced with the rest of the all-white 93rd Division, however, some saying "Hello, fellow," others saying "Hey, nigger," the "boys bonded pretty tight together—the captains and the sergeant knew they had a good corps."

Layton did not enjoy the Army. He had his own opinions about the officers. Colonel Hayward was "basically okay," he recalled, "he loved those fellas, street boys you could say." Ham Fish, everyone's favorite, was "gentle . . . understanding . . . proud of the men." Most important, Fish "liked music" and was not a stickler for nonretaliation when it came to fights with whites. Not all white officers ranked equally high in Layton's esteem. Lieutenant Colonel Woodell Pickering "wasn't a soldier . . . the men didn't like him." Nor did they like Captain Louis B. Candler, who carried out Pickering's orders.

Camp Spartanburg, South Carolina

The 15th New York was officially recognized as part of the U.S. Army on July 15, 1917. But instead of training like other militia, it was divided into small detachments and placed on guard duty in various parts of New York, New Jersey, and Pennsylvania. Colonel Hayward never stopped agitating for combat, protesting that the 15th New York were guarding camps while men of junior service were being prepared for overseas. Hayward's campaign paid off. In October, the regiment was reassembled and ordered to Camp Spartanburg, South Carolina, for twelve days of training before departing for France.

"I was sorry to learn that the Fifteenth Regiment has been ordered here . . . for, with their northern ideas about race equality, they will expect to be treated like white men," the mayor of Spartanburg told *The New York Times.* "I can say right here that they will not be treated as anything except negroes. We shall treat them exactly as we treat our resident negroes." A Spartanburg chamber of commerce official reiterated: "I can tell you for certain that if any of those colored soldiers go in any of our soda stores and the like and ask to be served they'll be knocked down. Somebody will throw a bottle. We don't allow negroes to use the same glass that a white man may later have to drink out of. We have our customs down here, and we aren't going to alter them."[85]

The day after they arrived in Spartanburg, Hayward assembled the entire company and urged them not to meet "the white citizens of Spartanburg upon the undignified plane of prejudice and brutality which had been so unfortunately advertised by Mayor Floyd, as the standard of the community." He appealed, "on grounds of self-respect," that the men not go where their presence was "not desired." And he warned them not to retaliate in case of physical abuse, but to report every incident, in detail, to him. "See to it . . . that if violence occurs, if blows are struck, that all of the violence and all of the blows are on one side, and that side is not our side."[86] The men were asked to raise their right hands, promising to refrain, despite provocation, from any kind of violence. Fish met with town officials. "I told them that if any of the town's citizens sought by force to interfere with the rights of the black troops under my command, I would immediately demand swift legal action to be initiated against the perpetrators. This quieted things down temporarily, but tensions remained high."[87]

Spartanburg did not like northern blacks, but it tolerated black music. The first Saturday evening after arrival, a band concert was given in the town square. "The Colonel and about a dozen of his most reliable officers attended that concert," wrote Arthur Little. "We didn't occupy seats. . . . With overcoat collars hooked . . . so as to hide the numerals on the crossed rifles of our blouse-collar-ornaments, we scattered through the audience. If disorder had been started in that assemblage every colored soldier present would have been able to find at least one officer's face that he knew. And our men, with their own trusted officers leading them, would never (and never did) go wrong." The concert was a success. But the next day, Captain Napoleon Bonaparte Marshall was insulted on a trolley car. "Captain Marshall, in civil life, is a lawyer. . . . He knew his rights. He was by no means lacking in appreciation of the wrongs of his race. But Captain Marshall had volunteered to help lick Germany, not to force a social or racial American revolution. So—Captain Marshall accepted the indignity, and got off the car."[88]

The Spartanburg "riot" began on a Sunday morning, when Jim Europe asked Regimental Drum Major Noble Sissle to "go over to the hotel and get every paper that has the words New York on it." Sissle told the story:

> When I went to the stand, I was roughly grabbed in the collar from behind, and before I realized what had happened my service hat was knocked from my head. A gruff voice roared, "Say, nigger, don't you know enough to take your hat off?" . . . I reached for my hat and as I did so received a kick accompanied by an oath. Lost for words, I stammered out: "Do you realize you are abusing a United States soldier and that is a government hat you knocked to the floor?" "Damn you and the government too," the man replied. "No nigger can come into my place without taking off his hat."[89]

Sissle left as soon as he could, but not before receiving three more kicks.

"Within a few seconds, however, the lobby of that hotel was in an uproar," reported Arthur Little. "Forty or fifty white soldiers, lounging there, had witnessed the outrage." There had already been incidents where white soldiers from New York's 7th Regiment had defended 15th New York soldiers from Spartanburg racists. Now whites from New York's 12th and 71st Regiments were in the hotel. "Let's kill the so and so, and pull his dirty old hotel down about his ears!" a white soldier shouted. "But the melee was quelled by a loud cry of 'ATTEN . . . TION!' " Little wrote, followed by an order to leave quietly, singly and in pairs. "The officer who had quelled that riot by the power and majesty of command was a black man, a full-blooded negro, 1st Lieutenant James Reese Europe." The man who had assaulted Sissle now turned on Europe: "Get out of this hotel—you blank blank blankity blank, how dare you step in here after I've just kicked your blank blank blankity of a blank side partner into the street!" Some of the 15th started out for Spartanburg but Hayward, on horseback, intercepted them and persuaded them to return to camp. He departed for Washington the same day, to urge the War Department, in person, to remove his men from Spartanburg.[90]

William Layton remembered being shocked by reports of the hotel manager's language. "Soldiers didn't curse in front of women," he said. Some members of the 15th wanted to "tear up the town." A notice appeared forbidding the men to go to Spartanburg. But Captain Fish promised to "straighten things up when they got to the other side," Layton recalled. "The boys felt they didn't want to fight for people who didn't want them in their town."

Hayward returned from Washington with Emmett J. Scott, having invited him to come to Spartanburg to speak to the regiment's NCOs. "My address to these men," wrote Scott, "was an appeal and admonition to do nothing that would bring dishonor or stain to the regiment or to the race which they represent." As Scott saw it, the War Department had three choices: 1. To stay in camp and face eruptions by white townspeople as well as black and white guardsmen. 2. To move the regiment to another camp "and thereby convey the intimation that whenever any community put forth sufficient pressure, the War Department would respond." 3. To send them overseas.The third choice was taken.[91]

On October 24, the 15th was ordered to Camp Whitman, New York, to prepare to set sail for Europe. "But trouble followed us," wrote Fish. They were stationed next to a white regiment from Alabama that wanted to refight the Civil War. "We thought the war was going to start right here in America rather than in the trenches of France," Fish said. The unarmed 15th borrowed ammunition from a white New York regiment. "After arming our soldiers, we told them if they were attacked they were to fight back; if they were fired on they were to fire back." It was not Spartanburg, but Fish feared a bloodbath: "Unfortunately around midnight a bugle was mistakenly sounded, calling the black troops to arms." Fish strapped on a revolver and ran into the darkness, where he bumped into three Alabama officers. "I told them that the black troops were armed and if attacked they would fight back, which would mean a massacre on both sides. I added that it was absolutely unnecessary for there to be an exchange of blood between the white and black soldiers; regardless of color, the soldiers were all Americans who had been called upon to fight a common enemy overseas." The Alabama officers agreed, and promised to do everything they could to prevent trouble. New York newspapers turned the story into "a major incident." It was "completely untrue," Fish wrote, that he had "challenged the Alabamans to a fistfight."[92]

"Colonel Hayward was a little slow at Camp Whitman," Layton said. "They didn't give blacks ammo, but Captain Fish gave us ammo and said if we were attacked we should shoot."

On the day they returned to Camp Dix, New Jersey, to prepare for embarkation, the 15th New York had another fight with white troops. "We wanted real guns," Layton said. Now there was a rumor that the regiment might be disbanded as "troublemakers," but thanks to Hayward's political clout, the 15th was finally "kicked" to France. The men were by now desperate to go overseas. They were going over to fight Germans, but they also hoped to square off with white Americans. Overseas meant vengeance.

"THE FRENCH ARE WONDERFUL"

In mid-December 1917, after numerous delays, the S.S. *Newark* finally steamed out of Hoboken, New Jersey. Outraged that the ship was crossing the Atlantic without destroyer protection against German U-boats, Ham Fish wrote to Franklin Roosevelt, assistant secretary of the Navy: "I am writing the following facts to you as a friend who has confidence in your discreetness and as an American who believes in your good judgement and ability to remedy a condition which in the near future will endanger the lives of thousands of American soldiers. . . . It was a great surprise to all of us, to find out that our convoy was not protected by destroyers. I have no desire to criticize anyone, and only hope to remedy the condition before it results in a disaster." It was customary, on American troopships, to keep blacks below the waterline even in U-boat-infested waters. Captain George C. Marshall (a future World War II general and the creator of the Marshall Plan) had been rather shocked to find, sailing to France, that black stevedores were assigned no lifeboats and were expected to use floating debris as rafts.[93]

The 15th New York arrived in Brest on an icy New Year's Day, 1918. The first black American combat troops to arrive in France marched off the boat singing. William Layton remembered being "scared to death" when the black sergeant grabbed him. "What's your name? Come here, you!" The captain wanted to know if Layton could bugle. To his great surprise Layton suddenly found himself both chief bugler of Company L and a corporal, although he was still paid as a private. The winter of 1918, with bitter cold and raging influenza, was known as Valley Forge. Acute shortages of clothing and boots plagued the frontline soldiers, but appeals to the War Department were rejected, "owing to need for supply of troops in the United States." At the expense of the AEF, Wilson was keeping knowledge of shortages from the public. There were also no training centers for troop replacements, because the government did not want civilians to think that it was preparing for great losses.

France was "bled white"; the morale of the country was "at a very low ebb," wrote Arthur Little. "Our first words of welcome from the population of the humble classes were words of protest at our coming. Why had we come? We could do nothing, now, but prolong the suffering of the nation! Germany was too strong. . . . If we had come sooner—perhaps; but now, it was too late."[94] They traveled in unheated railroad cars ("Quarante-huits"—forty men and eight horses) from Brest to St.-Nazaire, where, although neither officers nor men knew anything about handling cargo, they were put to work as stevedores and dam builders. Black stevedores, mostly southern, who by far outnumbered the entire 92nd Division, handled the greater percentage of the daily average of over 25,000 tons of cargo.[95]

St.-Nazaire was a racial war zone between black stevedores and white Marines pressed into stevedore duty. According to William Layton, St.-Nazaire Marines "began killing black soldiers one by one." The 15th New York retaliated, with mutual guerrilla warfare. "When a black was found dead, they killed a white soldier," he said in 1990, of events that were widely believed in but never officially verified. The answer, to the military high command ("since they like to fight"), was to send the 15th to the front. "But no American units would fight with us," Layton said. "Pershing wanted us to be stevedores, but we were fighting men." Now they spent all their time fighting white southerners over Frenchwomen in cafés. "We had Frenchwomen and Frenchwomen arguments with white soldiers waking up and going to sleep," he said. "The men were about ready to start a mutiny." After three months they complained to Hayward. "We were fighting men, and if we couldn't be put in battle, we preferred to go home."

Hayward wrote to General Pershing, asking for frontline service. Arthur Little suggested that Hayward request a personal interview: "You are without a doubt, the best fixer in the world; and if you can get to General Pershing, face to face, we'll get into the trenches within a week."[96]

Revolution

The Old Print Shop

Paul Revere's "Bloody Massacre": Crispus Attucks, the first popular martyr of the Revolution (who doesn't look black in this print), lies in the middle in a pool of blood. "Who set the example of guns?" John Hancock asked with a flourish. "Who taught the British soldier that he might be defeated? Who dared look into his eyes? I place, therefore, this Crispus Attucks in the foremost rank of the men who dared."

Photo courtesy New England Historic Genealogical Society

A State Department painting long thought to portray Barzillai Lew, the fifer-drummer of Bunker Hill. The portrait is now believed to be of his son, Barzillai Lew, Jr., also a musician-soldier. The Lew family have fought in every major American military engagement since the Revolution.

Yale University Art Gallery

Detail of John Trumbull's *The Battle of Bunker's Hill.* The black soldier is thought to be Peter Salem, a veteran of Concord Bridge and a hero of the day. Salem was responsible for the death of Major Pitcairn, the British commander who led the assault on Bunker Hill.

Anne S. K. Brown Military Collection, Brown University Library

A watercolor sketch of American soldiers at Yorktown by a French sublieutenant, Jean-Baptiste Antoine de Verger. The sketch includes, on the far left, a light infantryman of the 1st Rhode Island, the only all-black regiment in the otherwise integrated Continental Army.

Civil War

U.S. Military History Institute

Sergeant William Carney of the 54th Massachusetts, the first regiment of free northern blacks created after the Emancipation Proclamation. Carney, the first black winner of the newly created Medal of Honor, is shown here with the flag he rescued from the fallen Colonel Robert Gould Shaw at Fort Wagner in July 1863.

Moorland Spingarn Research Center, Howard University

Sergeant Major Lewis Douglass of the 54th Massachusetts, the eldest son of Frederick Douglass and, like his brother Charles, a survivor of Fort Wagner. "How I got out of that fight alive I cannot tell, but I am here," he wrote to his fiancée. "Remember if I die, I die in a good cause. I wish we had a hundred thousand colored troops. We would soon put an end to this war."

The Granger Collection

A Civil War recruiting poster for black soldiers.

Library of Congress

The 2nd U.S. Colored Artillery Battery, a rare black artillery unit, in action in Tennessee.

Library of Congress

A unit of the 107th U.S. Colored Infantry, which took part in the crucial capture of Fort Fisher in January 1865.

The United States Military Academy

Lieutenant Henry Ossian Flipper, class of 1877, the first black graduate of West Point. Through his courage and determination, Flipper won a measure of respect from his classmates and became a national celebrity. General Sherman himself led the ovation when Lt. Flipper received his diploma.

Collection of William Loren Katz

VOL. VII.–No. 163. APRIL 21, 1880. Price 10 Cents.

"What fools these Mortals be!" MIDSUMMER NIGHTS DREAM

Puck

PUBLISHED BY KEPPLER & SCHWARZMANN. NEW YORK OFFICE No. 21 – 23 WARREN ST.

RUNNING THE GAUNTLET.

SPECIAL COURSE FOR COLORED CADETS AT WEST POINT.

An April 1880 cover of *Puck*: a British view of West Point racism at the height of the Johnson Chestnut Whittaker controversy.

West Point cadet Charles Young, class of 1889, the third black graduate of the U.S. Military Academy. A hero of the Philippines and Mexico and a legendary Buffalo Soldier, Young hoped to lead black troops in World War I but was instead retired as a full colonel—the military couldn't countenance the thought of a black general.

Collection of William Loren Katz

The redoubtable Sergeant Horace W. Bivens of the 10th Cavalry, champion Army sharpshooter, who declined Buffalo Bill Cody's invitation to join his Wild West Show. Bivens is seen here with his famous messenger dog, Booth.

Collection of William Loren Katz

Exhausted but victorious members of the 10th Cavalry after the charge of San Juan Hill in July 1898.

Lieutenant Benjamin O. Davis of the U.S. Army cavalry in 1907. Davis became the Army's first black general and was the father of Benjamin O. Davis, Jr., who led America's first black fighter pilots in the Second World War.

Courtesy of Elnora Davis McLendon

Courtesy of Gordon Parks

Lieutenant Clem C. Parks of the 24th Infantry, a storied Indian-fighting regiment that also saw gallant action in the Spanish-American War. Sgt. Parks was the older brother of Gordon Parks and the uncle of Vietnam soldier David Parks.

Collection of William Loren Katz

Colonel Charles Young in Mexico during the Pancho Villa campaign in the spring of 1916, just before his forced retirement. Despite his marathon ride on his cavalry horse, Charlie, from Ohio to Washington, D.C., the War Department insisted he was "unfit" for further service.

WORLD WAR I

Lieutenant Errol Horne, my great-uncle, in the First World War.

U.S. Air Force

The intrepid American expatriate Eugene Bullard—boxer, acrobat, aviator, and spy. A hero of the French Foreign Legion, the French army, and the French air corps, Bullard was decorated in two world wars. At the time he received the French Legion of Honor in recognition of his heroism, he was back home in America, working as an elevator man.

Collection of William Miles

A poster featuring Lieutenant James Reese Europe of the 369th Regiment, whose famous band introduced American jazz to France.

Collection of William Miles

Lieutenant James Reese Europe and the 369th Regimental Band entertaining at a French hospital in September 1918.

Collection of William Miles

6 Division

Le 16 Mai 1918

Ordre N° 697

Le Général le Gallais Cdt la 16e D.I. cite à l'ordre de la Division les militaires du 369e R.I.U.S.

1. Johnson Henry, Nº Mle 1033-8, soldat à la Cie C:

"Se trouvant en sentinelle double de nuit et ayant été assailli par un groupe d'une douzaine d'allemands, en a mis un hors de combat à coups de fusil et blessé grièvement deux autres à coups de couteau. Bien qu'ayant reçu 3 blessures par balles de revolver et par grenades dès le début de l'action, a été au secours de son camarade blessé qui allait être emporté par l'ennemi et a continué la lutte jusqu'à la mise en fuite des allemands. A donné un magnifique exemple de courage et d'énergie."

2. Roberts Needham, Nº Mle 103369, soldat à la Cie C:

"Étant en sentinelle double de nuit, assailli et blessé grièvement à la jambe par un groupe d'allemands, a continué à lutter à coups de grenades, bien que tombé à terre, jusqu'à la mise en fuite de l'ennemi. Bon et brave soldat."

Le général a demandé que la citation du soldat Johnson soit transformée en citation à l'ordre de l'Armée.

P.A. Le Chef d'Etat Major, [signature] Le général Cdt la 16e D.I.

le Gallais

The official French citation for Sergeant Henry Johnson and Private Needham Roberts, whose heroic exploits during a German ambush made them, in May 1918, the first Americans to win the Croix de Guerre.

Corporal William Layton of the 369th Regiment, bugler and hero of the Meuse-Argonne offensive, wearing his Croix de Guerre.

Courtesy of William Layton

Courtesy of William Layton

Decorated members of the 369th Regiment returning home.

Photo by J. S. Cartier; courtesy of William Layton

Heywood K. Butt, William Layton, and Hamilton Fish, among the last surviving members of the 369th Regiment, photographed in 1987.

The Spanish Civil War

Courtesy of Vaughn Love

Captain Walter J. Love, World War I Army surgeon and the father of Vaughn Love.

Courtesy of Vaughn Love

Vaughn Love, veteran of the Abraham Lincoln Brigade, the integrated unit of American volunteers in the Spanish Civil War, also fought at Normandy Beach on D-Day.

Courtesy of Harry Fisher

Captain Oliver Law, black commander of integrated American troops of the Abraham Lincoln Brigade, overseeing an operation just before he was killed during the Brunete campaign in July 1937. The Spanish Civil War was the first war in which white Americans fought under black commanders.

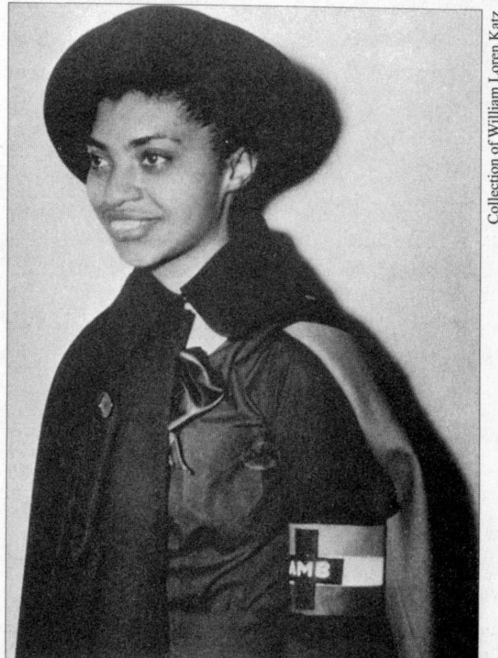

Collection of William Loren Katz

Harlem Hospital nurse Salaria Kee, the only black American woman volunteer in Spain. Kee was the hero of several well-known Spanish propaganda films, including *Heart of Spain*. She met her future husband, Patrick O'Reilly of the Irish Connolly Brigade, when he was her patient.

WORLD WAR II

Courtesy of William Miles

Dorie Miller, hero of Pearl Harbor, the first black winner of the Navy Cross and the first American hero of the Second World War.

U.S. Army photo

Members of the first class of Tuskegee Army Air Field graduates in 1942: George "Spanky" Roberts, Benjamin O. Davis, Jr., Charles H. DeBow, Lieutenant R. H. "Mother" Long (advanced flight instructor), Mac Ross, and Lemuel Custis.

Lena Horne at Tuskegee with members of the ground crew in 1943. She entertained all the black military units but was kicked out of the USO for refusing to sing at a camp where black GIs sat behind German POWs.

Library of Congress

Colonel Benjamin O. Davis, Jr., West Point class of 1936, commander of the Army Air Corps' first black fighter pilots, the 99th Pursuit Squadron and the 332nd Fighter Group—units known today as the Tuskegee Airmen—and Major Edward C. Gleed in Ramitelli, Italy, 1944.

U.S. Army photo

General Benjamin O. Davis, Sr., pins the Distinguished Flying Cross on his son, Colonel Benjamin O. Davis, Jr., in September 1944. At the start of World War II, there were only five black officers in the U.S. Armed Forces, three of whom were chaplains. The other two were the Benjamin O. Davises, father and son. After intense lobbying by black leaders, Davis senior became the first black general in the U.S. military.

Courtesy of Lee Archer

Captain Lee "Buddy" Archer in the cockpit of his plane *Ina, the Macon Belle,* named after his future wife. He grew up making model airplanes and knew the names of every World War I ace. In World War II, Archer became America's first black ace.

National Archives

Captain Lemuel R. Custis, of the first Tuskegee graduating class, and Captain Charles B. Hall, the first black pilot to shoot down a German plane.

Courtesy of Roscoe C. Brown, Jr.

Captain Roscoe C. Brown, Jr., in March 1945. He was one of the first Americans to shoot down a German jet. The War Department used film of Brown's jet encounter as combat training for new pilots.

Women's Army Corps

Charity Adams, the first black major in the Women's Army Corps, gets her gold oak leaves pinned on in September 1943. Major Adams was the highest-ranking and most important black woman in the U.S. military in World War II.

Major Charity Adams turns her command of Company 8 over to Lieutenant Alma Berry shortly before taking the 6888 to England.

Courtesy of Sallie Smith Jones

CLINIC RECEPTIONIST—
Cpl. Sallie Smith of Bluefiel
W. Va., of the Woman's Arm
Corps, is receptionist in the ey
ear, nose and throat clinic at th
Station Hospital at Camp For
rest, Tenn. (Photo by U. S. Arm
Signal Corps)

Courtesy of Sallie Smith Jones

Corporal (later Sergeant) Sallie Smith of the 6888th Central Postal Directory Battalion, in a newspaper clipping. She joined the WACs because it sounded exciting and because she hoped to be near her boyfriend in Italy. She went home to finish college on the GI Bill and became the first black woman to receive a master's degree from West Virginia University.

WORLD WAR II

Nineteen-year-old Carl Rowan, the son of a World War I veteran and the first black graduate of the Naval Reserves program, in 1944. Rowan was one of the first twenty black Navy officers in American history. Later he joined the administration of fellow Navy officer John F. Kennedy, who made him ambassador to Finland. He was a celebrated newspaper columnist until his death in 2000.

Courtesy of Vivien Murphy Rowan

Courtesy of William Pickens III

Lieutenant Harriet Pickens, one of the first two black WAVEs, was commissioned in December 1944. The daughter of William Pickens, a prominent NAACP official, she received not only a personal letter of congratulation from Eleanor Roosevelt but also endless GI fan mail. She was engaged throughout the war to my great-uncle John Burke Horne, a U.S. Army sergeant.

National Archives

"The Golden 13," the first black officers in the U.S. Navy. From left to right, top row: John W. Reagan, Jesse W. Arbor, Dalton L. Baugh, Frank C. Sublett. Second row: Graham E. Martin, Warrant Officer Charles B. Lear, Phillip S. Barnes, Reginald Goodwin. Third row: James E. Hare, Samuel E. Barnes, George Cooper, W. Sylvester White, Dennis D. Nelson II.

U.S.M.C. photo

Sergeant Gilbert H. "Hashmark" Johnson, one of the first black drill instructors of the Montford Point Marines, surveys a platoon of recruits in April 1943. He arrived at Montford Point in his naval uniform of Officer's Steward First Class and became one of the most feared and revered DIs in the corps.

U.S.M.C. photo

Members of the Marine 51st Defense Battalion pose with their gun, the *Lena Horne*, at Eniwetok in the South Pacific in 1945.

U.S.M.C. photo

Black Marines hit the beach at Iwo Jima on D-Day in February 1945.

Courtesy of Gene Doughty

Gene Doughty, squad leader and acting platoon sergeant of the Marine 8th Ammunition Company, celebrated his twenty-first birthday on Iwo Jima, "a hellish landscape," where he saw the flag raised over Mount Suribachi.

Courtesy of Bruce M. Wright

Infantry medic and poet Bruce M. Wright won his first Purple Heart in the third-wave assault on Omaha Beach in Normandy in June 1944. He won his second Purple Heart and a Bronze Star in Germany when he volunteered for the Battle of the Bulge integration experiment in December 1944. On his way home, he marched onto the troop ship wearing all his decorations. A white Navy officer sneered, "I didn't know niggers were fighting"—and Wright promptly walked off the ship and went AWOL in Paris. He returned to America in chains, but eventually became a New York State Supreme Court judge.

Courtesy of E. G. McConnell

Private E. G. McConnell, sixteen, a patriotic Boy Scout, volunteered with his parents' permission in 1942 and became a member of the 761st Tank Corps, the first "Black Panthers." He won a Purple Heart in the Battle of the Bulge.

McConnell left his integrated Queens, New York, Boy Scout troop for the segregated U.S. military.

Courtesy of E. G. McConnell

Courtesy of E. G. McConnell

E. G. McConnell's Sherman tank in November 1944. General Patton climbed on board and told McConnell to shoot everything he saw, even "old ladies."

Korea

U.S. Army photo

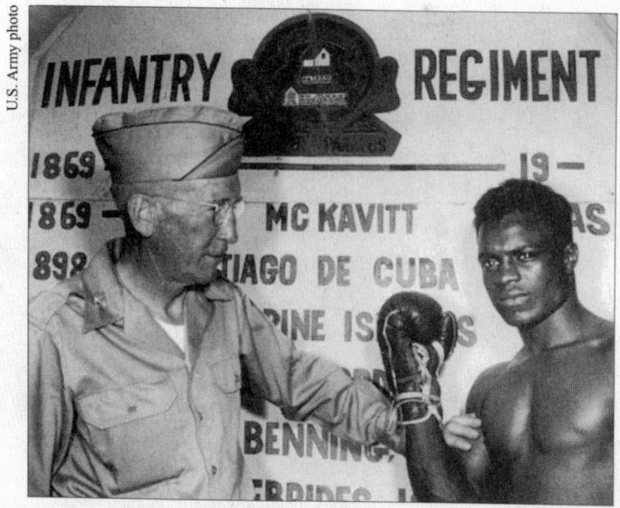

Colonel "Screaming Mike" Halloran and PFC Buffalo Simmons, a 24th Infantry boxer. The segregated Eighth Army in Japan paid more attention to black soldiers' athletic activity than to their military training.

U.S. Army photo

Troops of Company G, 24th Infantry, ready to move to the firing lines on July 18, 1950. Two days later they achieved the first victory of the Korean War, at Yechon.

U.S. Army photo

On August 6, 1950, Private First Class William Thompson became the first GI to win the Medal of Honor in Korea and the first black to win the medal since the Spanish-American War. His medal was awarded posthumously—and five months after the action, because his commander at first refused to submit the recommendation.

U.S. Army photo

Members of the mortar platoon of Company M, 24th Infantry, look happy in a picture taken just before the famed 24th was officially deactivated on October 1, 1951. It was the end of the segregated Army.

U.S. Army photo

Air power was decisive in the U.S. victory in the Korean War. Major Daniel "Chappie" James, a veteran of World War II, was one of the most illustrious of the new "fighter jocks" who switched from vintage Mustangs to jets in midwar. He became America's first black four-star general and went on to fly in Vietnam.

Tuskegee University Archives

"Black Man and Robin": Colonels Robin Olds and "Chappie" James celebrate the end of a successful mission at their base in Thailand.

U.S. Air Force Art Program

Colonel Fred V. Cherry's portrait hangs in the Pentagon. A pilot in the 35th Tactical Fighter Squadron, he was shot down over North Vietnam in October 1965 and became the first black American prisoner in the "Hanoi Hilton." He spent eight years as a POW. The image in the lower right corner shows Cherry in 1973 at Clark Air Force Base in the Philippines, having his first American cigarette since his capture.

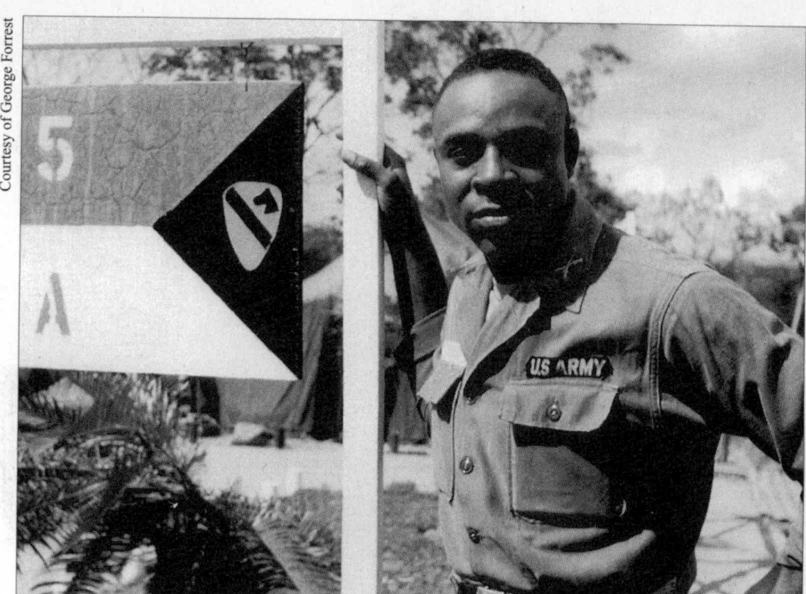

Courtesy of George Forrest

Lieutenant Colonel George Forrest, then a captain, whose famous football-trained six-hundred-yard run kept his unit from being overrun at Ia Drang in November 1965. Vietnam taught Forrest that there were many things he was willing to die for, but only a few he was willing to kill for.

Henri Huet, Wide World Photos

Black and white troops continued to share combat as well as comradeship after Ia Drang. These 1st Cavalry Division troops saw heavy fighting in 1966. While integration began with great wariness in Korea, in Vietnam black and white troops began to see each other as part of the same family.

Courtesy of George Brummell

George Brumell joined the Army in 1962 and served in Korea and Germany before being blinded by a land mine in Vietnam in June 1966. He made his blindness "a positive experience" and became National Field Service Director of the Blinded Veterans of America.

Courtesy of Gordon Parks

David Parks, a radio operator in E Company, 1st Battalion Mechanized Infantry (and the son of Gordon Parks), was wounded in Vietnam in 1967. He was disillusioned both by the war and by the antiwar movement. "I strongly felt that the men still fighting in Vietnam deserved our full support. . . . I had fought for my country and was in no way ashamed of it."

U.S. Army photo

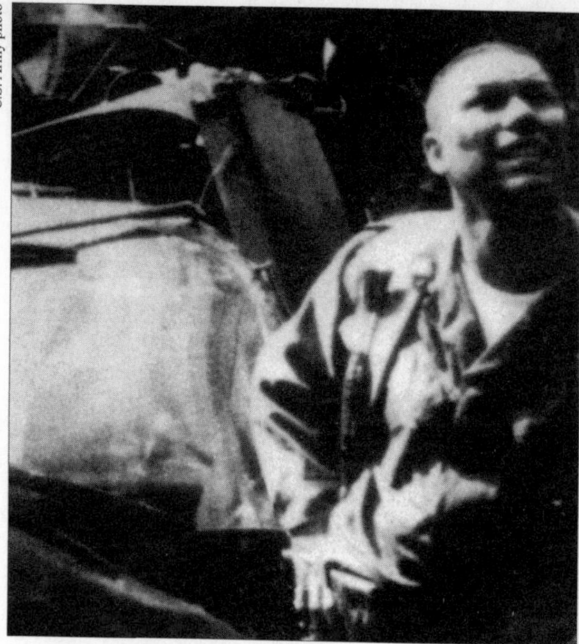

In November 1968, Major Colin Powell survived a helicopter crash in the jungle and helped pull others, including his commanding officer, from the wreck. By then Powell was beginning to realize that Army discipline and morale were deteriorating drastically. My Lai, that year, was a devastating consequence.

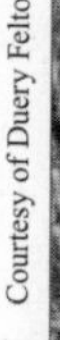

Courtesy of Duery Felton

Duery Felton saw some tough combat with the First Infantry Division near the Cambodian border in 1967. A U.S. tank nearly killed him—he heard a doctor say, "Specialist Felton, we're going to try to save your life." Felton later became curator of the Vietnam Veterans Memorial Collection.

Courtesy of Wayne Smith

Wayne Smith (*front, middle*), a combat medic in the Mekong Delta in 1969, later dedicated his life to helping veterans. He turned against the war, but reenlisted for a second tour of duty near the DMZ because he felt he was needed. "No one wanted to die alone in Vietnam," he said. "The men always said, 'Doc, stay with me.'"

DESERT STORM

U.S. government photo

General Norman Schwarzkopf's war room in Riyadh, Saudi Arabia, at the height of the Gulf War—(*left to right*) General Colin Powell, Secretary of Defense Richard Cheney, Schwarzkopf, and General Cal Waller.

Courtesy of Arthur Lamotte

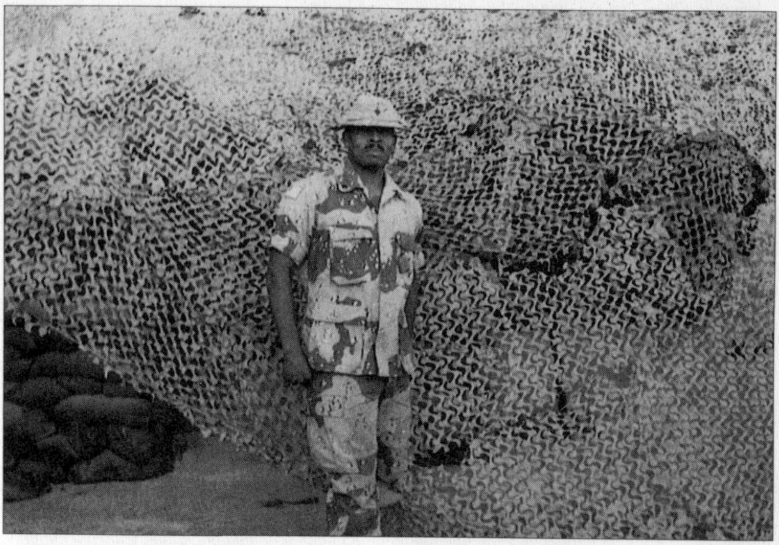

Staff Sergeant Arthur Lamotte of the 503rd Maintenance unit, a veteran of Panama's Operation "Just Cause," in support of frontline infantry at the start of the ground war in February 1991. The 503rd followed the infantry into Kuwait—for Lamotte, a place of oil fields in flames, burned-out vehicles, and unexploded mines.

U.S. government photo

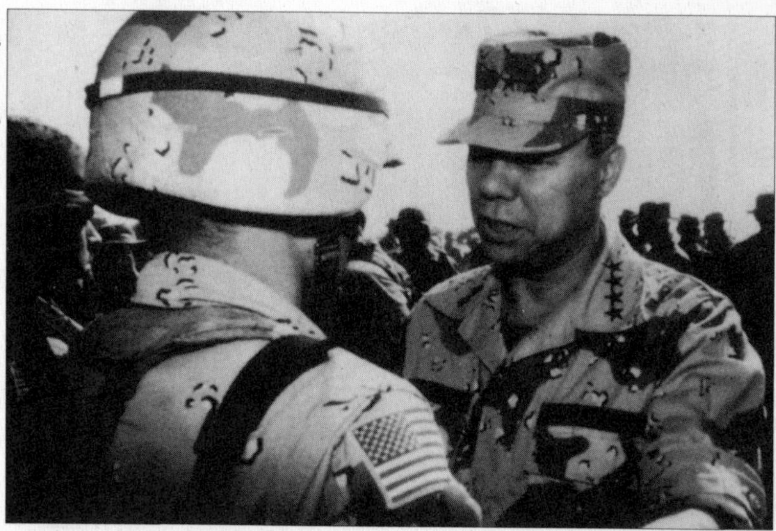

General Powell visiting troops in the field during Operation Desert Shield. "I know you want to know the answer to two questions," he told them. "What are we going to be doing here? And when are we going to go home?"

Courtesy of Flossie Satcher

Major Flossie Satcher faced her fears in the Gulf as a young lieutenant. She had joined the Army for travel and adventure, never expecting, as a mother of two, to find herself in the middle of a war. During her first months in Saudi Arabia she was "terribly scared," but she knew that her job was important and she was proud of her soldiers.

Courtesy of Ray and Kathleen Armstrong

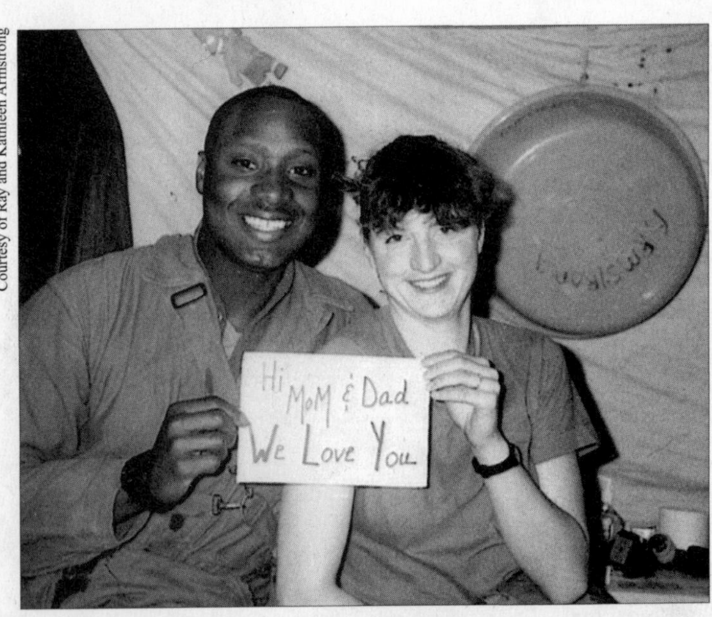

Staff Sergeants Ray and Kathleen Armstrong spent their honeymoon in Saudi Arabia. Their company served as the main support of the 2nd Cavalry Armored Regiment, supplying fuel to Bradley fighting vehicles, Abrams small tanks, and Apache, Cobra, and Black Hawk helicopters.

Epilogue

In January 1997, in a major military gesture of atonement for past racism, seven black winners of the Distinguished Service Cross in World War II received Medals of Honor. The Army provided photos of Lieutenant Vernon Baker, Staff Sergeant Edward Carter, Jr., Lieutenant John R. Fox, Major Charles L. Thomas, and Staff Sergeant Ruben Rivers. No pictures of Private First Class Willy F. James or Private George Watson were available. (All photos following courtesy of the U.S. Army)

Staff Sergeant Edward Carter, Jr.

Lieutenant John R. Fox

Major Charles J. Thomas

Staff Sergeant Ruben Rivers

Lieutenant Vernon Baker

Vernon Baker was the only living Medal of Honor recipient. "The only thing that I can say to those who are not here with me," he said, "is thank you, fellas, well done. And I will always remember you."

Little urged Hayward to impress Pershing with the regiment's medical record. Thanks to Little's "crankiness" on the subject, there had been no new case of venereal disease in three months. With soaring VD rates, the 15th's hygiene record had a propaganda purpose. The popular actor E. H. Sothern wrote to the *New York Herald:* "It is good to see the *Herald* and the *Telegram* declaring that sinister statements that our colored troops are abused by their officers is false. . . . I had the pleasure of being the guest of the Colonel and officers of the Old Fifteenth New York Infantry in France. . . . Colonel Hayward talked with great enthusiasm of his men and of certain prizes he had established for cleanliness and for perfection in equipment and behavior. He was especially proud of his regiment's record for health and gave his soldiers great credit for their discipline. His officers stood by and echoed his enthusiasm. We talked with the men who were equally proud of their colonel and his aides. There was no question of the genuine affection and regard these colored soldiers had for their officers."[97]

"Pershing was a pain in the neck," Layton remembered. "It made you sick. They didn't want black troops with whites. But Colonel Hayward made a little speech—and talked with a French general. And General Foch said, 'We'll take 'em, we need 'em.' So, he took them up to the frontline trenches with the Hundred and Sixty-first Infantry, French, and they were treated like they were gold. There was no bigotry or prejudice." The 369th had been sent to relieve the front lines of General Henri Gouraud's French Fourth Army at Châlons. The first regiment in U.S. history to serve as an integral part of a foreign army turned in their American military equipment and were trained with French rifles and machine guns. The French relied far more on machine guns, automatics, and grenades than on their inaccurate rifles, which, they admitted, were good only for holding bayonets, so effective in hand-to-hand combat. The regiment was also given French gas masks. ("The Germans' were better," Layton recalled; "when we caught a dead German, we took their gas mask off for ourselves.")

"The most wonderful thing in the world has happened to this regiment," Hayward wrote to a friend on March 18.

> We are now a combat unit—one of the regiments of a French Division in the French Army, assigned to a sector of trenches. . . . I loaded the wandering, saluting, laughing 15th N.Y., the only unit ever in France with a state name, on about a million of these little French cars, still carrying our State colors, and under sealed orders for the second half of the journey. . . . We went on and on for two days; passed the phony destination which had been announced as

> our destination, through great supply depots; passed acres and acres of piled up munitions; passed wonderfully camouflaged armored trains of big guns—the "long Toms" pointing up into the air; passed aviation centres where the aeroplanes looked like great flocks of birds; through miles of barbed wire entanglements; and finally stopped at a place I had never heard of . . . when I stepped off the train, the first thing I heard was the "boom-boom" of the big guns a few miles away. A French Staff Officer came up and asked me if I was the "Trois cent soixante-neuvième Régiment d'Infanterie, Américain"; and I allowed as I was . . . this was the nature of the passing of the old 15th New York.[98]

Hayward added: "There are no American troops anywhere near us, that I can find out, and we are 'les enfants perdus,' and glad of it. Our great American general simply put the black orphan in a basket, set it on the doorstep of the French, pulled the bell, and went away. I said this to a French colonel . . . and he said 'Weelcome leetle black babbie.' The French are wonderful—wonderful—wonderful."

JIM EUROPE AND HIS BAND: THE GOODWILL TOUR

"We were called the Fifteenth New York when we got on the boat in New Jersey; when we got off in France we were the Three Hundred Sixty-ninth Regiment," Layton said. The 369th was in the front lines for about a hundred days, with very little to eat. "The French were supposed to feed them, but they advanced too fast for the kitchen to keep up with them," Layton recalled. "They had very little food and water, but plenty of wine." Layton was not sent immediately to the front because, as a band member, he was about to travel more than two thousand miles to entertain Allied troops and French civilians. "Jim Europe and His Band! Some of those white folks would go to pieces," Layton recalled.

By virtue of age, Arthur Little was appointed band "godfather" for the goodwill tour. The commanding general of the region gave a speech. "He explained that where we were going, no American soldiers had as yet been; that, according to the impression left by us . . . so would rest the reputations of American soldiers in general. . . . He begged the men not to be the cause of the establishment, in the minds of French people, of a color line. He told the men that they were upon a mission of great importance; that they were not merely musicians and soldiers of the American Army but that they were representatives of the American nation."[99]

"All through France the same thing happened," Lieutenant Noble Sissle told a correspondent from the *St. Louis Post-Dispatch.* No one, from civilians to soldiers, could listen to Europe's band without wanting to dance. Even German prisoners of war "dropped their work to listen and pat their feet to the stirring American tunes."[100] Europe's band delighted the crowd with the "wah-wah" of their "talking trumpets" and mystified other musicians. Suspicious members of the French Garde Républicaine band actually examined the horns for hidden valves or chambers.

Back home, the Ziegfeld star Eddie Cantor sang "When Uncle Joe Steps Into France": "When they play the Memphis blues / They will use a lot of shoes / And fill them full of Darky gin / They'll rag their way right to Berlin." Other home-front titles were "When the Boys from Dixie Eat the Melon on the Rhine" and "Nigger War Bride Blues." Noble Sissle wrote the song that all the American soldiers sang: "To Hell with Germany."

"Lieutenant Europe was a fine fellow, quiet, with big eyes," Layton remembered. "But if someone hit a wrong note, he would find it in a few seconds and call you down. 'Big Jim' always said, 'I know there's a war on—but this band is going to play in Paris.' " In February 1918, Europe wrote to Eubie Blake: "Well, at present Eubie, I am a soldier in every sense of the word and must ONLY TAKE orders and be able to stand all sorts of hardships and make untold sacrifices. At the moment I am unable to do anything. My hands are tied and tied fast but if the war does not end me first sure as God made man I will be on top and so far on top that it will be impossible to pull me down." Europe had just received a glimpse of mortality. "Fitz was kind enough to send me the newspaper clipping of my good friend Vernon Castle. Can you imagine my grief. My one real and true friend gone." Captain Vernon Castle had been killed serving with the Canadian Air Corps.[101]

On Washington's Birthday, 1918, the band performed at the Nantes Opera House. The occasion proved to be of historic significance. All those present were French, with the exception of the band and the American general and his staff. "Most of the audience seated in the reserved sections were in evening dress," wrote Arthur Little.

> The galleries were crowded, and all standing room was occupied. I doubt if any first night or special performance at the Metropolitan Opera House in New York had ever, relatively, a more brilliant audience. . . . The French people knew no color line. All they seemed to want to know, that night, was that a great national holiday of their ally was being celebrated—and that made the celebration one of their own. The spirit of emotional enthusiasm had got into the blood of our men; and they played as they had never played before.[102]

"The program started with a French march, followed by favorite overtures and vocal selections, all of which were heartily applauded," reported the *St. Louis Post-Dispatch.*

> The second part of the program opened with "The Stars and Stripes Forever," the great Sousa march, and before the last note of the martial ending had been finished the house was ringing with applause. Next followed an arrangement of "plantation melodies" and then came the fireworks, "The Memphis Blues." Lieut. Europe, before raising his baton twitched his shoulders apparently to be sure that his tight-fitting military coat would stand the strain . . . The baton came down with a swoop that brought forth a soul-rousing crash. . . . Cornet and clarinet players began to manipulate notes in that typical rhythm (that rhythm which no artist has ever been able to put down on paper), as the drummers struck their stride their shoulders began shaking in time to their syncopated raps.

At this point, the correspondent continued, "the whole audience began to sway." Europe turned to the trombone players, "who sat impatiently waiting for their cue to have a 'jazz spasm' and they drew their slides out to the extremity and jerked them back with that characteristic crack." The audience, including the American general, erupted. "When the band had finished and the people were roaring with laughter, their faces wreathed in smiles, I was forced to say that this is just what France needs at this critical moment."[103]

In March, in Aix-les-Bains, the audience "rose en masse" when the announcement came that the band had been ordered to rejoin their regiment at the front. "Men and boys yelled and whistled," Arthur Little wrote. "Women cried. . . . Flags, hanging from the balcony . . . were torn loose and waved." The band was carried, rather than marched, to the troop train.[104]

THE FRONT: HENRY JOHNSON AND NEEDHAM ROBERTS AT THE MARNE

Ham Fish's fluent French had won him the friendship of the one-armed General Gouraud, the youngest general in the French army, and in mid-March, Jim Europe, Arthur Little, and the band joined Fish's company at the front: the Marne. "For the first time we saw a country devastated by modern warfare—wrecks of buildings, miles upon miles of meadow land torn and horribly disfigured by shell burst or by pick and shovel, the sole crop awaiting harvest, barbed wire entanglements," wrote Little. There were small wooden crosses "marking the graves of patriots of the supreme sacrifice—thousands and tens of thousands—some carrying a wreath of the tricolor of France, some bearing marks identifying the dead of Germany."[105]

Reaching the front in time for the Germans' April offensive, the 369th suffered its first artillery casualties on the five-mile hike from Châlons to the trenches. "Unfortunately, one of my men was wounded," Ham Fish wrote. "As I stood there watching him being placed on the stretcher, a German shell landed right on top of the stretcher, killing the wounded soldier and three of the stretcher bearers." Fish had discovered the "true horrors of war." Soon after, he saw six French soldiers killed when a German shell exploded near a poilu who was wearing a grenade belt. "The frontline position was actually an area with very deep trenches carved into the earth, surrounded and protected by numerous rows of barbed wire," Fish wrote. Outside of muddy and often gore-filled trenches, the men slept and ate in a maze of fifty-foot-long dugouts. Fish stressed the fact that (contrary to the spirit of Pershing's coming directive) he dined with Jim Europe "every evening."[106]

Europe, gassed on patrol duty, wrote his own wartime hit, "On Patrol in No Man's Land":

There's a minnenwurfer coming—Look out—(Bang)
Hear that roar, there's one more.
Stand fast, there's a very light.
Don't gasp or they'll find you all right.
Don't start to bombing with those hand grenades
There's a machine gun, holy spades!
Alert, gas, put on your mask. Adjust it correctly and hurry up fast.
Drop! there's a rocket for the Boche barrage.
Down, hug the ground, close as you can, don't stand.
Creep and crawl, follow me, that's all.
What do you hear? Nothing near, all is clear, don't fear.
That's the life of stroll when you take a patrol
Out in No Man's Land. Ain't it grand?
Out in No Man's Land.[107]

Europe's song is excellent combat reporting. But most black Americans called the Germans Bushes instead of Boches.

"When troops go into the front line to relieve other troops, there are many things that must be learned so that the new troops may be able to defend the new position, if attacked a few minutes after taking charge," wrote Sergeant Clinton Peterson, a 369th member who wrote a series of articles in 1919 for New York's white *Putnam County Courier.* Since none of the 369th's enlisted men spoke French, "we simply went and stood post beside them watching everything they did." All around were rotting corpses. "I shall never forget those fields covered with their silent motionless figures clad in the khaki of the United States, the horizon blue of France and the field gray of the Germans. Many of those bodies lay, for ten days in the hot sun before the pioneers, sappers and bombers, etc., came along to bury them, and to eat and sleep in such a place was not at all pleasant."

By May, the German onslaught appeared unstoppable. In some of the heaviest fighting of the war, the 369th was defending 20 percent of all territory held by American troops in the Champagne-Marne. That month, Henry Johnson, a former New York Central "Red-cap" porter from Albany, was promoted to sergeant. He was about to become the first American enlisted man to win the Croix de Guerre.

In the dark early morning of May 14, Sergeant Johnson and Private Needham Roberts were on outpost guard duty near an American-held bridge on the Aisne River when they heard the sound of wire clippers in the darkness. Shouting "Corporal of the Guard!" Johnson and Roberts threw an illuminating rocket—and were immediately hit by a volley of enemy grenades. It was a raiding party of some twenty Germans. Badly hurt and unable to rise, Roberts propped himself against the door of the dugout and began throwing grenades out into the darkness. Johnson, also wounded, did likewise. Then, armed only with a rifle and a bolo knife, Johnson confronted the enemy one by one as they entered the narrow enclosure, firing his first three shots at the first German who appeared. With no time to reload, Johnson swung his rifle butt at the next. "The German went down crying, in perfectly good Bowery English, 'The little black so and so has got me!' " To which (from Little's account of Johnson's report) Johnson replied, "Yas, an' dis little black so and so'll git yer 'gin—ef yer git up!"[108]

Meanwhile, Roberts was almost taken prisoner. But Johnson, leaping like "a wild cat" at the back of Roberts's helmetless captor, buried his bolo knife in the German's scalp. (A bolo knife, wrote Little, weighs "no less" than three pounds, with a blade of at least eight or nine inches.) The downed Bowery German then shot Johnson in the leg with his Lüger automatic. Johnson was hit, but still managed to disembowel his attacker with his knife. His hand-to-hand-combat skills frightened the Germans into retreat. "The enemy patrol was in a panic," Little wrote. Unbeknownst to Johnson and Roberts, their grenades had killed several Germans—the enemy's retreat could be followed later by "pools of blood." When the 369th relief party arrived, Johnson fainted. He was credited with killing at least four Germans and wounding some twenty-two.

Little showed the report on Johnson to visiting correspondents. "As they read, the only sounds in that little room were strange grunts and exhalations." The renowned war correspondent Irvin Cobb wondered how much training "that chap Henry Johnson" had before he "licked those Germans." Little replied that it was no more than "three weeks in theory." Cobb's story "The Battle of Henry Johnson" appeared a few days later on the front page of *The New York World.* By the next morning the Associated Press had spread the story of Henry Johnson all over America. Jim Europe was no longer the only hero of the 369th. "Our colored volunteers from Harlem had become, in a day, one of the most famous fighting regiments of the World War," Little wrote.[109] The Germans named them Hell Fighters.

Johnson and Roberts were both awarded the Croix de Guerre—Johnson's, a higher order, with gold leaf. Both men were cited by Pershing and by General Ferdinand Foch, of France, but they won no military recognition or honors from the United States.

FISH AND LAYTON AT BELLEAU WOOD, THE MEUSE-ARGONNE, AND METZ

Despite the heroism of soldiers like Johnson and Roberts, at the end of May the Germans were at Château-Thierry, less than fifty miles from Paris, and predicting imminent victory. By early June, as Americans began pouring into the lines, the German offensive would be stalled—but now the French army was demoralized and its men were deserting in droves. In early June, the 369th joined with two American divisions and twenty-five French divisions for the French counterattack at Belleau Wood, a costly Allied victory. Meeting heavy resistance on the front lines, a French general ordered the regiment to retire, but Hayward refused, pretending he did not understand. "My men never retire," he said. "They go forward or they die!" Prussians at Belleau Wood nicknamed the 369th the Black Watch. "We can't hold up against these men," a Prussian officer is said to have remarked. "They are devils! They smile while they kill and they won't be taken alive."[110]

In July, the 369th bore the brunt of the German offensive at Minaucourt. Fish wrote a "last letter" to his father: "My company will be in the first position to resist the tremendous concentration against us and I do not believe there is any chance of any of us surviving the first push. I am proud to be trusted with such a post of honor and have the greatest confidence in my own men to do their duty to the end."[111] This victory was less costly than expected—three men of Fish's company were killed, six were wounded, four others were poison gas casualties, and Fish's horse was killed. General Gouraud called the battle a "beautiful day" for France. ("We had the Americans as neighbors . . . they're first rate troops, fighting with intense *individual* passion," wrote the Jesuit priest Teilhard de Chardin, a French stretcher bearer.[112]) That month, Gouraud's troops captured 127 German soldiers and a German officer with plans of the next major attack—an artillery bombardment set for midnight on July 14–15, when it was assumed that the French would be too drunk to respond after celebrating Bastille Day. But moments before the scheduled German bombardment, Allied artillery began its own: the biggest in military history, with more than 2,500 French and American guns. The Allied counteroffensive was successful. By August, the Allies were winning.

In August (the same month as Pershing's racist directive), the AEF adopted a policy of having either all-black or all-white officers for black troops. Five black officers of the 369th, including Jim Europe, were transferred to the 92nd Division, although Europe later returned to the 369th as bandmaster. "Our colored officers were in the July fighting and did good work," wrote Hayward, "and I felt then and feel now that if colored officers are available and capable, they, and not white officers, should command colored troops. There is splendid material there. I sent away forty-two sergeants in France who were commissioned officers in other units. I would have sent others, but they declared they'd rather be sergeants in the Fifteenth than lieutenants or captains in other regiments."[113]

"When the battle had ended thirty percent of my regiment had suffered casualties," wrote Fish of the great Meuse-Argonne offensive of September 26. It was the turning point of the war, and the heaviest fighting for the 369th. All told, the regiment lost about eleven hundred men. Part of Fish's company was advancing rapidly against the enemy. Information was received that the Germans, planning to attack on both flanks, were leading them into a trap. Layton was ordered to take a message to Fish, warning him to stop and hold whatever ground was already taken. Layton took off with the message just as the Germans were beginning to lay down an artillery barrage. Scrambling along the banks of the Meuse, he was blown off a hill and gassed, but crawled the rest of the way to deliver the message. Taken to the hospital in St.-Nazaire with gas poisoning and shrapnel in his thumb, Layton heard the doctor say, "This man is too sick, send him to Brest." Fish won a Silver Star, and William Layton—along with the entire regiment—won the Croix de Guerre.[114]

The next thing Layton remembered was waking up in a hospital bed and being kissed by a nurse: "Something hit me on the cheek," Layton said. He "got around good" with the nurse, who called him Bébé. But he "woke up and went to sleep" with arguments with white soldiers. He pondered writing to the government about his corporal's rank and private's pay. "They took the shrapnel out of my thumb, bandaged it up, and put us on the road walking—they wouldn't let us lay around, they just kept us going all the time because of the gas," he said. "And when we went to recuperate, they sent us down to southern France. Vichy was like Florida here, a beautiful place. I had two or three girlfriends—and I wanted to stay in France because the scenery was so pretty."

Recovered, Layton rejoined his company for its last engagement, the liberation of Metz. The 369th became the first Allied troops to reach the Rhine. "You have collected the water of the Rhine in your hand and you have placed the 'Black Watch' along the river," wrote the French division commander to Hayward. "It is ours from now on, but no Frenchman ignores that it is to the Americans that we owe this conquest."[115]

Boyishly handsome, Layton sat for his photograph in uniform, wearing a battle ribbon and the Croix de Guerre. He came home on the passenger ship S.S. *France* in February 1919 to Camp Upton, New Jersey, where his Croix de Guerre was stolen from under his pillow when he went for a meal. After his discharge, he became a professional painter and interior decorator. He developed migrainelike headaches and "brown spots" on his chest and neck, but the doctor at the Veterans Administration clinic told him that he would "outgrow" the problems. He had twelve children, five of whom would serve in the military, including a World War II member of the Women's Army Corps. He was active in the American Legion, the Veterans of Foreign Wars, and the New Jersey chapter of the 369th Regiment Association.

Layton got his Croix de Guerre back in 1988, when a friend brought the loss to the attention of New Jersey congressman Peter Rodino, who petitioned the French government for a replacement. The medal arrived with an honor guard and a French military attaché. The presentation was made aboard a French carrier in New York harbor, sent to the U.S. to celebrate the seventieth anniversary of the November 11, 1918, armistice—and to thank the 369th. In an impressive color guard ceremony, with flags of both countries, Colonel Roger Lestac, president of the French Officers

Association, presented Layton with the new Croix de Guerre on behalf of the government of France. Layton was also awarded the Pour le Mérite. The medals were presented before representatives of the American Legion and the Veterans of Foreign Wars, and survivors of the 369th: Haywood Butt, James Jones, and the Honorable Hamilton Fish. The only recognition Layton received from America was a retroactive Purple Heart, awarded in 1936.

Chester Heywood and the 371st Infantry

The 371st Infantry of black South Carolina draftees followed the 369th to France in April 1918. They were the first draft regiment to sail from America, and the first draftees in the trenches. "Since the war many humorous stories have been told about colored soldiers," wrote Captain Chester D. Heywood, a white southerner and officer of the 371st. "Some of these are true, but the great majority picture Rastus as always 'hot footin' it' to the rear whenever a gun went off, or describe him as petrified with fright during all of his waking hours. Stories of their bravery and devotion to duty are rarely, if ever, told." Heywood hoped, in his book *Negro Combat Troops in the World War,* published in 1928, to give "a picture of colored combat troops who lived up to the best traditions of American soldiers."[116]

"The first intimation we had that the men had really arrived was the sound of distant yelling, catcalling, and laughter as our mob of embryo warriors was led through the crowds of convulsed white troops," he wrote.

> It was a sight never to be forgotten. They came with suit cases and sacks; with bundles and bandanna handkerchiefs full of food, clothing and knick-knacks. Many were barefoot. Some came with guitars and banjos hanging from their backs by strings and ropes. The halt, the lame, and the blind were there actually. Every colored derelict in certain districts must have been picked up when the draft order was received.

Heywood described the eventual metamorphosis: "The men were lighthearted and practically always in good spirits and were accustomed to taking orders and doing what they were told. Discipline was easily attained and necessarily strict, but just. Clean clothes, well-cooked food in quantity, systematic exercises and drill, regular hours, plus strict but intelligent and helpful discipline, soon worked wonders."[117]

War morale efforts placed great emphasis on the singing of patriotic songs. *Keep 'Em Singing and Nothing Can Lick 'Em* was an Army-produced film. The 371st rehearsed new Army songs twice a week—"Smiles," "There's a Long, Long, Trail A-Winding," and "Pack Up Your Troubles in Your Old Kit Bag," for instance. But spirituals—"Bye and Bye" and "Swing Low, Sweet Chariot"—were special. "I never expect again to hear such wonderful harmony," Heywood wrote. His men entertained ex-President Taft, visiting camp to lecture on "Why We Fight." But the 371st also became soldiers: "The marching and the close-order drill were excellent; the manual of arms unbelievably perfect. The men took the greatest pride in their uniforms and their equipment. Their salutes were snappy; their carriage soldierly; and we were all proud, not only of our individual companies, but of the regiment as a whole."[118]

The War Department decision, early in 1918, that the various provisional black infantry regiments, including the 371st, be assigned to depot brigades (labor) came as a "severe shock." Colonel Perry L. Miles, camp commander, sent a long telegram to the chief of staff, citing the regiment's rapid advancement and esprit de corps, and the great desirability of retaining it as a combat unit. The telegram was effective. The 371st was assigned to the 186th Infantry Brigade (Colored) of the 93rd Division—on the priority list for overseas duty. "Everybody talked overseas, A.E.F., France, the Boche," Heywood wrote, "and swanked about the camp and town as if they had already seen months of service in the trenches."[119]

In April, the regiment was off to France. The *Columbia Record* of South Carolina reported:

> The news comes from Mississippi that German spies have been at work there to disturb the Negroes. We do not know if any of them have been at work in this State, but if they have, their answer is to be found in the splendid showing of the 371st Infantry upon the streets of Columbia one day recently when this Regiment was marching through the city to receive a set of regimental colors presented by the people of that race. The Negroes of South Carolina are standing by. They are loyal, they are earnest, they are zealous. Sometimes they shame us in their exhibition of their understanding of the causes of this war and their determination to support the Government throughout. There are in that command officers from the best white families of South Carolina. They have a genuine affection for the men under their command and in their care. . . . This big, well-trained regiment is ready to go. Whenever the time

> comes, we wish the black boys of the 371st to know that the people of South Carolina appreciate the fact that they behaved beautifully while in the cantonment here, and we have yet to hear of the first unfavorable criticism of the conduct of Negro soldiers in Columbia.[120]

The 371st went directly from the troop train at Newport News to the *President Grant,* en route to Brest.

Like all black Americans, the 371st found France to be a different world. "The colored men were given different treatment from what they had been accustomed to receive from white people at home," wrote a white officer of the 371st.

> The French people could not grasp the idea of social discrimination on account of color. They said the colored men were soldiers, wearing the American uniform, and fighting in the common cause. . . . They received the men in their churches, and homes and places of entertainment. The men accepted this, and it did not appear strange to them. They seemed to understand that the customs over there were different from ours in the South, and let it go at that. I think these colored men, having made good soldiers, will now be more than anxious to make as good civilians, and that they will do so.[121]

In the spring of 1918, a group of semi-skeptical American correspondents went in pursuit of rumored black combat troops. "Word had come, no matter how, that Negro troops of ours were in the line," wrote Irvin Cobb. Cobb's "draft regiment from somewhere down South and another regiment from one of the Eastern States" were South Carolina's 371st and New York's 369th (where Cobb would discover the "Battle of Henry Johnson"). The push was on. Yanks were indeed coming, but journalists doubted that "colored troops were as yet facing the enemy across the barbed wire boundaries." They had seen black labor battalions "unloading ships and putting up warehouses and building depots and felling trees in the forests of France," but they had never seen black fighting men.

The reporters' quest for the 371st ended after a seven-hour "high-powered" car drive on the edge of the village of Rembercourt. "Right here from somewhere in the impending clutter of nondescript ruination we heard many voices singing all together. The song was a strange enough song for these surroundings. Once before in my life and only once have I heard it . . . on an island off the coast of Georgia. I don't think it ever had a name and the author of it had somehow got the Crucifixion and the Discovery of America confused in his mind." ("In Fo'teen Hunnerd an' Ninety-two / My Lawd begin his work to do! / In Fo'teen Hunnerd an' Ninety-three / Dey nailed my Saviour on de gallows tree.")[122]

The Night Raid of Avocourt

Fighting in the front lines from April to the Armistice, the 371st was attached to the famous 157th "Red Hand" Division of the French army. "From the moment of our arrival, the war became a reality," wrote Heywood. "The ruined houses and the distant but ominous booming of the guns on the Verdun battle front, gave a real meaning to our training now and brought the war home in a vivid way." The 371st was armed, equipped, and organized as a French infantry regiment. They started using French rations (with extra sugar instead of wine) in early May. Pay was still American—"Yanks" and Canadians were the highest paid Allies, who also included Chinese, Senegalese, and Arabs.

General Pershing's review, in the second week of May, was the 371st's last contact with the American high command—or any other American forces other than the black 372nd Infantry Regiment, also incorporated into a French division. Taking over the "ghost-filled" trenches of Verdun, the 371st went to the front in June in the Avocourt sector, as part of the French 157th Division. "At the moment when two American colored regiments join us I am bowing to their colors and I am wishing the best welcome to our new companions in arms," was the French general Goybet's translated message. French passwords were a problem, however. "Few of the officers, I think, could have pronounced the names accurately enough to satisfy any one demanding them and I am sure that our men were hopelessly at sea in their use," wrote Heywood. "I cannot remember that I was ever asked for a password by any of our men."[123]

In August, Heywood and some of the 371st participated in a carefully planned night raid at Avocourt. "This was our first experience in a French *coup de main* and we were out to learn all that we could. The group for this particular 'show' were all volunteers." The French volunteers consisted of one captain, two lieutenants, four sergeants, six corporals, and sixty enlisted men. The American volunteers were a white lieutenant and two black noncommissioned officers from the 371st, and one black lieutenant and two black noncommissioned officers from the 372nd. The commissioned officers, presumably including the black lieutenant, all messed together. "Our French chef was especially detailed from the division and we ate the best and drank the best that could be procured." ("If we had to be 'bumped off' later they were going to give us a good time while we lived," Heywood wrote.)[124]

The raid, in which German flares and machine-gun crossfire forced the men into shell holes, was "an utter failure." "We crawl from our dugout into the pitch black night," Heywood wrote; "there is silence now except for the angry growl of the German guns and the whine and crash of shells as they feel about the lines hoping to get some of us as we go out. We pay no attention to them. They seem as nothing compared to the tumult that still rings in our ears and throbs in our heads. Stumbling through the communicating trenches we are at last on the road . . . exhausted physically and nervously discouraged . . . knowing that all our work and planning has gone for naught, and wondering why; hoping for reports of the missing, the wounded and the dead." By Avocourt, French soldiers were said to be "sick of the war." They hoped—and by now expected—that the Americans would "finish it" in the fall.[125]

The Champagne Offensive

In September 1918, the 371st prepared to join the Champagne offensive, the "biggest show of all." "The roads are jammed with steady streams of traffic," wrote Heywood, "trucks by the hundreds, batteries of 75's, 155 Howitzers, 155 longs, machine-gun carts, cavalry, tanks, ammunition carts, ration carts, ambulances, officers' cars and lines of heavily laden infantry in columns of twos stumbling along in the ditches as they are pushed off the roads by the heavier traffic." The battle erupted on September 25, in the biggest artillery bombardment in the history of the world. "On the stroke of eleven that night, the whole front for miles seemed to explode in a crashing roar that words cannot describe," Heywood wrote. "It was wondrous—it was insanity and the fever of it gripped us all," wrote the French interpreter-instructor André Simonet.[126]

On September 26 and 27, the 371st were poised to attack Hill 188, a former German stronghold, when word came that the enemy wanted to surrender. A German NCO had come into camp, stating that he had thirty-five men who no longer wished "to risk their lives" for a "lost cause." On September 28, as the 371st moved toward the hill, confident of a fairly easy victory, Germans started climbing onto their trench parapets, their arms held up in surrender. The 371st advanced without firing. Suddenly, a whistle was blown and the Germans jumped back into their trenches and began shooting. The 371st had fallen for the "*Kamerad*" trick. The advancing Americans were virtually annihilated. But Corporal

Freddie Stowers and his squad continued on in the unrelenting fire to destroy the machine-gun emplacement that had inflicted at least 40 percent of his company's casualties. He was on his way, mortally wounded, toward another machine-gun position when he died. Thanks to Corporal Stowers, the new American attack succeeded: this time the Germans ran for real. "The final phase of this assault was extremely gruesome as our men could not be restrained from wreaking their vengeance upon the enemy who had so shamefully entrapped their comrades earlier that morning," wrote Heywood.[127] Corporal Freddie Stowers would be recommended, posthumously, for a Medal of Honor. He received it seventy-three years later, on April 24, 1991, from President George Bush.

They took Hill 188 in three days of battle, but some two-fifths of the regiment's enlisted men were killed. Colonel Perry L. Miles was ruefully reminded of Barry Pain's poem "The Army of the Dead":

> These men of ours, whom I saw in death on Hill 188, these black men who dignified death, who brought honor to their race and glory to our colors were not the misty shapes of a mere idea as were Pain's "Army of the Dead," but were the soldiers who helped to elevate our pride—the embattled men who rose from the cotton fields as symbolized on our Memorial Medal. Nevertheless, those lines of the poet accurately describe the serenity in death of those men of ours as I saw there. This episode will always remain as one of the deepest impressions made on me by war or life.[128]

The 371st lost more than half their men in the three-day battle. Three officers of the 371st won the Legion of Honor; thirty-four officers and eighty-nine enlisted men won the Croix de Guerre; and fourteen officers and twelve men won the American Distinguished Service Cross. A memorial obelisk, bearing the names of the fallen on four sides, was erected on the Champagne battlefield near Bussy Farm, by members of the 371st. It was purposely destroyed by Germans in World War II, because it reminded them of an ignoble defeat.

In October, General Goybet commended both the 371st and the 372nd: "Your troops have been admirable in their attack. You must be proud of your officers and men, and I consider it an honor to have had them under my command. . . . During these hard days, the division was at all times in advance of all other divisions of the Army Corps. I am sending you all my thanks. . . . I call on your wounded. Their morale is higher than my praise."[129]

Two Colored Women with the American Expeditionary Forces

Lieutenant P. E. Deckard, commander of the battalion's medical detachment, described the Champagne offensive as the "hardest task of the war." He and the second battalion surgeon worked until they "fell asleep on their feet" in shell-hole aid stations. "No medical men," wrote Deckard, "except those who have been in such a position, can begin to comprehend the appalling and helpless feeling that one suffers because of the sad limits that nature applies to one's physical endurance." Hugh O. Cook, a black YMCA volunteer from Kansas City, Missouri, worked with the 371st's gassed and wounded in the 3rd Battalion medical detachment aid station during the Champagne offensive until he himself was gassed and had to be evacuated. Heywood praised the YMCA, whose black workers were "the only one of all the American welfare units who came near us."[130]

The Wilson War Department, concerned with providing a "clean and wholesome environment" (meaning no women or alcohol) for soldiers behind the lines, requested that the Young Men's Christian Association be in charge of all post-exchange and entertainment services for the American Expeditionary Forces. "Y-huts" and "Y-secretaries" provided educational, athletic, religious, and social programs, with "separate but equal" facilities for blacks. Among the American welfare groups—the YMCA, the Red Cross, the Salvation Army, the Knights of Columbus, and the Jewish Welfare Board—only the Salvation Army received unqualified praise from all groups, and only the YMCA had black workers.

The main task of the YMCA was to provide basic educational classes for the many American soldiers who were illiterate or foreign-born or both. Although Emmett J. Scott claimed that the YMCA gave equal service to black and white, there was one Y-secretary for every 279 white soldiers, and one for every 1,267 black soldiers.[131] Seventy-five black "Y-secretaries," including three women, served the 140,000 black members of the AEF in France. New Yorkers Addie D. Hunton and Kathryn M. Johnson were two of the three black women Y-secretaries. Arriving in June 1918, they spent nearly fifteen months in France. They published *Two Colored Women with the American Expeditionary Forces* themselves, advertising for agents in *The Crisis*.

Kathryn Johnson was an Ohio-born teacher. Addie Hunton, who did most of the writing, was the daughter of the founder of the Negro Elks, a prominent member of the African Methodist Episcopal Church, and a YWCA youth leader. An American college graduate, she studied at Kaiser Wilhelm University in Strasbourg from 1908 to 1910. When her husband, the YMCA official William Hunton, died in 1916, she threw herself into war work. Traveling between Bordeaux, Brest, and St.-Nazaire, Hunton and Johnson had the longest active service of any black women in France.

"We entered a city of darkness and our taxicab literally felt its way to the hotel," wrote Hunton of Paris in June 1918. Their first impressions of the "bleeding, war-harassed city with its deadly foe pressing down upon it" were of women in black, and of wounded French soldiers, "heart-breaking in their poor torn bodies." There were sirens, air battles at night, and "Big Bertha" bombs by day. The face of the war was changing, however. "The day of the British and Belgian soldiers in Paris had almost passed," Hunton wrote, "that of the Americans scarce begun."[132]

As YMCA workers, they saw and heard the effects of racism on the ground, from men who "shed tears at their first sight of a colored woman in France." Hunton and Johnson were greeted with cries of "Ooh-la-la" from black soldiers. Although embarrassed, they "knew how genuine was the surprise of colored soldiers at the first sight of their own women in France, so we laughed back and waved them a welcome to the 'Y' hut." Offering hot chocolate, lemonade, and cake, they helped men write letters home, taught reading and writing, and established libraries. The Y hut at St.-Nazaire, with a fifteen-hundred-volume library serving nearly nine thousand men, was the largest for black troops. Hunton and Johnson taught stevedores and laborers to read and write. Huts of similar size for whites would have had at least six women and eight men. There were other "Colored" Y huts in Bordeaux, Brest, Le Mans, Marseilles, Joinville, and Orly.

"The service of the colored welfare workers was more or less clouded at all times with that biting and stinging thing which is ever shadowing us in our own country," wrote Hunton. "While the official heads of the YMCA in Paris were in every way considerate and courteous to its colored constituency, still there is no doubt that the attitude of many of the white secretaries in the field was to be deplored." A black female Y worker in Paris had been ordered home "on recommendation of Army officials in Bordeaux, who had brought from our southland their full measure of sectional prejudice . . . thus leaving three colored women to spread their influence as best they could among 150,000 men." Soldiers reported "No Negroes Allowed" signs on Y huts. When blacks were turned away from the scheduled performance of a black band, the band refused to play. There was also discrimination at base hospitals, where black officers were placed with privates instead of in private rooms as was their military right; and black soldiers were attended only after whites.[133]

In total, seventy-eight black men and nineteen black women served as Y secretaries in France. Three were cited for bravery: Matthew Bullock, who was under shell fire with the 369th Regiment; E. T. Banks, who went over the top with the 368th in Vienne and the Argonne; and Hugh O. Cook, who was gassed in the Champagne offensive with the 371st.

ARMISTICE

"At exactly 11 o'clock we came out into a clearing and as we did, a rocket went up from the heights behind us. We did not know it at that moment, but this was a signal that the war had ended," Chester D. Heywood wrote of the November 11, 1918, armistice.

> Suddenly from the line came a terrific burst of rifle and machine-gun fire and the crash of exploding grenades. We ran forward until we could see the front-line trenches and there standing up on the enemy parapets were groups of Germans yelling, dancing, throwing their little round caps in the air and acting like crazy men. We realized it was the Armistice. We stepped out into the open. I shall never forget the sensation. For months we had crouched like animals below ground and now for the first time, we stood up in broad daylight with the enemy in plain sight in front of us. There was no cheering and no display of excitement in our little group. We stood in a dazed silence unable to believe that at last the fighting was over.

Heywood came upon an Armistice "Sunday-school picnic": "In an open space behind a machine-gun emplacement were four of our men, three Boche and a woman. They were shaking hands with each other, trying to talk and all smoking American cigarettes and eating our reserve ration chocolate."[134]

The 371st, like the 369th, had had no real rest and no leave since they had arrived in France. "The enlisted men never had any leave granted for the reason that a leave area for colored troops had not been designated," Heywood wrote. "Instead of leaves G.H.Q. gave the colored regiments priority for return to the States." It was said that the early return of black regiments was due to the fact that the Secret Service, which was anyway terrified by the Russian Revolution, had discovered a "movement to stir up race hatred among these troops." In December, General Goybet said farewell to the 371st and 372nd Regiments, which had served with the 15th French Army: "Dear friends from America, when you have re-crossed the ocean, do not forget the Red Hand Division. Our pure brotherhood in arms has been consecrated in the blood of the brave. These bonds will never be severed."[135]

After the Armistice, the 371st and 372nd were denied permission by the American command to wear the Red Hand insignia on their uniforms.

THE BIG PARADE

The Croix de Guerre was pinned to the 369th's regimental colors on December 13, 1918, on the Plains of Münchhausen. "Recruited as fighting men, in ridicule; trained and mustered into Federal service, in more ridicule; sent to France as a safe political solution of a volcanic political problem; loaned to the French Army as another easy way out—these men had carried on," Major Arthur Little wrote.[136]

Within moments of arriving in Brest for the journey home, in what Little called "brutal morale baiting," a 369th private had his head split open by an American military policeman for taking the wrong direction to the latrine. An MP captain told Little of being "warned" that "the niggers" were "feeling their oats." They were instructed to deal quickly with the black soldiers, "so as not to have any trouble later on." The 369th may have been the most highly decorated American unit in the war, but MPs were instructed not to salute or stand at attention for the 369th's officers, white or black.[137]

They landed in New York harbor on February 17, 1919. No one, black or white, who saw the 369th come home from France ever forgot it. The homecoming parade up Fifth Avenue was the greatest black American celebration since Emancipation. Officially, it was the homecoming of the entire American Expeditionary Force. Banners read, "Our Heroes—Welcome Home." But Harlem's own 369th, in winter overcoats and tin hats, were the first troops to march under the "Victory Arch" at Fifth Avenue and Twenty-fifth Street. Specifically not invited to join the National Guard Farewell Parade of June 1917 (they would also not be invited to the Victory Parade of July 1919), the parade "orphans" had a unique moment of glory. America had never seen anything like the wave after wave of black men marching up Fifth Avenue in a phalanx, like the French army. Films and photographs of the marching 369th were shown throughout the country. Major Arthur Little was at the head of the 1st Battalion, about sixty paces behind Jim Europe's band. The reviewing stands were packed, and the sidewalks were overflowing. "During the entire progress of that seven mile march, I scarcely heard ten consecutive bars of music, so great were the roars of cheers, the applause, and the shouts of personal greeting!" Little added that on "the 17th of February, 1919, New York City knew no color line."[138]

At 110th Street and Fifth Avenue, the regiment turned jubilantly into Harlem. Hayward changed the phalanx formation to open platoon formation. "So far as might be possible," Little wrote, "the face and figure of each soldier boy must be made to stand out, for his loved ones to see and recognize." Marching up Lenox Avenue, the band played "Here Comes My Daddy Now!" Little reported, and "a quarter of a million of men, women, and children of the colored race went wild with a frenzy of pride and joy and love. For the final mile or so of our parade, about every fourth soldier of the ranks had a girl upon his arm—and we marched through Harlem singing and laughing."[139]

The band, instantly famous, was immediately sent to tour the country. "Their Glory Can Never Fade" handbills appeared—and posters: "Don't Miss This! The Band That Played the Hell Fighters On to Victory," with portraits of Jim Europe and Noble Sissle, "The Greatest Singer of His Race . . . America's Own 'Young Black Joe.' "

At Boston's Mechanic's Hall on May 9, 1919, during the intermission of the band's last concert of the tour, drummer Herbert Wright ("crazed with anger," wrote Sissle, "at what he considered an unfairness") stabbed Jim Europe. "Although Jim's wound seemed superficial, they couldn't stop the bleeding," Sissle wrote. The next day's headlines read "The Jazz King Is Dead." Irene Castle, a war widow, wrote to Sissle: "During the four years he played for Captain Castle and me, he originated many new tempos. . . . No inconsiderable part of our success was due to his wonderful playing and helpful suggestions. . . . I am sure that in his death the colored race has lost one of its most distinguished leaders, the music-loving public one of its most inspired composers, and a large host of Americans will, like myself, mourn the loss of a generous loyal friend."[140] When Hollywood later made a movie about the Castles, with Astaire and Rogers, the music director–orchestra leader was presented as white.

Riding in a car because of his war injuries, Sergeant Henry Johnson, the first enlisted American to win the Croix de Guerre, had been a star of the parade. (One eyewitness reported that Harlem crowds yelled out "Oh you Black Death! Oh you Black Death!") His heroic status was short-lived, however. Although Governor Alfred E. Smith met Johnson's train in Albany and gave a dinner in his honor, the monetary award and street dedication the governor proposed never materialized. There was not even a plaque in the Albany train station where Johnson worked as a porter, although the city named a bridge for the city's first white enlistee. Johnson joined Hayward on a Liberty Bond tour (to sell war bonds), but was run out of Texas for using the word "cracker" to describe a white. Permanently disabled, without disability pay, he died in poverty in Washington, D.C., in 1929.

J. E. Blanton, a black YMCA worker, witnessed the great July 14,

1919, victory parade in Paris. The 369th had been forbidden by American command to march. He published an angry dissent in *The Crisis,* in December 1919: "England had Canadians, Australians, Scotch, Londoners, Indians and Africans in the line. France had Frenchmen, Soudanese, Senegalese, Madagascans, Moroccans, and every other race that fought under her flag in line. Every nation had all the races that fought in the war, except the United States. Although there were over a thousand Negro troops here . . . the United States was represented only by white men."[141]

Welcome Home

The 367th Regiment of the 92nd Division provided a detail to load coal into the U.S.S. *Virginia,* bringing troops home from the war. When the job was finished, the men began to load their gear into the battleship for the voyage home. The ship's executive officer stopped them in their tracks, declaring that "no black soldier had ever embarked in an American battleship and that no one would." A tug took the men back to shore.[142]

Black troops did much of the war's cleanup. Nine thousand black soldiers had the job of reburying all the dead, with white soldiers as clerks. "It would be a gruesome, repulsive and unhealthy task, requiring weeks of incessant toil during the long heavy days of summer," wrote Hunton. American cemeteries were erected on or near the battlefields where the dead had fallen. Numerous labor battalions and the 813th, 815th, and 816th Pioneer Regiments performed the "most sacred" task of the war. Hard and terrible as the work was, wrote Hunton, it was "as naught compared with the trials of discrimination and injustices that seared their souls like hot iron." The Knights of Columbus put up a "No Colored" sign, and black soldiers, angry that they alone, not even German POWs, were left behind to rebury America's dead, razed the Knights' tent.[143]

"We regret that on October 1919 we will sail for our home in Petersburg, Va. United States of America where true democracy is enjoyed only by the white people," wrote a black private, William Hewlett, to W.E.B. Du Bois on August 26, 1919. "Why did black men die here in France 3300 miles from their home? Was it to make democracy safe for the white people in America, with the black race left out?"[144] In 1919, seventy-eight blacks were lynched. Fourteen were burned at the stake. Eleven of the victims were ex-soldiers. Race riots erupted that year in twenty-eight cities.[145]

In January 1920, *The Crisis* reprinted a letter from a Dr. John Hugh

Reynolds to the *Arkansas Gazette:* "We have a new Negro; he has come back from the war changed. . . . He has taken much credit to himself for our victory, and he has come back with a new sense of his importance and with aspirations, the realization of which means to overturn our traditional views and modes of life. A cardinal fact is that the Negro is not willing to take his old place and status before the war. In some cases he has come back with ideas of social and political equality."[146] Black Americans who had fought in France were perceived as different. But the Army remained the same, and the war ended as it began, with a racist American military message.

On the committee of white field-grade officers responding to a General Staff College query of March 1920 on "Use to be made of negroes in the U.S. military service" sat Lieutenant Colonel Allen J. Greer, who had written in 1919 that the 92nd Division had been a "danger" to no one but themselves and women. The committee issued a statement:

> As an individual the negro is docile, tractable, lighthearted, carefree, and good-natured. If unjustly treated he is likely to become surly and stubborn, though this is usually a temporary phase. He is careless, shiftless, irresponsible and secretive. He resents censure and is best handled with praise and by ridicule. He is immoral, untruthful, and his sense of right doing is relatively inferior. Crimes and convictions involving moral turpitude are nearly five to one as compared to convictions of whites on similar charges.[147]

Many members of the General Staff College Committee would play major roles in World War II.

* * *

The "New Negro" came home. He had fought to help change Europe. He was willing to fight to change America.

7 The "New Negro" and the Spanish Civil War

We didn't know too much about the Spaniards, but we knew that they were fighting against fascism, and that fascism was the enemy of all black aspirations.[1]

—*Vaughn Love, veteran of the Spanish Civil War*

"Red Summer" and the "New Negro"

Unlike black veterans of the Revolution or Civil War, World War I veterans, who fought for and came home to the most racist American political regime since before the Civil War, harbored a deep sense of pessimism about their country. They saw no national support (even in theory) for any measure of social justice for blacks. The Revolution had strengthened abolitionism; the Civil War had achieved Emancipation. The First World War did only one thing for black veterans: it gave them a new kind of anger.

Within four months of the 369th Regiment's triumphal Fifth Avenue parade, there were race wars in the streets of America. The summer of 1919 was known among blacks as Red Summer—"Red" for blood. Seventy-eight blacks were lynched in 1919: ten were veterans, several of whom were lynched in uniform. By the end of the year, there had been race riots in twenty-eight cities, North and South. But blacks were fighting back.

If we must die, let it not be like hogs
Hunted and penned in an inglorious spot. . . .
If we must die, O let us nobly die . . .
Like men we'll face the murderous, cowardly pack,
Pressed to the wall, dying, but fighting back.[2]

This was written by the poet Claude McKay, during the July 19, 1919, Washington, D.C., race riot. McKay, a "New Negro" recently arrived from his native Jamaica, believed in fighting back. A month later, W.E.B. Du Bois wrote: "They cheat us and mock us; they kill us and slay us; they deride our misery. When we plead for the naked protection of the law . . . they tell us to 'GO TO HELL!' . . . TO YOUR TENTS, O ISRAEL! And FIGHT, FIGHT, FIGHT for freedom."[3]

The First World War had not changed American racial policy, but it had changed the psychological profile of a generation. There was a new sense of disillusion and a widespread feeling that democracy, like the rest of the hypocritical old order, had failed. For many, especially in Europe, only the new orders of fascism and Communism offered any hope for the future. While some admired the new ideologies, most Americans preferred their "isms" homegrown. They would turn to extreme versions of Puritanism (Prohibition), to religious fundamentalism (as expressed in the Scopes trial), isolationism, and racism. In 1924, the Ku Klux Klan had 4.5 million members.[4] Racism was as American as apple pie. But black World War I veterans had tasted other fruit in France. Pessimistic as they were about their country, they were defiantly optimistic about themselves. No longer cornered and isolated, they were proven heroes in the larger world. They knew they had allies; and they knew they could fight back. Many blacks would do so through the Communist Party.

On the night of July 28, 1919, in the midst of the Chicago race riot, Haywood Hall and other black vets met at the 370th Regimental Armory. "It was rumored that Irishmen from west of the Wentworth Avenue dividing line were planning to invade the ghetto that night," Hall wrote in his autobiography, *Black Bolshevik*.[5] "We planned a defensive action to meet them." Fortunately for the Irish, the invasion never occurred. The "defensive action" of the 370th centered around the use of Army-issue 1903 Springfield rifles and a Browning submachine gun. "The Chicago rebellion of 1919 was a pivotal point in my life," Hall wrote.[6] "Always I had been hot-tempered and never took any insults lying down. This was even more true after the war." Now, influenced by his brother, Otto, also a veteran, he stepped into the class war, for the "battle" that changed his life, and joined Otto in the Communist Party.

The Red Summer was red in politics as well as blood. The Wilson administration had been terrified by the Russian Revolution. In 1919, the Palmer Raids—named for the U.S. attorney general, A. Mitchell Palmer, but directed by J. Edgar Hoover—initiated a systematic decade-long persecution of all shades of the American left. The socialist presidential candidate Eugene Debs was imprisoned; the Anarchists Sacco and Vanzetti were (as Damon Runyon put it) "fried"; and the twenty-six-year-old International Workers of the World was demolished. The IWW's "One Big Union" of Joe Hill and Big Bill Haywood had counted 100,000 black Wobblies.[7]

In 1922, Hamilton Fish, now a Republican U.S. representative from New York, spoke out in Congress (despite "hate inspired invectives" from southern Democrats) in favor of the Dyer Bill to make lynching a federal crime. "The colored man who went into war had in his heart the feeling that he was not only fighting to make the world safe for democracy but also to make this country safe for his own race," Fish said. "I have sworn to support the Constitution of the United States, and on that account, if for no other reason, it would be my sacred duty as a member of the House of Representatives to vote for a drastic anti-lynching bill to protect the lives of American citizens everywhere in the United States."[8]

The bill was defeated that year in the Senate, thanks to help from the Republican Warren G. Harding administration. (Harding himself confronted rumors that he was partly black by saying one of his ancestors may have "jumped the fence.") The Wilson administration had set the racial tone for both parties. Politically, the decade would end as it had begun, in assertions of white supremacy. In 1929, after polling every congressional wife and finding twelve who agreed to be cordial, the wife of the Republican president, Herbert Hoover, invited the wife of Oscar De Priest, the newly elected Chicago Republican congressman (the first black elected to Congress since 1901), to a congressional wives' tea.[9] In response, Senator Coleman Blease of South Carolina introduced a resolution stating that President and Mrs. Hoover should "remember that the house in which they are temporarily residing is the 'White House.' "[10]

As white supremacy flourished, so did the "New Negro" movement. An idea that had been developing at least since Reconstruction, the "New Negro" concept flowered between 1890 and 1920, when over two million blacks, fleeing post-Reconstruction Jim Crow and the law of the rope, moved north. Many black émigrés were educated children of Reconstruction. They supported civil rights organizations and became the backbone of black communities in large northern cities, of which New York City's Harlem was the most vibrant example.

"New Negroes" had a new sense of geographic identity. They saw themselves not only as American but also as *African*. In 1919 W.E.B. Du Bois went to Paris to organize the first NAACP-sponsored Pan-African Conference. At a time when former German territories in Africa were a postwar prize, the NAACP saw American blacks as leaders in the worldwide struggle for justice for the African people, and as proponents of

African culture. Throughout the 1920s, Neo-Africanism, or "negritude," flourished in the arts and politics. Darius Milhaud, Francis Poulenc, Arthur Honegger, and George Gershwin were among those who reflected their debt to the international phenomenon that was black music. Louis Armstrong, Bessie Smith, Edward Kennedy "Duke" Ellington, Josephine Baker, and James P. Johnson (composer of "Charleston!") were worldwide celebrities. Noble Sissle, veteran of the 369th Regiment, had become one of America's most popular composers ("I'm Just Wild About Harry!"). And Paul Robeson was an international theater star. Amid harsh political and social repression, black creativity flourished as never before. And so did black militancy.

In 1925, Dr. Ossian Sweet, a black physician, bought a house in a white neighborhood of Detroit. When he moved in, a white mob surrounded and stoned his house—and one of the mob was killed by a shot fired from inside the house. Sweet, his wife, their son, and ten friends were arrested. After a first hung jury, the NAACP hired the famed trial lawyer Clarence Darrow (who worked practically gratis), and a second jury acquitted everyone. That same year saw the great Howard University student strike against its white administration, over, among other things, compulsory military training. The philosopher Alain Locke, a Harvard graduate and the first black Rhodes Scholar, was dismissed from the faculty by Howard's white president for siding with the students. Locke's 1925 anthology, *The New Negro,* effectively defined the first quarter of the century as the "Renaissance" of the African diaspora.

BLACK EAGLES: BESSIE COLEMAN AND HUBERT JULIAN

Most black Americans in the 1920s had little interest in pan-Africanism, intellectual or otherwise. Those who could afford to flirt with such highfalutin ideas were far more likely to be interested in Wall Street. Bloated prosperity had created a new black middle class whose values, vices, and interests were those of mainstream America. The most consuming of these interests in the late 1920s was the new adventure of aviation. Teachers and planes were hard to come by for blacks who wanted to fly. Nevertheless, some black aviators, in World War biplanes, managed to capture America's attention—among them, Bessie Coleman and Hubert Julian.

The Texas-born Bessie Coleman's first exhibition flight was in 1922, before a large multiracial crowd in Chicago. The first black female licensed pilot, she had been inspired to fly by the war, but no American school would take her. Finally managing to work her way to France in 1921, she earned her wings in ten months. Back home, her subsequent barnstorming, circus, and carnival career was sponsored by Robert Sengstacke Abbott, publisher of the black *Chicago Defender,* whose antilynching motto, "If you must die, take at least one with you," led to its ban in many towns in Illinois. In 1923, Coleman piloted the largest airplane yet flown by a woman, a Benz-motored L.F.G. She was killed in 1926, at the age of thirty-three, falling out of her plane when it went into a steep dive during an exhibition test flight in Jacksonville, Florida. She wore no seat belt and had no parachute.

"Lieutenant" Hubert Eustace Fauntleroy Julian, a twenty-five-year-old Canadian Air Corps veteran and part-time recruiting officer for Marcus Garvey's Black Eagle Flying Corps, also came to public notice in 1922—as a parachutist, not as a pilot, when he jumped onto a Harlem rooftop to advertise a local optician. A relentless Jazz Age self-promoter, he jumped the next year while playing a saxophone. He missed his target, but the white press took notice. The *New York Telegram* called him the Black Eagle.[11] Early in 1924, he jumped onto the roof of the City College of New York to advertise a Harlem five-and-ten-cent store, and then announced plans for a solo seaplane flight from Harlem to Liberia. On July 4, 1924, wearing a sky-blue uniform—and after passing the hat for donations among some 25,000 well-wishers—he took off in his new Boeing hydroplane (still unpaid-for) from Harlem's 138th Street pier and almost instantly crashed into Flushing Bay, breaking his leg. Mocked in the white press, Julian's disastrous attempt at a transatlantic solo nevertheless predated Lindbergh's flight by a year. Harlem would boast that it had had a "Black Eagle" before there was a "Lone Eagle."

By the late 1920s and early 1930s, Chicago and Los Angeles were centers of serious black aviation, with schools for black pilots.

BLACK COMMUNISTS

In 1920, Lenin formally introduced the "Negro Question" at the Second Comintern Congress. The Communist International had resolved that the "Negro in the United States forms a well-defined subject caste, with a distinctly inferior economic, social and political status," wrote Will Herberg, in the famous 1932 anthology *Negro,* edited by the British Afrocentric heiress Nancy Cunard.[12] The caste status, wrote Herberg, so "advantageous to the ruling class from the viewpoint of economic profit and class power—is transformed into the corresponding class ideology—the 'theory' of the 'inherent' racial inferiority of the Negro." Only a "proletarian revolution" could accomplish what "the American bourgeois revolution that was the Civil War failed to do!" The Communist program championed the abolition of "peonage" and "serf conditions" for southern blacks. It took up the antilynching struggle, preached industrial equality, including the "organization of the unorganized and unskilled," and demanded the "complete social and political equality of the Negro race."

With such a program, why did so few blacks actually join the Communist Party? One reason may be that the Party was spiritually alien: if the Comintern resolution is any example, the Communists clearly had trouble talking to blacks in language they could relate to. Far more black intellectuals than workers and "peasants" would respond to Red overtures. Nevertheless, many blacks were Communist by inclination if not comprehension. ("The first slave who got off the boat turned left," the Harlem Renaissance poet Sterling Brown told me sometime in the early 1980s.) This natural inclination was underlined in a Harlem speech in 1919 by William Pickens, then a dean at Morgan State College and shortly to become a widely respected field secretary of the NAACP. "As for the Bolsheviks, it's injustice is making Bolshevism. . . . It's injustice that changes quiet inoffensive school-teachers and working-men into Bolsheviks, just as it is injustice is stirring up the colored people. . . . You know a tree by its fruits, and so you may know a country by what it produces. . . . Stop sowing injustice, and Bolshevism will cease growing."[13]

* * *

The American revolution may have been far off, but the black war veterans Haywood and Otto Hall were in its vanguard. For them, the NAACP was a bourgeois compromise, Garveyism was for utopian escapists, and capitalist prosperity was bunk. Otto Hall was among the first seven Americans in Moscow's prestigious new Lenin School for students from western Europe and North America. In 1921, Haywood Hall, who took the name of "Harry Haywood" to elude the FBI, was among the first foreigners invited to attend the new Stalin University for the Toilers of the East—known, American style, as Far East U.

The three-year course at Far East U was based on Lenin's development of Marx and Engels. Hall's classmates were Chinese, Japanese, Indian, North African, and Ashanti from the Gold Coast (Ghana). All Soviet university students, including foreigners, received full room and board, clothing, and a stipend. On Saturdays, all students helped at workers' cultural clubs, and worked on building the Moscow subways. According to Hall, there were eight blacks in a city of 4,500,000 people. One was Emma Harris, a middle-aged ex-vaudeville hoofer from Georgia, stranded in Moscow before the Revolution. Harris (known to white

Americans as the Moscow Mammy) married a Russian and became the madam of a high-class brothel. Antirevolutionary in sympathy, she hid White Russian officers in her establishment and was told by authorities that the only reason she was not shot was that she was black.[14]

By 1929, Otto Hall had been elected to the Central Committee of the Communist Party and was back in America helping to organize the Gastonia textile workers' strike in North Carolina, the Party's first mass action in the American South. Gastonia was a violent and bloody confrontation of police against workers. Otto Hall was on his way back to Gastonia from a nearby town when police attacked the strikers' tent colony and the chief of police was shot. Taking a collection to pay his railroad fare back to New York, white strikers orchestrated Hall's timely escape from a lynch mob. Fifteen union members, charged with murder, were defended by the Party's International Labor Defense.

In 1932, fifteen years after the Revolution, the Soviet Union was officially recognized by the U.S. government and became a new trading partner. The U.S. Chamber of Commerce opened a Moscow branch, and corporate and technical experts—among them American blacks—poured into Russia to offer U.S. know-how and expertise. A group of black agricultural scientists from Tuskegee Institute (including the son of Colonel Charles Young) went to Central Asia to teach cotton growing. Black and white Ford Motor Company mechanics arrived to help create an automobile assembly line. When white Ford mechanics refused to eat in the same dining room with the black mechanic Robert Robinson, the whites were expelled from the country. Robinson became a Soviet citizen, a move he soon regretted in the wake of the 1930s purges, when more than one million people disappeared. He would spend World War II under constant surveillance, and finally return to the United States in the 1970s.

The Depression made the black struggle both more integrated and more political. What Communists called economic determinism broke ethnic and racial barriers, even for noncommunists. The new anticommunist Congress of Industrial Organizations (CIO) organized big-industry workers across racial and gender lines. Throughout the 1930s racially integrated collective action was the norm, even in the South, where the short-lived Communist-organized Alabama Sharecroppers Union included a few whites. Official response to such integrated collectives was usually swift and brutal. In Washington, D.C., in the summer of 1932, soldiers led by the Army Chief of Staff, General Douglas MacArthur, violently attacked integrated World War I veteran "Bonus Marchers" (seeking their promised bonuses in full cash payments) and their families.

The Great Depression was a gift to the Communist International. In a decade that saw southern blacks lynched at the rate of one every three weeks, Communism appeared to address the twin problems of racism and economic oppression more forcefully than the NAACP. The Party's membership of blacks was low (it would hover between 7 and 8 percent throughout the 1930s and 1940s[15]) but its influence was high, despite W.E.B. Du Bois's emphatic rejection of Communism in *The Crisis* in 1931. Besides dealing forcefully with racism and economic oppression, Communism appealed to those who, like many in the 1930s, were seeking a better world. "To be a Communist," wrote the sociologist Nathan Glazer, speaking specifically of Jews, blacks, and immigrants, "meant to shed the limitations of one's social reality, and to join in a fraternity that transcended the divisions of the world."[16]

The small Communist Party U.S.A. would directly compete with the NAACP throughout the 1930s. A successful NAACP lobbying effort in 1930 to keep a racist judge, John J. Parker, off the Supreme Court encouraged subsequent NAACP legal assaults against segregated public schools. In 1931, the NAACP made a crucial mistake. On the grounds that young black men in Alabama were daily accused of rape by white women, the organization decided that there was nothing special in the case of nine young men accused of raping a white semi-prostitute who rode the boxcars with them. Unfortunately for the NAACP, the Scottsboro Boys became the civil rights defendants of the decade—assuring the influence and popularity of the Communist Party, which defended them.

Voting Democratic

"The Republican Party is the ship, all else is the sea," Frederick Douglass had said. The Republican Party collapsed with the crash, but its racial liberalism had already disappeared in the politics of Coolidge and Harding. The old high-minded party of Emancipation and Reconstruction was in new hands and new money, mostly western.

While many blacks identified with the Communist message, many more could separate the historical truth at the heart of the message from the dubious motives of the messenger. Throughout the 1930s, millions of ordinary black Americans would insist that it was possible to be "progressive" without being a Communist, to be prolabor without being anticapitalist, and to change America without a revolution. The ideas and the times came together in President Franklin D. Roosevelt's New Deal—a peaceful political revolution beginning in 1932, which found a middle road between totalitarian Communism and unfettered capitalism. It built bridges between capital and labor, and tried to build bridges between black and white.

Not only did New Deal legislation protect labor but black working people found a new spirit of inclusion in the labor movement itself—crystallized in the great 1935 Ford strike, led by Walter Reuther and the new CIO United Auto Workers. NAACP executive secretary Walter White had to convince black workers personally loyal to Henry Ford, who hired more blacks than any other automotive industrialist, not to act as strikebreakers.

"Gentlemen, the Pullman Company is ready to sign" was for the NAACP executive Roy Wilkins one of the most inspiring statements of the 1930s.[17] The words of capitulation, spoken in 1937 on behalf of the largest private employer of black labor in America, marked the end of a twelve-year contract wrangle and gave Wilkins the "faith that black people were making their way forward to equality." In 1925, A. Philip Randolph had been asked to help Pullman's ten thousand black railway employees in their struggle to win recognition for their own union, against a corrupt "company" union. (New Deal legislation would later outlaw company unions.) Randolph took the job and never commented on the potentially plausible story that Pullman had offered him a blank check for up to a million dollars, to give it up. Generically known as George, for the company's owner, George Pullman, Pullman porters were, next to the fictional Aunt Jemima and Uncle Ben, America's best-advertised blacks. Randolph's earliest Pullman victory, in 1926, was the right to a name tag: porters would no longer be penalized for not responding to the name of George. Under Randolph's leadership, the new Brotherhood of Sleeping Car Porters became one of the most influential black organizations in America until the late 1960s, when railway sleeping cars finally became obsolete.

Eleanor Roosevelt, FDR, and the New Deal

The political folklore of 1932 deemed America a "sick patient," afflicted with "a grave internal disorder" brought on by "Ol' Man Depression"—but "Old Doc New Deal" had the cure.[18] The treatment came labeled with governmental acronyms: NRA (National Recovery Act), PWA (Public Works Authority, or "Papa's Working Again"), WPA (Works Progress Administration, which hired jobless artists and craftsmen), CCC (Civilian Conservation Corps, which employed jobless youth), NYA (National Youth Administration, for young women and men), TVA (Tennessee Valley Authority, which harnessed the Tennessee River for electricity), FDIC (Federal Deposit Insurance Corporation, to guarantee bank deposits), HOLC (Home Owners Loan Corporation, to save homes from foreclosures), and SEC (Securities and Exchange Commission, to ensure truth in the sale of securities). Social Security and unemployment insurance were also brought into being, along with massive work-relief programs that transformed the landscape, as well as people's spirits. "Happy Days Are Here Again!" was the exuberant New Deal anthem.

Franklin Roosevelt was transformed by fate as well as by the circumstances of his times. Struck by polio at the age of thirty-nine, the young man who was once known as "Feather Duster" for his flightiness became a giant of history—with his own acronym, in keeping with the times. The man called FDR had enough confidence and charisma to convince Americans to take the medicine of the New Deal. Roosevelt and his wife (and cousin), Eleanor, were a team. Although their marriage was complicated, with infidelity on his part, Roosevelt told his son that Eleanor was the most "extraordinarily interesting" woman he had ever met.[19] Their mutual affection is clear from their letters. She, like most Americans, admired his leadership, and he clearly respected her judgment and intelligence. She was politically useful with groups whose support he needed but which he could not be seen to favor because of the rabid racism of the Party's southern wing. ("You kiss the Negroes and I'll kiss the Jews and we'll stay in the White House as long as we choose," went the doggerel.)

The Roosevelts played a masterly political balancing act. He veered right, she veered left. Eleanor Roosevelt believed that men pursued politics essentially for reasons of personal and public power, but that women sought power to meet human needs. Because he basically agreed with his wife's instincts, Roosevelt only rarely tried to curb her. "Lady," he had said when she asked him if he wanted her to stop, "this is a free country. Say what you think. If you get me in Dutch, I'll manage to get myself out. Anyway, the whole world knows I can't control you."[20] Each Roosevelt gave and grew in the White House; they were both elevated and altered by their times.

FDR did not do well with traditionally Republican blacks in 1932, when many preferred Herbert Hoover, his Republican rival. In Chicago, for instance, he got only 23 percent of the black vote. Two years later, a seismic political shift saw the black Chicago Republican Oscar De Priest replaced in Congress by the first black Democrat, Arthur Mitchell. Most Americans, including blacks, were getting behind Roosevelt—as much because of his wife, friend to the poor of every color, as because of his new economic programs.

Previously Eleanor Roosevelt had only known blacks as servants; now she made black friends. Her racial awakening was a product of her exhaustive travels around the country. (*Time* called her "Eleanor Everywhere.") Through her friendships with black leaders, fellow soldiers in the war against "Ol' Man Depression," she gained what one historian called "a crash course on the struggle of blacks against oppression."[21] She was a good student, for several reasons: her old-Republican roots, her settlement work among New York City's poor, and her own socially blighted childhood, which taught her never to treat anyone as inferior.

On January 26, 1934, Eleanor Roosevelt, in a quietly revolutionary gesture, arranged an informal dinner meeting with black leaders at the White House to discuss black participation in New Deal programs. Among the group invited to dinner that night (and to receive a brief cheery greeting from FDR in his wheelchair) was Walter White, the executive secretary of the NAACP. "I am a Negro," wrote White in his autobiography. "My skin is white, my eyes are blue, my hair is blond. The traits of my race are nowhere visible upon me." From a middle-class Atlanta family, White was one-sixty-fourth black—black according to the southern "one drop" rule. He learned the meaning of his racial heritage as a thirteen-year-old during the 1906 Atlanta race riot, when his father and his brothers armed themselves to protect the family. "Son, don't shoot until the first man puts his foot on the lawn and then—don't you miss!" his father had said.[22] As a student at Atlanta University, Walter White specialized in infiltrating lynch mobs for the NAACP. In 1918, he wrote a famous, searing, eyewitness account of the lynching of the pregnant Mary Turner, who was burned alive after her child was cut from her body and crushed underfoot.

Walter White became the leader of the NAACP in 1931, when James Weldon Johnson resigned because of ill health. Johnson had discovered White working at an Atlanta insurance agency. W.E.B. Du Bois made no secret of his disapproval. "Walter's direction was toward high-pressure salesmanship in Washington and around the country," wrote Roy Wilkins, then an NAACP field secretary; it was "an approach that mixed poorly with Dr. Du Bois's highbrow intellectual orientation."[23]

Roosevelt's administration had more black political appointees than any before it in American history. And Roosevelt had more black advisers than any president before him. There was an unofficial "Black Cabinet" of government appointees, whose recognized leader was Mary McLeod Bethune, director of Negro Affairs for the New Deal's National Youth Administration. Other members of the group, who met informally in Mrs. Bethune's home, were Edgar Brown, the black tennis champion, who served as adviser on Negro affairs in the Civilian Conservation Corps; Eugene Kinckle Jones, a professor and Urban League activist, adviser in the Department of Commerce; Lawrence Oxley, of the Division of Negro Labor in the U.S. Department of Labor; William Trent, race relations adviser to the Department of the Interior and the Public Works

Administration; Robert Vann, a lawyer and ex-Republican editor of the *Pittsburgh Courier,* serving as an assistant to the U.S. Attorney General; William Hastie, NAACP lawyer (and future first black federal judge), assistant solicitor in the Department of the Interior; and Dr. Frank Horne, my great-uncle, former assistant to Mrs. Bethune in the NYA, now an adviser in federal housing programs.

The Federal Council on Negro Affairs, an umbrella organization for all departments, gave blacks a theoretical voice in nearly every New Deal program, although it was usually ignored when programs were put into practice in the South. Nevertheless, by the end of the 1930s, 300,000 black youths were involved in National Youth Administration training programs; 250,000 were in the Civilian Conservation Corps; and the WPA was providing basic earnings for one million black families.[24]

Eleanor Roosevelt was almost singlehandedly responsible for helping blacks get a fairer share of the New Deal. On an inspection tour of southern New Deal programs, she found systemic bureaucratic discrimination against blacks. In 1935, thanks to his wife's prodding, Roosevelt signed an executive order barring discrimination in all WPA projects. Despite hostility in many quarters of the administration, Mrs. Roosevelt found allies, but she also inspired suspicion. In the autumn of 1935, a photograph of Mrs. Roosevelt accepting a bouquet of roses from a five-year-old black girl triggered a riot of hate propaganda in the South, denouncing her as a "Communist."[25] This was all good for the black vote, which, by the 1936 election, was entirely Roosevelt's.

Eleanor Roosevelt, so concerned with attacking problems directly, was also capable of the grand symbolic gesture. In 1938, in an Alabama auditorium that seated blacks on one side and whites on the other, she famously placed her chair in the middle. A year later, she publicly resigned from the Daughters of the American Revolution to protest their refusal to permit Marian Anderson to sing in Constitution Hall. The subsequent Easter Sunday concert at the Lincoln Memorial, arranged by Mrs. Roosevelt and Secretary of the Interior Harold L. Ickes, made Miss Anderson and the DAR (whom Langston Hughes called "Aryan hussies") known around the world. "For the first time," said one member of a 1939 delegation of black social workers visiting the Roosevelt home at Hyde Park, New York, "Negro men and women have reason to believe that their government does care."[26]

THE PEACETIME MILITARY

The New Deal kept the peacetime Army busy. Regular and reserve Army officers and Army NCOs directed the Civilian Conservation Corps. CCC camps employed jobless young men for basic environmental work in public parks and woodlands, in exchange for food, clothing, shelter, medical care, and a small salary. The law specified that race was not to be a factor in enrollment. Integrated camps were short-lived, however, as Army administrators enforced segregation, and replaced blacks only with other blacks.

While the four traditional black Army regiments, the Buffalo Soldier regiments, continued to be important to black America, they were slowly being rendered extinct. Throughout the 1920s, they were deprived of men in order to build up the postwar Air Corps. Vacancies in black units were not filled; instead, corresponding manpower units were transferred to the Air Corps and filled by whites. Many black companies were abolished, or converted from combat units to service units without a change of designation. The 10th Cavalry and 25th Infantry were both scheduled to be terminated entirely in favor of the Air Corps, but Walter White learned of the plan and protested. By 1938, the manpower policy had transformed the 10th Cavalry from a combat unit to part of the labor pool at Fort Leavenworth (where their families were not permitted to use any post facilities). Complaints resulted in an ersatz inquiry, which concluded that "the enlisted men of the 10th Cavalry are well taken care of, happy, contented, and possess a high state of morale."[27] There was also ambivalence among many blacks as to the wisdom of fighting both for the integrity of the Buffalo Soldiers, and for integration of the Army.

When the Army began formulating a definitive policy on black manpower at the end of World War I, segregation and racism were accepted as "fixed characteristics," and the Navy, which had basically stopped enlisting blacks after the war, was deemed the model to follow.[28] In the historic American Navy, ordinary seamen's ranks had been integrated, and so had gunner duties. With the end of World War I, blacks were eligible only for the stewards' branch. In 1923, the Navy stopped recruiting black stewards altogether, and began recruiting Filipinos. In 1933, perhaps for fear of Japanese infiltration, blacks were recruited again.

Most creators of military policy in the 1930s had been young officers in the time of Woodrow Wilson's War Department. These future leaders of World War II took their cue from the racist 1922 staff study (based on the notorious 1920 Army memo). Black manpower would be used only in proportion to the number of blacks in the nation and half of the blacks would be in regiment-sized-only combat units, which were easier to attach to white divisions. Some Army components, such as the Air Corps and the Signal Corps, refused to accept blacks at all. The Army claimed that "it was operating within a social framework which it did not create and which it did not have the power to alter in any significant manner."[29]

By June 1940, there were approximately four thousand blacks on active duty in the Army, about 1.5 percent of that service's total manpower.[30] The Navy had about the same proportion.

Ethiopia

America was not officially involved in either the Italian invasion of Ethiopia or the Spanish Civil War, but black Americans fought in both because they were struggles against fascism, which black Americans saw as global Jim Crow. When Hitler took the Saarland early in 1935, the first step in his plan to conquer Europe, Mussolini, ever competitive, looked to Africa. Declaring the Mediterranean "Mare Nostrum," on October 1, 1935, he sent his "African Legions" to take Ethiopia—where, in 1896, some twenty thousand Italian soldiers had suffered a humiliating defeat at the hands of stick- and spear-wielding natives at Adowa. Now Italian bombers blasted Adowa into ruins. The League of Nations declared Italy the aggressor, and imposed sanctions. Ethiopia's emperor, Haile Selassie, pleaded for international intervention, but the democracies remained neutral, and sanctions were ignored.

Despite Italian propaganda, which depicted Ethiopians as bloodthirsty savages, Italians claimed benevolent feelings toward them. The Italian Fascist song "Faccietta Nera" ("Little Black Girl") offered reassurance to an Ethiopian child that she would be safe under the Roman legions. But images of General Pietro Badoglio's huge mechanized army squaring off against barefoot warriors with spears did not make for good public relations. Neither did the Italian air force's bombing of unarmed villages, led by Mussolini's son-in-law, Count Galeazzo Ciano. Most Italians ignored international public opinion. Jingoism was high, wedding the "new order" of Fascism with nostalgia for Imperial Rome.

Ethiopia's plight—and the eloquence of Haile Selassie's address to the League of Nations—captured the heart of black America, and the world's imagination. Fascination with Emperor Haile Selassie, Ras Tafari, the Lion of Judah (who claimed to be a direct descendant of Solomon and the Queen of Sheba), produced an outpouring of sympathetic international mail, much of it addressed directly to the emperor. "I pray that you will deliver yourself from crucifixion," wrote a Los Angeles black woman, "and show the whites that they are not as civilized as they loudly assert themselves to be." Others advised the emperor to study Lawrence of Arabia's tactics against the Turks; to supply the Ethiopian army with bulletproof vests; and to join the British Empire. But the best advice came from a young man in Topeka, Kansas: "It seems to me that a head-on clash with the Italians would be disastrous. In my opinion the right course would be to allow them into the difficult and mountainous country where their heavy equipment would bog them down and engage them in what we call guerrilla warfare, the kind of tactic American Indians used to drive back the far better equipped pioneers."[31] Influenced or not by the writer from Kansas, the Ethiopians pursued this tactic with great success. Despite their overwhelming material supremacy, the Italians soon came to a standstill. Italian conscripts did not do well in up-close mountain fighting against warriors defending their native land.

In the Italian press, barely a hundred Swiss, Belgian, Greek, and Cuban military "advisers" to Ethiopia became thousands of "white mercenaries."[32] Count Hilaire du Berrier, of France, and Count Carl von Rosen, of Sweden (who flew from Stockholm to Addis Ababa in a plane fitted out as an ambulance), organized the Ethiopian Royal Air Corps. A small group of international pilots, under the direction of Mischa Babitcheff, half Ethiopian, half White Russian, used obsolescent World War I biplanes, useless in combat, to transport the emperor, ammunition, and medical teams. No black American is known to have fought in the ground war, but two black Americans were members of the essentially noncombat three-plane Ethiopian air force: the Chicago aviator John Robinson (one of the first group of blacks admitted to Curtiss Wright Flight Training School in 1930) and Hubert Julian, the 1920s "Black Eagle," who became an Ethiopian air corps colonel. Although Julian got the initial publicity, Robinson later won larger headlines in brave action against Mussolini's airmen. Julian, who cut a dashing figure with sword and white horse, eventually crashed the emperor's favorite plane—then came home complaining that Ethiopia was not "worth saving."[33]

"The one valid and concrete contribution made by the foreign contingent was that of doctors," wrote an Italian historian, Angelo Del Boca.[34] "They were the only members of this body to suffer for their devotion. . . . Theirs is the epic story still to be written of a handful of men, short of everything they needed, working ceaselessly under unimaginably difficult conditions to ease the sufferings of the wounded, many of whom were civilians." There were fifty doctors for 500,000 Ethiopian soldiers. American, Austrian, British, Dutch, Finnish, Greek, Norwegian, Polish, and Swedish Red Cross teams, along with the Egyptian Red Crescent, joined the Ethiopian Red Cross. Some medical workers were captured and tortured; others, including an American doctor, were killed. Blacks in America rallied to Ethiopia's cause, with black doctors and nurses of New York's Harlem Hospital organizing medical-supplies drives.

In June 1935, America's "Brown Bomber," Joe Louis, defeated the

Italian heavyweight Primo Carnera before a huge crowd at Yankee Stadium, to the delight of black Harlem and the consternation of neighboring Italian Harlem. It was, reported the *New York Herald Tribune,* "the first significant mixed heavyweight bout that has been staged in New York in modern times."[35] ("Mixed bouts" were considered dangerous to race relations.) For black Americans, it seemed a symbolic victory for Ethiopia. Roy Wilkins would call Louis's knockout three years later of the "superior Aryan" German boxer Max Schmeling, within a minute of the first round's opening bell in June 1938, the "shortest, sweetest moment of the entire thirties," a symbolic victory for all Americans.[36]

In Chicago, despite a ban by the notorious Mayor Edward Kelly and threats from Red Squad police, Harry Haywood's Southside Communists organized a huge Ethiopia demonstration. Denied permission for a street demonstration, Haywood's group moved the rally to the rooftops. The Southside Communists included two former soldiers, Oliver Law and Alonzo Watson. Law, a building-trade worker and veteran of the 24th Infantry (Buffalo Soldiers), was among those arrested for addressing the crowd from rooftops.[37]

"At this time when the politics of Italian fascism is to destroy the independence of small nations . . . when Japanese imperialism holds large portions of China under her iron heel, when German fascism is ready to plunge the whole world into a new war . . . when American imperialism oppresses a nation of Negro people," declared the perennial Communist Party U.S.A. vice presidential candidate, James Ford, "we can contrast the policy of the Soviet Union, where national minorities have been liberated and where the freedom of the peoples grow."[38] Ford, a black veteran of World War I, delivered his speech in 1935, a year of Moscow show trials and Stalin's bloody Party purge.

In May 1936, Italian troops finally captured Addis Ababa and Mussolini proclaimed, "At last Italy has her empire!"

At the Democratic National Convention that summer, Senator "Cotton Ed" Smith of South Carolina walked out when a black minister led a prayer. Smith refused to support "any political organization that looks upon the Negro and caters to him as a political and social equal."[39]

ARYAN SUPREMACY

Black Americans had been outraged in February 1934 by the sterilization in Nazi Germany of the so-called Rhineland bastards, children of German mothers and Senegalese occupation troops. Alfred Ploetz, the chief theorist of Germany's so-called racial hygiene system, hailed the United

States as a "bold leader in the realm of eugenics" because of its widespread ban on interracial marriage and its strict immigration laws.[40] Hitler had already saluted American "racial hygiene" in 1924 in *Mein Kampf,* which praised the eugenics-influenced Immigration Act passed that year under President Calvin Coolidge. The act barred "Negroes of African ancestry" from entry into the United States. Under the Nazis, most Afro-Germans, mainly of Cameroonian heritage, were either hounded out of Germany or sent to concentration camps, although a few were spared to make propaganda films for Africa. Germany's racism, like America's, managed a certain grim irony when it came to self-interest: Jim Crow laws in Washington, D.C., barred blacks from most restaurants and hotels, but exceptions might be made for *foreign* blacks, and Nazi Germany, which saw all Asians as inferior, considered the Japanese honorary Aryans.

The Berlin Olympic Games of 1936 were designed to be a racist spectacle. Germany's "pure Aryans" were programmed for overwhelming victory. Germany would win the most medals, with Japan, its Axis partner, in second place. But Jesse Owens, a black American sprinter and broad jumper from Ohio State University, was the only medal winner who mattered. American Jews, thanks to fascist sympathizers on the U.S. Olympic Committee, were not permitted to compete—but Owens belied Nazi racial myths by winning four gold medals. "I shall not shake hands with this negro," said Hitler to Baldur von Schirach (head of the Hitler Youth) as the stadium erupted with Owens's name and German Olympic athletes pointedly embraced him.[41]

SPAIN

Spain's Fascists had assumed an easy takeover in the simmering civil war that followed the exile of King Alfonso XIII in 1931, but they were stopped at the ballot box in 1936. Fascist interests (landowners, clergy, monarchists, and the military) had not counted on the stubbornness of what Hugh Thomas, in his monumental *The Spanish Civil War,* calls an "anxious group of middle-aged, middle-class liberals" who hated violence and "admired the pleasing, democratic ways of Britain, France and America."[42] Fascist interests had also not counted on the powerful allegiance to the Republic held by both workers and peasants. The February election between the Fascist National Front and the liberal-to-left Popular Front resulted in a Popular Front victory. Broadly speaking, the Popular Front, unlike the National Front, wanted to change Spain. Members of the coalition ranged from liberals who simply wanted to pull the country out of feudal monarchism (the intellectual elite and free-thinking city dwellers) to those who wanted some sort of revolution (trade unionists, mostly miners), and those with a special grievance (Catalan and Basque nationalists). Spain's small Communist Party was only one of several on the antifascist left, among whom the socialists were particularly strong. The new republic ignited extreme passions, pro and con.

In July 1936, the former Spanish army chief of staff, General Francisco Franco, who had been banished to the Canary Islands right after the election for declaring war on the Popular Front, attacked the southern mainland with the Spanish army of North Africa. This army was composed of Moroccan troops who had served under Franco. They were ferried to Cádiz by German transport planes in response to a plea from Franco to Hitler. While Spain's Fascism was less racially virulent (Spain having long assimilated Moors and Jews) than Germany's, it was equally anti-intellectual. "Down with intelligence! Long live death!" was a favorite motto of Franco's Spanish legionnaires.

"Though the rebels were well armed, they were few in number," wrote Thomas of Franco's forces. "In a place such as Seville, the large working-class population had to be terrified into acquiescence of the new order. . . . Hence, not only did the rebels feel bound to act with extraordinary ruthlessness towards their enemies, but also they had to act openly, and expose the bodies of those whom they killed to public gaze."[43] In the particularly bloody opening months of the war, Fascists killed democrats, liberals, and leftists of every persuasion—and Republicans, in an anticlerical fury, killed hundreds of priests and nuns.

While Franco had taken the southern cities of Córdoba and Seville and most of northwest Spain, the July 18 rebellion had failed in most of the major cities. With Franco nearing Madrid, the country's political and geographical center, the government of the Spanish Republic was moved to Valencia, on the Mediterranean coast. Most of southeast and central Spain and the Mediterranean cities of Barcelona and Valencia were still in Republican hands. The life of the Republic depended on Madrid, Barcelona, and Valencia, whose military units had remained loyal, producing legendary civilian commanders like Gustavo Durán (a composer) and Enrique Lister (a Communist quarry worker), who became generals. But Franco's military advantage soon became enormous. To the approximately 80 percent of the Spanish army who joined the rebellion were added ten thousand Germans, two divisions from Antonio Salazar's Portugal, and a hundred thousand Italian troops, fresh from Ethiopia.[44]

Desperate for arms, the Spanish government appealed to the international democratic community for arms sales. But the League of Nations nonintervention pact of August 1936, which Germany and Italy violated from the beginning, forbade the sale of arms to Spain. Only socialist Mexico, Czechoslovakia, and the USSR sold arms and/or matériel to Spain. Russia also sent some two thousand military advisers—most often identified as "Mexicans" named Ramón, to evade the nonintervention rule. The democracies, which basically hoped that Fascism and Communism would cancel each other out, remained neutral. Congress passed the Neutrality Act making it a crime for any U.S. citizen to go to Spain. Roosevelt later called American neutrality a "grave mistake." At the height of the war, a Gallup poll found that 75 percent of the American public favored a Republican victory.[45]

Spanish Rehearsal for World War was what the pro-Franco British writer Arnold Lunn called his 1937 eyewitness account of the war. Spain was indeed a German rehearsal for blitzkrieg and civilian bombing. Against a background of whitewashed villages and castanets, it was also a form of political theater—one in which Picasso painted the scenery, and the dialogue was written by (among others) Ernest Hemingway, George Orwell, and André Malraux. (Malraux helped organize French volunteers, including Antoine de Saint-Exupéry, for the Republican air force.) Spain inflamed romantics and offered up martyrs. "Or is it the suicide pact, the romantic / Death? Very well, I accept for / I am your choice, your decision. Yes I am Spain," wrote W. H. Auden. Fascists had "skulls of lead" and "patent leather souls," wrote the Spanish poet Federico García Lorca.[46] When Lorca was shot by a Franco firing squad in 1936, poets of the world volunteered—English, Irish, Cuban, Chilean, and American. Langston Hughes, with credentials secured by the French poet Louis Aragon to get him across the closed French border, became a war correspondent.

Spain was the first modern media war, as well as the first modern air war. Ruined cities, brave civilians, and "cry from the wall" posters were all captured by a new breed of hunter: the photojournalist. Newspaper and magazine action photography had been revolutionized since World War I. Americans saw the struggle from both sides. Henry Luce's *Time* and *Life* backed the Republic, while William Randolph Hearst's presses supported Franco. Radio gave the war a voice. The most powerful Spanish voice was that of a Republican woman, forty-year-old Dolores Ibarruri, a Communist parliamentary deputy from Asturias. Her voice helped give Spanish Communists influence in the war far beyond their numbers. Ibarruri won renown early, when one of Franco's four besieging generals famously predicted that Madrid would fall in a week, with help from a "fifth column" inside. She entered the popular lexicon with her response: "It is better to die on your feet than live on your knees." The wife and daughter of Basque miners, Ibarruri was radicalized in part by the death in infancy of four of her six children, for which she blamed the grinding poverty of miners' lives and Spain's feudal economic system. She helped her union-organizer husband and—educated and intelligent but too poor to fulfill a dream of becoming a teacher—she herself began to read Marx. Deeply religious as a girl, she wrote her first articles for the miners' newspaper during Holy Week, 1916, and signed herself "La Pasionaria." The name soon came to stand for her oratory.

The International Brigades

Needing to counter the damage of the nonintervention pact, Spain turned to the Communist International for help in procuring illegal arms from all over Europe, and raising a multinational volunteer army, the International Brigades. But Spain insisted, and the Soviet Union agreed, that it would be a Popular Front, not a Communist army. While most in fact were Communists, others were simply passionate antifascists. Stalin had not yet been revealed as a murderous despot; but Hitler was an open book with a clear message: "Today, Germany; tomorrow, the world!"

Some Americans had recognized the dangers of Fascism early on. For Jewish and black Americans, fighting to keep Fascism out of America's future, Communism seemed the only choice. And black Americans, while fighting for larger issues, could help avenge Ethiopia. (*This Ain't Ethiopia, But It'll Do* is the subtitle of Danny Duncan Collum and Victor A. Berch's *African Americans in the Spanish Civil War.*) Some 2,800 American men and women—numbers vary because of aliases—joined the Abraham Lincoln Brigade, the American unit of the International Brigades. Approximately nine hundred were Jewish. Only eighty to one hundred were black, but many would have leadership positions. Most of the white volunteers had no military training, but many blacks, older than the brigade's average of twenty-three, were World War I or National Guard veterans. Radicalized by American racism rather than by Marx or Lenin, most were Communists.

The five International Brigades—the 11th through 15th Brigades of the Republican army—were wrapped in socialist mystique. The German 11th Brigade of exiles and political concentration-camp escapees was called Ernst Thaelmann, for a jailed Communist labor leader. The 12th "Garibaldi" Brigade of Italian antifascists was named for the nineteenth-century revolutionary. The Balkan 13th "Dabrowsky" Brigade was named for an early-nineteenth-century Polish freedom fighter. The "Sixth of February" Franco-Belgian 14th Brigade recalled the Paris Commune of 1848.

The English-speaking 15th Brigade (plus an attached unit of Spanish-speaking volunteers from Latin America) was essentially four separate battalions—British, Canadian, Irish, and American. The Irish James Connolly Battalion, representing literary Dublin and the IRA (and including a Catholic priest), was separate by choice. They had refused to serve with the British. The British Saklatvala Battalion, named for an Indian Communist at Oxford, went by the more pronounceable "British Battalion." The large, bilingual Canadian Mackenzie-Papineau Battalion (named for the leaders of the 1837 rebellion) was known as the "Mac-Paps," and included Dr. Norman Bethune, creator of the blood bank (used for the first time in Spain), who helped organize Republican medical forces with support from Albert Einstein and the daughters of Marie Curie. The Americans voted to call themselves the Abraham Lincoln Battalion. At one point or another, American units included the George Washington Battalion, the John Brown and Frederick Douglass Field Artillery Companies, and the Tom Mooney Machine Gun Company. (The labor leader Tom Mooney was serving a life sentence for a 1916 bombing, for which he would be pardoned and released in 1939.)

On the grounds that a civilian army fought better if educated to the reasons for war, commissars were attached to every brigade to explain the importance of the battle in terms of the country and the world. The commissar idea was originally Spanish, not Russian. Commissars, whom some saw as fighting teachers, coaches, and cheerleaders, were also responsible for getting food and mail to the front lines and taking care of special needs. "First to advance and last to retreat," they had a high casualty rate. All International volunteers gave the fist-to-temple Popular Front salute (a variation on the Communist raised fist), greeted each other with "Salud," and called each other Comrade. Hemingway, who liked to be called Ernesto, copied their typical garb of beret, leather jacket, dirty corduroys, and espadrilles.

Political and philosophical unity aside, American volunteers were a study in racial, economic, and occupational diversity (among them were a ballet dancer, a Texas Ranger, and three self-described acrobats). Volunteers included the sons of a former governor of Ohio and of a mayor of Los Angeles, and the brother of a congressman from Wisconsin. James Lardner, son of Ring Lardner, would be the last American volunteer. Three O'Flaherty brothers from Boston volunteered together. A Japanese American antifascist, Jack Shirai, from San Francisco, became the Lincoln Brigade's cook, until he went absent without leave and was killed in battle. Fresh off a big strike, and flexing infant muscles, was a large contingent of merchant seamen, veterans of the labor wars of the new and integrated National Maritime Union. All the seamen, including the NMU's cofounder Bill Bailey, famous for ripping the swastika off the *Bremen* in

New York harbor in 1935, fought as infantrymen in Spain. Shaped by dust bowl hunger, labor wars, and lynching protests, Americans who went to Spain, black and white, represented the young hope of the American left.

Hugh Thomas found Americans "curiously innocent" beside the rest of the Brigades.[47] Americans who went to Spain in 1937, like those who went to France in 1917, were naïve about the nature of war. Most had never seen a rifle until their first battle. "They were younger than most of those in other brigades," he wrote. "Yet they fought with great gallantry, without artillery cover." That the vastly outmanned and outmachined Spanish Republic lasted three years was owing, foremost, to the heroism of the Spanish people and, secondarily, to Soviet material aid; but it was also owing, in great part, to the International Brigades, which saved for as long as possible the antifascist cities of Madrid, Valencia, and Barcelona. Many members of the Abraham Lincoln Brigade spent 120 consecutive days in the frontline trenches.

The first group of integrated American volunteers left New York the day after Christmas, 1936. With orders to talk to no one but their cabin mates, they sailed third class, with tickets paid by Communist organizations, on the *Normandie,* queen of the French Line. (Later volunteers, with passports stamped "Not valid for travel in Spain," would risk fines and prison terms.) Sharing a border with Spain, France was officially neutral, but Premier Léon Blum was a socialist, and his government was Popular Front. At Le Havre, the French customs officers, seeing camping gear, hiking boots, and leather jackets, passed the volunteers' bags with the Popular Front salute.

They registered in expensive Paris hotels, but actually stayed three and four to a room in working-class neighborhood hotels while waiting for orders from the International Brigades' travel committee, which included Josip Broz of Yugoslavia (the man who became Tito). The first volunteer group proceeded by train to Perpignan, near the Spanish border. Later volunteers, after the French border was closed, faced the terrifying eight-hour night climb over the Pyrenees—where most of the new camping gear was tossed away.

Black Lincolns: Oliver Law and Walter Garland

International Brigade Command disapproved of Americans who, espousing military democracy, insisted on choosing officers and noncommissioned officers only after they had proved themselves in battle. General André Marty, commander-in-chief of the International Brigades (and

French Communist hero of the Russian Revolution), considered them "spoiled children," and threatened to send them home.[48] Captain Robert Hale Merriman, a twenty-seven-year-old economics teaching fellow from Berkeley with a second lieutenant's commission from the University of Nevada ROTC, was appointed the Lincoln's commander. Merriman, who became the model for Robert Jordan in Hemingway's *For Whom the Bell Tolls,* convinced the Lincolns of the necessity of traditional military authority. He looked to the few men among them with military experience, including black volunteers Oliver Law and Walter Garland, to help turn the Lincolns into soldiers. Law and Garland became machine-gun section leaders, in charge of two of the company's four 1914 Russian Maxims.

The Lincoln commissar, Steve Nelson (a Croatian immigrant and Philadelphia dockworker), was on the committee that chose thirty-year-old Oliver Law as the third commander of the Abraham Lincoln Brigade. "More serious than jovial," he wrote of Law, "but never harsh; he was well-liked by his men . . . when soldiers were asked who might become an officer—ours was a very democratic army—his name always came up. It was spoken of him that he was calm under fire, dignified, respectful of his men and always given to thoughtful consideration of initiatives and military missions."[49] Charlie Nusser, a white vet, had a very Lincolnesque appraisal: "He was a courageous leader and a devoted anti-Fascist. He was also a regular guy."[50] The first black commander of an integrated American army, Law served for three months, until he was killed in action at Brunete.

"My first commander was Walter Garland, machine-gunner extraordinaire," wrote Milton Wolff, a white art student from Brooklyn who became the last Lincoln commander. "Whatever I learned about the Maxim (machine gun) he taught me. But more important . . . he instilled in me the conviction that we could go out there and take on the whole bloody, professional fascist Armies and kick the shit out of 'em."[51] Called El Lobo ("The Wolf") by both sides, Wolff was described by Hemingway as "tall as Lincoln, and as brave and as good a soldier as any that commanded battalions at Gettysburg."[52] His commander, Lieutenant Walter Garland, was a twenty-three-year-old ex–15th New York National Guardsman (369th Regiment) and a Harlem Communist Party activist. Garland would be wounded at Jarama and Brunete.

The most popular black Lincoln, wounded in the Ebro Retreats south of Barcelona, was dark, chubby-faced Eluard McDaniels, twenty-five. Known as El Fantastico because of his amazing grenade pitching, the sometime art student, longshoreman, and baseball player, the adopted son of the white San Francisco photographer Consuelo Kanaga, worried that he would not "sound like a Negro" in Spain.[53] Spanish peasants expressed a camaraderie with black Americans, because blacks had once been *esclavos,* slaves, as they also considered themselves to be.

Jarama and Pingarron

With less rudimentary basic training than most battalions, Lincolns were in the forefront at the Battles of Jarama and Brunete, extremely costly Republican victories that saved Madrid in the spring and summer of 1937. They became the most popular Internationals in Republican Spain, with the entire 15th Brigade soon fixed in the public imagination ("Viva la Quince Brigada!").

By February 1937, Madrid was in true danger. Fascists were about to cross the Jarama River, key to its southern defense. The Republican air force successfully took on German aircraft, but superior Fascist ground forces were defeating poorly trained British, French, and Balkan volunteers. Having spent a month drilling without rifles and ammunition, the Lincolns were called in as reinforcements. Many saw their first weapon the day they went into battle, on February 23, in an olive grove near Jarama's Pingarron Hill. They had been ordered to lead the attack on Pingarron—without air or artillery support. Merriman let each man take five practice shots at the side of a hill with the new Russian rifles and protested the lack of support to the International commanders, the Hungarian Colonel Gal (a nom de guerre) and the Yugoslavian Colonel Vladimir Copic. Told to obey orders "or else," Merriman ordered his men to prepare to go over the top, and wrote a farewell note to his wife: "Marian, dear, I love you! I am willing to die for my ideas. May I live for them and you!"[54] Instantly hit in the shoulder as he raised his arm for the men to follow him out of the trench, Merriman demanded that stretcher-bearers take him to confront Copic, who refused to see him. Meanwhile, the Lincolns continued suicidally over the top.

"Many got wounded just as they climbed the parapet to go over," wrote Pingarron veteran John Tisa.[55] "Some comrades from among the recent arrivals, uninformed and inexperienced, went over the top with full packs on their backs and charged toward the fascists. Many wounded men crawled back to the trenches safely; many were killed in the attempt." Five hundred Lincolns went into battle; many were wounded, and 127 were killed. The Fascists lost and retook Pingarron Hill three times. Republicans and Fascists each took about ten thousand casualties, or 25 percent losses on each side, during the monthlong battle. Madrid was saved in the spring of 1937. After Pingarron, the twice-wounded Walter Garland was promoted to lieutenant, as was Oliver Law.

Jarama's Battle of Pingarron had saved the Madrid–Valencia road, but the International Brigade commanders Gal and Copic were blamed for the deaths of many Americans. Copic handled the brigade "like an old apple woman with locomotor ataxia," Hemingway wrote to the poet Edwin Rolfe, a brigade member.[56] When Copic and Gal were later replaced, Hemingway enjoyed the rumor that they had been called to Moscow and shot. He considered General André Marty another "swine" who "ought to be shot," and was equally contemptuous of the lone American staff officer, Major Allan McNeil, formerly of the U.S. Army.

In February 1939, however, the second anniversary of Pingarron, Hemingway indelibly captured the essence of the war's idealism in his ode to the dead American volunteers: "The dead sleep cold in Spain tonight," he wrote. "For our dead are a part of the earth of Spain now and the earth of Spain can never die. . . . Those who have entered it honorably, and no men ever entered earth more honorably than those who died in Spain, have already achieved immortality."[57]

In a 1940 letter to Rolfe, Hemingway, at work on *For Whom the Bell Tolls,* wrote:

> Listen Ed . . . I miss the spanish war because life is fine and work (as now) the hardest thing to do. But it was fine to fight for something you believed in and be able to go straight to headquarters about pricks instead of having to suffer under them as when I was a kid [in World War I]. I wish the hell there was a war I could go to when I finish this book that I believe in. But there aint any such war. (You don't have to tell me there is the other always present war. I know about that. And I know, truly, I couldn't take the discipline.)[58]

For Rolfe, a committed Communist, the "always present" war was the class war. "I like the Communists when they're soldiers," Hemingway said. "I hate them when they're priests." Spain was Hemingway's last war. Although his wife Martha Gellhorn was a war correspondent, he spent most of World War II in Key West and Havana.

VAUGHN LOVE, JAMES YATES, AND SALARIA KEE

Too late for Pingarron, Vaughn Love and James Yates were two of the five black Americans who sailed February 20, 1937, on the *Ile de France,* with the largest contingent of Americans heading for Spain, three hundred out of eight hundred passengers. "Although we talked with each other and played poker, we all kept our destination a secret," Love wrote. Love and Yates, who dined with Hemingway, became my friends in the course of working on this book. Both had written of their experiences in Spain: Love in an unpublished memoir, and Yates in his published autobiography, *From Mississippi to Madrid,* which he sold on the streets of Greenwich Village, making friends as well as fans. They were both in their eighties, and still considered themselves revolutionaries. Yates, a bachelor, had a small bust of Lenin on the mantel of his neat, one-room, book-filled New York apartment.

The son of a World War I medical corps officer, Vaughn Love was the godson of World War I sergeant Henry Johnson, the first American soldier to win the Croix de Guerre. He had wanted to go to Ethiopia (although he had fewer illusions than most about Ethiopian democracy). Love's travel orders were to leave Paris for Marseilles with about two hundred other International volunteers aboard a Spanish freighter, awaiting a cargo of Russian wheat. The wheat arrived on the fourth day. That night "the ship eased out of the dock and suddenly came alive like a speedboat and lifted itself out of the water and headed for Barcelona," he wrote. The captain of the *Ciudad de Barcelona,* called "Ramón," was Russian, as was the entire crew. "We were all deep revolutionaries," Love said in a later interview. "We thought, 'We have to get to the front and kill these Fascists!' . . . I was through with the system. I knew it didn't work, and I was thinking in terms of changing society—to change the world." In Spain, Love joined the Washington Battalion, formed after the Battle of Pingarron as more Americans arrived. Its captain was Oliver Law.

James Yates, who left his native Mississippi for Chicago only two or three steps ahead of the Klan, became a railway union organizer and member of Harry Haywood's Ethiopia protests. Moving to New York, he joined the Communist Party—and saw his Chicago and Harlem friends Oliver Law, Alonzo Watson, Walter Garland, and Oscar Hunter leave for Spain without him. Yates had trouble getting a passport, because Mississippi did not keep records of black births. In Paris, he shared a hotel room with a Swede, an English Jew (who "talked like the king of England"), and a Nazi-hating German. He was "learning so much about people, and the world," that he felt his head would "split wide open," he wrote in his autobiography. He found the Champs-Elysées, and couldn't believe that he, "a poor fellow from Mississippi," was actually there.[59] But "painful memories of being constantly rejected" in his own country kept him from going into a café. Yates knew that he had to get over feeling like "half a man." How could he face bullets in Spain, if he "couldn't face a café filled with French people"? He conquered the café and, three days later, crossed the Pyrenees. Like most of the volunteers, he lightened his load during the climb. "When it came to my books—three battered paperbacks by Claude McKay Gorky, and Langston Hughes—I paused," wrote Yates. "I tried to fit them into my pockets, but they felt like pieces of lead. I fingered them regretfully, then pulled two out, letting them drop. They filtered down through the blackness. It was like a part of me falling." He had kept Langston Hughes.[60]

Republicans frowned on sexism as well as racism. There were women leaders in the Spanish government, and young Spanish women manned the barricades at the battle of Madrid University. Although women of the International Brigades were not in combat, many came under bombardment as doctors, nurses, and drivers in the front lines. Following her husband and brother to Spain, Evelyn Hutchins was the only woman driver of an ammunition truck.

Salaria Kee, a Harlem Hospital nurse who had collected medical supplies for Ethiopia, sailed to Spain in March 1937 with the second American medical unit, and became, at twenty-four, the only black nurse in the 15th Brigade. When black Lincolns heard of her arrival, a peseta was tossed to decide who would have the honor of welcoming her. Oliver Law won the toss, but the only decent uniform fit Doug Roach.[61] Kee met her future husband, Patrick O'Reilly of the Irish Connolly Brigade, when he was her patient. Their hospital marriage was performed by the Connolly Brigade's Catholic priest. A public relations gift, Kee appeared in two documentary films, *Heart of Spain* and *Return to Life.*

BRUNETE AND THE DEATH OF CAPTAIN LAW

Jarama and Pingarron had saved the Madrid–Valencia road, but Madrid was still surrounded on three sides. Brunete, a Fascist-held area some nineteen miles west of the capital, saw the first Republican offensive of the war. Its purpose was to relieve Madrid. Supported by over a hundred tanks and a hundred aircraft from Russia, British and American fighters spearheaded the July 5, 1937, attack. It would be a thirty-day battle; street by street, house by house, in hundred-degree heat. "Even the rivers ran dry," wrote Edwin Rolfe.[62] The Fascists had new troops and firepower. Brunete was a major defeat, and Americans suffered 50 percent casualties. Within days the Washingtons disbanded, and the two decimated units became one new Abraham Lincoln Brigade, with Captain Oliver Law as commander.

On July 10, the fifth day of the Brunete campaign, Lincoln commander Law was shot in the stomach and killed as he led an assault in the middle of a wheat field at Brunete's Mosquito Ridge. New Yorker Harry Fisher was there: "I heard the cries for first aid and the moans of the wounded and dying. . . . He was about twenty yards ahead of us, standing there yelling and waving his pistol. 'O.K., fellahs, let's go! Let's go! Let's keep it up. We can chase them off that hill. We can TAKE that hill. Come on!' He got hit just about then. That was the last I saw of him." To Fisher, it seemed that all the bullets were aimed directly at Law: "You could see the dust rising around him, where hundred of bullets seemed to be converging." Law's friend Jerry Weinberg crawled out and pulled him to the rear. He was placed on a stretcher under protest, and died soon after. His body was buried below Mosquito Ridge, marked with a piece of wood stating his age and race, and hung with his helmet. "Someday, the working class of America will properly acknowledge the role this brave Negro Communist played in the fight for freedom," said Commissar Steve Nelson in his eulogy.[63]

Vaughn Love was cited for conspicuous bravery at Brunete and sent to officers' training school (under a Russian captain named, as usual, Ramón). Walter Garland, wounded twice at Jarama, was shot in the knee at Brunete while going to the aid of a fallen comrade. "It was his inspiring leadership that made it possible for us to survive the 21 hellish days of Brunete and go on from there," wrote Milt Wolff.[64]

> Garland pulling the wounded Leo Kaufman off a hill and himself being wounded in the process, is a scene burned into my memory . . . him shouting for us to take cover as he lifted the frail Kaufman in his arms, a sniper peppering the exposed crest, and bringing Leo safely into the waiting arms of Sanidad and then Walter tying a handkerchief around his own wound and leading us on. . . . There was nothing that Captain Walter Garland could ask of me that I would not have done straightaway.

When he recuperated, Garland was sent to command the American training base at Tarazona. In late August, together with Langston Hughes and the Harlem Communist Louise Thompson, he made a special Madrid radio broadcast to raise black American support for Spain. In October, Garland was sent home to raise funds. Langston Hughes witnessed what his biographer Arnold Rampersad described as an inconceivable sight in America: white soldiers marching past a black base commander as he relinquished his post.

The Aragon Front: Paul Williams and James Peck

"When we got up with the Americans, they were lying under some olive trees along a little stream. The yellow dust of Aragon was blowing over them," Hemingway wrote of the Lincolns. "Since I saw them last spring, they have become soldiers." "This is a fine brigade we've got here," the Lincoln commander Merriman, new chief of staff of the International Brigades, told Martha Gellhorn. "Shock troops, now. You can tell a brigade is fine when they move it from front to front, in trucks, fast, to wherever the danger is."[65]

As "shock troops," Lincolns would be in the vanguard of two major 1937 diversionary offensives: in August on the Aragon front, in defense of Bilbao, the Basque capital, and at Teruel in December, in defense of Valencia. Aragon saw great loss of men as well as the loss, due to war damage, of most of the region's wheat crop—which meant hunger for the Republic. In August 1937, right after Brunete, the Republicans launched a diversionary offensive on the Aragon front, north and east of Madrid, to draw Fascist fire away from Bilbao. Fierce fighting continued in central Spain in defense of Madrid and in the province of Catalonia, whose capital, Barcelona, would become a last lifeline.

Crawford Morgan, from New York City's Hell's Kitchen neighborhood, was a runner for brigade headquarters until he was wounded in the leg on the Aragon front; he then drove a truck and was wounded again. He went to Spain at the age of twenty-six. "From the time I arrived in Spain until the time I left . . . I felt like a human being, like a man," Morgan told the authors of *African Americans in the Spanish Civil War*. "People didn't look at me with hatred in their eyes because I was black." In 1954, denying that fighting in Spain was un-American, Morgan was asked by the Subversive Activities Control Board if he would take up arms to fight America's "fascist tendencies." (The Subversive Activities Control Board was attempting, in response to a petition by U.S. Attorney General Herbert Brownell, to classify the Veterans of the Abraham Lincoln Brigade as a subversive organization.) "What you are asking me is, why don't I go out and be a stupid anarchist and get a machine gun," Morgan replied. "Now, maybe a lot of people would like for guys like us to do things like that, but we are only interested in freedom of speech, freedom of religion and equality. That is all any person requires, and we don't have it. But going out with arms, that is not the way to get it."[66]

At Aragon, black Americans saw action in the air for the first time. Paul Williams and James Peck were two of the thirty-one Americans trained by Russian "advisers" to fly with "La Gloriosa," the collective name of the Spanish airmen based around Madrid and Barcelona to protect those cities. Most of the army had joined Franco's rebellion, but 150 out of some 250 Spanish military pilots rallied behind the aviator hero Hidalgo de Cisneros, who became head of the Republican air force.[67] At the beginning of the war, before the Germans and Italians arrived, Republican air forces were stronger than the Fascists'. As German and Italian pilots joined Franco, French and Russians joined the Republic, but they were soon outnumbered. By mid-1938, the Republican air force would be relegated to coastal defense. Its final mission would be to fly government officials into exile in France.

Paul Williams was the only successful black aeronautical engineer in America in the 1930s. "We're Navy people," he said of his family in a March 1938 interview in the *Sunday Worker*.[68] His great-great-grandfather had fought with the Navy in the War of 1812; his grandfather served in the Union Navy in the Civil War. (Jacob Peterson, an earlier ancestor, had helped capture Benedict Arnold.) Williams grew up near a small airfield in Youngstown, Ohio. At sixteen, after helping a pilot repair a smashed ship, he was offered flying lessons, and after high school he entered Carnegie Tech to study aeronautical engineering. Later, at the Ohio School of Aeronautical Engineering, he designed his first commercial ship, a monoplane, for the Ohio Aero Company. Although he was the only black pilot at Ohio airfields, Williams found no prejudice. He formed a small company with three white pilots to produce a light dive-bomber for a government competition. "The small company lives and dies a quick death," he said. "It takes money to experiment." He then became a commercial test pilot, making good money for dangerous work—volunteering on the side to participate in Ohio flood relief, and to drop supplies to icebound islanders in northern Canada. The black Chicago congressman Oscar De Priest recommended him to the Navy, which accepted him with a special grade, Lieutenant Junior Class (which meant that he could not eat or fraternize with either commissioned officers or enlisted men). Williams left the service in 1935, to become an instructor in aeronautics for the Civilian Conservation Corps. He had just completed his second airplane, the WX21—"W" for Williams, "X" for experimental, "21" for 21st design—when he left for Spain, at the age of twenty-eight.

Williams and James Peck, the last Americans to join the Republican air force, had never met when they sailed for Spain together in August on the *Queen Mary*. (Lillian Hellman and Dorothy Parker were on the same boat, also bound for Spain.) Peck, a former University of Pittsburgh student, and professional drummer, was an aviation writer for white periodicals (his race went unmentioned). He had a commercial pilot's license, but his applications to both the Army and Navy flying schools were rejected. In a 1941 interview Peck said that the enemy in Spain "was a species of that thing which at home had kept me, a trained pilot, grounded, while keeping hundreds of thousands of other Negro youths from being what they wanted to be."[69] Peck, who often dined with Hemingway in Madrid, was one of America's three aces. He got four of his five verified kills on the Aragon front.

Paul Robeson at Teruel

Autumn brought victory and defeat on the Aragon front, but the winter of 1937–1938, the coldest winter in Spanish memory, saw a dreadful defeat at Teruel, north of Valencia. Teruel marked the beginning of the end of the Republic.

The Battle of Teruel, fought from December 1937 through February 1938, was another diversionary offensive to draw Fascists away from Barcelona. The soldiers fought in a blizzard with subzero weather; some had frostbitten fingers and toes that were later amputated. Half Republican, half Fascist, Teruel saw executions behind the lines on both sides against suspected enemy sympathizers. Like Brunete, it began with early Republican victories, and became a major defeat. More than fifteen thousand Republicans were killed or injured. The Lincolns, the Mac-Paps, and the British all suffered heavy losses.

At Christmas, Paul Robeson sang at the Teruel front. He brought "Ol' Man River," "Water Boy," and "Lonesome Road" to Spain and took home "Freiheit!" ("Freedom!"), the haunting song of the German Thaelmann Brigade; the unofficial International Brigade anthem, "Viva La Quince Brigada!" ("Long Live the 15th Brigade!"); and "Los Quatros Generales" ("The Four Generals"). Spain was a "major turning point" for Robeson. "Every artist, every scientist, must decide now where he stands," he had said six months earlier at a benefit for Basque refugee children at the Royal Albert Hall in London. "There is no standing above the conflict on Olympian heights. There are no impartial observers. . . . The artists must elect to fight for Freedom or Slavery. I have made my choice. I had no alternative."[70]

The "Retreats"

The spring and summer of 1938 brought the "Retreats"—with Lincolns as International shock troops in a Fascist offensive along the Ebro River, southwest of Barcelona. In March 1938, as Hitler was annexing Austria and Czechoslovakia, the International Retreats began at the towns of Belchite and Caspe, west of Barcelona on the other side of the Ebro River. Facing a full-scale Fascist onslaught, Lincolns were the last to leave Caspe. At Gandesa, there were 80,000 Republicans against 200,000 Fascists. The wild retreat across the Ebro was like a terrible dream—men, among them Major Robert Merriman, simply disappeared to be killed or captured. A lucky few made it across the river. "There wasn't a man who made the trip who didn't feel death walking by his side," wrote Milt Wolff, the last American to cross.[71]

By late summer 1938, with decimated ranks, three-quarters of the Lincolns were Spanish peasants. There were three thousand Internationals left, and fewer than 450 Americans—but Americans continued to volunteer. The last official volunteer was a twenty-three-year-old Paris *Herald Tribune* reporter, James Lardner (who ignored strong efforts to dissuade him, by Hemingway and the journalist Vincent Sheehan). Because of his famous father, the writer Ring Lardner, the Internationals tried to keep James out of combat, but he managed to get to the front. He was wounded in the thigh in early August, and vanished in the war's last offensive a month later.

On October 4, 1938, the Republican prime minister, Juan Negrín, officially withdrew the International Brigades from Spain. Two thousand surviving Internationals, including Captain Milt Wolff and two hundred other Americans, marched through flower-strewn streets on October 29 at the Barcelona farewell parade. "The people's salutation knew no bounds," wrote a Lincoln volunteer in a letter home.[72] "Girls broke through the lines and showered us with kisses. . . . The Negro comrades just couldn't march. They were actually besieged! Planes swooped down almost touching the tree-tops and threw leaflets with greetings to the Internationals. The soldiers of course were given flowers. They carried no arms at all. Even if the Fascists win, which I don't think, how can they hope to kill the memory of these days." People cried, "Viva los Internacionales!" and soldiers cried, "Viva la República!" André Malraux, seeing all Republican hope going with them, remarked to Vincent Sheehan that it was "toute la Révolution qui s'en allait" ("the entire Revolution was leaving").[73] The day ended with La Pasionaria telling the last Internationals that they were "history . . . legend . . . the heroic example of democracy's solidarity and universality."

Lincolns had a great sense of togetherness. Most returned to America in groups, on the *Normandie* or the *Paris.* For James Yates, it was a return to homegrown Jim Crow. The Lincolns walked out en masse when their New York City hotel refused to admit him. "I was doubly shocked to be hit so quickly," he wrote.[74] "The pain went as deep as any bullet could have done. I had the dizzy feeling that I was back in the trenches again. But this was another front. I was home."

Back Home

When America entered World War II in late 1941, surviving members of the Abraham Lincoln Brigade offered themselves as a unit to the U.S. government. Had they not been rejected, theirs would have been the only nonsegregated unit in the American military. Lincoln veterans suffered for being "red" as well as black. Officially labeled security risks, they were nonetheless admired by military command. Approximately six hundred of the surviving eighteen hundred Lincolns joined the armed forces. Some 400 went into the merchant marine; and nine, including Milt Wolff, joined the OSS, or Office of Strategic Services, the clandestine branch of the military. Lincoln vets would be killed in action at Guadalcanal, Leyte, Anzio, Omaha Beach, the Ardennes, and the Rhine; several were highly decorated. In the red-baiting 1950s, Lincoln vets who fought in World War II were forced to sue for the right to be buried at Arlington National Cemetery.

Salaria Kee, James Yates, Walter Garland, and Vaughn Love were among the black Lincolns who went to war again. Salaria Kee joined the Army Nurse Corps. James Yates joined the Signal Corps, and was the only one pulled out of his outfit to stay in America when the unit went overseas. Walter Garland, as a member of the 731st Military Police Battalion at Fort Wadsworth, Staten Island, taught mapmaking, mortar, and machine guns, and developed a new machine-gun sighting device, accepted, and used by the Army. Although he was asked to address a class of officers on the Brunete campaign, all of Garland's requests for combat duty were denied.

Vaughn Love joined the Quartermaster Corps. After one week of basic training at Camp Lee, Virginia, he became an acting corporal. (Infamous in World War I, where black soldiers froze to death in the winter of 1918, Camp Lee in World War II forbade black soldiers, under threat of court-martial, to enter certain stores in nearby Petersburg.) Within two weeks he was a regimental guard, with a citation for action above the call of duty. Remaining at Camp Lee after basic, he became a sergeant in charge of the only platoon not led by a second lieutenant, and was assigned to lecture staff officers on ground-troop defense against air and mechanized attack. There were no manuals; Love had learned everything from "Captain Ramón," his Russian advanced military training instructor in Spain. Later, when a U.S. Department of Orientation captain began a lecture before two assembled black Camp Lee regiments with the words, "Hitler is the greatest military genius who ever lived," Love stood up and said that he was "not a great military genius." Invited by the red-faced captain to "tell them all about it," Love described how the isolated Spanish Republic, under arms embargo, not only held Fascist armies at bay but inflicted heavy defeats. It was a matter of "will and dedication," he said, the "human element." Trained and dedicated soldiers were always superior to tanks and airplanes, he said. Love received cheers and a standing ovation for predicting that the Allies would "grind the German army to ashes." He considered himself America's first "commissar."

Informal charges of "discourtesy" were dismissed when Love's colonel, warning him to be more careful in the future, said that the entire staff agreed with him. But a first lieutenant "with no military skills" was now assigned to Love's platoon: Army intelligence had him under surveillance. He overheard a conversation about himself between a lieutenant and a captain. The lieutenant wondered why Love, a "number one sergeant," had an order on file forbidding him to carry arms outside the post. The captain answered that it probably had something to do with Love being a Spaniard and, therefore, "hotheaded." Love eventually went overseas, landing at Normandy's "Red Dog" Beach on D-Day.

In 1986, fifty years after the start of the war, 120 Lincoln Brigade veterans were invited to return to Spain, now a socialist monarchy, to become honorary citizens. In Madrid they met the ninety-one-year-old Dolores Ibarruri (returned from exile in the Soviet Union). "When the olive tree of peace puts forth its leaves again, entwined with the laurels of the Spanish Republic's victory—come back!" she had told the Lincolns in 1938. Now, James Yates kissed her and said, "Pasionaria, we are here!" Gathering on Mosquito Ridge, the group also paid homage to Captain Oliver Law.

8 World War II

THE DOUBLE V

The V for victory sign is being displayed prominently in all so-called democratic countries . . . then let we colored Americans adopt the double VV for a double victory. The first V for victory over our enemies from without, the second V for victory over our enemies from within. For surely those who perpetuate these ugly prejudices here are seeking to destroy our democratic form of government just as surely as the Axis forces.[1]

—*James G. Thompson, a cafeteria worker at Cessna Aircraft, from a letter written in January 1942 to the* Pittsburgh Courier

I. Peace

The Battle to Change the Jim Crow Military

In December 1941 Walter White, the executive secretary of the NAACP, sent a proposal to General George C. Marshall, the U.S. Army Chief of Staff, urging the creation of a volunteer Army division "open to all Americans irrespective of race, creed, color, or national origin."[2] White believed that such a division would "set a new and successful pattern of democracy." He was inspired by the actions of young Roger Starr, a recent graduate of Yale, who had read his article in the *Saturday Evening Post* about how discrimination against blacks in the army and private industry "was retarding our preparations for what everyone feared but understood was coming."[3] Starr told White that he planned to ask his draft board to let him serve with black troops, not as an officer but as an enlisted man. The NAACP released his letter to the press. Starr became something of a celebrity, and the NAACP was suddenly inundated with letters from other young whites pledging to follow Starr's example. Drafted in 1943, Starr was eventually dropped into China by the clandestine Office of Strategic Services (OSS), but his request to enlist in a black unit kept him out of officer candidate school and followed him wherever he was assigned in the Army.

"With elaborate casualness," Walter White mentioned his proposal for a nonsegregated division at a talk at the University of California at Berkeley in mid-1942.[4] "An avalanche of young men" poured down the aisle at the end of the meeting. "Ah want to be the first as a native of Jawja to volunteah for youah mixed division," a young southerner told White. "A lettah will be too slow—Ah'm goin to telegraph the Wah Depahtment." Despite "sympathetic support" from Assistant Secretary of War Robert P. Patterson, the War Department remained unmoved. "The tradition-bound and prejudice-indoctrinated majority," wrote White, felt that "we must not indulge in social experimentation in time of war."

Roy Wilkins, editor of *The Crisis,* had been "bleakly amused" in 1940 when the Nazi theorist Hans Habe described life for black Americans under a global Third Reich. "Germany would control their jobs and all forms of association that might lead to assimilation," Habe said. Voting, intermarriage, and access to all public accommodations (including roads, streetcars, and motion pictures) would be forbidden under the global Reich. Blacks would also be forbidden to serve in the military, except in labor battalions. For Wilkins, it could have been a page from American Jim Crow. "Negroes did not need us at the NAACP to tell them that it sounded pretty foolish to be against park benches marked JUDE in Berlin but to be *for* park benches marked COLORED in Tallahassee, Florida," Wilkins remarked in his autobiography, *Standing Fast.* "Negroes were not being sent to any concentration camps, of course," he wrote, "but what a thing to be thankful for."[5]

Home-front fascism was alive and well in America's 1940 military policy. The bases of that policy were the racist 1920 report on the use of black troops and a 1925 Army War College study stating that blacks were "physically unqualified for combat duty" because the black brain weighed ten ounces less than the white. Blacks, moreover, "subservient" by nature and believing themselves "inferior" to whites, were "susceptible to the influence of crowd psychology" and unable to control themselves in the face of danger. Thus, the War Department would not "intermingle colored and white enlisted personnel in the same regimental organization." Neither would it assign "colored Reserve Officers other than of the Medical Corps and Chaplains" to existing black combat units of the regular Army.[6]

What blacks called the "Negro is too dumb to fight" policy was backed by statistics. Twenty percent of blacks, and 74 percent of whites, had the highest Army grades of 1, 2, or 3. Eighty percent of blacks, and 26 percent of whites, were in 4 and 5, the lowest achieving grades. Seventy-five percent of black registrants came from southern states or border states, where four out of five blacks had not even completed the fourth grade of grammar school. Seventeen percent of blacks, as compared with 41 percent of whites, had graduated from high school.[7] The policy was to blame blacks themselves, rather than their limited educational and economic opportunities. The Secretary of War, Henry L. Stimson, was in favor of overlooking white illiteracy, however: "The Army had adopted rigid requirements for literacy mainly to keep down the number of colored troops and this is reacting badly in preventing us from getting some very good but illiterate [white] troops from the southern mountain states," he wrote in his diary.[8]

American racial policy in World War II is the story of the struggle between what Walter White called the "decent" and the "bigoted." Commander-in-Chief Franklin D. Roosevelt proved a master at juggling the two to serve both his better instincts and his political purposes. His wife was free to speak out, mostly because he agreed with her and because he famously, and usefully, could not "control" her. But no black issue, from making lynching a federal crime to desegregating the military, was more important than appeasing the southern wing of the Democratic Party.

Unfortunately, the day-to-day running of the war was in the hands of far less enlightened men than Roosevelt—men like Henry L. Stimson and the secretary of the Navy, Frank Knox. Stimson, whose diaries revealed his racial prejudice, had been secretary of state under Herbert Hoover. Frank Knox, a colonel in World War I, had been the publisher of the *Chicago Daily News* and was the Republican vice presidential candidate in 1936. As a Rough Rider in the Spanish-American War, Knox had fought side by side with black cavalry. He said at the time that he had never seen "braver men" anywhere, yet, invoking "tradition," would adamantly combat Roosevelt's efforts to integrate the Navy.

Eleanor Roosevelt took it upon herself in World War II, as she had in the Depression, to see to it that black civilians and service members got as fair a deal as possible. "The nation cannot expect the colored people to feel that the U.S. is worth defending if they continue to be treated as they are treated now," she said to a group of District of Columbia churchwomen shortly after the Japanese attack on Pearl Harbor.[9] "I am not agitating the race question," she said. "The race question is agitated because people will not act justly and fairly toward each other as human beings." In *No Ordinary Time,* her wonderful history of the Roosevelts during the war years, Doris Kearns Goodwin reports this exchange: "Looks like we're entertaining most of the blacks in the country tonight," remarked C. R. Smith, president of American Airlines, at a White House meeting.

"Well, C.R.," Mrs. Roosevelt replied, "you must remember that the President is their President also."[10]

Mrs. Roosevelt consistently brought black demands to the attention of those who could actually change things. In the first week of February 1943, she received a letter from Sergeant Henry Jones of the 349th Aviation Squadron, based at Carlsbad, California. The men in his unit were "loyal Americans," he wrote.[11] "The fact that we want to do our best for our country and to be valiant soldiers, seems to mean nothing to the Commanding Officer of our Post as indicated by the fact that 'Jim Crowism' is practiced on the very grounds of our camp." Complaints focused on discrimination in recreation and transportation. The post's theater had a thousand seats, but blacks were relegated to twenty seats in the last row. They could buy refreshments at the post exchange but, unlike white soldiers, they could not eat there. On buses to and from camp, blacks had half a row of seats in the back. Most were forced to walk. "We do not ask for special privileges," Jones wrote; "all we desire is to have equality; to be free to participate in all activities, means of transportation, privileges and amusements afforded any American soldier." There were 121 signatures on the letter.

Mrs. Roosevelt wrote to Henry Stimson, but received no reply. She then wrote so many letters to George Marshall on the subject that he assigned two members of his staff to respond. The War Department mandated segregation but it officially opposed "discrimination"—a fine line involving "treatment" rather than "condition." Marshall was persuaded to make changes. He may have been influenced by his World War I experience of discovering, en route to France, that black stevedores were not assigned lifeboats, but were expected to use floating debris.

On March 10, 1943, within a month of Jones's letter, the War Department officially banned segregation in all recreational facilities, "including theaters and post exchanges," in all services. "White" and "Colored Only" signs were also forbidden. In July 1944, the department finally directed that "all buses, trucks or other transportation owned and operated either by the government or by government instrumentality will be available to all military personnel regardless of race."[12] It also stated that "restricting personnel to certain sections of such transportation because of race will not be permitted either on or off a post camp, or station, regardless of local civilian custom."

The South was outraged. Blacks complained of beatings, shootings, and killing of those who disobeyed Jim Crow transportation rules. A black Army nurse, Lieutenant Nora Green, stationed at Tuskegee Army Air Forces training school in Alabama, was beaten and thrown into jail for refusing to move from a "white" bus seat while traveling from the base to the town. When the NAACP protested to the War Department and the Department of Justice, "Lieutenant Green was ordered not to talk about it," wrote Walter White, "and the case was hushed up."[13]

Carlsbad's Jim Crow regulations were no different from those in most camps, where black officers were routinely insulted and where black enlisted men, denied regular military privileges and recreational facilities, were excessively court-martialed and given "less than honorable" discharges. Blacks lived in separate, vastly inferior quarters. They received separate, often vastly inferior training, and were given vastly inferior weapons and equipment. In some Army camps, black soldiers were forced to sit behind German or Italian POWs for all entertainment, including United Service Organizations (USO) shows. The War Department argued that since it "could issue only one rule," the Jim Crow rule, which could apply "South and North alike," was most convenient.[14]

As in World War I, no blacks in World War II were awarded the Medal of Honor. Acts of black heroism, except the most undeniably extraordinary, were always overlooked—not by white commanders in the field, who were often surprisingly fair about frontline medal recommendations for black enlisted men, but by superior officers at headquarters, who usually filed the recommendations in wastebaskets. World War I was actually marginally better than World War II. Blacks who fought with the French in 1917–1918 were treated like soldiers and heroes, but the 500,000 black American men and women who served under their own flag in Europe, North Africa, and the Pacific in the 1940s would have bitter memories of the military. Despite Allied complaints and official War Department interdiction, the U.S. military enforced American-style racism wherever it went. Black GIs fought fascism on two fronts in World War II—at home and abroad, where, as often as not, the enemy wore an American uniform.

The Selective Service Act and the Election of 1940

On September 1, 1939, World War II broke out in Europe. Most Americans considered this less important than the issue of Roosevelt's coming third term. The 1940 election was far more preoccupying than the steady encroachment of Japan and Germany on their respective continents. By May 1940, having already taken Peking, Shanghai, Nanking, and Hangchou, Japan was determined to conquer China. The Nationalist leader Chiang Kai-shek had joined forces with the Communists Mao Tse-tung and Chou En-lai against the common foe. Germany looked equally unstoppable; it controlled Central and Eastern Europe and the Low Countries and was about to take France, where the entire British Expeditionary Forces, their backs to the sea, were trapped in the north at Dunkirk. In a miraculous nine-day amphibious evacuation, a military-civilian armada of pleasure boats, fishing boats, tugs, and battleships saved the beleaguered BEF. "We shall defend our island, whatever the cost may be," said Prime Minister Winston Churchill, with the clarion fervor that helped sustain the country through the worst of the Battle of Britain. "We shall never surrender, and even if . . . this island or a large part of it were subjugated and starving, then our Empire beyond the seas, armed and guarded by the British Fleet, would carry on the struggle until, in God's good time, the new world, with all its power and might, steps forth to the rescue and liberation of the old."

Despite vocal and well-financed isolationism, Americans had begun to understand that they would soon be joining the war. Roosevelt gave the order for rearmament in the summer of 1940. Late that summer, while Congress debated the new Selective Service Act, an NAACP-led drive against discrimination in the military went into high gear. The 230,000-man peacetime U.S. Army had fewer than 5,000 blacks. Senator Robert Wagner, a Democrat from New York, introduced an amendment declaring that no one could be denied the right to volunteer because of creed or color. Hamilton Fish introduced another amendment outlawing discrimination in the selection and training of men. Fish was an anti–New Deal isolationist but an ally of the NAACP. And Rayford W. Logan, who taught at Howard University and was chairman of the integrated Committee for the Participation of Negroes in National Defense, reiterated black demands for "equal opportunity" and black military service "in proportion to their numerical strength in the whole population."[15]

The military managed to circumvent Wagner's and Fish's nondiscriminatory language. In its final incarnation, the Selective Service Act stated that no man would be inducted unless he was "acceptable" to the Army and "until adequate provision shall be made for shelter, sanitary facilities, medical care and hospital accommodations." "Acceptable" could mean anything, and "adequate provision" meant segregation. Walter White and A. Philip Randolph asked to meet with Roosevelt to protest, but Steve Early, FDR's press secretary, chose not to respond to their request. When FDR signed the act on September 14, 1940, blacks flocked to recruitment centers only to be turned away because the Army had too few segregated facilities.

That same month, Eleanor Roosevelt spoke at the Brotherhood of Sleeping Car Porters convention, pledging her "faith, cooperation and energy" to make America a place of equality and opportunity for all. She received a standing ovation. That night she wrote to her husband about the need for a conference on "how the colored people can participate in the armed forces." "There is a growing feeling amongst the colored people," she wrote, "[that] they should be allowed to participate in any training that is going on in the aviation, army, navy. . . . This is going to be very bad politically besides being intrinsically wrong and I think you should ask that a meeting be held."[16]

The week of the Pullman convention, fifteen messmen who had joined the Navy on the promise of learning a trade wrote an open letter to the black newspaper the *Pittsburgh Courier.* "We sincerely hope to discourage any other colored boys who might have planned to join the Navy and make the same mistake we did," they wrote. "All they would become is seagoing bellhops, chambermaids and dishwashers. We take it upon ourselves to write this letter regardless of any action the Navy authorities may take. We know it could not possibly surpass the mental cruelty inflicted upon us on this ship."[17] Never given the opportunity to defend themselves in court, the signers were placed in the brig, indicted for conduct prejudicial to good order, and given dishonorable discharges. Hundreds of messmen immediately began protesting in open letters to black papers. Meanwhile, the Navy secretary, Knox, refused to let black reporters attend his press conferences.

Within a week of Mrs. Roosevelt's memo and the Navy messmen's letter a White House meeting was arranged to discuss military discrimination. White, Randolph, and T. Arnold Hill (former secretary of the Urban League) met with assistant secretary of war Robert Patterson, Knox, and the president. White and Randolph emphatically urged the "immediate and total abolition in the armed services of segregation based on race or color." Roosevelt, apparently sympathetic, promised to look into possible methods of "lessening, if not destroying, discrimination."[18] An NAACP memo urged that Army officers be assigned without regard to race, that specialized personnel like doctors and dentists be integrated, that Navy assignments other than menial services be opened to blacks, that blacks be placed on selective service boards, that aviation training centers for blacks be established, and that black civilian assistants be assigned to the secretaries of Navy and War.

"Why not put white and black regiments in the North side by side?" Roosevelt asked. Then, in case of war, "the thing gets sort of backed into."[19] Knox was discouraging. "We have a factor in the Navy," he said, "that is not so in the Army, and that is that these men live aboard ship. And in our history we don't take Negroes into a ship's company." Knox (who was, of course, wrong about U.S. naval history) remained adamant. Clearly somewhat desperate about his beloved Navy, Roosevelt suggested that "Negro bands" be put on ships to accustom white sailors to a black presence. The meeting ended in a stalemate but Roosevelt promised to reconvene. "According to [Patterson] it was a rather amusing affair—the President's gymnastics as to politics," wrote Secretary of War Stimson in his diary. "I saw the same thing happen 23 years ago when Woodrow Wilson yielded to the same sort of demand and appointed colored officers to several of the Divisions that went over to France, and the poor fellows made perfect fools of themselves. . . . Leadership is not embedded in the Negro race."

There was no second meeting—only silence from the White House. Then, on October 9, Steve Early announced the official new government policy on blacks in the Army and Navy. It gave with one hand and took away with the other. Yes, black strength in the Army would reflect the percentage of blacks in the population. Yes, black combat and noncombat units would be organized in every branch of the service, including the formerly barred-to-blacks Air Corps and Marines. Yes, blacks would have the opportunity to attend officer training schools. But all officers in present and future black units, except for three existing black regiments, would be white. And although blacks and whites would enjoy equality of *service,* they would not be integrated into the same regiments because that would "produce situations destructive to morale and detrimental to the preparation for national defense." Concessions had been granted, but not the ones White and Randolph really wanted. "Far from diminishing Jim Crowism," White wrote, "the new plan actually extended it."[20]

Roosevelt faced a race relations crisis in the election of 1940, when 19 percent of black men were still unemployed and some had come to refer to the New Deal as the "Dirty Deal." Many responded favorably to the Republican presidential candidate, Wendell Willkie. The 1940 Republican platform pledged that "discrimination must cease" and that blacks "be given a square deal in the economic and political life of this nation." The Democratic platform's less forthright pledge to "uphold due process and the equal protection of laws for every citizen regardless of race, creed, or color" was that party's first platform reference to blacks in the twentieth century. Angered by continuing military segregation, blacks were openly questioning Roosevelt's policies.

"I am an old campaigner and I love a good fight," Roosevelt said at the great Madison Square Garden rally of October 28, 1940, where he masterfully castigated Republican congressmen Joseph Martin, Bruce Barton, and Hamilton Fish for their anti-British isolationism, making a game of their names: "Martin, Barton, and Fish." Later that night Steve Early kicked James Sloan, a black New York City policeman, in the groin for blocking his path to the presidential train. Republicans had a field day. Early's victim proved to be a New Deal loyalist. "If anybody thinks they can turn me against our great President who has done so much for our race because of this thing they are mistaken," said Sloan, from his hospital bed.[21] While Steve Early was reported disconsolate at the possibility of costing FDR the black vote, black leadership seized the moment. "The Negroes are taking advantage of this period just before the election to try to get everything they can in the way of recognition from the Army," wrote Secretary Stimson in his diary.[22]

Black leaders had four demands. They wanted Judge William Hastie, the first black elevated to the federal bench, appointed assistant secretary in the War Department. They wanted Colonel Benjamin O. Davis, Sr., the highest-ranking black officer, promoted to brigadier general. They wanted Major Campbell C. Johnson, also black, named an assistant to the selective service director. And they wanted the desegregation of the armed forces. These demands were granted—except for desegregation.

Two of the great black trailblazers of World War II, Colonel Benjamin O. Davis, Sr., and Judge William Hastie, figured in the four demands of 1940. The third, Dr. Charles Drew, figured in the crucial background history of the war. Drew's research and development into the properties of blood radically advanced medicine and made a difference in life and death on the battlefield. Hastie and Drew, like Davis, came from prominent middle-class families in Washington, D.C. Hastie and Drew were also graduates of Dunbar High School, the best black high school in the country.

Benjamin O. Davis, Sr.

When World War II broke out, five of the five thousand black members of the U.S. Army were officers. Three of these were chaplains. The father-son duo of Colonel Benjamin O. Davis, Sr., and Captain Benjamin O. Davis, Jr., the latter the first black graduate of West Point since 1889, were the sole line officers.

Like most experienced black combat officers, Colonel Davis had sat out World War I in the Philippines. His career trajectory was typical, given the perceived necessity to avoid assigning a black officer to a position in which he would either command white enlisted men or outrank other white officers. Between 1905 and 1940, Davis was four times professor of military science and tactics at Wilberforce University. He was twice the U.S. military attaché in Liberia, and twice professor of military science and tactics at Tuskegee, where he stood ramrod straight on his front porch in a white dress uniform as the Ku Klux Klan paraded in front of his house. He was an instructor in the black 372nd Ohio National Guard, and, in 1938, commanding officer of New York's 369th National Guard Regiment (of World War I fame). As America's first black general, Davis commanded the 4th Cavalry Brigade, all black, with mostly white officers. He requested that his son, Captain Benjamin O. Davis, Jr., become his aide. General Davis would become a War Department troubleshooter in World War II. Most black soldiers regarded him as an Army public relations figure: they knew that there was little he could do within the military structure to change conditions.

WILLIAM HASTIE

Born into the black Republican middle class of Knoxville, Tennessee, William Hastie moved to Washington when his father took a job as a clerk in the U.S. Pension Office (an important job for a black). At Harvard Law School, his constitutional law professor, soon to be associate justice of the Supreme Court Felix Frankfurter, called him "not only the best colored man we have ever had but he is as good as all but three or four outstanding white men that have been here during the last twenty years." Hastie would not have been flattered. "This notion that Negroes have to be better than other people is about as disgusting as the notion that Negroes are inferior," he wrote in 1931, when he was twenty-seven. "As a matter of fact, I very much fear that they are rationalizations of the same thing."[23] Like the other Dunbar graduates, Hastie had been educated to believe in his own excellence. Self-confidence also came from belonging to Washington's education-oriented black middle class. Coming from a community that was both sophisticated and segregated, he had an acute understanding of the subtleties of racism.

Hastie returned to Washington after Harvard and became a partner in the Washington law firm of Charles Houston, a black World War I officer and civil rights activist. A member of Roosevelt's "black cabinet," Hastie served from 1933 to 1937 as assistant solicitor in the Department of Interior, under Harold Ickes. In 1937, Roosevelt appointed him federal judge of the U.S. District Court of the Virgin Islands, the first black federal judge in history. (He was then one of only 1,175 black lawyers in the United States.) Four years later he was appointed assistant secretary in the War Department. His job was to help develop policy on the fair and effective use of black manpower in the U.S. armed forces, but his office soon became the focal point for black GI mail decrying military racism. While his appointment was seen as a crucial step in achieving the integration of the armed forces, his strategy of "locating the problem, investigating it, and achieving quick remedial action" was effected "within the confines of segregation." There were some victories, however. Under pressure from Hastie and the NAACP, the War Department withdrew a January 1942 order from a Pennsylvania camp stating that "any association between the colored soldiers and white women, whether voluntary or not, would be considered rape."[24]

Hastie resigned from his War Department position in 1943 to protest continued segregation in Army and Air Force training. Between 1939 and 1949 he figured as co-counsel in twelve of the nineteen Supreme Court cases argued by Thurgood Marshall on behalf of the NAACP and the NAACP Legal Defense and Education Fund. "There were, in the forties, two citadels of civil rights in the United States," wrote Gilbert Ware, an early biographer. "One was the NAACP, the other was Howard University Law School; and both were what they were largely because of William Hastie."[25]

CHARLES DREW

One of America's 3,939 black physicians, Charles Drew was a classmate of Hastie's at Dunbar High School. Drew was Best Athlete (four letters) and Most Popular Student, and Hastie was valedictorian. They were classmates again at Amherst, where Drew won an athletic scholarship (and an honorable mention as the Eastern Division All-American halfback) and Hastie, again valedictorian, graduated magna cum laude.

Drew, whose mother was a Howard graduate, was born in his maternal grandmother's sixteen-room house on E Street in Washington, D.C. His father was the financial secretary and only black member of Local 85 of the Carpet and Linoleum Layers Union. With the red hair and freckles of his Irish grandfather, young Charles could almost pass for white. Later in life he would tell people that he had decided on medical school when an Amherst dean remarked, "Mr. Drew, Negro athletes are a dime a dozen."[26] Rejected by Howard University Medical School for deficiency in English credits, he enrolled instead at Montreal's McGill University—where, as "Charlie" Drew, he won Canadian championships in track and field. In 1935, after two years of internship and residency in Montreal, Drew became an assistant surgeon at Howard University's Freedmen's Hospital. The hospital's white chief surgeon, Dr. Edward L. Howes, recommended him for advanced training at Columbia University.

Midway through his first year at Columbia Presbyterian Hospital, Drew began to research blood chemistry and transfusion under Dr. John Scudder. By 1938, Scudder and Drew knew more about blood transfusion and preservation than anyone in the world. Drew wrote to his fiancée that he dreamed in his "wildest moments" of "playing some part in establishing a real school of thought among Negro physicians and guiding younger fellows to levels of accomplishment not yet attained by any of us."[27] Two years later Scudder and Drew developed their own blood bank at Presbyterian. In June 1940 Drew became the first black to receive the degree of doctor of science in medicine. His dissertation, "Banked Blood," was the size of the New York City telephone directory. Drew was set to return to Howard, but the war in Europe intervened.

In the late summer of 1940, John Scudder was invited to head the American Red Cross "Blood for Britain" program. He urged the Red Cross to give the job instead to Dr. Drew, who was also recommended by an old McGill friend, Dr. John Beattie, now chief of transfusion services for the British Royal Air Force. The Battle of Britain had shown the desperate need for banked blood in cities under aerial attack. "Blood for Britain" was actually blood plasma—blood protein and fluid without red blood cells—which Scudder and Drew had discovered to be more convenient and storable. Drew recommended that all plasma be processed in one laboratory and collected in refrigerated mobile units. (Thermo Control truck refrigeration was patented in 1940 by Frederick McKinley Jones, a black inventor whose portable cooling units were also used in the cockpits of B-29 bombers.) The first shipment of "Blood for Britain" left New York in August 1940. By January 1941, Britain was able to produce its own plasma. Drew now became director of the New York City Red Cross Blood Bank, in charge of blood collection for the U.S. armed forces.

The inevitable problem of what to do about "black blood" was confronted in the winter of 1941, when the military ordered white blood only. Blood segregation was mandated by the military—not the Red Cross. When blacks began to be wounded and killed in numbers, black donors' blood was collected for black use. In the meantime, blacks received blood from white donors. Drew was initially ineligible to donate blood for his own program.

"Dr. Drew is not known to have murmured" against the policy, said Dr. W. Montague Cobb, a black Amherst classmate. Others reported that he made one public statement. In any case, Drew resigned in the spring of 1941 and returned to Howard as a professor and chief of surgery. Perhaps he had decided not to protest because his eye was on another prize: he was creating his black medical "school of thought." As chief of staff to a generation of black physicians who called him Big Red, Drew was building esprit de corps in the black medical community. "In the individual accomplishments of each man lies the success or failure of the group as a whole," he wrote to a friend. "The success of the group as a whole is the basis for any tradition which we may create. The sense of belonging is of extraordinary importance. . . . The sense of continuously being an outsider requires the greatest type of moral courage to overcome before actual accomplishments can be begun."[28]

Drew remained an eternal outsider in the white medical community. He was a surgical consultant to the U.S. Surgeon General, the first black examiner for the American Board of Surgery, and a fellow of the U.S. chapter of the International College of Surgeons, but was rejected throughout his life for membership in the American Medical Association. He died in 1950, at the age of forty-six, in a car accident in North Carolina. In death, his extraordinary achievements were capped by the legend that Drew (like Bessie Smith) had died because a white hospital refused to admit him. The hospital did, in fact, admit black patients, although they were kept in the basement. And the three white attending physicians not only knew exactly who Drew was, but made extraordinary efforts to save his life. Nothing, including blood transfusions, could have succeeded.

LEND-LEASE, THE DEFENSE FUND, AND THE MARCH ON WASHINGTON

February 1941 was a dark time for Britain. At home, the Royal Air Force valiantly confronted the Luftwaffe as British civilians suffered relentless aerial bombardment. Abroad, British Tommies faced Field Marshal Erwin Rommel's vaunted, and so far victorious, Afrika Korps in North Africa, and Hong Kong was poised to fall to the Japanese.

"Sail on, O Ship of State! / Sail on, O Union, strong and great! / Humanity with all its fears, / With all the hopes of future years, / Is hanging breathless on thy fate!" read FDR's handwritten copy of a verse by Longfellow—delivered by his onetime rival Wendell Willkie to Prime Minister Churchill in February 1941. "Give us the tools and we will finish the job," Churchill replied with thunderous optimism in a worldwide broadcast.

Condemned by isolationist Republicans, the Lend-Lease Act of March 1941 allowed the President to transfer munitions and supplies from congressionally appropriated money to "the government of any country whose defense the President deems vital to the defense of the

U.S." Churchill called it "the most unsordid act in the history of any nation." As one Londoner put it, "Thank God! The tanks are coming."[29] Lend-Lease not only gave eleventh-hour support to the British, it enabled the defeat of the Germans in Russia, by financing the pivotal Red Army victory at Stalingrad. At the three-way Yalta conference of 1945, Stalin toasted Churchill as "the bravest governmental figure in the world," for standing alone against Hitler. And he saluted Roosevelt as the man "with the broadest conception of national interest; even though his country was not directly endangered, he had forged the instruments which led to the mobilization of the world against Hitler."[30] Roosevelt had first used his presidential powers to save America from the Depression. Now he used them to save the world from Germany and Japan. Lend-Lease was decidedly anti-isolationist, but it also reflected the miracle of American industry's seemingly overnight conversion from peacetime to wartime production.

* * *

"Negroes will be considered only as janitors," announced the general manager of North American Aviation in the spring of 1941. "We have not had a Negro working in 25 years and do not plan to start now," Standard Steel informed the Urban League. "It is not the policy of this company to employ other than of the Caucasian race," said California's Vultee Air.[31] Discrimination in the defense industry had become a major issue.

A. Philip Randolph decided to mobilize his troops. "You possess power, great power," he said, addressing the black community early in 1941. "The Negro stake in national defense is big. It consists of jobs, thousands of jobs. It consists of new industrial opportunities and hope. This is worth fighting for. . . . To this end we propose that 10,000 Negroes march on Washington." The march was scheduled for July 1, 1941. By the first week of June, there were march committees in eighteen cities, North and South. It appeared that blacks were prepared to go to Washington, "crying for their rights," wrote the young Washington journalist Murray Kempton, "to the boundless embarrassment not merely of politicians but of the arsenal of democracy which had forgotten them."[32]

In late May, Roosevelt wrote to William Knudsen and Sidney Hillman, the directors of the Office of Production Management, with a novel suggestion. Why not take "Negroes up to a certain percentage in factory order work?" he asked. "Judge them on *quality*—the first class Negroes are turned down for 3rd class white boys." Knudsen, the conservative head of General Motors, and Hillman, leader of the liberal and integrated Congress of Industrial Organizations, both turned him down. "If we set a percentage," they wrote, "it will immediately be open to dispute; quiet work with the contractors and the unions will bring better results."[33]

Although both Roosevelts were sympathetic to Randolph's demands, they were firmly opposed to the March on Washington and asked him repeatedly to call it off. Mrs. Roosevelt was emphatic: she called the march a "very grave mistake" and insisted that any "incident" could create "even more solid opposition" from certain groups in Congress. But Randolph continued to mobilize for July 1.

On June 18, Randolph and Walter White finally met with the president. Also at the White House that afternoon were Robert Patterson, Frank Knox, Knudsen, Hillman, and three New Deal liberals: Aubrey Williams, head of the National Youth Administration; New York City's mayor, Fiorello H. La Guardia; and Anna Rosenberg, the regional director of the Social Security Board for New York.

Bypassing the famous FDR charm, Randolph went straight to the point. The march would be called off only if the president issued an executive order banning segregation in defense industry jobs. "Well, Phil, you know I can't do that," Roosevelt had said. "In any event I couldn't do anything unless you called off this march of yours." The president asked Randolph how many people were expected. He was clearly stunned when Randolph told him that 100,000 marchers were ready to come. "It is clear that Mr. Randolph is not going to call off the march," said Mayor La Guardia, and he suggested they begin to "seek a formula." Despite angry opposition from Knudsen, Roosevelt asked Randolph to "make a draft of the kind of order" he wanted issued. The final order, written by a young government lawyer named Joseph Rauh, banned defense industry discrimination on the basis of race, color, creed, and national origin. Executive Order 8802, forbidding discrimination in industries holding government contracts for war production, and in training for jobs in war industries, was signed on June 25, less than a week before the scheduled march, which was then called off.[34]

Executive Order 8802 also established the Fair Employment Practices Commission. Responsible only to the president, the FEPC had the power to investigate and take action against discrimination. By early 1942, thanks to FEPC pressure, more than half of government contractors had committed themselves to integration. Black shipyard employment rose from six thousand to fourteen thousand in a year. In 1940 the aircraft industry had no blacks; by 1942 it had five thousand. Black women now had a choice between domestic service and war work, although they often had the worst jobs, working with ammunition, gunpowder, and poisonous plastics. The FEPC was effectively killed in 1944, when the agency was placed under the control of the southern-dominated Congress, which ultimately refused to fund it. But by the end of the war blacks, who had been 2.5 percent of workers in war production, made up nearly 10 percent—and black union enrollment had increased by 700,000.[35]

"The American people are united as never before in their determination to do a job and do it well," Roosevelt said in a radio address in October 1942, after a tour of defense factories. But he was disappointed that some employers were still reluctant to hire women, blacks, or older people. "We can no longer afford to indulge such prejudices or practices," he said. Home-front battlegrounds now included the urban North, where black and white southerners both flocked for defense work. One of the worst of the wartime race riots took place in Detroit in the spring of 1943, when 26,000 white Packard workers went on strike to protest black employment. (Walter White heard one striker yell that he would rather Hitler and Hirohito won the war than work next to a "nigger" on the assembly line.) Between May and August 1943, race riots in Detroit, Mobile, Los Angeles, and New York City left forty dead and twelve hundred injured. The Harlem riot in August, which began when a black soldier objected to the way a white policeman spoke to a black woman, saw five blacks killed, four hundred people of both races injured, and property damage estimated as high as $5 million.[36]

THE BLACK PRESS AND "DOUBLE V"

The black press was vital to black GIs, headlining military racism and serving as an outlet for their rage. It would be criticized for spotlighting acts of discrimination and equating them with Nazi practices, as well as for giving voice to black sympathy for Japan. ("If Japan goes down every black man's rights will go down with her," New York's *Amsterdam News* was quoted as saying in "Japanese Propaganda Among the Negro People," a 1939 confidential report prepared, according to the FBI, for the Chinese government.[37]) Critics of the black press included the president, the FBI, the Army, the Office of War Information, the Office of Censorship, the Office of Facts and Figures, the Post Office, and even many black GIs, who would blame it for "pushing" them into combat. Unlike its white counterpart, the black press had virtually no lucrative advertising accounts and depended on readership alone for survival. Charging hard at discrimination, black publications grew in circulation and influence during the war. In 1933 the average total circulation was 600,000; by 1940 that figure had more than doubled, to 1,276,600—and by the end of 1945 it would reach 1,808,060.

Military intelligence reported in January 1941 that John Sengstacke, publisher of the *Chicago Defender* and founder of the Negro Newspaper Publishers Association, had encouraged blacks to protest military discrimination by becoming conscientious objectors. In the summer of 1941, the *Defender* praised a speech by Dr. Harold M. Kingsley, of Chicago's Church of the Good Shepherd, in which he said that blacks must fight in any future war but must not give up the battle against discrimination at home. "It is sound wisdom," said Kingsley, "that we fight both of these battles at the same time."[38]

Sengstacke was one of twenty black columnists, editors, and publishers who met with General George C. Marshall and other Army officials on December 8, 1941—the meeting had been scheduled before Pearl Harbor—to discuss Army discrimination. Marshall impressed the group when he stated that he was "not personally satisfied" with the progress made toward ending discrimination in the Army. He praised black enlisted men and said a black division might be formed. Optimism turned to anger, however, when at the end of the meeting Colonel Eugene R. Householder read a prepared statement: "The Army is not a sociological laboratory," he said. "To be effective it must be organized and trained according to principles which will insure success. Experiments to meet the wishes and demands of the champions of every race and creed for the solution of their problems are a danger to efficiency, discipline and morale and would result in ultimate defeat."[39] This line—the official Army position on integration—was to be repeated many times.

In the spring of 1942, administrators of the Office of Facts and Figures, directed by the poet Archibald MacLeish, met with fifty black editors and civic leaders to discuss ways to improve morale among black civilians as well as military members. Despite directives opening all branches of the service to blacks, the Marines and Coast Guard still refused black enlistment, while the Navy still accepted blacks only as stewards and messmen. To add insult to injury, although the Red Cross had finally accepted blood from black donors—it stressed, under military orders, that their blood would be strictly segregated. Such headlines in the black press as "Red Cross Has No Use for Negro Blood" and "Negro Air Raid Warden Will Be Trained in Jim Crow Classes" raised government hackles. The FBI chief, J. Edgar Hoover, recommended voluntary press censorship. The black press had no intention of censoring itself—it planned to go further many times in any number of ways over the next decade, as the struggle for integration went from a dream to a reality.[40]

If the black press had a sometime enemy in FDR, it had a friend in Francis Biddle, the Justice Department solicitor general, who became the U.S. Attorney General in September 1941. "In so far as I can, by the use of the authority and the influence of my office, I intend to see that civil liberties in this country are protected," Biddle told *The New York Times* in 1941, "that we do not again fall into the disgraceful hysteria of witch hunts, strike breakings and minority persecutions which were such a dark chapter in our record of the last World War."[41] Biddle integrated the new Justice Department cafeteria, and instructed division heads to increase the number of black lawyers. Threatening to resign as an honorary member of the Federal Bar Association if blacks were excluded, he forced a policy change.

By mid-1942, the tide was turning on black morale and the black press began to relent. There were now blacks in the Air Corps, the Marines, the Coast Guard, and the Women's Army Auxiliary Corps. As racial policies changed, the Double V campaign was softened. Importantly, the black press got its first white advertisers. Philip Morris, Chesterfield and Old Gold cigarettes, Pepsi-Cola, Seagram's whiskey, Pabst Blue Ribbon beer, and Esso oil began advertising in the larger papers. The danger of sedition charges had passed. "The Negro press throughout the country, although they very properly protest, and passionately, against the wrongs done to members of their race, are loyal to their government and are all out for the war," Biddle said in a speech in Philadelphia in 1943.[42] It had been determined by the White House, as well as the Justice Department, that enemy propaganda would thrive if black papers were suppressed, because that would leave no source to which blacks could turn for news about themselves.

The black press had been campaigning for access to Roosevelt's press conferences since 1933, but it faced a veritable brick wall in Steve Early. Then, in the last week of May 1943, the administration made its first concession. Black reporters were admitted to the White House and the congressional press gallery for twenty-four hours, to cover the visit of Liberian president Edwin Barclay. In July, Biddle suggested to Roosevelt that a black reporter be admitted to White House press conferences. Roosevelt liked the idea.

On February 8, 1945, Harry S. McAlpin of the *Atlanta Daily World* became the first black correspondent accredited to a White House press conference. "I'm glad to see you, McAlpin, and very happy to have you here," Roosevelt said, reaching out his hand, and flashing a "genuine smile of friendliness" from the desk where he sat for press conferences, surrounded by standing reporters.[43] When Roosevelt died in April 1945, McAlpin was one of thirteen reporters allowed to cover the funeral service. Originally twelve whites were selected, but Jonathan Daniels, FDR's last press secretary, pointed out that a black should be included. Black editors and publishers met with President Harry Truman as soon as he assumed office, but black journalists were not admitted to the congressional press galleries until 1947.

II. War

Dorie Miller at Pearl Harbor

The first American hero of World War II was black. On December 7, 1941, at Pearl Harbor, Dorie Miller was a messman on the burning deck of the U.S.S. *West Virginia*. Miller, the shy twenty-two-year-old son of a Texas sharecropper, carried the ship's mortally wounded captain to safety, then manned an antiaircraft gun to bring down what witnesses said were four Japanese planes (officials listed two). Miller had never been taught to fire the antiaircraft gun; it was against Navy regulations for blacks to do so. Only when the ammunition was exhausted and the *Arizona* was sinking beneath him did he abandon ship. It took three months for his heroism to be officially recognized.

The first Navy dispatches from Pearl Harbor described him as an "unidentified Negro messman." Apparently embarrassed that the first hero of the war was black, the Navy found a white hero in Captain Colin Kelly, killed on December 9 in a crash-dive onto the Japanese battleship he had just bombed.[44] When Miller's name was officially released in March, the *Pittsburgh Courier* campaigned futilely for him to receive the Medal of Honor. In May, after considerable pressure from civil rights organizations, he became (to the disapproval of Secretary Knox) the first black to win the Navy Cross. It was presented by Admiral Chester W. Nimitz, commander of the U.S. Pacific Fleet.

In a front-page column, George Schuyler of the *Pittsburgh Courier* questioned why it had taken five months for the decoration to be awarded, and why Miller was not brought back to the United States, like white heroes, to boost morale and help sell war bonds. "The Navy finds Dorie Miller too important waiting tables in the Pacific to return him so that his people might see him."[45] Miller finally was sent home for a national war bond tour in December 1942, one year after Pearl Harbor. Returning to action, he remained a messman until he died on Thanksgiving Day, 1943, when all hands went down on the torpedoed carrier *Liscome Bay.* In the aftermath of Miller's heroics, Navy regulations were changed to require that all hands, including messmen and stewards, receive antiaircraft training. The U.S.S. *Harmon,* launched in 1943, was named for another Navy Cross messman, Leonard Roy Harmon, who had been killed a year earlier in the Battle of Guadalcanal.

AMERICA ENTERS THE WAR

Japan's attempt to destroy the U.S. Pacific fleet at Pearl Harbor caught the professional military, as well as ordinary citizens, by surprise. But America was quick to retaliate. Once it entered the war, it committed all its resources and manpower to secure a decisive victory. By early 1942, the Allied grand strategy was in place: to back Germany into a corner and to take back the Pacific, island by island. A great multinational army was envisioned to choke off Germany. Under British or American command, it would come from North Africa in the south, Britain in the north, and, eventually, Russia in the east. Whereas in World War I, Germany's opponents had reveled in national pride, in World War II they suppressed it. Allied forces, although fighting in national groups, were in many ways treated as a single unit. The term "United Nations" began to be used in 1942, the year that the twenty-six Allied nations pledged not to make separate peace treaties with the Axis powers.

The first half of 1942 was a terrible time for the Allies. Germany controlled most of continental Europe, and British and American soldiers and sailors were forced into a devastating two-thousand-mile retreat from the Philippines to Australia. Japan, which controlled much of China, now seized the Dutch East Indies, Kuala Lumpur, Burma, Singapore, Java, Rangoon, Mandalay, Corregidor, and Bataan—where, in the emergency of the Japanese invasion, elements of the black 25th Regiment fought side by side with white Marines.

Then, in 1942, the tide of war began to turn. Major General Jimmy Doolittle bombed Tokyo and other cities in Japan. The American Navy defeated Japan in the Coral Sea and at the pivotal Battle of Midway. And U.S. Marines landed on Guadalcanal, beginning the process of recapturing the Pacific islands. In Europe the RAF, which had won the Battle of Britain, bombed Berlin; by the end of 1943 there would be round-the-clock bombing of Germany. On the eastern front, in November 1942 the Red Army stopped the Germans at Stalingrad (where Hitler demanded a scorched-earth retreat). And that same month Field Marshal Bernard Montgomery, Commander of the Eighth Army, finally defeated Rommel's Afrika Korps at El Alamein.

In late 1942, 400,000 American troops landed in French North Africa, where all Allied armies were placed under the command of General Dwight D. Eisenhower, commander in chief of U.S. forces in the European theater. In July 1943, a multinational Allied force under British command landed in Sicily and captured Palermo. The Sicilian invasion forced Mussolini's ouster and replacement by Marshal Badoglio, a veteran of the Ethiopian War. (Mussolini later set up a short-lived puppet state in German-occupied northern Italy.) In September 1943, the Allies finally invaded mainland Italy and captured Salerno. Despite the heavy German counteroffensive and the rugged terrain, they swept past Anzio and Monte Cassino to capture Rome on June 4, 1944. It was the first Axis capital to fall. On June 6, D-Day, the greatest amphibious force in history hit the beaches of Normandy in occupied France, to establish a second front. On August 25, General Charles de Gaulle, head of the French Committee of National Liberation (the "Free French"), a World War I veteran who had refused to accept France's World War II capitulation, was given the courtesy of being the first Allied military leader to officially enter liberated Paris.

* * *

World War II, for black Americans, was a matter of "old" and "new." General Mark Clark's calling the black 92nd Division the "worst division in Europe" was old racism. Reputation aside, the 92nd fought and died, and won (belated) Medals of Honor, in Clark's Italian campaign. The 93rd Division, the 92nd's Pacific counterpart, saw action under General Douglas MacArthur on Bougainville and Morotai, but from Hawaii to Australia fought more white racists than Japanese. Despite their anger at military racism, black Americans were elated by the fact that blacks were going to war in revolutionary new ways: there were black fighter pilots, naval officers, Army (WACs) and Navy (WAVES) female personnel, Marines, paratroopers, and armored tank crews. They even won (as usual, belated) Medals of Honor, in integrated warfare during the Battle of the Bulge.

America's first black fighter pilots, the 332nd Fighter Group, led by Colonel Benjamin O. Davis, Jr., were in the battle for Sicily and the Italian peninsula, seeing action at Anzio and Monte Cassino. As fighter-escorts over Western Europe and the Balkans, the 332nd flew more combat missions than any other unit in Europe. The squadron's record was unmatched by any other escort group: in two hundred missions they never lost a single bomber. They were probably the first American pilots to meet and down German jets. They were certainly the only fighter pilots, of any color, ever to sink a destroyer with machine guns. Of the 450 black fighter pilots who saw combat during World War II, 65 were killed in action and 23 were shot down to become German prisoners of war. The 332nd Fighter Group won 3 Distinguished Unit Citations, 150 Distinguished Flying Crosses, a Silver Star, a Legion of Merit, 14 Bronze Stars, 744 Air Medals and Clusters, 8 Purple Hearts, and the Red Star of Yugoslavia.

America's first black Marines, joining the last military service to open its ranks to black volunteers, saw action in the South Pacific in 1944. Although 75 percent of the seventeen thousand new Marines had some college education, none became officers. They had been accepted in 1942 under segregated training conditions at the black Marine training center at Montford Point, North Carolina; only a token two Marine defense battalions—the 51st and 52nd—were trained for combat. The majority of black volunteers were trained either as messmen and stewards or for noncombat depot and ammunition companies. Depot companies loaded and unloaded ships and hauled supplies onto beaches during offensives. Ammunition companies loaded, unloaded, sorted, and guarded ammunition, moving it to frontline troops. Black Marine defense battalions in the South Pacific, though combat-trained, saw little action—but noncombat depot and ammunition companies, trained only with light weapons, fought and suffered casualties in the bloody battles for Saipan, Guam, Peleliu, Okinawa, and Iwo Jima. The nine black Marines killed and seventy-eight wounded in action during World War II were not supposed to have come into contact with the Japanese.[46]

America's first black armored combat unit, the 761st Tank Battalion, was called experimental, but General George S. Patton was happy to have them to reinforce his bogged-down Third Army just before the Battle of the Bulge. The 761st fought nonstop from October 31, 1944, to May 6, 1945, in four major Allied campaigns and six European countries. "The German army couldn't see how we could be in so many darned places," said one ex-tanker, Lieutenant Colonel Charles "Pop" Gates, in Studs Terkel's *The Good War*.[47] (The 730-member battalion, with ten white officers, was actually split into three companies, with companies split in two again.) The 761st, whose motto was "Come Out Fighting," spearheaded the American infantry advance through France, Belgium, Luxembourg, Holland, Germany, and Austria. In front all the way from the Saar Basin to the "Bulge" to the Siegfried Line, they beat the Russians to the Rhine, spending 183 consecutive days on the front line, more than any other armored battalion, and suffering a 50 percent casualty rate. They also won (belated) Medals of Honor. By November 1945, the 761st had the first black armored combat commander, Captain Ivan H. Harrison.

Although the U.S. military remained rigidly segregated throughout the war, the defense of Bastogne in the Battle of the Bulge saw a brief racial experiment. In January 1945, in the face of great losses and a strong German counteroffensive, a dramatic call went out to all black units for volunteers to replace fallen white GIs. More than four thousand men, mostly from service divisions, were enlisted. At first, volunteers were to be integrated as individuals into white units. But volunteer individuals soon became volunteer platoons: segregating a platoon was much easier than segregating one person. Black platoons were distributed among eleven combat divisions of the First and Seventh Armies, fighting in the crucial stages of the Battle of the Bulge and the subsequent Allied drive through Germany. Sixty-four percent of white troops had been skeptical when first informed of integrated platoons. Three months later, 77 percent were in favor of them.[48] Excellent reports appeared on black fighting abilities and black-white relations—but black combat volunteers were immediately (and unceremoniously) returned to their segregated units when the Battle of the Bulge was over.

Roosevelt had promised that black military strength would be 10 percent of the total military, reflecting the proportion of blacks in the United States generally. But three-quarters of blacks in the U.S. armed forces went into service and supply units. Although much of their duty was menial, much was also essential. Black troops built bridges, constructed airfields, drove trucks, and loaded and unloaded ships. Black engineering and transport groups, like the legendary Red Ball Express, built the great war highways: Burma's Stilwell Road and the Alaskan Highway.

More black noncombatants saw action than combat-trained black soldiers. The 387th Separate Engineer Battalion was not a combat unit, but three of its members won Silver Stars at the Anzio beachhead, where sixty-one men were wounded and eleven men and four officers were killed. The 320th Barrage Balloon Battalion was crucial to the initial assault at Omaha Beach. Huge barrage balloons, or blimps, to deter low-flying planes, were installed in the third wave to prevent Luftwaffe strafing.[49] Members of the 490th Port Battalion, a thousand-man unit of stevedores who landed at Utah Beach on D-Day, were awarded the Croix de Guerre and Bronze Arrowhead for their service to assault troops.

The 555th Parachute Infantry Battalion—the "Triple Nickels"—comprised America's first black paratroopers. Created in 1942, with all black officers, they never saw combat against Axis soldiers, but they did fight an old natural enemy of man. Sent to the Pacific Northwest in the spring of 1945 for the highly classified mission called Operation Firefly, the 555th became smoke jumpers. Firefly battled forest fires created by Japanese incendiary bombs hidden in silk and paper balloons that floated across the Pacific on the jet stream. The bombs' existence was kept secret from the public, to prevent panic. The 555th conducted more than twelve hundred individual jumps, putting out fires and defusing the bombs. The hot, dry summer of 1945 saw the Nickels fighting powerful Pacific Northwest forest fires as well. At the end of 1945, the 555th was administratively attached to General James Gavin's 82nd Airborne Division. They never saw combat with the 82nd, but Gavin insisted that they march in the January 1946 New York City victory parade with the division and wear its battle patches.[50]

The combined efforts of black leaders, the black press, and government and military reformers ultimately brought real change in the status of blacks in the military. Between 1941 and 1945, the number of black enlisted personnel grew from 5,000 to over 1,000,000, and the number of black officers grew from 5 to over 7,000.[51] Some 500,000 black men and women served overseas in North Africa, Europe, and the Pacific. The Army, with 701,678, had the largest black enlistment. The Army Air Force had 677,966 black enlisted men and 1,050 officers. Sixty-five thousand black men served in the Navy: 53 were officers, but 95 percent were still messmen or stewards at the end of 1945. There were 17,000 black men in the Marine Corps, and no black officers. There were 4 black officers and 4,000 black enlisted men in the Coast Guard. There were 4,000 black women in the Army and Navy, as members of the WACs (Women's Army Corps) and WAVES (Women Accepted for Volunteer Emergency Service).[52]

The quasi-civilian merchant marine was the most integrated of all World War II services. In 1942, the U.S.S. *Booker T. Washington* became the first U.S. merchant ship with a black captain: Hugh Mulzac, veteran of the British Royal Navy, the World War I merchant marine, and Marcus Garvey's Black Star Line. Although the Navy remained World War II's most segregated service, by the end of the war there was a black midshipman at Annapolis. Wesley A. Brown became the first black graduate of the Naval Academy in 1949. The final battle of military integration was yet to be won, but it had announced its coming in the "Bulge" experiment, as well as in the attitudes of many younger white combat officers.

THE PROPAGANDA WAR

The American public had to be sold on World War II. The Office of War Information (OWI) led the propaganda campaign, aimed at synchronizing popular culture with war goals. Initially led by Archibald MacLeish, writers included E. B. White, Malcolm Cowley, Reinhold Niebuhr, and Arthur M. Schlesinger, Jr. In terms of race, the best liberal intentions were always at odds with southern congressmen, who denounced "The Negro and the War," for example, an OWI effort written by Chandler Owen (World War I partner in socialism of A. Philip Randolph). Walking a fine racial line, the OWI also made a military training film, *Teamwork,* that depicted Germans trying to drive a wedge between otherwise friendly black and white Americans. The best propaganda films, because they used major studio talent, were Hollywood-made, government-commissioned documentaries. Among the best was Frank Capra's production *The Negro Soldier.* Beautifully made, with a cast of real soldiers and attractive nonactors, it was praised by blacks and whites alike and shown everywhere—except the South. *Why We Fight,* Capra's propaganda series (inspired in part by Leni Riefenstahl's Nazi epic *Triumph of the Will*), explained the war as a crusade. It was not merely a matter of helping friends or safeguarding interests; it was, in Churchill's words, a matter of saving "civilization as we know it."

While the powerful print media, such as Henry Luce's *Time* and *Life,* strongly supported black fighting men and favored an integrated military, Hollywood, the most important cultural outlet of all, studiously avoided putting black soldiers into war films. In early 1942, Walter White and Wendell Willkie began a campaign to purge Hollywood of *Birth of a Nation*–esque stereotyping. Preaching brotherhood abroad meant practicing it at home, was their message. David O. Selznick, Walter Wanger, and Darryl Zanuck arranged a meeting of Hollywood VIPs to discuss the issue. Blacks were not asking to be portrayed as heroes, it was pointed out, only as an integral part of the war effort. Willkie argued that many of America's allies disliked Hollywood's cartoon-stereotype depiction of people with dark skin. He also reminded his audience that many of those responsible for Hollywood films "belonged to a racial and religious group" that had been a target of Hitler. Few could have made this point, Walter White noted, "without giving offense," but Willkie was cheered—and *Variety* headlined, "Better Breaks for Negroes in H'Wood."[53]

White issued a "statement to the Negro public" stressing the importance of blacks being depicted as "normal human beings" instead of menials and comics. He wanted more roles for black actors, as well as black employment on the technical side of production. He added a gentle warning to "those actors in Hollywood who can only play comic or servant roles," hoping that they would not "spoil the opportunity" for change.[54] In 1942, with the proviso that she would not play menial or demeaning roles, my mother, Lena Horne, was signed by Metro-Goldwyn-Mayer to the first long-term Hollywood contract for a black player. Angry actors who specialized in comic or servant roles called her before a committee to give her a lecture on loyalty. How dare she refuse to play a maid? Everyone else played maids or servants. The only member of the committee to take her side was the first black Oscar winner, Hattie McDaniel ("Mammy" of *Gone With the Wind*).

Stereotyping was now exchanged for tokenism. The 1940s saw a step forward: 20th Century–Fox's *Crash Dive* (based on the life of Dorie Miller), Columbia's *Sahara,* Hitchcock's *Lifeboat,* and two Humphrey Bogart movies, *Bataan* and *Casablanca,* all featured dignified, *individual* black soldiers and civilians—among the first in American movies. (Bogart had volunteered to help the cause.) None of these movies could be shown intact in the South. Racially vigilant southern censors, who preferred stereotyping to tokenism, would cut blacks out of films until the 1960s. In 1943 two expensive, all-star black movie musicals, *Cabin in the Sky* and *Stormy Weather,* both starring my mother, were banned in the South except for black audiences. They were shown throughout the British fleet, but the American military labeled them for black soldiers only. (When she appeared later in otherwise all-white movies, her scenes were specially shot to be excised in the South.) Black GIs, left out of so much of wartime culture, were vocally grateful to Hollywood for giving them a black pinup. Lena Horne was equally grateful, but sorry and a little embarrassed that black GIs had only one.

Willkie's sudden death in 1944 put an end to the aggressive pursuit of racial balance in American movies. If Hollywood grudgingly acknowledged a black presence, real black heroism was completely ignored.

The Lonely Eagles: Benjamin O. Davis, Jr., and the 99th Pursuit Squadron

In January 1941, one day after a Howard University student named Yancey Williams threatened to sue the secretary of war to consider his Air Corps cadet training application, the Army announced the formation of the first black Air Corps unit, the 99th Pursuit Squadron. One-man pursuit flying was the most dangerous of all combat flying, but single-seat fighter pilot training worked best in terms of segregation. Bomber training, for example, would have necessitated separate black training facilities for bombardiers, navigators, and gunners.

With twenty-seven planes, thirty-three officer pilots, and four hundred enlisted technical crew, the 99th Pursuit Squadron was listed as "experimental." Black pilot candidates were chosen according to the same rigid criteria as whites; all were college graduates. Enlisted men had to have a mechanical background and college training. The new million-dollar Tuskegee Army Airfield in Alabama became the center of black World War II military aviation. The 99th Pursuit Squadron was the first unit of the future 332nd Fighter Group. Known to some white Americans as the Spookwaffe, they were also, less elegantly, called

Eleanor Roosevelt's niggers. They preferred to be known as the Lonely Eagles.

Black military flying officially began in 1939, when six black colleges were finally permitted to join the Civil Aeronautics Authority Civilian Pilot Training Program, or CPT, providing a pool of pilots for wartime emergency. Charles A. "Chief" Anderson, America's first black licensed pilot, headed the Tuskegee Institute program. In 1933, Anderson and his copilot, Dr. Albert E. Forsythe, had been the first black aviators to make a round-trip transcontinental flight. In 1934, Anderson and Forsythe were the first pilots of any color to go by airplane (as distinguished from a seaplane) from Miami to Nassau, the Bahamas. Anderson became a legendary trainer of future black fighter pilots. In March 1941, to the consternation of the white South, and of the First Lady's Secret Service agents, Chief Anderson gave a clearly delighted Eleanor Roosevelt her first and probably only spin in a two-seater with a black pilot.

One of the most important things to any fighter pilot, of any race or nationality, is style. Fighter pilot style, born in World War I, had already been refurbished by the time America entered the war. American pilots strove to combine the insouciance of General Claire Chennault's China-based Flying Tigers (inspiration for the comic strip "Terry and the Pirates") with the elan and raffish nicknames of Britain's Royal Air Force. The writer and airman Albert Murray remembered Tuskegee's white pilot instructors as a "wild group" of ex–Flying Tigers, but black American fighter pilots—like Charles "Buster" Hall, Lee "Buddy" Archer, Clarence "Lucky" Lester, Wendell "Hot Rock" Pruitt—put their own spin on daredevil panache. According to the 332nd pilot Lee "Buddy" Archer, whom I interviewed in 1990, most bombers flew twenty-five to fifty missions and most fighters flew fifty to seventy-five, but all black pilots flew at least a hundred. Archer himself flew 139.

A fighter pilot's style was only the outer expression of his "heart," best described in June 1943 by legendary ex–Flying Tiger Lieutenant Colonel Philip Cochran, a friend and mentor of the 332nd. "The fighting heart is what the fighter pilot has to have," said the thirty-three-year-old Cochran ("Flip Corkin" in "Terry and the Pirates") at a press conference in New York City.[55] "He must feel vicious, he has to want to fight. He's got to be exhilarated. We want him to go into the fight yelling and bouncing up and down in his seat. The fighting heart has to be inside right at the beginning."

Technical Sergeant John "Red" Connell, a white radio operator from Philadelphia, met the 332nd—known as Red Tails, for the red tailpieces of their silver-gray P-51 Mustangs—when he served as a waist gunner on a B-24 Liberator bomber over Europe in 1944. Fighter-escort duty required taking bombers up to their targets, waiting for them, and returning them to the rendezvous. "On a tough raid, maybe Munich, they would have to beat off fierce German fighter attack—you'd be shooting too," Connell, now an actor, told me over forty-five years later. The 332nd was "different" from other units. "You would look out the window off the wing and see your fighter coverage," he remembered. "Ordinary guys did a certain precision rollover to show you they were friendly, but the Red Tails would roll that wing over and over and float through the formation like dancers. If you didn't know who was in that plane, you *knew.* When you saw them you were happy. They were that hot, that good. They had class and finesse." There were many southerners on Connell's plane, but he never heard a racial remark from anyone. They were "respectful" of the Red Tails.

Conveniently for the Army Air Corps, Captain Benjamin O. Davis, Jr., had always wanted to fly. With Davis in command of the first black squadrons, there was no need for the Army to commission another black line officer.

Born in Washington, D.C., in 1912, Benjamin Davis, Jr., had been "overwhelmed" by his first flight, at a Washington air show in 1926. Lindbergh's flight across the Atlantic a year later capped his desire to fly. In October 1935, after receiving aviation training with his West Point class, he had applied for the Air Corps and passed the physical with flying colors. Despite his high class standing, Davis was rejected: he was informed that the Army Air Corps would have no black units. Six years later, when the Air Corps changed its policy, he failed his physical, having been diagnosed with epilepsy—under orders, doctors routinely failed all black Air Corps applicants. A second physical found him fit, although, at over six feet, he was tall for a pilot. (His fighter-pilot nickname was "The Thin Man.")

Davis graduated from West Point in 1936, sixty years after the first black graduate, Lieutenant Henry Ossian Flipper. In sixty years, West Point's racial mind-set had changed little. Davis's first month was deceptively peaceful; the only indication that he was unlike other "Beasts" was the fact that he lived alone in a room designed for two or three. He was friendly with the cadets across the hall and had even been "recognized" by upperclassmen. Recognition could be bestowed by any upperclassman on any plebe but was usually reserved for the end of the first year, when it was proffered in the context of a mass ceremony. Within days of Davis's arrival, Warren S. Everett, a first-year cadet from Wichita, Kansas (a home to Buffalo Soldiers), told him that he would "look out" for him.

Happening to meet Davis in the "sinks" (toilets), his "Beast" company commander, first classman Charlie Rich of West Virginia, told him if he continued in the future as he had begun, he would "get along all right."[56]

Everett and Rich spoke the last "few kind words" Davis heard at West Point. One evening at the end of the first month, as Davis was polishing his shoes and brass, he was informed with a rap on the door that there would be a meeting in the basement "sinks." "What are we going to do about the nigger?" he was stunned to hear just as he entered the basement. From that moment on, Davis was either invisible or insulted. No one spoke to him again for four years, except in the line of duty. The only exception was Charlie Rich, commander. Rich never became the promised friend, but he was at least always "neutral."

"Besides learning to withstand physical hardships, I had become hardened to personal abuse," Davis later wrote. "An impassive look in response to insult became one of my most useful strategies." Many upperclassmen made a point of "recognizing" Davis at the year-end ceremony. The next day he was "invisible" again. Cadets refused to eat with him, or to sit next to him on the way to football games. "The situation was ridiculous, but in no way funny," he wrote. "I had enough intelligence to know that complaints about my situation would not help me." Davis kept his letters home cheerful, asking for things just to get mail. He read voraciously, ran daily solo cross-country in all weather, and (for some "obscure psychological reason") ate an enormous amount of candy. "My father had taught me to be strong; he had endured adversity, and so could I."[57]

Davis could not fathom how Academy officials and cadets, "with their continually and vociferously stated belief in 'Duty, Honor, Country,' " could rationalize their treatment of him. Their aim was to drive him out of West Point, but he graduated thirty-fifth in a class of 276. (The future general William Westmoreland was among Davis's "silent" classmates.) Like Henry Flipper in the nineteenth century, Davis received prolonged applause at his graduation.

When Benjamin Davis married the beautiful Agatha Scott, who had visited him nearly every Saturday for two years and never met another cadet, at the West Point chapel a week after graduation, there was no arch of swords; no guests attended besides the immediate families. Davis and his young bride went to Fort Benning, Georgia, his first assignment, with nine of his West Point classmates. The silent treatment continued. No officer spoke to him except when duty required it, and no officer's wife spoke to Agatha. Davis received his first West Point "mea culpa" letter at Fort Benning. It came from an underclassman, Cadet J. P. Conner: "All I wanted to tell you was what a hell of a lot I thought of you and how nice it had been to know you the three years we were both here. The narrow mindedness of some people is astounding and I believe that this place instead of diminishing that quality in men, increases it."[58] Through the years, Davis would receive many such letters and apologies from classmates.

TUSK'GEE TRAINING: LEE "BUDDY" ARCHER AND CAPTAIN DAVIS

On March 7, 1942, after eight months of training, Lieutenants Lemuel Custis, Charles DeBow, George "Spanky" Roberts, and Mac Ross became the first black pilots of the newly named Army Air Force. Roberts (from West Virginia), Ross (Ohio), and DeBow (Indiana) were all college Civilian Pilot Training graduates. Custis, a Howard graduate from Connecticut, was a former policeman. The four were photographed with their white advanced training director, Lieutenant Robert M. "Mother" Long (short for "Mother Hen"). These four men, and others who joined them under the thirty-year-old Captain Davis, were idols of the black press, black America's favorite sons.

Every four and a half weeks, under a rigid quota system, a few new men entered pilot training. Tuskegee was soon producing more black pilots than the Air Force would allow itself to use. The 99th (with the 100th, 301st, and 302nd Squadrons) now became part of the 332nd Fighter Group, activated in mid-1942. A handful of blacks were eventually admitted to Air Corps Officers Training School in Miami. In 1942, Lieutenant Percy Sutton (a future borough president of Manhattan) was the first black to attend. When I interviewed him in 1990, Sutton told me that Clark Gable was the only white officer candidate to speak to him like a human being. "Don't let them get to you," Gable told him.

Lieutenant Lee "Buddy" Archer, one of nine children of a Harlem Tammany district leader, was one of Tuskegee's earliest recruits. He fell in love with flying at small barnstormer shows in Saratoga, in upstate New York, where his father went to gamble. He grew up making model airplanes and knew the names of World War I aces. In 1939, after graduating from Manhattan's integrated DeWitt Clinton High School and spending a year at New York University, the nineteen-year-old Archer and two white friends took the seven-hour Air Corps test. Grading was immediate, and Archer had the highest score, but the Air Corps rejected him and took his lower-scoring white friends. After he had taken the exam twice more, each time receiving a higher score than the one before, an honest young white lieutenant told him not to waste his time: there would be no blacks in the Air Corps. Archer was soon drafted into the Army.

Within three months of joining Camp Wheeler's 16th Training Battalion outside Macon, Georgia, he was an acting sergeant and a telegraphy instructor. There he met his future wife, the inspiration for his future fighter plane, *Ina, the Macon Belle.* With the creation of the 99th, the Air Corps asked Archer if he was "still interested." This time, he finished the seven-hour test in two hours.

Archer believed that the Tuskegee experiment was "designed to fail." Placing it in Alabama, he told me, was the proof. But the saboteurs had made a mistake. "If you're going to have a system designed to fail," he said, "you find failures to put into it." Archer's fellow candidates, mostly graduates of black colleges, had been taught not to fail. His first impression was that the other cadets were "arrogant and egotistical." But in class and training, watching Mother Long's "hair turn gray" as they took off and landed, the arrogance and egotism began to look like aggression and intelligence—perfect fighter-pilot attributes. Sporting a full-blown RAF mustache, Archer became first captain of the Tuskegee Cadet Corps, its best student, its best military man, and its best pilot.

The Tuskegee Army Airfield base commander was a reactionary West Point graduate, Colonel Frederick von Kimble. Kimble had replaced Major James A. "Straight Arrow" Ellison, who defied white townspeople by arming black military police. Kimble now disarmed the MPs and segregated the formerly integrated base. "For Colored Officers" and "For White Officers" signs were posted everywhere. In reverse discrimination, whites were now barred from the officers' club and the theater, because Ellison had already admitted blacks. When Kimble announced that no black officer would be promoted above the rank of captain as long as he was in command, the black press was notified and began an immediate campaign for his removal.

In mid-1942 Kimble was replaced by Lieutenant Colonel Noel F. Parrish. This time, the Air Force got it right. Parrish had studied black history and attended the Swedish sociologist Gunnar Myrdal's lectures on race relations at the University of Chicago. According to Davis, he was "eager to understand blacks and treat them on an equal man-to-man basis."[59] A native of Kentucky, Parrish did not try to change the system, but he "made it his business to ask black personnel what effect racial tensions were having upon them as individuals." Buddy Archer remembered: "Whenever I got mad at all white people and made plans to destroy them, I would meet someone like Parrish, or Mother Long. They were as fair as you could be under the system. They were crackers and rednecks, but they were *fair*." Parrish would become the only white member of the 99th Pursuit Squadron Veterans Association.

Benjamin Davis, Jr., became a colonel in mid-1942, the only black Air Force officer above the rank of captain. He had been promoted so swiftly that he skipped a grade; the Davises named their new dog Major. Davis believed that "within the bounds of segregation and racial prejudice"—not to mention obsolete equipment—the Air Force did a good job of training black combat pilots.[60] By July 1942, the men of the 99th were, in his opinion, as ready as they were "ever going to be." But their only mission seemed to be public relations. There were rumors that they would never see combat. Meanwhile, antagonism between black airfield personnel and the white town was reaching the boiling point. In early 1943, when town police attempted to seize the weapons of black MPs on Tuskegee property, a riot was barely averted. Far worse, the beating of black Tuskegee Army nurse Nora Greene in a bus incident nearly precipitated armed warfare. In March, Tuskegee's director, Frederick Patterson, turned to Eleanor Roosevelt. "Morale is disturbed by the fact that the 99th Pursuit Squadron trained for more than a year and is still at Tuskegee and virtually idle," he wrote.[61] Mrs. Roosevelt sent Patterson's letter to Secretary of War Stimson, with a covering note of her own: "This seems to me a really crucial situation." On April 5, the 99th was off to North Africa.

Sicily and D-Day Italy: Buster Hall and the First Kill

With the end of the costly but victorious Tunisian campaign, the squadron joined the rest of the Allies in the Mediterranean theater in preparing for the Sicilian campaign, the first step in the battle for Italy. They had received brand-new P-40s and a visit from Lieutenant Colonel Cochran, who, wrote Davis, "imbued all of us with his own very remarkable fighting spirit, and . . . taught us what to do and what not to do in aerial combat."[62] Based at Cap Bon, Tunisia, and attached to the white 33rd Fighter Group, they made their first combat sortie on June 2, over the heavily fortified Sicilian island of Pantelleria. The twelve-day assault on Pantelleria's air defenses marked the first time in any war that airpower alone had completely destroyed enemy resistance. But 99th pilots, flying as wingmen for the 33rd, saw no enemy in the first week—a bad omen. A fighter pilot's confidence depended on quick kill, evasion, and escape reflexes, all requiring practice. It would be another month before the 99th achieved its first victory.

On July 2, 1943, Buster Hall, escorting B-25s over Sicily, made the first 99th kill, bringing down a Focke-Wulf 190. There is a photograph of Hall, very young and slightly stunned, the first black American pilot to shoot down an enemy aircraft, holding a rare celebratory bottle of Coca-Cola instead of champagne. Louis R. Purnell, a member of the squadron, related the story of Hall's Coca-Cola in *Black Wings,* a publication of the National Air and Space Museum. "Although Charlie Hall was awarded the Distinguished Flying Cross," he said, "his most appreciated prize may well have been an ice-cold bottle of Coca-Cola." Purnell had obtained the precious bottle in Tunis, and upon arriving back at the 99th base, deposited it in the squadron safe. "The day of Charlie's victory," said Purnell, "we obtained a block of ice from a town that was fifteen miles from our base. We chilled the bottle of Coke in a one-gallon fruit juice can packed with ice. It was in the shade of a grove of olive trees that the bottle of Coke—probably the only one in the Mediterranean Theater of Operations—came to a well-deserved end."[63]

Hall's victory brought important visitors: Major General James H. Doolittle, Lieutenant General Carl Spaatz, and Supreme Allied Commander General Dwight D. Eisenhower. But Hall's victory was an exception, not the rule. The 99th's short-range P-40s kept them out of the initial invasion, and they spent the rest of the Sicilian campaign out of the war zone, covering shipping and escorting bombers to Salerno.

Sicily did not hold out for long. Now that they had secured a foothold in Italy, the Allies planned an all-out assault. The invasion of Italy (Italian D-Day), planned for September 9, necessitated the use of all available combat air units. The 99th was ordered to rejoin the 33rd Fighter Group. Colonel William "Spike" Momyer, the commander of the 33rd's P-40 squadrons, made life as difficult as possible for them—from giving pilots the wrong briefing times to publicly criticizing their low kill count. He then submitted a report to the Air Force stating that the 99th was "not of the fighting caliber of any squadron in this Group."[64]

Although they were known to have been out of the war zone, the failure of the 99th to gain "victories" was seized upon by critics as proof that the Tuskegee experiment had failed. Air Force Commanding General Henry H. "Hap" Arnold recommended to Army Chief of Staff Marshall that the 99th be removed from combat, that the 332nd be sent to a noncombat area, and that plans for a black bombardment group, the 477th, be shelved. In the late summer of 1943, Phil Cochran was the lone white voice in support of the squadron.

Benjamin Davis was called home at the height of the controversy, officially to take command of the 332nd Fighter Group but in reality to fight not just for the 99th but for the future of blacks in the Air Force. With his father by his side, Davis held a press conference at the Pentagon to condemn the idea that "the utilization of black men as pilots had to be regarded as an experiment." Apologizing for his own inadequacies as an unseasoned leader, Davis said that the 99th had gone for months without seeing the enemy, much less shooting at them.

Time reported the conference in its September 20, 1943, issue, with a photo of the grim-faced Davises. Calling Davis Junior "lath-straight," *Time* reported: "So little operational data on the 99th had reached Washington that it was impossible to form a conclusive opinion about its pilots. It has apparently seen little action, compared to many other units and seems to have done fairly well, that is as far as anyone would go," although "unofficial reports" from the Mediterranean theater suggested that the top air command was not altogether satisfied. Taking a liberal tone on integration, *Time* wrote: "Most thoughtful Army officers probably would agree that the Negro will never develop his potentialities as an airman or any other kind of soldier under the system of segregation in training." *Time* believed, however, that "the Negro pilot training experiment" would continue, proved or not—and black cadets would soon begin medium-bomber training classes. "This squadron, too, is an experiment, and will be one until a question as old as U.S. independence is answered: Is the Negro as good a soldier as the white man?"[65]

Later, Davis scored a decisive victory before the McCloy Commission, under Assistant Secretary of War John J. McCloy, on the employment of Negro troops. He pointed out that the "experiment" was, in fact, a "serious challenge" to the men of the 99th. "Our airmen considered themselves pioneers in every sense of the word, and every one of them was stared at when he landed at a new field because of the novelty of seeing a black pilot. And yet nothing mattered to them as long as no bad mark was registered against the squadron."[66] They would go through any ordeal, in garrison or combat, to prove their worth. Davis's spirited defense not only saved the 99th for combat but expanded the "experiment": the 477th Bomber Group was activated.

While Davis was at home the 99th, now led by Major George Roberts of the first Tuskegee graduating class, was reassigned to the 79th Fighter Group, where it finally saw combat. The 79th's commander, Colonel Earl Bates, was very different from Momyer. The 99th flew integrated missions and was treated like any other squadron in the group. On November 30, 1943, the 79th Fighter Group set a record of twenty-six missions—nine of which were flown by the 99th alone. Within weeks the 99th was flying thirty-six to forty-eight sorties a day. American air action enabled Montgomery's Eighth Army to finally establish an Italian beachhead, but Charlie Hall's victory four months earlier was still the only 99th "kill." Criticism seemed to have taken its toll on squadron morale. Within two months, however, at the Anzio beachhead, the 99th proved to itself and the Air Force that it could "fly and kill." And Anzio Beach was the key to Rome.

January 27 and 28, 1944, were two of the best Allied air combat days of the entire Italian campaign. Allied bombers counted fifty kills, and Allied fighters counted eighty-five—twelve of which belonged to the 99th. On January 27, outnumbered two to one, Captain Clarence Jamison's flight of twelve planes knocked out five German planes in less than five minutes, causing those remaining to turn and run. When they returned home to Naples's Capodicino airfield, each of the twelve pilots buzzed the field and made a slow victory roll. Later that day, Captain Lemuel Custis and Lieutenants Charles Bailey and Wilson Eagleson knocked out three more Germans. The next day, Lieutenants Lewis C. Smith and Robert Deiz each claimed one. And Buster Hall, owner of the first kill, knocked out two more enemy, winning the Distinguished Flying Cross. In the next two weeks, the 99th's total rose to twenty-four—a fighter-squadron record. The unit received an official commendation from the formerly inimical Hap Arnold.

Now recognized combat veterans, the 99th suddenly became, according to Major Roberts, "*the* outfit if you needed to have a bomb placed on a target."[67] The war correspondent Ernie Pyle, who brought the Sicilian campaign memorably home to America in the Scripps-Howard press, wrote of the 99th in his book *Brave Men* (1944): "Their job was to dive bomb, and not get caught in a fight. The 99th was very successful at this, and that's the way it should be."[68]

The 332nd at Selfridge Field and in Naples: Buddy Archer, Roscoe Brown, Jr., and Hot Rock Pruitt

While the 99th was winning its wings in the Mediterranean, the rest of the black units of the 332nd Fighter Group were at home with serious morale problems. In April 1943, they had been transferred from Tuskegee to Selfridge Field, outside Detroit. Selfridge was almost as bad as Tuskegee. The base commander, Colonel Robert R. "Jesus Bob" Selway, personally barred the 332nd pilots, under threat of arrest, from the Selfridge officers' club—this despite War Department A-R (Army Regulation) 210-10, specifically stating that all officers' clubs were open to all officers. Colonel Selway skirted the problem by calling all the black officers transients, even if they were assigned to the base. He directed Selfridge Women's Army Corps members not to walk the base unescorted because of the possible "threat" posed by black officers and enlisted men.[69] The pilots of the 332nd were angry, and they expressed their anger in the air. "We flew rather excitingly," Buddy Archer said. "They had other terms for it."

Detroit, scene of a race riot in June 1943, was even worse than the airfield. Black officers in downtown Detroit constantly confronted white soldiers who refused to salute. "Didn't you see me!" Lee Archer demanded of a nonsaluting white soldier. "Yes," the man replied. "Yes, what!" Archer barked. "Yes, sir! I was gonna salute, but she held my arm," indicating his girlfriend. Archer made the soldier salute, to his girlfriend's fury. When Colonel Davis finally assumed command of the 332nd in October 1943, racial tension was near eruption. "They decided to get us overseas," Archer said.

The 332nd arrived in Naples in February 1944. The Office of War Information had assigned the black photographer Gordon Parks to accompany and cover their mission, but at the last minute his papers were found to be "out of order," he told me when I spoke to him in 1990. A southern congressman had protested against publicizing black pilots at government expense.

In March, General Ira Eaker asked Davis to help him solve a serious problem. The Fifteenth Air Force was suffering a great loss of men and planes. Eaker's experience with the Eighth Air Force indicated that Germans were reluctant to attack escorted bombers, but the Fifteenth Air Force fighter pilots were averse to looking after bombers, preferring to pursue the kill. Escort flying was equally unpopular with black fighter pilots, but Davis made it clear to his men that they had no choice. "Our job is to protect and not be heroes," Archer remembered him saying. Any pilot who left his bombers to chase the enemy would be subject to court-martial. "White boys would leave their bombers in a minute to get a kill," Archer told me. "We couldn't do that." The 332nd became as good at defense as they were at offense.

The 332nd emblem was a fire-spitting black panther over a white star. "A lot of people didn't know we were black," Archer said. When one wounded B-24 could not make home base across the Adriatic, Archer nursed it to the 332nd. He "was in complete shock finding all these black people," Archer reported. But the enemy knew exactly who they were. "The colored boys have arrived," said the Nazi radio propagandists Axis Sally and Lord Haw-Haw—listing all the 332nd by name. The roster included Roscoe C. Brown, Jr., a future president of New York City's Bronx Community College; William Coleman, a future U.S. transportation secretary; and Coleman Young, a future mayor of Detroit.

The squadron's new Italian home was a villa in Ramitelli, in the hills above Naples. Pilots rose at six A.M. to fly combat missions two out of every three days for five weeks; then they rotated back to Naples for four or five days of "R and R." As Dr. Brown put it when I interviewed him in 1990, "R and R" meant "music, games, and women." Not welcome in the Naples overseas officers' club, the 332nd organized its own club, with a reputation for good music and beautiful women. The men of the 332nd found no prejudice among Italians. (Black GIs would be featured in the postliberation films of Roberto Rossellini and Vittorio De Sica.)

The 332nd saw heavy action in support of Allied ground troops converging on Rome in May 1944. The city finally fell on June 4, two days before the Normandy invasion. June was a busy month: Allied strategy was to keep the enemy fully occupied in Italy. On June 25, Captain Wendell Pruitt and Lieutenant Gwynne Peirson knocked out a German destroyer in Trieste harbor with machine guns—a feat unique in Air Force history. Pruitt hit the magazine, setting it on fire, and Peirson's coup de grâce created the explosion. Wing cameras furnished proof to the skeptical Fifteenth Air Force. Pruitt was awarded the Air Medal with six oak leaf clusters, and the Distinguished Flying Cross.

"Hot Rock" Pruitt was unofficially regarded as the best pilot in the outfit. Archer flew wing man for him. "No one could beat Pruitt and myself," Archer told me. "Wendell Pruitt was probably—no, positively—the most popular pilot in the 332nd," remembered the 332nd's intelligence officer Major Robert Pitts in Mary Penick Motley's *The Invisible Soldier*. "The second man would be Lee Archer. Both of these men had something very important in common. They were both top flyers, they were superb in the air, and they were veteran flyers, but both had time to talk to and give advice to a novice. They flew like birds but they kept their feet on the ground."[70]

Archer, who became the first black ace, practiced a philosophy he called nonchalant vigilance. "Never get comfortable; you get sloppy," he told me—but also never be less than nonchalant. Known as the Whistler, Archer always whistled or sang in his plane. His confidence that he could kill, evade, and escape in the air was total. He believed that nothing could hit him from the ground.

Pruitt was more of an artist. After each mission, when all the other pilots had landed, he would entertain the ground crew. "He would circle the base, tip his wings, go into chandelle and a couple of rolls," said Robert Pitts. "After about ten or fifteen minutes of beautiful flying he would come in for a perfect three-point landing. Any other pilot would have been chewed out by the boss." Pruitt was apparently the only pilot whom Colonel Davis could never severely reprimand. "Maybe it was because all the men on the ground and particularly his crew chief really loved the guy," said Pitts. "Everybody respected him, and he knew the guys that kept them flying would like to see a little show now and then."[71] In April 1945, Pruitt crashed and was killed in the midst of a victory roll at Tuskegee.

* * *

The spring of 1945 saw the final Allied assault on Germany as all fronts converged—north, south, and east. The 332nd took part in the all-out offensive against industry in the German-occupied Balkans, especially the vast and heavily defended Romanian oil fields at Ploeşti. On March 24, 1945, they took off on the longest mission in the history of the Fifteenth Air Force, escorting B-17 Flying Fortress bombers sixteen hundred miles round-trip from Italy to the Daimler-Benz tank factory in Berlin. On the way back, in a dogfight over Berlin, Captain Brown, Lieutenant Earl Lane, and Flight Officer Charles Brantley together shot down a new Messerschmitt 262 jet. "We were doing figure-eights over the bombers, and as we flew over Berlin, I noticed these streaks above us," Brown remembered when I interviewed him in 1990. "They were German jets. Instead of peeling up to meet them, we peeled down and then up and caught one of the 262s from underneath." After the war, the Defense Department used film of Brown's jet encounter as combat training for new pilots.

On March 31 and April 1, the 332nd shot down a total of twenty-five enemy planes. On April 26, they were responsible for the last four enemy kills in the Mediterranean theater. By this time, the 332nd under Davis had shot down 111 enemy aircraft, destroyed 150 other planes on the ground in strafing runs, and flown 1,578 combat missions, more than any other unit in Europe.

In their spare time during the war, Archer recalled, the men of the 332nd often discussed their future life and how they felt about America. They thought things would be different when they returned, that "there must be some appreciation for what they had done." But Buster Hall, winner of the Distinguished Flying Cross, and the first black American pilot to down an enemy plane, became a restaurant manager after the war. No airline or commercial transport company would give him a job. The story is typical of the racism they faced. In pursuits other than postwar civilian aviation, however, the story of almost every man was one of high achievement and success. Benjamin O. Davis, Jr., went on to supervise the fighter program of the U.S. Air Force worldwide during the Korean War, and, later, became a four-star Air Force general.

THE WOMEN'S ARMY CORPS: MAJOR CHARITY ADAMS, SERGEANT SALLIE, AND THE "SIX TRIPLE EIGHT"

The Army led the way for black women in the military. Approximately 130 black Army nurses and Red Cross women, and one large black Army Postal Directory Battalion of the Women's Army Corps went to England in World War II. The eight hundred black Army women of the 6888th Central Postal Directory Battalion, the "Six Triple Eight," who arrived in Britain in February 1945, were in charge of redirecting all "V-Mail" for Europe. Its mid-twenty-ish commander, Major Charity Adams, was the first black officer in the Women's Army Corps.

In June 1942 Charity Adams received what seemed to her to be an "invitation" to become a candidate for officer training in the new Women's Army Auxiliary Corps, the WAAC. (The WAAC would become the WAC in 1943.) Four years out of Wilberforce, Adams was a math and science teacher in Columbus, South Carolina. The tall, attractive daughter of a minister and a teacher believed that the Army would be "so pleased" to receive her application that she would "hear from some general within twenty-four hours," Adams wrote in her autobiography, *One Woman's Army.* After a week of silence, she turned her attention to graduate school at Ohio State University. She was about to board the train for Ohio when a telegram came "ordering" her to report immediately for a physical and an interview. The interview panel consisted of two "distinguished"-looking white middle-aged civilian women and an equally "distinguished" white colonel. Leaving the interview room, Adams heard one of the women say, "Let's take her and see if she is as good as she thinks she is."[72]

Fort Des Moines, Iowa, the WAAC training center, was an elegant old cavalry post, complete with golf course and officers with swagger sticks. Adams was the only black among the first twenty-five WAAC officer candidates from Ohio. The first stop was the mess hall, where she was followed by a swarm of media. "Every move we made was watched and recorded," she wrote. The first WAACs were big news—this was their introduction to the press. Adams's picture appeared in *Liberty* magazine.

The Ohio group had traveled to Fort Des Moines under integrated conditions, but on arrival black WAACs were placed in their own building. Although segregated, WAAC quarters were strictly equal. Black and white, WAACs received $21 a month in officer candidate pay. (Male candidates, black and white, received $50 a month.)

Living quarters were segregated, but training was not. White male officers and NCOs were responsible for all WAAC training. Fort Des Moines was more integrated than most camps. Black WAAC officer candidates encountered more sexism than racism from the men assigned to work with them: "Their problem," Adams wrote, "was having to train women." She could remember only one incident of racist behavior from a fellow officer candidate. After a gas mask drill, the women lined up to clean their individual masks, all with the same chemically treated cloth. One of the white women said that she could not use a cloth that had been used by "colored girls" because she had to put the mask on her face. "Absolute silence" followed her remark. No one offered another cloth. Red-faced, she used the offending cloth.

"We were thirty-nine different personalities, from different family backgrounds and different vocational experiences. . . . We were the ambitious, the patriotic, the adventurous. We were whomever our environments had made us, and that was what we had to contribute to the WAAC," wrote Adams of the 3rd Platoon of the 1st Company of trainees, the first black Women's Army Auxiliary Corps officers-to-be. They were married, single, divorced, engaged; college professors, housewives, and domestic workers. The uniform, the great equalizer, was a source of tremendous pride. The Army furnished everything, from toothbrushes to underwear (bras and girdles were pink, slips and panties khaki). The various shades of khaki and the "Hobby" hat, named for the WAAC director, Oveta Culp Hobby, were curiously flattering. Adams was photographed in all degrees of uniform, from Class A summer weight to winter dress uniform to fatigues. Publicity was the norm: WAACs were the public's darlings. They were photographed "eating, marching, at play, at rest, in quarters, in the company area, in classrooms, at the Coke machine, in the post exchange," Adams wrote.[73]

Classroom training, except for the omission of tactical studies, was basically the same as for male candidates, although math major Adams was disappointed to find that map reading was no snap. Physical training was even more challenging. No athlete, she was suddenly required to do handsprings and push-ups. Seven consecutive push-ups constituted a major victory. Making the perfect military bed was another problematic endeavor. "Inspection Day" became a weekly "test of whether we were tough enough to make it," she wrote. Close-order drill, surprisingly, was enjoyable. The "command" voice, however, was daunting. "Miss Adams, did I hear someone say something?" the lieutenant-in-charge had asked, the first time she barked a parade-ground command. Depending on who was addressing her, she was "Miss," "Auxiliary," "Private," "Officer Candidate" or "Soldier." Life had become a matter of the Army and "Before."

It was not easy, she wrote, but "in spite of everything, or because of it all, we were made into soldiers." Graduation day was August 29, 1942. The first WAAC Officer Candidate School class of 440 women included 40 black women. If the 3rd Platoon "colored girls" had not been graduated last, Charity Adams would, by virtue of alphabetical order, have been the first WAAC officer commissioned in World War II.[74]

Two black WAAC companies were formed: a basic training company and a specialist training company. Adams was appointed Fort Des Moines Basic Training Company commander. Male officers were removed from the company level, but remained regimental and battalion commanders. The tall (five feet, eight inches) Adams admired the six-foot-three-inch "slender blond" regimental commander, Major Joseph Fowler, in more ways than one. He was "a striking figure in his Cavalry uniform"; Adams envied his riding crop and wished she could carry one. She credited Fowler with most influencing her success as an Army officer. "He was military to the letter of the regulations, tolerated no foolishness, and gave none. He demanded the best of every member of his command and as a result kept all of us in a state of fear." Fowler invited Adams for a drink at the officers' club—to the outrage of the racist colonel, who did not believe in "race mixing." A nondrinker trying to think of a drink, Adams ordered Scotch with Coke. "Adams, don't ever let anyone else hear you say Scotch and Coke," Fowler said. "It's club soda or water."[75]

Because the few black WAACs could not be trained with whites, Adams and her officers trained four different companies, each with different duties, learning in short order what other officers assimilated over a much longer period. She believed that the training center produced "no better trained" troops in the Women's Army. Promoted to headquarters as the only black training supervisor, overseeing white as well as black troops, Adams socialized with her fellow supervisors, all white female officers.

Riding the Carolina Special for her first visit home in December 1942, Adams was on her way into the dining car for breakfast when the white steward put his arm against the door and announced that the car was full. She waited. A few minutes later, the steward announced, "All persons in uniform first." Adams stepped forward, but the steward put his arm across the door again and repeated angrily, "I said all persons in uniform first." Before she could answer, an angry southern male voice coming from a "very tall, very blond second lieutenant" said, "Well, what in hell do you think that is that she has on? Get your ——— arm down before I break it off for you." The lieutenant was red-faced with anger.

"What in the world are we fighting this damned war for? She's giving her service, too, and can eat anywhere I can. And, by Jesus, I am going to eat with her in this diner." By now Adams, rather alarmed, wondered what would happen next. The steward silently led her to a table for four in the middle of the car. The lieutenant followed, and sat down opposite her. The dining car was absolutely still until they were seated. When people began eating again, there was no sound except that of cutlery. The lieutenant continued his tirade against "crackers" and "cheap whites" who did not understand "what this war is all about." Breakfast over, he escorted Adams back to her seat, bowed, and left. He never introduced himself, and she never saw him again.[76]

By early summer of 1943, the public fascination with the WAACs was dissipating. Then a June 9 item in John O'Donnell's "Capitol Stuff" column of the *Washington Times-Herald* started the great WAAC contraceptive controversy: "Contraceptives and prophylactic equipment will be furnished to members of the WAACs according to a super secret agreement reached by the high ranking officers of the War Department and the WAAC chieftain, Mrs. William Pettus Hobby, wife of the publisher of the *Houston Post,*" said O'Donnell.[77] "The health of the girls in uniform and a determined feminine punch to smash through any out-moded double standards won the day. . . . It was a victory for the New Deal ladies who produced the cold turkey argument that the girls who want to go into uniform and fight what men have called the 'total war' have the same right here and abroad to indulge their passing fancies."

The next day, O'Donnell's column noted that Colonel Hobby had declared there was "no foundation of truth" to the contraceptive story. O'Donnell insisted, however, that the story came from "an intelligent and trustworthy official who swore that his eyes had passed over an official memorandum which dealt with this specific issue." On June 11, Secretary of War Stimson, with an interdenominational delegation of Protestant, Catholic, and Jewish clergy and two congresswomen, held a press conference to discuss "sinister rumors aimed at destroying the reputation of the WAACs through charges of immorality." Representative Edith Nourse Rogers, a Republican congresswoman from Massachusetts and author of the bill creating the WAACs, stated that "nothing could please Hitler more" than efforts to discredit the service, and American women in general. Charity Adams remembered the cartoons, dirty jokes, and "vile insinuations." WAACs were now seen either as providing "organized prostitution for the Army," or as women looking for "women associates."[78] But the WAACs had grown up. Big enough to discuss contraception, they were also big enough to finally join the Army. In the summer of 1943, the WAACs became the WACs, when "Auxiliary" was dropped from the corps name.

In the summer of 1943, Charity Adams became a major—a surprise event, with gold oak leaves and tears. It was now proposed that a separate black training regiment be created, to provide promotional opportunities for black officers. But Adams announced that she would not command such a unit. She wanted to make it as a WAC officer, "not as a Negro WAC officer." Her fellow black officers walked out of the meeting and refused to speak to her after she announced her decision. As suddenly as it had appeared, the plan for the "Negro regiment" was dropped.

That year, a black WAC colleague of Adams was beaten by whites in a southern railway waiting room, but Adams's own racist confrontations were never physical. When a white southern "lady," not wanting to share her sleeping car, demanded that one of the patrolling white military police "check" on Adams, he replied: "Ma'am, I am here in case of trouble, or a problem of some kind. There is no problem here. If I check, to use your word, that officer and she is not an imposter, I might not be a sergeant tomorrow. Besides an imposter would not pick a rank that high; there are too few WAC majors in the Army."[79] In November 1944, Adams was informed that she would be among the first group of WACs to attend U.S. Army Command and General Staff School at Fort Leavenworth, Kansas, the Army's highest level of schooling. She never got to Leavenworth. A month later, she was assigned to overseas duty.

Adams and black WAC Captain Abbie Noel Campbell flew Priority II (Priority I was reserved for the president and his top commanders) to Europe, final destination and assignment unknown, on a C-54 cargo plane with bucket seats. Adams and Campbell were two of three women among the nineteen passengers. The third woman was a civilian, who arrived with suitcases, hat boxes, and a cosmetics case, and ignored the black WACs. She would speak only to the most senior male VIP. The male passengers included military officers, civilian VIPs, and a war correspondent who wrote nonstop throughout the trip. A very young captain, doubtless thinking that "the three of us were the most lost souls in the group," attached himself to Adams and Campbell. Another man later made the group a foursome, dining together to stares on the Bermuda stopover.

Like most of their fellow passengers, Adams and Campbell carried sealed envelopes with instructions to open sometime after takeoff. About forty-five minutes over the ocean, envelopes began appearing, all fingered self-consciously. "I'm going to open this thing," said one man, breaking the ice. Reactions varied from surprise to pleasure to indifference. Adams and Campbell were "shocked" to discover that their secret orders were for London. In their bags they carried lists of places and people to see in Paris.

Arriving in England, Adams made her first and familiar observations (cold, fog, and people driving on the "wrong side" of the road) along with everyone else. "We had forgotten how strange we seemed, to military as well as civilian personnel." Salutes were slow in coming and, frequently, returned with great reluctance. "For most of the military personnel we encountered, accepting any Negro officer in the U.S. Army was hard enough, but accepting Negro women officers was a real burden." London, however, was different. "London was filled with representatives of all the Allies and neutrals, and every conceivable kind of uniform could be seen on the streets, worn by all races, colors, shapes, sizes, sexes, and religious persuasions." The V-2 bombs were also indiscriminate. Adams soon became as studiously cool as the Londoners: "It was only when the motor stopped that we held our breath." Every morning the streets had been cleared of the night's damage and destruction.[80]

Adams was now the commanding officer of the 6888th Central Postal Directory of the European Theater of Operations Postal Directory Service. Based at King Edward School in Birmingham, the Six Triple Eight was responsible for redirecting mail to all U.S. personnel in the European theater. Some seven million men and women (only the War Department knew the exact number), they included Red Cross workers, civilian specialists, and junketing congressmen as well as the uniformed military. But before Adams and Campbell could prepare for troop arrival, they were ordered to Paris to report to the commanding general of the European Theater of Operations, and to the ETO Women's Army Corps director. They were "invited"—that is, ordered—to dine with Lieutenant General John C. H. Lee, commanding general of the Services of Supply, or Com Z, in his elegant and expansive quarters at the Hôtel George V. There were twelve for dinner, including four WAC officers. "For strictly wartime female soldiers we were operating at a very high level," Adams wrote. "It was a great evening as we tried to relax and be socially proper as well as act according to military courtesy." During the course of dinner, General Lee turned and asked, "Adams, can your troops march?" (A classic question for black troops.) For an officer conscious of her "overseas duty efficiency report," there was only one answer: "Yes, sir, they are the best marching troops you will ever see."[81] Adams knew, regretfully, that she would have to prove her words or eat them. Her troops arrived in Birmingham on February 12. The general would be there on the fifteenth for review.

Fortunately, General Lee's parade was a great success. Photographs show a seemingly pleased Lee, short and bulky, standing next to a taller and seriously military Adams, equally bulky in her winter overcoat. The coated and Hobby-hatted troops themselves, marching in orderly precision, look confident and attractive, ready to go to work. "No mail, low morale" was the battalion motto. The Six Triple Eight worked seven days a week in three eight-hour shifts.

* * *

Pretty Sergeant Sallie Smith of Pocahontas, Virginia, joined the WACs in her second year at West Virginia's Bluefield State College because it sounded "exciting" and because she hoped to be near her boyfriend, who was based in Italy. She described her experience when I interviewed her in 1991. She remembered twenty-five to thirty in a stateroom, rough seas and seasickness with the rest of the Six Triple Eight, during the zigzag voyage to Glasgow on the *Ile de France*—where they were met on arrival by Brigadier General Benjamin O. Davis, Sr., of Headquarters Staff Com Z. In Glasgow, they boarded the train that night in a total blackout. The next morning, Smith was shocked by the bombing devastation in Birmingham. Press attention on their arrival was so enormous that Major Adams had to give instant public relations lessons to the troops.

Smith found the transition from civilian to military life traumatic. She hated drilling, she hated the lack of privacy, and she hated making military beds (though once she learned, she made them all her life). She felt that the black women officers played favorites but found Major Adams—known to the troops as "Big Ma"—tough but fair. Sallie Smith's sense of being "scared and far from home" was compounded by sirens, bombs, and orders to "take cover."

She was a supervisor of the directory search room, in charge of thirty-five women working at tables with boxes full of name cards. Every man in the ETO was in those boxes. They kept the locator cards up to date, and if a man died, wrote "deceased" on the card. Their responsibility was to forward and redirect mail and packages. Most civilians had no idea how to wrap packages. Damaged packages addressed to officers were usually confiscated by the civilian aides, or redirected to an enlisted man. British civilian aides called Smith "Sergeant Sallie." She felt no racism from the English, only a certain resentment about material goods. People would promise anything for a carton of cigarettes. Smith and her friends enjoyed sight-seeing (they were near Stratford-upon-Avon) and visiting pubs, but she rarely came in contact with any whites other than the "nice" German POWs who furnished straw for the beds and did everything around the school. There were dances with black GIs, but black officers seemed to feel "superior" to everyone—especially, Smith felt, to black enlisted women.

The English did not consider themselves bigots, professing to prefer those they called blacks, with their "nice manners," to those they called Yanks, "overpaid, oversexed, and over here." This was also true of the typical British soldier, as many military units were integrated with black British colonials. "During the summer of 1942 there was that Army order about keeping aloof from coloured troops to avoid the risk of rows with white US troops," wrote Dennis Sargent, of the British Signal Corps. "That, I'm glad to say, was very unfavourably received by the troops—both non combatants and Royal Engineers of the bomb-disposal company in which I was at the time. . . . 'Just like Hitler' was one typical RE [Royal Engineers] reaction to the order." An Office of War Information film called *Welcome to Britain* included a segment ("Lesson in Tact") in which an amiable old English lady invites a black and white GI to tea, as the narrator speaks: "Here is a problem. Let's be frank about it. There are less racial restrictions here. Just what you saw; an Englishwoman asking a Negro to tea. She was polite and so was he." But black soldiers' popularity in Britain would lessen with their length of stay and the degree of their popularity with English women. Approximately 130,000 black GIs went to Britain, the first arriving in mid-1942. By 1945, the British had tabulated at least 553 certifiable "brown babies."[82] (A 1990 British-made television documentary, *No Father, No Mother, No Uncle Sam,* interviewed several surviving "brown" British orphans.)

Adams's biggest racial battles were fought against the U.S. military. After a troop review mixup, a visiting general told her that he would order a "white first lieutenant" to show her how to run her unit. Not knowing which was worse, "white" or "first lieutenant," she responded, "Over my dead body, sir." The comment was grounds for court-martial. Just before midnight, an "advising" (warning) call came for Adams's adjutant: instructions had been received to draw up court-martial charges. The "advising" call meant that the general might consider an abject apology. Not abject in the least, Adams decided to draw up her own court-martial charges against the general, for disobeying a SHAEF directive cautioning all commanders about using language that stressed racial segregation. Admittedly stretching what had been a memorandum into a "directive," Adams figured she had nothing to lose and everything to gain. Three days later her adjutant received another call: charges had been dropped. By the end of the war, the general himself apologized: "It's been a long time since anyone challenged me, black or white, but you took me on," he told Adams. "You outsmarted me and I am proud that I know you."[83]

At midnight on April 12, 1945, Adams received the news of President Roosevelt's death from a Six Triple Eight telephone operator who got the signal from a Birmingham overseas operator in the process of putting through the call to Churchill at Downing Street. "The main reaction of Negro troops in the ETO," Adams wrote, "was to wonder whether we would get home again or, at best, whether we would have to remain in Europe until all white personnel were safely home."[84] She was the ranking American Army officer in Birmingham, so it was her responsibility to represent the United States at all memorial services for the commander in chief.

The Six Triple Eight was now reassigned to Rouen. The date of her preliminary trip, to inspect the new headquarters, May 7, was, as it turned out, V-E Day. Adams had no idea; she wondered why so many people were lining the tracks to wave and cheer as the boat train sped nonstop through towns and villages. From the moment she stepped off the train in Paris, her uniform was the target of victory hysteria. By the time she reached the U.S. billeting office—having been hugged, kissed, and forced to cede bits of her uniform—the lieutenant in charge could barely control his laughter.

With fighting over in the ETO, the Postal Directory unit was moved closer to the majority of troops. Their headquarters at Rouen was a small post originally built for Napoleon's army. They were a separate and self-sufficient unit, with the usual German POWs for labor and repair work. At Rouen the unit was besieged by black GIs, something that had not happened in Birmingham. "Major, there are 725 enlisted men for each enlisted woman and thirty-one male officers for each female officer," Adams was informed. When Adams replied, "I guess you mean in the ETO?," the noncom answered, "No, ma'am, I mean outside our gates." Troops were being routed through Rouen from the front, and there were white soldiers among the hordes. Without male MPs, the disorderly if cheerful crowds became a problem—solved in part by jujitsu lessons, volunteered by a D-Day veteran British paratrooper, for the unarmed female guards.

Sergeant Sallie Smith kept a copy of a newspaper story on Rouen (headlined "White Skin No 'Must' in France"): "The U.S. was never like this! This is the general feeling of Negro GIs stationed in and around this bomb-shattered French city, who have learned that the petite mademoiselles and the men of Rouen have no racial prejudices." The correspondent Hal Foust of the *Chicago Tribune* reported: "One sees Negro soldiers and French girls walking with their arms around each other in the city's streets." Foust interviewed a black D-Day veteran, Lieutenant

George Woody, of Danville, Virginia, a twenty-six-year-old officer of the 490th Port Battalion: "I know from personal experience as well as observation that the French family makes no distinction between colors in inviting United States soldiers into their homes. It is a contrast to the general custom in America which has a different cultural background. Unless conditions are changed in the United States we have lost the war for world-wide freedom."[85] Charity Adams also commented to Foust on interracial relations in Rouen: "It is regrettable that Americans are so race prejudiced that anything you write will offend many, each in light of his own prejudices. Yet the story should be written, as part of the history of the European war, as part of the current news of America's army still in Europe."

During her first month home, traveling by train in her uniform, Adams was lifting her suitcase to the overhead rack when a young black corporal moved forward to help. But as soon as he noticed her rank, he passed right by, muttering, "If she's strong enough to hold up those oak leaves, I guess she's strong enough to put her suitcase up on that rack."[86]

* * *

Sallie Smith briefly considered staying in France. Instead, she went home to finish college on the GI Bill, becoming the first black woman to receive a master's degree from West Virginia University. She married and divorced the boyfriend who had fought in Italy. She moved to New York City, intending to work on her doctoral degree, but instead worked in the CBS photography department, where she remained for thirty-five years.

Charity Adams retired from the service as a lieutenant colonel, the highest rank possible in the WAC, which by law could have only one full colonel: its director. The prospect of a peacetime job in the Pentagon did not appeal. She decided to go home and get on with her life, becoming a college dean and, in 1949, marrying a man she had first met in Rouen as a soldier. He studied medicine at the University of Zurich, where Adams studied at the Jungian Institute of Analytical Psychology. Back in America, she had two children and became an active participant in civic and corporate affairs. She had "accomplished much" since her military service, she wrote, having "opened a few doors, broken a few barriers," and, she hoped, "smoothed the way for the next generation."[87]

THE DESEGREGATION OF THE NAVY: THE GOLDEN THIRTEEN

The merchant marine, representing the war effort of America's civilian shipping fleet, was the only fully integrated service in the World War II

U.S. military. It was also one of the most perilous. Carrying everything from troops to food to fighter planes, merchant fleets of tough, squat "Liberty" ships dodged torpedoes back and forth across the Atlantic. The merchant marine casualty rate was second only to that of the Marine Corps. Some five thousand seamen were killed in 1942 alone, braving the Murmansk Run to the northern Soviet Union. (Humphrey Bogart's *Action in the North Atlantic* told the Murmansk story.) Quasi-civilian seamen, among them many members of the integrated National Maritime Union as well as veterans of Spain, refused to wear uniforms. Their only concession to the military was a badge on their caps. Hugh Mulzac, veteran of the World War I merchant navy and of Marcus Garvey's Black Star Line, was the first black captain in the U.S. merchant marines. His ship was the *Booker T. Washington.* (The *George Washington Carver,* another Liberty ship, was christened by Lena Horne in May 1943.) Officers serving under Mulzac on the *Booker T. Washington* included Joseph Williams, the first black graduate of the merchant marine officers academy, and John Beecher, the great-grandnephew of Harriet Beecher Stowe, who wrote the ship's history, *All Brave Sailors.* The oldest merchant seaman was William Lew, a sturdy seventy-eight-year-old, who volunteered in August 1943. Lew was the great-great-grandson of the black Revolutionary musician-soldier Barzillai Lew.

If the merchant marine was the most integrated service, the U.S. Navy continued to be the least. As a Harvard man and a former assistant secretary of the Navy, Roosevelt was profoundly critical in the spring of 1941 when Annapolis refused to let its lacrosse team play Harvard if Harvard's lone black player appeared on the field. Finally, stung by a January 1942 speech in which Wendell Willkie excoriated Navy racial policy as a "mockery" of democracy, Roosevelt wrote to Knox: "I think that with all the Navy activities the Bureau of Navigation might invent something that colored enlistees could do in addition to the rating of messmen." A Navy study board insisted that, because of close association on board ship, "members of the colored race be accepted only in the messman branch." Roosevelt told Knox that the report was unsatisfactory. "Officers of the U.S. Navy are not officers only but are American citizens," he wrote. "They should, therefore, be expected to recognize social and economic problems which are related to national welfare. . . . It is incumbent on all officers to recognize the fact that about 1/10th of the population of the United States is composed of members of the Negro race who are American citizens. . . . I [ask] you to return the recommendation of the General Board to that Board for further study and report."[88]

On April 7, 1942, Knox announced that 277 black volunteers per week would be accepted for enlistment, to be trained for general service, not just as stewards and messmen. The first-year goal was fourteen thousand blacks in service as clerks, gunners, signalmen, radio operators, ammunition handlers, and so on. They would be trained in segregated units, and could rise in rank no higher than petty officer. Except as stewards and messmen, they were still barred from seagoing duty.

It was a large step for the Navy, but the restrictions outraged blacks. The National Urban League's *Opportunity* magazine concluded that the service had chosen "to affirm the charge that Japan is making against America to the brown people . . . that the so-called Four Freedoms enunciated in the great 'Atlantic Charter' were for white men only."[89] (The "Four Freedoms," articulated by Roosevelt in January 1941, although not part of the Atlantic Charter, were freedom of speech, freedom of worship, freedom from want, and freedom from fear.)

Black enlistment began on June 1, 1942, at Camp Robert Smalls (named for the black Civil War naval hero), an isolated section of the Great Lakes Naval Training Center outside Chicago. Under the benevolent if paternalistic leadership of Lieutenant Commander Daniel Armstrong, an Annapolis grad whose father had founded the all-black Hampton Institute, black recruits received training that was in some respects superior to that of whites.

By February 1943, under the Selective Service Act, the Navy had a new quota of twelve hundred black sailors a month for general service, fifteen hundred for the messmen's branch. Approximately half of all blacks would be detailed to shore billets within the continental United States and most were assigned to ammunition and supply depots. In June and July 1943 there were two serious incidents of racial unrest, the first of many throughout the war: at a Virginia ammunition depot, and in a construction battalion on a Caribbean transport.

In their wake, a small "Special Program Unit" was created to deal with racial problems and coordinate policies for black sailors. Thirty-one-year-old Commander Christopher Sargent (a former member of Dean Acheson's law firm) was the unit's leader; a superior once called him "a philosopher who could not tolerate segregation." The Special Program Unit encouraged the training of a black shore patrol (Navy police), established a remedial training center with black faculty for illiterate draftees at Camp Robert Smalls, and got the Navy to rule that, except for special units, no black sailor could be assigned to maintenance or stevedore work in the continental United States. The unit was also responsible for two "experiments": the commissioning of the U.S.S. *Mason,* a destroyer escort with a crew of 196 black enlisted men and 44 white officers; and the assignment of 53 black seamen and 14 white officers to the submarine chaser PC 1264.[90] Both ships would eventually replace their white petty officers and some of their other officers with blacks. The crew of the *Mason* was recognized (fifty years later) for its heroism in battling ninety-mile-an-hour winds and forty-foot waves as an escort support ship to England in 1944. A convoy commander's recommendation of letters of commendation for the *Mason* had been "lost" in official channels.

By the fall of 1943, after congressional queries and much protest from civil rights organizations, the Navy began to examine the question of black officers. The Navy special assistant Adlai E. Stevenson, an Illinois lawyer and a future Democratic presidential candidate, was a strong advocate for black officers. There were then three roads to Navy commission: the Naval Academy at Annapolis; the V-12 reservist training program; and direct commission from enlisted ranks or civilian life. Annapolis remained closed to blacks until 1945, and only a few black V-12 reservists had been enlisted. The first sixteen black officer candidates to begin segregated training at Great Lakes on January 1, 1944, were chosen from among top enlisted personnel. They would receive only eight weeks of training—half the normal period.

Suspecting that they were being sabotaged, the candidates covered their windows with blankets after lights-out and continued studying, teaching one another what they knew. Their exam scores were so high that they were ordered retested. The second results were even higher: the best class scores ever recorded at Great Lakes. The Navy decided, however, that only twelve of the sixteen would be commissioned. Among the chosen twelve, ten had gone to college and two to technical schools. A thirteenth, with outstanding grades, was permitted to become a warrant officer. There was no graduation ceremony, but the men were commissioned on March 17, 1944, and photographed in a handsome group portrait for *Life* magazine. They were known as the Golden Thirteen: Ensigns Jess W. Arbor, Phillip S. Barnes, Samuel E. Barnes, Dalton L. Baught, George Cooper, Reginald Goodwin, James E. Hair, Graham E. Martin, Dennis D. Nelson II, John W. Reagan, Frank C. Sublett, and W. Sylvester White, and Warrant Officer Charles B. Lear. (Lena Horne had never heard such "roars of approval" in her life as when she made a 1944 appearance for black sailors at Great Lakes. She realized that the roars might not have been for her, but for her escort, Ensign Reginald Goodwin, one of the "Thirteen.") Upon receiving their commissions, each of the Golden Thirteen was officially designated "Deck Officers Limited—Only," a category usually reserved for officers whose physical or educational deficiencies kept them from performing all line-officer duties.[91]

In February 1944, after much opposition, the Special Program Unit, through the Bureau of Naval Personnel, published a pamphlet entitled "Guide to the Command of Negro Naval Personnel." Among its many controversial statements: "The Navy accepts no theories of racial differences in inborn ability, but expects that every man wearing its uniform be trained and used in accordance with his maximum individual capacity determined on the basis of individual performance."[92] The Navy eventually decided that maintaining duplicate training facilities was too expensive and desegregated officer training. By the end of the war there were some sixty black officers.

Frank Knox died in April 1944 and was replaced by his former undersecretary, James Forrestal, a Wall Street liberal and longtime member of the National Urban League. With the help of his special assistant Adlai Stevenson and the Special Program Unit's Christopher Sargent, Forrestal began moving the Navy toward integration. Too many blacks were relegated to shore jobs, he wrote; it seemed they had simply "swapped the waiter's apron for the stevedore's grappling hook." Forrestal concluded that the time had come to "expand the use of Negro personnel by assigning them to general sea duty." In the summer of 1944, he met with Admiral Ernest J. King, Chief of Naval Operations and Commander in Chief of the U.S. Fleet. Forrestal described the meeting to Lester Granger, a black member of the National Urban League, later Forrestal's special representative on Navy racial matters. "I don't think that our Navy Negro personnel are getting a square break," Forrestal told King. "I want to do something about it, but I can't do anything about it unless the officers are behind me. I want your help. What do you say?" Admiral King sat for a moment looking out the window, then replied, "You know, we say that we are a democracy and a democracy ought to have a democratic Navy." While he doubted the success of the efforts, King told Forrestal that he was behind him "all the way."[93]

Accepting arguments against integrating fighting ships in mid-war, Forrestal outlined an "experimental" plan for the integration of auxiliary ships, based on the merchant marine model: black signalmen, electricians, and boatswain's mates would mix with their white counterparts on tankers and troop transports. Forrestal presented this idea to Roosevelt in a letter in May 1944: "From a morale standpoint, the Negroes resent the fact that they are not assigned to general service billets at sea, and white personnel resent the fact that Negroes have been given less hazardous assignments." He explained that blacks would be used only on the larger auxiliaries and would make up not more than 10 percent of the ship's complement. If the plan worked, they would be used in small numbers on other ships, "as necessity indicates." The White House response was "OK, FDR."[94]

The experiment worked: official records indicated that black personnel had been "successfully absorbed in the ships' companies." The scheme was extended to smaller vessels with similar success.

Carl Rowan: Officer and Gentleman

Lieutenant Carl T. Rowan, one of a handful of black V-12 graduates, participated in the first integration experiments. The son of a World War I veteran, Rowan entered the V-12 program in Topeka in 1943—the lone black among 334 whites. The war was a "great liberator," he wrote in his autobiography, *Breaking Barriers.* It opened "new horizons of opportunity and potential achievement." Rowan's white roommate quipped that he was too busy trying to pass the physics course "to count the pigment" in his skin. The V-12 unit commander commended Rowan, the "lone Negro in a white world," for the "icy stare" with which he handled overt bigotry.

In 1944, Rowan was transferred to Northwestern University's V-12 program, but the university refused to permit a black to live on campus. Sent to the Oberlin College program, Rowan joined two other blacks. Oberlin, "citadel of liberalism," made them all roommates. Now there were "two separate worlds," and Rowan had no white friends. At New York City's Fort Schuyler Naval Reserve Midshipman School, he was one of three black "guinea pigs," but billeting was strictly alphabetical. Rowan's bunkmate, a Mississippi white, confessed before washing out ("sort of one Southern boy to another") that if anyone had told him that one day he would be "sitting beside a Nigra" and "not minding it," indeed "liking it and appreciating it," he would have "knocked somebody's teeth out." But there he was, sharing a final Hershey's bar with Rowan, and he wanted to wish him "luck." The change of heart was a two-way street. "As my bunkmate left, so did some of my bitterest feelings about my native South."[95]

At nineteen, Rowan was commissioned "an officer and gentleman" in the United States Navy. Unlike the "Golden Thirteen," he was qualified for officer duty anywhere, including oceangoing vessels. Fighting ships, however, remained off limits. He became a communications officer on the tanker U.S.S. *Mattole.* The commander's fitness report found Rowan "satisfactory," but recommended duties ashore as "administrator of colored personnel," or on a ship "manned by colored personnel." Transferred to a larger tanker, the U.S.S. *Chemung,* Rowan became deputy commander of the thirty-five-man communications crew, including two blacks. The men took orders from him "without protest or even the slightest hesitation." He credited the ship's commanding officer, C. K. Holzer, who had refused, despite an official advisory, to "prepare the crew" for a black officer. Holzer did not want the crew to think of Rowan as different from any other officer. "I'm a Navy man," he told Rowan. "We're in a war. To me, it's that stripe that counts—and the training and leadership that it's supposed to symbolize." Rowan appreciated the statement. "The skipper had shown an acute understanding of what I—and other Negroes—wanted: no special restrictions and no special favors; just the right to rise or fall on merit."[96]

After the war, fellow Navy man John F. Kennedy made Rowan deputy assistant secretary for public affairs in the State Department and, later, U.S. ambassador to Finland.

The Port Chicago Mutiny

On July 17, 1944, the Navy suffered the worst home front disaster of the war with the explosion of two military cargo ships at Port Chicago, California. Three hundred and twenty sailors were killed, including 202 black Navy ammunition loaders. The accident represented more than 15 percent of all black naval casualties—and the worst domestic loss of life—in World War II. Congress proposed compensation of up to $5,000 to families of victims, but Mississippi's Representative John Rankin objected because most of the prospective recipients were black. Maximum compensation was reduced to $3,000.[97]

Less than a month after the explosion, 258 of the surviving black seamen, denied the thirty-day leave granted to white survivors, refused to load ammunition at a nearby port under the same unsafe conditions, and were arrested. Fifty of those arrested were singled out and charged with mutiny, a crime punishable by death. Despite massive civilian protests, the war's largest demonstration of unified black anger, all the sailors were convicted and given long prison terms. "This is not fifty men on trial for mutiny," said the NAACP lawyer Thurgood Marshall, defending the accused sailors. "This is the Navy on trial for its whole vicious policy toward Negroes. . . . Negroes in the Navy don't mind loading ammunition. They just want to know why they are the only ones doing the loading!"[98] Thanks in large part to Marshall's efforts, forty-seven of the fifty protestors were released two years later.

Acknowledging that racism was responsible for the fact that only blacks had been assigned to load ammunition, but denying that prejudice tainted the fifty-year-old mutiny verdicts, in 1994 the Navy rejected a request to overturn the verdicts against the 258 original Port Chicago mutineers. In July 1999, fifty-five years after the explosion, the black Navy Veterans of the Great Lakes Naval Center and the NAACP were among those asking President Clinton to clear the names of the court-martialed sailors, for the sake of the last two known survivors. One was pardoned in December 1999.

The WAVES: Harriet Pickens and Frances Wills

On July 28, 1944, Navy Secretary Forrestal, overturning his predecessor's adamant refusal, recommended that black women be accepted into the Navy. Black WAVES (Women Accepted for Volunteer Emergency Services) would be trained on an integrated basis and assigned "wherever needed within the continental limits of the United States, preferably to stations where there are already Negro men."[99] The charge by the 1944 Republican presidential candidate, Thomas E. Dewey, that the White House discriminated against black women helped accelerate their enlistment. An October 1944 directive ordered the Navy, the Coast Guard, and the Marines to enroll black women on a nondiscriminatory basis.

The integration of black women into the Navy found a strong ally in the WAVES director, Captain Mildred H. McAfee, who in peacetime was president of Wellesley College, but she could not combat entrenched Navy racism. While the first Women's Auxiliary Army Corps officer candidate school class of 440 had included forty black women, the *last* training class of WAVES included only two: thirty-year-old Lieutenant, junior grade, Harriet Pickens, and twenty-six-year-old Ensign Frances Wills. Both New Yorkers, they graduated from training at Smith College on December 21, 1944. Despite the handicap of joining the class when one-third of the eight-week course was over, Pickens, daughter of the highly respected NAACP official William Pickens, graduated third. She received a personal letter of congratulation from Eleanor Roosevelt—and endless GI fan mail. A "poor soldier somewhere in the South Pacific" hoped she would write; another, from "somewhere in the ETO," asked her to say "hello to all the girls in your outfit"; and one, "lonesome goodness knows," was looking to correspond with "a cute little WAVE." Lieutenant Harriet Pickens (engaged to my great-uncle Sergeant John Burke Horne) was a distinct public relations asset for the Navy.

Within six months of graduation, seventy-two black women were enlisted in Navy basic training and Pickens and Wills were part of the officer personnel aboard the "U.S.S. *Hunter*." The "*Hunter*" was not a ship, but a group of buildings leased from Hunter College in New York City, where WAVE boots (new recruits), including thirty-two blacks, were trained on an integrated basis. Wills continued to train incoming WAVES, and Pickens had supervisory and public relations assignments.

In January 1945, Phyllis Mae Daly became the first black member of the Navy Nurse Corps. Six more black nurses were eventually commissioned. The Coast Guard accepted a small number of black female enlistees, but the Marine Corps Women's Reserve did not enroll blacks until 1949.

THE MONTFORD POINT MARINES: "THE CHOSEN FEW"— EDGAR HUFF, GILBERT "HASHMARK" JOHNSON, BILL DOWNEY

"The Negro race has every opportunity now to satisfy its aspirations for combat, in the Army," said Marine Corps Commandant Major General Thomas Holcomb in January 1942. "And their desire to enter the naval service is largely, I think to break into a club that doesn't want them."[100] Grudgingly bowing to government pressure, the Marines were the last military service to accept black volunteers. General Ray A. Robinson complained to a Selective Service officer: "Eleanor says we gotta take in Negroes, and we are just scared to death; we've never had any; we don't know how to handle them; are afraid of them." The Selective Service officer promised to help Robinson "get good ones": "I'll get the word around that if you want to die young, join the Marines. So anybody that joins [has] got to be pretty good!" Robinson later admitted that they got "some awfully good Negroes." The black recruits, 75 percent of whom had some college education, included specialized technicians, teachers, ROTC grads, and even Army professionals who had relinquished commissions for the Corps. But there would be no black Marine officers, despite the superior quality of these recruits.

Montford Point Marine training center, in North Carolina, was home to the first black Marines. A token two defense battalions (seacoast artillery, antiaircraft artillery, and infantry and tank units for overseas base defense)—the 51st and 52nd—would be trained for combat. The rest of the seventeen thousand black Marines were trained for the noncombat messmen and stewards branches and for depot and ammunition companies. Depot and ammunition companies, which often served in the line of fire hauling supplies onto beaches during offensives and guarding and delivering ammo, were trained only in the use of light firearms. From October 1943 until September 1944, one ammunition company and two depot companies were organized every month at Montford Point. The Marines had discovered a useful role for the new, unwanted black recruits. Placing them in formerly white labor battalions as Pacific support troops would, according to Marine leadership, free more white Marines for fighting.

The Montford Point Marines, like the Tuskegee Airmen, were named for their segregated training camp. Montford Point, in the Sea Islands of black Civil War history, was a swampy, mosquito-ridden, snake- and bear-infested forest behind Camp Lejeune. The nearest civilization was Jacksonville, North Carolina, a sand-and-palmetto coastal town. Despite general hostility, Montford had a relatively benign white command staff. Black Marines respected Colonel Samuel A. Woods, Jr., the first commanding officer of the 51st Composite Defense Battalion, a veteran of World War I who had fought in China, Cuba, the Philippines, and the Dominican Republic. Drill instructors, also old-line Marine types, were chosen from among the least openly racist. Nevertheless, the traditional welcome to Marine recruits—"I'm going to make you wish you had never joined this damn Marine Corps"—was given new significance for Montford Pointers.

"Are you sure you want to join the Marines?" the recruiting officer asked twenty-two-year-old Edgar R. Huff of Gadsden, Alabama. It was June 1942; Huff had read in the paper that qualified blacks would be admitted. "Sergeant, I am more sure I want to join the Marines than about anything else in my life."[101] The recruiting sergeant walked to the window, looked out, then turned and said, "Well, I'll take a chance on you." Huff, who stood over six feet tall and weighed nearly two hundred pounds, enlisted "from a log cabin in the cornfields of Alabama" with a quarter in his pocket, a quarter he was to carry for thirty years, for good luck. "I wanted to be a Marine because I had always heard that the Marine Corps was the toughest outfit going, and so I wanted to be a member of the best organization," said Huff in a later interview with the authors of *Blacks in the Marine Corps.*[102] His father, Edgar R. Huff, Sr., a World War I veteran who grew up among Alabama Creek Indians and was fluent in their language, had served in Signal Corps Intelligence and died from mustard gas in France.

"You may as well go over the hill, or go home tonight," white DIs yelled at the black recruits standing at attention in their undershorts at one A.M. on the second night of boot camp, "because you'll never make good Marines!" They stood at attention for two hours, as mosquitoes attacked. When they were finally allowed to return to their huts, several began to pack. "Unpack your bags, men!" said Huff, calling a meeting and making the first of his many speeches. "They want us to fail," he went on. "Don't let anybody push you out of the Marines . . . hold on like a bull dog on a bone. Don't let our race down; they are depending on us to succeed. Unpack your bags and stick to it like men." A black Marine who survived boot camp, Huff believed, "could go through hell singing a song."[103]

Huff dropped out of school in the tenth grade because his widowed mother, a domestic, had been fired by her white employers when she needed a major operation. As a Marine recruit, he passed his high school equivalency test and also enjoyed "regular balanced meals, electric lights, running water and an inside bath" for the first time in his life. Boot camp, for Huff, built "muscles, alertness, discipline, courtesy and military pride."[104] By the end of November 1942, after eight weeks of the "purity" of boot camp nutrition, the recruit platoons found that beer and candy bars made them sick.

The Marine Corps decided to develop black noncommissioned officers. Exceptional black recruits were singled out as acting "jacks," or drill instructors. In January 1943, Private Edgar R. Huff, promoted to private first class, became the first black Marine NCO. A month later, Huff recommended that a fellow Alabaman, Private Gilbert Johnson, also be promoted. Johnson, with two years of college and sixteen years' combined service in the Army and Navy, should have been promoted faster than Huff, but was considered "outspoken." Johnson was thirty-seven when he arrived at Montford Point, and was so impressive in his naval uniform (officer's steward, First Class) with three stripes up and three stripes down his arm (thus his nickname, "Hashmark"), that Huff stood at attention until Johnson said, "Son, sit down." Huff had never seen anyone so "squared away." Over time the two would become best friends; they married identical-twin sisters.

By May 1943, black sergeants and drill instructors were in charge of all training platoons at Montford. "Hashmark," now Sergeant Johnson, was chief DI. Other black NCOs were George A. Jackson, a former Army lieutenant, and John T. Pridgen, a veteran of the 10th Cavalry. Arvin L. "Tony" Ghazlo, a former bodyguard and jujitsu instructor from Philadelphia, and his assistant Ernest "Judo" Jones became senior instructors in bayonet and in unarmed combat for all black recruits. Many recruits believed that with black NCOs boot camp became even tougher. Johnson admitted to being something of an "ogre," but the goal—to shape in a few weeks "a type of Marine fully qualified in every respect to wear that much cherished Globe and Anchor"—was "nearly impossible."[105]

Everyone had been awed when Huff, a "rangy-built dude" with a "high-pitched voice," became the Marine Corps' first "real live Negro Private First Class," wrote Bill Downey, then a private in the 16th Platoon, in *Uncle Sam Must Be Losing the War.* Recruits had been told to salute anything, "even a zebra," that had a stripe. "The first time we saw our black PFC we followed him around like cubs," he wrote. "We were so proud of our PFC that we saluted the man at every corner of the company area." Downey, whose grandfather had been the first black policeman in Iowa, enlisted from his hometown, Des Moines, after reading a newspaper headline that "Marines are suffering 50 percent casualties on Guadalcanal." The trip to Montford was Downey's first time in the South. Traveling in the "cattle car," with no bathroom and no food, he noticed a black Army officer with an "aura of withdrawn dignity," reading a paperback as if he were in the Jim Crow car "by choice."[106]

The 16th Platoon had been in limbo for nearly a month, waiting for enough recruits to begin training. Meanwhile, they had no uniforms, no equipment, no boots or shoes. The men cleaned toilets and hauled garbage in civilian clothes—some in zoot suits. They were forced to stand naked at attention in the sun for hours, so that "mosquitoes could feast," and ordered to memorize the Marine Corps manual, with more laws and rules than the Constitution. For the first ten days, Downey believed that the chief drill instructor's intent was to drive recruits either to "commit suicide or go mad." The white chief DI was, oddly, named Sergeant Germany. Downey remembered his first words: "I did not come here to make friends. I came here to undertake the impossible assignment of making Marines out of you goddam people. When the first load of y'all got here it made me want to puke, then go get drunk. The material gets worse with each platoon. The Marine Corps is not for cooks and janitors. Which is about all you son of a bitchin' people are qualified to do as far as I can see. Just remember that I am going to try and get as much out of you people as I would from a platoon of white recruits. If I have to kill you to do it then you are dead. . . . My name is Sergeant Germany. I'm a red-necked peckerwood and I hate a goddamn nigger."[107]

The platoon, completely at Sergeant Germany's mercy, felt an "acrid hatred" of its drill instructor, "much more than the animosity of black for white or the hatred of the oppressed for the oppressor," Downey wrote. Midway through boot camp, Germany was abruptly transferred to the South Pacific. Downey remembered his farewell to the troops: "You people are about as far along as a patient man can take you. . . . There are buds of leadership among you. . . . This has been an interesting two and a half months. You ain't the worst bunch I ever seen." Later, hearing that Germany had been killed in the first wave during the assault on Peleliu, they all raised bottles "to a bad-assed redneck son-of-a-bitch!" Soon after, Downey himself made PFC.[108]

* * *

In the summer of 1943, Major General Henry L. Larsen, the new Camp Lejeune commander, was invited to a Montford "boxing smoker" (so called because officers smoked cigars), where he delivered an unforgettable speech to the assembled Montford troops. Having just returned "from the hellish battles of Guadalcanal," he was stunned by the new Marine Corps: "Dogs in the infantry to serve as sentries. Women in the Marines. Then when I saw YOU people in uniforms—Uncle Sam surely must be losing the war."[109] The response of the black troops was immediate and tumultuous. At least one white witness was equally unhappy. "It broke my heart," the musician and composer Bobby Troup recalled when I spoke to him in 1991. In 1943, he was twenty-five-year-old Lieutenant Robert W. Troup, Jr., of New York City, camp recreation director and band organizer.

Black USO shows, intramural sports, and, especially, music were Montford's morale boosters. Men who had played with Count Basie, Cab Calloway, Duke Ellington, and Erskine Hawkins were in the 51st Battalion Band. Lieutenant Troup, the band organizer, was a jazz musician, the composer of such hits as "Daddy, I Want a Diamond Ring" (on the 1941 Hit Parade for fourteen weeks), "Snootie Little Cutie" (a Tommy Dorsey favorite), and "(Get Your Kicks on) Route 66." He was most popular at Montford, however, for a song called "Jacksonville": "Take me away from Jacksonville, 'cause I've had my fill and that's no lie. / Jacksonville stood still while the rest of the world went by." In Downey's words, the men of the 51st considered Troup "the best paddy [white] on the base" and "would have followed him to hell if he had asked." Troup was not big on discipline; the men called him Bobby within earshot: No one in the Marine Corps was supposed to call a lieutenant by his first name . . . but Bobby Troup kept playing like the only thing that would upset him was if someone tried to take away his piano." Troup was a reminder to Downey "that there were still civilized white men in the world."[110]

Despite rumors that no black Marines would actually see combat, the new commanding officer, Lieutenant Colonel Floyd A. Stephenson, recommended in mid-1943 that the 51st become a regular heavy defense battalion. Now they were separated from the rest of the unit for intensive training. The men of the 51st were wary of Marine Corps promises, however: "We went through the motions of training to become a composite defense battalion but none of us had many illusions left," Downey wrote. "We felt the 51st had been a front for getting blacks to enlist so they could be used as servants and stevedores. . . . The general anger and resentment for being hoodwinked into thinking we would someday be a crack combat Marine force became a catalyst. We began to work harder and even stayed up nights to improve our defense battalion skills. We would make them notice us if we had to declare a war of our own."[111]

In September 1943, the 51st Defense Battalion moved out of the main Montford Point area to special quarters at Camp Knox. The last use of Camp Knox, formerly belonging to the Civilian Conservation Corps, had been war dog training, and the quarters were badly in need of repair, but the move was popular with the battalion. As the only black Marine unit engaged in extensive combat training, the men felt that they were "a bit different [from], superior even" to the rest of Montford Point. Morale soared with the arrival of brand-new 155mm artillery guns—"not the tools of a work battalion." The guns were named Lena Horne, Joe Louis, and Zombie. The men had seen such guns in movie newsreels but never dreamed of having them.

"When the new pieces were assigned to gun crews," wrote Downey, "the guys were so excited they worked all one weekend sandbagging their guns into mock positions." With artillery placed toward the ocean, and target ships towed by small Navy craft, the first shot fired by black Marines in U.S. history was a direct hit on a moving target on the ocean off Onslow Beach. The beach, of course, was otherwise off limits to blacks. "Discrimination had become such a way of life we tried to take it in our stride, although inside it was a festering sore that refused to heal," wrote Downey. "To retain our sensibility we put all our energy in our work."[112]

The 51st became known as a hotshot shooting outfit. Words like "remarkable" and "unbelievable" were heard and passed on to the company. A young white Marine whose jeep Downey helped tow out of the sand reported that everyone had heard that the 51st was a "hot outfit," but "the brass didn't want the outside world to know."[113] In November 1943, on the last day of gunnery training, with more military brass on the beach than ever before, the men broke all existing coastal and antiaircraft firing records. The achievement remained a secret, but their scores shot them into the war. They were sent overseas. In January 1944, they were on their way to the Pacific.

* * *

"This is a troop train of the United States Marines on their way to a port of disembarkment," a lieutenant argued with a southern sheriff who refused to let the men get off the train for food. "I don't give a good goddam if them niggers is going to Tokyo," the sheriff replied. "They ain't goin' to eat in Atlanta, Georgia, with white folks." When one of the officers returned with news that German POWs were eating in the station cafeteria, the men wanted to empty the train and take the station apart. "It was so frustrating that some of the guys actually wept," Downey wrote. "There was no place to hide their tears or their shame."[114]

San Diego was almost as bad. Proudly wearing new shoulder patches, red ovals with a blue 90mm antiaircraft gun superimposed over a large white "51," they disrupted the show when they were told that they would have to sit in the back at the open-air movie. Morale fell further when the weapons and equipment the battalion had brought from Montford were turned in to San Diego quartermasters. The men feared a noncombat assignment. But on February 11, 1944, they sailed for Nanumea and Funafuti, the Ellice Islands, to relieve the white 7th Defense Battalion. Eager to leave, the 7th were "never so glad to see black people in their lives."[115]

The 51st got their first look at Marine life in the Pacific. "We must have looked as strange to them as they did to us," Downey wrote. "Their dress violated all Corps rules and should have been good for at least two hundred years imprisonment. . . . All dungarees were cut off at the knees. Their shoes were slashed open at the toes and along the sides. Everyone was bearded, mustachioed and bushy-headed. Shirts looked like vests."[116] The 51st was in the field, but there would be little combat: the unit's job was to maintain and defend island airfields. The greatest dangers, the men were told, were mildew, fungus, and warts.

Funafuti itself, which no one had heard of (Tarawa, Bougainville, and Midway were the islands in the news), was a disappointment. About three miles long, three-quarters of a mile wide at its widest, and with a maximum elevation of twelve feet, its chief vegetation was coconut trees. The island was populated by lizards, rats, and mosquitoes, its human elements consisting of a small British Colonial Office detachment, American sailors, Marines, a company of Seabees (Navy construction battalions), and a few Polynesian women. "There was no doubt we were being dumped," wrote Downey. "As sure as the Gilberts and the Marshalls were stepping stones to Japan, Funafuti was heading the other way." The Japanese radio propagandist Tokyo Rose echoed his sentiments: "I beseech you black men of the Marines to listen to me. Don't you know you are being used? They make you do the menial work and fill your head with lies about the Japanese people being your enemies. . . . Please don't hate us for killing you and your black brothers. Especially those of your black brothers who at this very minute work as stevedores for the whites on Japanese islands north of your base." They liked

Rose. She played the best jazz in the Pacific—Ellington, Basie, and the Benny Goodman trio.[117]

Funafuti was followed, six months later, by Eniwetok atoll, "the general shape of a dead whale," with all vegetation "blasted off." This time the 51st took over the weapons and equipment of the 10th Antiaircraft Battalion. The Seabees on Eniwetok kept busy making "Japanese souvenirs": swords from American bayonets, and flags out of parachute silk. The men of the 51st sharpened their gunnery talents; according to the record books, they were the best gunners in the Corps. But the first black combat Marines spent nineteen months in the Pacific, until the war's end, without seeing combat.[118]

The only black Marines to see combat were not combat troops. Members of the 3rd Marine Ammunition Company and 18th and 20th Depot Companies hit the beach on D-Day Saipan—June 15, 1944. The island was the first target in the Japanese-held Mariana Islands. Men from the 3rd Ammo Company helped repulse an enemy counterattack during the night and were credited with knocking out a Japanese machine gun. An exploding mortar shell produced four 18th Depot Company casualties as they unloaded ammunition and other supplies. "My company landed about 2 p.m. on D-Day," wrote the 20th's commander, Captain William C. Adams. "We were the third wave, and all hell was breaking when we came in. It was still touch and go when we hit shore, and it took some time to establish a foothold. My men performed excellently. Among my own company casualties, my orderly was killed." Adams's orderly, Private Kenneth J. Tibbs, trained as a noncombatant, was the first black Marine killed in action in World War II.[119]

The Marine Corps and the national press recognized the actions of black Marines on Saipan. "The Negro Marines are no longer on trial," said the Marine commandant, General Alexander Vandegrift. "They are Marines, period." *Time* reported: "Negro Marines, under fire for the first time, have rated a universal 4.0 on Saipan."[120] The 3rd Ammunition and 18th, 19th, and 20th Depot were included in the 4th Marine Division Presidential Unit Citation. Black Marines of the 2nd and 4th Ammunition Companies were also in the thick of the recapture of Guam in July 1944, and were included in the Navy Unit Citation.

The recapture of Guam did not mark the end of encounters with the Japanese. Two black Marine companies took part in the bloody battle for the island of Peleliu in September. The 11th Depot Company, with seventeen men wounded, had the highest casualty rate of any black Marine unit. In December, Private First Class Luther Woodward of the 4th Ammunition Company earned the highest decoration won by a black Marine.

Following fresh footprints near the ammunition dump he was guarding, he crawled through thick brush and spotted six Japanese. He immediately opened fire, killing one and wounding another before they fled. Returning to camp, he got five Marines to join him in hunting down the enemy. Woodward killed two more Japanese. He was awarded the Bronze Star, later upgraded to Silver.

GENE DOUGHTY AND THE 8TH AMMO AT IWO JIMA

In February 1945, twenty-year-old squad leader and acting platoon sergeant Gene Doughty and the 8th Ammunition Company were transported to Guam aboard an LST (Landing Ship, Tank). A "floating hearse," Doughty called it when I interviewed him in 1990, "the worst transport ship that any soldier, Marine or Navy man would want to be on, particularly heading for a combat zone." The men of the 8th had no idea where they were going, but they knew that "something big" was up. Their destination was Iwo Jima in the Marianas, halfway between Tokyo and U.S. Air Force bases on Saipan, the site of the largest Marine amphibious operation in the Pacific.

The 8th Ammo landed after the first assault wave, just before sunset on D-Day plus 5, in the face of flying bullets, shell fire, and long-range-gun fire. All they saw on the beach were dead bodies and black volcanic ash. To Doughty it was a "hellish" landscape. Seasoned fighters who had seen Tarawa said it was "nothing like this." Outnumbered 5th Division Marines faced intense mortar fire from enemy soldiers dug into caves with labyrinthine tunnels and underground transits. With one landing beach for armada and assault troops, the Americans were easy targets. It took Doughty forty-five minutes to dig a foxhole in the black ash, and even that did not protect from shells.

Five days after landing, Doughty and the 8th Ammo saw six Marines from the 2nd Battalion, under heavy enemy fire, raise the American flag on Mount Suribachi, a long-inactive volcano. A mile away, the Americans on the beach applauded and cheered. (The flag raising was done twice, once for real and again for the famous photograph—both times under fire.) From February 19 to March 25, Marines and Japanese battled for Iwo Jima. Black Marine service and supply troops saw more action than the white 3rd Division, waiting offshore.

The "time for heroism," said Doughty, came on D-Day plus 25, when "all hell broke loose." That night, a company of Japanese sprang on Doughty's unit and made for the ammunition they were guarding. They came from underground, although the Marines had believed that all caves were sealed. Some of the Japanese appeared to be unarmed; others carried spears, anything they could fight with. Korean slave laborers fought with bare hands, the Japanese having forbidden them weapons. Doughty could see that these were "much fiercer fighters" than American troops: highly disciplined, and trained to kill at the cost of their own lives. They seemed to come wave on wave, from skirmishes to minor engagements to pocket battles. Fighting in the dark, Doughty and his men had no idea how many they were killing. At sunrise, he could not believe his eyes. His men had killed a full company or more. Private Harold Smith was killed and two other 8th Ammo men were wounded. Private Vardell Donaldson of the 36th Depot was also killed, and two members of the 36th were wounded. Black Seabees were used as medical corpsmen, so that white corpsmen would not have to touch black Marines.

Twelve black Marines were wounded and three were killed in the first month of the battle for Iwo, the single fiercest contest in the Pacific. All told, more than six thousand Marines were killed and close to twenty thousand wounded, the most in a single Pacific encounter in World War II. Captain Robert C. Johnson, commander of the Seabees, called it "the most expensive piece of real estate the United States has ever purchased. We paid 550 lives and 2,500 wounded for every square mile."[121] Two men of the 36th Depot were awarded Bronze Stars for "heroic achievement against the enemy." The secretary of the Navy announced that support units of the V Amphibious Corps were authorized to wear the Navy Unit Commendation ribbon.

When the Marines left Iwo, black Seabees and the 8th Ammo stayed behind for graves registration, a function traditionally reserved for black troops. Sunday, March 3, 1945, was a day Doughty would never forget. A Navy supply ship arrived, and the men were invited on board for bacon and eggs, milk, toast, and coffee. Doughty remembered feeling "so grateful to be alive and to have fresh food." The Navy left a portable shower unit, and the Seabees rigged a hot sulfur shower from a natural underground lava spring. It was Doughty's twenty-first birthday. He felt the shower was "God's blessing."

* * *

The battle for Okinawa, the last Japanese island bastion, lasted from April 1 until June 21, 1945. Three black ammunition companies, the 1st, 3rd, and 12th, and four depot companies, the 5th, 18th, 37th, and 38th, were at Okinawa D-Day. Fourteen black Marines were wounded in the campaign; one, Steward Second Class Warren N. McGrew, Jr., was killed. The island was declared secure, but there was little letup for black troops: Okinawa was to be the principal supply and staging area for the invasion of Japan.

President Roosevelt died on April 12. The war in Europe was over on May 7. Now four Marine divisions were preparing for the October 1 invasion of the Japanese mainland. But the Marines' war was unexpectedly brought to an end in August. Hiroshima and the atomic bomb were beyond Doughty's "wildest dreams." He believed that dropping the bomb was a wise decision: "America never could have successfully invaded the Japanese mainland," he told me in 1990. "They had one-man submarines everywhere. Everyone was kamikaze—little children would be strapped in grenades."

Back home, on November 10, 1945, Private First Class Frederick C. Branch became the first black commissioned reserve officer in the U.S. Marine Corps. Shortly after, however, the Corps abolished its combat-lacking, but record-breaking, black antiaircraft units. "So long as social conditions make segregation desirable," reported Lieutenant Colonel Thomas C. Moore to the Marine Corps commandant, "it is believed that Negro Marines would be more advantageously employed in almost any other type unit."[122]

The Marines were perhaps the fiercest in their resistance to integration. The Army, fighting in Europe, was confronted with such dire manpower shortages that shortly before the end, in an ad hoc field experiment, black soldiers were asked to volunteer for integrated combat.

"INTEGRATION": THE BATTLE OF THE BULGE

In December 1944, in the midst of the fiercest fighting of the Ardennes offensive, Lieutenant General John C. H. Lee officially suggested that black service troops be permitted to volunteer for combat. Desperately needing manpower, Eisenhower agreed (as did Generals George Patton and Omar Bradley), and Lee's Com Z issued a late-December circular calling for black volunteers. The call was limited to privates who had some infantry training in the upper four categories of the Army General Classification Test. Noncommissioned officers wishing to apply would have to accept a rank reduction. "It is planned to assign you without regard to color or race to the units where assistance is most needed," read the appeal, "and to give you the opportunity of fighting shoulder to shoulder to bring about victory."[123] General Benjamin O. Davis, Sr., drafted the directive. "Yesterday," he wrote to his wife, "I secured a decision from the High Command which I think is the greatest since the enactment of the Constitutional Amendments following the emancipation."[124] Two thousand two hundred and twenty-one black troops volunteered for combat in December 1944, to fill in for white troops already killed in the ongoing Battle of the Bulge.

The "invitation," worded as if it resulted from War Department beneficence rather than urgent need, was a definite policy departure—too much so, as it turned out, for the Supreme Headquarters American Expeditionary Force (SHAEF) under Eisenhower in Paris. Advised by Lieutenant General Walter Bedell Smith to warn the War Department that civil rights spokesmen might seize the moment to demand wider integration, Eisenhower revised Davis's circular.[125] The black volunteers would be trained in *platoons*—not as "individuals." They would remain in segregated groups, to which white commanders could assign white platoon sergeants and white platoon and squad leaders. Although it was no longer a serious issue, "integration" nevertheless made a point. An Army poll revealed that while only 33 percent of white officers had favored integration before the experiment, 77 percent favored it after. Among white enlisted men, the figures were 35 percent and 77 percent.[126]

Alan Morrison was the only black correspondent for the military newspaper *Stars and Stripes.* In a postwar article in *Ebony,* he wrote: "When the news reached Washington that Negro and white Americans were battling the enemy in mixed companies, tempers flared on Capitol Hill and the War Department brusquely cabled European Theater headquarters for an 'explanation' of this violation of American racial policy."[127] A December 1944 letter to Mississippi's notoriously racist Senator Theodore Bilbo from Robert Byrd, a future U.S. senator from West Virginia, indicated the depth of white-supremacist reaction. "Integration of the Negro into White regiments is the very thing for which the Negro intelligentsia is striving and such a move would serve only to lower the efficiency of the fighting units and the morale of the average white serviceman as well," Byrd wrote.

> I am a typical American, a southerner, and 27 years of age, and never in this world will I be convinced that race mixing in any field is good. All the social "do-gooders," the philanthropic "greats" of this day, the reds and the pinks . . . the disciples of Eleanor . . . the pleas by Sinatra . . . can never alter my convictions on this question. . . . I am loyal to my country and know but reverence to her flag, BUT I shall never submit to fight beneath that banner with a negro by my side. Rather I should die a thousand times, and see old Glory trampled in the dirt never to rise again, than to see this beloved land of ours become degraded by race mongrels, a throw back to the blackest specimen from the wilds.[128]

Unlike the black soldiers with whom he would "never submit to fight," Byrd did not serve in the military in World War II.

The twenty-five-year-old black infantry medic Bruce M. Wright heard the Lee-Eisenhower announcement in Cardiff, Wales. Wright was insulted, he told me in our 1990 interview, by the message of "To Our Negro Troops": "You may now fight at the side of your white brothers who have borne the brunt of combat." Black GIs knew of the manpower shortage. Wright volunteered to leave his service unit for combat, "hoping to prove something, hoping that things would be better." He was one of three blacks assigned to K Company, 26th Regiment, 1st Infantry, and their welcome was memorable. "I never thought I'd live to see the day when a nigger would wear the Big Red One," said a "short, angry" white captain, as remembered by Wright in his autobiography, *Black Robes, White Justice.*[129]

Wright had been drafted in 1942, in his second year at New York's Fordham Law School. Sent to basic training at Camp Rucker in Alabama, he earned ninety days in the stockade for protesting a two A.M. order for black troops to put out a fire started in the woods by a white artillery unit's target practice. Wright wrote letters to *The New York Times* about racism at Rucker, and to the black New York City congressman Adam Clayton Powell, Jr., requesting help for a transfer. He found out later that none of the letters had left camp. Having studied pre-med at Lincoln University, he became a quartermaster battalion medic and, in February 1943, was sent overseas to England, Scotland, and Wales. In Swansea, before the black Red Cross was created, he became the object of a southern white Red Cross hostess's "fancy." More important, he befriended an English soldier who shared his interest in Dylan Thomas. Wright's new friend had worked for a publishing house. "I will see what I can do with this," he said, taking some of Wright's poetry. Several months later, Wright went to a German airport to meet a jeep with fifty copies of his collected verse, *From the Shaken Tower,* which described, in traditional poet-soldier fashion, idealism destroyed by war.

As an infantry medic, Wright had participated in the third-wave assault at Omaha Beach on D-Day, June 6, 1944. As the landing craft hit the beach against a backdrop of hills belching fire and smoke, he saw panicked men drowning in four feet of water. He would never forget the sight. Wright won his first Purple Heart in Normandy, and was out of combat for thirty days in an English hospital. He won his second Purple Heart and first Bronze Star in Germany, wearing the Big Red One, in the aftermath of the "Bulge." In *Black Robes, White Justice,* Wright never speaks about his medals or how he won them; but he told me about them in 1990. Under counterattack on a lonely road, with German machine guns firing from the top of hill, he heard a white soldier say, "Oh, shit,

I'm hit." Always called when someone was hurt, Wright took off his pack and crawled under covering fire through a mine field, to a man who had been hit in the stomach by German dumdum (expanding) bullets. He put antiseptic powder on the wound and covered the man with his body until the attack subsided. The Bronze Star and a battlefield promotion came together. Three weeks later, he received a note from Missouri: "Thanks to the colored boy who tried to save my Jim." When the unit first moved to Germany, Wright informally defended black GIs accused of rape and other crimes. An officer told him, "If you'd forget race problems you'd make a good corporal."

Wright was in Czechoslovakia in May 1945 when he learned that the European war was over. He wrote a poem, "Journey to a Parallel":

I remember the tired tumult of my urges
and the sun shining, and the dust, and the clouds,
and how I turned my rifle down;
I remember a cow stinking in the street
and a woman sweeping dung,
With Prague and Pilsen just forty kilometers;
I recall that songs were sung, attention stood, allegiance reasserted,
and I saw two colonels cry.
There was the first night of awkward peace
with pillows
trimmed in Slavic lace and lettered "schlafe wohl,"
and hugged into humanity;
I trembled and felt quite old.

The 1st Infantry was reassigned to duty at the Nuremburg war crimes trial, but all black volunteers were taken out of the integrated units and sent to a redeployment camp outside Paris to dig sewage trenches with German prisoners of war. On some labor details, Germans drove trucks and supervised black American soldiers.

The assignment was in direct violation of Eisenhower's promise that those who had fought in line divisions as infantrymen would never have to serve in quartermaster units again. Wright joined thirty black soldiers in protest. They dug foxholes and slept outside camp perimeters. When they were accused of insurrection, he posted an open letter "To whom it may concern":

> All of the men who were combat men, and who were assured and reassured that they would never again have to serve in the Quarter-

> master, are completely demoralized by the impotence of the promises which were made them. They volunteered for combat infantry at a time when they felt that their country needed them, and at a time when no one knew just how successful von Runstedt's Ardennes offensive would be. Now they are being neglected and cast off, much in the manner of cheap shoes which are no longer serviceable.[130]

Wright's posted open letters, often signed "Adgee Taitor," were famous. He was accused of inciting to riot. Let off lightly because of his medals and combat record, he was reassigned to a laundry unit, from which he went AWOL. He spent his second tour in an Army prison.

Wright may have been sent to prison, but his letter eventually made its way to Paris. Sergeant Herbert L. Wheeldin, another veteran of the "Bulge" experiment, took the letter to Eisenhower's headquarters. Wheeldin belonged to the black 5th Platoon, assigned to the white 310th Infantry Regiment, 78th Division, among the first Americans to cross the Rhine. "The fighting had no more stopped than we found they were taking men out of platoons and sending them to labor battalions scheduled for shipment to the Pacific," Wheeldin said in a postwar interview. But every man was a combat veteran, entitled to a trip home and a thirty-day furlough before being sent back into combat. Borrowing clean quartermaster corps uniforms, and sticking some papers under their arms to make themselves look official, Wheeldin and friends "borrowed" a jeep and drove straight to Paris and into the SHAEF courtyard. Ducking past the door of the officer on duty, and marching past the paratrooper outside Eisenhower's offices, they knocked on the door and stood there as if they "belonged." Surprisingly, they found a sympathetic colonel. He listened, made a few phone calls, and managed to get the men of the 5th Platoon home.

When Wright was finally sent home, he marched onto the troop ship with his duffel bag and a typewriter he had "liberated" in Czechoslovakia, wearing all his medals and decorations, including a combat infantryman's badge. A Navy officer sneered, "I didn't know niggers were fighting." Wright turned around, walked right off the ship, and went AWOL again, in Paris. He found his way to Léopold Sédar Senghor, the poet and future president of Senegal, who looked after him and fed him. Wright was caught eighteen months later, and again those who found him did not believe his medals were genuine. When they proved to be so, Wright was assigned to barracks instead of the stockade, but he was put in chains aboard the troop train to Ostend and the ship that would take him back to Fort Dix.

Back in the States, Wright graduated from New York University Law School on the GI Bill and became a judge in the New York State Supreme Court, known to his enemies as "Turn-'Em-Loose Bruce" for what they perceived as his excessive sympathies for the accused.

The 761st Tank Battalion: E. G. McConnell and the "Black Panthers"

In late October 1944, with his Third Army bogged down in France's Saar Basin, General George S. Patton, Jr., needed replacements. The only combat armored units still in America were black. Of three "experimental" black battalions on maneuvers in Texas, Patton chose the 761st, welcoming them to Normandy on November 2, 1944, in typical "Blood and Guts" style: "Men, you're the first Negro tankers to ever fight in the American Army. I would never have asked for you if you weren't good. I have nothing but the best in my Army. I don't care what color you are, so long as you go up there and kill those Kraut sonsabitches. Everyone has their eyes on you and is expecting great things from you. Most of all, your race is looking forward to you. Don't let them down, and, damn you, don't let me down."[131] Afterward, Patton climbed aboard Private E. G. McConnell's tank to examine the new 76mm cannon. McConnell, remembering Patton in our 1991 interview, found him "dapper as he could be—pearl-handled revolver and all." "Listen, boy," Patton said, "I want you to shoot every damn thing you see—little children, old ladies, everybody you see." McConnell's response was "Yes sir!"

A "very patriotic" sixteen-year-old ex–Boy Scout from Queens, McConnell had volunteered for the tank corps in 1942, enlisting with parental permission. He went to training camp in his first pair of long pants, and was embarrassed when his mother asked the sergeant to look after him. Camp Upton was McConnell's first taste of discrimination. Soon after his arrival an order for black soldiers to perform KP (kitchen patrol) duty for whites was rescinded after black protest. It was withdrawn, McConnell believed, only because Joe Louis was stationed at Upton and authorities feared publicity. With Boy Scout resourcefulness, McConnell started his own laundry business, charging fifty cents for a "suntan" shirt and pants with military crease. He was so successful he eventually hired an assistant.

When they moved by train to Fort Knox after basic training at Upton, the unit was ordered to pull down the shades, for Kentucky whites were in the habit of shooting at passing black troops. At Fort Knox and, later, at Army Command Training School at Camp Claiborne, Louisiana, McConnell learned enough about maintaining motorcycles and other wheeled vehicles to become an accomplished mechanic. He also, at age seventeen, became disillusioned with the Army and with military and civilian racism. When he was promoted to corporal, he handed one stripe back in protest against the system.

McConnell had enlisted to fight; he wanted to get out of maintenance. In September 1944, choosing to risk a summary court-martial on his first furlough home, he stayed three days after leave to see his father, back from a California defense job. He was given six months in the stockade with some tank corps pals who had stayed with him. They were released under "company arrest" twenty-nine days later, to join the 761st when it went overseas.

A Sherman tank with a 76mm gun weighs thirty-five tons and requires a five- or six-man crew: driver, assistant driver, bow gunner, turret gunner, cannoneer, radio operator, and commander. McConnell, still under company arrest, was trained to handle all positions. In late October 1944, four months after D-Day, the 761st crossed the Channel to Normandy and Omaha Beach. As their tanks rolled out onto shore, they saw the wreckage of D-Day ships, tanks, and trucks, and of German bunkers. The 761st had been assigned to the 26th Infantry Division of Patton's Third Army, now stalled in front of Metz in the upper Saar Basin. They were welcomed on October 31 by Major General Willard S. Paul, 26th Infantry commander: "I am damned glad to have you with us. We have been expecting you for a long time, and I am sure that you are going to give a good account of yourselves. I've got a big hill up there that I want you to take, and I believe that you are going to do a great job of it."[132] Two days later, standing atop the same half-track as General Paul, Patton gave his "kill those Kraut sonsabitches" speech.

November 8, 1944, D-Day in the Saar Basin, found the 761st leading 26th Division infantrymen toward the town of Bezange-la-Petite and Hill 253 (General Paul's "big hill"), through a landscape of snow, sleet, and mud. "A" Company's popular young white captain, David J. Williams II, author of *Hit Hard* (a 761st history), described himself as "a young punk out of Yale who also changed as the action went along." He knew no blacks except for the family maid and chauffeur, and considered himself a "most unlikely candidate" for black troops. "But I got my manhood with them," he later told *The New York Times*. "These guys were better than heroes because they weren't supposed to be able to fight, and they were treated worse than lepers. I can tell you, it took a rare sort of character to go out there and do what they did. I used to ask myself, why the hell should these guys fight? Why?"[133]

Rolling in a mile and a half behind Williams, E. G. McConnell saw

"A" Company "slaughtered," and white infantrymen sprawled all over the ground by the German counteroffensive. Private Clifford C. Adams, a medic from Waco, Texas, was the first of the 761st to be killed—hit by an exploding shell while rendering aid to an injured soldier. Captain Garland N. Adamson, the battalion surgeon, operated on a wounded tanker while shells fell around him. Staff Sergeant Ruben Rivers of Tecumseh, Oklahoma, opened the way for the capture of the town and the hill by climbing out of his tank under heavy fire to dismantle a roadblock. One of the acknowledged heroes of the 761st, Rivers would be responsible for more than three hundred German deaths between the towns of Hampont and Guebling alone. "Rivers led the way!" became a byword for bravery. Whenever his company attacked, Rivers's tank was always first into a town. But Rivers met his fate at Guebling, where his head was blown off. He won a posthumous Silver Star. Fifty years later, Captain David Williams, himself a Silver Star winner, joined Rivers's family in a campaign to have him awarded the Medal of Honor. According to Williams, Rivers refused morphine and even evacuation when his leg was torn to the bone by shrapnel. "You need me," Rivers said. "We did need him," said Williams. "Only he got killed."[134]

* * *

As three Third Army divisions slowly encircled the town of Metz, the 26th Infantry, the Ninth Air Force, and the 761st Tankers were closing off all entrances and exits. Resistance was stiff, and every inch was contested, even as the enemy withdrew. Five out of eleven tanks were lost at Honskirch on November 25. The night before that battle, McConnell dreamed that he had been killed. The next day the town was so familiar that he was convinced he had been there before. Then his tank was hit several times and he was knocked out, wounded in the head and arm. Waking up in a ditch, he thought he was dead or blind: his eyes were closed by blood. V-mail wadded in his helmet probably saved his life. When medics tried to put him in a jeep, he insisted on walking. "Get the other guys," he said. Forced onto the jeep, he found hundreds of moaning and crying wounded at the aid station, and a stack of bodies five feet high.

A two-star general visited the hospital, passing all the beds and greeting each man. At McConnell's bed, the general said, "What's wrong with you, boy? Got the clap?" McConnell was too stunned and angry to respond, but a white 26th Infantry man in the next bed said, "Hey, General, if he got it, he got it from your mother." When the general returned later that day with McConnell's Purple Heart, McConnell held up a comic book in front of his face (normally he never looked at them), as the general read his commendation and placed his medal on the bed. McConnell was reassigned to the quartermasters after his wounds healed, but he demanded to return to the 761st, hitching his way back to the front.

In early December, Company "B" broke through the French Maginot Line at Achen and Etting. Next stop was the Reich. Major General M. S. Eddy commended the unit for the "speed with which they adapted themselves to the front line under most adverse weather conditions," and the "gallantry with which they faced some of Germany's finest troops."[135] On December 11, the exhausted 26th Infantry was relieved. Infantry front lines were sent back to rest every three or four weeks, but there was no rest for the 761st. "Never once," remembered E. G. McConnell in 1991, "never once a shower truck. We washed with snow. Never once a Red Cross doughnut truck." McConnell refused ever to contribute to the Red Cross, because it "totally ignored" black GIs.

The unrelieved 761st and the green 87th crossed into Germany just as the order came to turn around and dash back to the Ardennes and Belgium for the Battle of the Bulge. On Christmas Eve, in two to four feet of snow and ice, the 761st was streaming northward, around and above beleaguered Bastogne, joining Lieutenant General Courtney S. Hodges's First Army. The 761st encountered what was left of the gradually retreating 13th SS Panzers. The Germans made their toughest stand at Tillet, but after five furious days, during which neither side yielded an inch, they began to retreat. The men of the 761st and the 87th had helped push Karl von Runstedt's army sixty miles back into Germany. Now they were following the Germans into their own land.

In March, joining the 103rd Infantry in Alsace-Lorraine, the 761st was ready to crack the Siegfried Line, the zone of heavy fortifications built in Germany directly in front of the Maginot Line, and make for the Rhine. They rode so far and fast along icy mountain curves that they were soon out of range of their own artillery. But the 761st and the 103rd overran retreating enemy columns. After knocking out Siegfried defenses at Reisdorf, tankers from "C" Company of the 761st shared celebratory fried eggs with infantrymen of the 103rd's 409th Regiment. In the fifteen miles between Reisdorf and Klingenmunster—the latter on the far side of the mountains, beyond the Siegfried Line—"C" Company took out two antitank guns, twenty-four pillboxes, and nine machine-gun nests. They killed 265 Germans and captured 1,450. They had faced elements of fourteen different German divisions.

With white infantry riding the tanks or flanking them in the woods, the 761st set off across Germany to capture a thousand SS troops of the

Mountain Division, "liberate" camera factories and a cognac factory, and find beds to sleep in for the first time in months. Two platoons of the 761st, led by Second Lieutenants Frank C. Cochrane and Moses E. Dade, took part in the fighting that led to the capture of Hermann Göring's castle. Germans were surrendering by the thousands—though one fanatical SS trooper pulled a razor and slashed his throat before an American tank. Coburg, the ancient capital of Saxe-Coburg, fell on April 12, 1945. The 761st ate a victory dinner of fresh eggs, chicken, and wine in the square, beneath the monument to Coburg's black patron saint, St. Maurice of the third-century Theban Legion. Two days later, after much resistance, Bayreuth fell. The German defeat was imminent.

The 761st crossed the Danube on April 27. The next morning, they were the sole armored spearhead of the assault on Regensburg, future headquarters for Patton and the Third Army. They were now instructed to move toward Austria and a "destination unknown." The order finally came in early May: "You will advance to the Enns River, and you will wait there for the Russians." The entire 761st crossed into Austria on May 4 and headed for Steyr, on the Enns. Marshal Ivan Konev's First Ukrainian Front arrived on May 6. It was the great meeting of East and West, a hugely photographed and celebrated event. Between March 31 and May 6, the 761st took 106,926 prisoners, an average daily rate of 2,813, including twenty German generals. They also liberated the Gunskirchen concentration camp.[136]

Major General E. H. Hughes, a former personal aide to Eisenhower, recommended the 761st for the Distinguished Unit Citation, but Eisenhower refused to sign the recommendation—although at least twelve white units to which the 761st had been attached did receive citations.

In 1978, after much campaigning on the part of 761st veterans, President Carter finally signed the Distinguished Unit Citation. The 761st was commended for "extraordinary heroism" in "operating far in advance of friendly artillery" and encountering "the fiercest of enemy resistance in the most heavily defended area of the war theater." They were also cited for spearheading the attack on the Siegfried Line: "The accomplishments of the 761st were truly magnificent as the successful crossing of the Rhine River into Germany was totally dependent upon the accomplishment of their mission."

When the movie *Patton* was released in 1970, no mention was made of the 761st. Patton had called on them in America's darkest hour. They had "come out fighting," staying longer on the front line than any other armored battalion, and riding deeper into Germany. But only one black was portrayed in the film: Patton's orderly.

"LIBERATORS"

"On April 11, 1945, I was liberated in Buchenwald at the age of 17, when the spark of life was almost extinguished," wrote the concentration camp survivor Benjamin Bender in an April 1985 letter to *The New York Times*. "The recollections are still vivid—black soldiers of the Third Army, tall and strong, crying like babies, carrying the emaciated bodies of the liberated prisoners." Bender was particularly struck by his liberators' tears. "In Buchenwald they didn't cry," he said, "they moaned like wounded animals."[137] He wrote the same words in a polite letter to President Ronald Reagan at the time of Reagan's controversial visit to a military cemetery containing SS graves in Bitburg, Germany. The last of his middle-class Polish Jewish family, Bender was one of five or ten survivors from a group of approximately two thousand, the rest of whom were murdered two days before liberation. To Bender, his black American liberators were "giants"—"not from this planet." In his memoir, *Glimpses,* he described his first sight of them: "The huge roll call square was full of American soldiers, General Patton's best, tall black men, six footers, with colorful scarves around their necks. I had never seen black men before. They were unreal to me."[138]

"The most moving moment of my life was the day the Americans arrived, a few hours after the SS had fled," wrote Elie Wiesel, a Buchenwald survivor and Nobel laureate, in *The New York Times* on April 11, 1989. "It was the morning of April 11. I will always remember with love a big black soldier. He was crying like a child—tears of all the pain in the world and all the rage. Everyone who was there that day will forever feel a sentiment of gratitude to the American soldiers who liberated us."[139]

In October 1991, the New York public television station WNET brought together thirty camp survivors and forty black veterans to see the documentary film *Liberators: Fighting on Two Fronts in World War II.* The film dealt with the 761st Tank Battalion and the 183rd Combat Engineers and the liberation of Buchenwald and Dachau. The film's creators, the respected black documentary filmmaker William Miles (creator of *Men of Bronze,* on World War I's 369th Regiment) and Nina Rosenblum, whose father had photographed the liberation of Dachau, hoped that the film might help repair damaged black-Jewish relations. In the film, some "survivors and liberators," including Benjamin Bender and the 761st veteran E. G. McConnell, traveled to Buchenwald.

By February 1993, *Liberators* was being called a fraud. An article by Jeffrey Goldberg in *The New Republic,* calling the film *The Exaggerators,* pointed out that the 761st was miles away in the west, at Coburg, on

April 11, when Patton's 4th Armored Division liberated Buchenwald.[140] E. G. McConnell was quoted in a *New York Post* editorial attacking *Liberators,* as calling the film "a lie." "We were nowhere near those camps when they were liberated," he said.[141] He claimed that he had stopped collaborating with the filmmakers when he realized that they were "faking material." The editorial went on to state that several survivors who had said they were freed by black soldiers now no longer remembered when they first saw them, although they never retracted the fact that black soldiers were, indeed, their liberators.

By September 1993, WNET had withdrawn *Liberators* as "seriously flawed"; it would no longer be distributed or shown at public gatherings, nor would videotapes be sold. WNET did not question the film's premise—that black Americans were involved in liberating concentration camps—but "there are details, names of towns, locations of concentration camps, that through oral history and documentation and lack of documentation put some question as to who's got it right."[142] It was agreed that the 761st did participate in the liberation of several smaller camps, but not Buchenwald or Dachau.

Despite its withdrawal of the film, WNET/Channel 13 produced a report to answer the most critical challenges. Throughout combat, the 761st were attached to various other units, some of which did indeed participate in the liberation of Buchenwald and Dachau. (As Pop Gates had said in *The Good War,* "The German Army couldn't see how we could be in so many darned places.") Black veterans had described running their tank into the Dachau gate; one had photographs he had taken; another had kept in touch with a family of Jewish prisoners who invited him back to Germany to visit them. The report also uncovered why E. G. McConnell had so adamantly denied being present at the camps: at the time of liberation, he was recovering from the shell wound that won him a Purple Heart. The film narration states that "two veterans of the 761st Tank Battalion returned to Buchenwald with Ben Bender, who was imprisoned there." Critics took this to mean that McConnell had been there before. "All the film meant was that McDonnell was accompanying Bender, as a representative of the 761st," the producers said of the careless wording. The film's producers questioned why the entire film had to be censored, when they might simply have corrected problems by changing a few words or a few sequences.

* * *

In 1945, black veterans once again came home to a country where they could be lynched for wearing a uniform. America was the same, but veterans, again, were different. In 1918, many black vets had looked to Communism for ways to change their country. In 1945, they looked to democracy, coming home to use the Declaration of Independence, the Bill of Rights, and the Constitution to nourish the frail shoots of civil rights and to make sure that black soldiers would never again fight and die for a country that did not treat them like Americans.

9 Korea

TRANSITION

The great pity of it all was that so many good men had to die needlessly because the U.S. Army refused to send qualified white combat soldiers as replacements to a black infantry regiment, even in desperate combat.[1]

—*Lieutenant Colonel Charles M. Bussey, author of* Firefight at Yechon: Courage and Racism in the Korean War

Changing the System

In April 1945, while black American fighter pilots of the 332nd Fighter Squadron were shooting down the last enemy aircraft over the Mediterranean, 101 black Air Force officers of their sister unit, the 477th Bombardment Group, were shooting down military injustice at home. The 101 pilots were arrested at Freeman Field, Indiana, for staging group sit-ins at the illegally barred-to-blacks officers' club. A-R 210-10, passed in December 1940, opened all officers' clubs to all officers on post. Freeman Field's commander, "Jesus Bob" Selway, had labeled black officers "transients" at Michigan's Selfridge Field; now, once again, he evaded the law, this time by calling all black officers "trainees," including the flight surgeon and the chaplain.[2]

The Freeman action was strictly by the book and according to military regulations. Advised by the NAACP as well as their own barracks lawyer, Lieutenant William Coleman, Jr., the men expected arrest and pledged themselves to nonviolence. The "Freeman Field 101" were forerunners of the civil rights movement.

Of the 101 officers who were arrested, only Lieutenants Roger Terry, Marsden A. Thompson, and Shirley R. Clinton were tried. Terry, accused of shoving a superior officer, was charged under Article 64, which comprised military crimes punishable by death. The three became a black cause célèbre. Their mothers wrote to congressmen. It was Colonel Selway who broke the law, blacks maintained, not the three young officers.

The court agreed. Thompson and Clinton were acquitted, and Terry was merely fined $150 for the "shove."[3] The victory was complete when the Air Force chief, Hap Arnold, replaced the white command structure at Freeman Field, including Selway, with black officers. Taking over at Freeman, Colonel Benjamin O. Davis, Jr., became the first black commander of a U.S. Army air base.

* * *

In May 1945, U.S. Army commanders around the world responded to Assistant Secretary of War John J. McCloy's request for performance reports on black units and recommendations on postwar racial policy. Truman Gibson, a black civilian War Department aide, convinced McCloy and Robert Patterson, now secretary of the Army, that while they were rating black troop performance, they should also assess how segregation affected that performance.

McCloy's request resulted in a near carbon copy of the infamous 1920 Staff College memorandum. Black GIs, like their doughboy counterparts, were described as mentally inferior, afraid of the enemy (and the dark), and adversely affected by cold weather. Joseph T. McNarney, commanding general in the Mediterranean Theater of Operations, was the only one to dissent. The "colored soldier individually can be made into a good combat man," he said, but "segregated units" were a failure.[4] McNarney urged immediate experiments in integrating blacks into white squads.

Three general officers, under General Alvan C. Gillem, Jr., were now ordered to study Army racial policy and prepare a report on how the restructured military could use blacks most efficiently. The Gillem Board's report, "Utilization of Negro Manpower in the Postwar Army Policy," filed in April 1946, recommended that the military "eliminate, at the earliest possible moment, any special considerations based on race."

Despite such fine words, the Gillem Report sent a mixed message. Integration of units was recommended for duty hours only; off-duty housing, for example, would remain segregated. Moreover, manpower would be used "without regard to antecedents of race" only at an "unknown date" against an "undetermined aggressor."[5] Three months after the new policy was announced, a group of black publishers took a fact-finding trip to Europe to examine post-Gillem Army conditions. Except for two generals, no white officer had even heard of the report. There were no integrated units in Europe, and there were no black military police in Germany. "To accept the racial prejudices of the German people," wrote Marcus Ray, Truman Gibson's successor at the War Department, in his "Report of Tour of European Installations," "is to negate the very ideals we have made part of our reeducation program in Germany."[6]

The Gillem Report seemed to have no effect on the Army. The proposed universal military training bill of 1947, which mandated registration for the draft, made no mention of integration.

A. Philip Randolph, once again, was at the forefront of change. Believing that blacks should refuse to serve in a segregated military, he vowed to "openly counsel, abet and aid" resistance to the draft and refusal to register. When asked whether this was treason, he responded that a higher law applied. His League for Non-Violent Civil Disobedience against Military Segregation called on blacks and whites alike not to register. An NAACP poll of black college students found that 71 percent were sympathetic to civil disobedience against the draft.[7]

Truman's response was to form, by executive order, the first presidential committee on civil rights, with Charles E. Wilson, the president of General Electric, as chairman. The committee's 1947 report, "To Secure These Rights," was everything blacks had hoped for. It condemned segregation wherever it existed, and labeled "separate but equal" a myth. It recommended federal antilynching laws, a permanent Fair Employment Practices Commission, a full civil rights division in the U.S. Justice Department, and action "to end immediately discrimination and segregation based on race, color, creed or national origin," in all branches of the Armed Forces.[8]

PRESIDENT TRUMAN AND EXECUTIVE ORDER 9981

After the war, to the consternation of the white South, blacks began to insist on their legal right to vote. Theodore Bilbo of Mississippi (where textbooks for black schools deleted all references to voting and elections) called on "red-blooded Anglo-Saxon" southerners to stop blacks from voting by "any means." "If you don't know what that means," Bilbo added, "you are not up on your persuasive measures."[9]

"The first nigger to vote will never vote again," read a sign on a black church during the July 1946 Georgia primaries. A war veteran named Macio Snipes, the only black to vote in Taylor County, Georgia, was dragged from his house and shot to death. In Monroe, Georgia, two days after the election, two black veterans and their wives were taken from a car by a mob of white men. All four were shot, with about sixty bullets pumped into their bodies. "My God! I had no idea it was as terrible as that! We've got to do something," said Truman, when Walter White informed him of the Georgia murders.[10] Truman, a World War I officer, had been sickened earlier that year by the beating and blinding in South Carolina of Sergeant Isaac Woodard, a black soldier in uniform on his way home from the Pacific. The rash of postwar racial atrocities had converted Truman, formerly satisfied with the racial status quo, into a civil rights activist. Though it was motivated by basic border-state fairness and a strong sense of the meaning of democracy, Truman's position was seen by many as radical. "I believe in the brotherhood of man; not merely the brotherhood of white men, but the brotherhood of all men before the law," he had said in a 1940 Missouri speech. "If any class or race can be permanently set apart from, or pushed down below the rest in political and civil rights, so may any other class or race when it shall incur the displeasure of its more powerful associates, and we may say farewell to the principles on which we count our safety."[11]

As part of Kansas City's Pendergast machine, Truman had inherited the black vote and developed a surprisingly liberal civil rights record. Opponents tried to insinuate that he was a closet Klansman, but a *Pittsburgh Courier* investigation of 1944 found that the Klan had opposed him as far back as the 1920s. "If his personal relationships with Negroes and Negro problems have been few, they seem at least to have been fair," said the *Courier.*[12]

In October 1947, the NAACP presented to the United Nations a 154-page "Statement on the Denial of Human Rights to Minorities in the Case of Citizens of Negro Descent in the U.S.A., and an Appeal to the United Nations for Redress." The U.N. had invited the NAACP to send representatives to the historic first San Francisco meeting in 1945, when Walter White and W.E.B. Du Bois proposed the abolition of colonialism and supported the Chinese-Soviet proposal that colonial independence be guaranteed in the U.N. Charter. America's allies in the U.N. were beginning to hit hard on race, as were cold war propagandists. "The top dog in a world which is over half colored ought to clean his own house," Truman said in his characteristic Missouri way.[13]

On February 2, 1948, Truman sent the first ever Civil Rights Message to Congress. Prepared by his adviser Clark Clifford, it presented a comprehensive program—including statehood for Hawaii and Alaska, home rule and suffrage for the District of Columbia, and settlement of the claims of Japanese Americans arising out of their wartime internment. It also proposed a federal antilynching law, a permanent Fair Employment Practices Commission on Civil Rights, a joint congressional committee on civil rights, and a civil rights division in the Department of Justice. It promised to strengthen existing civil rights laws and protect everyone's right to vote. And it asked the secretary of defense to put an end to military discrimination as soon as possible.[14] But: "There is race prejudice in this country," said General Eisenhower, reflecting basic military opinion, in an April appearance before the Senate Armed Services Committee. "When you pass a law to get somebody to like someone, you have trouble."[15]

Although Truman sincerely believed that military segregation was wrong, by 1948 his motives were not entirely disinterested. He was a political pragmatist as well as a man of principle, and he needed the northern black vote. In the election that year he not only faced the Republican Thomas E. Dewey—whose platform was opposed to "the idea of racial segregation in the armed forces of the U.S."—but also stood between the right and left in his own Democratic Party. On the right, the "Dixiecrats," led by South Carolina's Strom Thurmond, violently attacked his civil rights efforts. On the left, the Progressive Party, under former (1941–1945) vice president Henry Wallace (the New Deal secretary of agriculture), maintained that American restrictions against blacks, Jews, and new immigrants made the world laugh at its "pretension to democracy." Calling for a presidential proclamation to deny federal funds to "any state or local authority which withholds opportunities or benefits for reasons of race, creed, color, sex, or national origin," the Progressive platform also urged an end to "all forms of discrimination in the armed services and federal employment."[16]

Truman's civil rights positions "committed the Democratic party to a historic enterprise from which there was no turning back, the quest for equal rights for all Americans," as Clark Clifford wrote in retrospect. "At the same time, the identification of the Democrats with the struggle for civil rights would be the primary factor that drove the South into the Republican column in most subsequent Presidential elections."[17] In 1948 this phenomenon was known as the southern backlash.

On July 26, 1948, Truman issued Executive Order 9981. One of the first federal actions against discrimination in America, it established a precedent for future presidents seeking to bypass a hostile Congress. Order 9981 stated in part: "It is hereby declared to be the policy of the President that there shall be equality of treatment and opportunity for all persons in the armed services without regard to race, color, religion, or national origin. This policy shall be put into effect as rapidly as possible, having due regard to the time required to effectuate any necessary changes without impairing efficiency or morale."[18]

Eisenhower had led the way in protest. The Army establishment, with its very southern mind-set, followed suit. "Separate but equal" was necessary to national defense, said the Army, asserting that its policy rested on "equality of opportunity on the basis of segregation." General Omar Bradley declared that the Army was no place for social experiments. And because the assistant secretary feared that the next step would be "integration of Negroes into Regular Army units as individuals," the secretary of the Army, Kenneth Royall, rejected the requests of northern governors like Luther W. Youngdahl of Minnesota and Thomas E. Dewey of New York to integrate their state National Guards.[19]

Lieutenant General Julius Becton, a black veteran of World War II, recalled his experience as a young reserve lieutenant at the Aberdeen, Maryland, Proving Ground in 1948, when the base commander assembled all the officers to read Executive Order 9981. "Now, gentlemen," the commander announced when he had finished reading, "as long as I'm in command, there will be no changes."[20]

But the Navy and the new Air Force, both formerly closed to blacks, had comparatively little trouble integrating. This was in large measure thanks to their leadership. Under James V. Forrestal, the Navy had declared itself integrated as early as February 1947, a full year before Order 9981. "Effective immediately, all restrictions governing the types of assignments for which Negro naval personnel are eligible are hereby lifted," announced the Navy ordinance. "In the utilization of housing, messing and other facilities, no special or unusual provisions will be made for the accommodation of Negroes."[21] In 1949, Wesley A. Brown became the first black graduate of Annapolis. There was still a vast difference between Navy policy and practice, however. Besides a few black officers, the majority of blacks in the Navy would remain stewards and messmen.

Freeman Field had been the wake-up call for the Air Force, which had been separated from the Army in 1947 in a major military restructuring. The Air Force secretary, Stuart Symington, had long expressed the belief that segregation was wasteful and inefficient. In December 1949, the Air Force announced that integrated units, already in use, had doubled in number between June and August, with no racial conflicts. Air Force integration was the "swiftest and most amazing upset of racial policy in the history of the U.S. military," *Ebony* proclaimed.[22]

Not everyone was pleased. Strom Thurmond launched an official protest when integrated Air Force ROTC barracks for summer cadets opened at Alabama's Maxwell Air Force Base. Ignoring him and others, the Air Force was soon operating and maintaining large islands of integration with their own housing, schools, stores, and places of recreation in the midst of strictly Jim Crow southern communities.

Two years of unyielding pressure—and a war—finally forced the

Army and Marines to obey Truman's order. The President's Committee on Equality of Treatment and Opportunity in the Armed Services, under a Catholic New Dealer, Charles Fahy, had been established in September 1948 to give the reluctant Army a push. The Fahy Committee attacked the Army's contention that segregation was neither discriminatory nor inefficient. And it recommended that all jobs be opened on the basis of qualification, without regard to race, that black quotas for Army schools be abolished, that all Army school graduates be assigned without regard to race, and that the 10 percent ceiling on black enlistment be abolished. With the Army fearful of a service overloaded with uneducated blacks, the quota issue remained unresolved. But the Army finally agreed to gradual integration, starting with skilled blacks and working its way down. Enlistment quotas were finally done away with in March 1950. "Freedom to Serve," the final Fahy report, was submitted to Truman on May 22 of that year.

It was just in time to respond to the alarming, frustratingly vague intelligence that began reaching the State Department in late May and early June: that the armed forces of "some Communist power" were expected to go into action soon, "somewhere."[23]

The Cold War

Less than five years after World War II, the geopolitical face of the world had changed. Former wartime allies had become enemies, and former enemies had become the staunchest friends. In 1946, Winston Churchill announced at Fulton, Missouri, that an "iron curtain" of Communism was descending over Eastern Europe. With the defeat in 1949 of Chiang Kai-shek by the Communist forces of Mao Tse-tung, it was clear that a similar "bamboo curtain" might be descending over Asia.

Korea was the last place anyone expected to go to war over. Japan, home to the Far East Command and the imperial splendor of General Douglas MacArthur, was the place that really mattered. Beyond imparting its own credo of freedom and democracy, America had little interest in Korea. Early in 1950, the secretary of state, Dean Acheson, had even remarked that Korea was outside America's "defense perimeter."[24] "If the best minds in the world had set out to find us the worst possible location in the world to fight this damnable war, politically and militarily," Acheson told a journalist, "the unanimous choice would have been Korea."[25]

Terrible as it was for freedom and democracy, North Korea's invasion of the South on June 25, 1950, was a plus for the Republican Party. It was the perfect outrage, coming so soon after the fall of China, for the House and Senate Republican minority to blame on the "soft-on-Communism" Democrats, whom the Republican senator Joseph R. McCarthy of Wisconsin, the most strident public voice of anticommunism, called "commiecrats." Many Republicans saw Acheson's "defense perimeter" remarks as an open invitation to North Korea to cross the 38th Parallel and invade the South.[26] European policy might look good, with the economic success of the Marshall Plan and the military success of the U.S.-led Berlin airlift against the Soviet blockade, but someone had "lost" China—and now seemed to be giving away Korea. Republicans blamed Mao's victory and the spread of Communism on FDR's so-called giveaway at Yalta in February 1945, when Stalin was thought to have duped the dying president into selling out Eastern Europe and Asia. "We know that at Yalta we were betrayed," said McCarthy. "We know that since Yalta, the leaders of this Government, by design or ignorance, have continued to betray us. . . . We also know that the same men who betrayed America are still leading America. The traitors must no longer lead the betrayed."[27]

What Republicans did not say, by design or ignorance, was that Stalin was not the source of the greatest pressure on Roosevelt at Yalta. The pressure on Roosevelt came from the U.S. military. Early in 1945, with the atom bomb still an unknown, the American military was desperate to get Russia into the war against Japan. Ceding part of Japan's former Korean labor colony to Russia seemed a small price to pay. At the end of the war, the United States accepted the Japanese surrender of Korea south of the 38th Parallel, and the USSR accepted the surrender to the north. North Korea bordered China and Russia, so South Korea had been half expected to fall into the Soviet orbit anyway.

Coming too soon after what World War II veterans called the Big War, Korea became the "Forgotten War," and "the war no one wanted." Except among a few old soldiers, like the grizzled sergeant in James Brady's *The Coldest War,* who remarked, "It ain't much but it's the only war we got,"[28] Korea was especially unwelcome in the U.S. military. By 1950, postwar cutbacks and new spending priorities in nuclear and jet capability had reduced general military strength and readiness to levels almost as low as those of 1940. No one wanted a war in Asia; all combat readiness was directed toward Eastern Europe. More important, no one wanted to risk war with Russia or China.

After Hiroshima and Nagasaki and the successful Soviet atomic test of 1949, any third world war was expected to be a nuclear Armageddon. Only those who would come to be known as "Strangeloves" on either side actually wanted the superpowers to fight it out. Korea represented a place (as Vietnam would later) where they could let off steam through old-fashioned nonnuclear warfare. The policy of creating a small war to stop a "total" war was known as limited warfare, which did not mean limited killing. In three years of war some three million people died on both sides; almost two million were Korean civilians. About 900,000 Chinese troops died, and some 37,000 Americans (an estimate lower than the postwar figure of 54,000).[29]

THE COLD WAR AT HOME: MCCARTHYISM AND THE ARMY

Despite the death toll, Korea was less important militarily than symbolically, for good and ill. On the positive side, it demonstrated America's determination to support the United Nations, and, as Truman had promised, to defend friendly nations in their struggle against Soviet domination. On the negative side, it fed into and fueled a new Red scare, McCarthyism.

From the beginning Communism was a domestic issue as well as an international one. As U.S. soldiers fought real Communists in Korea, the U.S. Congress, through the House Committee on Un-American Activities, or HUAC, fought real or imagined Communists back home. HUAC had been looking for subversion in the arts and entertainment since the late 1930s, to little general interest. They finally made headlines in 1947 with the "Hollywood Ten": writers, directors, and producers accused of putting Communist propaganda into their movies. The writer Dalton Trumbo (a Spanish Civil War veteran) and the director Edward Dmytryk came under fire for having Ginger Rogers's character say "Share and share alike, that's democracy," in the popular film *Tender Comrade.* (Not, as the title might imply, about love on a Soviet collective, but an adaptation from a novel of the same name about war wives sharing a house while their husbands are overseas.) Bartley Crum, the noted attorney for the Hollywood Ten, saw the case as a straightforward First Amendment issue. "In the words of the Supreme Court," Crum said, "if there is any fixed star in the constitutional constellation, it is that no official can prescribe or force citizens to confess what is orthodox in politics or religion. . . . It is indeed an honor to serve these men in defense of Americanism."[30] Almost overnight, the case degenerated into accusations, denunciations, witch-hunts, and ruined careers. Blacklists sprang up in nearly every walk of American life, but Hollywood's made the headlines.

The Red scare of the late 1940s and '50s was much bigger than the similar outbreak of Red-baiting under Attorney General Palmer in World War I. This time, ordinary citizens were appointing themselves anti-Red watchdogs and naming names on the basis of hysteria, hearsay, and malice.

In 1948, HUAC left Hollywood for Washington and bigger headlines, investigating Communists in the State Department. Now came high drama: a face-off between two very different men. Ex-Communist Whittaker Chambers, a rumpled former editor of the *New Masses* and writer for the *Daily Worker,* was a sometime Russian agent who quit the Party in the late 1930s and became an editor at *Time.* Chambers accused the highly attractive and socially impeccable Alger Hiss, head of the Carnegie Endowment for International Peace, of not only being a Communist but passing secrets to Moscow. Hiss, a member of the foreign policy establishment, adamantly denied both accusations, and the question of his guilt divided America. Hiss featured prominently in the confirmation hearings of Dean Acheson, a favorite Republican target, as secretary of state. An official of the State Department from 1936 until 1946, Hiss had briefly worked under Acheson. And he had been part of the American delegation sent to Yalta in 1945 to draft the United Nations Charter.

In 1949, eleven Communists were found guilty of seeking to overthrow the U.S. government. Over Truman's veto, Congress passed the McCarran Act a year later, calling for severe restrictions against Communism in every form, and the registration of all Communist organizations and individuals. "Who lost China?" was the political question of the moment. In consequence, McCarthy (who had recently been voted worst member of the Senate by the Washington press corps) needed only to announce, as he did in early 1950, that he had a list of the names of 203 known State Department Communists in his pocket, to set off a purge of old China hands. The number of McCarthy's State Department Communists would vary, ranging from 205 to 57.

Eisenhower's election was the beginning of the end for McCarthy, whom Ike despised for his attacks on General George Marshall before the election. (He wanted to make an anti-McCarthy speech but his advisers would not permit it.) With Eisenhower in office, the Republicans no longer needed McCarthy. His power in the Senate was waning. Besides, he had begun to bite the hand that fed him, enraging John Foster Dulles by denouncing the nomination of Charles Bohlen, Dulles's choice, as ambassador to Moscow.

The 1950 election was one of the ugliest in memory. Republicans in general had been happy to use McCarthy tactics against their opponents. "Joe [Stalin] likes him and he likes Joe," said George Smathers in Florida, victorious against Senator Claude Pepper.[31] Richard Nixon's defeat of the Democrat Helen Gahagan Douglas in California was textbook Red-baiting. "We'll name them as they jump out of windows," Senator Karl Mundt of South Dakota had said when asked, after a friend of Alger Hiss had committed suicide, to name more Communists. "Keep talking,"

Senator Robert Taft had said to McCarthy, "and if one case doesn't work out, proceed with another."[32] Secretary of State Acheson received so many death threats that his home was placed under guard.

In the end, as David Halberstam wrote, McCarthy produced little beyond "fear and headlines"—but great fear and big headlines.[33] The headlines finally turned against him with his fateful and fatal search for Communists in the Army. Black-and-white television was not kind to beetle-browed, sweating politicians with five o'clock shadows and thuggish manners. The nation watched McCarthy self-destruct on ABC live television. In the midst of the Army hearings of January 10, 1954, McCarthy announced out of the blue that there was a Communist connection in the background of a young staff member of Army counsel Joseph Welch. Shaking with indignation, Welch, a crusty New Englander, finally and memorably asked, "Have you no sense of decency, sir, at long last?" The Senate would censure McCarthy later that year. The press began to ignore him. In May 1957 he was dead, having done damage that, sadly, would long outlive him.

The Cold War also raged among black Americans. Paul Robeson, one of America's most admired artists and unapologetic left-wingers, was the focus of attention. His statement at the 1949 Paris Congress of the World Partisans of Peace had been instantly controversial. "Our will to fight for peace is strong," he said. "We shall not make war on anyone. We shall not make war on the Soviet Union." Controversial as his actual words were, according to Robeson's biographer Martin Bauml Duberman, a widely distributed AP dispatch purporting to "quote" Robeson was false. He had never said that it was "unthinkable that American Negroes would go to war on behalf of those who have oppressed us for generations against a country [the Soviet Union] which in one generation has raised our people to the full dignity of mankind."[34]

Vilified by the right, Robeson was equally attacked by left and center. Among his critics were Eleanor Roosevelt, now a civil rights and U.N. activist, A. Philip Randolph, Roy Wilkins of the NAACP, and Jackie Robinson. Appearing before HUAC with a statement written by Lester Granger of the Urban League, Robinson scorned Robeson's political ideology, but found areas of agreement. "The fact that it is a Communist who denounces injustice in the courts, police brutality, and lynching when it happens doesn't change the truth of his charges," he said.[35] Robinson also believed in fighting American racial discrimination, but "we can win our fight without the Communists and we don't want their help." Robeson now joined the artist Rockwell Kent, the writer Howard Fast, the Protestant clergyman Richard Morford (head of the National Council of American-Soviet Friendship), the philanthropist and writer

Corliss Lamont, and other prominent members of the left in having his passport revoked. The State Department deemed his travel abroad "contrary to the best interests of the United States." Robeson's passport was restored in 1958, when the Supreme Court ruled that the State Department had no right to deny any individual a passport because of his "beliefs and associations."[36]

SERGEANT EDWARD CARTER

Edward Carter, not a household name like Robeson, was also caught in a web of ideological suspicion. As Sergeant Edward Carter, he had been one of World War II America's nine black Distinguished Service Cross winners. His claim to HUAC's attention, however, was that he was a veteran of the Abraham Lincoln Brigade. The California-born son of missionaries, with a black American father and an East Indian mother, Carter grew up in Shanghai and was the product of a Chinese military school. Looking for a war, or maybe just on the run from a missionary household, he first tried to join Chiang Kai-shek's Chinese Nationalist Army, which kicked him out for being underage. He then made for Manila, only to be rejected by the U.S. Army. Finally, working his way to Marseilles on a merchant ship, he volunteered for Spain. Joining the U.S. Army, at last, in World War II, he became a hero of the Battle of the Bulge.

By 1947, with work for black vets hard to find, Sergeant First Class Carter had reenlisted, becoming a weapons instructor in a new black National Guard engineering unit. It was a plum assignment. In 1949, just before his automatic reenlistment, he was shocked to suddenly receive an honorable discharge, with papers stamped "Not permitted to re-enlist without permission of the adjutant general." After consulting the NAACP, which declined the case as a matter of civil liberties rather than civil rights, Carter found support in a young American Civil Liberties Union lawyer, Herbert Levy. But the Army refused to answer Levy's request for a statement of the charges. "I have always been loyal and faithful to the land of my birth," wrote Carter, in a letter to Levy in which he enclosed his Distinguished Service Cross, asking him to return it to President Truman. "I ask for justice," he wrote, decrying his Kafkaesque situation. "This could not be a democracy. There must be some mistake." Six months later, in a letter to another ACLU lawyer, Levy wrote that the Army rejected Carter "purely on the basis of a directive to do so by the Central Intelligence Agency, which itself did not disclose the reasons to the adjutant general."[37]

"This thing just took on a life of its own," Levy told the writer Joseph L. Galloway in 1999. This "thing" was what Levy called the "national hysteria" about Communism. "It was guilt by association. It was un-American, but it was being done by the House Un-American Activities Committee."[38] Carter now exchanged work that he knew and loved for one of the worst possible jobs, as a vulcanizer in a tire factory. He began drinking. Finally, in 1953, he asked the ACLU to close the case. In late 1962, he was diagnosed with lung cancer (probably job-related, if not job-inflicted). He died a year later, and was buried in Los Angeles National Cemetery.

Thanks to the Freedom of Information Act, Carter's family later discovered that because he was a Lincoln vet he had been investigated by Army Intelligence from the day of his enlistment in 1942. While Carter considered himself an antifascist rather than a Communist, in McCarthy terms he was a "fellow traveler." His file was trivial (he read *Popular Mechanics;* he was a Mason). Only two items were listed under "adverse information": his membership in the Lincoln Brigade, and his speaking knowledge of Hindustani and Mandarin Chinese. (The file never mentioned that his mother was Indian and that he was raised in China.) Nevertheless, the CIA soon came to agree with Carter's self-assessment; according to the file, he had twice been officially cleared of being "potentially subversive," in 1943 and 1950. But the information was either not passed on by the CIA or ignored by the Army.

In 1999, Carter's World War II Distinguished Service Cross was upgraded to a belated Medal of Honor.

KOREAN SURPRISE

"This is war against the United Nations," said the U.N.'s first secretary general, Trygve Lie of Norway, when Acheson informed him, late in the night of June 24, 1950, that North Korean troops had crossed the 38th Parallel and had taken the city of Seoul.[39] The next day an emergency session of the U.N. Security Council approved the American resolution calling the invasion a breach of world peace and calling on member nations to come to South Korea's aid. Passage of the resolution had been possible only because the Soviet delegation, angry at the U.N.'s refusal to replace the Nationalist Chinese delegation with one from the People's Republic of China, was boycotting the Security Council. On June 27, President Truman ordered U.S. air support for South Korean ground forces, and sent the Seventh Fleet to the Strait of Taiwan as a show of strength, to deter mainland China from involvement. (Meanwhile, Acheson also recommended increased aid to the French, to shore up anticommunism in Indochina.)

Despite America's swift response, Truman regarded Korea as a possible Russian trick to distract the United States in Asia while it prepared for something major in Europe. This was not the first occasion in his lifetime, Truman wrote, "when the strong had attacked the weak"; he cited the pre–World War II invasions of Manchuria, Ethiopia, and Austria.[40] The only way to stop World War III, he believed, would be to make Korea a "limited war." Steering clear of both Russia and China, America would aim only to restore the 38th Parallel.

Acheson believed that to avoid the Korean conflict would be bad for U.S. power and prestige. "Prestige," to Acheson, was "the shadow cast by power, which is of great deterrent importance."[41] The United States did not necessarily require total victory, "but rather to see that the attack failed." This was the goal of limited warfare. The ensuing war was a proxy superpower confrontation, with South and North Korea standing in for the United States and the USSR. Unfortunately, no one stood in for Korean civilians or the fighting troops. Overwhelmingly led by the United States, opposition to North Korea was officially a partnership among the United Nations, the United States, and South Korea—joined by eighteen other western countries, four of which contributed medical contingents only. Eight Republic of Korea (ROK) divisions, seven U.S. divisions (as well as airpower), and one division from the British Commonwealth (comprising the United Kingdom, Canada, Australia, and New Zealand) were joined by Belgian, Colombian, Greek, Dutch, and Filipino battalions, and a Turkish brigade.

In Tokyo, General MacArthur initially called the North Korean invasion a "mere border incident," one that would soon blow over. By June 29, however, he had come to the conclusion that even with American air support, ROK troops would never be capable of pushing the North Korean People's Army back across the 38th Parallel. Given full command over all Korean military operations on July 2, MacArthur asked for ground troops. Rejecting Chiang Kai-shek's offer of Taiwan-based troops as too threatening to Mao, Truman authorized the use of two American occupation divisions from Japan, insisting, to MacArthur's extreme disapproval, that U.S. planes and vessels were not to be sent north of the Parallel.

At first most of the American military agreed with MacArthur that the invasion was only an "incident"—at most, a prelude to a very short war. But the combination of overwhelming North Korean manpower—in some places it outnumbered the opposition by as much as twenty to one—and Russian tanks drove South Korean and U.N. troops back to a tiny Dunkirk-like perimeter around the port of Pusan, at the southern end of the peninsula. The allies retreated to Pusan in raging monsoons, hundred-degree-plus weather, and equally raging dysentery in the ranks. It was a catastrophe. Casualties were as high as 30 percent. American and ROK forces "had no tanks, no artillery, or any weapons capable of slowing the Russian tanks," wrote David McCullough in *Truman*. "World War II bazookas bounced off the Russian tanks like stones."[42]

"At the beginning of the Korean conflict, the U.S. Army did not perform well," wrote Lieutenant Colonel Charles M. Bussey, then a twenty-nine-year-old captain and the commander of the 77th Engineer Combat Company, in *Firefight at Yechon: Courage and Racism in the Korean War*. "The Eighth Army blamed its debacles on the ROK divisions," he wrote. "The 25th Infantry Division blamed its inadequacies on its Negro troops."[43] The 24th Infantry Regiment (the last Buffalo Soldier regiment, not to be confused with its mother unit, the 25th Infantry Division) was the only all-black infantry regiment in Korea. The 77th Combat Engineers (which would have a good Korea record) followed the 24th Infantry to within seven miles of the Yalu River border between South Korea and China, fighting beside the 24th from July 13, 1950, to October 1, 1951. The 77th Engineers and 159th Field Artillery, highly trained specialized black units, avoided controversy because Korea was first and foremost an infantryman's war. According to Bussey, failure was the fault of the Army, not of black GIs who had never been trained for night fighting and were not physically fit for the hostile Korean environment. The Army "had not trained [them] to change our tactics from mass attacks to guerrilla warfare from one day to the next and from massive tank actions to individual combat with handmade knives from one hour to the next."[44]

Blamed for American failure, blacks were doubly disillusioned in Korea. Truman had integrated the armed forces in 1948, but as of 1950, blacks were still fighting and dying in the same old segregated and racist Army.

GIFU: THE SEGREGATED ARMY IN JAPAN

As of June 1950, the Eighth Army in Japan had not yet begun to desegregate. Eighth Army racism started at the top. General Douglas MacArthur's chief of staff was Major General Edward M. Almond, the actively racist commander of World War II's ill-fated 92nd Division. "A devout anti-black bigot" was how Clay Blair, author of *The Forgotten War*, described him.[45] Almond would act out his racism in Korea, resegregating successfully integrated units and refusing to approve medals for black soldiers. In February 1951, when General Matthew B. Ridgway, the commander of the Eighth Army, ordered a Silver Star for Forrest Walker, a black 2nd

Division company commander, Almond blocked the medal and transferred Walker to an all-black unit.

The 24th Infantry, part of the 25th Division's Japanese occupation force since 1945, was stationed at Gifu, halfway between Tokyo and Kobe. Blacks considered Gifu their own "little world" within the larger structure of segregation. "Good living was the order of the day," recalled Bussey. Occupation duty meant "occupying the best of Japanese commercial, residential, and recreational facilities, holding the glass in one hand and a Japanese girlfriend, or 'moosimae,' in the other." The only fighting for U.S. soldiers, he wrote, "was negotiating a price for a single night's pleasure . . . or for Noritake china and Mikimoto pearls."[46] In 1948, the Eighth Army assigned the 24th to provide security for Kobe Base, with battalions on alternating guard duty. Venereal disease, black-market crime, and drugs now became major problems.

According to Clay Blair, the 24th had been sent to Gifu because "Ned Almond wanted the blacks out of sight and in one place."[47] The four-thousand-man 24th Infantry was the last officially designated all-black active-duty regiment in the U.S. Army. A "segregated holding unit" for all blacks in the Pacific, it was the only regiment in Far East Command with three battalions.[48] By 1950, blacks made up 10 percent of the Army, with the vast majority still in service and supply units. Punished and court-martialed out of all proportion to their infractions, they lived and trained under completely segregated conditions. Even so-called combat troops like the 24th trained only half a day, with poorly maintained war-surplus weapons, and never at night or in winter conditions. "On paper," wrote Clay Blair, the 24th was the strongest and best-equipped unit in the Far East Command, but most Army brass "subscribed to the widespread view in the Army that 'Negroes won't fight.' "[49]

While the white command structure did not encourage actual military training, it did, in Old Army style, encourage pride of unit. Colonel "Screaming Mike" Halloran, the 24th's white commander, boasted of regimental athletic teams (especially the Army's heavyweight boxing champion) and the marching band, which performed throughout Japan. It was hardly the stuff of warfare, but it made the paternalistic Halloran highly popular with black enlisted men—and much less popular with black officers.

Although the 24th Infantry had many black officers, mostly because they had few other places to go, they never commanded or supervised white officers. Black Eighth Army lieutenants and captains led only at platoon and company levels, while whites held field-grade positions of major and above. Most black majors were still chaplains or headquarters staff. Blacks in command positions remained rare. Army personnel officers still seemed to believe that black troops served best under white southerners. With few exceptions, black officers ranked the white senior officers in the regiment as being of very low caliber. Black officers believed that white officers tolerated weaknesses in black troops that would be penalized among whites, simply because blacks were not expected to do any better. There was "a climate of cover-up, benign neglect, acceptance of inadequate performance," agreed a white intelligence officer.[50]

"The Army of occupation was in bad shape," wrote Bussey. "The general physical condition of the troops was poor, morale was low, and the general level of intelligence was reduced."[51]

Most black officers were aware of the regiment's shortcomings, none more so than Lieutenant Colonel Forest Lofton, the highest-ranking black officer in the 24th and one of the few black field-grade officers in the Army. Commander of the 1st Battalion, Lofton asked more of his men, and was consequently less popular than "Screaming Mike" Halloran. When Lofton headed Gifu's drug eradication efforts early in 1950, the men resented his harsh measures (which included prison and Army discharge). Informed that the 24th was about to be committed to combat, Lofton told Colonel Horton V. White (Halloran's successor) that "he wanted no part of that." The regiment was neither trained nor prepared for war, he said, and he requested reassignment. He remained at Gifu as commander of the detachment that maintained the base while the regiment was in Korea. Because Lofton never made his feelings public, black soldiers assumed that his reassignment was another case of white prejudice against black officers.[52]

Early in July 1950, the 24th, accompanied by three other black combat units—the 159th Field Artillery Battalion, the 77th Engineer Combat Company, and the 512th Military Police Company—was rushed to Korea, along with two companies of the white 1st Battalion, 21st Infantry. Basically untrained for combat, they were among the earliest troops to go to war, and they expected to be back in Japan within a few weeks. (Officers were told to pack dress uniforms for the "big parade" anticipated very soon in Seoul.) Thus, most American soldiers saw extended, nearly unrelieved, frontline service from July 1950 to October 1951, in temperatures ranging from one hundred-plus degrees to twenty below zero, in the same summer uniforms. Despite poor equipment, Russian tanks, and the NKPA (whose ranks included veterans of the Maoist side of the Chinese civil war), both the first American ground victory and the war's first Medal of Honor were won by black troops of the 24th Infantry.

Charles Bussey at Yechon

On July 20, 1950, ten days after landing at Pusan, three black units of the 25th Infantry Division—the 24th Infantry, the 77th Engineers, and the 159th Field Artillery—were ordered to recapture the town of Yechon, north of Pusan on the Naktong River in South Korea. The sixteen-hour battle, led by L Company and the black paratrooper Bradley Briggs, a veteran of the World War II "Triple Nickels," was the first combat assignment ever for most of the 24th. Clay Blair calls it a "textbook assault." With light American casualties, the 24th fought off NKPA troops, holding the town until the ROK army could take control. In a widely publicized dispatch, Tom Lambert, the Associated Press correspondent who accompanied the 24th to Yechon, called it "the first sizable American ground victory in the Korean War."[53] Yechon and the black regiments were hailed in the *Congressional Record* ("First United States Victory in Korea Won by Negro GIs") and in newspaper headlines around the country. "It was the first South Korean city restored to friendly hands by American troops," wrote the historian of the 25th Division. "Although it was not a tremendous victory, many believed it symbolic of the liberation of South Korea." For Clay Blair, the victory "was reason for blacks to celebrate, but Yechon was not long remembered."[54]

The 24th, acknowledged on all sides to be poorly trained and ill prepared, had proved at Yechon that they could fight. As the war became a matter of swiftly shifting victory and defeat, Yechon's importance would fade, and even its existence would be doubted. In his official Army history of the first six months of the Korean War, *South to the Naktong, North to the Yalu,* author Roy Appleman dismissed the idea that a battle had taken place at Yechon at all. Veterans believed that the 24th's victory at Yechon was denied because the Army did not want its first Korean War heroes to be black.

"I was there, and it was a battle as far as I was concerned, and it was a victory, too," wrote Charles Bussey. A World War II fighter pilot and son of a World War I veteran, Bussey joined the 25th Division in Japan in January 1950. He had rejoined the Army two years earlier, hoping to be transferred to the Air Force. (His Air Force orders would arrive in late December 1950, when the 25th Division was dug in on the Imjin River. The assistant division commander refused to let him go because there was no black replacement.) "I will remember Yechon for another hundred years. Even in my nightmares I've never seen carnage, death, and destruction to equal—even to approach—that of 20 July 1950."[55]

There was no question about Yechon in the mind of Major General

William Kean, the 25th Division's commander, who gave Bussey a Purple Heart and a Silver Star for "killing a number of North Koreans." General Kean told Bussey to regard the Silver Star as a "down payment" on a Medal of Honor. It would have made him the first black officer (though not the first black soldier) in American history to receive that honor. General Kean's recommendation, submitted by the company's first sergeant, was sent upward but never made it past General Almond's headquarters.

Lieutenant Colonel John T. Corley was another white officer for whom there was no question about Yechon. Later, when he commanded the 24th Infantry, his rallying cry was "Remember Yechon!" "The 24th Infantry Regiment performed extremely well for Colonel Corley," wrote Bussey. "Leadership seemed more important to him than skin color in determining success in battle." A highly decorated World War II combat veteran, Corley, who was considered tough but fair, was Bussey's "whiskey friend" at Kaesong: they shared bottles, "Big War" stories, and candor. Corley translated Army racial policy for his friend: "Company level command for blacks, okay. Battalion-level command, maybe in six to eight years."[56]

Corley was equally "honest" on the subject of medals. As the commander in the field, Corley made medal recommendations to General Kean. "I only recommended you for the Silver Star for the job you did at Yechon," he said, "and I only recommended a Bronze Star for your rescue of Lieutenant Lenon and his people [an earlier Bussey exploit]. The Distinguished Service Cross was appropriate for the Lenon rescue. . . . So was the Congressional Medal of Honor for Yechon. If you were white, you'd have gotten them both. You'd be a hero in song and fable. . . . You will note there are no black heroes, except maybe for Jackie Robinson and baseball." He told Bussey he was dangerous to the military establishment: "I cannot allow you to become a hero, no matter how worthy. I reduced the size of the battalion that you saved to a group, and I reduced the number of men you killed so that finally the job was only worth the Silver Star." While admitting that Bussey was his "kind of soldier," his "kind of man," Corley feared that as a Medal of Honor winner, he would "flaunt it." Taking a long swig from Corley's bottle, Bussey compared a "bigot" to a "bastard" and walked away. He only drank with friends.

"It was an ugly, emotional encounter," Bussey recalled, "but I was prepared to face a lifetime of abuse at the hands of Corley's ilk. I could handle it. I could thrive on it. Medals are of extremely short life, like their recipients."[57] Bussey would be invalided out of the Army in 1951. By then, he had received the Silver Star, the Legion of Merit, the Bronze Star, the Air Medal, the Purple Heart, and the Army Commendation

Medal. The Army denied that he had ever been recommended for a Medal of Honor.

DAVID CARLISLE, ROBERT GREEN, AND WILLIAM THOMPSON

"West Point never produced better men," Charles Bussey wrote of Lieutenants David Carlisle and Robert W. Green. They arrived in Yechon in July directly after graduation, to serve under Bussey in the 77th Engineers. Carlisle and Green, Californians, were the first two blacks from west of the Mississippi to graduate from West Point. They were also the first two black West Pointers in the Army Corps of Engineers. David Carlisle was the son of a Croix de Guerre–winning World War I first sergeant. Robert Green was the son of a former Buffalo Soldier, the 9th Cavalry's Lieutenant John Green, a veteran of the Philippines.

When he entered West Point in July 1946, Carlisle shared a suite with three white roommates. When Green moved in about ten days later, the whites were moved out. "It gave the segregation signal," he said when I spoke to him in 1993. Comparing the West Point years of General Benjamin Davis, Jr. (1932–1936), to his own (1946–1950), Carlisle said that Davis had suffered 100 percent racism, while he and Green had faced about 50 percent. Like Davis, the abuse he endured was verbal, never physical. But unlike Davis, Carlisle had a white "protector," the "beast" barracks platoon leader Leroy Majesky, the "best damn officer in the U.S. Army," who interceded as much as he could with racist upperclassmen. Majesky was killed in Korea. Carlisle had only two or three friends, including Green. They fought on the front lines together in Korea for fifteen months, when the average combat time for white officers was six to nine months. Carlisle went from platoon leader to commander of the 77th, establishing a rule that officers could not be rotated out before men. He believed that most segregation ended at West Point right after Korea, about 1954.

West Point graduated ten other blacks between Davis in 1936, and Carlisle and Green in 1950. General Roscoe Robinson, Jr., class of 1951, would become the Army's first black four-star general. He saw action in Korea and Vietnam, receiving his fourth star in 1982, when he became the U.S. representative to NATO's military committee. The main academic auditorium at West Point was renamed for General Robinson in 2001.

On August 6 at Masan, some twenty miles south of Yechon, 24th Infantry Private First Class William H. Thompson refused to join his company as it withdrew. Staying at his machine gun, he laid down covering fire until everyone was out; he was mortally wounded. Thompson became the first GI to win the Medal of Honor in Korea and the first black Medal of Honor winner since the Spanish-American War. But he was not officially recommended for his medal until January 4, 1951, almost five months after his heroic death. Lieutenant Colonel Melvin Blair, Thompson's commander, refused at first to submit the recommendation.[58]

AIRPOWER: DANIEL "CHAPPIE" JAMES, JR.

With ground troops initially in disarray, the Air Force would have the first and almost the only early Korean victories. "Air power was the decisive factor in the Korean War," wrote General Benjamin O. Davis, Jr. "It was air power that blunted the first North Korean attacks in the early days and later prevented the expulsion of United Nations forces."[59] Major Daniel "Chappie" James, Jr., was one of the most illustrious of the new "fighter jocks" who switched from World War II–vintage P-51 Mustangs to jets in mid-war. He became the first black commander of an integrated Air Force squadron, and the first black four-star general. (His Air Force fourth star came seven years before that of the Army's Robinson.)

One of seventeen children, James grew up near the Pensacola, Florida, Naval Air Base and always wanted to fly. Pilots used to take him up in return for odd jobs and chores. He became a civilian pilot teacher while waiting to make the Air Force Tuskegee quota. At six feet, four inches and over two hundred pounds, James was too big to be a fighter pilot, but he was a natural for General Davis's all-black 477th Bombardment Group. The 477th was activated in January 1944 and, thanks to the usual foot-dragging on black bomber training, remained stateside throughout the war. As a young lieutenant, James took part in the officers' club sit-ins. "We would start by going into the club . . . and ordering a drink and the bartender would say, 'I can't serve you here. We just can't serve you here, this is the Supervisory Officers' Club,' " he remembered in J. Alfred Phelps's *Chappie.* "We would reply, 'Well then, we'll sit here until you serve us.' Then they would close the bar. We would leave and later one of our white friends would call us and say, 'Hey, they just opened the bar, come on back.' We would dash back up, and as soon as we walked in again they said the bar was closed."[60]

By the end of the war, with Air Force integration under way, James had made it his goal to "get with an integrated outfit and prove that I was one of the best fighter pilots around." In September 1949, he got his chance with the 12th Fighter-Bomber Squadron at Clark Field, in the Philippines. There was intense hostility toward James and his family from white pilots (and their wives). But he ranked first in rocketry, second in bombing accuracy, and was one of the top ground gunners in the group, as well as a basketball and baseball star; his fighter-pilot skills and confident, jovial personality eventually won the squadron over. "After a month or so it would have taken an incredible bigot to dislike Chappie James," said Colonel Frank Buzze.[61] In the spring of 1950, James won the Distinguished Service Medal when, suffering from severe burns and fractured vertebrae, he pulled a fellow pilot from a runway jet crash. After months of hospitalization, he rejoined his squadron in Korea in August 1950.

The Korean War saw fierce air-to-ground combat; planes flew low, providing the infantry with ground support: bullets, bombs, rockets, and napalm. Although fighter jets had begun to appear, the original plane of choice in Korea was the P-51 Mustang. James flew eight missions a day. He had a black panther painted on his flight helmet, his call sign was Black Leader, and his integrated flight team was called Black Flight. James's job was to provide tactical support for ground crews, strafing at treetop level so as to destroy trains, enemy supply lines, and Russian T-34 tanks. In October 1950, he was flying in close support of ground forces in Namchonjom, North Korea, attacking only a few yards in front of friendly troops. Calling strike after strike until all ammunition was spent, he was responsible for over one hundred North Korean dead. After the battle he was awarded the Distinguished Flying Cross, and promoted to captain.

But watching American pilots from the ground, then nineteen-year-old Sergeant David Hackworth (who, after fighting in Korea and Vietnam, became both a colonel and America's most decorated living soldier) was not always impressed with their accuracy. "On one occasion," he wrote in his autobiography, *About Face,* not casting specific reflection on Chappie James, "American fighter planes must have concluded that the hordes of desperate civilians were Chinese columns moving south; P-51s had strafed the refugees, and for at least a mile there were dead littered across the road. Retreating vehicles had to push the bodies out of the way." Infantrymen, wrote Hackworth, believed that "it was only the guys on the ground who saw and understood the real horrors of war."[62]

The 24th at Notorious Battle Mountain

Late on the night of August 31, 1950, during the high-water mark of the North Korean offensive, the attacking NKPA forced the 24th Infantry to withdraw from Hill 625, "Battle Mountain," on the southern tip of the

Pusan perimeter. Army records state that even before the North Koreans opened fire, the 24th was seized with "mass hysteria" and ran at the first sight of the enemy, repeatedly defying white superiors' orders to stand and fight. Desertion, abandonment of weapons and equipment, and self-inflicted wounds were reported to be rampant. The men of the 24th were accused of running away. "Two battalions [of the 24th] evaporated in the face of the enemy, and a large part of them repeated this performance four nights later," wrote Roy Appleman. Clay Blair described the official Army history of the 24th Infantry at Battle Mountain as the "most scathing indictment of an Army regiment (black or white) ever published."[63] The 24th was called the "Bugout Brigade" and the "Runnin' 24th," by sister units as well as by the press.

In the face of the North Korean onslaught, many poorly trained white units and soldiers also performed poorly. "Everybody was running," said Thurgood Marshall of the NAACP, which sought to aid the many black GIs who received court-martial convictions during the war. But blacks were the easiest targets of blame. Suffering terrible morale, still segregated in a nominally integrated military, the 24th eventually fulfilled everyone's worst expectations, caught between racists who blamed them for U.S. losses and others who saw them as a stumbling block to integration.

The accusation of cowardice seriously tarnished the reputation of a once-proud regiment, but those who had been there fiercely contested it. "My company didn't disappear," said a Battle Mountain company commander, Roger Walden, in a 1989 interview in the *Los Angeles Times*. "We were up there all night long, fighting." Walden disputed Appleman's "bug-out" account. "The North Koreans pushed through with so much force it just disrupted everything, but I saw no one break and run," he said. "We were catching hell and the next sector over was pretty well mauled." Walden's company suffered fifty casualties out of about 130 men.[64]

David Carlisle, who was there as a young lieutenant, later recalled that the 24th fought "magnificently" at Battle Mountain, despite poor leadership, sweltering heat, and lack of water. "The onus is on the white officers to prove that they led properly," he said. "On this night the regimental commander bugged out and if the black soldiers withdrew, they were withdrawing to catch up with their regimental commander, who was panic stricken and running away from the action himself."[65] Charles Bussey agreed: "The regimental commander led them out. His battalion commanders were all with him. It was not a matter of the troops breaking and running. They went out under leadership. And they went back and retook it the next day."[66]

"The 24th Infantry Regiment lost and regained that hill for nearly forty-five days," wrote Bussey. "They had no baths, very little drinking water, and seldom did they have clean clothes. Sunset provided the only respite from the hellfire of the sun. It was a stinking conflict, with numerous changes of commanders at battalion and company level. It was impossible for the troops to identify with their officers or vice versa." The North Koreans were willing to take great losses to achieve victory. "Pound for pound the North Korean soldier was as good as any in the world," Bussey wrote. "He was tremendously motivated and probably the best mortarman on the planet." But the NKPA paid "an awesome price" for every inch of Battle Mountain. Their casualty rate was devastating, thanks to barbed wire laced with 77th Engineer antipersonnel mines. When troops complained about decaying enemy bodies, engineers provided quicklime for disposal. The American walking wounded, often returned to their units before they were healed, created another morale problem. Replacements were mostly eighteen- to twenty-year-olds trained in technical services, with no combat experience. "It didn't matter if they were properly trained or were qualified in the proper skills," Bussey wrote. "It only mattered that they were black."[67]

* * *

Battle Mountain was one of a succession of defeats in late August and early September that led General MacArthur to go public with his quarrels with President Truman and to achieve one of the most daring victories of his military career. Furious with Truman for rejecting Taiwanese troops and for keeping him out of the North, MacArthur even used the word "appeasement," which he later grudgingly semi-retracted, in a speech to the Veterans of Foreign Wars. On September 15, 1950, he roundly won the public relations battle, and cemented his image as a military hero, with the spectacular landing at Inchon. Directing the action from Tokyo, he sent Marines from the Korea Strait to an amazing Yellow Sea amphibious landing—possible only two days a month because of tides—at Inchon, just southwest of Seoul. Inchon, behind enemy lines, saw some thirty thousand to forty thousand North Korean casualties; U.S. casualties were 536 dead, 2,550 wounded, and 65 missing. The tide of war had turned, and victory seemed at last within reach.

THE THANKSGIVING SUPRISE AND THE 9TH INFANTRY

The direction of the war having changed, America's attitude changed with it. Instead of merely restoring the 38th Parallel, the military mission was now to unite the country under the American-dominated South Korean leader, Syngman Rhee. Truman and MacArthur, who could agree on very little, did agree on this—but Truman again established restrictions. American planes could now bomb the North, but there would be no air or naval action against China, and only South Korean troops could cross the 38th Parallel to fight in the North near the Chinese border at the Yalu. On October 15, to make sure that MacArthur understood his limits, Truman flew seven thousand miles to Wake Island in the Pacific to reiterate them. MacArthur firmly assured the president that China would never intervene on behalf of North Korea.

By mid-October, North Korean forces had been expelled from the South, and United Nations troops had invaded the North. Troops of the American Eighth Army's 25th Division, including three black units—the 24th Infantry, the 77th Engineers, and the 159th Field Artillery—were exactly where Truman had ordered them not to be: above the 38th Parallel facing the Yalu River and China. They were seeking out substantial outposts of resistance near the border, along the Chongchon River. They were in for a Thanksgiving surprise.

On November 23, as it was making its way to the Yalu, the 25th Division was suddenly informed that at least two Chinese divisions and part of a North Korean division were directly in front of them and heading their way. Intelligence estimates were that they faced a combined enemy force of about 34,000 men.[68] Highly indoctrinated Communist Chinese army troops had already crossed the Yalu, attacking in strength along the Chongchon, disconcerting the stunned American troops by screaming and blowing bugles as they attacked. Within forty-eight hours of the initial Chinese onslaught, about a thousand U.S. troops were killed or wounded. It was the beginning of the largest retreat in U.S. Army history. On November 27, MacArthur, who had been urging the men to fight on, sent a cable to Washington: "We face an entirely new war."[69] Defeat had apparently been snatched from the jaws of victory. As the United States withdrew, Chinese soldiers, essentially having taken over the North Korean army, broke through the 38th Parallel, to claim Seoul.

First Lieutenant Ellison C. Wynn, of the 9th Infantry, the first integrated regiment in Korea, was one of the few black officers awarded the Distinguished Service Cross in that war. When the Chinese crossed the Yalu, the 9th were badly hit. Owing to a shortage of replacements and a liberal commanding officer, about half of the 129 men of B Company, 9th Infantry, were black. On the night of November 25, that officer, William C. Wallace, was seriously wounded, so the executive officer, Wynn, was in command. Fierce fighting continued throughout the night, and when the battle ended, Wynn was left with only thirty-four soldiers in his company. When the ammunition ran out, he began throwing rocks and canned

C Rations at the enemy, until a grenade blew away part of his face and he finally staggered to the rear.[70]

Truman had called Korea a "police action." To the swamped U.S. troops fighting in minus-20-degree cold (many wearing the same summer uniforms they had worn a few months earlier in 120-degree-plus heat without water) it was more like war. "It was a frigid, brutal, soul-destroying time," wrote Hackworth, who as a young NCO had envied the Chinese their down mittens, trousers, and jackets, and the white coats that blended into the snow.[71] Despite jets, warships, tanks, heavy weapons, and (in their first use) helicopters, it was an infantryman's war. David Douglas Duncan's combat photos for *Life* captured the Valley Forge–like physical distress and low morale of America's infantry in the terrible winter of 1950–1951.

THE RETURN AND RISE OF CHAPPIE JAMES

The war entered a decidedly different phase after a scathing attack by Communist Chinese forces at Chongchon in late November 1950. MacArthur demanded vengeance for the sneak attack, even requesting nuclear weapons and permission to bomb and blockade China. (Mao Tse-tung's entry into the war was apparently more personal than political. He sent Chinese "volunteers" only after his favorite son was killed in a U.S. bombing raid on the North Korean capital of Pyongyang.) Publicly contradicting Truman yet again, on March 20, 1951, MacArthur wrote to the Republican leader of the House, urging the use of Taiwanese forces. On April 11, raising a firestorm of political criticism, Truman dismissed MacArthur as supreme commander of the U.N. forces in Korea and replaced him with General Matthew B. Ridgway. MacArthur may have been "senior to everyone but God" in the American military, but Truman, who called him "Mr. Prima Donna," was commander in chief.[72]

When the Chinese entered the war in November, Russian-made MiGs came with them. Although outnumbered five to one by MiGs, the Air Force, turning to jets, won nine out of ten dogfights. As a jet pilot, Chappie James performed unarmed reconnaissance over North Korea. Later, in the midst of a "milk run" (a vertical dive at more than seven hundred miles an hour, followed by a quick climb to 43,000 feet) he was shot out of his plane by North Korean gunners. "When the big stuff hits you it's like being slugged," he said, "and you can no longer hold onto your mount or [get it] to do your bidding."[73] Bailing out behind enemy lines, James was rescued by a Marine Corps tank crew.

In late December 1950, having completed one hundred Korean combat missions, James was sent back to the Philippines, to train pilots on their way to war. By 1952 he was a major. A year later he became the first black Air Force officer commanding an integrated fighter squadron in the continental United States. (A Cape Cod landlord near the Otis Air Force Base in Massachusetts, where he commanded the squadron, still refused to rent him a house.) By 1957 James was a lieutenant colonel in the Pentagon, on his way, with a few detours, to becoming a general. In 1960, he became director of operations for the 81st Tactical Fighter Wing, based in England, under the command of Colonel Robin Olds. Olds was an ex–West Point football star, a movie star's husband (Ella Raines), and a triple ace (fifteen kills). As "Black Man and Robin," James and Olds would be a famous Vietnam team, part of the 8th Tactical Fighter Wing "Wolf Pack."

One of the few black combat-jet pilots in Korea (and later in Vietnam), James, though almost universally popular, was considered extremely tough on black officers. "None of his black guys ever made a mistake," a white aide remembered. "They got rewarded but they had to work harder to get rewarded." Often the man in the middle, James was criticized by college-age blacks as a prominent apologist for the war in Vietnam. When he won his first star, in 1970, several disgruntled white Air Force colonels complained that he was promoted only because he was black. Nevertheless, in 1975 he became the first black four-star general and succeeded General Lucius D. Clay at North American Air Defense Command (NORAD) in Colorado Springs, where he got phone calls from strangers worried about "the black man who could start a nuclear war."[74] He tried to reassure callers that there were actually no "buttons" to push at NORAD to start a war. James retired in January 1978, and died of a heart attack a month later. He was buried at Arlington National Cemetery.

Army Integration: General Kean, Sergeant Charlton, and the End of the 24th

While American soldiers were fighting a segregated war, integrated training began at home. In August 1950, two months after war was declared, the post commander of the Army training center at Fort Jackson, South Carolina, found that he had so many recruits that it was "totally impractical to sort them out" in terms of race. He began integrated training strictly on his own.[75] It worked so well that the Army made Fort Jackson a model. Black soldiers were now assigned wherever they were needed. Fears of conflict between black and white troops proved groundless, and integrated units achieved high performance ratings.

By September, possibly because of both the disastrous failure of the segregated 24th Infantry and the heroism of the integrated 9th Infantry on Battle Mountain, the Army was finally ready for integration. Calling the 24th "untrustworthy" and "incapable of carrying out missions expected of an Infantry regiment," Major General Kean said that he wanted the unit removed and its men reassigned on a not-more-than-10-percent-quota basis to white Eighth Army units. Making it clear that his charges were directed at the unit, not at individuals, Kean feared that "continued use of this Regiment in combat will jeopardize the United Nations war effort in Korea." Kean had concluded that the combat value of black soldiers would never be realized unless they were integrated into white units. Even some powerful southerners on the House and Senate Armed Services Committees, like Senator Richard Russell and Representative Carl Vinson, both of Georgia, were finally willing to admit the manpower waste in overstrength black units, when white units lacked men because blacks could not replace them. And morale was so obviously low among black troops that MacArthur had started his own investigation. Far East Command reported that "Negro soldiers can and do fight well when integrated," but MacArthur was dismissed before the investigation was completed.[76]

In the spring of 1951, General Ridgway, who believed that segregation was not only "un-American and un-Christian" but "inefficient" and "improper," formally asked permission to racially integrate forces in Korea. "Project Clear," a separate 1951 Army think tank report, concluded that integration enhanced military effectiveness, while segregation undermined it. The Army chief of personnel, General Anthony C. McAuliffe (hero of Bastogne, which saw 1945-style integration), endorsed the findings of Project Clear and ordered immediate integration with "minimum press publicity."[77]

Lieutenant General Julius Becton, who was wounded three times in Korea and became the first black officer to command a combat corps, remembered being a young officer in early 1951, when gradual division integration brought him one of the first white replacements. Becton's first thought, he told me in 1993, was "Don't let anything happen to him!"

On July 26, 1951, the Army announced that integration would be completed in about six months in Japan, Korea, and Okinawa—and that the all-black 24th Infantry would be disbanded.

Some white veterans agreed with the assessment, but blamed the system. " 'When the Chinese yell "banzai," the Deuce-Four says "goodbye" and heads south' was how we described our mutual sister unit, as month after month we carried its load," wrote David Hackworth. "It had not always been that way; in fact, the Deuce-Four had been responsible for the first significant American ground victory of the war. . . . But the regiment had been bloodied since then." Hackworth decried the loss of many of the 24th's "fine" black NCOs, most of whom were replaced by white NCOs "unable or unwilling to bond with the troops—and vice versa"; the 24th, he said, "had gone to hell in a hand basket." While the regiment "certainly had its share of Medals of Honor, Distinguished Service Crosses, and Silver Stars, as a fighting organization, its leadership was too thin and its combat scars too many."[78]

As controversy swirled around the 24th, Sergeant Cornelius H. Charlton received the regiment's second posthumous Medal of Honor. He was killed on June 2, 1951, after a series of exploits demonstrating "indomitable courage, superb leadership and gallant self-sacrifice" while leading a platoon attack on a Communist-held ridge near Chipo-Ri. When his white commanding officer was seriously wounded, Charlton took command of his platoon and spearheaded three separate assaults up the steep ridge. He personally wiped out several enemy positions with grenades and rifle fire and, wounded in the chest by a grenade, waved away medics so he could single-handedly go after a group of Chinese on a far ridge. Holding his chest wound with one hand and an M-1 carbine with the other, he raced into the fire to be killed by an enemy grenade.

"My boy's death makes a liar out of Paul Robeson, who said the Negroes would never fight for their country against the Communists," said Charlton's father, a West Virginia coal miner.[79] Charlton had been buried in a black cemetery in Beckley, West Virginia, when Congress awarded him the Medal of Honor in 1952. Because of what was later called "administrative oversight," the Army did not offer to rebury him with full military honors at Arlington. When it did finally propose to move his remains there, in 1989, Charlton's family rejected the offer. "They say it was an administrative error," his brother told the *Los Angeles Times* in 1990, "but I say it was discrimination."[80] Local American Legion members now proposed that Charlton be moved from the small black graveyard to the American Legion cemetery. "Any man who gave his life to this nation should be recognized," said John Shumate, a Navy World War II veteran who was the president of Beckley's all-white American Legion Post No. 32.[81] Charlton was reburied on March 10, 1989, attended by an assistant secretary of state, a local congressman, two Army generals, and a full honor guard from Fort Knox. He was the only black among the 251 other soldiers on top of the hill in the American Legion cemetery.

* * *

The 24th Infantry was deactivated on October 1, 1951, its colors retired. It had been a victim of its friends as well as its enemies. Its enemies wanted to end the 24th; its friends wanted to end segregation.

THE END OF THE WAR

Seoul changed hands four times in the course of the war. As victories and defeats moved back and forth, so did peace talks. Dwight Eisenhower became president in January 1953 with a clear mandate to end the war, as he had tacitly promised to do. The new secretary of state, John Foster Dulles, now practiced "brinksmanship," threatening to unleash both Chiang Kai-shek and nuclear weapons if North Korea did not go to the peace table. On March 5, Stalin suddenly died, and the Soviet attitude changed completely. By March 10, his successor, Georgi M. Malenkov, proposed an exchange of wounded and sick POWs; Malenkov hoped that this would "lead to a smooth settlement of the entire question of prisoners of war, thereby achieving an armistice in Korea, for which people throughout the world are longing."[82]

Similar messages came from Kim Il Sung of North Korea and Chou En-lai of China. Although fighting continued along the truce line, talks resumed at Panmunjon in late May. The only barrier to peace now was Syngman Rhee, who declared that South Korea would permit no concessions at all to the North and, moreover, demanded a united country under the South. Declaring martial law, Rhee forbade all military and civilian personnel from working for the U.N. But a humiliating ROK defeat, combined with threats and promises from Washington, finally brought Rhee into line. The Korean armistice was signed on July 27, 1953. After so much terrible loss on both sides, the end of the war was a stalemate. The Panmunjon armistice sent North Korea back to the 38th Parallel, approximately where it had been when the war began.

AFTERWARD

David Carlisle left the Army in 1951, having begun to suffer from asthma in Korea. As a civilian, he began a one-man crusade to vindicate the 24th Infantry. He wanted Yechon declared a victory, and he wanted to erase the stigma of cowardice from Battle Mountain. The 24th Infantry Regiment Association was founded in 1975, to actively pursue the rewriting of the official Army history of the war. In response to persistent lobbying, a revised edition of Appleman's 1961 history was published by the Department of the Army in 1968. The words "if indeed it was an action at all" were deleted—but Yechon was not declared a victory. The Army "danced around" the subject until 1987, Carlisle said, when he enlisted Lieutenant General Colin Powell and Secretary of Defense Caspar Weinberger of the Reagan administration, as well as Democratic representatives Augustus Hawkins and Les Aspin. Aspin was chairman of the House Armed Services Committee. The secretary of the Army, John Marsh, Jr., directed Army historians to prepare a new history of the 24th, and ordered a review of the regiment's performance.

By 1988, the tide seemed to be shifting in favor of vindication. Congress adopted a resolution honoring the 24th Infantry's historic triumphs, from 1869 to 1951. Yechon was finally declared an unequivocal "victory," and the resolution stated that the Army was "currently investigating the historical accounts of this battle in an attempt to set the record straight."[83] In response to a directive from Marsh, Colonel John Cash, a black Korean veteran and military historian, was assigned to begin a new history of the 24th in Korea. The Distinguished Military Graduate (i.e., best in his class) of the Rutgers University ROTC program, Cash was an infantry officer and former West Point history professor who had held command and staff positions in Korea, Vietnam, Brazil, and El Salvador. The author of an oral history of the Vietnam War, and a former senior Latin America analyst with the Defense Intelligence Agency, he considered one of the challenges of the job to put his blackness in his "hip pocket" and "function as an Army officer, as an historian."[84]

In October 1989, six 24th Infantry veterans accompanied Cash on a two-week fact-finding trip to South Korea, primarily to reexamine the 24th's performance at Battle Mountain and to substantiate Bussey's claim to the Medal of Honor. Both goals proved elusive. "When I first got into this project, I thought that racism would explain it all, but as I've gotten into the facts and the personalities, it's not that simple," Cash told the *Los Angeles Times* in November 1989. Veterans of the 24th had "set out on a painful journey to erase a record of shame," the *Times* said—but instead of cleansing the record, "the inquiry raised new questions and deepened these veterans' pains."[85]

Cash's research would uncover the murder of an old Korean peasant (one soldier bet another that he could hit him at six hundred yards with a single rifle shot), a gang rape (widely known throughout the division, but never reported), and the mass surrender to the Chinese of an entire 24th company (136 men had been asked by their black commander whether they preferred to fight or show the white flag). Interviews with over 250 vets produced overwhelming evidence that some soldiers did run from the enemy, particularly in the first months of the war. But Cash also found that the official history had failed to give the 24th credit for later "textbook operations," particularly in two river crossings in March and April of 1951, in difficult terrain under harsh enemy fire. And it in no way reflected the heavy 24th Infantry casualties, suffered in protecting white units farther down the line.

Bussey's Medal of Honor remained equally problematic. Historians of Korea maintained that records of the time reveal no mass killings, and no eyewitnesses came forth. Men and officers in Army units around Yechon claimed never to have heard of Bussey's exploit. "It's hard to believe. All that action and nobody notified me?" said one retired major general, Oliver Dillard, who had been a twenty-three-year-old black 24th Infantry company commander at Yechon on the day of Bussey's supposed deed.[86]

The veterans of the 24th won no clear victory in their struggle to salvage military honor. *Black Soldier, White Army,* the second official Army history, by William T. Bowers, William M. Hammond, and George MacGarrigle (based on the research of Colonel Cash, who had retired), was eventually published in 1996. Unfortunately, it reached a conclusion similar to Roy Appleman's protested first history: "Many fought well but others fled. In that light, the regiment's achievements—during the first weeks of the war, in the breakout from the Pusan Perimeter, at the Han and Hant'an River crossings, and elsewhere—bear a special mark. They underscore the courage, resilience, and determination of those among the unit's members who chose to do their duty, to fight in the face of adversity, and to prevail."[87]

* * *

In June 2000, fifty years after the start of the war, the leaders of North and South Korea met in an extraordinary summit in Pyongyang to try to reconcile their differences and take the first steps toward future reunification. There were still some 37,000 U.S. troops in South Korea, and North Korea was branded a rogue state, suspected of developing long-range missiles and nuclear weapons. But North and South agreed for the first time since the war to hold regular high-level talks, and North and South Koreans would be permitted to exchange visits. Some veterans, South Korean and American, were disappointed that South Korea had scaled back, in deference to the thirty thousand or more North Koreans killed there, its plans for a huge commemorative parade and a reenactment of the Inchon landing. But the black New York congressman Charles Rangel, who was part of the official delegation and had won a Bronze Star and a Purple Heart in Korea, felt otherwise. "When countries have been at war for 50 years and when they are concentrating on peace rather than war," he said, "I would think that doves and olive leaves are a little more important than parades and display of military power."[88]

* * *

Korea saw the birth of a new American military, integrated (more or less) from top to bottom during the administration of a president, Eisenhower, who had once publicly supported segregation. In October 1953, the Army announced that 95 percent of black troops had been integrated into white units; the last segregated units were dissolved in 1954. After Korea, the military commitment to integration was so deep that President Eisenhower claimed to have started the process himself at the Battle of the Bulge. (He had, sort of.) It had been a quiet revolution, without the predicted bloodshed. Integration began slowly, but once it began, the military, going strictly by the book, never looked back. Both the Jim Crow Army and Jim Crow society were coming to an end.

Unfortunately, the Cold War was still raging. If Korea was the new military's difficult birth, then Vietnam would be its stormy adolescence—inchoate and anarchic on the home front as well as on the battlefield.

10 Vietnam

THE 1960s

They did what they thought their country needed them to do.

—Lieutenant Colonel George Forrest (ret.), speaking with the author about GIs in Vietnam

May 1954

On May 7, 1954, the French outpost at Dienbienphu, in an isolated valley near the Laotian border of Vietnam, fell to the Communist Vietminh after a fifty-six-day siege. It was a victory for Vietminh leader Ho Chi Minh, who had briefly lived in Harlem in 1918 and attended meetings of Marcus Garvey's Universal Negro Improvement Association. Working closely with the American OSS in World War II, during the Japanese occupation of Vietnam, Ho Chi Minh sought U.S. help after the war and used the words of the American Declaration of Independence in his own freedom charter. "All men are created equal," read the Vietnamese declaration of independence. "They are endowed by their Creator with certain unalienable rights, among these are Life, Liberty and the pursuit of Happiness." After the war, however, the United States supported France when it sought to restore its colonial hold. Vietnam became a Cold War battlefield, and the United States paid for most of the disastrous eight-year effort. The French people grew increasingly frustrated with "the dirty war," as it had come to be called, and the debacle at Dienbienphu ended nearly a century of colonial rule. But the subsequent peace agreement represented only a brief pause in a war that continued for another two decades.

America's Vietnamese entanglement really began in July 1941, when Japan seized Vietnam, Cambodia, and Laos, the three countries that made up French Indochina. Roosevelt saw Japan's occupation as a threat to the U.S. rubber supply and froze Japanese assets in America—a major step toward Pearl Harbor. He favored independence for Indochina after the war. "France has had the country—thirty million inhabitants—for nearly one hundred years and the people are worse off than they were at the beginning," he said to Secretary of State Cordell Hull in 1943. "The people of Indochina are entitled to something better than that." Unfortunately, as Arthur M. Schlesinger, Jr., wrote in *The Bitter Heritage: Vietnam and American Democracy 1941–1966,* the idea "died with him."[1]

France reasserted its colonial power, and Ho Chi Minh and his forces (veterans of underground warfare against the Japanese) fought back. In 1950, the United States denounced Ho as "an agent of world communism" and called the French war "an integral part of the world-wide resistance by the Free Nations to Communist attempts at conquest and subversion."[2] By 1951 there was full-fledged war in Indochina. Political, if not public, debate grew.

"We have allied ourselves to the desperate effort of a French regime to hang on to the remnants of empire," said Representative John F. Kennedy in 1951. "To check the southern drive of communism makes sense but not only through reliance on the force of arms. The task is rather to build a strong native non-communist sentiment within those areas and rely on that as a spearhead of defense rather than upon the legions of General de Lattre [who commanded the French forces in Indochina]. To do this apart from and in defiance of innately nationalistic aims spells foredoomed failure. . . . Without the support of the native population, there is no hope of success in any of the countries of Southeast Asia."[3]

By 1952, the Vietminh were everywhere, and receiving arms and matériel from the Soviet Union. In September 1953, President Dwight D. Eisenhower sent a thirty-five-member military and economic mission to Saigon as the specter of a Communist victory grew. "The French are going to win," said Admiral Arthur Radford, the chairman of the Joint Chiefs of Staff, echoing what French and American officials had been saying for two years.[4]

"I am frankly of the belief that no amount of American military assistance in Indochina can conquer . . . 'an enemy of the people' which has the sympathy and covert support of the people," said Kennedy—then a U.S. senator—in 1954. "For the United States to intervene unilaterally and to send troops into the most difficult terrain in the world, with the Chinese able to pour in unlimited manpower, would mean that we would face a situation which would be far more difficult than even what we encountered in Korea. It seems to me that it would be a hopeless situation." Many congressional Democrats would ask, along with Kennedy, "whether all or a part of Indochina is absolutely essential to the security of Asia and the free world."

Senator Lyndon B. Johnson was so disturbed by the conflicting and confusing Indochina policy in 1954 that he believed "we should turn our eyes from abroad and look homeward." In full Cold War cry, however, Secretary of State John Foster Dulles declared neutrality "immoral."[5]

The debate grew louder in the spring of 1954, when Dienbienphu was under siege and a French nurse, Geneviève de la Gaillard, the "Angel of Dienbienphu," became a U.S. media celebrity. Americans thought the war was a French enterprise, even though between 1950 and 1954 the United States paid for 80 percent of it—some $2 billion. In any case, the events of May 1954 led most Americans to think they had heard the last of Vietnam, wherever it was.

★ ★ ★

Ten days after the fall of Dienbienphu, the U.S. Supreme Court ruled unanimously in *Brown v. Board of Education* that segregated schools were unconstitutional and "inherently unequal." *Brown* was the culmination of over twenty years of effort by the NAACP Legal Defense team, under Thurgood Marshall, to desegregate tax-supported education. The next two decades in America would see both the first full flowering of the new civil rights movement, and its brutal demise.

The war in Vietnam and the civil rights movement, each with its own long history, became intertwined in May 1954. They would be joined for the next twenty years. What united them was the U.S. military. Segregation had been abolished in military base schools as well as Veterans Administration hospitals in 1953, the year before *Brown.* (The year after *Brown* saw two egregious civil rights crimes in Mississippi: the murder on August 13, 1955, of a World War II veteran, Lamar Smith, shot and killed for registering voters; and, two weeks later, the torture death of fourteen-year-old Emmett Till.) The U.S. military was becoming a model of racial integration in an otherwise segregated country. The post-Korea military became an attractive career prospect for young black men, many of whom would eventually find themselves in Vietnam.

COLIN POWELL AND THE LITTLE ROCK NINE

In February 1954, three months before Dienbienphu and *Brown v. Board of Education,* sixteen-year-old Colin Powell registered for his first semester at the City College of New York. (He had also been accepted by New York University, but NYU cost $750 a year and CCNY cost $10.) After a brief interest in the School of Engineering, he soon changed his major to geology.

Powell's parents were well-educated, middle-class Jamaican immigrants and devout members of the Anglican Church. A majority population in their own country, with mostly absentee white landlords, black Jamaicans did not suffer the crippling racist oppressions of their North American cousins. Caribbean immigrants had a history of success in America that generally surpassed native blacks. As early as 1901, they owned 20 percent of Harlem businesses. By 1991, the earnings of first-generation English-speaking West Indian immigrants topped those of native-born whites as well as blacks.[6] The Powells in America were themselves part of an extended family of high achievers.

When Colin Powell was four and a half years old, Air Force Captain Colin Kelly, Jr., killed bombing a Japanese warship two days after Pearl Harbor, became the first publicized hero of World War II. Hearing about Kelly, Powell, one of the youngest among the Bronx neighborhood boys who played "war," not only changed the pronunciation of his name to match, but also decided to become a soldier when he grew up. As a young teenager during the Korean War, he kept his military dream.

Geology aside, Colin Powell's real major, in which he always received A's (thus keeping his grade-point average up), was the Reserve Officer Training Corps—and especially the elite "Pershing Rifles" ROTC fraternity. "The discipline, the structure, the camaraderie, the sense of belonging were what I craved," Powell wrote in his autobiography, *My American Journey.* "I became a leader almost immediately. I found a selflessness within our ranks that reminded me of the caring atmosphere within my family. Race, color, background, income meant nothing. The PRs would go the limit for each other and for the group. If this was what soldiering was all about, then maybe I wanted to be a soldier."[7] The Pershings, like all fraternities, recruited pledges with beer and pornographic movies. When Powell became the Pershing pledge officer, he replaced the porn with movies of drill competitions. He became cadet colonel—the highest ROTC rank—and Distinguished Military Graduate.

His father had not been happy in 1957 to see young Powell go to ROTC summer camp at Fort Bragg, North Carolina. Powell Senior was nervous about the South in general. Racial violence had erupted in Alabama in January in the wake of the Supreme Court's decision that supported the Montgomery bus boycott, inspired by Rosa Parks and led by the Reverend Martin Luther King, Jr. Bombs had exploded in four black churches and in the homes of ministers. Willie Edwards, Jr., a black Montgomery man, had been lynched.

Powell, warned by his father not to stray from the base, was named "Best Cadet, Company D," and was second-best cadet for the entire camp. He felt "marvelous" about the latter honor until a white supply sergeant told him why he was not number one. "You think these Southern

ROTC instructors are going to go back to their colleges and say the best kid here was a Negro?"[8] Powell was more "stunned" than angry. "I did not want to believe that my worth could be diminished by the color of my skin," he wrote. "Wasn't it possible that [the highest-ranked cadet] was simply better than Cadet Powell?"

Powell returned from Fort Bragg to start his junior year at City College just as the "Little Rock Nine" were setting off for high school. It was the birth of the civil rights youth crusade, which already counted seven-year-old Linda Brown, the lead plaintiff in the school desegregation suit. On September 4, 1957, in direct defiance of *Brown v. Board of Education,* Governor Orval Faubus called out the Arkansas National Guard to keep nine black teenagers from entering Little Rock High School. Faubus might have been successful, except that NBC television's John Chancellor happened to be there to make Little Rock a national drama, bringing the civil rights struggle into American living rooms for the first time. Television gave civil rights a powerful new nonviolent weapon.

Frowning behind dark glasses, fifteen-year-old Elizabeth Eckford clutched her schoolbooks closer and maintained, in her starched back-to-school dress, an implacable dignity. It was real life; and it was great television—featuring Elizabeth, her hate-contorted tormentors, and a Good Samaritan. Americans watched a racial drama unfold, with a black hero and white villains—and, suddenly, a white hero. It gave the civil rights movement a human face, and it allowed whites to feel both bad and good about themselves. All alone in a sea of frenzied, epithet-spewing white women, Elizabeth, dignified but clearly terrified, seemed about to be overwhelmed. Suddenly, pushing her way through the mob without saying a word, came a sturdy middle-aged white woman to lead Elizabeth to the relative safety of a nearby bus stop bench and a clutch of reporters. (The *New York Times* man, Benjamin Fine, was taken off the story for being seen on television patting Eckford on the shoulder.) The brave white woman, whose name was Grace Lorch, stood stolidly between Eckford and the surprised and somewhat deflated mob, until the first bus arrived and she took the young girl home.

Elizabeth Eckford was not quite the lamb tossed to the wolves that she appeared on television. She had actually been trained for months on how to behave in the face of verbal violence and invective. Her tutor was Daisy Bates, the courageous longtime president of the Arkansas chapter of the NAACP, den mother and guardian angel to the Little Rock Nine. (Mrs. Bates, who had suffered rocks through her window and a burning cross on her roof in the course of the struggle, also saw the financial ruin of the *Arkansas State Press,* the pro–civil rights weekly she published with her husband, L. C. Bates.) Importantly for Eckford, Mrs. Bates had encouraged her charges to wear dark glasses, in case they were frightened or began to cry.

Eisenhower was not noted for his sympathy for civil rights, but Faubus had angered him by flouting the law and encouraging mob violence. (Harry Ashmore's front-page editorials in the Arkansas *Gazette,* supporting the students and castigating Faubus, won him a Pulitzer Prize.) Never one to take half measures when it came to a military objective, Eisenhower mobilized units of the 101st Airborne Division to guarantee the safe integration of Little Rock High School. "Our personal opinions about the decision have no bearing on the matter of enforcement," he said in a national television address. "Mob rule cannot be allowed to override the decisions of our courts."[9]

When the Little Rock Nine were finally admitted to high school, each was assigned a personal bodyguard from the 101st Airborne. Melba Patillo Beals, then fifteen, remembered her bodyguards in Juan Williams's history of the civil rights movement, *Eyes on the Prize.* "The troops were wonderful. They were disciplined, they were attentive, they were caring, they didn't baby us, but they were there."[10] A year later, Eisenhower's staff said no when Daisy Bates asked if she could bring the nine young people to meet the president.

COLIN POWELL, COLD WARRIOR: 1959–1960

Powell graduated from CCNY in 1959 and entered the Army, soon finding himself on the front lines of the Cold War in West Germany, where he served two years with the 3rd Armored Division. His first platoon sergeant was a veteran white NCO from Alabama, whose race was initially a cause of concern. "I need not have worried," Powell wrote. "My color made no difference to Edwards; I could have been black, white, or candy-striped for all he cared. I was his lieutenant, and his job was to break in new lieutenants and take care of them."[11] By the end of 1960, he was the only lieutenant in the battalion to command a company; that job was usually held by a captain.

In Germany, Powell continued to experience the bonds of military brotherhood that he had first found in the Pershing Rifles. "You can serve thirty-five years in the Army and rise to the top, yet your first assignment always stands out as the most unforgettable," he wrote later, "the one against which all future posts are measured. That is what Gelnhausen meant to me. It marked the beginning of lifelong friendships among my class of lieutenants."[12] Foremost among this group was Lieutenant Joe Schwar, a white classmate who turned up later in Powell's life, under very different circumstances.

"For black GIs, especially those out of the South, Germany was a breath of freedom—they could go where they wanted, eat where they wanted, and date whom they wanted, just like other people. . . . The dollar was strong, the beer good, and the German people friendly, since we were all that stood between them and the Red hordes. War, at least the Cold War in West Germany, was not hell."

War may not have been hell in Germany, but life was hellish for blacks in certain parts of the United States. A twenty-three-year-old named Mack Parker, who had spent two years in the peacetime Army, was lynched near Poplarville, Mississippi, in 1959, accused of raping a white woman who admitted that she was unsure whether Parker was her actual attacker. As his Army service merited, Parker's coffin was covered with an American flag. But Poplarville whites were so outraged that they protested to the Veterans Administration, which ultimately demanded that his sister return the flag.[13]

Vietnam: 1954–1959

Between 1954 and 1959, while Colin Powell was learning to be a soldier, the United States spent $2.3 billion in Vietnam.

Even before Dienbienphu fell, it had been apparent to the Eisenhower administration that the days of the French in Indochina were numbered and that Ho Chi Minh was on his way to leadership once they had gone. In Cold War terms, it was a dangerous situation, and Washington turned to an Air Force general, Edward G. Lansdale, a Cold War hero who was credited with masterminding the suppression of the Hukbalahap rebels in the postwar Philippines. (Like the Vietnamese Communists, the Huks fought the Japanese in World War II with the American OSS.) Lansdale had what Neil Sheehan in *A Bright Shining Lie* called "a mystique, a reputation for being able to perform miracles."[14] Lansdale arrived in Saigon on June 1, 1954, just as the Vietminh blew up an ammunition dump at Tan Son Nhut airport to celebrate the Dienbienphu victory. His instructions were to make the best of a very bad situation and to report directly to the top in Washington, via the CIA.

Under the terms of the Geneva agreement of July 22, 1954, Vietnam was provisionally partitioned at the 17th Parallel, with Hanoi the capital in the North and Saigon the capital in the South. The agreement called for elections in July 1956 to elect the leader of a single, unified Vietnam. The United States did not sign the treaty. Instead, policy makers in Washington set about making the partition permanent.

Lansdale and his superiors did not look forward to the 1956 election.

President Eisenhower himself observed that if an election did take place, Ho Chi Minh would certainly win, with as much as 80 percent of the vote. There was no doubt that Ho, who had stirred Vietnamese patriotism by vanquishing the French colonialists, had more charisma than the man Washington had chosen to back as the new head of a new government in Saigon, the aloof and often enigmatic Ngo Dinh Diem. He and his family were Roman Catholics, a minority in Buddhist Vietnam but under the French a favored and powerful minority. There was little in Diem's background to qualify him to lead a country, but his anti-Communist credentials were in good order.

Lansdale, backed by copious U.S. assistance in money and matériel, coached Diem as he eliminated his immediate rivals—including religious sects, river pirates, and ambitious military leaders. Lansdale also helped orchestrate Operation Exodus in the summer and autumn of 1954, in which nearly a million people were relocated from the North to the South. Two-thirds of them were Catholic, and many had been alarmed to see the French army prepare to leave. In the South they provided an instant and powerful bloc of political support for Diem.

Once Diem had established his authority, he set about rounding up Vietminh who were still numerous in the South, as well as ordinary citizens who had supported the Vietminh, who were even more numerous. Eventually, while American propaganda portrayed him as a champion of democracy, Diem's security forces imprisoned, tortured, and killed Vietnamese by the thousands.

In the North, a disastrous land-reform program in 1955 and 1956 killed, by some estimates, as many as 100,000 people. Afterward, living conditions improved, and the well-trained army that had defeated the French remained intact. Ho Chi Minh and his colleagues kept an eye on developments in the South.

In January 1955, the United States established MAAG, the Military Assistance and Advisory Group, in Saigon, and American advisers began training a South Vietnamese army. By July, Diem was confident enough to denounce the Geneva agreements and say that he would not cooperate with elections in 1956. In Washington, officials approved of Diem's decision (and, privately, Lansdale's skill in bringing it about). In October 1955 Diem declared himself president of the Republic of Vietnam. By then, thanks mostly to Lansdale, the political landscape had changed completely. South Vietnam was a going concern and Diem was the undisputed power in Saigon. A potential Cold War defeat had been turned into a Cold War standoff.

In 1957, a low-level guerrilla war ignited in the South as former

Vietminh guerrillas and others antagonized and threatened by Diem's repression took up arms against his regime. Between 1957 and 1960, guerrilla forces expanded from two thousand to ten thousand; each year they captured thousands of weapons from the Saigon forces. Diem grew even more repressive and shrugged off American suggestions that he change his policies.

On July 8, 1959, guerrillas killed two American advisers (there were fewer than five hundred in Vietnam at the time), Major Dale Buis and Sergeant Chester Ovnand, at Bien Hoa. Eventually, the names of more than 58,000 Americans appeared on the Vietnam memorial in Washington, D.C.

CIVIL RIGHTS 1960

By 1960, the Reverend James Lawson, a young black minister in Nashville who had studied Gandhi's techniques in India, was giving student workshops in nonviolent philosophy and strategy across the South. The young black South, in great numbers, was being recruited to learn the techniques of passive resistance and mass nonviolent protest. Massive action, Gandhi taught, was the safest form of nonviolent protest. Lawson joined others, including the Reverend Martin Luther King, Jr., to become part of a group of black and white southern ministers influenced by Gandhi and pacifism.

The first mass action began in a deceptively small way on February 1, 1960, when four black Greensboro, North Carolina, college students (one in his ROTC uniform) walked into a Woolworth's, made some purchases, and sat down at a lunch counter. They were refused service, but refused to move. The staff closed the counter rather than serve them. It was the first sit-in since that of the World War II–era Freeman Field pilots. In the following weeks, larger and larger groups of young men and women (including whites) would sit passively at counters while whites jeered, poked, and spit at them. Within a year, some seventy thousand young people in more than a hundred southern cities had sat in, and several thousand of them had been arrested. In the North, integrated student groups began to picket already integrated northern Woolworth's. Growing out of the sit-ins, the college-aged members of the Student Nonviolent Coordinating Committee (SNCC) acted as radically pacifist, faith-oriented civil rights shock troops.* "They have shown that the new

*While all SNCC members in the early 1960s, who included Julian Bond, Tom Hayden, Robert Moses, James Forman, and John Lewis, adhered to nonviolence, some questioned the principle's efficacy even then. "You can't kill a snake by kissing it to death," a young white southern male SNCC member said in my presence at the 1961 National Student Association Conference at the University of Wisconsin.

way for Americans to stand up for their rights is to sit down," said 1960's Democratic presidential candidate, John F. Kennedy, that spring.[15]

A month before the 1960 election, Martin Luther King, Jr., was sentenced to four months in a rural Georgia penitentiary for driving without a Georgia license. The physical danger to King was clear to both presidential candidates. While the Republican, Richard M. Nixon, called the Justice Department to see if King's rights had been violated, John F. Kennedy and his brother Robert made calls to Georgia officials, including the governor and the major of Atlanta, promising to make no triumphant public statement if King was released. The King family released news of Kennedy's private sympathy call to Mrs. King, just as her husband was being freed. Martin Luther King, Sr., now urged blacks to "take off" their Nixon buttons. Kennedy won the election that year with 68 percent of the black vote.

Kennedy created the most racially liberal administration in American history. A combat-wounded World War II veteran, he questioned aloud during his inaugural parade why there were so few black faces among the Coast Guard. Kennedy appointed Thurgood Marshall to the U.S. Court of Appeals in the Second Circuit. Members of FDR's unofficial New Deal "Black Cabinet" now became official members of JFK's "New Frontier." Robert Weaver, as administrator of the Federal Housing and Home Finance Agency, became the highest-ranking black government official in history. James B. Parsons became the first black federal district judge in the continental United States. (William Hastie had served in the Virgin Islands.) And Carl Rowan, one of the first black naval officers of World War II, became a White House spokesperson, as well as ambassador to Finland. The Kennedys also had the first black guests at official White House dinners since Theodore Roosevelt was publicly castigated for inviting Booker T. Washington. (Black New Dealers who dined at the White House had attended unofficial evenings.)

Like Truman, Kennedy bypassed Congress and made full use of his executive powers in the civil rights area. He first used the words "affirmative action" in his 1961 executive order on Title VII of the Civil Rights Act of 1960, referring to possible remedies for unlawful discrimination in employment. An executive order that same year created the President's Committee on Equal Employment Opportunity; a 1962 order forbade racial or religious discrimination in federally financed housing. Kennedy talked about making the world safe for "democracy, diversity and personal distinction." Kennedy's presidency also saw the first black honor guard at the Tomb of the Unknown Soldier.

In 1962, Kennedy's Committee on Equal Opportunity in the Armed Forces, the Gesell Committee, extended the military desegregation process. The committee's revolutionary directive, issued by Secretary of Defense Robert McNamara, stated that military commanders must oppose discriminatory practices affecting military personnel and their dependents—both on and *off* base. Individual racism and racist commanders continued to exist, but openly racist attitudes were now what might be called distinctly non-career-enhancing. Black servicemen found new opportunities in promotions, service schools, and civilian communities. Thanks to Kennedy, the early 1960s were a good time for blacks in the military.

COLIN POWELL: FROM FORT BRAGG TO VIETNAM

In January 1961, after two years in Germany, Lieutenant Colin Powell returned to the 1st Battle Group, 4th Infantry, 2nd Infantry Brigade at Fort Devens, Massachusetts. His three-year service obligation ended in the summer of 1961, but for a young black, he wrote, "no other avenue in American society offered so much opportunity," and "nothing counted so much as the fact that I loved what I was doing." Despite his parents' misgivings that the Army was not a real job, he never considered not reenlisting.[16]

Powell was at Fort Devens in November 1961, when he met Alma Johnson, the beautiful daughter of a Birmingham, Alabama, high school principal, on a blind date. Alma was attending graduate school in Boston, and Powell was immediately smitten. They were married in the summer of 1962, right after Powell received word that he was going to Vietnam. With some sixty black homes and churches bombed since the end of World War II, Birmingham had become known to blacks, who lived in daily fear, as Bombingham. At first, Powell's father, with his horror of the South, refused to attend the wedding, but Powell's sister and her white husband shamed him out of his fear by announcing that they, an interracial couple, intended to go.

Driving to Fort Bragg a month after the wedding for the Military Assistance Training Advisor course at Bragg's Unconventional Warfare Center, the Powells could not find a gas station bathroom to use. Trying to find a habitable furnished rental in the black neighborhood of Fayetteville, North Carolina, was even worse. Help came in the form of Joe Schwar, with whom Powell had served in Germany.

Alma Powell had been surprised by the social integration among Army couples. Now she was astounded when Schwar and his wife invited them to share their small government-issue house on the post, dislodging two of their three sons from a bedroom. To Alma, who was newly pregnant, the Schwars' kindness meant so much that she would name her firstborn Michael Kevin, for Kevin Michael Schwar, one of the boys evicted.

In the fall of 1962, as the Cuban missile crisis unfolded and violence erupted at the University of Mississippi when James Meredith tried to become the first black to enroll, both Schwar and Powell received early promotions to captain. The adviser course finished shortly before Christmas. The Powells left for Birmingham, where Alma would live while Colin was overseas. Two days before Christmas, Powell left for Vietnam.

* * *

In Vietnam, the Vietcong were becoming more successful every day as Diem's inept and corrupt Army surrendered more weapons and territory. Vice President Lyndon B. Johnson visited Vietnam in May 1961. "The basic decision in Southeast Asia is here," he reported. "We must decide whether to help these countries to the best of our ability or throw in the towel and pull back our defenses to San Francisco. . . . More important, we would say to the world in this case that we don't live up to our treaties and don't stand by our friends. This is not my concept. I recommend that we move forward promptly with a major effort to help these countries defend themselves. . . . American combat troop involvement is not only not required, it is not desirable."[17]

The security situation continued to deteriorate as the Vietcong grew stronger. General Maxwell Taylor and presidential adviser Walt W. Rostow returned from Vietnam in October 1961, recommending that U.S. combat troops go to Vietnam, posing as flood relief forces, but Kennedy said no. "They want a force of American troops," he complained. "They say it's necessary in order to restore confidence and maintain morale. But it will be just like Berlin. The troops will march in; the bands will play; the crowds will cheer; and in four days everyone will have forgotten. Then we will be told we have to send in more troops. It's like taking a drink. The effect wears off, and you have to take another."[18]

In February 1962 the U.S. Military Assistance Command in Vietnam (MACV, pronounced "Mac-Vee") was established in Saigon. In April, the Pentagon verified that U.S. pilots were flying combat missions and that U.S. soldiers were actually fighting Vietcong. Vietnam was a "very real war" with deep U.S. commitment, wrote Homer Bigart of *The New York Times.* "The struggle will go on at least ten years, in the opinion of some observers, and severely test American patience."[19] In July 1962, in an interview with Bernard Fall, Ho Chi Minh also predicted that the war might "perhaps take ten years." "I think the Americans greatly underestimate the determination of the Vietnamese people," he said. "The Vietnamese people always have shown great determination when they were faced with a foreign invader."[20] In December 1960, there were approximately eight hundred U.S. military personnel in Vietnam. By December 1962 there were 11,300.

* * *

A few days after Christmas, 1962, Captain Colin Powell headed north to the tropical forests of the A Shau Valley, along the Laotian border, as field adviser to a four-hundred-man infantry battalion of the Army of the Republic of Vietnam (ARVN). Most of the critical fighting at the time was far from the A Shau, in the Mekong Delta. Powell's base, near the primitive beginnings of the Ho Chi Minh Trail, was remote and isolated. His initial sensations were of "towering" over his South Vietnamese troops—and of being a perfect target. He asked himself the eternal military question, "What the hell am I doing here?" He was there as an "American presence," he determined, to help push the Vietcong out of the A Shau.[21]

Powell had arrived just before the disastrous January 2, 1963, battle at Ap Bac in the Delta. Reporters, including Neil Sheehan of United Press International, told what had happened: "Angry United States military advisers charged today that Vietnamese infantrymen refused direct orders to advance during Wednesday's battle at Ap Bac and that an American Army captain had been killed while out front pleading with them to attack," Sheehan wrote.[22] The Vietcong had scored a major military victory.

Powell was making similar discoveries. He was also finding out that no one, especially leaders in Washington, seemed to understand the Vietcong or know how to fight them. And he was learning new lessons of brutality.

Operation Grasshopper was Powell's first mission. The battalion moved out in the predawn of February 7, 1963. "Soon the long green line of troops was swallowed up by the dark jungle," he wrote. "I felt a tingling anticipation. A force of armed men moving into the unknown has a certain power, even a touch of majesty, although the squealing pigs and cackling chickens accompanying us in wicker baskets detracted somewhat from the martial aura."[23] Every day in the thick tropical forest was an endless obstacle course. The Vietcong's trails were sown with punji sticks (bamboo stakes smeared with buffalo dung to cause pain and infection). The mile-long single column of ARVN soldiers was an obvious tactical mistake, but ARVN officers politely ignored Powell's advice for three or four parallel columns. On the sixth day of the march, Powell heard his first incoming fire. The VC had attacked, killing one man and wounding another before quickly disappearing. The message calling for a helicopter to evacuate the casualties was tapped out in old-fashioned Morse code. Powell found that his battle "exhilaration" had evaporated. "This was not war movies on a Saturday afternoon; it was real, and it was ugly." It was also incompetent.

Powell always carried a pencil and a GI-issue pocket notebook, as he had been taught to do at Fort Benning. Typical entry: "10 Feb.: Rain. Located evacuated village; destroyed houses and 100 K [kilos] rice, 20 k corn." Ronson and Zippo lighters were used to burn houses and crops. The peasants would lose more crops as helicopters delivered chemical herbicide, a forerunner of Agent Orange. "Why were we torching houses and destroying crops?" At the time, it was considered "counterinsurgency at the cutting edge," Powell wrote. As he entered information matter-of-factly in his diary in 1962–1963, Powell, conditioned to obey and to believe in the "wisdom of superiors," had "no qualms": "It all made sense in those days."[24]

Although Powell and his troops were ambushed almost daily, after two months they had still not seen the enemy. Deciding, in best infantry-officer style, to take the offensive as ARVN troops just "stood around" after an attack, Powell shouted, "Follow me!," as mandated by Benning, and took off into the jungle. No one followed. "Captain, come back!" the men called. Powell turned back. But he found it "maddening" to be ambushed daily by a "phantom enemy." He found Vietnam a "baffling" war. Most of the time, they "could not even find" the Vietcong.[25]

In May 1963, as government control of the countryside was collapsing and the Vietcong feasted on U.S. weapons taken from the ARVN, Powell's men ambushed and killed their first VC, a slight man wearing black "pajamas" and rubber-tire sandals. The ARVN were eager for more "kills," since this seemed to be what Americans wanted, Powell wrote. They were forever "proving" kills by displaying patches of blood. Powell stressed that a dead body was required. Soon after the first kill, a Vietnamese lieutenant excitedly reported another, but the body was too far away to carry back. He would bring proof. The lieutenant returned with a handkerchief. Opening it, Powell "gaped" to find a pair of freshly cut ears. He now stipulated that "KIA" meant a whole body—no more mutilation of the enemy.

Powell's officer's quarters consisted of a thatched hut of bamboo and grass, complete with dirt floor, frame cot, and huge rats. Americans called the base camp the "A Shau Hilton." The only camp diversion was waiting for the twice-weekly helicopter delivery of mail, cigarettes, and paperback books. Powell's anticipation was "almost sexual." He read F. Scott Fitzgerald's *Tender Is the Night,* Carson McCullers's *The Heart Is a Lonely Hunter,* John Hersey's *The Child Buyer,* Wallace Stegner's *Shooting Star,* Cornelius Ryan's *The Longest Day,* and many whodunits. But he was waiting every moment for Alma's "baby letter." Regimental headquarters at Quang Tri had been alerted to open at once an envelope marked "baby letter" and radio the message to Powell. But the baby letter never arrived. On April 3, the day after a VC mortar attack in which he was nearly killed, Powell read a letter from his mother saying how happy they were about "the baby." Michael Kevin Powell had been born March 23, nearly two weeks earlier. Alma's letter was back at Quang Tri, sitting in a stack of undelivered mail. Life now seemed "more valuable" and survival "more critical." Powell was determined to "make it through the year."[26]

The informal motto of American policy had become "Sink or swim with Ngo Dinh Diem," but America's hand-picked leader was becoming as much of a problem as the VC. In May 1963, Diem ordered his troops to fire into a crowd of Buddhists in Hue who were displaying flags to mark the Buddha's 2,587th birthday. Nine people were killed. To protest the deaths, the Venerable Thich Quang Duc, a Buddhist monk, sat down in the lotus position in a Saigon street and set himself on fire. Quang Duc's was the first of seven Buddhist suicides in 1963. Diem's response was to declare martial law and raid Buddhist temples. His notorious sister-in-law, the beautiful Madame Ngo Dinh Nhu, spoke derisively of "barbecued monks." To the Buddhist majority, Diem and his sister-in-law more than ever represented the religion of colonial oppression. His actions (and her words) caused Washington to question Diem's ability to prevent a Communist takeover. The United States tacitly informed some generals plotting to overthrow him that it would not oppose a coup.

On another frustrating operation near the Laotian border in July, Powell stepped on a punji stick and was briefly hospitalized. He had only four months left in country, so his field duties were over. Back at 1st ARVN Division headquarters, he was not happy with what he saw in the upper ranks of the Vietnamese military. While ARVN foot soldiers were "brave and uncomplaining" and most of the officers and NCOs in his battalion were "dedicated, able professionals," at headquarters "incompetence, corruption and flashy uniforms" were the norm. "Were these the people . . . for whom ARVN grunts were dying in the A Shau Valley?"[27]

The "credibility gap" was growing. "The corner has definitely been turned toward victory in Vietnam," said the U.S. Defense Department in May. "South Vietnam is on its way to victory over communist guerillas," said American ambassador Frederick Nolting, Jr., in June 1963. "I can safely say the end of the war is in sight," said General Paul Harkins, head of the American Military Assistance Command, in October.[28] These were the same sort of self-delusional lies that the French and Americans had told before Dienbienphu.

Journalists covered the disasters of the war close-up and also reported the views of candid American military advisers, who contradicted the official, cheerful assessments. Neil Sheehan, David Halberstam of *The New York Times,* Merton Perry of *Time* and, later, *Newsweek,* and François Sully of *Newsweek* often found themselves attacked by the military. "Why don't you get on the team?" Admiral Harry Felt demanded of an Associated Press reporter.[29]

Meanwhile, Powell had learned that his assignment after Vietnam was Benning's Infantry Officers Advanced Course. A captain for only seven months, he was told not to be surprised if he received "an early promotion to major." On November 1, 1963, he was in Saigon, ready to be processed home. Driving to the Tan Son Nhut airport to ship his gear, he suddenly found himself in the midst of a coup. That day the Diem government was overthrown by a group of officers, led by General Duong Van Minh. The next day, November 2, Diem and his brother and chief adviser, Ngo Dinh Nhu, were murdered.

Powell left Vietnam shortly after. Waiting for an afternoon flight to Birmingham, sitting in an airport in Nashville and leafing through a magazine, he saw people clustered around a TV set. President Kennedy had been assassinated in Dallas. "Three weeks before, I had been in Vietnam on the day that that country's president had been assassinated," he wrote. "This afternoon, the President of my country had been murdered. And while I had been off fighting for my country, four little black girls had been killed by a bomb planted in Birmingham's 16th Street Baptist Church. I had returned home, it seemed, to a world turned upside down."[30]

Civil Rights and Powell in Georgia

In the spring of 1963, shortly after Michael Kevin Powell was born, Martin Luther King, Jr., brought the "Children's Crusade" to Alma Powell's hometown. In boycotts and mass marches, hundreds of protestors, including King, were arrested. "Freedom is never voluntarily given by the oppressor; it must be demanded by the oppressed," he said in the "Letter from a Birmingham Jail," responding to white ministers who urged him to be more patient.

That May, thousands of children, including six-year-olds, walked through the police dogs and fire hoses of Birmingham's police chief, Eugene "Bull" Connor, to protest Jim Crow. They were arrested and memorably captured by the world media. The Kennedy administration saw the jailing of children as a potential political disaster with international repercussions. Federal mediators were immediately sent to Birmingham to twist the arms of the city's white businessmen, who, already hurting from the black boycott, ultimately agreed to integrate downtown facilities and hire blacks in stores where they shopped.

On June 12, 1963, President Kennedy addressed the nation on radio and television. "A great change is at hand," he said, "and our . . . obligation is to make that revolution, that change, peaceful and constructive for all." Kennedy called the civil rights campaign a "moral crisis." That same night, thirty-eight-year-old World War II veteran Medgar Evers, Mississippi's first NAACP field secretary, was shot and killed outside his home by Byron De La Beckwith, a White Citizens Council member. (A few days earlier my mother had planned to stay with the Everses when she appeared at a Jackson NAACP rally organized by Evers, but he had apologetically explained that recent bomb damage made that impossible.) The day Evers was buried in Arlington National Cemetery, Kennedy sent a bill to Congress guaranteeing equal rights in public accommodations, and giving the U.S. Attorney General power to sue for enforcement of the Fourteenth and Fifteenth Amendments.

At the end of August 1963 Martin Luther King led the March on Washington and electrified the world with his "I Have a Dream" speech. Two weeks later, four Sunday school girls were killed in the bombing of Birmingham's Sixteenth Street Baptist Church. The deaths of Denise McNair, aged eleven, and Addie Mae Collins, Carole Robertson, and Cynthia Wesley, all aged fourteen, perhaps more than any other event of the period, caused American whites to side with their black fellow citizens. Public support for civil rights legislation soared.

Powell's parents had tried to persuade Alma to leave Birmingham, but she elected to stay in her own war zone, where her father sat up nights with a shotgun across his lap to defend his home. And she kept all of this out of her letters to her husband.

* * *

In the spring of 1964, back at Fort Benning and looking for a house to rent in Columbus, Georgia, Colin Powell stopped to buy a hamburger at a drive-in restaurant. The waitress asked if he was Puerto Rican or African. When Powell said, "I'm a Negro. I'm an American. And I'm an Army officer," she refused to serve him. Apologizing for company policy, she offered to serve him from the back. "I'm not that hungry," Powell snapped, and burned rubber leaving the restaurant. "I wasn't even trying to sit-in. All I wanted was a hamburger," he told *Parade* magazine in 1989.[31] After the passage of the 1964 Civil Rights Act, five months later, which forbade discrimination in public accommodations and employment, he returned to the restaurant and got a hamburger. And he and Alma settled into Benning.

(Powell would be strongly criticized for this incident in 1989 by Peter Bailey, a former president of the New York chapter of the National Association of Black Journalists. "An African-American officer who hadn't hesitated to fight Asians in Vietnam and who, from the tone of his speech, is ready to throw down with anyone who challenges the United States, was unwilling to fight against the racism practiced by a restaurant in Georgia. To have joined in the struggle against racist brutality in 1963 might have cost him advancement in the military. It was a price he was not prepared to pay."[32] In a 1991 interview in *The Guardian Weekly,* Powell addressed his reasons for fighting the civil rights battle on his own terms: "Because of my position and the things I was doing in my career, in my life, I didn't have a chance to participate in that struggle in an active way. I did it my own way, by my own example, and by helping other people who were coming along as best I could. But you better believe that I identified with that struggle, and continue to identify with that struggle."[33])

The conflict erupted in 1964 over voting rights, during the Mississippi Freedom Summer, and raged on into 1965. The voting campaign was the last southern battle, the last integrated battle, and the bloodiest battle of all. It began with the arrival in Mississippi of one thousand mostly white college students to register black voters and teach in "Freedom Schools." On the very first day of Freedom Summer, three voting rights workers—James Chaney, who was black, and Andrew Goodman and Michael Schwerner, both white—were kidnapped and murdered.

LBJ's Vietnam: The Question of U.S. Troops

In 1964, President Lyndon B. Johnson had no doubts about the gravity of the problem in Vietnam that was now his.

From the start, his policy was to stave off Communist takeover by means of increased U.S. military participation and a variety of covert programs, including harassment attacks on North Vietnam. He named General William C. Westmoreland (West Point, 1936—the class that "silenced" Benjamin O. Davis, Jr.) the new commander of MACV.

Johnson realized how misleading the optimism of Westmoreland's predecessors had been—and how the removal of Diem had created even more problems. In January, General Nguyen Khanh ousted the original coup makers with a coup of his own and other military officers jockeyed for position. Through the winter and spring the Vietcong continued to seize weapons and expand the areas they controlled. The prospect that Hanoi would take over South Vietnam grew, even if few Americans paid much attention.

On May 27, 1964, LBJ called his old friend Senator Richard Russell of Georgia to discuss the Vietnam problem. Here is an excerpt from their conversation:

RUSSELL: You'd look pretty good, I guess, going in there with all the troops and sending them all in there, but I tell you it'll be the most expensive venture this country ever went into.

LBJ: I've got a little old sergeant that works for me over at the house, and he's got six children and I just put him up as the United States Army, Air Force, and Navy every time I think about making this decision and think about sending that father of those six kids in there. And what the hell are we going to get out of his doing it? And it just makes the chills run up my back.[34]

During that year's election campaign, Johnson criticized the bellicosity of his Republican rival, Senator Barry Goldwater, even as he and his advisers increased U.S. involvement in covert operations. In public, Johnson said he was adamant that there be no big American war in Vietnam. "Some others are eager to enlarge the conflict," he said. "They call upon us to supply American boys to do the job that Asian boys should do. They ask us to take reckless actions which might risk the lives of millions and engulf much of Asia."[35] But in the end, that is just what he did.

* * *

By June 1964 Pentagon officers were drawing up plans to bomb North Vietnam, and in July South Vietnamese commandos began a program of covert harassment attacks along the coast of North Vietnam. Then, on August 2, 1964, North Vietnamese patrol boats attacked a U.S. Navy destroyer in the Gulf of Tonkin in the vicinity of the covert operations. Two days later a second incident was reported, but, as became clear over time, it probably never happened. Johnson seized on the opportunity, condemned (and exaggerated) the incidents, and did not mention the covert,

U.S.-backed operations against the North Vietnamese coast that had probably provoked them.

On August 5, three days after the first incident, Johnson ordered bombers to attack an oil depot and other installations in North Vietnam.

Johnson, a master politician, acted like an offended "dove" and managed to push the Gulf of Tonkin Resolution through Congress. The Resolution authorized him "to take all necessary measures" including the use of force to assist any member or protocol state of the Southeast Asia Collective Defense Treaty requesting assistance in defense of its freedom.

It was the equivalent of a declaration of war in that Johnson could now take whatever warlike actions he wanted without getting the approval of Congress. In a bitter irony, Congress passed the Civil Rights Act of 1964, the sweeping legislation that changed America profoundly (and allowed Colin Powell to buy his hamburger), at almost the same time. Once again, the war in Vietnam and the civil rights movement meshed, with events just a short time apart propelling each other forward.

In September, Johnson continued to reiterate his public opposition to enlarging the conflict, portraying Goldwater as someone whose Vietnam policy risked nuclear war. "We are not going north and we are not going south," he said. "We are going to continue to try to get them to save their own freedom with their own men, with our leadership and our officer direction, and such equipment as we can furnish them."[36]

After his landslide election, Johnson concentrated on planning for what he had always condemned as folly: putting in U.S. combat troops.

SELMA AND THE VOTING RIGHTS ACT

In February and March 1965 most headlines were about war and civil rights. Bombing was renewed in the North and Marines, the first U.S. combat troops, landed in Danang. Political turmoil engulfed Saigon. Malcolm X was assassinated in February in New York. And twenty-six-year-old Jimmy Lee Jackson of Selma, Alabama, was shot and killed by a white state trooper during a voting rights demonstration.

Early in 1965, Martin Luther King brought the voting rights battle to Selma. It was the movement's last great stand. On March 7, demonstrators began a march from Selma to Montgomery, the state capital, to confront Governor George Wallace. Brutally beaten back at the Edmund Pettus Bridge before they even left Selma, the marchers endured a bloody confrontation with mounted state troopers. Television told the Selma story, as bulletins interrupted network programs. "When that thing happened at the foot of the bridge, it looked like war," said Selma's mayor,

Joseph Smitherman, in a later interview. "That went out all over the country. And the people, the wrath of the nation came down on us."[37]

King now rallied prominent clergymen, black and white, by telegram for another march from Selma to Montgomery, on March 21. On March 9, the day King's telegrams went out, the Reverend James Reeb, a white Unitarian minister from Boston, was beaten to death on a Selma street. Reeb's death roused concerned clergy all over the country. The second Selma march became, like the March on Washington, an iconic civil rights event: under billowing American flags, a seemingly endless line of people, walking along the side of the Selma-to-Montgomery highway. This time the marchers, including many prominent clergy, were protected by the police as well as the media. They entered Montgomery on the twenty-fifth, singing "We Shall Overcome." Later that day, Viola Liuzzo, a white Catholic mother of five from Michigan who had volunteered to drive people back to Selma, was shot and killed by Klansmen as she transported marchers in her car.

Selma marked the end of nonviolence. As the battle for civil rights moved north, it became increasingly angry. Frustrated urban youths, imprisoned by poverty rather than Jim Crow laws, took their fury and frustration into the streets over four consecutive summers of ghetto rioting. The summer of 1965 saw the worst riot in decades, when thirty-four people were killed during several days of rioting in Watts, the black ghetto of Los Angeles. This, too, was broadcast into American living rooms.

Despite his Nobel Peace Prize (won in 1964) and his enormous influence, some blacks seemed to be distancing themselves from Martin Luther King. Turning their backs on King's Christian message, more and more were embracing Islam. In 1965 Cassius Clay, an Olympic gold medalist who was the world heavyweight boxing champion, converted to Islam and took the name Muhammad Ali. Rejecting both nonviolence and integration, the black northerner Stokely Carmichael, the new leader of the formerly southern-led and integrated SNCC, called for "Black Power"—just as angry northern black youth had begun to burn their own inner cities.

In August, under pressure from Johnson as well as public opinion, Congress passed the Voting Rights Act of 1965, dismantling the last legal basis of Jim Crow. "We shall overcome!" said President Johnson, when he signed the bill. He had been one of only three southern senators (the others were Albert Gore, Sr., and Estes Kefauver) who refused to sign the 1956 "Southern Manifesto" against school desegregation. "Freedom is not enough," he said in a 1965 speech at Howard University. "You will not take a person who for years has been hobbled by chains and liberate him, bring him up to the starting line of a race and then say you're free to compete with all the others, and still justly believe that you have been completely fair."

POWELL AT FORT BENNING

Colin Powell had completed the Infantry Officers Advanced Course in May 1965, ranking first among infantrymen but third in his two-hundred-man class, behind a tanker and an artilleryman. He then received what he called "a coveted assignment," to teach in the school from which he had just graduated. Powell called the instructors' course "*the* pivotal learning experience of my life." This time he graduated first, without question. "Instructors taught the officers who would be leading the troops in battle," he wrote, "not a mission the Army entrusted lightly." He was now promoted to major—in less than eight years, rather than the normal ten to eleven. To be an instructor in the Infantry Officers Advanced Course was "an impressive career credential," wrote Powell, and it was also militarily vital. "When I left Southeast Asia," he wrote, "it had still been a Vietnamese conflict involving some 16,000 American advisors. By the time I was asked to join the Infantry School faculty, the American involvement had begun to approach 300,000 troops, and the Army needed to produce more officers."[38]

And what an Amy it was—a model of integration and high morale, with little or no racial tensions. Participants in the first integrated-at-the-outset American war since the Revolution stood in stark contrast to civilian society in 1965.

JOHN CASH AND HAL MOORE

At Fort Benning, where Powell was in the class ahead of his, Captain John Cash—the same John Cash who, years later, would be asked to investigate the history of the 24th Infantry in Korea—heard the buzz that the war was getting bigger. Eager to get there, he went to the personnel officer, who called the Pentagon and granted Cash his wish. Informed that he had a war and a company command, Cash bought the biggest bottle of champagne he could find and took it home to his young, pregnant wife. He recalled nearly thirty years later that she was far less happy about the lucky "ticket punch" than he was.

John Cash, like Colin Powell and so many others, believed that there was no better place for a confident young black man in America than the military. Military morale was "tremendous," he said. And the racial atmosphere, crucial for morale as well as career advancement, was "sweetness and light." It was an Army in which, in many ways, race no longer seemed to matter, especially as combat intensified. "It was a *great* Army," Cash said.

Cash spent most of his first Vietnam tour, in 1965–1966, as a captain in Colonel Harold G. Moore's 1st Battalion of the 7th Cavalry. A dashing unit, redolent with history, it was Custer's old command. With cavalry panache and helicopter speed, the "First of the Seventh" was the best battalion in the brigade—with "quality leadership," Cash said. The best kind of commander, Colonel Moore, tall and taciturn, was a soldier's soldier who respected his troops with no eye to color. His motto, stated in his book, *We Were Soldiers Once . . . and Young,* written with Joseph L. Galloway, was "Loyalty flows down."[39] Cash said he would have given his life for Moore, who taught him "what it was to be a soldier."

Moore called his 1965 soldiers the "Kennedy class," meaning the class that heard Kennedy's call to ask what they could do for their country. The Army that was great in race relations and morale was also great in idealism and courage. This great Army and Vietnam collided in the battle of Ia Drang, the first large-scale confrontation of the war, and the subject of the Moore-Galloway book. "John F. Kennedy waited for us on a hill in Arlington National Cemetery," wrote Moore and Galloway, "and in time we came by the thousands to fill those slopes with our white marble markers and to ask on the murmur of the wind if that was truly the future he had envisioned for us."[40]

One of the few black company commanders in the division, Cash was as idealistic and eager as his brother officers from West Point, the Citadel, and college ROTC programs as varied as Rutgers, Duquesne, and Yale. He was also as much of a cold warrior. Not only was South Vietnam a "bulwark against Communism," he believed, but America was "going to kick ass." Cash had seen helicopters "blot out the sun." The United States "had everything," he told me. He fully believed that when the Vietcong saw Americans, they would "turn and run."

CALVIN BOUKNIGHT, DENNIS DEAL, GEORGE FORREST, AND MILTON OLIVE

Twenty-four-year-old Specialist 5 Calvin Bouknight, a black trooper from Washington, D.C., and twenty-three-year-old Second Lieutenant Dennis Deal, a white ROTC graduate of Duquesne University, were two more members of Moore's "Kennedy Class." As Deal told me much later, his first impression of Bouknight, quiet and frail, with a high-pitched voice and delicate mannerisms, had been that he was "a weak sister." As it turned out, the platoon was lucky to get him. A senior battalion medic, Bouknight had treated Colonel Moore's acute sinus problem back at base, but most of his duties revolved around infantry-style foot problems: checking blisters, abrasions, signs of infection. Sleeping without a mosquito net was an Article 15 offense and daily malaria pills were mandatory. But some men preferred malaria to combat. Bouknight handed out the "horse" pills and every Sunday, platoon leaders watched each man swallow his pill. At the end of one Sunday, Bouknight had an extra pill. It turned out that Deal had forgotten to take his. Bouknight gave Deal the worst "ass-chewing" of his life—proving then, as he would later in combat, that there was nothing weak about him.

Twenty-six-year-old Captain George Forrest, commander of Alpha Company, 1st Battalion of the 5th Cavalry, was another gung ho "Kennedy Class" officer. As a black officer, he told me, he was happy in the Army, because the Army judged him only by his ability to "do the job." The second of three brothers, Forrest was the son of a Chesapeake and Potomac Telephone line foreman. His father's greatest gift had been to teach him how to "interact," how to "establish rapport and trust" with people. "When the other people do not look like you," his father had said, "the onus is on you to prove your worth." ("Kids today say 'I don't have to prove myself to anybody,' " Forrest said. "This is not true.") Forrest learned from his father that "black men have to be twice as good, twice as smart, and three times as lucky." "Discipline, organization, and the fact that everything is written down," he said, "is why the military is such a successful endeavor."

An ROTC graduate of Morgan State University, Forrest was not the best student, having been sidetracked by football, basketball, and track. He graduated in 1960 and married a college classmate, choosing the military for job security. Joining Benning's basic officer course in January 1961, he moved on to Fort Ord and, later, to Germany with the 1st Infantry Division. His first efficiency report came from a white commanding officer from Mississippi: "This is an outstanding Negro officer," he wrote. Forrest was considered a "phenomenon," but he wanted to be seen as an officer, not a "Negro officer." In 1963, he was chosen for the "Old Guard," the presidential Honor Guard in Washington, based at Fort Meyer. He served at Kennedy's funeral.

Back at Benning, Forrest joined the test unit 11th Air Assault Division, the future 1st Cavalry (Airmobile). In August 1965, he went to Vietnam. There were no black brigade or battalion commanders in the 1st

Cavalry, but Forrest was one of several black combat company commanders, four of whom were Morgan State grads and fraternity brothers. A quarter of his company was black or Latino. Race was "not a problem" for Forrest.

* * *

On October 22, 1965, two weeks before his nineteenth birthday, PFC Milton L. Olive III was on a search-and-destroy mission with the 173rd Airborne Brigade when he chose to save his fellow soldiers by falling on a live grenade and absorbing its blast with his body. A product of Chicago parochial schools, Olive became the first black enlisted man to win the Medal of Honor in Vietnam.

IA DRANG: JOHN CASH, RON BARROW, AND SPECIALIST 5 CALVIN BOUKNIGHT

During 1965, American troop strength in Vietnam increased to 200,000. From the start, Westmoreland wanted a big-battle war and one of his favorite sites turned out to be the jungle of the border areas of the Central Highlands, where North Vietnamese regulars were stepping up infiltration. The trouble for American troops was that their North Vietnamese enemy wanted to fight there as well, and they usually chose the time and place. Indeed, the enemy set the tempo for the war all over Vietnam. "By the second decade after World War II, the dominant characteristics of the senior leadership of the American armed forces had become professional arrogance, lack of imagination, and moral and intellectual insensitivity," wrote Neil Sheehan in *A Bright Shining Lie.*[41] In picking Westmoreland, that senior leadership had picked one of their own—and one result was the battle of the Ia Drang valley in November 1965, a four-day meat grinder that did not have to happen, in which the blunders of senior leadership betrayed the valor of the officers and men who had to carry out their orders.

Westmoreland underestimated and belittled the enemy in part because they were so *folkloric,* with their rations of rice, their "Ho Chi Minh sandals," their "Red Diaries," and their whistles and bugles. According to Colonel Hal Moore, every soldier at Ia Drang was a hero and a patriot. (Even the enemy was "worthy." "We who killed them," he wrote of the North Vietnamese, "pray that their bones were recovered from that wild, desolate place where we left them, and taken home for decent and honorable burial.") Patriotism was "one kind of love" for Moore, but another "far more transcendent" came on the battlefield. "We discovered in that depressing, hellish place where death was our constant companion that we loved each other," he wrote (in a stirring and evocative book in which the only way to tell a soldier's race is through photographs). "We killed for each other, we died for each other. And in time we came to love each other as brothers."[42]

* * *

Landing Zone X-Ray, where the battle began, was about the size of a football field and ringed by brush. "Relatively flat and open as seen from above," as John Cash wrote later, the place "took on a different appearance when viewed by the infantrymen on the ground." (Cash heard the battle unfold over field radios, as 3rd Brigade assistant operations officer at the Catecka tea plantation headquarters of Colonel Thomas W. Brown. In 1970, the Army published his official history of the battle in *Seven Firefights in Vietnam.*)[43]

Down at rifleman level, the place was a baking nightmare of razor-sharp elephant grass as high as five feet, interspersed with equally high termite hills. Once the battalion had been inserted, troops would explore the nearby hills and mountains, looking for North Vietnamese regulars to kill. The trouble was, the North Vietnamese had their own plan. "They practically lit flares for us to come in there," John Paul Vann, the legendary American adviser in Vietnam and the subject of Neil Sheehan's *A Bright Shining Lie,* summed it up for David Halberstam.[44]

No sooner had Moore and some elements of his battalion landed than the NVA, who had thousands of troops massed near the edges of the LZ (Landing Zone) and in the nearby hills, pounced.

Lieutenant Dennis Deal's platoon was trapped in a hailstorm of bullets; anyone who stood up was shot at. It was Deal's first combat experience. There were wounded all around, some twelve to fifteen men, when Deal felt a foot stepping on his back. "Calvin was getting up," he recalled when we spoke some thirty years later. Calvin Bouknight, the 3rd Platoon medic, was the only man on his feet. If Deal had known what Bouknight was going to do, he would have ordered him to stop. Using his body to shield a wounded man, Bouknight knelt on one knee to provide first aid. It was the most "extraordinary heroism" Deal had ever witnessed. That morning, before the X-Ray landing, he had asked Bouknight to reconsider his refusal to carry a weapon. "I don't believe in killing," Bouknight had said. He was a conscientious objector, and refused to carry a weapon.

Deal thought that Bouknight knew he was going to die. Being "zapped" was inevitable, Deal said. "He knew the situation—he saw guys on their knees being shot down." Miraculously, the medic was able to patch up two or three men. Finally, less than five minutes after he began to treat the wounded, Bouknight was shot in the center of his spine. Deal saw that he was in "deep, deep trouble," probably "an instant paraplegic." At considerable personal risk, two soldiers (both white) ran up and carried Bouknight back for evacuation. Deal could see that Bouknight was in "utter agony," with tears streaming down his face. "You're gonna make it, Calvin," he told him.

The two soldiers who ran over to Bouknight were friends of Ron Barrow, a white trooper from Snow Hill, North Carolina, who had known Bouknight back at Benning: the medic had found Barrow a doctor when he was sick. When I spoke to him in 1996, Barrow recalled being pinned down in the elephant grass under heavy fire. He was watching people rise, and fall again as they were hit, when he heard his friend Todd call out, "Barrow, I believe Hines is dead—there's blood running out of his ears." Hines, a friend, had been shot between the eyes. "You stay down," Barrow had shouted to Todd. Then Barrow saw someone running to a man who was hit. It was Bouknight. He saw the medic work on one man, then jump up again. "Finally, I didn't see him anymore for a few moments," he said. Crawling through the grass, he found Bouknight lying on his back, conscious. "Barrow, I've been hit," he said. "Give me a shot." The men had each been issued one prepared morphine needle. Bouknight told Barrow where to hit him in the leg. It took about thirty seconds, and Barrow thought he had died. Then, Barrow's two buddies "sort of staggered" over to carry Bouknight back to cover. Barrow had only two weeks left in service. He managed to stay alive and make it home.

"Sarge, I didn't make it," were Bouknight's first, and last, words to the medical platoon sergeant at the aid station. "The Scriptures say that there is no greater love than to lay down your life for your friends," Moore wrote. "This is what Calvin Bouknight did in that fire-filled jungle."[45] Back at An Khe after the battle, the battalion constructed a chapel to honor Bouknight and William B. Mitchell, another platoon medic, also killed at X-Ray.

* * *

For John Cash, at 3rd Brigade field headquarters, Catecka tea plantation, the atmosphere was "terrible," like a "morgue." The casualty count noted on the blackboard kept getting higher. "There were guys crying, they had all come over on the boat together," he told me. Cash heard Moore on the radio asking for reinforcements. He estimated that he was up against five hundred to six hundred North Vietnamese, with more on the way.

But Moore's men fought alone the rest of the day, as volunteer helicopter crews came in regularly, under fire, to evacuate the dead and wounded. In an early evening lull, Joseph Galloway of United Press International became the first reporter on the scene. He had hitched a ride on a helicopter carrying reinforcements, ammunition, water, and medical supplies. Moore welcomed Galloway. He believed that the "American people had a right to know what their sons were doing in this war."[46]

The next morning's attack killed forty-two Americans and wounded nearly twenty more in hand-to-hand combat. Moore called in the code phrase "Broken Arrow" ("American unit in danger of being overrun") and thought of Custer. Now B-52s out of Guam dropped bombs and fighters delivered napalm into the hills above X-Ray, where the North Vietnamese were massing to attack. It was the first time that strategic bombers had flown in *tactical* support of American ground troops.

Two days after the battle started, it ebbed away, as the North Vietnamese seemed to pull back. Moore refused to leave X-Ray until battalion rear headquarters radioed him that all his men, dead or alive, "had been fully accounted for and evacuated." Moore and Galloway cried together. "Go tell America what these brave men did," Moore told the journalist; "tell them how their sons died."[47]

George Forrest at Ia Drang

As Moore and the other survivors prepared to return to base camp, replacements and reinforcements arrived, including Captain George Forrest's Alpha Company, 1st Battalion, 5th Cavalry. Shortly afterward, the fresh troops were ordered to walk from X-Ray to LZ Albany, a clearing about two miles away where they were supposed to be picked up by helicopters. Instead, they walked into the second and even bloodier phase of the Ia Drang battle, in which 155 Americans were killed and another 121 wounded in close, fierce combat. More Americans were killed on the misbegotten march toward Albany than in any other single confrontation in Vietnam.

"What the heck am I doing here?" was Captain Forrest's first thought on arriving at X-Ray to be briefed by Moore, who was "composed and under control, like lieutenant colonels are supposed to be." Forrest was nervous, he told me. He had been a company commander for three months. This was his first experience of combat, all part of the "absolute confusion" of his first days in Vietnam. Going into X-Ray under small-arms fire was something he would never forget. "There must have been about a thousand rotting bodies out there, starting at about twenty feet, surrounding the giant circle of foxholes."

Forrest felt well trained, but mentally unprepared. He would rely on his "god-blessed" NCOs, "older guys, leadership people." Forrest found that senior NCOs with combat experience had a "calming effect" on company commanders as well as troops. His platoon leaders were all "boys" out of Officer Candidate School and ROTC, but two of his top sergeants, both black, were veterans of Korea. Both would be killed on the way to Albany.

Like X-Ray, the disaster of Albany was the result of military blunders. At mid-morning on February 18, Lieutenant Colonel Robert McDade, commander of the operation, ordered all units to leave X-Ray and proceed to the Albany landing zone in a single, foolhardy column with no flanking protection (like Colin Powell's ARVN in the A Shau). Forrest's unit was at the rear. "I had no idea what guys in front were doing," he told me. He was worried about his men. It was unbearably hot; they had been up for two nights in a row and were not as alert as they should have been. Compounding the first blunder, McDade, in a move Forrest called "most unusual" and others called "disastrous," suddenly called all company leaders forward to the head of the column, to discuss the capture of two NVA "scouts." Having all the company leaders in one place was as bad as giving credence to so-called captured NVA scouts. Forrest, more than five hundred yards in the rear, moved forward through McDade's other units with his two radiomen. He did not like what he saw. "I saw guys sitting around smoking, drinking water," he said, "not in a position to respond."

The small-arms fire began almost as soon as Forrest reached the command post. The "scouts" were actually an NVA advance guard. Forrest saw the situation as a classic ambush, "just like the Indian wars."

When the first rounds came in, Forrest did not wait to be dismissed by McDade. He immediately started running back to his company. "George Forrest's run down that six-hundred-yard-long gauntlet of fire, miraculously unscathed," Moore and Galloway wrote, "and the forming of his men into a defensive perimeter, helped keep Alpha Company, 1st Battalion, 5th Cavalry from sharing the fate of Charlie, Delta, and Headquarters companies of the 2nd Battalion in the middle of the column." Specialist 4 James Young, in Forrest's company, told Moore and Galloway: "Our company commander, Captain Forrest, came running along our line. He was stopping and telling everybody where to go. He acted as though he was immune to the enemy fire. I don't know how he kept from getting hit."[48]

Back at Catecka, despite terrible X-Ray casualties, there was still a sense of victory and euphoria. John Cash, on duty as assistant operations officer, was writing a letter to his wife. Suddenly, the sergeant manning the radio said, "Sir, something is going on." He was hearing calls for fire support from all over. "We are surrounded!" he heard somebody say. At one point, McDade could be heard crying. Colonel Brown, 3rd Brigade commander, grabbed the radio and barked, "Get hold of yourself!" But everyone at Catecka was crying, Cash remembered. Good friends were being killed. "They knew the guys," he told me.

Thirty years later, Forrest claimed that the famous "run" (for which he was grateful to football) was not heroism so much as a compulsion to return to the safest place he knew—his unit. "It had nothing to do with goals and objectives, I just wanted to get back to people I knew," he said. He was under fire almost constantly. "My two outstanding young radio ops were both killed on the way back." Forrest had never seen killing up close before. But he saw men killed right and left on that run, when he expected at every moment that it would be "me too." The troops were being overrun in hand-to-hand combat with the North Vietnamese. And, Forrest knew, air support would be severely limited because the fighting was so close that it would be hard to hit the enemy without hitting friends.

Being last in the column turned out to be lucky. Forrest moved his group off the main trail and "circled the wagons." Everything outside was "bad guys." Unfortunately, some of the guys outside were Americans. The kill zone was right where Forrest's men were sitting—"immediate and quick." They soon lost radio contact with nearly everybody. Meanwhile the Air Force, as one soldier on the ground put it, seemed to be "dropping everything but the atom bomb."[49]

U.S. relief patrols and helicopters began arriving at daybreak. Out of 111 men in Forrest's company, seventeen were killed and forty-two or forty-three were wounded.

Back at base, John Cash was stunned by the extent of the casualties. The "Daily Bulletin's" kill figures had previously been in twos and threes. After X-Ray and Albany it was six pages long. It was then that Cash wrote to his wife that he was "not cut out to be infantry." But he got his company command a month later. Dennis Deal was in the company. Thirty years later, Deal said that Cash taught him "how to be an officer."

* * *

During the four days of fighting, 234 Americans were killed. Enemy dead were estimated at some two thousand and on that basis Westmoreland declared the battle a "victory." The slaughter confirmed his faith in attrition and the importance of "body count" as a measure of success in the war. "Westmoreland seemed to have no clue of the carnage," Forrest said in 1995. "They talked about 'heavy enemy casualties' and 'light to moderate friendly casualties.' Westmoreland and the Pentagon turned warriors into bounty hunters," he said. "You can't fight a war based on body count. You fight to gain territory or establish military objectives. There was no mission—no grand strategy. Stopping dominoes is not enough. MacArthur or Patton would have quit under the circumstances."

" 'Victory' is one of those words," wrote David Hackworth, the Korean hero who became a legendary combat leader in Vietnam, "as hard to define as 'light,' 'moderate,' and 'heavy,' three more of those words that MACV had chosen as the official words to describe friendly combat casualties to the press corps and the folks back home. These words would have pleased Humpty-Dumpty sitting on his wall in the world inside Alice's looking glass: 'When *I* use a word,' he'd said, 'it means just what I choose it to mean—neither more nor less.' "[50]

At Ia Drang, Hackworth wrote in his memoir, the enemy learned how to "hug the belt" of U.S. troops, "to come in as close as they could in order to neutralize the killing power of our artillery and air support." At Ia Drang, the North Vietnamese "learned how to fight us. And looked at in this way, even if the battle was an unprecedented victory for the Americans in our war of attrition, it was an equally unprecedented victory for our enemy in their protracted guerrilla war."[51]

A week after Ia Drang, Westmoreland asked for 41,500 more U.S. troops.[52]

* * *

Ward Just provided this description of a reconnaissance unit of the 101st Airborne Brigade in the Central Highlands in June 1966. They were "a rugged and motley lot," Just wrote, "unshaven, dirty, unlettered, mean, nervous. . . . Some . . . had the spirit of buccaneers, fugitives from a safe society. They liked the adventure and the weapons. . . . Half the platoon was Negro."[53] Blacks volunteered for elite combat units out of proportion to their numbers, especially in the early years of the war. Of the 47,193 combat deaths in Vietnam, blacks accounted for 12.1 percent.[54]

Major Colin Powell at Fort Benning and Leavenworth

Now a member of the Infantry School faculty, Major Colin Powell had a growing family. His daughter Linda was born in April, and Benning was turning out to be a good place for young black families. Powell calls this "one of the happiest" periods of his life. "For an infantryman Fort Benning . . . holds a sentimental place," he wrote. "The bachelor lieutenant sows his wild oats, gets married, makes captain, gets orders to the career course, and brings his wife to Fort Benning, often her first post." Racial relations at Benning were excellent (despite the fact that most of Powell's white peers were confused and disturbed by the civil rights movement). "We visited each other in our look-alike houses, small two- and three-bedroom ranches set on concrete slabs."

Although life at Benning was completely integrated, Powell developed new respect and esteem for black officers from the South.

> During my growing-up years, I had never felt uncomfortable around whites; I never considered myself less valuable. Different, yes; inferior, never. These Southern blacks had never been told anything else. Through the years that followed, as I watched them rise in the Army, my admiration grew. Most of them simply refused to carry the baggage that racists tried to pile on their backs. The day they put on the same uniform as everybody else, they began to consider themselves as good as anyone else. And, fortunately, they had joined the most democratic institution in America, where they could rise or fall on merit.[55]

In 1966, Captain Tony Mavroudis, a Greek American from Queens, who had been Powell's Pershing Rifle buddy, was killed in a firefight. A few months earlier Mavroudis had practically lived with the Powell family as a Benning bachelor while taking the advanced officer course. With his death, Powell told Alma to be prepared for his own Vietnam orders.

But Powell remained at Benning until the spring of 1967. Then he was assigned to Army Command and General Staff College at Fort Leavenworth, where students earn the military equivalent of a master's degree. Not all majors were chosen for Leavenworth; it was the track for future generals. At Leavenworth, Powell felt the "pulse of history." He was thrilled to walk in the footsteps of Custer, Sheridan, Eisenhower, and Patton. Leavenworth was where a battalion-level infantry officer experienced a "larger canvas of warfare." At the end of thirty-eight weeks he would be expected to know "how to move a division of twelve to fifteen thousand men by train or road, how to feed it, supply it, and, above all, fight it."[56]

* * *

While Powell was at Benning, more and more U.S. troops poured into Vietnam; casualties on both sides rose, with no end in sight. The enemy continued to set the tempo of the war, determining when and where to engage.

In 1966, Secretary of Defense McNamara instituted "Project 100,000," which he portrayed as part of President Johnson's Great Society program. McNamara's initiative drafted 100,000 men a year who otherwise would have been rejected, mainly for low grades on mental aptitude tests. McNamara asserted that his motive was to help disadvantaged young men. As Charles C. Moskos and John Sibley Butler report in their authoritative *All That We Can Be: Black Leadership and Racial Integration the Army Way,* "Whether wartime conscripts would have welcomed this kind of assistance is questionable, but the fact is that Project 100,000 quadrupled the number of entrants from the lowest mental aptitude test groups. Blacks accounted for a disproportionate 36 percent of the program's conscripts, while half were high school dropouts."[57] Moskos and Butler add, "A disproportionate number [of the Project 100,000 draftees] were assigned to the combat arms. Unexpectedly, Project 100,000 men did only marginally worse than other recruits in completing their tours, although they received noticeably fewer promotions."[58]

Meanwhile, military operations uprooted millions of Vietnamese civilians. Some Americans were taking count of that toll. Besides creating a generation of refugees, American weapons were killing and wounding uncounted Vietnamese children. "I have witnessed modern war in nine countries, but I have never seen a war like the one in South Vietnam," wrote correspondent Martha Gellhorn.[59] With bombs and napalm falling indiscriminately, civilian casualties often outweighed the military. Hundreds of children were killed monthly, and some two thousand a month were orphaned. The correspondent Jonathan Schell heard American officers sing a song that was a macabre comment on civilian casualties.

Bomb the schools and churches.
Bomb the rice fields, too.
Show the children in the courtyards
What napalm can do.[60]

American officials constantly reported progress and tried to dress up the puppets who ran the Saigon government as national leaders. Most notable was the new premier, Nguyen Cao Ky, a flamboyant pilot famous for his flashy flight suits and his glamorous wife.

At the same time LBJ denounced critics of the war, calling them "callous or timid . . . blind to experience and deaf to hope." He spoke of "nervous Nellies" who broke "under the strain" and turned on "their leaders, their country, and their own fighting men." Vietnam was inspiring the largest outpourings of public antiwar feeling in American history. "The war began as a struggle for the soul of Vietnam: will it end as a struggle for the soul of America?" asked Arthur M. Schlesinger, Jr., in 1966.[61]

COLONEL FRED CHERRY, P.O.W.

Colonel Fred V. Cherry, one of eight children of a Virginia truck farmer, whose boyhood hero had been the Tuskegee Airman Lucky Lester, graduated in 1951 from Virginia Union College, where he majored in biology. Just before graduating, Cherry took a battery of flight school tests at Langley Air Force Base. He was the only black in a group of twenty, and he received the highest overall score. He wanted to be a Navy pilot but the obvious racism of Navy recruiters turned him off. Joining the Air Force instead, he flew thirty-five missions in Korea, deep behind enemy lines, in F-89G fighter-bombers.

For several months in 1965, as a fighter pilot in the 35th Tactical Fighter Squadron, based in Thailand, he flew bombing missions over North Vietnam. In October 1965, he was shot down and became the forty-third American pilot captured in the North—and the first black. He was taken to Hoa Lo Prison, the "Hanoi Hilton." He told his story to Wallace Terry, a *Time* correspondent, who reported on the black experience in Vietnam. Cherry's story was one of the many oral histories collected in his seminal book, *Bloods.*

Cherry's cell in the Hanoi Hilton had "the biggest rats you ever saw in your life." Every morning he was taken to the place Americans called Heartbreak, a torture chamber with built-in leg irons. Cherry was soon moved to Cu Loc Prison outside Hanoi (known as the Zoo), where he got a cellmate: Lieutenant Porter Halyburton, a white Navy pilot from Tennessee shot down five days before him. They mistrusted each other instantly. Cherry thought that Halyburton was a French spy working for the Communists and Halyburton had a problem believing that Cherry was a flier. He had learned in the Navy that "blacks couldn't fly because they had a depth-perception problem." At first they "played games." Halyburton changed the name of his ship; Cherry told Halyburton no more than he told the Vietnamese. But eventually they began to trust each other.

In February 1966, four months after becoming a prisoner of war, Cherry, whose shoulder was wounded when he was captured, underwent surgery. He was put into a torso cast to his hip, with no medication and no treatment. The incisions quickly got infected. He fell in and out of consciousness, and was totally immobile. "Hally was feeding me," he told Wallace Terry. "Hally would take me to the wash area, hold me up against the wall while he manipulated his towel, wet it, soap it, and wash my whole body. . . . I would tell him when I had to go to the bucket." Delirious and delusional, Cherry imagined that "little men" were working on his chest, "fixing his air conditioning."[62]

In March he went to the hospital to have the cast taken off. His weight was down from 135 to 80 pounds. The other Americans thought they would never see him alive again. "When they took the cast off, a lot of skin came off with it. Then they washed me down with gasoline out of a beer bottle . . . when I came to, they were slapping my arteries. Then they gave me a blood transfusion, fed me intravenously, and sent my butt right back to Hally." He had two more operations, one in April, from which he got a bad infection, and another in July, on a night when all the other Americans were being marched through the streets of Hanoi. "This time there was no anesthetic," he said. "They just took a scalpel and cut away the dead flesh, scraping at the infection on the bones. . . . It was the worst straight pain I had yet known. They had my face covered with a sheet. And they kept raising it to see if I'm going to beg for mercy, going to scream. And each time they look down at me, I would look at them and smile."[63]

When Cherry got back to his cell, blood was running down to his feet. Halyburton put him in his bunk, and they both cried. Four days later, Halyburton was removed from the cell and they wept again. "I never hated to lose anybody so much in my entire life. . . . He was responsible for my life."

Cherry was now tortured twice a day. He began to cough up great clots of blood. He had yet another operation—then was sent back to camp and kept in solitary for fifty-three weeks. The interrogators wanted tapes and written statements denouncing the war and the U.S. government, and telling young GIs, especially blacks, that they should not be fighting an American imperialist war. Cherry's four- and five-hour daily interrogations were led by a good guy–bad guy team. The good guy, called Stag ("Sharper Than the Average Gook"), had read *Raisin in the Sun* and *Invisible Man,* and he knew more about Malcolm X and Stokely Carmichael than Cherry did. The Vietnamese could not understand why a "colored man" was not on the side of other "colored." "If they are going to kill me, they are going to have to kill me," he thought. "I'm just not going to denounce my government or shame my people." Meanwhile, Cherry's wound did not heal and he was hemorrhaging daily. There was another operation, to remove the infected stitches and clean up the wound. This was followed by more infection, until he was finally given antibiotics.

No matter how "rough the tortures" or "how sick" he became, Cherry never wanted to "quit" or take his own life. "I would just pray to the Supreme Being each morning for the best mind to get through the interrogations, and then give thanks each night for makin' it through the day." Prisoners tapped the letter "C" for "church" from wall to wall through the camp, and everyone stopped for silent prayer.

When the men were allowed to get together, they devised a movie committee. "Bradley Smith, a Navy guy, could give you the best movie reviews you could ever hope for in your life . . . last almost as long as the movie. You could just close your eyes and see it." Other prisoners did the same thing with horse races and sex. Cherry had "fantasy affairs with the most beautiful women in the world." He raced cars, flew in air-to-air combat, and calculated bomb releases. And he re-created picnics with his children.[64]

GEORGE BRUMMELL: "I HAD TO PROVE MYSELF"

George Brummell was born in 1944 and was raised by his grandmother in Federalsburg, Maryland, along with a brother who was nine years older. He said he was a "mischievous" youth who never got in any serious trouble. At seventeen, as a senior in high school, the husband of an older woman with whom he was involved threatened to kill him. That was one good reason to join the Army. But he had another as well. He had grown up without any adult male presence in the house and, he said, "I had to prove myself, to show that I could do it."

Brummell signed up in February 1962 and after basic training went to Korea. In 1963, he spent about ninety days on temporary duty in Germany and, back in the United States, was assigned to Fort Hood, in Killeen, Texas. "We always said that Killeen means 'Kill each and every nigger,' " Brummell remembered. "Even though you're in uniform, fighting for and representing the United States, you still had to be bothered by this stuff," he said, referring to the off-base segregation and racial hostility. He and a buddy drove from Killeen to Savannah during a short leave. Somewhere in Mississippi, in the middle of the night, they pulled up at a small store to buy a Coke and some crackers. Brummell, who had been driving in his socks, encountered three white men sitting around a wood-burning stove. "Hey, nigger soldier boy, didn't John F. Kennedy buy you no boots?" one of them asked.

Brummell reenlisted in February 1964; then he went to Fort Devens, and—like Colin Powell—met and married his wife there. His next assignment, in 1965, was Hawaii, where he excelled at the NCO Academy, the last stop before Vietnam. Brummell was one of the youngest E5s (buck sergeant) in the Army and a thoroughly "strac," or spectacularly squared-away, soldier.

"I did pretty well in the military," Brummell said.

Whenever he went to a new assignment, Brummell said, "I would always try to find some really sharp soldier—I'd look around—and I would use that person as a role model." In Hawaii, that role model was a white sergeant from West Virginia with more time in uniform than Brummell (and a stint in Vietnam) named Theodore Belcher. "I could not let that white boy outsoldier me," Brummell said. "We used to hang out in Hawaii. We were good friends, best buddies."

In Vietnam, Brummell and Belcher worked closely again. "We were probably the sharpest guys in the outfit," Brummell recalled. Aside from one incident with a white platoon sergeant who called him "nigger," Brummell, like most in the 1965 Army, found the racial climate generally healthy. Belcher was one of several white friends.

They saw plenty of combat and also learned an important fact of Vietnam life. Base camps could be as dangerous as the field. Brummell was sure he heard digging sounds under U.S. positions in Cu Chi, but superior officers ignored his reports. The Cu Chi tunnels, an elaborate underground maze of hiding places, combat hospitals, and escape passages for the enemy, became one of postwar Vietnam's leading tourist attractions.

In June 1966, an antitank mine exploded near Brummell, killing the company commander and three GIs and wreaking havoc on Brummell. The blast blew off his clothes, and various wounds left him covered with blood. "From the time I was hit, I was conscious throughout the whole ordeal," Brummell said. "No one knew who the hell this person—me—was. It's amazing. I'd seen it in combat situations. You can be right next to somebody and an explosion goes off and you say, 'Now who the hell was that?' My face was messed up. I was numb."

The medic was at his side immediately. Brummell could not speak; he felt bubbles in his mouth. The medic kept working on him as a helicopter approached. Brummell felt red ants on his body.

"God bless helicopters," Brummell said. "God bless morphine."

Brummell moved through a series of hospitals, his face, arms, and much of his body swathed in bandages. Back in the United States, he heard two doctors talking about him, and only then realized the extent of his wounds. "They mentioned 'this blind man.' They were talking about me," he said. He had thought his eyes were only bandaged. "Then depression set in."

He spent five months in the hospital at Fort Sam Houston, his wife there with him. "I cannot downplay the importance of support," he said. He started mobility training and occupational therapy. His wife's steadfastness was "part of the incentive to go to school, instead of just sitting at home drawing a check. I wanted to do something where the kids could see me as a positive role model. Also, I'm adventurous and I love challenges." Brummell and his wife had three children and were divorced in 1981.

In 1980, after seven and a half years of study, Brummell earned a bachelor's degree in social work from the University of Akron. He started work on a master's at Case Western but in 1984 dropped his studies and took a job with the Blinded Veterans Association, a nonprofit veterans service organization. "People were not breaking their necks to hire blind, black people," Brummell said as he recalled his decision. "It was an opportunity, and I took advanatage of it. I've been doing it ever since, having a ball." In due course, Brummell became national field service director of the BVA, a demanding job involving extensive travel from his office in Washington.

"I try to make blindness work for me in a positive way," he said. "I could not have done as good a job as a sighted person as I am doing as a blind person. I probably would have been distracted in other ways." Blindness, he said, had become a "positive experience." Brummell remarried in 1995.

One day when Brummell was in West Virginia on veterans' affairs business he decided to track down Belcher, his "best buddy" from his days in uniform. "I thought you were dead," said Belcher, who had not seen Brummell since he was being lifted aboard the medical evacuation helicopter. Belcher himself served two tours in Vietnam, and raised a family. The two old buddies—"Kennedy soldiers," as Hal Moore called the soldiers of their era—got together, drank beer, and talked for four days. And that was just the beginning of their reunion. "Every time we get together now—he and his wonderful family—and I do it whenever I can, it's a family affair. We love each other," Brummell said.

DAVID PARKS: "IF THIS IS WHAT WE'RE FIGHTING . . ."

In 1966, in the midst of growing antiwar protests and the turmoil of the civil rights movement, David Parks, sheltered by a famous father and a middle-class life, joined the Army and volunteered to go to Vietnam. His father, the celebrated photographer Gordon Parks, told him that "he didn't want any heroes in the family." But when it was clear that David's mind was made up, he advised him to keep a journal. Parks thought going to war was a "rite of passage," and he believed in his country's mission.

Parks arrived in January 1967 and went to the field as a radio operator in E Company, 1st Battalion, Mechanized Infantry. "Seen very little action so far," he wrote in his journal on January 11, 1967. "Captured a couple of VC. They were children, not more than fifteen or sixteen years old, short and skinny. If this is what we're fighting, I wonder why the war is taking so long."[65]

"The FO's [forward observer's] job is one of the hairiest in a mortar platoon," Parks wrote on January 31, 1967. "He's on more patrols because an FO is required to be with the patrolling squad at all times. . . . The odds are against him. Sgt. Paulson hand-picks the men for this job. So far he's fingered only Negroes and Puerto Ricans. I think he's trying to tell us something." Racism abounded in a variety of forms—toward blacks, toward Latinos, and above all, toward the Vietnamese. "This is a real poor country," wrote Parks. "Everywhere you go people are on their knees begging. Some of the Whiteys dig this sort of thing and make a game of it. . . . Someone throws a piece of bread on the road. The kids go for it like a pack of wolves. Often one of them gets hit by a track [armored vehicle] or several get hurt in the scramble. It's a bad scene. You never see a soul [a black man] do anything like that."[66]

Within two months, Parks found himself becoming hardened. "I think I'm getting a little too casual about death. This morning we were out on patrol with an ARVN unit when we spotted a guy . . . sitting inside the tree line. The ARVN sergeant suspected he was a VC and he tries to question him, but the guy tried to get away. The ARVN just gunned him down with his carbine; I don't even remember that he told him to halt." When he found himself eating a can of C Rations a few minutes after seeing the man's "guts spilling into the mud," Parks began to worry.[67] On March 11, a week after his twenty-third birthday, a mine went off, driving shrapnel into his forehead and getting him a Purple Heart and dizzy spells for the rest of his time in Vietnam. Within a week he was back with his company.

"It seems the villagers complained about our company's looting and burning their homes," he wrote in early April. "They are right to a great extent. The dead bodies . . . didn't help us any." Men in his company had tied five dead Vietnamese to the back of their armored vehicles "in revenge for our guys who were killed and castrated." Most of the men, including Parks, "resented what a few others have done to us," but "we are part of the company." A general from headquarters choppered in to call them "a pack of thieves and untrained dogs," telling their captain that if he could not exercise more control over his men he would be demoted. Parks's unit was ordered out of the area, but this brought no changes. Two months later, when a black soldier shot a civilian in front of his three children, his commanding officer told the soldier not to worry, that he was just doing his job. Parks could not stop thinking about the children.

"They'll hate us for the rest of their lives," he wrote. "And who can blame them?"[68]

Parks went home in September, eighty days early because of his wound, a changed young man. "When I came into the army I had no questions, but I am leaving with some," he wrote. "Back in basic they told us over and over again that these people needed help . . . that we had promised them our help, and that we couldn't go back on them. Well, there were times when it seemed we were doing them more harm than good."[69]

Parks began photographing weekend antiwar protests in New York and Washington—classwork at the Rochester Institute of Technology, where he studied film and photography. "I was shaken by the hate slogans that were shouted at the soldiers and police. . . . I strongly felt that the men still fighting in Vietnam deserved our full support. . . . I had fought and killed many Vietcong; I didn't allow myself to feel as though I were an outright murderer. . . . I had fought for my country and was in no way ashamed of it." Parks believed that the GI suffered "double and irreconcilable alienation." Americans made Parks and other veterans feel guilty for the killing they had done on their behalf. Parks blamed himself for "letting the American government use him for material gains."[70]

In Washington, at the Pentagon, Parks saw soldiers (most of them just back from Vietnam) being bombarded with bottles and rocks. Some had tears in their eyes; several had laid down their arms. Others stood their ground—and one, without orders, tossed a tear gas grenade into the crowd. "The crowd scattered briefly, regrouped and surged forward," Parks wrote. "I was carried forward with such force that I was unable to use my camera. I could only watch as the soldiers were overrun, and I found the experience more devastating than any I had known in Vietnam." In Vietnam, Parks had known the enemy. In Washington he found the enemy hard to define. "When the crowd reached the steps of the Pentagon, the protesters seemed to go berserk. They thrust their arms upward and screamed obscenities as though they had conquered the enemy. The soldiers didn't retaliate because they were tired, sick and broken. I couldn't take pictures. It was impossible to do anything." Parks was deeply depressed. "I hated what I had seen and I hated America for it."[71]

GI Diary, David Parks's Vietnam journal, was published in 1968. In a postscript to the reprint, published in 1983, Parks describes the America he came home to. "There were still a few hawks who favored the war, and my book did not present a favorable view of our position in Vietnam. On the other hand, the doves had problems with my favorable attitude toward an army that I felt had made a better man of me." One 1968 critic complained that Parks never "lets you forget his color" and that the book "reeks" with sensitivity on the subject. "While serving in Vietnam, I had problems with whites," Parks wrote in 1983, "but the problems didn't compare with the racism I encountered when I returned to America. Perhaps the most positive thing that came out of the war was the comradeship that developed between black and white combat soldiers. . . . We needed each other. 'Charlie' was the enemy, and olive green was the only color that mattered."[72]

* * *

In 1967, President Johnson asked Congress to pass a bill banning discrimination in the sale and rental of housing. At the same time, he created the National Advisory Commission on Civil Disorders, under Governor Otto Kerner of Illinois. He also named Thurgood Marshall as the first black justice of the U.S. Supreme Court. But the summer of 1967 saw the frightening face of Black Power. In July, H. Rap Brown urged blacks in Washington, D.C., to "get you some guns." "The white man is your enemy," he said. "You got to destroy your enemy."[73]

Martin Luther King had been speaking out against the war since 1965. In April 1967 he made it clear, in a speech at Riverside Church in New York City, that he opposed the war not just because of the disparity in black and white draft statistics and the fact that the war was bankrupting poverty programs. King said he feared for "the health of our land" and for the American soul—lest it become "totally poisoned" by the war.

"Somehow this madness must cease," he said. "We must stop now. I speak as a child of God and brother to the suffering poor of Vietnam. I speak for the poor of America who are paying the double price of smashed hopes at home and death and corruption in Vietnam."[74]

Another American icon, Muhammad Ali, refused to be inducted into the Army that year. The World Boxing Association stripped him of his championship and barred him from fighting in the United States for four years. Nineteen sixty-seven saw more and more demonstrations against the war, while fighting intensified throughout Vietnam.

U.S. troop levels neared the 500,000 mark and the war appeared to be stalemated. Late in the year, there were highly publicized and very bloody pitched battles in the highlands and along the Laotian border; U.S. infantry units and Marines were engaged exactly where their enemy wanted to fight.

* * *

On October 31, 1967, at Ap Dong, thirty-year-old Captain Riley Leroy Pitts of the 25th Infantry Division was pinned down in the jungle under heavy fire. Pitts, an ROTC graduate of Wichita State University, displayed nearly superhuman indifference to incoming fire; at one moment in the firefight he grabbed an enemy hand grenade and threw it back—and when it bounced back toward U.S. troops, he fell on it. It failed to explode. Eventually, a rocket-propelled grenade hit him, killing him instantly. He became the first black officer in American history to win a Medal of Honor.

During 1967, 9,300 Americans were killed in Vietnam. Nevertheless, according to Westmoreland the prognosis was excellent. In November, in Washington, he proclaimed "the enemy's hopes are bankrupt." The general told Congress and the press in emphatic terms that the United States on the threshold of 1968 was becoming more and more successful all the time.[75]

1968

"The morning of February 1, 1968, I came out of the bedroom, put on the coffeepot and turned on the TV news," wrote Colin Powell, still at Leavenworth. "I was stunned. There on the screen were American GIs fighting on the grounds of the U.S. embassy and ARVN forces battling before the Presidential Palace in the heart of Saigon." It was the Tet offensive: the Vietcong and the NVA had launched coordinated attacks against Saigon, Danang, Hué, Pleiku, Kontum, Can Tho, and provincial and district capitals the length and breadth of South Vietnam.

It was a "punch in the gut" for America, Powell wrote, but "in cold military terms" a massive defeat for the VC and the North Vietnamese, who were driven out of every town they struck with enormous losses. "It did not matter how many of the enemy we killed," Powell wrote. "The North simply started sending in its regular army units to counter the losses."[76]

The Tet offensive shattered the credibility of Johnson and Westmoreland, and more bad news followed. The siege of the Khe Sanh Marine base, which had begun in January, grew very grim. The press raised the specter of Dienbienphu and there was talk of nuclear weapons. Indeed, even before the siege began, Westmoreland had ordered a study of the feasibility of using nuclear weapons in the area, but Washington officials ordered him to stop.[77]

Popular support for LBJ's policies ebbed as the fighting became more and more savage. On March 16, Robert F. Kennedy announced his candidacy for the presidency, opposing Johnson and also Senator Eugene McCarthy, whose popularity among the young was surging. That same day in Vietnam, U.S. troops of the Americal Division massacred hundreds of Vietnamese civilians at My Lai in Quang Ngai province, killing until they were interrupted by a U.S. helicopter crew who attempted to save some of the wounded Vietnamese children. The incident became known to the general public in the autumn of 1969.

Antiwar demonstrations spread across the country. On March 31, Johnson stunned the world by announcing that he would not seek reelection in November. He also announced a partial bombing halt and said he would seek peace talks, and, presumably, a negotiated end to the war. On April 4, Martin Luther King was assassinated in Memphis and 125 American cities instantly erupted in flaming violence.

"The death of Martin Luther King intruded on the war in a way that no other outside event had ever done," wrote Michael Herr in his stunning and endlessly resonant Vietnam memoir, *Dispatches*. "In the days that followed, there were a number of small, scattered riots, one or two stabbings, all of it denied officially." Herr almost lost a friend: a black staff sergeant from Alabama with whom he had dinner the night before King was killed refused to speak to him. The sergeant went to the press tent later and told him that "it shouldn't happen that way." Herr and the sergeant went outside to share a bottle of scotch. The sergeant was in a state of near despair. "Even before King's murder he had seen what this might someday mean," Herr wrote. He wondered if he would have to turn his guns on his own people. "That was it," Herr continued. "There was hardly a black NCO anywhere who wasn't having to deal with that." The man started to cry. "Oh, man," he said to Herr. "This war gets old."[78]

On June 6, after winning the California Democratic primary, Robert Kennedy died from an assassin's bullet. Visibly changing in the years between 1963 and 1968, the former counsel for Senator McCarthy had become a committed liberal reformer who also appealed to blue-collar conservatives, creating, from this duality, the most populist political coalition since FDR. For a few months in 1968, fusing opposition to the war with support for civil rights, Robert Kennedy was the focus of whatever hope remained for integration and peace. Many believed that he would heal America and end the war. The crowd that lined the tracks, saluting, holding flags and babies, and waving hands and handkerchiefs at the passing of Kennedy's funeral train was entirely integrated and largely blue-collar.

The Democratic National Convention in Chicago was turned into a bloody spectacle in which Chicago police violently assaulted antiwar demonstrators and Vice President Hubert Humphrey defeated Eugene McCarthy.

By the fall of 1968, almost no one wanted war anymore. Richard Nixon campaigned for president on a "secret" (and nonexistent) plan to end the war and the "southern strategy," which involved exploiting white backlash against the civil rights movement. In a campaign film, Nixon appealed to "forgotten Americans." Joe McGinniss, author of *The Selling of the President,* watched the film being made. "They provide most of the soldiers who died to keep us free," Nixon said, as a close-up photo of a young black soldier in Vietnam appeared on the screen. Nixon's adviser Leonard Garment shook his head at an early viewing. "We can't show a Negro just as RN's saying 'most of the soldiers who died to keep us free,' " he said. "That's been one of their big claims all along—that the draft is unfair to them—and this could be interpreted in a way that would make us appear to be taking their side." The black soldier was replaced with a white one.[79]

POWELL AND MY LAI

At Leavenworth during the Tet offensive and the murder of Martin Luther King, Major Colin Powell must have felt far from both war fronts. He and his fellow black officers understood the riots and the bitterness of black GIs, but they were "professionals first," he wrote, with a duty to "oath" and "country." They regarded black radicals with uneasiness. "We were not eager to see the country burned down," Powell wrote. "We were doing too well in it."[80]

In July 1968, Powell left Fort Leavenworth Army Command and General Staff College to return to Vietnam as executive officer, 3rd Battalion, 1st Infantry, 11th Infantry Brigade, Americal Division, in Quang Ngai province.

It had been five years since Powell had been in Vietnam, but the "end was nowhere in sight," he wrote. "Deterioration of discipline and morale was obvious." The burning of houses and crops was only part of the violent norm. Nguyen Cao Ky, the former air marshal who was now vice president of South Vietnam, had stated that his only hero was Hitler. "This was the man for whose regime three, four, even five hundred Americans were dying every week in 1968," Powell wrote. Both blacks and whites increasingly resented the authority that kept them in Vietnam for a "dangerous and unclear" purpose.

In the summer of 1968, Powell moved his cot every night, partly to thwart the Vietcong, partly to avoid "attacks on authority from within the battalion itself." "Fragging" (the killing of officers by fragmentation grenade) had entered the Vietnam lexicon. From a career point of view, it appeared that Colin Powell was in the wrong division. The Americal was widely considered to be the worst U.S. division in Vietnam, in terms of leadership and performance.[81]

Powell got a lucky break shortly after he got to Vietnam, when *Army Times* published a story about his Leavenworth graduating class and it was read by the Americal commander, Major General Charles M. Gettys. "I've got the number two Leavenworth graduate in my division and he's stuck out in the boonies as a battalion exec?" he said. "Bring him up here. I want him as my plans officer." The job of plans officer, or "G-3," usually went to a lieutenant colonel; Powell would be the only G-3 in Vietnam who was a major. Overnight, he went from "looking after eight hundred men" to "planning warfare for nearly eighteen thousand troops, artillery units, aviation battalions, and a fleet of 450 helicopters." The story in *Army Times* was "luck," Powell later told Carl Rowan. "But finishing No. 2 at Leavenworth was hard work. Hard work generates good luck—and opportunities."[82]

Powell was lucky again when, still the only major among lieutenant colonels, he was chosen to brief Westmoreland's successor, Creighton Abrams, a man widely seen inside and out of the Army as far more capable and candid than his predecessor. During World War II Abrams was a tank commander who fought through German lines to relieve the 101st Airborne at Bastogne in the Battle of the Bulge. Briefing was (and is) an art form in the Army and Powell was a master. He used no notes, having memorized an extraordinary amount of information. Afterward, Abrams asked Gettys, "Who's that young major?"

In November 1968, a helicopter carrying Powell and several others crashed in the jungle. "When we crashed I didn't think about anything but leaving," he said in a later interview. "I hit the belt, jumped, and ran a few feet. Then I turned around and realized the helicopter was starting to smoke while the men were still in there." Ignoring his own fear that the gas tank might explode, he pulled several people—including his barely conscious division commander, the chief of staff, and the pilot—from the smoldering craft. He made four trips back and forth. "I wasn't alone," he said. "Others were doing it. It wasn't anything too heroic."[83] He was awarded the Soldier's Medal.

* * *

The Americal's area of operation included populated districts where U.S. firepower caused enormous numbers of civilian casualties throughout the war. In one episode, on March 16, 1968, a unit of the 11th Brigade reported a body count of 128 enemy dead on the Batangan Peninsula, without capture of any weapons. Westmoreland's command awarded the unit a special commendation for the large "body count." In fact, the dead were all civilians and residents of My Lai.

In mid-March 1969, while he was at the Chu Lai division headquarters, Powell received a visit from the MACV inspector general's office regarding division operational journals for March 1968. He was asked to look for "an unusual number of enemy killed on any day."[84] Powell was mystified, but sensed that the investigator already knew what he would find. It turned out that the investigator, prompted by evidence gathered by a GI named Ronald Ridenhour, was probing reports that the commendation-winning action had in fact been a massacre of innocent civilians, including many old people and children. Powell maintained that this was the first he had heard of such an event.

But did Powell know about My Lai before mid-March of 1969? Charles Lane, a journalist, tracked Powell's actions in regard to what happened at My Lai and in its aftermath. The Army's credo, wrote Lane, was "Duty, Honor, Country." But its "unstated code" was "Don't rock the boat." Lane accused Powell of being one of the "nonrockers"—of choosing expediency over ethics.

In April 1995, in an article in *The New Republic* entitled "The Legend of Colin Powell: Anatomy of an Establishment Career," Lane described the My Lai massacre as "the moral and professional nadir of the post–World War II U.S. Army."[85] Lane claimed that Powell knew about My Lai as early as November 1968, when Specialist 4 Tom Glen of the 11th Infantry Brigade—already known to grunts as the Butcher's Brigade—revealed his concerns in a letter to Creighton Abrams. Glen did not name My Lai, although he had heard accounts of the episode through GI talk; he wrote that murder and torture in general were common and seemingly "sanctioned." By December 9, 1968, Lane claimed, the letter had "worked its way through Army channels" to Major Powell, who was ordered to check the letter out and report within three days with a suggested reply. According to Lane, Powell did not question Glen but instead relied on Glen's commander, who stated falsely (according to Glen) that Glen was a "rear-guard" type who could not have witnessed the capture and torture of enemy prisoners. Powell's December 13 memo thus affirmed that Glen's charges were false—excepting, perhaps, for "isolated instances"—and that abuses were punished rather than tolerated. The memo criticized Glen: he should have come forward earlier and he should have included specifics on which to base an inquiry. "If Powell had been morally engaged by Glen's letter and taken it upon himself to seek and report the truth, the trail might have led all the way to My Lai," wrote Lane.

While attacking Powell, Lane also said that "most officers would have written just what Powell did; he may even sincerely have believed it." Powell, whose "only cause in life" was the Army, is ultimately excused for being a soldier. "Of course there was a war on, and as deputy G-3 in the largest division in the Army, Powell had much else on his mind," Lane wrote. "He had no formal duty or authority to get to the bottom of the matter." By military lights, Powell had followed standard operating procedure: protect the system at all costs. Not culpable for anything that happened, he had performed in a predictable bureaucratic fashion. The Army did not investigate My Lai until it could not ignore a detailed letter about the massacre, written by the ex-grunt Ridenhour to government officials, including his congressman, Morris Udall of Arizona, who asked for an investigation. Ridenhour, like Glen, had not been at My Lai; his letter was based on information from eyewitnesses. In November 1969, Lieutenant William Calley, under whose orders the massacre was carried out, was formally charged with mass murder. The 128-victim count was only partial; there were actually 347 victims. A court-martial found Calley guilty and sentenced him to life in prison. President Richard Nixon reduced the sentence to three years of house arrest.

Black GIs, like their white counterparts, were less likely to blame Calley for the My Lai massacre than to blame the system. "This dude, Lieutenant Calley, really didn't do nothing, man," Specialist 4 Charles Strong, a machine-gunner in Calley's Americal Division from July 1969 to July 1970, told Wallace Terry in *Bloods.* "I know, because I used to be in the field. He didn't do that on his own to My Lai. He was told to do that."[86]

* * *

Powell's second tour ended in 1969. "Judged solely in professional terms, it was a success," he wrote. As his "perspective enlarged," however, he came to see that "euphemisms, lies, and self-deception" were eroding the "bedrock of principle and conviction" that he had brought to Vietnam. Readiness and training reports were routinely inflated, "to please and conceal rather than to evaluate and correct." The powers that be seemed to believe that "by manipulating words, we could change the truth." Powell was also offended by the "wholesale" distribution of medals and awards. "A corrosive careerism had infected the Army; and I was part of it."

For Powell, My Lai was "an appalling example" of much of what went wrong in Vietnam. The Army desperately needed something by which to measure success. Rarely able to measure territory gained, or objectives accomplished, "bodies became the measure," he wrote. "Because the war had dragged on for so long, not everyone commissioned was really officer material." And "shake-and-bake sergeants" were replacing professional NCOs. Too many unprepared officers and noncoms led to "breakdowns in morale, discipline, and professional judgment," Powell wrote. It also led to "horrors like My Lai," as troops "became numb to what appeared to be endless and mindless slaughter."[87]

CAPTAIN NEIL R. BROOKS

As Colin Powell ended his second tour of Vietnam, so did Air Force Captain Neil R. Brooks, a descendant of Bunker Hill veteran Barzillai Lew. When I tried to figure out his great-great relationship, he laughed and said, "Just say I'm the seventh generation." Like his eminent ancestor, he was Massachusetts born and raised. Like Colin Powell, he was Distinguished Graduate of his 1964 Officer's Training School class.

From 1964 to 1967, as lieutenant and captain, he spent the war at Clark Air Force Base in the Philippines, as assistant director of administrative services for the 13th Air Force—responsible for all administrative services in the Philippines, Thailand, and Taiwan, with support for bases in Vietnam. He was part of what made the Air Force function. He spent the rest of the 1960s and the 1970s in command manpower management positions at Langley Air Force Base in Virginia and at Andrews in Maryland. Brooks went on to the Pentagon, from 1983 to 1986, and served in the office of the Joint Chiefs of Staff, where he became the U.S. representative to the North Atlantic Treaty Organization and a lieutenant colonel. When he retired in 1986, he received his fifth Air Force Meritorious Service Medal. He opened his own management consulting firm.

THE 1968 ARMY: "BLOODS"

By 1968, the Army had the same race problems as American society. Confederate flags proliferated and black soldiers began more and more to opt for Black Power. A few months after King's death, a riot broke out at the Long Binh Army stockade between mostly black prisoners and mostly white military police. The escalation and continuation of the war had brought in many more urban black draftees, already veterans of the strife at home. The new draftees of 1966 and 1967, who landed in Vietnam in 1968, were different from every other black American soldier in history—they wanted to be recognized, above all, as "black."

Wallace Terry, the *Time* magazine reporter, understood that the black GI of 1968 was different. "The war had used up the professionals who found in military service fuller and fairer employment . . . and who found in uniform a supreme test of their black manhood," wrote Terry in *Bloods.*

> Replacing the careerists were black draftees, many just steps removed from marching in the Civil Rights Movement or rioting in the rebellions that swept the urban ghettos from Harlem to Watts. All were filled with a new sense of black pride and purpose. They spoke loudest against the discrimination they encountered on the battlefield in decorations, promotions and duty assignments. They chose not to overlook the racial insults, cross-burnings and Confederate flags of their white comrades. They called for unity among black brothers on the battlefield to protest these indignities and provide mutual support. And they called themselves "Bloods."[88]

"In this highly controversial and exhaustively documented war, the Negro and particularly the Negro fighting man, has attained a sudden visibility," wrote Thomas A. Johnson in April 1968 in *The New York Times,* "a visibility his forefathers never realized while fighting in past American wars." A black correspondent, Johnson was with the Marines in February during the monthlong battle for Hué. One of Vietnam's many ironies for Johnson was that ordinary black soldiers, especially frontline teenagers, had no idea that blacks had served in previous American wars. "They feel they're the first Negroes to fight because their history books told only of white soldiers, and their movies showed that John Wayne and Errol Flynn won all American wars," a black intelligence officer on Westmoreland's staff told Johnson.[89]

Merrill Dorsey, PFC: "You're Not Going to Make It in No Marine Corps . . ."

Just as many young Americans sought to avoid the draft, others were eager to get into uniform and go to Vietnam.

Merrill Dorsey saw a Marine Corps uniform in the window of a recruiting office in Catonsville, Maryland, when he was a little boy and resolved that one day he would be a Marine. But when he was thirteen years old a car accident severely damaged and deformed his left foot. Dorsey underwent seven operations; doctors told him that standing up was going to be difficult for the rest of his life, let alone running and jumping, which were out of the question. "But my mind kept on saying, 'You can deal with this,' " Dorsey said.

In 1968, when he was eighteen, Dorsey went to sign up with the

Marines. "I had to lie during the physical test," he said. "Well, I didn't lie, I just decided I wasn't going to take my socks off."

Dorsey had no interest in the debate about Vietnam. "The thing was to prove to my father that I could do what I wanted to do," he said. "When he found out I was going in he said, 'You're not going to make it in no Marine Corps.' Whatever he said I could not do, I wanted to prove that I could do. He asked me about my foot and I said no one asked and I didn't show it."

Dorsey excelled at the Parris Island boot camp and returned home a full-fledged Marine. His family did not believe him, and accused him of being AWOL. Dorsey showed them his travel papers for a training assignment at Camp Lejeune and left.

He returned home again a few weeks later and got married to his pregnant girlfriend, Theresa. "Wrong thing to do. But, me being a gentleman, quote, unquote, it was the right thing to do," he said. "I felt very, very proud. I was a gungho Marine. I was going to protect my country and my people would be very happy. But all that got to be hogwash."

Dorsey's disillusionment began when he was assigned to communications school at Lejeune, whose graduates would be entrusted with calling in air strikes and artillery bombardments, and whose errors could be disastrous. When his class sat down for its final exam, the instructor wrote all the answers on the blackboard. The course had to produce bodies to go to Vietnam, trained or not. Dorsey protested, and he was reassigned to more infantry training, with special attention to detecting booby traps. "I wound up being a winner. Day or night, I could always find them," he said.

In early 1969, baby daughter Theresa arrived, and shortly afterward Dorsey left for Vietnam, where he was assigned to an area not far from Danang that he called "booby trap heaven." He performed very well in combat, but his disillusionment deepened. "Vietnam was a big mistake for everybody who was there," he said. The more he came to know his fellow Marines, he said, the more he realized that "basically a lot of them had nowhere to go. Most people had been in trouble on the outside—black and white. This was not what I imagined this whole thing was about."

Dorsey echoed the views of many other Marines, black and white, about the racial atmosphere. "At times, there was lots of conflict. But when we did what we were supposed to be doing, everybody just did it," Dorsey said, referring to time in the field when a booby trap or enemy ambush could erupt at any moment.

Dorsey longed for news from home but never got any mail. One day he learned why. A white Marine from Alabama was hiding it, presumably out of malice. "I confronted him and he pushed me back. I'm only a hundred twenty-five pounds, so you can push me back, but I can hold up my own," Dorsey said. They fought and Dorsey refused the help of two black Marines. "This had to be a battle between him and me—and I don't believe in saying I can't do it."

The mailman knocked Dorsey down again and again. "He said, 'Dorsey, just stay down,' but I was right back up again. I got a couple of good licks in, but that was all I got. He knocked me down again. Afterward, I got my mail from him and he and I became friends. I felt I got my message across."

After nearly six months in Vietnam, Dorsey was wounded and a Marine officer saw his naked left foot while he was in a hospital. Despite Dorsey's superb performance as a Marine, and his fervent desire to return to his unit, he was going home. One could not have a foot like Dorsey's and still be a Marine, the officer said.

"He was trying to help me but I didn't want his help," Dorsey said. "You go back home, you're just a piece of shit. I always wanted to be this and then here comes this officer."

The Marines sent Dorsey to a hospital near his home in Maryland, but he did not tell his family he had returned. A Navy enlisted man on the hospital staff, noting Dorsey's name, inadvertently brought Dorsey up to date on his domestic scene, as he described his girlfriend, a woman named Theresa Dorsey, whom Dorsey recognized as his wife.

Dorsey eventually told the couple that he bore them no hostility. As he recalled: "I said, 'I'm not mad at you. I didn't expect anybody to be a little saint when you've got a man thousands of miles away. I'm shocked but I'm not shocked.' " He refused to accept his father's seriously offered advice to "shoot both of them." He had no desire to hurt anyone. "After Vietnam, I didn't understand what the hell was going on back here—everybody fighting with each other."

In the years immediately after his return, Dorsey suffered from depression and sometimes considered suicide. But the responsibilities of helping raise his daughter "helped me bring myself back," he said—and made him realize how much he enjoyed working with children. He became part of a team at the John F. Kennedy Institute, a facility affiliated with Johns Hopkins University, for the care of disturbed and handicapped children. He stayed for fifteen years, doing everything from clerical work to counseling troubled youngsters. He became the resident manager of a condominium in Washington, D.C., and Dorsey and his girlfriend helped look after his granddaughter, Latoya.

"I don't regret one day, not one second of the time I was in the Corps," Dorsey said. "The training has stayed with me through life. At my lowest moments over the years, I pray and then Marine Corps training kicks in, with the most important lesson: respect yourself."

DUERY FELTON, JR., AND THE VIETNAM MEMORIAL

Duery Felton, Jr., born and bred in the District of Columbia, was nineteen in 1967. He tried to follow his father and uncle and join the Navy, in which they had served in World War II, but was turned down because of a heart murmur. By the time he took his draft physical, however, the murmur was "cured," as he said later, and he entered the Army.

In basic training at Fort Gordon, Georgia, there was keen awareness of the war at home. A white drill sergeant from the South told all black draftees from Washington, Philadelphia, and New York to step forward. Felton and many other "brothers" from the urban centers where there had been violence promptly did so. "I'm going to keep an eye on you boys," the sergeant warned.

In Vietnam, Felton was a radio operator with the 1st Infantry Division, operating very close to the Cambodian border. He saw plenty of action. As a radio operator, he made friends with voices. Sometimes he never met the people he heard, but he regarded them as a "family." It was "weird," he recalled, "to hear people on the radio fighting for their lives." After several months in-country, a freak accident nearly killed him. A tank snagged part of his radio gear and dragged Felton alongside, crushing his face against the side of a bridge and nearly severing his tongue. Shortly afterward, in an Army field hospital, Felton heard a doctor say, "Specialist Felton, we're going to try to save your life." He was given pencil and paper and managed to write a note to his mother. He quoted Job: "Naked I came into this world and naked I will leave it . . . Blessed is the Lord." He survived, and was furious when he learned that the Red Cross had failed to deliver his note.

Back home, at the illustrious Walter Reed Hospital, racial tension ran high, Felton recalled, and one day there was even a mini–race riot, in the recreation room. "My Girl" by The Temptations was playing, and the record began to skip. Some white patients started to cheer the malfunction, and soon there was a brawl, black against white. "People in body casts, in wheelchairs, on crutches, carrying IV bags on them, were all fighting," he recalled.

Felton saw plenty of racism in Vietnam but, years later, he had other memories as well. Once, air turbulence nearly threw him out of a combat-loaded helicopter. He said he can still see the single white arm that reached out and kept him from falling into the jungle below; it remains a powerful memory. When he was injured, it was a white man from Oklahoma who liked to sing Motown and who was one of his closest friends in the field who held his hand and helped him to the medevac helicopter. That friend was later killed in action.

Felton, like many other vets, anticipated the dedication of the Vietnam Veterans Memorial in Washington, D.C. In early 1982, when construction workers were pouring concrete for the foundations of the memorial, a Navy officer threw his dead brother's Purple Heart into the concrete. No sooner had the memorial—"The Wall"—opened, on Memorial Day 1982, than visitors began leaving other items, and transforming the site into a shrine.

"At first, National Park Service rangers did not know what to do with the things they were finding each day," writes Thomas B. Allen in the preface to *Offerings at the Wall,* a book of photographs of these artifacts.[90] "The rangers gathered up flags and roses, letters and teddy bears, toy cars and birthday cards, dog tags and service medals, cans of C rations and packets of Army-issue toilet paper."

"I have two daughters myself now," wrote one GI, including with his letter a photo of a North Vietnamese man with a young girl. "I perceive you as a brave soldier defending his homeland. Above all else, I can now respect the importance that life held for you. . . . Forgive me, Sir." Another veteran enclosed his Narcotics Anonymous ring. "I learned fear. I learned to be ALONE. . . . I learned to kill—no—I learned it was OK to kill. . . . I came home and nothing worked—my family did not want me—they were—ARE—afraid of me. I am afraid of me. I pray for your forgiveness for my life/lies."[91]

In 1983, Duery Felton became one of the Vietnam-veteran volunteers who help the Park Service catalog objects. Sealed letters are never opened and marijuana joints are confiscated, but everything else is cataloged. Veterans like Felton can explain that the helmet graffiti "Don't Shoot, I'm Short" was not about the man's height, but that he was down to the last of his 365 days in Vietnam (or 395, for Marines). In 1989, Felton became curator of the Vietnam Veterans Memorial Collection.

Designer Maya Lin's mysterious masterwork, conceived when she was a twenty-year-old Yale senior, is, like the Lincoln Memorial, a national monument that does not separate the living from the dead. Thomas B. Allen calls the Vietnam Wall "a place where people can feel what Lincoln called the mystic chords of memory, stretching from every battlefield and patriot grave, to every living heart and hearthstone, all over this broad land."[92] The Lincoln Memorial, infused with one man's immense, thoughtful serenity, and the Vietnam Veterans Memorial, starkly recalling the many, are both alive in the spirit. When I touched Calvin Bouknight's name on the Wall, I knew him.

* * *

By the summer of 1969, the first U.S. military units were withdrawn. But even while the overall U.S. troop level had begun to decline, fresh draftees still arrived every day to replace GIs who had finished their tours in the remaining units. And casualties remained appalling. The June 27, 1969, issue of *Life* magazine carried on its cover a single face and the words "The Faces of the American Dead in Vietnam/One Week's Toll." Inside, on twelve pages, were 217 photos (and twenty-five names without photos) of the 242 U.S. troops killed in Vietnam between May 28 and June 3, 1969. It looked like a yearbook of the dead. Under each man's photo was his name, age, rank, branch of service, and hometown. Twenty-six of the dead appeared to be black and another eight Hispanic. Most were about twenty years old, but fifty-one of the 242 who had been killed were teenagers, eighteen or nineteen years old. It was a portrait of young Middle America, and the dramatic display helped intensify opposition to the draft as well as to the war. While peace talks continued in Paris, Nixon pursued the "Vietnamization" of the war. "Vietnamization" meant reducing the number of U.S. ground troops, and turning the brunt of the fighting over to the ARVN, and supporting it with U.S. air strikes. Nixon ordered secret bombing of Cambodia in March 1969. In August, he sent his national security adviser, Henry Kissinger, to Paris to begin secret discussions with the North Vietnamese. In September, Ho Chi Minh died. Two massive antiwar demonstrations occurred in Washington that autumn, before the revelation in November of the My Lai massacre.

WAYNE SMITH: "NO ONE WANTED TO DIE ALONE IN VIETNAM"

Wayne Smith was born in 1951 and grew up in an integrated, working-class neighborhood in Providence, Rhode Island. His "awareness of race" came when he was eight or nine, when he saw his father thrash a white man who called him "nigger." "I felt fear," Smith recalled. "But it was thrilling, too. It's hard to explain."

His father died when he was ten. "My mom taught us good values, to treat people as they treated us, and to judge them on who they were and how they treated us," he said. Another lesson was "always excel." Smith went to a Catholic school and recalls the time as almost idyllic. Nevertheless, as he approached graduation more and more people he knew from school, or the neighborhood, were getting killed in Vietnam. "My mom believed and I believed it was the right thing to do to serve in the military," he said. "To fight for one's country was not dishonorable." Smith's older sister protested against the war, but his mother told him something he could never forget. " 'Wayne, the government really isn't going to lie to us,' she said. You can tell how gullible I was. Every now and then I will remind her." Smith wanted to be a doctor.

In November 1968, with a white high school friend, he joined the Army on "the buddy system," a recruitment ploy that promised buddies would serve together. "The deal didn't hold," he said, and after basic training his white friend got a safe, stateside office job and Smith was assigned to train to be a combat medic, and go to Vietnam.

At Fort Dix, he met blacks his age who had never heard of Rhode Island and never talked to a white person. "Basic training was a horrible revelation," he said, as he recalled his process of disillusionment. "I couldn't understand how an American Army trying to motivate people to fight an enemy could be so brutal to their own people. Nothing was safe. It was all about survival." Two black sergeants regularly attacked black recruits "to show whites they would treat us as badly or worse than whites," he said.

On May 15, 1969, three months after his eighteenth birthday, he got his orders to Vietnam. "I'm going to war. I wondered . . . would I, could I kill? What kind of person am I going to be? What scared me more than anything was being a coward. Under no circumstances would I be a coward," Smith said.

Smith spent more than two months at Dong Tam, headquarters for the U.S. 9th Infantry Division, part of an Army unit on a Navy ship that treated wounded flown back from the field. Then he went to the field himself as a medic with an infantry unit, "immersed in the slosh" of the Mekong Delta and constantly exposed to ambush and booby traps. Smith carried a weapon but "did not want to kill anyone."

Soon after he arrived, "guys went down like bowling pins" when a series of mines exploded. Smith performed a tracheotomy in a rice paddy. "I helped save a life," he said. "I felt a tremendous sense of pride." Smith saved other lives and saw his share of heavy combat.

"In combat, there were many brothers," Smith said. "Combat was soulsville. But what mattered was not black or white." In the field, racism among the troops was never an issue. "Are you down?" was the only question. "No one wanted to die alone in Vietnam," he said. "The men always said, 'Doc, stay with me.' " Smith was very proud of his work. "I was vital," he said. "As a medic, and as a humanitarian, I saved lives. No one was killed in my platoon while I was the medic."

Smith had white buddies but his black pride deepened. He realized that he was "part of a continuum. I'm another black man who fought for his country. Black men have been in all the wars. We didn't see them in the movies, but we knew they were there."

Smith recalled the pleasures of a day or two back at base, after coming out of combat. "Some of the brothers would gather at a bunker, listen to some music, have a little bit of something to drink, maybe a little smoke, and talk about life," he said. "What we were going to do when we got home—when we got back to the world! How we were going to change things, get rid of all those drug dealers and pimps—and produce equality. Some of the finest people I've met in my entire life were in that combat unit. We were very close."

Smith saw a priest offering mass in a small clearing. "We're going out to kill and he's blessing us, giving us communion," thought the former altar boy at the time. "That was a stake in the heart of my value of religion. . . . There were so many contradictions. I was hurt emotionally."

Smith's disillusionment deepened in the midst of pervasive racism, including the routine reference throughout the military to all Vietnamese as dinks and gooks, which made it easier, he said, to "psych you up to kill."

"I came home for thirty days leave and it was one of the worst mistakes I ever made. I came home and it was stranger than going to Vietnam," Smith said. "My value system changed. Much of what I believed in was a lie. I knew I would never practice medicine. I had no understanding of the future at all. The problem was that I stuffed it inside. I couldn't express—how can you express . . . I did not have the capacity to express the pain."

While he was home, a woman in the neighborhood gave a party in Wayne's honor at her house. Wayne went to a bar before going to the party and decided to bring along a woman—a "floozy," in a sequined dress. "It was a disaster," Wayne said. The basketball coach was on hand but Wayne ignored him and all the other old friends. He locked himself in the bathroom. "Nightmarish. I couldn't wait to get back to Vietnam," he said.

In April 1970 Smith was assigned to the 1/5 Mech, as a rear-area medic at Dong Ha, a former Marine base near the DMZ. It was a grim time. "I lost much of my belief," he said. "The saying was 'Fuck it, it don't mean nothing.' That was a good guard against almost everything, an attitude that lasted for some time."

"I did not have a delayed reaction to Vietnam. I started my meltdown in-country," he said.

Three weeks out of the Army, he and two pals got together and one of them ended up dead. Wayne and the other survivor were charged with manslaughter. The dead man's mother testified on Wayne's behalf but he was convicted and sentenced to ten years in prison. He was twenty years old.

"Talk about blessed," Smith said in describing that time. Just as he entered jail, an experimental program sponsored by Roger Williams College was being introduced in Rhode Island. It provided a college education for selected inmates who would in turn teach other inmates at least enough to get a GED. Smith was one of the participants in the program during the three years he spent behind bars.

"I survived very well in prison," Smith recalled. "I was prepared by the Army." He also got a degree in psychology, and became one of the first advocates for Vietnam vets. One way or another, that has been his life's work ever since. A few years ago, the judge who sentenced him to ten years in jail just after he had returned from Vietnam made it clear how much Smith's life had changed. His work as a therapist and advocate for veterans had been so successful that the judge asked Smith to testify on his behalf when the judge was trying to get promoted. Smith is now executive director of the Justice Project, in Washington, D.C., a research and advocacy group for people (including veterans) in need on a variety of issues.

Blaxploitation and Disaffection

The war in Vietnam came home with a vengeance in the spring of 1970, when the invasion of Cambodia ignited huge protests at colleges around the country. The antiwar movement had become a battle between young and old. Antistudent violence escalated on May 4, when four students at a Kent State University antiwar rally were killed by Ohio National Guard troops. Within a week, protests and boycotts closed down more than four hundred campuses across the country. On May 15, two students were killed by police during an antiwar protest at predominantly black Jackson State College, in Mississippi. Thirty-seven university presidents, in a signed letter of protest, blamed Nixon's policies for alienating the nation's youth.

"Blaxploitation" films—featuring a new kind of black hero, armed and lethal, often just back from Vietnam—entered pop culture in the early 1970s. Even "good guys," like Richard (*Shaft*) Roundtree and Pam

(*Coffy*) Grier, were "bad." "Unlike Sidney Poitier—the Sixties embodiment of noble striving in his white shirt, dark suit and tie—the blaxploitation guys and gals are as funky as their multicolored bell-bottoms and two-toned platform shoes," wrote the critic Nelson George.[93] "Their state-of-the-art threads seem to free them to live as large and insolent as we all dream we might."

In Vietnam the black GI style that began in 1968 flourished for the next several years, as the entire Army changed. In October 1970, John Saar of *Life* wrote about an Army "in evolution"—an Army "trying to adjust to the winding-down war in Vietnam." It was also an Army that was becoming more and more disaffected. "Old ideas of dress, behavior, discipline and rank no longer apply," Saar wrote. "Virtually no draftee wants to be fighting in Vietnam anyway, and in return for his reluctant participation he demands, and gets, personal freedoms that would have driven a MacArthur or a Patton apoplectic." The new Army was one "in which all questions—including 'Why?'—are permissible."[94]

GIs wore peace-symbol medallions and inscribed "FTA" ("F—— the Army") on their helmets. Stories about troops refusing direct orders appeared in the press, as did accounts of "fraggings," or murder of officers who appeared to risk their men's lives unnecessarily. Marijuana had long been popular and in 1970 and 1971 very powerful heroin, known as scag, flooded Vietnam and reached thousands of young soldiers, black and white.

The war was clearly not going to be won, but casualties continued, many from mines and booby traps. "In the past four or five months, there appears to have been a four- or fivefold increase in multiple amputees," the chief medical officer of a hospital ship told James Sterba of *The New York Times Magazine* in October 1970.[95] "I hope this is all incredible some day. Right now, it's all too credible."

Faced with black GIs in Vietnam in 1971 who wanted to be "black," the military, eager to defuse anger, went along. It established race relations seminars and compromised on "black pride" symbols such as Afros, street talk, and ritual "soul" handshakes, called daps. (Connoisseurs knew the difference between the Long Binh dap and the Bien Hoa dap.) "In the beginning, you know, we used to dap sort of quietly on the side," a black soldier told *Newsweek* in January 1971. "But then, wow, it looked like it annoyed some of the white guys. So the idea got around to dap a little louder, do it a little more."[96]

In February 1971, South Vietnamese troops with U.S. air and helicopter support invaded Laos. By April, the U.S. death toll in Vietnam was 45,019. In June 1971, Daniel Ellsberg, a State Department official who had served in Vietnam in the mid-1960s, gave copies of the "Pentagon Papers," a top-secret Defense Department study of U.S. decision making in Vietnam, to *The New York Times* and other newspapers. Ellsberg was indicted on various espionage, theft, and conspiracy charges, although these were later dismissed. Meanwhile, the papers made it clear that over the years policy makers had consistently and deliberately lied to Congress and the American people about Vietnam.

POWELL AT THE PENTAGON: THE CARLISLE SURVEY AND THE BASE ARMY

In 1971 a semisecret document began to circulate among military professionals. It was the Carlisle War College Survey of 450 lieutenant colonels, most of whom had served in Vietnam. The Carlisle Survey concluded that the Army had generated an environment in Vietnam that "disregarded or discouraged the growth of long-term qualities of moral strength." There were no scapegoats, not even politicians; Vietnam was the Army's "own mess," wrote Colin Powell, who studied the document carefully at the time.

On the promotion list for lieutenant colonel, Powell was now in the Pentagon, on the staff of Lieutenant General William E. DePuy, the Army's assistant vice chief of staff and a leading advocate of the Carlisle Survey. In what Powell called a "hush-hush" meeting early in 1972, DePuy's group faced some unpleasant facts. The military was becoming unpopular, and Congress was tightening the budget. DePuy ordered Powell to "take a couple of bright guys and start rethinking the unthinkable": a 500,000-man Army, something not seen since 1940.[97]

Powell's group created the outlines for a "Base Army," a paring down of personnel to the level just below which America could not defend itself. When word leaked to Pentagon seniors, however, the idea was instantly shelved. (The "Base Army" would reappear some twenty years later in the Persian Gulf—under the leadership of one of its creators.)

Powell now reached a "turning point" in his career. In 1971, he began a prestigious year as a White House Fellow, with trips to the Soviet Union and China. It was not a sabbatical he sought; he had been drafted into it by the infantry, which wanted a strong candidate to join the other talented Fellows. The fellowship was exciting and, besides, Powell was worried that "the American military had become alienated from its own people." He thought it would be good for "the civilian world to see that military officers did not have horns."[98] The terrible gulf between civilians and the military created by Vietnam had sadly been brought home to Powell in

June 1972, when his alma mater, like many colleges and universities, abolished its ROTC program.

JOHN CASH RETURNS TO VIETNAM

John Cash returned to Vietnam in 1972, seven years after Ia Drang, serving in Thailand and Vietnam as a historian on special missions for the Office of the Chief of Military History. As a professional soldier, Cash was beginning to sense that "the people at the top had no clear idea what they wanted." He was stunned when Army doctors told him that his trusted black first sergeant had a three-cap-a-day heroin habit. According to Cash, by 1972, Army doctors were writing to *Stars and Stripes* that most of their time was spent dealing with drug overdoses.

Race relations appeared to have made a "180-degree turn" since the assassination of Martin Luther King. Influenced by King, Cash now saw the war as part of the "race story." He was also beginning to hear accounts of atrocities, which he refused to believe that American soldiers could commit. Then his wife sent him pictures of Americans using water torture on a Vietcong prisoner.

The Vietcong had "good leadership," Cash said. "And their motive was so different." For Cash, the Vietcong were the perfect demonstration of "minimum means, maximum gains." He had seen "skinny and dehydrated" VC soldiers come back fighting after a B-52 air strike that leveled an area the size of a football field; they sent sniper fire out of the devastation three nights later. Cash had never wanted to admit to himself, he told me, that Vietnam might be a civil war, but it was becoming increasingly difficult to believe all the "bulwark-against-Communism" propaganda. "Nothing is more dangerous," he said, "than an enemy with his head screwed on right, and motivation—an enemy who is prepared to die." Cash had seen the best and the worst of the Army, and the war went on.

THE END OF THE WAR

In January 1972, President Nixon announced that Henry Kissinger had for some time been carrying on secret negotiations with the North Vietnamese about ending the war. In February, Nixon and Kissinger visited Mao Tse-tung and Chou En-lai in China, again raising hopes for peace. As U.S. troop levels and casualties declined, Vietnam receded from the headlines. But the war came back with startling ferocity at the end of March with the Easter Offensive, in which the North Vietnamese sent the ARVN reeling in panicky, headlong flight in several parts of the country.

Nixon bombed Hanoi and Haiphong and mined Haiphong harbor. Only massive tactical B-52 strikes kept the rampaging NVA at bay before the fighting ebbed away.

In the midst of the offensive, Nixon operatives broke into the Watergate offices of the Democratic National Committee and were promptly caught. The incident attracted little attention at the time and was not a significant issue in the presidential campaign. Democratic presidential candidate George McGovern ran on a pledge to end the fighting and the bombing immediately and to get out of Vietnam. Nixon and Kissinger talked up negotiations during the summer and by October they had a plan that was acceptable to North Vietnam but not to the Saigon regime. Despite President Nguyen Van Thieu's objections, Kissinger announced that "peace is at hand" shortly before election day. Nixon trounced McGovern, but the war did not end. Thieu continued to balk at signing the treaty, which sounded like a death warrant for his regime. To reassure the Saigon regime that the United States was still its ally, Nixon and Kissinger unleashed a mammoth, eleven-day B-52 assault on North Vietnam at Christmas time, killing many civilians, including some patients at the Bach Mai civilian hospital in Hanoi. North Vietnamese antiaircraft fire shot down some of the bombers and more U.S. pilots became POWs.

On January 27, 1973, in Paris, the war in Vietnam came to its official end (as did the draft in the United States). Representatives of the contenders—the United States, North Vietnam, the Saigon regime, and the Vietcong, otherwise known as the Provisional Revolutionary Government—signed a peace treaty with several provisions. There was to be an immediate cease-fire and POW exchange, and all remaining U.S. troops had to leave Vietnam within sixty days. North Vietnam was not to reinforce its troops in South Vietnam, or to seek reunification by other than peaceful means. Fred Cherry and the other American POWs came home. On March 29, 1973, the last planeload of U.S. troops lifted off from Tan Son Nhut airfield. It was the first time in a hundred years that there were no foreign troops in Vietnam.

In fact, some fifty U.S. military attachés remained and there was no doubt that the war would continue, as it did in Cambodia, where heavy U.S. bombing went on until August 14, 1973, when Congress ordered it stopped. On the surface at least, the war entered a lull, during which the North sent men and supplies toward the South in great quantities on the Ho Chi Minh trail.

Thieu's Saigon regime clung to the hope that the United States would always rescue it, peace agreement or not, with B-52 strikes, if the North Vietnamese decided to mount an offensive. But Richard Nixon's options in Vietnam narrowed as the Watergate scandal deepened. Nixon resigned on August 9, 1974, and Vice-President Gerald Ford became the thirty-eighth president. He pardoned Nixon on September 8. A week later, Ford signed the Vietnam War Clemency Act, offering repatriation and pardon to all draft resisters and military deserters in exchange for two years of public service, and an oath of allegiance. (Only about 22,000 of the 124,000 eligible acted on the offer.)[99] President Carter issued a blanket pardon to draft resisters the day after his inauguration in 1977.

While Nixon was president, nearly 21,000 Americans were killed in Vietnam, and another 53,000 were seriously wounded. We will never know how many casualties occurred throughout Indochina during the war.

On March 11, 1975, North Vietnamese forces captured Ban Me Thuot, in the Central Highlands, and touched off a rout. ARVN units disintegrated. By March 25, northern troops had seized Hue. By March 30 they had Danang and were headed for Saigon. In Cambodia, the Khmer Rouge were closing in on Phnom Penh. The U.S. embassy staff pulled out on April 13 and the Khmer Rouge entered the city four days later. Thieu and other top Saigon officials fled on April 25 and the last American officials in Vietnam lifted off from the roof of the Saigon embassy on April 29. The next day, North Vietnamese tanks clanked past the embassy and toward Thieu's palace. The war was over.

GOING HOME

"Back in the World now, and a lot of us aren't making it," wrote Michael Herr toward the end of *Dispatches.* Career officers and soldiers who returned home were assimilated and welcomed on bases: the professional military protected its own. But many draftees, returning to civilian communities, found an indifferent welcome at best. "When I got back to the real world, it seemed nobody cared that you'd been to Vietnam," one vet complained to Wallace Terry. "As a matter of fact, everybody would be wondering where have you been for so long. They would say, how did you lose your leg? In a fight? A car wreck? Anything but Vietnam."[100] Others felt so unwelcome and so alienated that they turned to the counterculture, or to crime. And others still fought inner demons.

Black and white Vietnam vets would find that they often had more in common with each other than with civilians of either race. Both agreed that coming home was, in its own way, as hard as combat. They agreed that the war had changed them. They agreed that Hollywood usually "got it wrong." There would always be the military argument over the "winnable" and "unwinnable" war. But most recognized that the war (winnable or unwinnable) came close to destroying the moral fabric of the military as well as the country. Hands down, this had been the worst American war. The future American military byword would be "No more Vietnams."

Afterward: Fred Cherry and George Forrest

Fred Cherry got his first letter from home in 1970, from his sister. He never heard from his wife. When he finally came home, in 1973, his wife—who had told his children that he was dead, spent his back pay, and had a child with another man—refused to divorce him. She "wanted the checks to keep coming." Cherry sued the Air Force for negligence in handling his money, and the U.S. Court of Claims awarded him $150,000. He reached the rank of full colonel two months before his release from North Vietnam, and he received the Air Force Cross, two Bronze Stars, and two Purple Hearts. He had already been awarded the Distinguished Flying Cross and the Silver Star.

Fred Cherry and Porter Halyburton kept in touch. Halyburton spent two weeks with Cherry in 1977 while doing research at the Pentagon for his master's degree. "We talked about how we looked at each other the first time we met," Cherry said. "We talked about what we learned from each other. . . . We rehashed the whole thing. Naturally, I thanked him again for really, really saving my life." Cherry retired in 1981, with a dashing Air Force portrait on display in the Pentagon. Back home in Suffolk, Virginia, he established the Colonel Fred Victor Cherry Scholarship Fund to help capable young people get money for college. Speaking across the country for the Tuskegee Airmen's Association, he told young black men to study engineering, science, and technology—hoping, as he told Wallace Terry, that one might "walk across a field one day, look up at an airplane, like I did so long, long ago, and say, 'I'm going to fly. I'm going to be a fighter pilot.' "[101]

* * *

"Over the years, scarcely a day has gone by that his name has not floated over my mind," Dennis Deal said of Calvin Bouknight. He assumed that Bouknight had won a Silver Star, but when he finally managed to track down his family for the first Ia Drang survivors' reunion, in November 1993, he discovered that Bouknight's only medal had been a Purple Heart. Deal and Bravo Company's commander, John D. Herren, were among those campaigning for a posthumous Medal of Honor. Their chances of success were slim because of the time lapse and loss of witnesses, until Herren found another witness, Ron Barrow—who had never heard from anyone in the battalion until November 1994, when he went to his first reunion. (It was like a "homecoming," he told me.)

In 1993, George Forrest and several other survivors returned to Ia Drang with Moore and Galloway, on a trip televised by ABC's *Day One.* Forrest was nervous about going back, and nervous about being the only black on the trip. He wondered how he would interact, but he made "new" old friends. Meeting one of the NVA survivors of the Ia Drang battle, Forrest learned that his former enemy's greatest memory of war was the death of his fourteen-year-old godson. Forrest saw the common thread between them: love of their men and ability to survive. "Their stories are the same as ours," he said.

Forrest, who worked with at-risk youth in the Maryland public school system, believed that he was permitted to return from the Vietnam War to take a message to young people "who accept mediocrity" and to teach them to strive for more. In memory of "seventeen guys who could have been absolute national treasures," he said, he kept his Silver Star, Legion of Merit, several Bronze Stars, Vietnam Cross for Gallantry, and other decorations on the wall in his office. "These were gallant, noble, afraid young men, not drug-infested crazies," he said. "They did what they thought their country needed them to do."

For twenty-eight years, Forrest carried "a big albatross" of guilt about Vietnam: "It was a dirty war, and you're responsible." He "did no normal vet stuff," joined no veterans' organizations. He could not talk about Albany with anyone, not even his father. Then Joe Galloway called and urged Forrest to talk about his memories. Forrest felt as if he had finally come "out of the closet" about Vietnam. He finally forgave himself. "It's a humbling feeling, when men at reunions now come up and say 'Captain, I am sitting here now because you did A, B, or C'—although it doesn't help the dead." Forrest finally came to believe that he also did what he thought his country needed him to do. Returning to X-Ray, he felt that his seventeen dead were watching him and telling him to "let go." Vietnam taught Forrest that there was much he was willing to die for, but only a short list of what he was willing to kill for.

11 Desert Storm

SWEET RESTORATION

We had given America a clear win at low casualties in a noble cause, and the American people fell in love again with their armed forces.[1]

—*General Colin Powell,* My American Journey

For an African-American, the military is the fairest place to reach goals based on potential. In the military, standards are very clear. If you are good and you've met the standards you will be promoted.

—*Lieutenant General Calvin Waller, deputy commander of Operation Desert Storm, in interview with author*

No More Vietnams: The New Army

After its harsh birth in Korea and its stormy Vietnamese adolescence, the New Army finally came of age in a small war in the Persian Gulf: "Operation Desert Storm." The battle to save oil-rich Kuwait from Iraq's Saddam Hussein was in a sense the American military's revenge for Vietnam. It was a success. The sins of Vietnam, both domestic and military, were seen to be washed away in the Gulf. It was, in the words of the journalist Charles Lane, the "sweet restoration of the Army as a harmonious, winning family, unsullied by Vietnam."[2]

Although led by Vietnam veterans, Desert Storm was everything Vietnam was not. It was swift, victorious, and popular, with few U.S. casualties and high troop morale. The times were also different. Worldwide war nostalgia was rife: 1989 marked the fiftieth anniversary of the Second World War's start, and at the end of a decade noticeably devoid of idealism or self-sacrifice, Americans seemed to be looking for heroes. They found them in the New Army, the All Volunteer Force, encamped under dusty camouflage in the "sandbox" of Saudi Arabia.

The largest U.S. force fielded since Vietnam was unlike any military organization in American history. Integrated and coed, the All Volunteer

Force represented brand-new demographics. With more minorities and more women, the volunteer Army was older; service members were more likely to be married, more professedly religious, more economically homogeneous, and much better educated than any previous U.S. military. It was a "citizens' army." Ninety-five percent were high school graduates, as compared to 75 percent of the population at large. Far better trained than Vietnam draftees, Gulf War troops saw little overt drug or alcohol abuse, almost nonexistent overt racism, and no fragging. America's Gulf warriors seemed, for the mad minute of the war, to represent democracy's golden mean as well as a new golden age of the American military.

The Gulf War was a military hybrid: it combined World War II nostalgia with Spanish-American War–style jingoism and Star Wars technology. The only thing missing was idealism. While "poor little Kuwait" was hardly a bastion of democracy, Hitlerizing Iraq's Saddam Hussein was easy. Like the "splendid little war" in Cuba at the end of the nineteenth century, the hundred-hour war in the Persian Gulf was good for blacks. As in the Spanish-American War, black soldiers were held up as heroes.

Sadly, the postwar backlash was also similar. Within a year of San Juan Hill, southern revisionism ruled the Army as well as the country. Within a year of Desert Storm, blacks were the villains of affirmative action, and U.S. race relations had deteriorated once again.

The media accused the military of allowing only "managed news," which doubtless reflected the military's fear of Vietnam-era freedom of reporting. Managed or not, the media coverage of U.S. troops was overwhelming, and black soldiers were extremely visible heroes. *Life*—published weekly instead of monthly for the war's duration—recaptured the sentimental mastery of its World War II incarnation. "Heroes All," declared the March 11, 1991, end-of-the-war cover, with a picture of General H. Norman Schwarzkopf surrounded by four GIs, three of whom were black. In response to those (black and white) who questioned why the military comprised such a large percentage of blacks, Colin Powell wrote, "Let the rest of American society open its doors to African-Americans, and give them the opportunities they now enjoyed in the armed forces."[3]

No war in U.S. history had seen more blacks in leadership positions—from General Colin Powell, chairman of the Joint Chiefs of Staff, to the Desert Storm deputy commander Lieutenant General Calvin Waller, to three members of the Patriot missile crew decorated for shooting down Scud missiles over Riyadh. Blacks, about 12 percent of the U.S. population, made up 20 percent of the total U.S. troops in the Gulf: some

30 percent of the Army, 22 percent of the Navy, 17 percent of the front-line Marines, and 13 percent of the Air Force.[4] They were 48 percent of all Army enlisted women, and 40 percent of women in the Gulf. Of the 266 American soldiers killed in the Gulf War, 15 percent were black.[5] Eighteen-year-old black Army private Robert D. Talley of Newark, New Jersey, killed in a "friendly fire" incident, was the youngest soldier to die in the Gulf. The oldest soldier to lose his life was a fifty-eight-year-old black veteran of Korea, First Sergeant Joseph Murphy of New York's 102nd Maintenance National Guard Unit.

Desert Storm proved that conservative values like duty, honor, and respect for the uniform could coexist with liberal values like equality of treatment and opportunity, striking a perfect balance between stability and change. Post-Vietnam integration, like all military integration, was a process of evolution, not revolution. Like most American inspirations for the good, it combined morality and expediency, flourishing under the combined encouragement of President Jimmy Carter's commitment to civil rights and President Ronald Reagan's commitment to military spending. It could not have succeeded without the military's own commitment to fairness and affirmative action. Doors of opportunity had been opened to blacks and, within limits, women, but crossing the threshold remained a matter of individual ability. Respect for the uniform was key. The uniform had no race or gender; green was the great equalizer. The military had learned the lessons of Vietnam and the new troops were treated and trained like unhyphenated Americans.

By 1973, when the All Volunteer Force was born, the unofficial Army motto was "No more Vietnams." No more drafts, with their economic loopholes, leaving, in the main, the bottommost strata of society to serve. Uncle Sam now wanted *motivation,* not just bodies. The military wanted young people who were looking for job training, travel opportunities, and college funds; in an extension of the GI Bill, it offered as much as $25,000 per recruit for college tuition. In the years immediately after the Vietnam War, when most middle-class American youths had come to profoundly distrust the military, it was predicted that the volunteer service would attract disproportionately high numbers of minorities. ROTC recruitment had stepped up at black colleges after white campus units closed in the wake of Vietnam protests. In 1973, blacks formed about 17 percent of the enlisted military as a whole. By the late 1970s, the proportion had nearly doubled.[6]

The new black volunteers were a far cry from Vietnam's angry draftees. The military was now attracting, in general, better-educated and better-motivated blacks than whites. A Congressional Budget Office study showed that black recruits generally came from areas with above-average black incomes and education, while similar areas for white recruits were "underrepresented."[7] In 1986, thanks to Reagan's military buildup, the Army spent $76.9 million on advertising.[8] The new Army slogan, "Be all you can be!" was deliberately crafted as an equal-opportunity appeal. Like their white counterparts, blacks saw military service as an opportunity, rather than a burden. Some were even surprised to learn, at the start of Desert Storm, that real war was part of the contract.

Clifford Alexander

Clifford L. Alexander, the first black secretary of the Army, appointed in 1977 by President Carter, was an important civilian father of the AVF. A Harvard graduate and former Washington lawyer, Alexander had served as a special consultant on civil rights to Lyndon Johnson. He was justly proud of his tenure in office. Opening the Army to minorities and women, he mandated equal treatment, and made sure, he told me, that personnel were trained for "full civilian employment opportunities." He was the first secretary of the Army to have a woman officer on his team and to choose a woman as a special assistant. Under his leadership, the Department of the Army had the first female general counsel in the Defense Department. And he opened the ranks of general to blacks. "A list of general officer candidates is submitted to the secretary by an Army board," Alexander said, explaining the procedure. He sent the first list he ever received back to the board and asked them to reexamine the records because there were no black candidates. When he took office there were nine black generals; by the time he left in 1981, there were thirty—including Army nurse Hazel Winifred Johnson, the first black woman general, and Colin Powell.

Powell and Clausewitz

In 1974, just back from Korea, where he served for a year under the command of the legendary General Henry "The Gunfighter" Emerson, Lieutenant Colonel Powell was selected for the National War College at Fort McNair, the Harvard of the military. Lieutenant General Julius Becton had not met Powell in 1974 when, as president of the Selection Board, he recommended him. "He was not all that strong academically," Becton told me, "but his Efficiency Reports were sterling." Efficiency Reports are the all-important officer's report card that can make or break a career.

The War College accepted about 140 students a year, split equally among the services and including civilians from the State Department, the U.S. Information Agency, and the CIA. Powell called his discovery at the War College of Carl von Clausewitz, the nineteenth-century Prussian political philosopher, "an awakening." "War is nothing but the extension of politics by other means," wrote Clausewitz in his classic 1833 text *On War.* "Clausewitz's greatest lesson for my profession was that the soldier, for all his patriotism, valor, and skill, forms just one leg in a triad," Powell wrote. "Without all three legs engaged, the military, the government, and the people, the centerpiece cannot stand."[9] It was the perfect post-Vietnam response to war. During the war in Vietnam, one leg was missing: a large proportion of the American people were distinctly disengaged from the military and the government.

In mid-1976, halfway through War College, Powell received accelerated promotion to full colonel and command of the 2nd Brigade, 101st Airborne Division (the "Screaming Eagles"), at Fort Campbell, Kentucky. At thirty-nine, he was the youngest in his War College class to make colonel, and one of only two Army officers in the class chosen for brigade command. He was also the oldest man to qualify for air assault school. None of his fellow infantry brigade commanders could pass the test, which included rappelling out of helicopters and making twelve-mile forced marches. On the Clausewitz track, he was assigned to the Pentagon a year later as senior military assistant to Carter's deputy secretary of defense, going to Iran three months before the fall of the Shah. In December 1978, when he was forty-two, he became a brigadier general. He was the youngest general in the Army.

At mandatory brigadier general "charm school," the Army Chief of Staff told Powell's class of fifty-two men that half might make major general, ten might make lieutenant general, and maybe four would have four stars. At the formal promotion ceremony, the Department of Defense protocol officer presented Powell with a framed quotation from Abraham Lincoln on the Confederate capture of a general and some horses: "I can make a brigadier general in five minutes. But it's not so easy to replace one hundred and ten horses." An envelope was taped to the back of the frame: "Not to be opened for ten years." In 1989, when he was already chairman of the Joint Chiefs, Powell would open the envelope to read, "You will become Chief of Staff of the Army."[10]

In the Pentagon when the Reagan administration came in, Powell stayed to assist Frank Carlucci, the deputy secretary of defense under Caspar Weinberger. Carlucci asked him to resign his commission and become undersecretary of the Army. But Powell chose to remain in service as the assistant commander of the 4th Infantry Division at Fort Carson, Colorado. He almost retired with one star thanks to his commanding officer there: Major General John W. Hudachek, whom General Julius Becton suspected, as he told me later, of being a borderline racist.

Powell had served under Hudachek in Vietnam in the Americal Division, infamous for My Lai. Now, as his deputy, Powell received a career-killing Efficiency Report, his first unfavorable report. Hudachek gave Powell a "no confidence" rating as a commander (although he rated Alma Powell high, considering her "fully capable of representing the Army and supporting her husband wherever he may be assigned").[11] Powell took out his civilian résumé and thought about early retirement. Fortunately, two friends intervened. General Becton and General Richard Cavazos, a Mexican-American hero of Korea, met on an airplane and started talking about Powell. They decided, according to Becton, to make sure that the "powers that were" knew the facts of Powell's case. According to Powell, the "powers" had already gotten the message. "It came down to the fact that the generals knew the officer being rated and they knew the officer who had rated him," he wrote in his memoir.[12]

In 1982, Powell was named deputy commanding general of the U.S. Army Combined Arms Combat Development Activity (CACDA), at Fort Leavenworth, Kansas. At CACDA, which ensures that the different Army schools (infantry, armor, and air defense) train as a team, Powell's assignment was to design a smaller, faster, more lightly equipped mobile infantry—particularly useful in Third World conflicts.

He also had the promise of a second star. Powell had always loved Leavenworth's history. Now Alma Powell had a mansion fit for a "general's lady," a house formerly inhabited by Mrs. William Tecumseh Sherman, Mrs. Philip Sheridan, and Mrs. George Armstrong Custer (and said to be haunted by Mrs. Sheridan's ghost). Powell met the Buffalo Soldiers in the flesh at Leavenworth. A local barber, "Old Sarge" Jalester Linton of the 10th Cavalry, was a repository of black military history. When Powell asked Linton how Leavenworth commemorated the Buffalo Soldiers, the answer was 9th and 10th Cavalry Avenues: "two dirt roads and an abandoned trailer park," which Powell discovered by accident when he was jogging.[13] He began lobbying the post historian to build a fitting Buffalo Soldier memorial. Just before the start of the Gulf War, Powell attended a groundbreaking ceremony for a monument at Fort Leavenworth to the black 9th and 10th Horse Cavalry Association.

In early 1983, still at Leavenworth, Powell was asked by General John Wickham, the new Army Chief of Staff, to lead a one-month crash study with thirteen of the brightest lieutenant colonels and colonels on where the Army ought to be in the next four years. The Powell group's response was called Project 14 (because of the group's fourteen members). Recommending what Powell called "some modest course corrections," it stressed the importance of guaranteeing no more failures. Short on specific proposals, Project 14 basically boiled down to the edict that the Army must win cleanly next time. The Army existed to win battles and wars, "not just to manage itself well," Powell explained later. "If we expected to restore the nation's confidence in us, we had to succeed in the next test of arms."[14]

Back at the Pentagon by the summer, Powell became senior military assistant to Weinberger, who was now secretary of defense. Weinberger dealt with policy, but Powell was "the real Secretary of Defense," the former assistant defense secretary Michael Pillsbury told *New York Newsday.*[15] If Powell could not make a meeting, Weinberger "simply canceled the meeting." In the fall of 1983, Powell and Weinberger faced a series of challenges. The Russian downing of a Korean commercial airplane in September was followed by the bombing of the U.S. Marine barracks in Lebanon on October 23; 241 Marines were killed. Powell and Weinberger agreed that the Marines, with no clear mission, should not have been there in the first place. Operation Urgent Fury, the possibly diversionary invasion of Grenada, came two days later.

The disaster in Lebanon had a profound impact on Weinberger, who responded by developing guidelines to ensure that U.S. troops never be put in the line of fire without a clear mission. In November 1984 he announced his six-point test for the use of U.S. combat forces abroad:

1. Commit only if allied vital interests are at stake.
2. A commitment having been made, use all resources necessary to win.
3. Go in only with clear political and military objectives.
4. Be ready to change the commitment if the objectives change.
5. Only take on commitments that Congress and the American people will support.
6. Commit U.S. forces only as a last resort.

"In short, is the national interest at stake?" asked Powell. "If the answer is yes, go in, and go in to win. Otherwise, stay out."[16]

Powell writes that he was the first to warn Weinberger in 1985 about the developing National Security Council plan to sell antiaircraft missiles to Iran in exchange for the release of American hostages—a plan championed by the national security adviser, Admiral John M. Poindexter, and his aide Major Oliver North. Powell opposed the plan. "Colin felt strongly that you do not negotiate with terrorists, and that if we were ever going to talk to Iran, it had to be with authoritative figures, not in the shadows," a former White House official told *The New York Times.*[17] But when the order came from Reagan to send the missiles to Iran, Powell obeyed. He was not held responsible for following orders in the Iran-Contra scandal. By warning Weinberger and Poindexter in writing of the necessity to inform Congress of the arms transfer, he had saved the Army's integrity as well as his own—but both had been badly served by politics.

Powell asked to return to the field in the wake of Iran-Contra. In July 1986 he was given a third star and a prize command, V Corps, based in Frankfurt. There his immediate superior, General Glenn Otis, commander of all U.S. forces in Europe, was also a black three-star general. But Powell stayed in Frankfurt for only six months. The Reagan administration was under heavy attack for the Iran-Contra affair; after Powell had refused three requests to return, Reagan himself finally called to say that he was needed "to help Frank Carlucci straighten out the mess at the NSC." He had no choice but to return to Washington, "get out the old civvies, and move into a White House cubicle about the size of the bathroom" at V Corps.[18] As the president's deputy assistant for national affairs, Powell now played the role of ambassador and mediator between the Pentagon, the State Department, and the CIA. And he helped shore up the scandal-damaged National Security Council.

In November 1987 Powell became the first black national security adviser, replacing Frank Carlucci, who had become defense secretary. He was responsible for coordinating the Ronald Reagan–Mikhail Gorbachev Washington summit that resulted in the signing of a treaty to destroy all intermediate-range nuclear weapons. He and Reagan got along well. According to observers, Powell overlooked Reagan's occasional racial insensitivity as a holdover from an earlier time. Like most Americans, he was dazzled by the president's charisma and struck by "the paradox of warmth and detachment Reagan seemed to generate simultaneously, as if there could be such a thing as impersonal intimacy."[19] (A gift Reagan may have learned as a radio announcer.) Sometimes, the two men would "just philosophize," sharing a "mutual amazement" at how far each had come despite his mediocre academic achievement.[20] Reagan's famed detachment was most apparent during meetings: after opening with a joke, he "listened carefully and asked a few questions, but gave no guidance."[21] According to Bob Woodward, Powell enjoyed the stress of his job but was taking two medications for high blood pressure. If he told

Reagan he didn't have to worry about something, Woodward wrote, "the President would soon be happily gazing out the window into the Rose Garden."[22] Before leaving office, Reagan awarded Powell his fourth star.

WEST POINT: GENERAL FRED A. GORDON

Nineteen eighty-seven was the hundredth anniversary of Lieutenant Henry Flipper's graduation from West Point. That year, forty-seven-year-old Brigadier General Fred A. Gordon became the first black commandant of West Point, surely a sign of closure for historic outrages against black cadets. A bust of Flipper was dedicated, and "Buffalo Soldiers Field" was created on the site of the old barracks where, between 1907 and 1946, a detachment of the black 10th Cavalry had served as West Point riding and tactics instructors. The West Point Veterinary Clinic was renamed for Sergeant Robert P. Johnson, the West Point–born son of a Buffalo Soldier who spent over twenty years as an Academy instructor in communications and tank and infantry tactics.

I met General Gordon in December 1989. (In the same year, Kristin Baker, daughter of an Army colonel, became the first female captain of the West Point Corps of Cadets.) It was perfect West Point weather, gray skies heavy with snow. It began to snow, in fact, as we sat in front of the fireplace in the gracious old Commandant's House high above the Hudson. West Point was a "premier assignment," Fred Gordon said. "There are over two hundred brigadier generals, but only one Commandant of Cadets."

Born in Alabama and raised in Michigan, Gordon graduated from West Point in 1962. His first assignment was the Canal Zone, as a field artillery second lieutenant, just in time for anti-American riots. Starting in 1966, as a young captain, he had two tours of duty in Vietnam and a postwar tour in Korea. He attended both the Armed Forces Staff College and the National War College. In the Clausewitz track, as a soldier-politician in 1980, he was in Washington as executive officer in the office of the U.S. Army chief of legislative liaison. In 1982 he became commander of division artillery of the 7th Infantry, at Fort Ord. He was still there when he made brigadier. "Making brigadier is the *hard* part of military life," Gordon said. "They look at over two thousand colonels and select forty-three." In 1984, when he became a general, there were about thirty other black generals in the Army. "We all knew each other's names, if not personally," he said. By 1989, there were "too many to ever know them all." Gordon believed that affirmative action helped him, as it "has helped anyone who is black in any situation," but he also insisted that in the end it boiled down to "professional competence on the individual level." A generalship entails impressive baggage, for generals, like royalty, travel with their own flags. Flag rank means "you're good at your profession," Gordon said.

In 1986, while back at Fort Ord as assistant division commander, Gordon received a call from an old West Point friend asking if he would like to be commandant of the Academy. Gordon (who knew of at least two other candidates) was interviewed in January 1987, and appointed. The media attention was more than his wife, Marcia, liked. Pretty Marcia Gordon was an Army brat, the daughter and granddaughter of Buffalo Soldiers. Her grandfather had been with the 9th Cavalry in the Philippines in 1905 when he met her grandmother, who became one of the many Filipina war brides at Fort Riley, Kansas. Marcia's mother had seven sisters, several of whom married black soldiers. One uncle, a lieutenant in the 24th Infantry, became a prisoner of war in Korea. Marcia's brother was a Marine. There was "no other way of life." She "wouldn't know what to do," she said, if she "suddenly had a place to call home."

Marcia Gordon's father, Chief Warrant Officer Alfred E. Stewart, had been a member of the 9th Cavalry just before World War II. He saw his division disbanded early in 1942 when the unit went overseas. "We were still the Second Cavalry Division at our overseas staging area at Camp Patrick Henry, Virginia," Stewart told me. "We didn't know that we had been disbanded as a division, until the ship reached Casablanca," he said, when their boots and horses were taken away. Men and black officers (mostly medical) were separated and sent to service units. Stewart joined the 117th Quartermaster Battalion, based in Naples. He tried civilian life after the war, but like most professional soldiers found it boring. Reenlisting in the Army, he went to West Point as a communications and tactical training instructor in 1956, the year that Fred Gordon entered the Academy as a cadet. Stewart knew that his future son-in-law "had something special," but never dreamed that he would return as commandant.

Marines: "Devil Dogs" and Women

In the spring of 1989, my husband and I went to Parris Island, South Carolina, to attend our nephew's Marine Corps boot camp graduation. Marine Corps boot camp is a great leveler in more ways than one. The grads all looked alike. This was not just because of the newly hatched military pates; it was a product of the expression on their faces. As they jogged toward us two by two in the balmy Sea Island sunset the evening before graduation, it was difficult to see racial differences. They were a single glowing unit of health, will, and contained energy. "Devil Dogs": a fearsome fighting machine. "The Army teaches you to defend yourself," said one young graduate; "the Marines teach you to kill." After thirteen weeks of boot camp, they could see their families and pollute their bodies again with junk food. Having also suffered weeks of time disorientation and sleep deprivation, the grads were sent to bed early after their ritual ingestion of sugar, salt, and fat. The drill instructors now invited the families to an NCO Club beer party. Lean and tautly muscled to a man, these famous strikers of terror were all smiles and charm. "Our job is to break them down and build them up again," said Sergeant Simpson, our nephew's young black DI, almost apologetically. Sergeant Simpson was a Marine Corps boxer, whose life was spared because he was away at a match when five members of his family, all members of the Marine Corps, were killed in the 1983 Beirut barracks bombing.

The next morning at graduation, lined up in starched khakis on the sweltering parade ground, several "Devil Dogs" keeled over, to be silently swept away by ambulance crews. Only the two top grads wore Marine blues. They were a matched pair: the same height, with the same shoulders-to-waist triangular physique and the same handsome chiseled faces under wide-brimmed caps. A living Marine poster: one was black, the other white. Despite heat, flies, mosquitoes, and heads cracking asphalt, the top two stood at rigid attention, swords in hand, all through the ceremony.

So much for racial assimilation. Gender assimilation was another matter. Or was it? Marine Corps basic training remained sexually segregated. We discovered that the "Semper Fi" spirit was genderless, however, in the Beaufort, South Carolina, airport. Beaufort—sand, mosquitoes, heat, humidity, and antebellum mansions—is black Civil War history writ large. Its Sea Island breezes fell on the 54th Massachusetts, the 1st South Carolina Volunteers, and Miss Charlotte Forten and Captain Robert Smalls. Beaufort, gateway to Parris Island, is where we saw the person whom I, momentarily regressing to the prefeminist past, pointed out to my husband as a "lady Marine." Actually, she was proof positive that there are only Marines. Wearing combat boots and fatigue cap and trousers, she ambled through the narrow ticket area as if casually claiming the territory. She walked exactly like John Wayne—if Wayne had been a five-foot-four, 110-pound, very attractive young woman with a blond ponytail. With aviator shades under pushed-forward cap, and white T-shirt sleeves folded over golden biceps, she radiated contained power and something like intimidation. All anyone in the area wanted to do was get out of her way. A pair of white male civilians, seemingly local, eyed her with furtive suspicion as they, like all of us, shrank toward the wall. My husband and I, visitors from the North, were frankly awed. We had never seen a woman of such supreme confidence and such undeniable glamour. Her dog tags looked like fashion accessories. She reminded us of a movie star. My husband said, "Jessica Lange." Jessica Lange, we agreed, as Rambo.

Powell and Bush

Before he became president, George Bush had been less of a White House insider than Powell, who was short-listed for vice president in the 1988 election by a few columnists and politicians. A real war hero, not a movie hero, Bush wanted all the details and made his own decisions. Bush and Powell respected each other, they were in agreement on arms control, and Mrs. Bush (unlike Mrs. Reagan) asked Powell to call her by her first name. But Bush wanted to bring his own men to the White House. Bush offered Powell his choice: he could be CIA head or State Department number two—but not national security adviser. "It was a sad day," Powell later told Carl Rowan: watching Bush's inauguration on television at home, he absentmindedly picked up his White House phone to find that it was dead.

Powell almost left the Army. He had a million-dollar speaking-tour offer and two daughters in college. He made two lists; there were many reasons to stay in the Army and only one reason to leave—money. "If you want to come home to the Army, we have a job for you," said General Carl Vuono, the Chief of Staff. The job was a big one. Powell returned to the Army as head of Forces Command, Fort McPherson, Georgia, overseeing some one million active-duty Army members as well as reservists and National Guardsmen prepared to defend the continental United States and Alaska, or go wherever conventional warfare erupted. He was at Forces Command for six months. In August 1989, Bush named him chairman of the Joint Chiefs of Staff.

In his first public speech after becoming chairman, Powell told the National Association of Black Journalists that his appointment would not have been possible "without the sacrifices of those black soldiers who served this great nation in war for over two hundred years." Paying respect to the generation closest to his own, he named Generals Chappie James, Frank Peterson, Roscoe Robinson, Julius Becton, and Bernard Randolph (Air Force Systems Command chief), and Major General Harry Brooks. Besides these officers, who demonstrated "that we could do it as well as anybody," he praised "all those NCOs and soldiers who have served their nation so well." The real story, Powell said, was that he had climbed well and hard and "over the cliff," but always "on the backs and the contributions of those who went before me."[23]

Powell not only symbolized America's post-Vietnam military renaissance, he single-handedly, and almost immediately, inspired a new American appreciation for black fighting men. Unfortunately, it was a time when many black Vietnam vets were not doing well. Nearly two decades after the end of the war, blacks, who had fought in disproportionate numbers, were still suffering disproportionate postwar ills. "Some 17 percent of veterans diagnosed with post traumatic stress disorder are black," said George F. Sanders, vice chairman of the Federation of Minority Veterans, in July 1989.[24] About 275,000 black soldiers served in Vietnam. As many as 30 percent of all homeless veterans in major cities were black, and black vets were three times likelier than whites to be unemployed.

"Universally liked and respected," said an anonymous black colonel speaking of Powell a few months after he became chairman. He gave his colleague high marks for "a mind like a steel trap" and praised his "cool, sure handling of press briefings" as "more than impressive." While other generals were better field officers, he said, Powell was best suited for "the job of interacting between Congress and the White House." Alma Powell was the perfect general's wife, he added, knowing how to "fulfill her key social roles in old-fashioned Army style." Acknowledging that "officers don't live in the real world," he insisted that "Army tradition has served black America well—you learn to deal with the situation, turn it around, and make it a positive force. You always have to make split-second decisions on how to react; it's character-building."

The Chairman

The new chairman faced a media blitz. With the "best smile" since Ike and (according to *Time*) "teddy-bear good looks," the public was hooked.[25] He was a family man who liked to tinker with old cars. Possibly heeding Lord Chesterfield's advice to always "speak the language of the company you are in," he seemed the master of assimilation. "At the Pentagon he is spit and polish," wrote *The New York Times*. "On Capitol Hill, he is the affable soldier-statesman. In the White House, he is the punctilious military adviser who offers political and diplomatic analysis."[26] The *Times* also mentioned his "legendary icy self-control" (although there were rumors of a formidable private temper).

Powell was the first black chairman of the Joint Chiefs, and the first from the reserves. His color was the major news of his appointment, but it was in many ways only a sociological bonus. He had ranked first or second in every Army test of skill and leadership since his ROTC years. He had always been very good, very lucky, and very attractive to important mentors. Many saw his appointment as the end of military racism. Yet despite his singular talents, his career would never have taken off without the push of affirmative action in the 1970s. "If affirmative action means programs that provide equal opportunity, then I am all for it," Powell wrote.

> If it leads to preferential treatment or helps those who no longer need help, I am opposed. I benefited from equal opportunity and affirmative action in the Army, but I was not shown preference. The Army, as a matter of fairness, made sure that performance would be the only measure of advancement. When equal performance does not result in equal advancement, then something is wrong with the system, and our leaders have an obligation to fix it.[27]

In 1986, Powell's predecessor, Admiral William J. Crowe, Jr., became the first chairman of the Joint Chiefs to receive new congressionally mandated powers as principal military adviser to the secretary of defense, the National Security Council, and the president. But Colin Powell, standing at the apex of the American military renaissance, would be regarded by many as the most powerful and influential chairman in the history of the Joint Chiefs. The New Military had favorably announced itself in the early-1980s brushfires of the Philippines, El Salvador, and Liberia, and the 1983 invitational invasion of Grenada. Powell now put the stamp of his powerful presence on two larger conflicts. The first, in late 1989, was Operation Just Cause, the invasion of Panama.

Panama, the Powell Doctrine, and the New Base Army

The failed coup attempt against Panama's Manuel Antonio Noriega in October 1989 was the first major crisis of the Bush administration. Powell had been Joint Chiefs chairman for barely twenty-four hours. As Reagan's national security adviser, he had not believed that Panama was worth military intervention. Noriega had been on the payrolls of the CIA and the Defense Intelligence Agency since the mid-1960s. His backers, including George Bush, regarded him as a useful asset, especially when he collaborated with Oliver North in various schemes to help the Contras. By 1987, his crimes, known and tolerated by the Reagan and Bush administrations, became public and Noriega, a drug dealer and murderer, was notorious. By 1989, his violations of the Panama Canal Treaties had become an embarrassing political problem for George Bush, who publicly shook his fist at the man he had called Tony when Bush was CIA director and later, vice president. Noriega (rather in the manner of Pancho Villa) publicly laughed at him. On December 20, 1989, Operation Just Cause solved Bush's problem.

Now Powell, armed with maps and easels, became a TV star as he described "a 'mini Normandy invasion' involving some 25,000 men and women who would walk, swim, ride, fly and jump."[28] But some of the capabilities the military now displayed were "more Cecil B. DeMille than Eisenhower." Some were even superfluous. The Stealth fighter-bomber, for example: Panama had no air defenses. For Powell, Panama confirmed every Clausewitzian lesson: "Have a clear political objective and stick to it. Use all the force necessary, and do not apologize for going in big if that is what it takes. Decisive force ends wars quickly and in the long run saves lives."[29]

When Just Cause began, Noriega went into hiding. U.S. helicopters, C-130 gunships, and armored units assaulted his headquarters, which was situated in El Chorrillo (home of the boxer Roberto Durán), a poor, densely populated area of wooden houses, more like shacks, dating back to the digging of the Panama Canal. Most of its people were dark-skinned. U.S. troops received virtually no opposition, but civilian casualties reached around a thousand.

Staff Sergeant Arthur Lamotte of Louisiana, then a twenty-two-year-old private and trained mechanic, went to Panama as support for the military police. He had joined the Army for money for school and to see the world—and, also, he told me, because his father had insisted. "You need to learn responsibility," the elder Lamotte, a Vietnam veteran of the Navy, had said, recommending at least one tour of military duty. Sergeant Lamotte believed his father was right. "I had a rough background," he said; "I was going the wrong way." At first, even in the military, he "stayed in trouble." He had no one to say, "This is what you need to do to get promoted." Then one day a sergeant pulled him aside to say, "You think I don't know what you're going through?" He made PFC very soon after. He knew that if he ever reached a rank that could make a difference, he would help people coming up. He would show them the ropes and tell them "that they needed to see the world." "Once they see conditions in other parts of the world they will know how good they have it." He had never expected to be anywhere near combat, however. In Panama, following MPs who were clearing out street blockades near where Noriega was hiding, he was shocked when his unit was shot at by civilians. Lamotte was not afraid, but he had joined a peacetime military in which fighting wars had been the least part of the inducement to enlist.

The day of the coup attempt, Powell finally met a man whose face he had once seen every day. "I used to keep your picture on my desk in Frankfurt," Powell told the new Soviet minister of defense, General Dmitri Yazov, former commander of the Soviet 8th Guards Army, which had faced Powell's V Corps across the Fulda in Germany. "Yes, and I kept your picture on my desk," Yazov had responded.[30] Shortly before the actual start of the Panama invasion, while pumping his stationary bicycle (a gift from Arnold Schwarzenegger), Powell suddenly had a clear vision of his mission. His job was to solve America's new military problem: what to do when you lose "your Best Enemy."

Powell's answer was twofold: "Strategic Overview—1994," in which he considered the military's next four years; and the restoration of the 1973 "Base Army." Powell envisioned a "new order" defined by the flow of information, capital, technology, and goods "rather than by armies glaring at each other across borders." The new Base Army, rapidly mobile (with no reserves), would be prepared for three types of conventional warfare: an Atlantic Force, of armored units and planes; a scaled-down Pacific Force, of Army, Navy, and Air; and a light Contingency Force, for small-scale Third World threats. Predicting the next four years, Powell saw 40 percent Soviet military budget cuts, and a "defensive posture only" Russian military. He saw no Warsaw Pact, no East Germany, and no Soviet forces in Eastern Europe; Cuba would be "isolated, irrelevant." Korea, Lebanon, the Philippines, and the Persian Gulf would be persistent trouble spots, however—with "potential U.S. involvement" in Korea or the Persian Gulf.[31]

"Strategic Overview—1994" and the plan for a Base Army called for deep military cuts across the board. Congress was mandating Pentagon cuts of between $10 billion and $13 billion. "Across-the-board cuts" meant everything from cutting personnel to closing bases to closing or downsizing ROTC units to cutting recruitment advertising and, possibly, even veterans' benefits. The Army, most manpower heavy of the services, would be most affected by personnel cuts. "The changes envisioned were enormous," Powell wrote, "from a total active duty strength of 2.1 million down to 1.6 million." The Army would be reduced from 1.65 million troops to about 521,000.[32] In concrete terms, its recruiting efforts were already hampered by an advertising budget shrunk to $60 million in 1990 from $76.9 million in 1986.[33] Base closings meant the loss of thousands of civilian and military jobs.

Arguments flared: should personnel be cut, or should weapons programs? Critics feared that blacks would suffer disproportionately in the first case. "Conservatively 60,000 blacks will be discharged during the next year or two," wrote David Carlisle, a commander of Korea's last all-black combat unit.[34] "Save the boys, not the toys," wrote Colonel David Hackworth, now retired. "As we close out this century, we'll have invisible bombers to clobber invisible enemies, new nuclear missiles galore and more high-tech subs, ships, planes and Star War goodies, too. . . . As usual, the wrong stuff for most probable wars." Arguing that "boys not toys win wars," Hackworth used a Vietnam analogy: "The world's mightiest military power was defeated by warriors who were light on hardware but heavy on guts and know-how."[35]

Many civilians were pleased by the projected cuts, which in turn promised to create a so-called peace dividend. Seen by conservatives as a chance to cut taxes and send new money into the private sector, the peace dividend was seen by liberals as an opportunity to address social problems like education, housing, and drug control. But downsizing had few friends in the military, especially among blacks. "What does the nation lose if the military no longer serves as a channel for upward mobility for those at the bottom of the social ladder, especially members of minority groups?" asked Peter Applebome in *The New York Times* in May 1990.[36]

Powell at the Pentagon

On July 26, 1990, a day of cloudless Washington heat, I went to the Pentagon to meet General Powell. Inside the cool foyer of the Pentagon's River Entrance there was a sense, as in many older Washington buildings, of nineteenth-century American grandeur: classical statues and brass cuspidors. There was very little, beyond patched-on twentieth-century metal detectors, to hint at the real twenty-first-century Pentagon buzzing away beneath the ground. The crowd in the foyer could have been Sandburg petitioners waiting to see Lincoln, except that there was nothing nineteenth-century about Captain Robin Crumm—young and attractive in a crisply skirted Air Force uniform. (A scenario typical of the New Army: Captain Crumm had an Air Force husband.) Colonel William Smullen, her boss, Powell's information officer, was wearing Ivy League civvies. He kept his beribboned uniform in a clear plastic bag on the rack in his small, cluttered office. Smullen was the perfect information officer, intelligent, affable, and discreetly forthcoming. His glowing praise of Powell seemed heartfelt.

The chairman's office overlooked the Potomac. There were framed prints and memorabilia, comfortable sofas, and a large desk in front of a wall of books. In the manner of Jefferson and Hemingway, the general was working at a stand-up desk by one of the tall windows as we came in. He strode over, in short-sleeved khaki and modest ribbons, to clasp my hand, just as Air Force Master Sergeant Joe Fallon snapped the obligatory commemorative photograph. Colonel Smullen and I discreetly synchronized our tape recorders. A big man with a quiet voice, Powell seemed at once relaxed and brisk, warm and detached—those qualities that he himself ascribed to Ronald Reagan. Four-star generals, like presidents and movie stars, need personae to draw the public close, but not too close. In the new, user-friendly Army, Powell successfully balanced military rigor with easy civilian friendliness.

"The Defense Department has been ordered to get smaller, and to spend less," he said when I asked about cuts. "We need to get a lot smaller over a period of time—take in fewer and encourage others to leave sooner than later through education incentives." It was not a happy prospect for anyone, he admitted, stressing his own discomfort at the closings of ROTC units. Young people and their parents, schools and communities had written to him to protest.

"Why not cut hardware instead of men?" I asked.

"If you get rid of manpower, put someone off the rolls," he explained, "you save instantly, it's cost-effective. If you get rid of hardware, you don't save instantly; it takes maybe three years." He admitted that there would be "fewer opportunities for everyone, white and black," but he did not think that blacks would suffer disproportionately. I asked what advice he might have for my nephew in the Marine Corps. "Tell him to stay good."

"Social problems mean performance problems," Powell said when I asked how the military had accomplished what civilians seemed unable, or unwilling, to do about racism, sexism, and drugs. "The Army is not paid to solve social problems," he stressed, but it did so automatically simply "by taking in some one hundred and thirty thousand young people every year and sending them back to their communities better trained and better disciplined and drug free." Social problems for the Army were problems of "function and performance," he went on. "Whether people are uneducated, or on drugs, the efficiency needs of the military require the ability and worth of every single person in the organization. The Army knows that race problems and segregation don't win battles. The military could court-martial someone for being a racist. We believe in what we say; the Army does not have a dual standard. We require that people play by our rules—and they are stern rules."

Powell showed me his prized mementos: a shotgun from Mikhail

Gorbachev, a bottle of Panamanian *cerveza,* some old pieces of Soviet missile, and a signed (Reagan, Gorbachev, et al.) Soviet copy of the INF (Intermediate-Range Nuclear Forces) Treaty. Although he did not attend the Military Academy, West Point swords hung on the wall, accompanied by a print of Lieutenant Henry Flipper in the Indian Wars. There were mementos of the 54th Massachusetts, the 24th Infantry at San Juan Hill, and the Triple Nickels of World War II. Powell believed in the importance of black history. Blacks must not be allowed to "drop out of the story," he said. I asked what he planned to do with all these items when he left the chairmanship. "Oh, probably toss them in a box," he said, with a laugh. Scheduled for a forty-five-minute interview, I was given an hour. I would never have imagined that the country was in the midst of a military crisis. Most of America, including me, had no idea that the Iraqi situation had become critical.

In his book Powell describes having appointments the day before the invasion of Panama: meeting a high school student who wanted to interview a "famous person" and having lunch with an Annapolis midshipman. "I went through these innocent encounters as scheduled to make my day look normal and thus protect the security of Just Cause." My interview was probably one of those "innocent encounters."

OPERATION DESERT SHIELD

"The Iraqi army had made me uncomfortable ever since Iraq and Iran ended their bloody eight-year war in 1988," Powell wrote in *My American Journey.*[37] "Once Saddam, with an army over one million men strong, no longer had Iran to worry about, I feared he would look for mischief somewhere else." There are three ways to tell if the enemy is about to attack, Powell had written some nine months earlier in his "Strategic Overview": "Is artillery moving forward? Are they laying down communications? Are troops being reinforced with fuel and ammunition?" By July 31, 1990, all three were clearly happening in southern Iraq, where 100,000 Iraqi troops, including the elite Republican Guard with hundreds of new Soviet tanks, were amassed on the border with Kuwait. Powell was concerned enough to call General Norman Schwarzkopf at MacDill Air Force Base, in Tampa.

As commander in chief of Central Command, Schwarzkopf was responsible for military activities in southern Asia, the Horn of Africa, and the Middle East. A situation in which Iraq was the aggressor was his "worst case" Mideast scenario. "The world's fourth-largest army," he wrote, "was sitting just north of oil fields whose output was essential to the industrialized world." Fortunately, Schwarzkopf was not entirely unprepared. Although the Pentagon, envisioning a Red Army attack upon Iranian oil fields, had ordered training for a war in the Zagros Mountains of northern Iran, Schwarzkopf believed that this was a mistake. He already had an ally in Powell.* Importantly, Powell agreed with him that training for war in the Zagros Mountains was unrealistic, and that stockpiling equipment for that war (which called for shipping petroleum *to* the Middle East because Iranian refineries could not be counted on) was a "gigantic" waste of money.

By July 1990, the United States changed the plans of its annual computer-simulated war game, code-named Internal Look. Under the Schwarzkopf-planned scenario, Iraq, not the Soviet Union, was now the enemy—possibly taking on Saudi Arabia. Internal Look determined that Saudi Arabia could be defended against Iraq, but at great cost. That week, the Pentagon-simulated war games began to look like the reality on the ground. On July 17 Saddam Hussein, who had an enormous war debt and was hoping to raise oil prices, publicly threatened Kuwait and the United Arab Emirates with war. He accused them of putting a "poisoned dagger" into Iraq's back by exceeding production quotas set by OPEC and driving down the price of oil. The first reports of unusual troop movement north of Kuwait began coming in that day.

On August 2, Iraq crossed the border to invade Kuwait. Schwarzkopf, in Tampa, heard the news from Central Command's satellite radio intelligence team in the American embassy. He was about to call Powell, just as Powell called him to come to Washington to brief the president.

"I think we'd go to war over Saudi Arabia," Powell told Schwarzkopf just before the meeting, "but I doubt we'd go to war over Kuwait."[39] Seeming to bear out Powell's belief, later that day Bush adamantly informed a pool of TV reporters that the United States was "not discussing intervention."[40]

On August 3 Schwarzkopf explained to the president and the National Security Council just why Iraq figured in a worst-case scenario. In size, Saddam Hussein's standing army ranked behind only China's, the Soviet Union's, and Vietnam's. (The U.S. armed forces ranked seventh.) Iraq had 900,000 men in sixty-three divisions, including eight of the Republican Guard, and an arsenal of international weapons: Soviet tanks,

---

*"In discussions about the future of the Army, it was often Powell and Schwarzkopf against many of our colleagues," Schwarzkopf wrote. "We argued that, because the Army could no longer expect to go to war against the Soviets, we should rethink the way we were structured and equipped—before Congress did it for us."[38]

South African heavy artillery, Chinese and Soviet rocket launchers, Chinese and French antiship missiles, Soviet bombers, and French Mirage fighters.[41] Unmentioned by Schwarzkopf in this arsenal was what the CIA estimated to be at least a thousand tons of chemical weapons.

Schwarzkopf stressed that his contingency plans concerned only the defense of Kuwait. If the United States wanted to *remove* Iraq from Kuwait it would have to go on the offensive—meaning the use of many more troops and the expenditure of much more time. Conscious, like his friend Powell, of the lessons of Vietnam, Schwarzkopf intended that Central Command be prepared for all possibilities. "The U.S. military in Vietnam had been accused of regularly sugar-coating the truth in an effort to please the President," he wrote, "and on the basis of bad information the President had made some disastrous decisions. We were not going to repeat that mistake. Every shred of information we gave the President would be the most accurate we had, even if it reflected unfavorably."[42]

The next day, in a National Security Council meeting attended by Bush, Defense Secretary Richard B. Cheney, William Webster of the CIA, Deputy Secretary of State Lawrence Eagleburger, and others, Powell asked "if it was worth going to war to liberate Kuwait." Calling this "a Clausewitzian question which I posed so that the military would know what preparations it might have to make," Powell detected "a chill in the room."[43] Although fluent in warlord-militarese ("We will chase him, and we will find him," he had said of Noriega; "First we're going to cut it off, then we're going to kill it," he would say of the Iraqi army), like most Clausewitzians Powell was generally less hawkish than his civilian bosses. He would be criticized as "cautious." He was not alone. Even the famously volatile Schwarzkopf was considered "hesitant to fight" by some in the Bush White House.[44] The former Joint Chiefs chairman Admiral Crowe urged caution in testimony before the Senate Armed Services Committee a few months later: "Our dislike for Hussein seems to have crowded out many other considerations. I would argue that we should give sanctions a fair chance. . . . If, in fact, the sanctions will work in 12 to 18 months instead of six months, the trade-off of avoiding war with its attendant sacrifices and uncertainties, would, in my estimation be more than worth it."[45] One of the lessons learned by the best of the Vietnam War officers, but seemingly not by many politicians, was not to consider "cautious" a necessarily dishonorable epithet.

The scenario took a turn for the worse on August 5, when the Iraqi Republican Guard began massing tanks and artillery on the Saudi Arabian border. Now Bush declared unilaterally that the invasion of Kuwait "will not stand." In a matter of days, the United States had gone from "not discussing intervention" to committing itself to the liberation of

Kuwait and the greater matter of defending Saudi Arabia. Cheney and Schwarzkopf flew there to brief King Fahd. Schwarzkopf wanted to be sure that "the king understood that we were talking about flooding his airfields, harbors, and military bases with tens of thousands more Americans than Saudi Arabia had ever seen."[46] Two days later, the first U.S. fighter planes landed.

America would be "ready to move from the deterrent to the defensive phase by early September," Powell told Bush in the second week of August. By about December 1, with some 184,000 troops in place, he said, "there would be no doubt that we could defend Saudi Arabia."[47] By the third week of August, the defensive operation in the Gulf had a name: Operation Desert Shield.

Bush had determined in early August that America's diplomatic efforts should be "massive" in order to mobilize world opinion against Iraq. The UN condemned the invasion that month and officially voted to use force to expel Iraqi forces in November. Meanwhile, Bush and Secretary of State James Baker, having won an essential agreement by China and Russia not to block the proposal, marshaled an international coalition. Personnel, matériel, or both would come from Afghanistan, Argentina, Australia, Bahrain, Bangladesh, Belgium, Britain, Canada, Czechoslovakia, Denmark, Egypt, France, Greece, Italy, Kuwait, Morocco, the Netherlands, New Zealand, Niger, Norway, Oman, Pakistan, the Philippines, Poland, Qatar, Romania, Saudi Arabia, Spain, Senegal, Singapore, Sierra Leone, South Korea, Sweden, Syria, Turkey, and the United States. The latter would provide by far the most troops: 540,000.[48]

"We had been planning for this kind of war on a grand scale for years at NATO," wrote Powell. "But we had assumed it would be fought amid hills and forests against a Soviet enemy, not across sand dunes against an Arab foe." Even Arab friends could make life difficult for non-Arab troops. The Saudi Arabian ambassador, Prince Bandar, explained the rules. U.S. troops could not wear visible crucifixes, nor could they bring Bibles into the country. (But Saudi officials would look the other way if Bibles were flown directly to air bases.) U.S. Jewish troops could hold no religious services on Saudi soil. (Helicopters would take them to the Persian Gulf, for services on U.S. ships.) There could be no alcohol. On the subject of "sexual hanky-panky between an American and a Saudi," Powell wrote, he and Bandar had a "gentlemen's agreement."[49] The American would be spirited out of the country for U.S. punishment, before Islamic law took hold. U.S. women in T-shirts driving vehicles proved to be the only insurmountable problem. (Saudi women inspired by Americans to drive were promptly arrested in Riyadh.)

Despite preparations for war, James Baker, Admiral Crowe, and

General Powell stood firmly on the side of sanctions. Powell believed that containment—he called it strangulation—would work best in dealing with Saddam Hussein. But Bush, influenced by Britain's Margaret Thatcher, was set on war. ("This is no time to go wobbly, George," she had reportedly said.) Never ones to rush into war, and always needing clear political goals, once Clausewitzians were committed they were firm on two points: conflicts should be as brief as possible, and they should be resoundingly victorious. Richard Cheney called this the "don't-screw-around school of military strategy."[50]

American troops began arriving in Saudi Arabia in early September. Staff Sergeant Arthur Lamotte, veteran of Panama and member of the 503rd Maintenance Company, arrived in the Gulf from Fort Bragg in that initial wave. His first thoughts, he told me, were about Vietnam, not Panama. He wondered if the Gulf War would be anything like his father's war. He also wondered if their chemical warfare training would work. After an initial stint of guard duty, Lamotte's unit moved to its desert compound, where it was in constant danger from snipers and booby traps.

Powell visited American troops on October 21. "I know you want to know the answer to two questions," he told them. "What are we going to be doing here? And when are we going to go home? I can't give you the answers to those questions, we are giving our political leaders time to work this out." He worried about the troops' patience. "Troops would fight for each other and for certain core values: national survival, the lives of American citizens," he wrote later. "They would fight for their leaders—presidents, even generals, if the reasoning was presented clearly and honestly."[51] But it was "problematical," he believed, whether they would fight for long for another country, like Kuwait, or simply to punish a Saddam. Ten days later Bush decided to double the number of U.S. forces in Saudi Arabia, sending three more aircraft carriers, a second Marine division, and the tank-heavy VII Corps from Germany. He kept the decision secret until after the midterm elections that November, however. In mid-November it was determined that the target date for the ground war would be sometime in mid-February.

MAJOR FLOSSIE SATCHER

Major Flossie Satcher was a twenty-five-year-old First Lieutenant in October 1990 when she went to Saudi Arabia as part of the 24th Ordnance Company, based at Hunter Army Air Field in Georgia. The 24th Ordnance provided ammunition for the 24th Infantry Division. Lieutenant Satcher grew up in Mississippi, "in the country," as she told me. As a high school senior, she heard her friends and classmates talking about the Reserves and how "exciting" it was. Enlisting in the Mississippi National Guard, she won a ROTC scholarship to Jackson State University and went into the Army at twenty-one, right after graduation. She had never been out of Mississippi. She was looking for "travel" and "adventure." Like most reservists of her generation, never in her life did she expect to go to war. War was inconceivable. Her mother had agreed to her enlistment only on her promise that there would never be a war. More important, she was the single mother of eighteen-month-old twin daughters.

She was also the personification of Army values. Values, she told me, "just like" those instilled in her as a child by her mother and her church. There was no choice; she had made a commitment to the military. She was very positive about her Army experience and happy to be a soldier. Her financial situation was better than those of most of her high school and college friends. She was ready, if not exactly happy, to go. She knew "never to question the mission and to obey all legal orders." She left the twins with her mother. She was a first lieutenant, she had found excitement and adventure—but she was very afraid.

As a company commander, she slept by herself in a small tent next to the operations (company headquarters) tent, away from the company area. She was afraid to leave the tent at night. When she first arrived there had been an infiltration scare—a possible enemy in the area had been heard on the radio, but never found. Although her support unit was noncombat, as an officer she had been issued an M-16 rifle and a pistol; she kept them both pointed toward the entrance of the tent at all times. She also spent her nights in terror of attack by Scuds or chemical weapons. Every time a Scud missile was fired toward Dhahran, it came in right over their heads.

The daytime was easier. Because she had always played sports, she had a sense of discipline, which the Army reinforced. She felt good about her personal contribution to the war effort. She understood the purpose of the mission. Before they were deployed, the battalion commander had explained what they were doing and what the mission was going to be. She knew that her job was to support the combat military, and to "support each other and our country." "I was proud of my soldiers," she told me. They were doing a good job. Her "customers" had commended them. (Support units called their main units "customers," and the customer was always right.)

Sixteen percent of the women serving in the Gulf were single parents. Colonel M. Richard Fragala, a consultant for psychiatry to the Air Force surgeon general, said that most of the 3,800 Air Force women in the Gulf had carried out their mission admirably. Some, however, mostly among those with children under the age of two, had to be sent back to the United States. They had become "very vulnerable to stress during the deployment," he told *The New York Times*.[52] (Major Satcher's nighttime fears may well have resulted from her vulnerability to stress.) One of the women killed in the Gulf, twenty-seven-year-old Sergeant Tracey Brogdon of the Florida Army National Guard, was the mother of a six-year-old son.

STAFF SERGEANT RAY ARMSTRONG

Staff Sergeants Ray and Kathleen Armstrong basically spent their honeymoon in the Gulf. The Armstrongs had met at Fort Drum, New York, where they were both in the 240th Quartermaster Company. They had married in July 1990, delaying their honeymoon for an expected tour of duty in Germany together. Instead, in November, their company was in Saudi Arabia as the main support of the 2nd Cavalry Armored Regiment. At first, they slept in separate tents. Once they were detached to the 2nd Cavalry, they shared a pup tent but had individual vehicles and rifles. Ray and Kathleen had the same job: to supply fuel to Bradley Fighting Vehicles, Abrams tanks, and Apache, Cobra, and Black Hawk helicopters.

Ray Armstrong, from Cleveland and the son of a minister, won a college football scholarship, but broke the same arm four times and could no longer play. Enlisting to earn education money, he planned to get out in five years, but "stayed on the train" because he was happy. He "loved to go to work." When he first went in, the NCOs were all Vietnam vets who really took care of their soldiers. "They loved them like family," he said. In what he described as his only bad Army experience, a racist captain at Fort Drum, Armstrong believed, kept him from being promoted to sergeant first class because his marriage was interracial. On the other hand, Fort Drum's commander, General Norman Burnett, the "best white man" he ever knew, taught him that not all whites were racists. The best part of his Army experience, he said, was "dealing with people of different cultures and background."

"GUARDIAN CITY": THE NATIONAL GUARDS

Few large National Guard units served in Vietnam, but 53,000 National Guardsmen, out of 540,000 total U.S. troops, went to the Gulf. All told, 142,000 Army reservists were made active, in the biggest call-up since Korea. The reservists in the Gulf were generally men and women with technical expertise, including pilots, doctors, truck drivers, and water purification specialists. Many would find themselves too close to combat for comfort.

New York's 719th Transportation Company, formerly the 369th Infantry Regiment, World War I's "Harlem Hell Fighters," was the first National Guard unit from New York to reach Saudi Arabia. Home was still the grand old 369th Regiment Armory on upper Fifth Avenue; the marbled walls were inscribed with names of places like Minaucourt, Vosges, and Maison-en-Champagne and lined with photos of winners of the Croix de Guerre. Captain Dennis Bush, a New York City police officer, was commander of the mostly black and Hispanic company. Most of the unit were civil servants, including New York City transit employees, sanitation workers, teachers, and firefighters and police officers. Many were Vietnam vets. Their average age was forty, although the range was twenty-two to fifty-five. The 719th went to Saudi Arabia in early November 1990, in support of the 101st Air Assault Division. Their corner of the Saudi Arabian sandbox was called Guardian City, named for both the National Guard and the Guardians, a black police fraternal organization. The 719th camp had signs reading "El Barrio," "Puerto Rico," and "Seventh Avenue, Harlem." Their major duty was driving semitrailers and keeping the front lines supplied with everything from computers to armored personnel carriers. The company included one female officer and twelve enlisted women. Sergeant Alvie Grimes, an accountant, joined the Guards in 1983 for extra pay. "It's a good cause," she said. "I never expected to be here. I've been enjoying the benefits for seven years, and now it's time to do what I was trained to do."[53]

* * *

In December, on Powell's second visit to Saudi Arabia, he was mobbed for autographs. Now he told all troops to be ready for war.

LIEUTENANT GENERAL CALVIN WALLER

"This Army of ours in the Gulf War was absolutely superb—not perfect, but superb," Lieutenant General Calvin Waller told me. "It was the best Army that I ever saw." Waller was deputy commander of Desert Storm. "For an African American, the military is the fairest place to reach goals based on potential," he said. "In the military, standards are very clear, if you are good and if you've met the standards you will be promoted." Waller's two earliest mentors, both white officers, "didn't know what to do" with him until they saw his "leadership ability, and ability to get things done."

Powell, Schwarzkopf, and Waller, three "fathers" of Desert Storm, had all been young officers in Vietnam. Their career tracks had run nearly parallel. Powell and Schwarzkopf had both been "fast burner" (Army slang for overachievers) Vietnam advisers. Waller and Schwarzkopf had been classmates at Fort Leavenworth. Powell and Waller had worked together daily at the Pentagon in the late 1970s and early 1980s, when both were senior military assistants at the Defense Department. Schwarzkopf had been Waller's commanding officer at General Staff College. They served together again in the early 1980s, when Schwarzkopf (with three stars) was commander, and Waller (with two stars) was his chief of staff.

Waller was chosen as Schwarzkopf's deputy, according to Michael R. Gordon and General Bernard Trainor, authors of *The Generals' War,* partly to act as a "steadying influence" on Schwarzkopf's difficult temperament.[54] Many generals, including Eisenhower and Powell, were known for terrible tempers, but Schwarzkopf's was volcanic. Cheney, for example, called him "something of a screamer"; although he was famously avuncular and benign with enlisted personnel, senior as well as junior officers quaked before his tirades.

When Waller arrived in Riyadh in December 1990 to help plan the upcoming offensive, he found a demoralized general staff, afraid to risk Schwarzkopf's disapproval. Waller was able to defuse tense situations simply by taking charge of whatever the problem was. "I'll take care of it," he would say. "Now let's move on to something else." Sometimes, he would simply kick Schwarzkopf's boot under the table to calm him down. Powell was another who seemed to be able to handle the volatile commander. "How's the CINC [commander in chief] doing?" he would ask Waller. "His hair still on fire?"[55]

As chief of American and Allied ground forces, Cal Waller was to deal with troop and equipment delays, as well as with interservice rivalry. (Air Force generals were not always considered team players.) He also dealt with conflicts between Schwarzkopf and the Army high command. Schwarzkopf had already told Bush that reversing an invasion was one of the most difficult military tasks. It would take eight to twelve months for U.S. forces to be up to strength to remove Saddam Hussein's army from Kuwait. Waller made unwelcome headlines that December when he told a group of journalists that the Army would not be ready to launch a ground offensive until mid-February at the earliest, instead of the January 15 deadline set for Saddam's withdrawal by the UN. According to Bob Woodward's *The Commanders,* Powell was furious. But Secretary Cheney felt that Waller, unused to dealing with the media, "had been thrown to the wolves."[56]

On January 12, Congress officially authorized the use of force in the

Persian Gulf. Three days later, the United Nations deadline for Iraqi withdrawal from Kuwait came and went.

Just before the war began, Powell saw a copy of a cable from Ambassador Charles Freeman in Saudi Arabia: "For a range of reasons, we cannot pursue Iraq's unconditional surrender and occupation by us. It is not in our interest to destroy Iraq or weaken it to the point that Iran and/or Syria are not constrained by it."[57] That is, the military ideal of a "spectacular" win was tempered somewhat by diplomatic concerns. "If the United States goes to war against Iraq, it could cause a heck of a backlash in the Arab world," Freeman had told Schwarzkopf in early October. "I'm not sure anyone in Washington has given that enough thought."[58] Schwarzkopf realized that two conditions were necessary to placate the Arab world. "First, Arab forces in significant numbers had to fight by our side; second, we had to win." In the event of a ground war against Iraq, he determined that Arab forces must be the ones to liberate Kuwait City. Diplomatic concerns might be assuaged, but a Clausewitzian principle was broken. War began without clear agreement as to the objectives of the mission. Was it to simply remove Iraqi forces from Kuwait? Or, as most Americans believed and Bush all but said, to destroy the regime of Saddam Hussein?

Operation Desert Storm

In the first days of the war, Schwarzkopf copied out a quote from the *Memoirs of General William T. Sherman:* "War is the remedy our enemies have chosen. And I say let us give them all they want."

When the air campaign against Iraq began on January 17, Schwarzkopf suggested that the operation, heretofore known by its defensive name of Desert Shield, be changed to the offensive Desert Storm. And he sent a message to the troops:

> Soldiers, sailors, airmen, and Marines of United States Central Command. This morning at 0300 we launched Operation Desert Storm, an offensive campaign that will enforce United Nations resolutions that Iraq must cease its rape and pillage of its weaker neighbor and withdraw its forces from Kuwait. The President, the Congress, the American people, and indeed the world stand united in their support for your actions. . . . My confidence in you is total. Our cause is just! Now you must be the thunder and lightning of Desert Storm. May God be with you, your loved ones at home, and our country.[59]

By the end of the first day, U.S. bombs had destroyed every known Scud missile site in western Iraq, and only two U.S. planes had been downed. The Scud missile was, in Powell's words, "a cheap, inaccurate Soviet weapon of destruction" that had proved an effective terror weapon against civilians in the Iran-Iraq War.[60]

The air campaign, plotted by Air Force Colonel John A. Warden III, was based on Clausewitz's idea that every warring state had a "center of gravity"—defined by Warden as "the point where the enemy is most vulnerable and the point where an attack will have the best chance of being decisive." According to Warden, Iraq's "center" was made up of five concentric circles (drawn on a blackboard): 1. "Iraqi leadership," 2. "petroleum and electricity targets," 3. "Iraqi infrastructure" (particularly transportation), 4. "the Iraqi population," and 5. "Saddam's fielded military force."[61]

Flying to Tampa to confer with Schwarzkopf, Warden wondered how to "excite an infantry officer" about an air campaign. "You have a chance," he told the CINC, "to achieve a victory equivalent to or greater than MacArthur's Inchon landing—by executing an air Inchon in Iraq." Despite such visions, Schwarzkopf did not believe that strategic air strikes alone would get Saddam out of Kuwait. (Vietnam had demonstrated the limitations of air power.) He listened to Warden's plans, but his "imprint on the allied air campaign was virtually nil," wrote Rick Atkinson in *Crusade.* Schwarzkopf's life, Atkinson wrote, had "revolved around the clash of ground armies." Throughout the fall he had concentrated on dealing with the ground, specifically with the Iraqi Republican Guard, Saddam's best troops. The main ground attack force mission, personally dictated by Schwarzkopf, was "attack deep to destroy Republican Guard armored mechanized forces."[62]

* * *

On the first day of war, Powell thought of a saying of Robert E. Lee: "It is well that war is so terrible, or we should grow too fond of it." He realized how much, like all professional soldiers, he loved preparing for war and he had to remind himself that this was real, and that many Americans would not be coming back. If Clausewitz had all the answers for waging war, Powell now discovered that Fred Iklé, who had been Reagan's undersecretary of defense for policy, had all the answers for ending war. Powell read Iklé's *Every War Must End* just before Desert Storm began. "Thus it can happen that military men, while skillfully planning their intricate operations and coordinating complicated maneuvers, remain curiously blind in failing to perceive that it is the outcome of the war, not the outcome of the campaigns within it, that determines how well their plans serve their nation's interests," wrote Iklé. For Powell, this was a perfect description of Vietnam. He did not want it to happen in the Gulf.

On the second day, Powell and Cheney briefed the press. "I explained the battle plan," Powell wrote. "We were using our airpower first to destroy the Iraqis' air defense system and their command, control, and communications to render the enemy deaf, dumb, and blind. We then intended to tear apart the logistics supporting their army in Kuwait, including Iraqi military installations, factories, and storage depots." Powell was proud of his punch line: "Our strategy in going after this army is very simple. First we are going to cut it off, and then we are going to kill it."[63]

The second day also saw retaliatory Scud missile attacks on Israel (against which, the Israelis soon claimed, U.S. Patriot missiles seemed ineffective). On January 19, two American fighter pilots were shot down during a hastily planned mission to attack missile storage bunkers in western Iraq. Ten days later, after an initially quiet response to the opening of the air campaign, an Iraqi armored division attacked along the Saudi-Kuwaiti border, overwhelming the Saudi army at Al Khafji—a setback that King Fahd, in his fury, blamed on Schwarzkopf. Fortunately, Americans helped Saudi Arabia regain Al Khafji without agreeing to King Fahd's request to level the city rather than let it remain another day in enemy hands.

Despite initial heavy Scud attacks on Riyadh, by the last week in January, Schwarzkopf wrote, "the skies over Iraq belonged to the coalition." And "we were accomplishing exactly what we had set out to do: cripple Iraq's military system while leaving its agriculture and commerce intact and its civilian population largely unharmed."[64]

FIRST LIEUTENANT PHOEBE JETER AND SPECIALIST MELISSA RATHBUN-NEALY

On the night of January 21, a twenty-seven-year-old black first lieutenant, Phoebe Jeter of Sharon, South Carolina, the only woman to direct the launch of a Patriot missile during the war, shot down a Scud aimed at Riyadh. She told her story to *People*. There had been "no time to think" when she saw the "TBM" (tactical ballistic missile) on her "green scope" coming directly at them. "All around I could hear the BOOM! BOOM! BOOM! of other Patriot units beginning to fire. The van began to rock." There were so many Scuds, Jeter said, that her scope "looked like popcorn." The attack, which looked to people outside the van like something from *Star Wars,* lasted less than five minutes but seemed much longer.

Jeter, who remembered to put her gas mask on only halfway through the attack, said that she used to be "scared of the dark" before she joined the Army. "When we all started congratulating each other later on about how well we did, about the four Scuds the Patriots took down that night, I felt so proud," she said. "I thought to myself, 'I can do anything. Anything I put my mind to, I can do.' "[65]

* * *

On January 31, twenty-year-old Melissa Rathbun-Nealy, a member of a transportation battalion based along northern Saudi Arabia's Trans-Arabian Pipeline highway, became the first woman to be missing in action in American history, and the first female POW since World War II. Rathbun-Nealy, of Grand Rapids, Michigan, was white, but had been raised in a predominantly black environment. "If you heard her voice on the phone, you would never know she was white," her mother told *Life,* which put Melissa on its March 18 cover, hugging General Schwarzkopf.[66]

Melissa's parents, a former Roman Catholic nun and a former Roman Catholic brother, were Grand Rapids public school teachers. When whites began fleeing the inner city, the Rathbuns stayed. Melissa sang in the school choir, opposed drug and alcohol use, and joined the ROTC to earn money for college. She wrote to her parents from Saudi Arabia: "I'm so scared over here. . . . I just pray that it is God's will for me to survive this ordeal."

Shot in the arm when captured, Melissa was in captivity for thirty-two days. Her parents received letters of support from all over the world. Her Iraqi captors called her as "brave as Sylvester Stallone and as beautiful as Brooke Shields." Melissa regarded her captors, according to *Life,* as "the nicest people." (Off the record, they were rumored not to have been "nice" at all.) She reported crying only three times and wanted to be out before her twenty-first birthday—which she celebrated on the plane flying home.

Soon after her release, Melissa married a black fellow soldier, Specialist 4 Michael Coleman. She had received volumes of sympathetic mail on the subject of her capture; now she received a barrage of hate mail (mostly from her hometown), so much of it that she would no longer grant interviews, for fear of generating more.

Thirty-five thousand American women had served in World War I, ten thousand of them overseas. Nearly 400,000 served in World War II, where military nurses in the Pacific became prisoners of war. About 7,500, mostly nurses, served in Vietnam. Some 30,000 women served in

Desert Storm, about 6 percent of the 540,000 U.S. forces. Two women became prisoners of war; twenty-one were wounded in action; and fifteen, of ranks from private to major (black and white) died, five of them in hostile action. None of the women were nurses. They were pilots, truck drivers, MPs, water purification experts, and West Point graduates. In the new semi-egalitarian military, women could not, by federal law, serve in direct combat (on warships, in attack aircraft, or in ground combat units), but they were increasingly serving in combat support groups perilously near the front. Thanks to the performance of women in the Gulf, in 1991 Congress, while still barring women from combat positions in the infantry, enacted measures to permit but not require women to enter the Air Force, Navy, Army, and Marines to become combat pilots. Among the American women killed in hostile action, Major Marie Rossi was an Army helicopter pilot.

"No Blood for Oil"

As America's "Best Enemy" collapsed abroad, "We Shall Overcome," the black American civil rights anthem, rang out in Wenceslas and Tiananmen squares and at the Berlin Wall. At home, however, the vocabulary of civil rights had been co-opted by its enemies. Americans should now be judged by the "content of their character," not "the color of their skin," said conservatives—quoting Martin Luther King. This meant no "preferential treatment" for minorities. Now "welfare queens" were seen as taking food from the mouths of poor white children, and affirmative action was seen as snatching diplomas from the hands of poor white students. In 1975, 32 percent of black Americans lived 50 percent below the poverty level—in 1992, 49 percent lived 50 percent below the poverty level.[67] It was hard to see how affirmative action was keeping whites from educational opportunities.

Despite the achievements of extraordinary black individuals and the unprecedented successes of some members of the new black middle class, blacks, like many others in the 1980s, had separated into haves and have-nots, with many of the have-nots either on urban streets or in prison. Poor black Americans had come to the end of a decade that featured southern solutions to economic and social problems, solutions proposed by ex-Dixiecrats now calling themselves conservative Republicans.

The percentage of those who agreed in a national poll that "we are spending too much on welfare programs in this country" rose from 61 percent in 1969 to 81 percent in 1980.[68] A January 1991 National Opinion Research Center survey indicated that many white Americans held ingrained derogatory and stereotypical images of blacks. While the poll indicated more tolerance in some areas (on the subject of interracial marriage, for example), most of the white Americans surveyed rated black Americans as lazy, prone to violence, and less intelligent than themselves. Fifty-one percent also rated blacks as less patriotic.[69] When the survey was released, blacks, some 12 percent of the population, were 30 percent of U.S. forces in the Gulf War.

Never, before Desert Storm, had blacks held military positions of such prominence. And never before were so many blacks united in antiwar feeling before war even began. Some blacks regarded the war as part of the pattern of U.S. action against Third World people of color, as in Grenada, Libya, and Panama. Jesse Jackson, Coretta Scott King, and Eleanor Holmes Norton, the District of Columbia's delegate to Congress, were among the many black leaders who strongly criticized the war. Blacks, in general, were angry with Bush. His racially charged election campaign, his restriction of minority college scholarships, and his veto of the 1990 Civil Rights Bill happened long before bombs fell on Baghdad. (George Bush was only the third president in U.S. history to veto civil rights legislation. The other two were Andrew Johnson and Ronald Reagan.)

The idea of "economic conscription" was central to black protest. It was a "class issue more than a race issue," the retired Army sergeant father of a black Naval Reserve medic told *The Washington Post* in December 1990.[70] "I couldn't afford to send him to college . . . this was the only means he could go to school. I don't think he should be penalized . . . for me not being a millionaire . . . if you got the money your kid doesn't have to go." Four members of Congress had children in the Gulf. No one in Bush's cabinet did.

And black communities were losing the best and the brightest to the new, smarter Army. So many were already lost to drugs and crime; now they would lose the good ones, the future, to war. Charles Moskos, a military sociologist, stated in *The New York Times* in January 1991 that there was "scarcely a black church or inner-city school where someone does not know at least one person, if not a lot of people, in the Gulf."[71] Father George H. Clements of Holy Angels Roman Catholic Church, a black Chicago parish, reported that 104 members, or relatives of members, were in the Gulf. A black radio host in Chicago, Ty Wansly, who received taped messages from soldiers in the Gulf, saw "a pretty pervasive feeling of alienation" among black GIs. "Very little news of discontent reached the public," Wansly said, "because the mainstream media ignored stories that would interrupt the furious cadence of war drums."[72]

On the other hand, in February 1991 John Lewis, a black Georgia congressman, and the black *Washington Post* journalist Juan Williams visited Saudi Arabia. Williams reported "very high morale" and a "great degree of interracial cooperation, a much greater sense of family, a greater sense of togetherness among the military people than I see in civilian life."[73] He wondered why a number of prominent black leaders were casting the war in "racial terms," seeming "determined to drive a wedge between black America and its troops in combat as well as mainstream America, which is strong in its support of Operation Desert Storm." (About one-third of Desert Storm's combat NCOs were black.)

In the early days of the war, tens of thousands of men and women demonstrated against the war on college campuses and in Washington and other cities across America. The vote authorizing the president to use force to expel Iraq from Kuwait was relatively close. But the protests "fizzled" because the war was a "quick success," said Mitchell Stephens, of the department of journalism and mass communication at New York University. "Many base their opposition to wars on principle . . . the bulk of the American people typically seem to base their support or opposition on another consideration: how well a war is going."[74]

The Ground Campaign

The successful air phase of the Gulf War lasted thirty-eight days. The ground war, launched in mid-February, lasted all of four.

On February 8, Cheney and Powell went to Riyadh for a final review of ground-war plans. Just before the trip Cheney had asked Powell a somewhat unnerving question on the subject of "Prefix 5," the military code for nuclear-weapons potential. "Let's not even think about nukes," Powell replied. "You know we're not going to let that genie loose." "Of course not," Cheney responded. "But take a look to be thorough and just out of curiosity." The resulting top secret "look," indicating that to seriously damage even a single armored division dispersed in the desert would require too many small tactical nuclear weapons, confirmed whatever doubts Powell had concerning the practicality of nukes on the battlefield. They left for Riyadh with Cheney hopeful that Schwarzkopf had "an offensive plan with a little imagination this time."[75]

"At bottom, neither Powell nor I wanted a ground war," Schwarzkopf confessed in retrospect. "We agreed that if the United States could get a rapid withdrawal we would urge our leaders to take it. Though we hadn't literally defeated Saddam on the battlefield, in the eyes of the world—including the Arab world—under the circumstances a rapid withdrawal would be a defeat for Iraq." Like Powell, Schwarzkopf was suspicious of Washington "hawks." "These were the guys who had seen John Wayne in *The Green Berets,* they'd seen *Rambo,* they'd seen *Patton,* and it was very easy for them to pound their desks and say, 'By God, we've got to go in there and kick ass! Gotta punish that son of a bitch!' "[76]

Nevertheless, on February 8, Schwarzkopf told Cheney and Powell that he was ready. "We had moved entire divisions so far forward that it took a long time even by airplane and helicopter to get to them," he wrote." "Where once had been nothing but desert, a pipeline, and an occasional Bedouin tent, there now were seas of camouflage . . . that I knew concealed thousands of tons of food, spare parts, fuel, water, and munitions for the offensive." Saudi Arabian troops and U.S. Marines were poised on the eastern end of the Saudi-Kuwaiti border, Egyptians spearheaded the pan-Arab corps on the western end, and the U.S. VII Corps was arriving from Germany to tactical assembly areas near the front. The U.S. Navy had its big guns ready in the Persian Gulf, and British troops and French Legionnaires were in position. The assembled force was enormous, and strategic air strikes had already accomplished their vital mission. But there were always ground-war variables. As the air campaign moved from striking government buildings and infrastructure to bombing Iraqi forces, the Republican Guard *and* their tanks simply went underground into bunkers.

The air campaign reached its final "center of gravity" on February 13, with the targeted strike on the Al Firdos air raid bunker in a Baghdad suburb, which killed more than two hundred civilians and led to immediate restrictions on strategic bombing. Meanwhile, a broadcasting and leafleting campaign continued to urge Iraqi troops to defect, advising them to "March towards Mecca," the direction of the U.S. front lines.[77]

Schwarzkopf and Powell were both under pressure—Powell from civilian hawks and Schwarzkopf from commanders in the field who wanted more time. With Powell as the semi-harassed mediator, Washington and the U.S. command in Riyadh agreed on February 24 for the opening of the ground war.

On February 21, with the failure of Russian attempts to coax Iraq out of Kuwait, Bush set a new deadline for Iraqi withdrawal: noon on February 23. On the day of the deadline, U.S. Army Special Forces troops were inserted deep inside Iraq, and Stealth fighters attacked Iraqi intelligence headquarters (unaware that that American POWs were inside). The ground war began the next day.

At four A.M. Saudi time on February 24, the first Marines, led by M-60 tanks and Cobra helicopters and followed by thousands of troops in armored carriers and Humvees, crossed the Saudi-Kuwaiti border in darkness and cold rain, under covering fire from 155mm howitzers. Schwarzkopf laid out three strategic goals: "to kick Iraq out of Kuwait, to support our Arab allies in the liberation of Kuwait City, and to destroy the invading forces so Saddam could never use them again."[78]

At six A.M. Saudi time, President Bush appeared on television to declare that "the liberation of Kuwait has now entered a final phase." The Kuwaiti resistance reported that the Iraqis were destroying Kuwait City, with explosions throughout the city. The Arab liberators of the Kuwaiti capital were on their way: two Saudi armored brigades and a combined pan-Arab brigade, the victors of Al Khafji. Some three hundred miles to the west, a French light armored division and a brigade from the 82nd Airborne were on their way to Al Salman air base, home of the Scuds that fell on Riyadh. Thirty miles east of Al Salman, the biggest helicopter assault in history, slightly delayed by rain and fog, was about to begin.

"More than three hundred Apache, Cobra, Blackhawk, Huey, and Chinook helicopters, piloted by men and women, were transporting an entire brigade with its humvees, howitzers, and tons of fuel and ammunition fifty miles into Iraq," wrote Schwarzkopf, describing the late-twentieth-century version of wagons, pack horses, and mules. "They were to set up a huge firebase from which attack helicopters could easily strike the Euphrates valley." The *main* attack force, with sixteen hundred heavy tanks, was waiting on the Saudi border. It had three objectives: to free Kuwait City, the job of the pan-Arab corps; to destroy the Republican Guard, the job of VII Corps; and to close Iraqi escape routes in the Euphrates valley, the job of General Barry McCaffrey's 24th Infantry Division of the XVIII Airborne Corps.

On learning that the Iraqis had blown up Kuwait City's desalinization plant, the capital's only source of drinking water, Schwarzkopf was sure the invaders were ready to leave the city as well as Kuwait. In order to catch them, he had to speed up the main attack, which would now erupt at three P.M. Saudi time. "The Iraqi army, having demonstrated little aptitude for the simpler requisites of warfare," wrote Rick Atkinson, "now faced the most difficult of military maneuvers: a withdrawal under fire."[79] By mid-morning, coalition troops had reported little real opposition and taken many prisoners of war. "After firing a few shots," wrote Schwarzkopf, "the Iraqis just climbed out of trenches and gave themselves up." By the second day of the ground war the Marines had so many prisoners, and so few trucks available to transport them, that they were simply taking their weapons and pointing south, directing them to "Walk that way." At the end of the first day of ground warfare there were eight U.S. dead, and twenty-seven wounded, and more than thirteen thousand Iraqi prisoners. "The campaign had shifted from deliberate attack to what tacticians call an exploitation," wrote Schwarzkopf, "in which an army pursues a faltering enemy, forcing it to fight in hopes of precipitating a total collapse."

But bad news came on the second day: VII Corps, whose job was to take out the Republican Guard, was, alone of the entire main attack force, behind schedule. The long-term success of Operation Desert Storm depended upon the success of VII Corps. "Did VII Corps stop for the night?" asked an angry Schwarzkopf. "Until we'd destroyed the Republican Guard," he wrote, "our job was only half done, and all of us felt the window of opportunity rapidly slamming shut."[80] Worse news came from Al Khobar in Saudi Arabia: the U.S. Army barracks had been destroyed by a Scud attack that killed twenty-eight U.S. soldiers and wounded ninety-eight. "The casualty list presented a harsh reality of our modern army," wrote Powell: "women were among the victims."[81] Twenty-year-old Private Adrienne Mitchell, a black member of a noncombat Army Supply Unit, was one of three women killed when the missile fell on the coed barracks. "I did 30 years [and] didn't get a scratch," her retired Air Force master sergeant father told *Newsweek.* "My daughter's been in for five months, and she's dead."[82]

By noon Saudi time on February 26, VII Corps was finally in the thick of the fight, having almost destroyed one Republican Guard division, the Tawakalna, and driven two others, the Medina and Hammurabi, into retreat toward Basra, Iraq. The enemy was being driven directly into what the Air Force called the kill box—the four-lane highway leading from Kuwait City to Basra. "We bombed the hell out of every convoy we could find," wrote Schwarzkopf. Between air strikes Americans flew overhead, telling Iraqis in Arabic, "Get out of your vehicles, leave them behind, and you will not die."

Meanwhile, U.S. Marines and the pan-Arab brigades were linking up to liberate Kuwait City. As forces that did not speak the same language began to converge on the battleground, incidents of friendly fire—called blue-on-blue attacks by the military—were an increasing danger. Now VII Corps fought off the elusive Medina Division all night and Kuwaiti, Saudi, Egyptian, and other Arab forces officially liberated Kuwait City on the morning of February 27. That afternoon Powell told Schwarzkopf to think about "wrapping up" the war. The United States already had, in Powell's words, a "prisoner catch" of up to seventy thousand. "The doves are starting to complain about all the damage you're doing," Schwarzkopf reported Powell as saying.[83] For public relations purposes, Washington wanted the war to last an even one hundred hours.

Cal Waller was astounded when Powell called Schwarzkopf, at two a.m. Saudi time on February 28, to say that George Bush had decided to announce a cease-fire. The last Waller had heard, the cease-fire was "a matter for discussion, not a fait accompli." Waller thought that the idea of a hundred-hour war was "bullshit." "You go argue with them," Schwarzkopf had said. Waller knew that the war was coming to an end, but from an "operational point of view," he believed it should not have ended until both escape routes were blocked by allied ground troops and the Republican Guard was destroyed.

The debate over how far to advance into Iraq was already in full cry. Bush's characterization of Saddam Hussein as the devil incarnate did not help Americans to understand why he was allowed to stay in power, but the danger of destabilizing the Arab world was brought up in every debate. Meanwhile, the last Iraqi escape route, the highway from Kuwait City to Basra, had become what Powell called "a shooting gallery" for U.S. planes; the media were calling it the Highway of Death. "The road was choked with fleeing soldiers and littered with the charred hulks of nearly fifteen hundred military and civilian vehicles," Powell wrote. Inside many of those vehicles were the bodies of Iraqi soldiers who had ignored or failed to hear the coalition message to flee. Powell and Schwarzkopf agreed that TV coverage made it look like "slaughter for slaughter's sake."[84]

Flossie Satcher: The Highway of Death

To supply ammunition close up, Major Flossie Satcher's unit had followed the 24th Infantry Division into Iraq. She would never forget the odor of the Highway of Death. Having grown up in the Mississippi countryside, she was reminded of the smell of burning hair off hogs, but stronger and worse. At the tail end of the line, they saw burning vehicles and bodies on fire. The desert wind was so strong that she knew that she was inhaling floating particles of burning bodies. It would have been the worst feeling she had ever had, except that she had gone home in December, on emergency leave, to have her mother die three days after she arrived. She felt that her mother's death had somehow prepared her for the experience of seeing the burning bodies in Iraq.

When she finally returned home six months after the ground offensive, her children had forgotten her. "They wouldn't come near me, they didn't want to live with me," she said. She felt full of grief and pain at having abandoned her children. It took about a month to regain their confidence. It was the most terrible feeling she had ever known, by far the worst aspect of the Gulf War.

When the war ended, Major Satcher was happy to get back home, but she agreed later with soldiers who said that they had not finished the job they set out to do. When I asked how being in the Army had changed her life, she said it had made her "braver."

The End of the War

"When President Bush gave the word, the tanks lined up," said Staff Sergeant Ray Armstrong. "When it was called off, we were one hour and thirty minutes from Baghdad." Armstrong, whose 240th Quartermaster Company had followed the 2nd Cavalry into Kuwait City and seen total destruction, was not at all satisfied with the end of the war. "It was a political situation," he told me. The Army had become too "political" about many things, he believed. Armstrong was not opposed to women in the military; he had a female squad leader who "cussed" more than he did, but he "wouldn't baby anybody—male or female." If he did, he said, "the Army could not live up to its name." His wife retired from the Army when her enlistment was up. "Kathleen got scared after Desert Storm," he told me; "it took a toll on her family." He was never afraid in the Gulf. "Everybody's gotta die, nothing is guaranteed," he said. Armstrong planned to retire in 2001, after twenty years, and go back to Cleveland as a Ford Motor Company supervisor.

Staff Sergeant Lamotte believed that the United States had waited too long before sending in ground troops. "It was a long buildup for a short war," he told me. "They accomplished what they had to do, get the Iraqis out of Kuwait, but Saddam was still there. They should have gone in and gotten it over with," he said, "like Panama"—and stayed until they captured Saddam, as they had Noriega. As a mechanic, Lamotte was in support of the frontline infantry at the start of the ground war. The mission of the 503rd Maintenance was to get supplies to the front and fix broken vehicles. They followed the infantry into Kuwait—for Lamotte, a place of burning oil fields, burned-out vehicles, unexploded mines, and bodies and limbs.

In a matter of some six days, U.S. and coalition forces had liberated Kuwait; 75 percent of the Iraqi army had deserted or surrendered; the Republican Guard had been routed; Iraq was basically bombed back to the Stone Age; and Kuwait was on the brink of ecological disaster because of burning oil wells. One hundred forty-seven Americans had died in combat. Two hundred thirty-six had died in accidents and of other causes, including many caught in friendly fire. A tentative U.S. estimate of Iraqi losses would be 100,000 killed and 300,000 wounded.[85] What looked like "slaughter" to Powell and Schwarzkopf was, in fact, an all-out battle and rout of the sort that Clausewitz called *die Schlacht,* "the slaughter."

* * *

By the end of the war, members of New York's 719th Transportation Company were complaining that their unit had been broken up, stripped of much of its equipment, and moved into frontline positions without proper preparation or training. The Army showed little sympathy. "National Guard units, like any other Army units, will be positioned wherever they must go to perform their unit mission," said the Army spokesman in Riyadh. "If their mission requires going to the front lines, that's where they go." A family support group protested the placing of Guards troops so near the front. "They should not be out in the desert at their age," said Linda E. Williams, head of the group.[86] "They are weekend warriors who are not prepared to be in a ground war. It is almost like suicide." While the World War II veteran William DeFossett of the 369th Veterans Association called the complainers "perennial troublemakers," New Army recruitment, for both reserves and active military, rarely, if ever, stressed the going-to-war aspects of enlistment. Reservists became even more unhappy when a disproportionate number (mostly support, mechanical, transport, or specialist groups) had to stay in the Gulf after most combat units went home. (Because of cuts in personnel, the armed forces were using reservists more and more, and would do so again in Bosnia and Kosovo.)

* * *

At the end of the war, *Newsweek* reported that Desert Storm had won the military new stature "as an institution of opportunity for American blacks." "The question we need to be asking as a society," said the black military sociologist John Sibley Butler, "is how we have raised two generations of white middle-class youth who have no sense of service to their country." General Cal Waller preferred to address the issue of young black civilians: "What are our leaders doing in our communities to get our young black males off drugs? What are they doing to keep them in school or from dying in the streets."[87]

"We wanted to complete what we had set out to do," Waller told me in 1994. "But once we were told what the decision was, we didn't scream and yell. We said okay. We could have 'fallen on our sabers.' " Waller believed that America was justified in going to war. He also believed, despite the precipitous ending, that the mandated mission—"to push everybody back to the sea, capture the equipment, and destroy the Republican Guard"—had been completed. He was proud of all the forces and their "magnificent" accomplishment. "The military just never imagined that Saddam could remain in power," he said.

Waller retired from the military in 1991 to become senior vice president of an environmental technology company, responsible for cleaning up Rocky Flats, Colorado, home of nuclear triggers. He died of a heart attack four years later, at the age of fifty-eight.

* * *

Powell faced a media barrage in May 1991 with the publication of Bob Woodward's *The Commanders,* which implied that he was a "reluctant warrior," privately opposed to the president and responsible for turning the troops back away from Baghdad. "The military impulse to end the war as soon as a 'victory' was achieved, to get out as quickly as possible," wrote Gordon and Trainor in *The Generals' War,* "limited American military power as an instrument for shaping and enforcing the peace."[88]

In response to critics, Powell agreed that more tanks and Republican Guards escaped than expected. And "possibly the escape hatch needed another two or three days to close," but "we met the Iraqi army in the field, and while fulfilling the United Nations' objectives, dealt it a crushing defeat and left it less than half of what it had been." Powell was happy to quote the judgment of the military historian John Keegan: "The Gulf War, whatever it is now fashionable to say, was a triumph of incisive planning and almost faultless execution." It fulfilled, according to Keegan, the highest purpose of military action: "the use of force in the cause of order."[89]

The Big Parade

The victory parade in June in New York City was a blizzard of ticker tape, confetti, and balloons. Powell and Schwarzkopf (who both refused bulletproof vests as adding to girth) sat on the backs of open cars, in the Lindbergh and MacArthur tradition. "The celebrations were no doubt out of proportion to the achievement," Powell wrote. "We had not fought another World War II. Yet, after the stalemate of Korea and the long agony in Southeast Asia, the country was hungry for victory. We had given America a clear win at low casualties in a noble cause, and the American people fell in love again with their armed forces. The way I look at it, if we got too much adulation for this one, it made up for the neglect the troops had experienced coming home from those other wars."

Petty Officer Harold Mansfield, Jr.

"Today, I am going to introduce you to someone very special who is fighting for us so that we can be free," was how John Roberts, a white fourth-grade teacher in a predominantly black and Hispanic school, asked his class to "adopt" Navy Petty Officer Harold Mansfield, Jr., at the start of the war.[90] Mansfield's mother, Connie, had been Roberts's fellow teacher in the same Oklahoma City grade school. Connie Mansfield's husband had died eleven months before her son went to the Gulf, and Roberts wanted to "cheer her up." The children wrote letters to Mansfield, kept his picture on the bulletin board, and drew pictures of the U.S.S. *Saratoga.* A Catholic priest came to bless his picture so that he would be safe in the Gulf. When Mansfield came home in April, the class gave him a party, with popping balloons, and a cake with a design of the *Saratoga.* There were hugs and speeches, and many of the boys said that they wanted to be like Mansfield when they grew up. He impressed the children even further by demonstrating his Gulf War job, writing flight information backward so people on the flight deck could read it. On clear laminated plastic, Mansfield wrote "Everyone can be a hero" backward. He talked about the importance of getting an education—and he talked about his engagement.

Three weeks later, the class learned that Mansfield had been shot dead in a Florida grocery store parking lot by a member of the white supremacist Church of the Creator, one of the most active and sophisticated of the new Web-based hate groups. Roberts wrote "white supremacist" on the blackboard, and told the children to look up "supremacist" in the dictionary. Their first reactions were violent: they wanted to "fry" Mansfield's killer in the electric chair or drown him. Seeking a positive outlet for their rage, Roberts suggested that the children write to him instead. "Why did you kill our hero?" they asked again and again. One child wrote, "I hope you stay in jail forever." Another wrote, "I don't think Mr. Roberts has forgiven you and I don't think some of the children have forgiven you, but I forgive you. I just wish you hadn't killed Harold." About twenty children went to the funeral, each carrying a rose for Connie Mansfield. "Mr. Roberts, we went from balloons to bullets," said one of the children.

Revisionism and "Gulf War Syndrome"

Like most shining moments, the Gulf War glow proved illusory as well as brief. Saddam Hussein remained in power, despite the immense suffering of great numbers of innocent Iraqis, not to mention hundreds of thousands of Kurds and Shi'ite Muslims who rose against him. Critics of the war decried the decision to destroy Baghdad's infrastructure, water, and electricity; and they blamed continuing economic sanctions for contributing to the malnutrition and disease of most of Iraq's children. More militaristic critics insisted that the war had ended too soon, and that the ending was badly planned.

At the same time, a mysterious "Gulf War syndrome" was turning heroes into victims. Smoke from burning oil wells, insecticides, poison gas released by allied bombing, and anti–nerve gas pills were variously blamed. But, the Pentagon insisted, based on studies by the National Institutes of Health and the Defense Science Board, there was no "single disease syndrome" and no "persuasive evidence" of chemical or biological weapons exposure in Gulf War vets. The Defense Science Board study, known as the Lederberg Report, claimed that the entire vet health problem was "stress." According to a report published in the August 1995 issue of *Playboy,* Dr. Joshua Lederberg, the report's author, a Nobel laureate, was himself director-at-large of the American Type Culture Collection, a U.S. toxin exporter that had shipped large quantities of poisons to Iraq in the 1980s—including anthrax, botulism, brucella, and *E. coli.*[91]

Colonel Herb Smith, the wartime U.S. Army health liaison to Saudi Arabia, told *Playboy*'s reporter, Kate McKenna, that he saw "hundreds of dead camels, sheep and birds" spread out across the Kuwaiti desert. The bodies bore no bullet holes or other apparent injuries, and there were dead flies on the carcasses; it was a field-manual depiction of poisoning. Smith also recalled the constant ringing of chemical-weapons alarms, as well as the pervasive black smoke of oil well fires that, McKenna wrote, made soldiers spit up fuel oil and sneeze axle grease. Within a few months in the Gulf, Smith himself had swollen lymph nodes and flulike symptoms. Within two years of service in the Gulf, the once healthy Green Beret was confined to a wheelchair with autoimmune disease, organic brain disease, muscle degeneration, and heart, blood, and bone disorders. Finding a cure or even the nature of "Gulf War syndrome" seemed elusive.

In 1995, as the Pentagon finally officially admitted that the Vietnam-era defoliant Agent Orange caused birth defects, it also firmly proclaimed that there was no Gulf War syndrome, despite the nearly seventy thousand sick veterans of Desert Storm, many of whose children had genetic defects. In August 1995, the administration of President Clinton urged the Pentagon to get to the bottom of the problem. In April 1996, researchers at the University of Texas and Duke University announced that animal tests had confirmed that Gulf insect repellent and anti–nerve gas chemicals, harmless when used individually, were highly toxic and damaging to the nervous system when used in combination. There was no "single disease," but the combination of vaccines, pills, and lotions, compounded by the release of toxic chemicals in fuel oil fires, seems to have been responsible for the devastating symptoms of Gulf War syndrome.In any case, its victims were casualties of war.

In March 1997, Olivia and Frederick Fowler, a black Gulf War veteran couple from Laurel, Mississippi, were featured in a *Ladies' Home Journal* story. Olivia Fowler reported that an informal survey of her own National Guard unit revealed that thirteen out of fifteen babies born since the conflict, counting her own, had serious health problems, including birth defects and physical abnormalities.[92] That same year, the now-discharged Melissa Rathbun-Nealy Coleman, the first American servicewoman to be a prisoner of war, announced that she was suffering chronic health problems that had only developed after the Gulf War.

"Something's making 'em sick," said General H. Norman Schwarzkopf. He wondered if allied bombings of Iraqi frontline positions might have destroyed chemical weapons bunkers and thus exposed U.S. troops to poison gas.[93]

Role Model

In a 1904 Boston address, Booker T. Washington worried that the world heard too much about blacks who were charged with crime or lynched. He complained that "too often those who write and speak most concerning the Negro have never come in contact with him in his higher and better selves." In the light of alarming early 1990s statistics on young black males (dead, in jail, or on drugs), the question of role models became important. Although the media continued to focus on blacks as either criminals or victims, Colin Powell, the new role model, was obviously neither.

Powell claimed that he was not a victim of racism, because he made racism "someone else's" problem. "Others may use my race against me, but I will never use it against myself," he wrote. "My blackness has been a source of pride, strength, and inspiration, and so has my being an American." Having seen West Africa and Nelson Mandela's South Africa, he believed that black children should know about their heritage. They should learn about black writers, poets, musicians, scientists, and artists. But they should also know the "Greek origins of democracy," the "British origins of our judicial system," and the "contributions to our national tapestry of Americans of all kinds and colors."[94] A completely assimilated American, Powell had no need to separate his race from his nationality.

Older black role models have soared higher on philosophical or creative planes, but none in a certain sense has ever had so much power. No one, not even Frederick Douglass or Martin Luther King, Jr., had such high rank. People looked at Powell and saw stars. He wore the "suit of lights" for the last time in September 1993, for his retirement ceremony on the Fort Myer parade ground. Guests included cousins, Pershing Rifles buddies, former defense secretaries Richard Cheney and Caspar Weinberger, George and Barbara Bush, Dan and Marilyn Quayle, Vice President Al Gore and Tipper Gore, and President and Mrs. Clinton. Alma Powell, model military wife, received the Army's Decoration for Distinguished Civilian Service. And Powell received his second Presidential Medal of Freedom, "with Distinction." "I had benefited beyond my wildest hopes from all that is good in this country, and I had overcome its lingering faults," he wrote. "I had found something to do with my life that was honorable and useful, that I could do well, and that I loved doing. That is rare good fortune in anyone's life. My only regret was that I could not do it all over again."[95]

The Army and the Streets

Only under extraordinary conditions, like wars or natural disasters, does government request or even suggest military standards of behavior for ordinary citizens. Arguably, the state of young black men in America at the millennium could be termed a natural disaster; it could even, considering the number of guns at large, be termed a state of war. Young black America at the end of the 1990s was clearly in need of enormous spiritual and physical "disaster" aid. Many agreed that conditions might be extraordinary enough among black youths for ordinary citizens to step in where government feared to go. That meant initiating community-based volunteer efforts, with relatively little government involvement. It required a certain sacrifice of time, money, and service.

Nearly half of those who applied to join the military in the closing years of the 1990s were rejected. Inner-city youths were rejected most often. Recruits had to have a high school diploma with no major criminal convictions, and they had to pass the Armed Services Vocational Aptitude test, including a prequalifying multiple-choice test to assure that they could read and calculate at a tenth-grade level. The military was, in fact, closing inner-city recruitment centers. When asked whether the military was abandoning inner-city kids, Sergeant First Class Terry Graves, a black recruiter, said, "No—I think it is society that is leaving behind the inner city by not educating these kids. They get out of high school and they've got nowhere to go, not even the Army."[96]

The months immediately preceding and following Desert Storm saw much discussion of launching a home-front war on social problems. "Let's put a turbine under all this euphoria and use it to clean up our problems over here," said the entrepreneur and sometime presidential candidate Ross Perot.[97] The idea was to get out of uniform and get into volunteerism. More and more veterans were going into education, crime prevention, and other forms of community service. Ex-soldiers, ideally, would wage urban warfare on poverty, racism, drugs, and inadequate education. Black vets were particularly addressed. "The war on drugs? Street crime? Oil spills? Toxic chemical pollution? Ask black vets," said George F. Sanders, vice chairman of the Federation of Minority Veterans, in a 1989 interview. "They are trained in command, discipline, organization and communications. And they want to work."[98] Colin Powell was also high on the vets' potential. "Every year 135,000 young men and women, better trained and better disciplined, enter the community," he said in 1990. "We provide one heck of a social service to this country. We take in a couple of hundred thousand kids a year who generally hope to better themselves." When they return to civilian life they are much more responsible and have a "better sense of order in their lives, of self-discipline and self-appreciation."[99]

Powell also believed in the creative peacetime use of military standards. "I saw for myself during 35 years in the military what happens when you take young people, provide a nurturing, structured environment and give them leaders to look up to," he said.[100] "I've since wondered what would happen if only we could make that model available to every kid." Traveling the country, Powell had seen "deeply troubling" social, cultural, and racial divides. "There are problems government can't solve," he wrote, "so it's up to the rest of us—before it's too late." In the years between his retirement and his appointment as George W. Bush's Secretary of State, Powell devoted himself to the problem of education and opportunity for young people, launching a campaign to involve more Americans in community service.

"Everyone should function as member of society for two to three years—as teachers, nurses, police, et cetera," General Waller told me, stressing his belief in some form of mandatory universal public service. He recommended a role for the military based on the 1930s Army-run Civilian Conservation Corps, which put unemployed urban youth, among others, to useful work in a healthy environment. "You owe it to your country," he said; "it does not need to hurt the tax base." He believed that "protestations of devotion" to flag and country should be backed up by a bit of "sacrifice," by giving something back. "What can we do for our country, in return for what it has done for us?" asked William F. Buckley, Jr., in a 1990 *New York Times* op-ed piece. "The person who has given a year in behalf of someone or something else, is himself better for the experience."[101]

The President's Summit for America's Future of April 1997 seemed to be the happy combination of volunteerism with government help. "Citizen service belongs to no party, no ideology," said Bill Clinton at the January 1997 ceremony announcing the Summit. It was an occasion "suffused with the soft glow of bipartisanship," wrote Todd S. Purdum in *The New York Times,* with Colin Powell standing between Presidents Clinton and Bush. The purpose of the summit, held in Philadelphia, was to bring citizen groups, foundations, and corporations from every state together with the government to "scale up and leverage up" existing volunteer programs around the country. Summit goals included connecting at-risk children with caring adults; providing safe places for children to go after school; providing health care for uninsured children; educating them in a marketable skill; and encouraging volunteer community service, so that young people could give something back. Powell described the Summit as the union of George Bush's "points of light" volunteerism and Bill Clinton's Americorps program, which awarded college tuition for community service. Clinton proclaimed that the era of "big government" was over, and the era of "big citizen" was just beginning.[102]

* * *

The military is very good at solving tactical and logistic problems. It also has learned, almost despite itself, how to solve social problems. What better environment for young people than one that is based not on military action, but on the military ethos: one that imposes disciplines, skills, and values beneficial to the community as well as the individual?

One of General Powell's favorite stories on the speech circuit is a conversation between the TV correspondent Sam Donaldson and a young black tank platoon soldier on the eve of Desert Storm. "How do you think the battle will go? Are you afraid?" Donaldson asked.

"We'll do okay, we're well trained," the soldier answered. "I'm not afraid," he added, "because I'm with my family." The other platoon members, men and women of all races, shouted, "Tell him again. He didn't hear you!" The soldier reiterated, "This is my family and we take care of each other."[103]

Epilogue

The Gulf War, with the ascendancy of General Colin Powell as its centerpiece, marked the historical zenith of the black American military experience. Newly aware that blacks had an honorable military history, the American public had a new appreciation for black Desert Storm heroes. For the military, it was a watershed moment. In recognizing a distinguished black military past, the military was forced to acknowledge its own past racism. After the Gulf War, in the most radical step in its slow but steady evolvement from preaching democracy to practicing it, the military was ready not only to celebrate its black heroes but also to apologize for past injustices. Because the history was long, and the injustices rife, belated rewards for a job well done came only to a representative handful. The few, most of them long dead, would have to stand in for the many. These brave men were honored throughout the 1990s in ceremonies that evoked tears, pride, and some anger as the government and the military made their mea culpas.

* * *

In July 1994, a memorial was dedicated in Concord, California, to the 320 sailors, mostly black ammunition loaders, who were killed in the Port Chicago Naval Magazine explosion of July 1944, the deadliest military accident on U.S. soil in World War II. Five years later, eighty-year-old Freddie Meeks, one of two surviving members of the fifty sailors convicted of mutiny after the explosion, was pardoned by President Clinton. While the Navy denied that the convictions for mutiny were motivated by racism, it admitted that racism made blacks ammunition loaders. Meeks, who served only seventeen months of his fifteen-year sentence thanks to Thurgood Marshall's defense, was proven not to have mutinied but, in fact, to have volunteered for other duty. "I knew God was keeping me around for something," he said in an interview. "But I am just sorry so many of the others are not around to see it."[1]

* * *

In 1995, more than one hundred years after he had been dismissed from West Point, accused of beating, slashing, and tying himself to his bed,

Johnson C. Whittaker finally received his Army commission. After years of lobbying by his descendants, the cause was finally taken up by Senator Ernest F. Hollings of South Carolina (the state where Whittaker had been a slave). "Johnson Whittaker was a rare individual, a pathfinder, a man who through courage, example and perseverance, paved the way for future generations of African Americans," said President Clinton at a ceremony in the Roosevelt Room of the White House attended by Whittaker's seventy-seven-year-old granddaughter, a retired teacher, and his teenage great-great-grandchildren. Whittaker himself became a teacher (Ralph Ellison was one of his students) and a lawyer in Oklahoma City. His Bible, seized in evidence during his court-martial and kept in the National Archives ever since, was presented to his family. The inscription he had written as a second-year cadet was fading but still legible: "Try never to injure another by word, by act, or by look, even. Forgive as soon as you are injured, and forget as soon as you forgive."[2] Four years later, Lieutenant Henry Flipper, West Point's first black graduate (and Whittaker's philosophical soul mate), who was dismissed from the Army on false embezzlement charges, received a presidential pardon from Clinton, a president who put great stakes in healing divisions between blacks and whites in America.

* * *

In 1995, the Air Force announced that the official reprimands against 101 black Tuskegee Air officers who sat in at the illegally segregated white officers' club at Freeman Field, Indiana, in 1945 would be expunged from their records. In 1997, Walterboro, South Carolina, which had shown greater hospitality in World War II to German and Italian POWs than to black American pilots, honored the Tuskegee Airmen with a monument. Charles Dryden, a former Tuskegee pilot, considered it significant that "the town that was so hostile to us back then is now apologizing for what they did to us American patriots."[3] In 1945, Dryden had been so enraged by Walterboro racism that he made mock strafing runs over the town in his P-38 fighter and was dismissed from the service.

* * *

In 1998, five black infantry volunteers of the Battle of the Bulge, who had been returned to their segregated labor units without their combat service noted in their records, received belated Bronze Stars. That same year, eighty-five-year-old General Benjamin O. Davis, Jr., of the Tuskegee Airmen, received his fourth star after years of lobbying by the men who'd flown under him.

* * *

"I'd give my immortal soul for that medal," General George S. Patton once said of the Medal of Honor. The nation's highest award for valor, bestowed only by the president, was symbolically the most important mea culpa of them all. It was at last bestowed upon Corporal Freddie Stowers of the First World War's 371st Regiment. The Army admitted it had made a "mistake." Stowers's commanding officer had recommended him for the Medal of Honor in September 1918 for actions on the infamous Hill 188 during the Champagne Offensive, when 40 percent of his company were casualties. In May 1991, President Bush presented the Medal of Honor to Freddie Stowers's eighty-eight-year-old sister. Staff Sergeant Douglas Warren of the 101st Airborne Division, his great-great-nephew, was flown in from Saudi Arabia to be part of the East Room ceremony.

The quest for Freddie Stowers's Medal of Honor began in 1985, when Leroy Ramsay, a teacher and historian in Albany, decided to find out why no blacks had been awarded Medals of Honor in the first and second world wars when they had won them in all previous and subsequent wars. In 1988, Congressman Mickey Leland of Texas and Congressman Joseph J. DioGuardi of New York, influenced by Ramsay, introduced legislation to confer posthumous Medals of Honor on two home-state heroes: Sergeant Henry Johnson, who fought in New York's 369th Regiment in the First World War, and Navy messman Dorie Miller of Waco, Texas, the first American hero of the Second World War.

Why award just two, Secretary of Defense Frank Carlucci had asked, when many more might be overlooked? It was decided, to the disappointment of Representatives Leland and DioGuardi, to consider only veterans of the World War II Army. Shaw University, founded in North Carolina by the family of Civil War hero Robert Gould Shaw, won an Army grant in 1995 to look into potential Medal of Honor candidates. Concentrating on the nine black winners of the Distinguished Service Cross, with all references to race deleted, an Army board selected seven men to receive the nation's highest award for heroism under fire.

On January 13, 1997, President Clinton stood beneath Gilbert Stuart's full-length portrait of George Washington in the East Room of the White House to bestow, in a simple but eloquent ceremony, the belated medals. Joseph L. Galloway, co-author of *We Were Soldiers Once . . . and Young,* described the recognition as the "last act of a grateful nation's half-century commemoration of the Allied victory in World War II." It was also a "simple and long-delayed act of justice."[4] Accepting the medals were brothers, sisters, widows, and children. Only one veteran among the seven was alive to receive his own gold medal, with its sky-blue ribbon, in its glass and wood presentation case.

"History has been made whole today," Clinton said, "and our nation is bestowing honor on those who have long deserved it." The men who were honored that day almost all died on the battlefields of France, Germany, and Italy, and in the Pacific, giving their lives to protect their men and their regiments.

Private George Watson of the 29th Quartermaster Regiment was the first black winner of the Distinguished Service Cross in World War II. He was cited for actions aboard a torpedoed troopship off New Guinea in 1944. Watson stayed in the water to help soldiers who could not swim to a nearby life raft and drowned in the suction of the sinking ship.

First Lieutenant John R. Fox of the 366th Infantry, 92nd Division, was cited for actions in 1944 at Serchio, Italy, where the 92nd Division won its bad reputation. He was killed calling in artillery on his own forward observation post to stop an enemy advance after a white officer had refused to believe a black patrol team's sighting of Germans. Asked what the day meant to her, Fox's widow, Arlene, who had wept silently when she received his medal, replied, "I think it's more than just what it means to this family. I think it sends a little wake-up call, that when a man does his duty, his color isn't important."[5]

Staff Sergeant Ruben Rivers of the 761st Tank Corps was cited for actions outside Guebling, France, in 1944, when, although gravely wounded, he refused evacuation and even morphine because he had spotted enemy positions and vowed to keep on fighting. "Rivers led the way!" was the company byword. He had led the way until, finally, his head was blown off by a German shell. His commander, Captain David J. Williams, recommended him for a Medal of Honor in 1944, but he was awarded a posthumous Silver Star at the time. Williams, for whom Rivers's Medal of Honor became a crusade, attended the 1997 ceremony.

Major Charles L. Thomas of the 614th Tank Destroyer Battalion was cited for actions in Climbach, France, in 1944, when, as a lieutenant, he volunteered to lead a task force to storm a village five miles from the German border. Stopped by an onslaught of direct enemy fire, he continued to shoot his machine gun from the top of the armored scout car. Despite multiple gunshot wounds in the chest, leg, and arm, he refused to be evacuated until he had set up antitank guns and determined that his junior officer was in full control of the situation.

Staff Sergeant Edward Carter, Jr., of the 56th Armored Infantry, 12th Armored Division, was cited for actions in Germany in 1945. A veteran of the Spanish Civil War, Carter volunteered in the Battle of the Bulge to lead a three-man patrol team to report on the source of the small arms and bazooka fire that was hitting his tank. When one of his men was killed, he ordered the other two back and went on alone. He finally fell after being shot five times. When an eight-man German patrol came to certify his death, Carter suddenly sprang back to life. Opening fire with his Thompson machine gun, he instantly killed six of the eight men. He used the other two as prisoner-shields to get back across an open field to his unit. According to Joseph Galloway, Carter's commanding officer "couldn't believe his eyes."[6] (Clinton later apologized to Carter's family when he discovered that 1950s Red-baiting had kept him from reenlistment in the Army despite the fact that the FBI had twice cleared him of potential subversion.)

Private First Class Willy F. James of the 415th Infantry Regiment was cited for actions in Lippoldsberg, Germany, in 1945. James volunteered to go forward to pinpoint enemy positions, making his way across approximately two hundred yards of open area under furious enemy crossfire. Finally, pinned down and exposed, he lay on the ground and observed enemy positions. Then, utterly indifferent to his own safety, he made it back some three hundred yards to give a full report, before volunteering again to lead an assault squad on the key enemy position. He was killed shortly after, going to the aid of his wounded platoon leader.

Lieutenant Vernon Baker of the 370th Regiment, 92nd Division, was cited for actions in Italy in 1945 at Castel Aghinolfi, where, leading an advance on a German-held castle, he single-handedly killed eight Germans, and destroyed an enemy observation post and an enemy dugout. Then, with about two-thirds of the twenty-five men with him killed or injured by enemy machine-gun and mortar fire, he volunteered to cover the withdrawal of the walking wounded and, in the process, destroyed two enemy machine-gun emplacements. Baker's commanding officer had recommended him for a Medal of Honor at the time. He was the only one of the seven honored men who was still living.

"I was a soldier and I had a job to do," Vernon Baker said of his heroism. But he admitted that risking his life for his country, while serving in a segregated unit, was "kind of rough." "I was an angry young man," he said. "We were all angry. But we had a job to do, and we did it." He never lost hope in the possibility of change. "I knew things would get better, and I'm glad to say that I'm here to see it," he said. "The only thing that I can say to those that are not here with me is, thank you, fellas, well done. And I will always remember you."[7]

They were patriots, each and every one of them, few of whom knew at the time that they were part of a long history.

Acknowledgments

This book could not have been written without the many veterans who were willing to share their stories with me. I am forever grateful to these remarkable men and women—especially the following:

From World War I: Hamilton Fish, Sr., and William O. Layton. From the Spanish Civil War: Harry Fisher, Moe Fishman, Vaughn Love, Charles Nusser, Barney Rucker, Moe Sussman, and James Yates. From World War II: Lee Archer, Roscoe C. Brown, Jr., Anne Chaney, John Connell, Benjamin O. Davis, Jr., Gene Doughty, William DeFossett, Clarence Hall, Sallie M. Jones, E. G. McConnell, Roger Starr, Alfred E. Steward, Percy Sutton, Bobby Troup, Franklin R. Williams, and Bruce Wright. From Korea: Julius Becton, James Brady, David Carlisle, William Dandridge, David Hackworth, and Charles Rangel. From Vietnam: Ron Barrow, Neil R. Brooks, George Brummell, John A. Cash, Robert L. Clewell, Dennis Deal, Merrill Dorsey, Duery Felton, Jr., George Forrest, David Hackworth (again), Harold A. Moore, and Wayne Smith. From Operation Desert Storm: Raymond Armstrong, Arthur LaMotte, Flossie Satcher, and Calvin Waller.

My thanks to General Colin L. Powell, who was so generous with his time, and to Colonel William Smullen and Captain Robin Crumm.

I would also like to thank General and Mrs. Fred A. Gordon for their gracious hospitality at West Point. And I am grateful to Sheila Biles and Suzanne Christoff of the Special Collections and Archives Division of the United States Military Academy, and to Andrea Hamburger of the Directorate of Academy Relations, and Major Sharon Waddell of the Directorate of Information Management. I want to thank Brendalyn Carter, Major Tom Collins, and Major Ryan Yantis of the Army Public Affairs Office of the Pentagon, the U.S. Army Military District of Washington Public Affairs Office, Fort McNair, and the U.S. Army Center of Military History. I want to thank Karin Martinez of the Army Public Affairs Office of the 10th Mountain Division, Fort Drum, New York. And I want to thank Beverly Lyall of the Department of the Navy Nimitz Library, of the United Naval Academy. I would also like to thank Clifford L. Alexander. And special thanks to Paul W. Bucha of the Congressional Medal of Honor Society.

I want to thank Alice Adamcyzk, Aisha Al Adawija, Diana La Chataniere, Betty Odabashian, and Roberta Y. Yancy of the Schomburg Center for Research in Black Culture of the New York Public Library. And thanks to Crawford Doyle Books, Liberation Book Store, the Madison Avenue Bookshop, the Military Bookman, the Revolutionary Bookstore, the Unity Book Store, the National Archives, and NBC News. I am grateful, also, to the Museum of Afro-American History, the W.E.B. Du Bois Institute for Afro-American Research of Harvard University, and the Vietnam Veterans Memorial Collection.

I am deeply grateful for the invaluable help and encouragement provided by members of the following organizations: the Band of Brothers, the Black Lions, the Blinded Veterans Association, the Comancheros, the Daughters of the American Revolution, the 8th Field Depot and 8th Service Regiment (United States Marine Corps), the 1st Battalion of the 7th Cavalry, the Justice Project, the Liberandos, the Montford Point Marine Association, the National Maritime Union, the 9th & 10th (Horse) Cavalry Association, the Patriots Memorial, the Rocks, the 761st Tank Battalion, the 77th Combat Engineer Company, the 6888 Postal Battalion of the Women's Army Corps, the Sons of the American Revolution, the 332nd Fighter Group, the 367th Heavy Bombardment Group, the 369th Regiment Veterans Association, the 10th Mountain Division, the Veterans of the Abraham Lincoln Brigade, the Vietnam Veterans of America, and the Vietnam Veterans Foundation.

For each war, I relied on the time, analyses, advice, and singular perspectives of many people. Very special thanks go to Anka Begley, Louis Begley, James Brady, Roscoe Brown, Jr., Sterling Brown, Colonel John A. Cash, James Chace, Matt Clark, Barbara Epstein, Moe Fishman, Frances FitzGerald, Thomas Fleming, David R. Fromkin, Joseph L. Galloway, Colonel David Hackworth, Brooke Hayward, Arthur Loeb, Gita Mehta, Albert Murray, Arthur M. Schlesinger, Jr., Jean Kennedy Smith, Lewis Sorley, James Sterba, Richard Stolley, General Calvin Waller, and James Yates.

In the category of special interest in specific wars, I am forever grateful to the following:

For the Revolution: Mae and Frank Bonitto, Neil R. Brooks, and Dr. Harold E. Pierce and the Hon. Lawrence W. Pierce for introducing me to their Revolutionary ancestors, Barzillai Lew and Adam Pierce. Thanks also to Maurice Barboza and Lena Ferguson of the Patriot's Memorial.

For the Civil War: David Mortimer, Richard Newman, Edwin Redkey, Harry Sedgwick, and Miss Ruth Y. Jones, the great-grand niece of Frederick Douglass (whose spirit, she said, was still at home in her Cambridge, Massachusetts, house).

For the Buffalo Soldiers: Joann Brown, Leon D. Curry, H.D.S. Greenway, Franklin J. Henderson, J. Anthony Lukas, Lani Russell, and the Toy Soldier Gallery, Inc.

For World War I: Adele Logan Alexander, James Du Bose, Hamilton Fish, Lydia Ambrogio Fish, William Miles, Robert Paxton, George Stevens, Jr., and Edward Tuck.

For the Spanish Civil War: Nelly Baker, Tibby Brooks, Barney Josephson, Jack McCusker, Eric Simonoff, and the memories and resources of the Veterans of the Abraham Lincoln Brigade. I am profoundly grateful to Una G. Mulzac for memories of her father, Captain Hugh Mulzac.

For World War II: Jack Hogan (for memories of the Four Chaplains), Lena Horne, Elnora Davis McClendon, Gordon Parks, Vivien Murphy Rowan, William Rowe, Roger Starr, and William Zinsser. I am grateful to William R. Pickens III for access to the papers of Lieutenant Harriet Pickens. And I am grateful to Benjamin Bender, for his memories of the liberation of Buchenwald.

For Korea: James Chace, Colonel David Hackworth, Richard Holbrooke, and Rep. Charles Rangel.

For Vietnam: Frances FitzGerald, Joseph L. Galloway, Colonel David Hackworth, Bobby Muller, Wayne Smith, Lewis Sorley, James Sterba, and Erik Villard.

For Desert Storm: Karin Martinez.

I read many books before and while I was writing this book (many are mentioned in the endnotes). The "open sesame" experience was Edmund Wilson's *Patriotic Gore,* studies on Civil War literature, which gave me a model for every war. It made me know that, whenever possible, I wanted to hear people's voices.

I want to mention a special bibliography, the books that "spoke" to me the most. I urge anyone who reads this to read them.

For the Revolution: Thomas Fleming's *Liberty!*; Sidney Kaplan and Emma Nogrady Kaplan's *The Black Presence in the Era of the American Revolution;* Albert Murray's *The Onmi-Americans;* William Cooper Nell's *The Colored Patriots of the American Revolution;* Benjamin Quarles' *The Negro in the American Revolution;* and *The Image of the Black in Western Art,* published by the Menil Foundation, Inc.

For the Civil War: Peter Burchard's *One Gallant Rush;* W. J. Cash's *The Mind of the South;* the *Narrative of the Life of Frederick Douglass;* Luis F. Emilio's *A Brave Black Regiment: The Journal of Charlotte L. Forten;* John Hope Franklin's *Race and History: Selected Essays 1938–1988; On the Altar of Freedom, the Letters of James Gooding; Behind the Scenes,* by Elizabeth Keckley (an ex-slave, and confidante of both Mrs. Abraham Lincoln and Mrs. Jefferson Davis): James M. McPherson's *The Negro's Civil War;* Carl Sandburg's *Abraham Lincoln: The War Years* (awe-inspiring, if not fact-filled); and Harriet Beecher Stowe's *Uncle Tom's Cabin.*

For the Buffalo Soldiers: Herschel V. Cashin's *Under Fire with the 10th Cavalry;* Edward M. Coffman's *The Old Army;* Frances FitzGerald's *America Revised;* Henry O. Flipper's *The Colored Cadet at West Point;* William Loren Katz's *The Black West;* Richard Severo and Lewis Milford's *The Wages of War;* and Walter J. Stevens's *Chip on My Shoulder.*

For World War I: P. J. Carisella and James W. Ryan's *Black Swallow of Death;* Chester D. Heywood's *Negro Combat Troops in the World War;* Harry Haywood's *Black Bolshevik;* Addie D. Hunton and Kathryn H. Johnson's *Two Colored Women with the American Expeditionary Forces;* Robert Kimball and William Bolcom's *Reminiscing with Sissle and Blake;* Arthur W. Little's *From Harlem to the Rhine;* Kelly Miller's *History of the World War for Human Rights;* and Emmett J. Scott's *Official History of the American Negro in the World War.*

For the Spanish Civil War: *African-Americans in the Spanish Civil War,* edited by Danny Duncan Collum and Victor A. Berch; Nancy Cunard's *Negro; Death in the Olive Groves,* by Arthur H. Landis; Marian Merriman and Warren Lerude's *American Commander in Spain: Robert Hale Merriman and the Abraham Lincoln Brigade;* George Orwell's *Homage to Catalonia;* Hugh Thomas's *The Spanish Civil War;* and James Yates's *From Mississippi to Madrid.*

For World War II: *Benjamin O. Davis, Jr.,* an autobiography; Bill Downey's *Uncle Sam Must Be Losing the War;* Charity Adams Early's *One Woman's Army;* Doris Kearns Goodwin's *No Ordinary Time* (awe-inspiring and fact-filled, too); Nelson Peery's *Black Fire;* Carl Rowan's *Breaking Barriers;* Patrick S. Washburn's *A Question of Sedition;* and Walter White's *A Man Called White.*

For Korea: *The Forgotten War* by Clay Blair; *The Coldest War* by James Brady; *Firefight at Yechon* by Lieutenant Colonel Charles M. Bussey; *Acheson* by James Chace; *About Face* by Colonel David Hackworth; *The Fifties* by David Halberstam; and *Truman* by David McCullough.

For Vietnam: Frances FitzGerald's *Fire in the Lake;* Michael Herr's *Dispatches;* Stanley Karnow's *Vietnam;* the Library of America's *Reporting Vietnam;* Arthur M. Schlesinger, Jr.'s, *The Bitter Heritage: Vietnam and American Democracy 1941–1966;* General Harold G. Moore and Joseph L. Galloway's *We Were Soldiers Once . . . and Young;* David Parks's *GI Diary;* General Colin L. Powell's *My American Journey;* and Wallace Terry's *Bloods.*

For Civil Rights: *Free at Last: History of the Civil Rights Movement and Those Who Died in the Struggle,* edited by the Civil Rights Project of the Southern Poverty Law Center; David Halberstam's *The Children;* and Juan Williams's *Eyes on the Prize* (companion to the PBS documentary).

For the Gulf War: Rick Atkinson's *Crusade;* General Colin L. Powell's *My American Journey;* and General H. Norman Schwarzkopf's *It Doesn't Take a Hero.*

I have discussed this project with friends over the years; sometimes they did not know how valuable their apparently casual comments were. I am grateful to these conversationalists: Terry Adams, Alice Arlen, Arthur Ashe, Rev. William Bergen, S.J., Bernard Berkowitz, Boaty Boatwright, Belinda Breese, Colin Campbell, Carol Craig, Constance Curry, Kitty D'Alessio, Jean Douglas, Boker Doyle, Susanna Doyle, Inger Elliott, Osborn Elliott, Gloria Emerson, Ken Emerson, Linda Francke, Barbara Gelia, Barbara Goldsmith, Adolph Green, Arthur T. Hadley, Louise Hirschfeld, Penny Janeway, Hannah Kaiser, Robert G. Kaiser, Frances Kiernan, Arthur Kretchmer, Rev. George Kuhn, Joseph Lelyveld, Arthur Loeb, Sr., Mary Jo Lynch, O.P., Hon. Thurgood Marshall, John Regan "Tex" McCrary, David McCullough, Mildred Newman, Phyllis Newman, Rev. Charles O'Byrne, S.J., Mike O'Neill, Sidney Offit, Peter Osnos, Hal Prince, Judy Prince, Martie Proffitt, Nicholas C. Proffitt, St. Clair Pugh, Tracy Quinn, Betty Rollin, Cathy Romine, Alexandra Schlesinger, Marion Lapsley Schwarz, Deborah Scroggins, Geoff Shandler, William Shawcross, Annette Tappert, Elliott Taylor, Julie Taylor, Camille Troy, Lily Tuck, Shelley Wanger, and Barbara Watson.

I am grateful for the special assistance of Jamie Brogan, Heather Haebe, Sarah Hogan, David R. Levine, Marci Lovitch, Barbara E. McMullen, and John F. McMullen.

I am extremely grateful for crucial art and photographic help from the following: Anne Burns Images; Elmer D. Jones; the collection and private archives of William Loren Katz; Harry Koundakjian, Richard Pyle, and Chuck Zoeller of the Associated Press; and Richard Stolley of *Life.* With special thanks to Anita Dickhuth for her discerning eye.

At Random House I am especially grateful for the patient efforts on my behalf of Benjamin Dreyer and Amelia Zalcman, and for their kindness. I want to thank Deborah Foley. And I want to thank Jolanta Benal, the copy editor. And I am forever grateful for the intelligence, taste, perception and energy of my editor, Joy de Menil.

I want to thank my friend and agent, Lynn Nesbit.

And finally, exuberant thanks and love to my family—which includes Buckleys, Cannavales, Hornes, Joneses, Lumets, Montantes, and Rosenfelds.

Notes

Introduction

1. Bernard C. Nalty, *Strength for the Fight* (New York: Free Press, 1986), p. 99.
2. Danny Duncan Collum, ed., *African Americans in the Spanish Civil War* (New York: G. K. Hall & Co., 1992), p. 85.
3. Richard Rohr, Center for Action and Contemplation, Albuquerque, New Mexico.
4. Albert Murray, *The Omni-Americans: New Perspectives on Black Experience and American Culture* (New York: Outerbridge & Dienstfrey, 1970), p. 21.

1: The Revolution

1. William Cooper Nell, *Colored Patriots of the American Revolution* (Salem, N.H.: Ayer, 1986, reprinted from 1855), p. 129.
2. Sidney Kaplan and Emma Nogrady Kaplan, *The Black Presence in the Era of the American Revolution* (Amherst: University of Massachusetts Press, 1989), p. 8.
3. Thomas Fleming, *Liberty!* (New York: Penguin, 1997), p. 74.
4. Kaplan and Kaplan, *The Black Presence in the Era of the American Revolution,* p. 6.
5. Ibid., p. 8.
6. Erwin Randolph Parson, ed., *In Perspective of the Black American Veteran* (Albany, N.Y.: Elramco Enterprises, 1991), p. 56.
7. Kaplan and Kaplan, *The Black Presence in the Era of the American Revolution,* pp. 9–10.
8. Peter M. Bergman, ed., *The Chronological History of the Negro in America* (New York: New American Library, 1969), p. 48.
9. Benjamin Quarles, *The Negro in the American Revolution* (New York: W. W. Norton & Co., 1973, reprint from 1961), p. ix.
10. Fleming, *Liberty!,* p. 152.
11. Esmond Wright, *Fabric of Freedom* (New York: Hill & Wang, 1961), p. 105.
12. Quarles, *The Negro in the American Revolution,* pp. 39–40.
13. Bergman, *The Chronological History of the Negro in America,* p. 41.
14. Ibid., p. 44.
15. Quarles, *The Negro in the American Revolution,* p. 37.
16. Bergman, *The Chronological History of the Negro in America,* p. 46.
17. Kaplan and Kaplan, *The Black Presence in the Era of the American Revolution,* p. 203.
18. Ibid., p. 15.
19. Eric Foner, *Tom Paine and the American Revolution* (New York: Oxford University Press, 1976), p. 73.
20. Fleming, *Liberty!,* p. 106.
21. Curt Johnson, *Battles of the American Revolution* (New York: Bonanza Books, 1975), p. 33.
22. Howard H. Peckham, *The War for Independence* (Chicago: University of Chicago Press, 1958), p. 10.
23. A. J. Langguth, *Patriots: The Men Who Started the American Revolution* (New York: Simon & Schuster, 1988), p. 251.
24. Johnson, *Battles of the American Revolution,* p. 33.
25. Bergman, *The Chronological History of the Negro in America,* p. 51.
26. Richard Newman, *Black Preacher to White America* (Brooklyn: Carlson Publishing, 1990), pp. 9–15.
27. Langguth, *Patriots,* p. 233.
28. Phillip T. Drotning, *Black Heroes in Our Nation's History* (New York: Cowles, 1969), p. 23.
29. Kaplan and Kaplan, *The Black Presence in the Era of the American Revolution,* p. 17.
30. Revolutionary War Pension File M20461, Commonwealth of Massachusetts, Office of Secretary, Revolutionary War service of Barzillai Lew.
31. Fleming, *Liberty!,* p. 140.

32. Kaplan and Kaplan, *The Black Presence in the Era of the American Revolution,* p. 21.
33. Ibid., pp. 22–23.
34. Drotning, *Black Heroes in Our Nation's History,* p. 26; Bergman, *The Chronological History of the Negro in America,* p. 51; Kaplan and Kaplan, *The Black Presence in the Era of the American Revolution,* pp. 19, 60.
35. Sam Dennison, *Scandalize My Name* (New York: Garland Publishing, 1982), pp. 8–9.
36. Peckham, *The War for Independence,* p. 27.
37. Quarles, *The Negro in the American Revolution,* p. 72.
38. Ibid., p. 15.
39. Ibid., pp. 14–15.
40. Kaplan and Kaplan, *The Black Presence in the Era of the American Revolution,* p. 185.
41. Foner, *Tom Paine and the American Revolution,* p. 79.
42. Quarles, *The Negro in the American Revolution,* p. 25n.
43. Kaplan and Kaplan, *The Black Presence in the Era of the American Revolution,* p. 77.
44. Quarles, *The Negro in the American Revolution,* p. 16.
45. Newman, *Black Preacher to White America,* pp. 18–19.
46. Fleming, *Liberty!,* p. 186.
47. Herbert Aptheker, *The Negro in the American Revolution* (Secaucus, N.J.: Citadel Press, 1973), p. 96.
48. *Ebony Patriots* (New York: New York University, Institute of Afro-American Affairs, 1976), pp. 4–6.
49. Fleming, *Liberty!,* p. 327; Ira D. Gruber, "America's First Battle: Long Island, 27 August 1776," in *America's First Battles,* 1776–1965, ed. Charles E. Heller and William A. Sofft (Lawrence: University Press of Kansas, 1986), pp. 1–32; Don Higginbotham, *The War of American Independence, Military Attitudes, Policies, and Practice, 1763–1789* (New York: Macmillan, 1973), pp. 148–62.
50. Kaplan and Kaplan, *The Black Presence in the Era of the American Revolution,* p. 29.
51. Ibid., pp. 52–54.
52. Peckham, *The War for Independence,* pp. 55–57.
53. Kaplan and Kaplan, *The Black Presence in the Era of the American Revolution,* p. 26.
54. Peckham, *The War for Independence,* p. 77.
55. Lerone Bennett, Jr., *Before the Mayflower* (New York: Penguin Books, 1978; reprinted from 1962), p. 58.
56. E. Merrill Beach, *From Valley Forge to Freedom* (Chester, Conn.: Pequot Press, 1975), p. 11.
57. Peckham, *The War for Independence,* p. 82.
58. Beach, *From Valley Forge to Freedom,* pp. 12–13.
59. Nell, *Colored Patriots of the American Revolution,* p. 388.
60. Bernard C. Nalty, *Strength for the Fight* (New York: Free Press, 1986), p. 4.
61. William Stewart and Theophilus Stewart, *Gouldtown* (Philadelphia: J. B. Lippincott, 1913), p. 63.
62. Kaplan and Kaplan, *The Black Presence in the Era of the American Revolution,* pp. 64–65.
63. Nell, *Colored Patriots of the American Revolution,* p. 129.
64. Kaplan and Kaplan, *The Black Presence in the Era of the American Revolution,* p. 65.
65. Nell, *Colored Patriots of the American Revolution,* p. 127.
66. Peckham, *The War for Independence,* p. 129.
67. Wright, *Fabric of Freedom,* pp. 148–49.
68. Quarles, *The Negro in the American Revolution,* p. 60.
69. Bergman, *The Chronological History of the Negro in America,* pp. 56–57.
70. Quarles, *The Negro in the American Revolution,* p. 140.
71. Ibid., p. 80.
72. Kaplan and Kaplan, *The Black Presence in the Era of the American Revolution,* p. 61.
73. Fleming, *Liberty!,* p. 302.
74. Kaplan and Kaplan, *The Black Presence in the Era of the American Revolution,* p. 56.
75. Johnson, *Battles of the American Revolution,* p. 118.
76. Ibid., p. 120.
77. Fleming, *Liberty!,* p. 334.
78. Quarles, *The Negro in the American Revolution,* p. 94.
79. Johnson, *Battles of the American Revolution,* p. 122.
80. Fleming, *Liberty!,* p. 334.
81. Kaplan and Kaplan, *The Black Presence in the Era of the American Revolution,* p. 63.
82. Drotning, *Black Heroes in Our Nation's History,* p. 29.
83. Fleming, *Liberty!,* p. 335.
84. Peckham, *The War for Independence,* p. 197.
85. Quarles, *The Negro in the American Revolution,* p. 168.
86. Ibid., p. 165.
87. David O. White, *Connecticut's Black Soldiers* (Chester, Conn.: Pequot Press, 1973), p. 42.
88. Bennett, *Before the Mayflower,* p. 62.

89. Ken Ringle, "Freeing the Slaves and His Conscience," *The Washington Post National Weekly Edition,* July 28–August 4, 1991.
90. Andrew Billingsley, *Black Families in White America* (Englewood Cliffs, N.J.: Prentice-Hall, 1968), p. 59.
91. Bennett, *Before the Mayflower,* p. 62.
92. Bergman, *The Chronological History of the Negro in America,* p. 63.
93. Kaplan and Kaplan, *The Black Presence in the Era of the American Revolution,* pp. 36–37.
94. Thomas Jefferson, *Notes on the State of Virginia* (New York: Penguin, 1999), pp. 145–47.
95. Kaplan and Kaplan, *The Black Presence in the Era of the American Revolution,* pp. 145–47.
96. Jefferson, *Notes on the State of Virginia,* pp. 168–69.
97. Fleming, *Liberty!,* p. 365.
98. Bergman, *The Chronological History of the Negro in America,* p. 64.
99. Wright, *Fabric of Freedom,* pp. 177–78.
100. Nell, *Colored Patriots of the American Revolution,* p. 128.

2: The War of 1812

1. Peter M. Bergman, ed., *The Chronological History of the Negro in America* (New York: New American Library, 1969), p. 87.
2. Lerone Bennett, Jr., *Before the Mayflower* (New York: Penguin Books, 1978; reprinted from 1962), pp. 98–99.
3. Ibid., p. 105.
4. Ibid., pp. 110–11.
5. Esmond Wright, *Fabric of Freedom* (New York: Hill & Wang, 1961), p. 245.
6. Roger Butterfield, *The American Past* (New York: Simon & Schuster, 1957), p. 70.
7. Bergman, *The Chronological History of the Negro in America,* p. 82.
8. Saunders Redding, *They Came in Chains* (Philadelphia: J. B. Lippincott, 1950), pp. 49–50.
9. Herbert Aptheker, *A Documentary History of the Negro People in the United States,* vol. 1 (Secaucus, N.J.: Citadel Press, 1951), pp. 45–46.
10. Ibid., pp. 50–51.
11. Bergman, *The Chronological History of the Negro in America,* pp. 94–95.
12. Ibid., p. 93.
13. Sidney Kaplan and Emma Nogrady Kaplan, *The Black Presence in the Era of the American Revolution* (Amherst: University of Massachusetts Press, 1989), p. 149.
14. Samuel Eliot Morison, *Dissent in Three American Wars* (Cambridge, Mass.: Harvard University Press, 1970), p. 3.
15. Butterfield, *The American Past,* p. 52.
16. Phillip T. Drotning, *Black Heroes in Our Nation's History* (New York: Cowles, 1969), p. 33.
17. Morison, *Dissent in Three American Wars,* p. 3.
18. Bergman, *The Chronological History of the Negro in America,* p. 96.
19. Drotning, *Black Heroes in Our Nation's History,* p. 37.
20. Ibid., pp. 35–36.
21. Sam Dennison, *Scandalize My Name* (New York: Garland Publishing, 1982), p. 28.
22. Drotning, *Black Heroes in Our Nation's History,* p. 39.
23. Bergman, *The Chronological History of the Negro in America,* p. 71.
24. Drotning, *Black Heroes in Our Nation's History,* p. 42.
25. Ibid.
26. Ibid., p. 43.
27. Rayford W. Logan and Michael R. Winston, *Dictionary of American Negro Biography* (New York: W. W. Norton & Co., 1982), p. 543.
28. Drotning, *Black Heroes in Our Nation's History,* p. 46.
29. Logan and Winston, *Dictionary of American Negro Biography,* p. 544.
30. Drotning, *Black Heroes in Our Nation's History,* p. 48.
31. Benjamin Quarles, *The Negro in the Making of America* (New York: W. W. Norton & Co., 1973; reprinted from 1961), p. 91.
32. Logan and Winston, *Dictionary of American Negro Biography,* p. 544.
33. John Hope Franklin, *Race and History* (Baton Rouge: Louisiana State University Press, 1989), pp. 136–37.
34. Aptheker, *A Documentary History of the Negro People in the United States,* p. 71.
35. Bergman, *The Chronological History of the Negro in America,* p. 111.
36. Jack D. Foner, *Blacks and the Military in American History* (New York: Praeger, 1974), p. 27.
37. Bergman, *The Chronological History of the Negro in America,* p. 112.
38. Aptheker, *A Documentary History of the Negro People in the United States,* p. 76.
39. William Cooper Nell, *Colored Patriots of the American Revolution* (Salem, N.H.: Ayer, 1986; reprinted from 1855), p. 245.

40. Aptheker, *A Documentary History of the Negro People in the United States,* p. 76.
41. Bennett, *Before the Mayflower,* p. 115.
42. Vincent Harding, *There Is a River* (New York: Harcourt Brace Jovanovich, 1981), p. 71.
43. Franklin, *Race and History,* p. 99.

3: The Civil War

1. David W. Blight, *Frederick Douglass' Civil War* (Baton Rouge: Louisiana State University Press, 1989), p. 161.
2. Albert Fried, *John Brown's Journey* (Garden City, N.Y.: Doubleday, 1978), pp. 135–37.
3. Peter Burchard, *One Gallant Rush* (New York: St. Martin's Press, 1965), p. 6.
4. Merton L. Dillon, *The Abolitionists* (New York: W. W. Norton & Co., 1974), p. 29.
5. Oliver Wendell Holmes, from *Two Poems to Harriet Beecher Stowe,* June 14, 1882, cited in *John Brown's Raid,* National Park Service History Series (Washington, D.C., Office of Publications, National Park Service, Department of the Interior, 1974).
6. Julius Lester, *To Be a Slave* (New York: Scholastic, 1968), p. 129.
7. Alexis de Tocqueville, *Democracy in America,* quoted in John Hope Franklin, *Race and History: Selected Essays 1938–1988* (Baton Rouge: Louisiana State University Press, 1989), p. 93.
8. William Wells Brown, *The Black Man* (Salem, N.H.: Ayer, 1992; reprint from 1865), p. 17.
9. Lester, *To Be a Slave,* pp. 36–37.
10. W. J. Cash, *The Mind of the South* (New York: Doubleday, 1956), p. 78.
11. Quoted in Franklin, *Race and History: Selected Essays 1938–1988,* pp. 102–3.
12. Ibid., p. 103.
13. Bernard C. Nalty, *Strength for the Fight* (New York: Free Press, 1986), p. 26.
14. Roger Butterfield, *The American Past* (New York: Simon & Schuster, 1947), p. 81.
15. Jean Strouse, *Morgan* (New York: Random House, 1999), p. 61.
16. William Lloyd Garrison, preface to Frederick Douglass, *Narrative of the Life of Frederick Douglass* (Garden City, N.Y.: Doubleday, 1973; reprinted from 1845), p. xix.
17. Frederick Douglass, *Life and Times of Frederick Douglass* (New York: Collier Books, 1962), p. 213.
18. Ibid., p. 469.
19. Nat Brandt, *The Town That Started the Civil War* (Syracuse, N.Y.: Syracuse University Press, 1990), p. 28.
20. Ibid., p. 55.
21. Douglass, *Narrative of the Life of Frederick Douglass,* p. x.
22. Ibid., p. 36.
23. Albert Murray, *The Omni-Americans: New Perspectives of Black Experience and American Culture* (New York: Outerbridge & Dienstfrey, 1970), p. 20.
24. Douglass, *Life and Times,* p. 222.
25. Ibid., p. 68.
26. Butterfield, *The American Past,* p. 103.
27. Ibid., p. 111.
28. James Mellon, *Bullwhip Days: The Slaves Remember* (New York: Weidenfeld & Nicolson, 1988), p. 65.
29. Sarah H. Bradford, *Scenes in the Life of Harriet Tubman* (Salem, N.H.: Ayer, 1988; reprint from 1869), p. 10.
30. Ibid., pp. 19–20.
31. Ibid., p. 7.
32. Ibid., p. 22.
33. Lester, *To Be a Slave,* p. 94.
34. Sidney Kaplan and Emma Nogrady Kaplan, *The Black Presence in the Era of the American Revolution* (Amherst: University of Massachusetts Press, 1989), p. 44.
35. Ibid.
36. William Cooper Nell, *Colored Patriots of the American Revolution* (Salem, N.H.: Ayer, 1986; reprint from 1855), preface.
37. Butterfield, *The American Past,* p. 145.
38. Ibid., p. 143.
39. Eric Foner, *Free Soil, Free Labor, Free Men* (London: Oxford University Press, 1970), p. 34.
40. Butterfield, *The American Past,* p. 143.
41. Douglass, *Life and Times,* p. 273.
42. Ibid., p. 319.
43. Stephen B. Oates, *To Purge This Land with Blood* (New York, Harper & Row, 1970), p. 299.
44. Rayford W. Logan and Michael R. Winston, *Dictionary of American Negro Biography* (New York: W. W. Norton & Co., 1982), p. 130.
45. Oates, *To Purge This Land with Blood,* p. 338.
46. Ibid., p. 306.

47. Edmund Wilson, *Patriotic Gore* (Boston: Northeastern University Press, 1984; reprint from 1962), p. 244.
48. Andrew Carroll, ed., *Letters of a Nation* (New York: Kodansha International, 1997), p. 108.
49. Oates, *To Purge This Land with Blood,* p. 351.
50. Ibid., p. 358.
51. Ibid., p. 356.
52. Abraham Lincoln, *Selected Speeches and Writings* (New York: Library of America, 1992), p. 131.
53. James M. McPherson, *Battle Cry of Freedom: The Civil War Era* (New York: Ballantine Books, 1988), p. 244.
54. Richard Wheeler, *Witness to Gettysburg* (Toronto: Penguin Books Canada, 1987), p. 88.
55. Carl Sandburg, *Abraham Lincoln: The War Years* (New York: Dell, 1954; reprint from 1939), p. 520.
56. E. B. Long, *The Civil War Day by Day* (Garden City, N.Y.: Doubleday, 1971), pp. 700, 725.
57. McPherson, *Battle Cry of Freedom,* p. 835.
58. Blight, *Frederick Douglass' Civil War,* p. 154.
59. James M. McPherson, *The Negro's Civil War* (New York: Pantheon, 1965), p. 148.
60. Dudley Taylor Cornish, *The Sable Arm* (Lawrence: University Press of Kansas, 1987), p. 69.
61. Ibid., p. 72.
62. Ibid., p. 77.
63. Elizabeth Keckley, *Behind the Scenes* (New York: The New York Printing Co., 1868), p. 146.
64. Cornish, *The Sable Arm,* p. 45.
65. McPherson, *The Negro's Civil War,* pp. 168–171.
66. Thomas Wentworth Higginson, *Army Life in a Black Regiment* (New York: W. W. Norton & Co., 1984; reprint from 1869), pp. 18–19.
67. Ibid., p. 21.
68. Brown, *The Black Man,* p. 179.
69. Sandburg, *Abraham Lincoln: The War Years,* p. 225.
70. McPherson, *The Negro's Civil War,* p. 184.
71. "This Week in History," *City Sun* (Brooklyn, N.Y.), September 26–October 2, 1990.
72. Douglass, *Life and Times,* p. 353.
73. McPherson, *The Negro's Civil War,* p. 50.
74. Luis F. Emilio, *A Brave Black Regiment* (Salem, N.H.: Ayer, 1990; reprint from 1894), p. 14.
75. Ibid., pp. 21–22.
76. Ibid., p. 3.
77. Burchard, *One Gallant Rush,* pp. 5, 43.
78. Ibid., pp. 72–75.
79. Ira A. Berlin, Joseph E. Reidy, and Leslie Rowland, eds., *Freedom* (Cambridge, Eng.: Cambridge University Press, 1982), p. 337.
80. Virginia M. Adams, ed., *On the Altar of Freedom: Letters of James Gooding* (Amherst: University of Massachusetts Press, 1991), pp. 5–7.
81. McPherson, *The Negro's Civil War,* p. 169.
82. Cornish, *The Sable Arm,* p. 141.
83. Ibid., p. 192.
84. Ibid., p. ix.
85. Martin Robinson Delany, "The Condition, Elevation, Emigration and Destiny of the Colored People of the United States, Politically Considered" (Salem, N.H.: Ayer, 1988; reprinted from 1852), pp. 183, 209.
86. Lerone Bennett, Jr., *Before the Mayflower* (New York: Penguin Books, 1978; reprinted from 1962), p. 149.
87. Joseph T. Glatthaar, *Forged in Battle: The Civil War Alliance of Black Soldiers and White Officers* (New York: Free Press, 1990), p. 30.
88. McPherson, *The Negro's Civil War,* p. 231.
89. Ibid., p. 185.
90. Ibid., p. 186.
91. Ibid.
92. Emilio, *A Brave Black Regiment,* p. 31.
93. Burchard, *One Gallant Rush,* p. 93.
94. Ibid., pp. 93–94.
95. Adams, ed., *On the Altar of Freedom,* p. 30.
96. Emilio, *A Brave Black Regiment,* pp. 47–48.
97. Burchard, *One Gallant Rush,* p. 116.
98. Ray Allen Billington, ed., *The Journal of Charlotte L. Forten* (New York: W. W. Norton & Co., 1981), p. 212.
99. Emilio, *A Brave Black Regiment,* p. 60.
100. Burchard, *One Gallant Rush,* p. 126.
101. Ibid., p. 133.

102. Berlin, Reidy, and Rowland, *Freedom,* p. 534.
103. Burchard, *One Gallant Rush,* p. 135.
104. Emilio, *A Brave Black Regiment,* p. 92.
105. Logan and Winston, *Dictionary of American Negro Biography,* p. 91.
106. Adams, ed., *On the Altar of Freedom,* pp. 38–39.
107. Carroll, ed., *Letters of a Nation,* p. 116.
108. Emilio, *A Brave Black Regiment,* p. 103.
109. Burchard, *One Gallant Rush,* p. 143.
110. Emilio, *A Brave Black Regiment,* p. 401.
111. Albert D. Richardson, *The Secret Service* (Hartford, Conn.: Books for Libraries Press, 1971; reprint from 1865), p. 415.
112. *Photographic History of the Civil War* (Secaucus, N.J.: Blue and Grey Press, 1987, reprint from 1911), vol. 4, pp. 230–32.
113. Emilio, *A Brave Black Regiment,* p. 415.
114. Sandburg, *Abraham Lincoln: The War Years,* p. 423.
115. Carroll, ed., *Letters of a Nation,* p. 117.
116. Emilio, *A Brave Black Regiment,* p. 406.
117. McPherson, *The Negro's Civil War,* pp. 71–72.
118. Louis Auchincloss, ed., *The Hone & Strong Diaries of Old Manhattan* (New York: Abbeville Press, 1989), pp. 221–22.
119. Alexander H. Newton, *Out of the Briars* (Miami: Mnemosyne, 1969; reprinted from 1910), p. 31.
120. McPherson, *The Negro's Civil War,* p. 163.
121. Abraham Lincoln, letter to James C. Conkling, August 26, 1863. In *Selected Speeches and Writings,* pp. 392–93.
122. McPherson, *The Negro's Civil War,* p. 209.
123. Richard A. Long, ed., *Black Writers and the American Civil War* (Secaucus, N.J.: Blue and Grey Press, 1988), p. 37.
124. Ibid., p. 42.
125. Cornish, *The Sable Arm,* p. 173.
126. Ibid., p. 174.
127. John M. Taylor, "The Crater," *The Quarterly Journal of Military History,* Winter 1998, pp. 31–39.
128. Noah Andre Trudeau, *Like Men of War* (Boston: Little, Brown and Co., 1998), p. 249.
129. R.J.M. Blackett, ed., *Thomas Morris Chester, Black Civil War Correspondent* (Baton Rouge: Louisiana State University Press, 1989), p. 140.
130. Robert A. Webb, "The Greater 'Glory' Behind the Movie," *The Washington Post National Weekly Edition,* February 26–March 4, 1990.
131. The Reverend Henry McNeal Turner, "Rocked in the Cradle of Consternation," edited by Edwin S. Redkey, *American Heritage,* October–November 1980, pp. 70–79.
132. David Herbert Donald, *Liberty and Union* (Lexington, Mass.: D. C. Heath and Co., 1978), p. 149.
133. Cornish, *The Sable Arm,* p. 282.
134. Blackett, *Thomas Morris Chester, Black Civil War Correspondent,* p. 314.
135. Ibid., p. 294.
136. Keckley, *Behind the Scenes,* pp. 165–66.
137. Blackett, *Thomas Morris Chester, Black Civil War Correspondent,* p. 295.
138. Trudeau, *Like Men of War,* p. 450.
139. McPherson, *The Negro's Civil War,* p. 237; Long, *The Civil War Day by Day,* p. 708.

4: Buffalo Soldiers I

1. Herschel V. Cashin, *Under Fire with the Tenth Cavalry* (New York: Bellwether Publishing, 1970; reprint from 1899), p. 26.
2. Henry Ossian Flipper, *The Colored Cadet at West Point* (Salem, N.H.: Ayer, 1986; reprint from 1878), p. 196.
3. Richard Drinnon, *Facing West* (New York: New American Library, 1980), p. 329.
4. Evan S. Connell, *Son of the Morning Star* (New York: Harper & Row, 1984), p. 127.
5. Drinnon, *Facing West,* p. 199.
6. Edward M. Coffman, *The Old Army* (New York: Oxford University Press, 1986), p. 389.
7. Ibid., p. 369.
8. William Loren Katz, *The Black West* (Garden City, N.Y.: Doubleday, 1973), p. 224.
9. Connell, *Son of the Morning Star,* pp. 13–14.
10. Ibid., p. 126.
11. Phillip T. Drotning, *Black Heroes in Our Nation's History* (New York: Cowles, 1969), p. 95.
12. Drinnon, *Facing West,* pp. 214–15.

13. Drotning, *Black Heroes in Our Nation's History,* p. 103.
14. William G. Muller, *The Twenty Fourth Infantry Past and Present* (Fort Collins, Colo.: The Old Army Press, 1972; reprint from 1922), unpaginated. The material cited appears on the sixth through eighth pages.
15. Ibid., p. 11.
16. Drotning, *Black Heroes in Our Nation's History,* p. 105.
17. Coffman, *The Old Army,* p. 368.
18. Edmund Wilson, *Patriotic Gore* (Boston: Northeastern University Press, 1984; reprint from 1962), p. 576.
19. Sam Dennison, *Scandalize My Name* (New York: Garland, 1982), p. 243.
20. Geoffrey C. Ward, Ric Burns, and Ken Burns, *The Civil War* (New York: Knopf, 1990), p. 382.
21. W.E.B. Du Bois, *Black Reconstruction in America* (New York: Atheneum, 1962; reprint from 1935), p. 136.
22. Peter M. Bergman, ed., *The Chronological History of the Negro in America* (New York: New American Library, 1969), p. 255.
23. Richard Nelson Current, *Old Thad Stevens* (Westport, Conn.: Greenwood Press, 1942), p. 320.
24. Flipper, *The Colored Cadet at West Point,* p. 306.
25. U.S. Military Academy Archives, West Point, New York.
26. Flipper, *The Colored Cadet at West Point,* pp. 290–91.
27. Ibid., p. 316.
28. Ibid., pp. 37, 165.
29. Ibid., p. 286.
30. Ibid., pp. 47, 268.
31. Ibid., pp. 121, 148, 233.
32. Ibid., pp. 106, 128, 135.
33. Ibid., pp. 151, 174.
34. Ibid., pp. 171, 226.
35. Ibid., pp. 4, 173, 239.
36. *The New York Times,* June 15, 1877.
37. Flipper, *The Colored Cadet at West Point,* pp. 249, 253–54.
38. Coffman, *The Old Army,* p. 231.
39. Flipper, *The Colored Cadet at West Point,* p. 251.
40. Coffman, *The Old Army,* p. 367.
41. Drotning, *Black Heroes in Our Nation's History,* p. 106.
42. John H. Nankivell, *History of the 25th Infantry 1869–1926* (Fort Collins, Colo.: The Old Army Press, 1972), p. 35.
43. David Maraniss, "Due Recognition and Reward," *The Washington Post Magazine,* January 20, 1991, p. 20.
44. Ibid.
45. David Stout, "First Black from West Point Gains Pardon," *The New York Times,* Feb. 20, 1999.
46. Connell, *Son of the Morning Star,* pp. 25–27.
47. Ibid., p. 26.
48. "Seeking Fair Deal for a Black Cadet," *The New York Times,* January 31, 1994.
49. Lerone Bennett, Jr., *Before the Mayflower* (New York: Penguin Books, 1978; reprinted from 1962), pp. 213, 221.
50. Coffman, *The Old Army,* p. 228.
51. Cashin, *Under Fire with the Tenth Cavalry,* p. 41.
52. Ibid., pp. 42–43.
53. Nankivell, *History of the 25th Infantry,* p. 48.
54. W. Augustus Low and Virgil A. Clift, *Encyclopedia of Black America* (New York: Da Capo Press, 1984), p. 839.
55. Ray Stannard Baker, *Following the Color Line* (Williamstown, Mass.: Corner House Publishers, 1973; reprint from 1904), p. 225.
56. John D. Weaver, *The Brownsville Raid* (New York: W. W. Norton & Co., 1973), p. 99.
57. Herbert Aptheker, ed., *A Documentary History of the Negro People in the United States,* vol. 2 (New York: Citadel Press, 1968), p. 907.
58. Rayford W. Logan and Michael R. Winston, *Dictionary of American Negro Biography* (New York: W. W. Norton & Co., 1982), p. 245.

5: Buffalo Soldiers II

1. Phillip T. Drotning, *Black Heroes in Our Nation's History* (New York: Cowles, 1969), p. 133.
2. Marvin E. Fletcher, *The Black Soldier and Officer in the United States Army 1891–1917* (Columbia: University of Missouri Press, 1974), p. 33.
3. John H. Nankivell, *History of the 25th Infantry 1869–1926* (Fort Collins, Colo.: The Old Army Press, 1972), p. 66.

4. William G. Muller, *The Twenty Fourth Infantry Past and Present* (Fort Collins, Colo.: The Old Army Press, 1972; reprint from 1922), unpaginated.
5. Herschel V. Cashin, *Under Fire with the Tenth Cavalry* (New York: Bellwether Publishing, 1970; reprint from 1899), p. 120.
6. William Hilary Coston, *The Spanish-American War Volunteer* (Freeport, N.Y.: Books for Libraries Press, 1971; reprint from 1899), p. 9.
7. Peter Harrington, "You Supply the Pictures, I'll Supply the War," *Quarterly Journal of Military History,* vol. 10, no. 4 (Summer 1998), p. 52.
8. Ibid.
9. Cashin, *Under Fire with the Tenth Cavalry,* p. 279.
10. Edmund Morris, *The Rise of Theodore Roosevelt* (New York: Ballantine Books, 1979), p. 12.
11. Cashin, *Under Fire with the Tenth Cavalry,* p. 76.
12. Ibid., p. 160.
13. Ibid., p. 80.
14. Ibid., p. 140.
15. Ibid., p. 276.
16. Ibid., p. 126.
17. Ibid., p. 128.
18. Ibid., pp. 128–29.
19. Ibid., p. 160.
20. Ibid., p. 208.
21. Ibid., p. 93.
22. William Loren Katz, *The Black West* (Garden City, N.Y.: Doubleday, 1973), pp. 275–76.
23. Fletcher, *The Black Soldier and Officer in the United States Army,* p. 45.
24. Cashin, *Under Fire with the Tenth Cavalry,* p. 161.
25. Ibid., p. 159.
26. Ibid., p. 209.
27. Fletcher, *The Black Soldier and Officer in the United States Army,* p. 41.
28. Cashin, *Under Fire with the Tenth Cavalry,* p. 176.
29. Ibid., p. 332.
30. Ibid., p. 224.
31. Cashin, *Under Fire with the Tenth Cavalry,* p. 177.
32. Fletcher, *The Black Soldier and Officer in the United States Army,* p. 42.
33. Morris, *The Rise of Theodore Roosevelt,* p. 658.
34. Cashin, *Under Fire with the Tenth Cavalry,* p. 105.
35. Ibid.
36. Muller, *The Twenty Fourth Infantry Regiment Past and Present,* p. 30.
37. Coston, *The Spanish-American War Volunteer,* pp. 55–56.
38. Walter J. Stevens, *Chip on My Shoulder* (Boston: Measor, 1946), pp. 48–50.
39. Ibid., pp. 56–58.
40. Ibid., pp. 66–67.
41. Ibid., p. 68.
42. Ibid., pp. 73, 198–99.
43. Fletcher, *The Black Soldier and Officer in the United States Army,* p. 63.
44. Marvin E. Fletcher, *America's First Black General* (Lawrence: University of Kansas Press, 1989), p. 22.
45. Richard Severo and Lewis Milford, *The Wages of War* (New York: Simon & Schuster, 1989), p. 223.
46. Ibid., pp. 216–27.
47. Ibid., pp. 213–14.
48. Ibid., pp. 222–23.
49. Leon Litwack and August Meier, ed., *Black Leaders of the Nineteenth Century* (Chicago: University of Illinois Press, 1988), pp. 270–71.
50. Fletcher, *The Black Soldier and Officer in the United States Army,* p. 49.
51. Nankivell, *History of the Twenty Fifth Infantry,* pp. 101–2.
52. Fletcher, *The Black Soldier and Officer in the United States Army,* p. 50.
53. Ibid., p. 51.
54. Clinton Cox, "The Civilized vs. the Savage: A Powerful Myth," *The City Sun* (Brooklyn, N.Y.), May 1–7, 1991.
55. Clinton Cox, "Monkey Business, Past and Present," *The City Sun* (Brooklyn, N.Y.), March 6–12, 1991.
56. Severo and Milford, *The Wages of War,* p. 219.
57. Ibid., p. 216.
58. Ibid., pp. 217–20.
59. Cox, "Monkey Business, Past and Present."
60. Severo and Milford, *The Wages of War,* p. 220.
61. Stanley Karnow, *In Our Image: America's Empire in the Philippines* (Random House, 1989), p. 267.

62. Rayford W. Logan and Michael R. Winston, *Dictionary of American Negro Biography* (New York: W. W. Norton & Co., 1982), p. 218.
63. Sam Dennis, *Scandalize My Name* (New York: Garland Publishing, 1982), p. 347.
64. John D. Weaver, *The Brownsville Raid* (New York: W. W. Norton & Co., 1970), p. 19.
65. Ibid., p. 78.
66. Bernard C. Nalty, *Strength for the Fight* (New York: The Free Press, 1986), p. 94.
67. Weaver, *The Brownsville Raid,* p. 248.
68. Fletcher, *The Black Soldier and Officer in the United States Army,* p. 144.
69. Weaver, *The Brownsville Raid,* p. 274.

6: The World War

1. *The Crisis,* May 1919, pp. 16–17.
2. Michel Fabre, *From Harlem to Paris: Black American Writers in France* (Chicago: University of Illinois Press, 1991), p. 48.
3. Emmett J. Scott, *Official History of the American Negro in the World War* (New York: Arno Press, 1969; reprint from 1919), p. 118.
4. Byron Farwell, *Over There* (New York: W. W. Norton & Co., 1999), p. 149.
5. Scott, *Official History of the American Negro in the World War,* pp. 276–77.
6. Winston Churchill, *The World Crisis* (New York: Scribners, 1923–31), cited in Farwell, *Over There,* p. 121.
7. John Keegan, *The First World War* (New York: Knopf, 1999), p. 52.
8. Farwell, *Over There,* p. 128.
9. Ibid., p. 119.
10. Ibid., p. 37.
11. Keegan, *The First World War,* p. 411.
12. Farwell, *Over There,* p. 168.
13. Ibid., p. 22.
14. P. J. Carisella and James W. Ryan, *Black Swallow of Death* (Boston: Marlborough House, 1972), p. 8.
15. Ibid., p. 60.
16. Ibid., pp. 70, 113.
17. Keegan, *The First World War,* p. 135.
18. Carisella and Ryan, *Black Swallow of Death,* pp. 85–105.
19. Ibid., p. 102.
20. Ibid., pp. 117–18.
21. Ibid., p. 135.
22. Ibid., p. 150.
23. Ibid., p. 211.
24. Ibid., p. 266.
25. Ibid., p. 118.
26. Ibid., p. 169.
27. Ibid., pp. 13, 198.
28. Langston Hughes, *The Big Sea* (New York: Thunder's Mouth Press, 1986; reprint from 1940), p. 160.
29. Carisella and Ryan, *Black Swallow of Death,* pp. 231–32.
30. Ibid., p. 247.
31. Ibid., p. 256.
32. Scott, *Official History of the American Negro in the World War,* p. 34.
33. Bernard C. Nalty, *Strength for the Fight* (New York: Free Press, 1986), p. 110.
34. Walter J. Stevens, *Chip on My Shoulder* (Boston: Measor, 1946), pp. 178–79.
35. Rayford W. Logan and Michael R. Winston, *Dictionary of American Negro Biography* (New York: W. W. Norton & Co., 1982), p. 679.
36. Scott, *Official History of the American Negro in the World War,* pp. 37–38.
37. Ibid., p. 67.
38. Peter M. Bergman, ed., *The Chronological History of the Negro in America* (New York: New American Library, 1969), p. 382.
39. Scott, *Official History of the American Negro in the World War,* p. 84.
40. David M. Tucker, *Lieutenant Lee of Beale Street* (Nashville: Vanderbilt University Press, 1971), p. 31.
41. Scott, *Official History of the American Negro in the World War,* p. 430.
42. Jack D. Foner, *Blacks and the Military in American History* (New York: Praeger, 1974), p. 118.
43. Scott, *Official History of the American Negro in the World War,* p. 439.
44. Ibid., pp. 35–50.
45. Ibid., p. 59.
46. Ibid., p. 105.

47. Foner, *Blacks and the Military in American History,* p. 119.
48. Scott, *Official History of the American Negro in the World War,* pp. 62–63, 104, 108.
49. Kelly Miller, *History of the World War for Human Rights* (New York: Negro University Press, 1969; reprint from 1919), pp. 537–38.
50. Scott, *Official History of the American Negro in the World War,* p. 99.
51. Ibid., pp. 431–33.
52. Adele Logan Alexander, *Homelands and Waterway* (New York: Pantheon, 1999), p. 412.
53. Tucker, *Lieutenant Lee of Beale Street,* p. 38.
54. Addie D. Hunton and Kathryn H. Johnson, *Two Colored Women with the American Expeditionary Forces* (Brooklyn: Brooklyn Eagle Press, 1918), p. 47.
55. *The Crisis,* December 1919, p. 46.
56. Farwell, *Over There,* p. 157.
57. Nalty, *Strength for the Fight,* p. 123.
58. Foner, *Blacks and the Military in American History,* p. 124.
59. Scott, *Official History of the American Negro in the World War,* pp. 167, 188.
60. Ibid., pp. 280, 296–97.
61. *The Crisis,* July 1918.
62. Sally Hanley, *A. Philip Randolph* (New York: Chelsea House Publishers, 1989), p. 35.
63. Farwell, *Over There,* p. 134.
64. Scott, *Official History of the American Negro in the World War,* p. 75.
65. Harry Haywood, *Black Bolshevik* (Chicago: Liberator Press, 1978), p. 44.
66. Ibid., pp. 42–51.
67. Ibid., pp. 39, 42, 52.
68. Hunton and Johnson, *Two Colored Women with the American Expeditionary Forces,* p. 79.
69. Arthur W. Little, *From Harlem to the Rhine* (New York: Covici-Friede Publishers, 1936), p. xi.
70. Ibid., p. 3.
71. Farwell, *Over There,* p. 144.
72. Hamilton Fish, *Memoir of an American Patriot* (Washington, D.C.: Regnery Gateway, 1991), p. 26.
73. Little, *From Harlem to the Rhine,* pp. 13–14.
74. Fish, *Memoir of an American Patriot,* p. 32.
75. Little, *From Harlem to the Rhine,* pp. 27, 239, 256.
76. Ibid., p. 108.
77. Robert Kimball and William Bolcom, *Reminiscing with Sissle and Blake* (New York: Viking Press, 1973), p. 60.
78. Ibid., pp. 59–61.
79. Ibid., p. 63.
80. Little, *From Harlem to the Rhine,* p. 116.
81. Kimball and Bolcom, *Reminiscing with Sissle and Blake,* p. 35.
82. Little, *From Harlem to the Rhine,* p. 14.
83. Ibid., p. 13.
84. Ibid., p. 46.
85. Ibid., pp. 49–50.
86. Ibid., pp. 54–55.
87. Fish, *Memoir of an American Patriot,* p. 27.
88. Little, *From Harlem to the Rhine,* p. 55.
89. Kimball and Bolcom, *Reminiscing with Sissle and Blake,* p. 65.
90. Little, *From Harlem to the Rhine,* pp. 68–69.
91. Scott, *Official History of the American Negro in the World War,* pp. 80–81.
92. Fish, *Memoir of an American Patriot,* pp. 26–27.
93. Farwell, *Over There,* pp. 82, 90.
94. Little, *From Harlem to the Rhine,* p. 185.
95. Scott, *Official History of the American Negro in the World War,* p. 323.
96. Little, *From Harlem to the Rhine,* p. 101.
97. Ibid., pp. 132–33.
98. Ibid., p. 146.
99. Ibid., p. 130.
100. Kimball and Bolcom, *Reminiscing with Sissle and Blake,* pp. 67–68.
101. Ibid., p. 66.
102. Little, *From Harlem to the Rhine,* p. 128.
103. Kimball and Bolcom, *Reminiscing with Sissle and Blake,* p. 68.
104. Little, *From Harlem to the Rhine,* p. 138.
105. Ibid., p. 142.
106. Fish, *Memoir of an American Patriot,* pp. 28–29.
107. Kimball and Bolcom, *Reminiscing with Sissle and Blake,* p. 78.
108. Little, *From Harlem to the Rhine,* p. 195.
109. Ibid., pp. 195–201.
110. Scott, *Official History of the American Negro in the World War,* p. 208.

111. Fish, *Memoir of an American Patriot,* p. 30.
112. Farwell, *Over There,* p. 183.
113. Scott, *Official History of the American Negro in the World War,* p. 213.
114. Fish, *Memoir of an American Patriot,* p. 30.
115. Little, *From Harlem to the Rhine,* p. 336.
116. Chester D. Heywood, *Negro Combat Troops in the World War* (Worcester, Mass.: Commonwealth Press, 1928), foreword.
117. Ibid., pp. 3–10.
118. Ibid., p. 12.
119. Ibid., p. 13.
120. Ibid., p. 24.
121. Ibid., pp. 43–45.
122. Ibid., pp. 33, 57.
123. Ibid., p. 113.
124. Ibid., p. 116.
125. Ibid., pp. 156–60.
126. Ibid., pp. 163–69.
127. Ibid., p. 177.
128. Ibid., p. 181.
129. Ibid., pp. 189, 242.
130. Hunton and Johnson, *Two Colored Women with the American Expeditionary Forces,* p. 24.
131. Ibid., pp. 17–18.
132. Ibid., pp. 15, 24.
133. Heywood, *Negro Combat Troops in the World War,* pp. 222–24.
134. Ibid., pp. 231–39.
135. Little, *From Harlem to the Rhine,* p. 350.
136. Ibid., p. 352.
137. Ibid., p. 361.
138. Ibid.
139. Ibid., p. 362.
140. Kimball and Bolcom, *Reminiscing with Sissle and Blake,* p. 72.
141. *The Crisis,* December 1920.
142. Nalty, *Strength for the Fight,* p. 123.
143. Hunton and Johnson, *Two Colored Women with the American Expeditionary Forces,* pp. 234–35.
144. Fabre, *From Harlem to Paris,* p. 53.
145. *The Crisis,* February 1920.
146. *The Crisis,* January 1920, p. 142.
147. Mary Penick Motley, *The Invisible Soldier* (Detroit: Wayne State University Press, 1987), p. 16.

7: The "New Negro" and the Spanish Civil War

1. Danny Duncan Collum, ed., *African Americans in the Spanish Civil War* (New York: G. K. Hall & Co., 1992), p. 85.
2. Claude McKay, *Selected Poems* (New York: Harcourt, Brace & World, 1953), p. 36.
3. *The Crisis,* August 1919, p. 179.
4. Peter M. Bergman, ed., *The Chronological History of the Negro in America* (New York: New American Library, 1969), p. 411.
5. Harry Haywood, *Black Bolshevik* (Chicago: Liberator Press, 1978), p. 81.
6. Ibid., p. 83.
7. Bergman, *The Chronological History of the Negro in America,* p. 414.
8. Hamilton Fish, *Memoir of an American Patriot* (Washington, D.C.: Regnery Gateway, 1991), p. 33.
9. Blanche Wiesen Cook, *Eleanor Roosevelt.* Vol. 2, *1933–1938* (New York: Viking, 1999), p. 19.
10. Bergman, *The Chronological History of the Negro in America,* p. 441.
11. David Levering Lewis, *When Harlem Was in Vogue* (New York: Knopf, 1981), p. 111.
12. Nancy Cunard, ed., *Negro* (New York: Frederick Ungar Publishing, 1970; reprinted from 1934), pp. 132–35.
13. Herbert Aptheker, ed., *A Documentary History of the Negro People in the United States,* vol. 3 (Secaucus, N.J., Citadel Press, 1977), p. 299.
14. Allison Blakely, *Russia and the Negro* (Washington, D.C.: Howard University Press, 1986), p. 83.
15. Nathan Glazer, *The Social Basis of American Communism* (Westport, Conn.: Greenwood Press Publishers, 1961), p. 175.
16. Ibid., p. 168.
17. Roy Wilkins, *Standing Fast* (New York: Penguin Books, 1982), p. 164.
18. Doris Kearns Goodwin, *No Ordinary Time* (New York: Simon & Schuster, 1994), p. 481.

19. Ibid., p. 568.
20. Cook, *Eleanor Roosevelt,* p. 37.
21. Goodwin, *No Ordinary Time,* p. 162.
22. Walter White, *A Man Called White* (New York: Viking Press, 1948), pp. 3, 11.
23. Wilkins, *Standing Fast,* p. 153.
24. Goodwin, *No Ordinary Time,* p. 163.
25. Cook, *Eleanor Roosevelt,* p. 292.
26. Goodwin, *No Ordinary Time,* p. 163.
27. Bernard C. Nalty, *Strength for the Fight* (New York: Free Press, 1986), pp. 131–32.
28. Richard M. Dalfiume, *Desegregation of the U.S. Armed Forces* (Columbia: University of Missouri Press, 1969), p. 22.
29. Ibid., p. 24.
30. Morris J. MacGregor, Jr., *Integration of the Armed Forces 1940–1965* (Washington, D.C.: Center of Military History, United States Army, 1989), p. 67.
31. Angelo Del Boca, *The Ethiopian War* (Chicago: University of Chicago Press, 1969), pp. 96–97.
32. Ibid., p. 85.
33. Jay Maeder, "Place in the Sun: The Black Eagle, 1935," New York *Daily News,* May 17, 1998.
34. Del Boca, *The Ethiopian War,* pp. 92–94.
35. "Louis-Carnera Bout Draws 15,000 Negroes, 1,300 Police," *The New York Herald Tribune,* June 23, 1935.
36. Wilkins, *Standing Fast,* p. 164.
37. William Loren Katz and Marc Crawford, *The Lincoln Brigade* (New York: Atheneum, 1989), p. 14.
38. James W. Ford, *The Negro and the Democratic Front* (New York: International Publishers, 1938), pp. 165–66.
39. Bergman, *The Chronological History of the Negro in America,* p. 474.
40. Peter A. Quinn, "Closet Full of Bones," *America* magazine, February 18, 1995.
41. Duff Hart-Davis, *Hitler's Games* (New York: Harper & Row, 1986), p. 177.
42. Hugh Thomas, *The Spanish Civil War* (New York: Harper & Row, 1961), p. 3.
43. Ibid., p. 166.
44. Arthur H. Landis, *Death in the Olive Groves* (New York: Paragon House, 1989), p. xx.
45. Ibid., p. 221.
46. Federico García Lorca, "The Ballad of the Spanish Civil Guard," translated by Langston Hughes. Quoted in *Paul Robeson: The Life and Times of a Free Black Man,* by Virginia Hamilton (New York, Harper & Row, 1974), p. 78.
47. Thomas, *The Spanish Civil War,* p. 380.
48. Marion Merriman and Warren Lerude, *American Commander in Spain* (Reno: University of Nevada Press, 1986), p. 86.
49. Katz and Crawford, *The Lincoln Brigade,* p. 33.
50. Charlie Nusser, letter to author, May 21, 1993.
51. Joe Brandt, ed., *Black Americans in the Spanish People's War Against Fascism* (New York: International Publishers, n.d.), p. 31.
52. Don Lawson, *The Abraham Lincoln Brigade* (New York: Crowell, 1989), p. 15.
53. Collum, *African Americans in the Spanish Civil War,* p. 30.
54. Merriman and Lerude, *American Commander in Spain,* p. 96.
55. Ibid., p. 109.
56. Cary Nelson and Jefferson Hendricks, *Edwin Rolfe* (Urbana: University of Illinois Press, 1990), p. 91.
57. Ernest Hemingway, "On the American Dead in Spain," *New Masses,* February 14, 1939.
58. Nelson and Hendricks, *Edwin Rolfe,* p. 91.
59. James Yates, *Mississippi to Madrid* (Seattle: Open Hand Publishing, 1989), p. 106.
60. Ibid., pp. 105–6, 112.
61. Ibid., p. 129.
62. Lawson, *The Abraham Lincoln Brigade,* p. 71.
63. Brandt, *Black Americans in the Spanish People's War Against Fascism,* p. 53.
64. Ibid., p. 32.
65. Lawson, *The Abraham Lincoln Brigade,* p. 85.
66. Collum, *African Americans in the Spanish Civil War,* pp. 175–79.
67. James W. Cortada, *Historical Dictionary of the Spanish Civil War* (Westport, Conn.: Greenwood Press, 1982), p. 258.
68. Herbert Steiner, "Bailing Out," *The Sunday Worker,* March 6, 1938.
69. Collum, *African Americans in the Spanish Civil War,* p. 89.
70. Martin Bauml Duberman, *Paul Robeson* (New York: Knopf, 1988), p. 212.
71. Lawson, *The Abraham Lincoln Brigade,* p. 111.
72. Letter from Veterans of Abraham Lincoln Brigade, 60th Anniversary Luncheon, April 21, 1996. In author's possession.
73. Landis, *Death in the Olive Groves,* p. 218.
74. Yates, *Mississippi to Madrid,* p. 160.

8: World War II

1. Patrick S. Washburn, *A Question of Sedition* (New York: Oxford University Press, 1986), p. 55.
2. Walter White, *A Man Called White* (New York: Viking Press, 1948), p. 220.
3. Roger Starr, letter to author, 1999.
4. White, *A Man Called White,* p. 222.
5. Roy Wilkins, *Standing Fast* (New York: Penguin Books, 1982), pp. 176–84.
6. Richard M. Dalfiume, *Desegregation of the U.S. Armed Forces* (Columbia: University of Missouri Press, 1969), pp. 2, 39.
7. Doris Kearns Goodwin, *No Ordinary Time* (New York: Simon & Schuster, 1994), pp. 566–67.
8. Dalfiume, *Desegregation of the U.S. Armed Forces,* p. 57.
9. Goodwin, *No Ordinary Time,* p. 328.
10. Ibid., p. 627.
11. Ibid., p. 422.
12. Ibid., p. 521.
13. White, *A Man Called White,* p. 223.
14. Phillip McGuire, *He Too Spoke for Democracy* (New York: Greenwood Press, 1988), p. 61.
15. Bernard C. Nalty, *Strength for the Fight* (New York: Free Press, 1986), p. 136.
16. Goodwin, *No Ordinary Time,* p. 168.
17. Ibid., p. 166.
18. White, *A Man Called White,* pp. 186–87.
19. Goodwin, *No Ordinary Time,* p. 168.
20. White, *A Man Called White,* p. 187.
21. Goodwin, *No Ordinary Time,* p. 86.
22. Dalfiume, *Desegregation of the U.S. Armed Forces,* p. 42.
23. McGuire, *He Too Spoke for Democracy,* p. xiii.
24. Washburn, *A Question of Sedition,* p. 59.
25. McGuire, *He Too Spoke for Democracy,* p. xiv.
26. Charles E. Wynes, *Charles Richard Drew* (Chicago: University of Illinois Press, 1988), p. 16.
27. Ibid., p. 51.
28. Ibid., pp. 70–79.
29. Goodwin, *No Ordinary Time,* p. 214.
30. Ibid., p. 582.
31. Ibid., p. 247.
32. Ibid., p. 248.
33. Ibid., p. 249.
34. Ibid., pp. 250–51.
35. Ibid., pp. 370, 540.
36. Ibid., p. 373.
37. Washburn, *A Question of Sedition,* p. 32.
38. Ibid., pp. 38–39.
39. Ibid., p. 57.
40. Ibid., p. 108.
41. Ibid., p. 51.
42. Ibid., p. 186.
43. Ibid., p. 200.
44. Goodwin, *No Ordinary Time,* p. 329.
45. Washburn, *A Question of Sedition,* p. 54.
46. Henry I. Shaw, Jr., and Ralph W. Donnelly, *Blacks in the Marine Corps* (Washington, D.C.: History and Museums Division, Headquarters, U.S. Marine Corps, 1975), p. 1.
47. Studs Terkel, *The Good War* (New York: Ballantine Books, 1984), p. 264.
48. Dalfiume, *Desegregation of the U.S. Armed Forces,* p. 100.
49. Stephen Ambrose, *D-Day* (New York: Simon & Schuster, 1994), p. 372.
50. Patrick K. O'Donnell, *Beyond Valor* (New York: Free Press, 2000), p. 180.
51. Peter M. Bergman, ed., *The Chronological History of the Negro in America* (New York: New American Library, 1969), p. 495.
52. Ibid., pp. 495, 508.
53. Thomas Cripps, *Slow Fade to Black* (London: Oxford University Press, 1977), p. 349.
54. Ibid., p. 387.
55. Jay Maeder, "Fighting Heart, Flip Corkin, 1943," New York *Daily News,* June 15, 1998.
56. Benjamin O. Davis, Jr., *Benjamin O. Davis, Jr.: American* (Washington, D.C.: Smithsonian Institution Press, 1991), p. 26.
57. Ibid., pp. 28–29, 36–37.
58. Ibid., p. 59.
59. Ibid., p. 76.
60. Ibid., p. 89.
61. Goodwin, *No Ordinary Time,* p. 423.

62. Davis, *Benjamin O. Davis, Jr.: American,* p. 97.
63. Von Hardesty and Dominick Pisano, *Black Wings* (Washington, D.C.: National Air and Space Museum, Smithsonian Institution, 1983), p. 39.
64. Robert A. Rose, *Lonely Eagles* (Los Angeles: Tuskegee Airmen, 1976), p. 61.
65. *Time,* September 20, 1943.
66. Davis, *Benjamin O. Davis, Jr.: American,* p. 106.
67. Tony Brown, "America's Black Air Force," *Tony Brown's Journal,* January/March, 1983.
68. Rose, *Lonely Eagles,* p. 60.
69. Alan M. Osur, *Blacks in the Army Air Forces During World War II* (New York: Arno Press, 1980), p. 56.
70. Mary Penick Motley, *The Invisible Soldier* (Detroit: Wayne State University Press, 1987), p. 206.
71. Ibid.
72. Charity Adams Early, *One Woman's Army* (College Station: Texas A & M University Press, 1989), p. 12.
73. Ibid., pp. 23–32.
74. Ibid., pp. 34–39.
75. Ibid., pp. 55–56, 107.
76. Ibid., pp. 60–62.
77. John O'Donnell, "Capitol Stuff," *Washington Times-Herald,* June 9, 1943.
78. Early, *One Woman's Army,* p. 70.
79. Ibid., p. 104.
80. Ibid., pp. 134–35.
81. Ibid., pp. 138–39.
82. Graham Smith, *When Jim Crow Met John Bull* (New York: St. Martin's Press, 1987), pp. 61, 88, 208.
83. Early, *One Woman's Army,* pp. 160, 192.
84 Ibid., p. 174.
85. Undated news clip (given by Sallie Smith Jones to author).
86. Early, *One Woman's Army,* p. 187.
87. Ibid., p. 214.
88. Goodwin, *No Ordinary Time,* pp. 249, 329–30.
89. Morris J. MacGregor, Jr., *Integration of the Armed Forces 1940–1965* (Washington, D.C.: Center of Military History, United States Army, 1989), p. 67.
90. Ibid., pp. 176–77.
91. Ibid., p. 82.
92. Ibid., p. 84.
93. Goodwin, *No Ordinary Time,* p. 523; MacGregor, *Integration of the Armed Forces 1940–1965,* pp. 88–89.
94. MacGregor, *Integration of the Armed Forces 1940–1965,* p. 85.
95. Carl T. Rowan, *Breaking Barriers* (Boston: Little, Brown & Co., 1981), pp. 43–55.
96. Ibid., p. 53.
97. Robert L. Allen, *The Port Chicago Mutiny* (New York: Warner Books, 1989), p. 67.
98. Ibid., p. 119.
99. MacGregor, *Integration of the Armed Forces 1940–1965,* p. 87.
100. Shaw and Donnelly, *Blacks in the Marine Corps,* p. 1.
101. Jesse J. Johnson, *Roots of Two Black Marine Sergeants Major* (Hampton, Va.: Carver Publishing, 1978), p. 18.
102. Shaw and Donnelly, *Blacks in the Marine Corps,* p. 3.
103. Johnson, *Roots of Two Black Marine Sergeants Major,* p. 47.
104. Ibid., p. 46.
105. Ibid., p. 11.
106. Bill Downey, *Uncle Sam Must Be Losing the War* (San Francisco: Strawberry Hill Press, 1982), p. 79.
107. Ibid., pp. 34–39.
108. Ibid., p. 80.
109. Shaw and Donnelly, *Blacks in the Marine Corps,* p. 13.
110. Downey, *Uncle Sam Must Be Losing the War,* p. 54.
111. Ibid., p. 124.
112. Ibid., pp. 127–29.
113. Ibid., p. 133.
114. Ibid., p. 152.
115. Shaw and Donnelly, *Blacks in the Marine Corps,* p. 20.
116. Downey, *Uncle Sam Must Be Losing the War,* p. 169.
117. Ibid., p. 168.
118. Ibid., p. 198.
119. Shaw and Donnelly, *Blacks in the Marine Corps,* p. 34.

120. Ibid., p. 35.
121. Alvin M. Josephy, Jr., "Iwo Jima," *American Heritage,* June–July 1981, p. 101.
122. Shaw and Donnelly, *Blacks in the Marine Corps,* p. 28.
123. Dalfiume, *Desegregation of the U.S. Armed Forces,* p. 99.
124. Marvin E. Fletcher, *America's First Black General* (Lawrence: University Press of Kansas, 1989), p. 139.
125. Nalty, *Strength for the Fight,* p. 176.
126. White, *A Man Called White,* p. 250.
127. Allan Morrison, undated *Ebony* magazine clip given by Bruce Wright to author.
128. Smith, *When Jim Crow Met John Bull,* p. 225.
129. Bruce M. Wright, *Black Robes, White Justice* (Secaucus, N.J.: Lyle Stuart, 1987), p. 43.
130. Wright, undated letter written in Giessen, Germany. Copy in author's possession.
131. Trezzvant W. Anderson, *Come Out Fighting* (Long Island, N.Y.: 761st Tank Battalion and Allied Veterans Association, 1979; reprinted from 1945), p. 21.
132. Ibid.
133. C. Gerald Fraser, "Book Recalls Black World War II Tank Battalion," *The New York Times,* September 5, 1983.
134. Richard Bernstein, "Comrades and Family Fighting to Honor a Hero," *The New York Times,* March 28, 1993.
135. Anderson, *Come Out Fighting,* p. 37.
136. Ibid., pp. 71–89.
137. Benjamin Bender, letter to the editor, *The New York Times,* April 22, 1985.
138. Benjamin Bender, *Glimpses* (Berkeley, Calif.: North Atlantic Books, 1995), p. 161.
139. Elie Wiesel, *The New York Times,* April 11, 1989.
140. Jeffrey Goldberg, "Black Soldiers and Buchenwald: The Exaggerators," *The New Republic,* February 8, 1993, p. 15.
141. *New York Post,* February 3, 1993.
142. Joseph B. Treastor, "WNET Inquiry Finds No Proof Black Unit Freed 2 Nazi Camps," *The New York Times,* February 12, 1993.

9: Korea

1. Charles M. Bussey, *Firefight at Yechon: Courage and Racism in the Korean War* (Washington, D.C.: Brassey's, 1991), p. 163.
2. Charles E. Francis, *The Tuskegee Airmen* (Boston: Branden Publishing Company, 1988), p. 205.
3. Alan M. Osur, *Blacks in the Air Force During World War II* (New York: Arno Press, 1980), p. 121.
4. Richard M. Dalfiume, *Desegregation of the U.S. Armed Forces* (Columbia: University of Missouri Press), p. 149.
5. Ibid., pp. 150–51.
6. Ibid., p. 153.
7. Ibid., pp. 164–69.
8. Ibid., p. 156.
9. Ibid., pp. 133–34.
10. Walter White, *A Man Called White* (New York: Viking Press, 1948), p. 331.
11. David McCullough, *Truman* (New York: Simon & Schuster, 1992), p. 247.
12. Dalfiume, *Desegregation of the U.S. Armed Forces,* p. 141.
13. Ibid., p. 138.
14. Clark Clifford with Richard Holbrook, *Counsel to the President* (New York: Random House, 1991), pp. 205–6.
15. Ibid., p. 167.
16. Peter M. Bergman, *The Chronological History of the Negro in America* (New York: New American Library, 1969), p. 518.
17. Clifford, *Counsel to the President,* pp. 203–4.
18. Dalfiume, *Desegregation of the U.S. Armed Forces,* p. 171.
19. Ibid., pp. 151, 160, 172.
20. Joseph L. Galloway, "The Last of the Buffalo Soldiers," *U.S. News and World Report,* May 6, 1996, p. 45.
21. Dalfiume, *Desegregation of the U.S. Armed Forces,* pp. 102–3.
22. Ibid., p. 195.
23. James Chace, *Acheson* (New York: Simon & Schuster, 1998), p. 280.
24. Ibid., p. 269.
25. David Halberstam, *The Fifties* (New York: Fawcett Columbine, 1993), p. 63.
26. Chace, *Acheson,* p. 269.
27. Halberstam, *The Fifties,* p. 17.
28. James Brady, *The Coldest War* (New York: St. Martin's Press, 1990), p. 2.

29. Clay Blair, *The Forgotten War* (New York: Times Books, 1987), pp. 975–76.
30. Patricia Bosworth, *Anything Your Little Heart Desires* (New York: Simon & Schuster, 1997), p. 224.
31. Halberstam, *The Fifties,* pp. 52–54.
32. Chace, *Acheson,* p. 237.
33. Halberstam, *The Fifties,* p. 54.
34. Martin Bauml Duberman, *Paul Robeson* (New York: Knopf, 1988), p. 342.
35. Ibid., p. 360.
36. Virginia Hamilton, *Paul Robeson* (New York: Harper & Row, 1974), pp. 159, 182.
37. Joseph L. Galloway, "A Soldier's Story," *U.S. News and World Report,* May 31, 1999, pp. 44–52.
38. Ibid., p. 53.
39. Chace, *Acheson,* p. 282.
40. Ibid., p. 284.
41. Ibid., p. 283.
42. McCullough, *Truman,* p. 787.
43. Bussey, *Firefight at Yechon,* p. 72.
44. Ibid., p. 89.
45. Blair, *The Forgotten War,* p. 648.
46. Bussey, *Firefight at Yechon,* pp. 41–42.
47. Blair, *The Forgotten War,* p. 151.
48. William T. Bowers, William M. Hammond, and George L. MacGarrigle, *Black Soldier, White Army: The 24th Infantry in Korea* (Washington, D.C.: United States Army Center of Military History, 1996), p. 71.
49. Blair, *The Forgotten War,* p. 147.
50. Bowers, et al., *Black Soldier, White Army,* p. 45.
51. Bussey, *Firefight at Yechon,* p. 43.
52. Bowers, et al., *Black Soldier, White Army,* p. 54.
53. Blair, *The Forgotten War,* p. 152.
54. *Congressional Record,* vol. 96, pt. 8, 24 July 1950, p. 10866; Blair, *The Forgotten War,* p. 153.
55. Bussey, *Firefight at Yechon,* pp. 99, 107.
56. Ibid., p. 213.
57. Ibid., pp. 213–15.
58. Bowers, et al., *Black Soldier, White Army,* p. 130.
59. Benjamin O. Davis, Jr., *Benjamin O. Davis, Jr.: American* (Washington, D.C.: Smithsonian Institution Press, 1991), p. 183.
60. J. Alfred Phelps, *Chappie* (Novato, Calif.: Presidio Press, 1991), p. 63.
61. Ibid., pp. 181–83.
62. Colonel David Hackworth, *About Face* (New York: Simon & Schuster, 1989), p. 54.
63. Blair, *The Forgotten War,* p. 242.
64. John M. Broder, "Army: Blacks Look Back at Record in Korea," *Los Angeles Times,* November 15, 1989.
65. J. Paul Scicchitano, "All Black Regiment Struggles to Reclaim Its Lost Reputation," *Army Times,* August 21, 1989, p. 15.
66. Bussey, *Firefight at Yechon,* p. 159.
67. Ibid., pp. 159–62.
68. Bowers, et al., *Black Soldier, White Army,* pp. 92–93.
69. Chace, *Acheson,* p. 303.
70. Blair, *The Forgotten War,* p. 444.
71. Hackworth, *About Face,* p. 53.
72. Stanley Weintraub, *MacArthur's War* (New York: Free Press, 2000), p. 1.
73. Phelps, *Chappie,* p. 189.
74. Ibid., p. 302.
75. Bowers, et al., *Black Soldier, White Army,* p. xiii.
76. Morris J. MacGregor, Jr., *Integration of the Armed Forces 1940–1965* (Washington, D.C.: Center of Military History, United States Army, 1981), pp. 436–39.
77. Bernard C. Nalty, *Strength for the Fight* (New York: Free Press, 1986), p. 260.
78. Hackworth, *About Face,* p. 92.
79. Stephen John Williams, "Last Heroics of an All-Black Army Unit," *The City Sun* (Brooklyn, N.Y.), July 11–17, 1990.
80. Shawn Pogatchnik, "After 39 Years, a Town Honors Its Black Hero," *Los Angeles Times,* May 28, 1990.
81. Juan Osuna, "Forgotten Hero Buried with Full Honors," *Register-Herald* (Beckley, W. Va.), March 11, 1990.
82. Blair, *The Forgotten War,* p. 971.
83. *Congressional Record,* vol. 134, October 21, 1988, no. 151.
84. Scicchitano, "All Black Regiment Struggles."
85. Broder, "Army: Blacks Look Back at Record in Korea."

86. Ibid.
87 Bowers, et al., *Black Soldier, White Army,* p. 270.
88. Calvin Sims, "War Memories Temper Korean Euphoria," *The New York Times,* June 25, 2000.

10: Vietnam

1. Arthur M. Schlesinger, Jr., *The Bitter Heritage: Vietnam and American Democracy 1941–1966* (Boston: Houghton Mifflin, 1966), pp. 2–3.
2. Ibid., p. 4.
3. Ibid., p. 7.
4. Ibid., p. 8.
5. Ibid., pp. 8–9, 15.
6. David Hatchett, "What Are the Secrets of the West Indian Success Story?" *The Crisis,* May 1991, vol. 98, no. 5, p. 21.
7. Colin Powell, *My American Journey* (New York: Random House, 1995), p. 28.
8. Ibid., p. 34.
9. Juan Williams, *Eyes on the Prize: America's Civil Rights Years 1954–1965* (New York: Viking, 1987), p. 107.
10. Ibid., p. 110.
11. Powell, *My American Journey,* p. 51.
12. Ibid., p. 53.
13. Sara Bullard, executive ed., *Free At Last* (Montgomery, Ala.: Civil Rights Education Project, Southern Poverty Law Center), p. 46.
14. Neil Sheehan, *A Bright Shining Lie: John Paul Vann and America in Vietnam* (New York: Random House, 1988), p. 134.
15. Williams, *Eyes on the Prize,* p. 135.
16. Powell, *My American Journey,* p. 61.
17. Schlesinger, *The Bitter Heritage,* p. 21.
18. Stanley Karnow, *Vietnam, A History* (New York: Penguin Books, 1984), pp. 21–22, 694.
19. Homer Bigart, "A 'Very Real War' in Vietnam—and the Deep U.S. Commitment," *The New York Times,* February 25, 1962; in *Reporting Vietnam: 1959–1969* (hereinafter *Reporting Vietnam*), edited by the Library of America (New York: Library of America, 1998), p. 32.
20. Bernard B. Fall, "Master of the Red Jab," *The Saturday Evening Post,* November 24, 1962; in *Reporting Vietnam,* p. 47.
21. Powell, *My American Journey,* pp. 80–81.
22. Neil Sheehan, "Vietnamese Ignored U.S. Battle Order," *The Washington Post,* January 7, 1963, in *Reporting Vietnam,* p. 68.
23. Powell, *My American Journey,* pp. 83–84.
24. Ibid., pp. 86–87.
25. Ibid., p. 89.
26. Ibid., p. 95.
27. Ibid., p. 101.
28. Schlesinger, *The Bitter Heritage,* p. 25.
29. Sheehan, *A Bright Shining Lie,* p. 26.
30. Powell, *My American Journey,* p. 104.
31. David Wallechinsky, "Have a Vision," *Parade,* August 13, 1989, p. 4.
32. A. Peter Bailey, "Seeing Stars and Taking Note," *The City Sun* (Brooklyn, N.Y.), August 23–29, 1989, p. 34.
33. Martin Walker, "A Buffalo Soldier on the Brink," *The Guardian Weekly,* February 24, 1991, p. 11.
34. Michael R. Beschloss, *Taking Charge: The Johnson White House Tapes* (New York: Simon & Schuster, 1997), pp. 363, 364, 368, 369.
35. Schlesinger, *The Bitter Heritage,* p. 29.
36. Ibid.
37. Williams, *Eyes on the Prize,* p. 273.
38. Powell, *My American Journey,* p. 116.
39. Lieutenant General Harold G. Moore (Ret.) and Joseph L. Galloway, *We Were Soldiers Once . . . and Young* (New York: Harper Perennial, 1993), p. 20.
40. Ibid., p. xix.
41. Sheehan, *A Bright Shining Lie,* p. 285.
42. Moore and Galloway, *We Were Soldiers Once,* pp. xviii–xix.
43. John Cash, *Seven Firefights in Vietnam* (Washington, D.C.: Office of the Chief of Military History, United States Army, 1970), p. 11.
44. David Halberstam, "Requiem for the Cold War," *Playboy,* January 1994, p. 168.
45. Moore and Galloway, *We Were Soldiers Once,* p. 137.

46. Ibid., p. 157.
47. Ibid., p. 268.
48. Ibid., pp. 279, 286.
49. Ibid., p. 316.
50. Colonel David Hackworth, *About Face* (New York: Simon & Schuster, 1989), p. 487.
51. Ibid., p. 488.
52. Sheehan, *A Bright Shining Lie,* p. 579.
53. Ward S. Just, "Reconnaissance," from *To What End: Report from Vietnam, 1968,* in *Reporting Vietnam,* p. 266.
54. Charles C. Moskos and John Sibley Butler, *All That We Can Be: Black Leadership and Racial Integration the Army Way* (New York: Basic Books, 1996) p. 8.
55. Powell, *My American Journey,* pp. 114–15.
56. Ibid., p. 122.
57. Moskos and Butler, *All That We Can Be,* p. 79.
58. Ibid.
59. Martha Gellhorn, "Suffer the Little Children . . ." *Ladies' Home Journal,* January 1967, in *Reporting Vietnam,* p. 287.
60. Jonathan Schell, from *The Military Half: An Account of the Destruction in Quang Ngai and Quang Tin, 1968,* in *Reporting Vietnam,* p. 409.
61. Schlesinger, *The Bitter Heritage,* p. 118.
62. Wallace Terry, *Bloods: An Oral History of the Vietnam War by Black Veterans* (New York: Ballantine Books, 1984), p. 274.
63. Ibid., p. 280.
64. Ibid., pp. 283–86.
65. David Parks, *GI Diary* (Washington, D.C.: Howard University Press, 1984; reprint from 1968), pp. 1, 52, 133.
66. Ibid., pp. 71, 76.
67. Ibid., p. 83.
68. Ibid., pp. 98–99, 111.
69. Ibid., p. 121.
70. Ibid., pp. 134–35.
71. Ibid., p. 135.
72. Ibid., p. 137.
73. Peter M. Bergman, ed., *The Chronological History of the Negro in America* (New York: New American Library, 1969), p. 604.
74. Speech by Martin Luther King, April 4, 1967, at meeting of Clergy and Laity Concerned at Riverside Church, New York City, in *I Have a Dream: Writings and Speeches That Changed the World by Martin Luther King,* edited by James M. Washington (San Francisco: Harper and Co., 1992).
75. Karnow, *Vietnam, A History,* p. 532.
76. Powell, *My American Journey,* pp. 122–23.
77. Karnow, *Vietnam, A History,* p. 552.
78. Michael Herr, *Dispatches* (New York: Avon, 1978), p. 159.
79. Joe McGinniss, from *The Selling of the President 1968,* in *Reporting Vietnam,* p. 663.
80. Powell, *My American Journey,* p. 124.
81. Ibid., pp. 132–33, 135.
82. Carl Rowan, "Called to Service: The Colin Powell Story," *Reader's Digest,* December 1989, p. 125.
83. Ken Adelman, "Ground Zero," *The Washingtonian,* May 1990, p. 70.
84. Powell, *My American Journey,* p. 142.
85. Charles Lane, "The Legend of Colin Powell: Anatomy of an Establishment Career," *The New Republic,* April 17, 1995, p. 20.
86. Terry, *Bloods,* p. 53.
87. Powell, *My American Journey,* pp. 144–45.
88. Terry, *Bloods,* p. xiv.
89. Thomas A. Johnson, "The U.S. Negro in Vietnam," *The New York Times,* April 29, 1968, in *Reporting Vietnam,* p. 615.
90. Walton Rawls, ed., *Offerings at the Wall* (Atlanta: Turner Publishing, 1995), p. 5.
91. Ibid., p. 8.
92. Ibid., p. 15.
93. Nelson George, "fools, suckas & baadasssss brothers," in *Rolling Stone: The Seventies* (New York: Rolling Stone Press, 1998), p. 58.
94. John Saar, "You Can't Just Hand Out Orders," *Life,* October 23, 1970, in *Reporting Vietnam,* p. 153.
95. James Sterba, "Scraps of Paper from Vietnam," *The New York Times Magazine,* October 18, 1970, in *Reporting Vietnam,* p. 145.
96. "The Troubled U.S. Army in Vietnam," *Newsweek,* January, 11, 1971, p. 37.

97. Powell, *My American Journey,* pp. 155–57.
98. Ibid., p. 162.
99. Karnow, *Vietnam, A History,* p. 701.
100. Terry, *Bloods,* p. 181.
101. Ibid., pp. 290–91.

11: Desert Storm

1. Colin Powell, *My American Journey* (New York: Random House, 1995), p. 532.
2. Charles Lane, "The Legend of Colin Powell: Anatomy of an Establishment Career," *The New Republic,* April 17, 1995, p. 28.
3. Powell, *My American Journey,* p. 501.
4. Jack Sirica, "The Face and Race of Desert Shield," *New York Newsday,* December 26, 1990.
5. Steven A. Holmes, "Military Moves to Aid Racial Harmony," *The New York Times,* April 5, 1995.
6. Charles C. Moskos and John Sibley Butler, *All That We Can Be* (New York: Basic Books, 1996), p. 33.
7. Sirica, "The Face and Race of Desert Shield."
8. Peter Applebome, "As Armed Forces Cut Back, Some Lose a Way Up in Life," *The New York Times,* May 7, 1990.
9. Powell, *My American Journey,* p. 208.
10. Ibid., pp. 243–44.
11. Ibid., p. 270.
12. Ibid., p. 273.
13. Ibid., pp. 276, 278.
14. Ibid., p. 279.
15. Patrick J. Sloyan, "The Success of Colin Powell," *New York Newsday,* August 11, 1989.
16. Powell, *My American Journey,* p. 303.
17. Michael R. Gordon, "Vital for the Invasion: Politically Attuned General," *The New York Times,* December 25, 1989.
18. Powell, *My American Journey,* pp. 330–31.
19. Ibid., p. 298.
20. David Wallechinsky, "It Can Be Done," *Parade,* August 13, 1989.
21. Powell, *My American Journey,* p. 334.
22. Bob Woodward, *The Commanders* (New York: Simon & Schuster, 1991), p. 49.
23. Remarks by Colin Powell, Commander in Chief Forces Command, to the National Association of Black Journalists, New York City, August 17, 1989.
24. George F. Sanders, "Black Vet's War Goes On," New York *Daily News,* July 30, 1989.
25. Barrett Seaman, "A Complete Soldier Makes It," *Time,* August 21, 1989, p. 24.
26. Gordon, "Vital for the Invasion: Politically Attuned General."
27. Colin Powell, *My American Journey,* p. 608.
28. Kevin Buckley, *Panama: The Whole Story* (New York: Simon & Schuster, 1991), p. 230.
29. Colin Powell, *My American Journey,* p. 434.
30. Ibid., p. 419.
31. Ibid., p. 436.
32. John Barry, "The Coming Cutbacks in Military Money," *Newsweek,* March 18, 1991, p. 42.
33. Peter Applebome, "As Armed Forces Cut Back, Some Lose a Way Up in Life."
34. David Carlisle, "As the Army Cuts Back . . . ," *The New York Times,* July 4, 1990.
35. Colonel David Hackworth, "Save the Boys, Not the Toys," *Newsweek,* August 6, 1990, p. 8.
36. Peter Applebome, "As Armed Forces Cut Back, Some Lose a Way Up in Life."
37. Powell, *My American Journey,* pp. 459–61.
38. General H. Norman Schwarzkopf, *It Doesn't Take a Hero* (New York: Bantam Books, 1993), pp. 332–35.
39. Ibid., p. 344.
40. Woodward, *The Commanders,* p. 225.
41. Schwarzkopf, *It Doesn't Take a Hero,* p. 349.
42. Ibid., p. 347.
43. Powell, *My American Journey,* p. 464.
44. Rick Atkinson, *Crusade* (Boston: Houghton Mifflin, 1993), p. 111.
45. Woodward, *The Commanders,* p. 332.
46. Schwarzkopf, *It Doesn't Take a Hero,* p. 353.
47. Powell, *My American Journey,* p. 469.
48. Eric Schmitt with Michael R. Gordon, "Tensions Bedeviled Allies All the Way to Kuwait," *The New York Times,* March 24, 1991.
49. Powell, *My American Journey,* pp. 474–79.
50. Atkinson, *Crusade,* pp. 83, 113.

51. Woodward, *The Commanders,* p. 311.
52. Jon Nordheimer, "Women's Roles in Combat: The War Resumes," *The New York Times,* May 26, 1991.
53. George James, "From Harlem to Saudi Arabia," *The New York Times,* November 25, 1990.
54. Michael R. Gordon and General Bernard Trainor, *The Generals' War* (Boston: Little, Brown & Co., 1995), p. 187.
55. Atkinson, *Crusade,* pp. 68, 73, 94.
56. Woodward, *The Commanders,* p. 346.
57. Powell, *My American Journey,* p. 527.
58. Schwarzkopf, *It Doesn't Take a Hero,* p. 412.
59. Ibid., pp. 479–80.
60. Powell, *My American Journey,* p. 511.
61. Atkinson, *Crusade,* pp. 58–59.
62. Ibid., pp. 59–60, 107–8.
63. Powell, *My American Journey,* pp. 509, 519.
64. Schwarzkopf, *It Doesn't Take a Hero,* p. 494.
65. "Tales From the Front," *People,* 1991, p. 60.
66. Lisa Grunwald, "MIA," *Life,* March 18, 1991.
67. William Julius Wilson, *When Work Disappears: The World of the New Urban Poor* (New York: Vintage Books, 1996), p. 156.
68. Ibid., p. 161.
69. National Opinion Research Center Poll, Chicago, January 1991.
70. Lynne Duke, "If War Comes Will Blacks Pay More Than Their Fair Share?" *The Washington Post National Weekly Edition,* December 10–16, 1990, p. 31.
71. "Blacks Wary of Their Big Role as Troops," *The New York Times,* January 25, 1991.
72. Salim Muwakkil, "Religious Bullying, Racism Corrode Troop Relations," *In These Times,* February 20–26, 1991.
73. Juan Williams, "Black Troops, Black Leaders and the War in the Gulf," *The Washington Post National Weekly Edition,* January 28–February 3, 1991.
74. "Why the Protest Against the Gulf War Fizzled," *New York Newsday,* March 27, 1991.
75. Powell, *My American Journey,* pp. 485–86.
76. Schwarzkopf, *It Doesn't Take a Hero,* pp. 416, 514.
77. Ibid., pp. 491–506.
78. Ibid., pp. 523–24.
79. Atkinson, *Crusade,* p. 437.
80. Schwarzkopf, *It Doesn't Take a Hero,* pp. 524–28, 539.
81. Powell, *My American Journey,* p. 515.
82. "The Heroes Remembered," *Newsweek,* March 11, 1991, p. 74.
83. Schwarzkopf, *It Doesn't Take a Hero,* pp. 540–42.
84. Powell, *My American Journey,* p. 520.
85. Patrick E. Tyler, "Iraq's War Total Estimated by U.S.," *The New York Times,* June 5, 1991.
86. Chris Hedges, "Harlem's Guard Troops Complain of Treatment," *The New York Times,* February 23, 1991.
87. Bill Turque, "The Battle for Respect," *Newsweek,* March 11, 1991, p. 55.
88. Gordon and Trainor, *The Generals' War,* p. 469.
89. Powell, *My American Journey,* pp. 526–28.
90. John Roberts, "Why Did You Kill Our Hero?" *Teaching Tolerance,* Southern Poverty Law Center, Spring 1992, p. 14.
91. Kate McKenna, "The Curse of Desert Storm," *Playboy,* August 1991, p. 64.
92. Kathryn Casey, "Soldiers of Misfortune," *Ladies' Home Journal,* March 1997, p. 148.
93. Richard Sisk, "Gen. Leans to Gulf Poison-Gas Theory," New York *Daily News,* January 30, 1997.
94. Powell, *My American Journey,* p. 534.
95. Ibid., p. 591.
96. Thomas E. Ricks, "U.S. Infantry Surprise: It's Now Mostly White; Blacks Now Hold Office Jobs," *The Wall Street Journal,* January 6, 1997.
97. *Life,* March 18, 1991.
98. George F. Sanders, "Black Vet's War Goes On," New York *Daily News,* July 30, 1989.
99. Ken Adelman, "Ground Zero," *The Washingtonian,* May 1990, pp. 70–71.
100. Colin Powell, "Why Service Matters," *Newsweek,* February 3, 1997, p. 36.
101. William F. Buckley, Jr., "National Debt, National Service," *The New York Times,* October 18, 1990.
102. "Clinton, Bush and Powell to Share Ideas About Volunteerism," *The New York Times,* January 25, 1997.
103. Powell, *My American Journey,* p. 611.

Epilogue

1. William Glaberson, "Sailor from Mutiny in '44 Wins a Presidential Pardon," *The New York Times,* December 24, 1999.
2. Todd S. Purdum, "Black Cadet Gets a Posthumous Commission," *The New York Times,* July 25, 1995.
3. "South Carolina Honors Tuskegee Airmen with a Monument," *The New York Times,* May 27, 1995.
4. Joseph L. Galloway, "Debt of Honor," *U.S. News & World Report,* May 6, 1996.
5. James Bennet, "Medals of Honor Awarded at Last to Black World War II Soldiers," *The New York Times,* January 14, 1997.
6. Joseph L. Galloway, "A Soldier's Story," *U.S. News & World Report,* May 31, 1999.
7. Bennet, "Medals of Honor Awarded at Last."

Index

About the Type

This book was set in Times New Roman, designed by Stanley Morrison specifically for *The Times* of London. The typeface was introduced in the newspaper in 1932. Times New Roman has had its greatest success in the United States as a book and commercial typeface rather than one used in newspapers.